Eating Disorders: Medical Care, Complications and Management

Eating Disorders: Medical Care, Complications and Management

Edited by Walter Williamson

hayle medical

New York

Hayle Medical,
750 Third Avenue, 9th Floor,
New York, NY 10017, USA

Visit us on the World Wide Web at:
www.haylemedical.com

ISBN: 978-1-63241-588-2

Printed in China.

Cataloging-in-Publication Data

Eating disorders : medical care, complications and management / edited by Walter Williamson.
p. cm.
Includes bibliographical references and index.
ISBN 978-1-63241-588-2
1. Eating disorders. 2. Eating disorders--Treatment. 3. Medical care.
I. Williamson, Walter.
RC552.E18 E28 2019
616.852 6--dc23

Table of Contents

Preface

An eating disorder is a mental disorder in which a person's mental and physical health takes a toll owing to abnormal eating habits. Eating disorders may be in the form of binge eating, anorexia nervosa, bulimia nervosa, pica, rumination disorder, etc. Substance abuse, anxiety disorders and depression are common manifestations of eating disorders. The treatment of eating disorders depends on the type and severity of the disorder. Exercising, counseling, proper diet and medication can have positive outcomes. Cognitive behavioral therapy, art therapy, dialectical behavior therapy, music therapy, recreation therapy, nutrition counseling, etc. may also be recommended for the management of eating disorders. Often, it is seen that eating disorders can lead to complications such as miscarriages, relapse and attachment insecurity. This book explores all the important aspects of eating disorders in the modern day scenario. It strives to provide a fair idea about the complications of eating disorders along with their medical care and management strategies. It will serve as a valuable source of reference for graduate and post-graduate students.

This book is the end result of constructive efforts and intensive research done by experts in this field. The aim of this book is to enlighten the readers with recent information in this area of research. The information provided in this profound book would serve as a valuable reference to students and researchers in this field.

At the end, I would like to thank all the authors for devoting their precious time and providing their valuable contribution to this book. I would also like to express my gratitude to my fellow colleagues who encouraged me throughout the process.

Editor

1

The coexistence of psychiatric and gastrointestinal problems in children with restrictive eating in a nationwide Swedish twin study

Jakob Täljemark[1*], Maria Råstam[1,2], Paul Lichtenstein[3], Henrik Anckarsäter[4] and Nóra Kerekes[5]

Abstract

Background: Restrictive eating problems are rare in children but overrepresented in those with neurodevelopmental problems. Comorbidities decrease wellbeing in affected individuals but research in the area is relatively scarce. This study describes phenotypes, regarding psychiatric and gastrointestinal comorbidities, in children with restrictive eating problems.

Methods: A parental telephone interview was conducted in 9- or 12-year old twins (n = 19,130) in the Child and Adolescent Twin Study in Sweden. Cases of restrictive eating problems and comorbid problems were established using the Autism, Tics-AD/HD and other Comorbidities inventory, parental reports of comorbidity as well as data from a national patient register. In restrictive eating problem cases, presence of psychiatric and gastrointestinal comorbidity was mapped individually in probands and their co-twin. Two-tailed Mann–Whitney U tests were used to test differences in the mean number of coexisting disorders between boys and girls. Odds ratios were used to compare prevalence figures between individuals with or without restrictive eating problems, and Fisher exact test was used to establish significance.

Results: Prevalence of restrictive eating problems was 0.6% (concordant in 15% monozygotic and 3% of dizygotic twins). The presence of restrictive eating problems drastically increased odds of all psychiatric problems, especially autism spectrum disorder in both sexes (odds ratio = 11.9 in boys, odds ratio = 10.1 in girls), obsessive-compulsive disorder in boys (odds ratio = 11.6) and oppositional defiant disorder in girls (odds ratio = 9.22). Comorbid gastrointestinal problems, such as lactose intolerance (odds ratio = 4.43) and constipation (odds ratio = 2.91), were the most frequent in girls. Boy co-twins to a proband with restrictive eating problems generally had more psychiatric problems than girl co-twins and more girl co-twins had neither somatic nor any psychiatric problems at all.

Conclusions: In children with restrictive eating problems odds of all coexisting psychiatric problems and gastrointestinal problems are significantly increased. The study shows the importance of considering comorbidities in clinical assessment of children with restrictive eating problems.

Keywords: Restrictive eating problem, Neurodevelopmental problem, Psychiatric problem, Gastrointestinal problem, Twin study

* Correspondence: jakob.taljemark@med.lu.se
[1]Lund University, Medical Faculty, Department of Clinical Sciences Lund, Child and Adolescent Psychiatry, Baravägen 1, S-221 85 Lund, Sweden
Full list of author information is available at the end of the article

Plain English Summary

Restrictive eating problems, where children do not get enough nutrition through their diet, are rare overall but more common in children with psychiatric problems. This study investigated which psychiatric and gastro-intestinal problems (problems related to the stomach and the intestines) are also present, and how often, in children who have restrictive eating problems. We also studied what type of problems the twin-pair of a child with restrictive eating problems has.

We found that six in every 1000 children (9 or 12-year-olds) in a nation-wide general population had severe restrictive eating problems. The chance that both twins had this problem was much higher in identical (one egg) twins, suggesting that severe restrictive eating problems are partially inherited.

If a child had restrictive eating problems, risks were high that he/she also had other psychiatric problems. The risk for autism spectrum disorders was very high in girls and boys with restrictive eating problems. Even problems with digestion were frequent in these children, for example lactose intolerance and constipation were often occurring.

The results from this study show how important it is for health care professionals to assess for both psychiatric and gastrointestinal problems in children with severe restrictive eating problems.

Background

In children and adolescents, a diagnosis of a formal eating disorder is at the extreme end of a broader spectrum of abnormal eating attitudes and behaviors [1]. Younger children often present with sub-threshold heterogeneous disordered eating symptoms [2] and relative to adolescents or adults, few children meet threshold criteria for specific eating disorders. New diagnostic categories introduced in the Diagnostic and Statistical Manual of Mental Disorders, 5th ed (DSM-5) [3] increase the number of individuals diagnosable with specific feeding and eating disorders by introduction of new diagnoses e.g. Avoidant/Restrictive Food Intake Disorder (ARFID) [2]. This study focuses on eating problems that differ from ARFID: included cases in this study are prepubertal children that have significant problems with restrictive eating as well as fear of gaining weight.

It is known that childhood restrictive eating is a risk factor for developing formal eating disorders including anorexia nervosa (AN) later on [4, 5]. In a previous study, using data from the Child and Adolescent Twin Study in Sweden (CATSS) study but from a different birth cohort, restrictive eating in prepubertal children was found to be more common in children with neurodevelopmental problems such as attention deficit hyperactivity disorder or autism spectrum disorder, particularly if the two conditions co-existed [6]. The present study investigates a wider range of psychiatric comorbidities than the original study, and explores physical comorbidity for children with restrictive eating problems. While links between restrictive eating problems (REP) and obsessive-compulsive disorder are well described for adolescents [7], there is less data on these patterns in children. Data on the association between REP and externalizing behavioral problems (oppositional defiant disorder and conduct disorder) are scarce for all ages.

Gastrointestinal symptoms are often reported in cases of formal eating disorders in children and adolescents, with constipation the most common complaint in cases of eating disorders with restrictive eating [8]. Gastrointestinal symptoms appear more common in ARFID than in AN or bulimia nervosa (BN) [9]. There are however few studies aiming to describe the wide range of comorbid gastrointestinal conditions to restrictive eating problems.

To better understand the function and symptom load in cases of clinically relevant eating problems it is essential to understand which other disorders coexist and what implications this overlap has for individuals. We hypothesised that middle school aged children with restrictive eating resulting in low weight would have an increased risk for adverse mental and somatic health problems compared to the rest of their peers. The aims of this study are twofold:

(1) To characterize the REP-phenotype by concurrently describing seven different possible coexisting psychiatric and five different gastrointestinal problems in probands.

(2) To compare the rates of the coexisting mental disorders and somatic disorders in REP-discordant monozygotic versus dizygotic co-twins, in order to illustrate the full range of phenotypical expressions of shared genetic and environmental effects.

Methods

Participants

The study participants were recruited from the ongoing longitudinal Child and Adolescent Twin Study in Sweden (CATSS) [10]. Data in this study was collected from the CATSS 9/12 sub-study launched in 2004. In CATSS 9/12, all parents of Swedish twins were invited to participate in a telephone interview regarding aspects of their children's mental and physical health and social circumstances in connection with their children's 9th (or 12th - for the first three years of the study only) birthdays. The overall response rate was 80% [10]. In 2013 the CATSS 9/12 was linked to the National Patient Register, which encompasses data on all Swedish psychiatric inpatient care since 1987 and since 2001 it also comprises information from outpatient consultations with specialist physicians.

Data from parental interviews performed with the birth cohorts between 1992 and 2000 of CATSS 9/12 was used in the present study. It included information on 19,130 children (51% boys), of whom 28.2% were monozygotic (MZ) twins, 35.3% dizygotic (DZ) same sex (ss) and 34.3% DZ different sex (ds) twins, while 2.2% had unknown zygosity. Zygosity was determined with the help of a panel of 49 single nucleotide polymorphisms using the children's saliva samples [11]. When DNA was not available, a previously developed algorithm of questions was used. Only twins with >95% probability of being correctly classified were assigned zygosity by this method, and thus 2.2% (420 twins) were excluded on the basis that their zygosity was unknown, leaving 18,710 children. A further 43 children with chromosomal aberration (ICD-10 Q85, Q90–99) and 284 with brain damage (ICD-10 G00-G39, G45-G46, G80-G94, Q00-Q04) based on information from the National Patient Register were excluded resulting in a final study population of 18,383. For twin-pair analyses we further excluded twins without their co-twin, therefore those results are based on 9046 twin pairs (18,092 children). Among the 95 children with REP identified, five children were excluded as the data file did not contain information about their or their co-twins' psychiatric and/or somatic health, leaving 90 children with REP for the co-twin analyses. Five of them were concordant pairs for REP, therefore co-twin analyses are presented for 85 probands with REP.

Measures

REP was defined in two different ways, (a) through the eating module in the Autism, Tics-AD/HD and other Disorders (A-TAC) inventory, and (b) by direct questions to parent relating to earlier diagnosis of clinical eating disorder.

a.) *The Autism, Tics-AD/HD and other Disorders (A-TAC)* inventory: This inventory has been described in more detail elsewhere [12]. In short, it is a questionnaire developed for use in large-scale epidemiological research to investigate child psychiatric problems based on criteria stated in the Diagnostic and Statistical Manual of Mental Disorders, 4th ed, text rev. (DSM-IV-R) [13] and can be carried out as a parental phone interview. The eating module in A-TAC screens for restrictive eating problems and includes two questions: "has (s)he ever failed to gain enough weight for more than a year?" and "has (s)he seemed fearful of gaining weight or growing fat?". Questions addressing specific symptoms or characteristics in A-TAC may be answered by the response categories "no" (score 0), "yes, to some extent" (score 0.5), and "yes" (score 1.0). REP by A-TAC was defined as scoring at least one and a half points (≥1.5) on the collapsed score for these two questions.

b.) *Restrictive eating problems diagnostic question in CATSS*: the CATSS telephone interview also contains two specific questions that are worded "has your child ever received a diagnosis of anorexia nervosa/ bulimia nervosa?" A positive answer to the first of these two questions qualified the child to be included in the REP group.

Definition of coexisting disorders

Other coexisting disorders were defined via (i) the relevant 'diagnostic module' on the A-TAC using validated low cutoffs for each, or by (ii) recognition in the National Patient Register.

(i) *A-TAC diagnoses:* In the A-TAC, screening cutoffs with high sensitivity but lower specificity have been validated for Autism Spectrum Disorder (ASD), Attention Deficit and Hyperactivity Disorder (ADHD), Learning Disorder (LD), Tics Disorder (TD) [12] and conduct disorder (CD) [14]. For oppositional defiant disorder (ODD) a validated high cutoff [14] was used in the present study, because the low specificity of the low cutoff would result in an unreasonable high prevalence of ODD. Beside validity, the internal reliability of the scales has also been established previously with Cronbach's α for ASD 0.86, ADHD 0.92, TD 0.57, ODD 0.75 and CD 0.61 [10]. Obsessive-Compulsive Disorder (OCD) has not been included in previous A-TAC validation studies [12, 14] [15]. However, the questions of the OCD module show good agreement with clinical practice [16].

(ii) *National patient register:* The National Patient Register encompasses data regarding clinical diagnoses from all psychiatric inpatient care since 1987 and since 2001 the register also comprises information from outpatient consultations with psychiatry specialist physicians. From the National Patient Register, information about ICD-10 diagnoses of ASD, ADHD, LD, TD, ODD, OCD and CD were also collected.

Identification of somatic problems

The identified somatic problems were: celiac disease, lactose intolerance, other food or nutritional allergies (apart from celiac disease or lactose intolerance, from now on referred to as "food allergy"), diarrhea and constipation. The telephone interview questions regarding gastrointestinal conditions are straight forward yes or no questions, e.g. "does (s)he have or has (s)he ever had lactose intolerance (celiac disease; other food allergy)?" or "does (s)he have or has (s)he ever had problems with prolonged periods of diarrhea (constipation) growing up?". Answers are coded for "yes" as "1" and for "no" as "0", while the alternatives "do not know" or "do not wish to answer" are coded as missing values.

Statistical methods

The statistical analysis was made using IBM SPSS Statistics version 22.

Among 85 children with REP available for twin pair analyses, there were five pairs where both twins had REP (concordant pairs for REP). In these pairs the proband was defined randomly. This resulted in 80 REP probands with known zygosity. For each of these probands and their co-twins coexisting problems were plotted separately for gender and for zygosity class. Concordance rate was defined as the percentage of co-twins meeting criteria for REP. Two-tailed Mann–Whitney U tests were used to test differences in the mean number of coexisting disorders between boys and girls.

The odds ratio (OR) for psychiatric problems and gastrointestinal problems was calculated for REP by comparison of the prevalence in this group to individuals without REP, and using Fisher exact test to establish significance.

Results

Prevalence of restrictive eating problems

In total, 95 children (40 boys, 55 girls) fulfilled criteria for REP corresponding to a population prevalence of 0.6% with a male–female ratio of 1 to 1.4. Of these 95 children 94 were identified from the A-TAC interview and 3 by parental reports about existing diagnosis of AN (2 of them by both). There were no parental reports about bulimic behavior.

Coexisting problems in children with restrictive eating problems

Table 1 summarizes the prevalence of defined psychiatric and gastrointestinal problems in those boys and girls who were selected for REP. The most prevalent co-existing psychiatric problems were ADHD and LD (both present in almost 36% of children with REP), and the most prevalent co-existing gastrointestinal problems were constipation (in 22% of children with REP) followed by lactose intolerance and food allergies (each in about 12% of children with REP). Generally, there was a strong trend towards boys with REP having a higher prevalence of other psychiatric problems than girls with REP (mean composite number of psychiatric diagnoses 1.90 in boys, 1.09 in girls, $p = 0.051$) (Table 1). For specific conditions, significantly more boys than girls with REP had co-existing ASD, ADHD, TD or OCD. Coexisting gastrointestinal problems did not differ significantly between boys and girls.

When defining the odds of having another psychiatric or gastrointestinal problem in a child with REP, the prevalence of defined psychiatric and gastrointestinal problems in the group of children with REP was compared to the prevalence found in children without REP (controls,

Table 1 Prevalence and composite number of comorbid psychiatric and gastrointestinal problems in boys and girls with restrictive eating problems (REP) according to A-TAC ($n = 95$)

	REP ($n = 95$)	Boys with REP ($n = 40$)[a]	Girls with REP ($n = 55$)[b]	p of gender difference
ASD	22 (23.2%)	14 (35.0%)	8 (14.5%)	0.027
ADHD	34 (35.8%)	20 (50%)	14 (25.4%)	0.018
LD	34 (35.8%)	16 (40%)	18 (32.7%)	0.519
TD	10 (10.6%)	8 (20%)	2 (3.6%)	0.015
OCD	9 (9.5%)	7 (17.5%)	2 (3.6%)	0.033
ODD	14 (14.7%)	5 (12.5%)	9 (16.3%)	0.771
CD	15 (15.8%)	8 (20%)	7 (12.7%)	0.399
Composite[¤] (SD)	1.45 (1.78)	1.90 (2.0)	1.09 (1.54)	0.051
Celiac disease	2 (2.1%)	0 (0.0%)	2 (3.6%)	0.506
Lactose intolerance	12 (12.6%)	5 (12.5%)	7 (12.7%)	1.00
Food allergy	11 (11.6%)	5 (12.5%)	6 (10.9%)	1.00
Constipation	21 (22.1%)	5 (12.5%)	16 (29.1%)	0.079
Diarrhea	5 (5.3%)	3 (7.5%)	2 (3.6%)	0.646
Composite* (SD)	0.49 (0.73)	0.43 (0.69)	0.53 (0.76)	0.505

ASD autism spectrum disorder, *ADHD* attention deficit hyperactivity disorder, *LD* learning disorder, *TD* tics disorder, *OCD* obsessive compulsive disorder, *ODD* oppositional defiant disorder, *CD* conduct disorder, *A-TAC* The Autism-Tics, AD/HD and other Comorbidities inventory

¤Composite: Mean number of assigned psychiatric diagnoses ASD, ADHD, LD, TD, OCD, ODD, CD

*Composite: Mean number of assigned gastrointestinal problems celiac disease, lactose intolerance, food allergy, constipation, diarrhea

[a] $n = 39$ for composite measure of psychiatric problems because of missing information for a boy in TD; $n = 37$ for composite measure of somatic problems based on missing data for three boys in lactose intolerance, food allergy and diarrhea

[b] $n = 51$ for composite measure of somatic problems based on missing information for four girls in celiac disease, lactose intolerance (2) and diarrhea

Table 2 Prevalence of psychiatric and gastrointestinal problems in the population of children with restrictive eating problems (REP) and in those without REP, separately presented by genders

	Boys without REP (*n* = 9305)	Boys with REP (*n* = 40)	Odds ratio	Girls without REP (*n* = 8956)	Girls with REP (*n* = 55)	Odds ratio
ASD	402 (4.3%)	14 (16.9%)	11.91 (6.17–22.9) $p < 0.001$	149 (1.7%)	8 (14.5%)	10.06 (4.67–21.65) $p < 0.001$
ADHD	1213 (13.0%)	20 (31.5%)	6.66 (3.57–12.41) $p < 0.001$	576 (6.4%)	14 (25.5%)	4.96 (2.69–9.15) $p < 0.001$
LD	1557 (16.7%)	16 (28.1%)	3.32 (1.76–6.26) $p < 0.001$	1130 (12.6%)	18 (32.7%)	3.37 (1.91–5.94) $p < 0.001$
TD	412 (4.4%)	8 (13.6%)	5.57 (2.54–12.19) $p < 0.001$	154 (1.7%)	2 (3.6%)	2.16 (0.52–8.93) $p = 0.247$
OCD	167 (1.8%)	7 (11.2%)	11.61 (5.96–26.61) $p < 0.001$	126 (1.4%)	2 (3.6%)	2.65 (0.64–10.97) $p = 0.184$
ODD	322 (3.5%)	5 (12.5%)	3.98 (1.55–10.23) $p = 0.001$	186 (2.1%)	9 (16.4%)	9.22 (4.45–19.10) $p < 0.001$
CD	465 (5.0%)	8 (20.0%)	4.75 (2.18–10.36) $p = 0.001$	262 (2.9%)	7 (12.7%)	4.84 (2.17–10.79) $p = 0.001$
Celiac disease	78 (0.8%)	0 (0%)	0	125 (1.4%)	2 (3.6%)	2.71 (0.65–11.25) $p = 0.177$
Lactose intolerance	535 (5.7%)	5 (12.5%)	2.39 (0.93–6.13) $p = 0.074$	449 (5.0%)	7 (12.7%)	2.91 (1.30–6.49) $p = 0.016$
Food allergy	811 (8.7%)	5 (12.5%)	1.53 (0.60–3.92) $p = 0.387$	721 (8.1%)	6 (10.9%)	1.39 (0.59–3.26) $p = 0.452$
Constipation	543 (5.8%)	5 (12.5%)	2.30 (0.90–5.89) $p = 0.083$	756 (8.4%)	16 (29.1%)	4.43 (2.46–8.00) $p < 0.001$
Diarrhea	357 (3.8%)	3 (7.5%)	2.08 (0.64–6.79) $p = 0.190$	233 (2.6%)	2 (3.6%)	1.44 (0.35–5.93) $p = 0.653$

ASD autism spectrum disorder, *ADHD* attention deficit hyperactivity disorder, *LD* learning disorder, *TD* tics disorder, *OCD* obsessive compulsive disorder, *ODD* oppositional defiant disorder, *CD* conduct disorder

n = 18,261) (Table 2). Generally, the odds significantly increased of all co-existing psychiatric problems in children (both boys and girls) with REP, except for girls to have with REP co-existing TD or OCD. The relative risk for a boy with REP to have another psychiatric problem was elevated three to twelvefold and most markedly elevated for the co-existence of ASD (OR = 11.9, $p < 0.001$) and OCD (OR = 11.6 $p < 0.001$). For a girl with REP the odds of having comorbid psychiatric problems was elevated two to tenfold, most markedly for the co-existence of ASD (OR = 10.1, $p > 0.001$). The odds for a girl with REP to have ODD was nine-fold increased (OR = 9.22, $p > 0.001$) compared to controls, and higher than for a boy with REP.

Boys were generally less affected by gastrointestinal problems than girls. In a girl with REP the odds were almost tripled for co-existing lactose intolerance (OR = 2.91 $p < 0.001$) and more than fourfold increased for constipation (OR = 4.43, $p < 0.001$).

Psychiatric and somatic problems in co-twins of probands with restrictive eating problems

Three of 20 MZ pairs (15%) were concordant for REP (10% MZ boy, 20% MZ girl), while in DZ there were 2 of 65 pairs (3.1%) where both twins had REP (0% DZss boy, 0%DZss girl, 9% DZds co-twin girl, 0% DZds co-twin boy).

Girl co-twins to a proband with REP more often had REP than a boy co-twin. Boy co-twins however more often had other psychiatric problems (ADHD, ASD, LD, TD, OCD, ODD or CD). 70% of MZ boy co-twins and 40% of MZ girl co-twins to a proband with REP had some psychiatric problem (REP and/or other psychiatric problem), leaving 30% of MZ boy and 60% of MZ girl co-twins without any psychiatric problem (Fig. 1). Around half of the DZ co-twins (43–58%) had no psychiatric problems (no REP and no other psychiatric problems) (Fig. 1).

One of four co-twins to a proband with REP had somatic problems. This prevalence was five times higher than the occurrence of somatic problems in control children (5%) and two and a half time higher than it was in probands with REP (9.8%). Similar proportions of boy and girl co-twins had (i) somatic problems, (ii) somatic problems only (i.e. no psychiatric problems) and (iii) neither psychiatric nor somatic complaints (around 40%) (Table 3).

Discussion

Summary of main findings

The prevalence of REP was 0.6% with a male to female ratio of 1 to 1.4. Individuals with REP had a higher prevalence of psychiatric problems than controls. The odds of comorbidity were increased for all studied

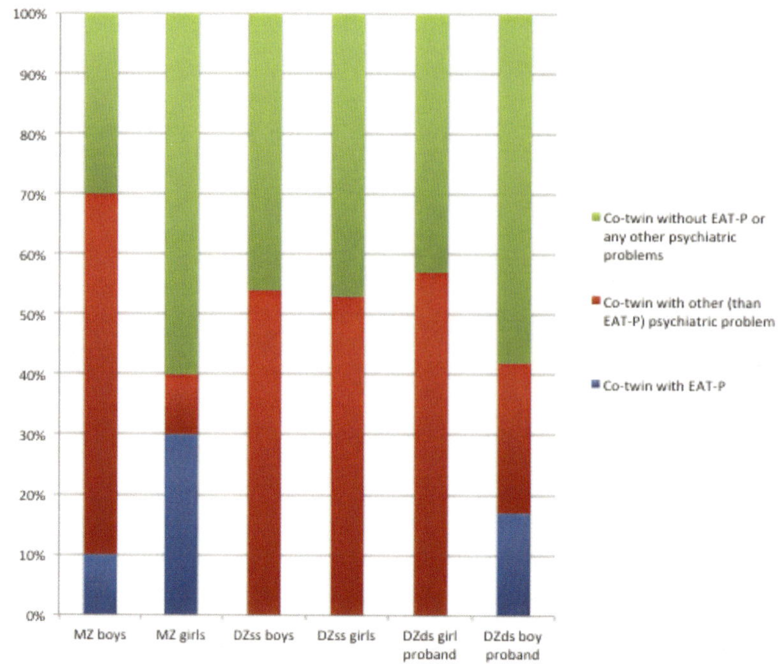

Fig. 1 Sibling recurrence rates of REP and other psychiatric problems in co-twins of probands with REP according to proband zygosity (*MZ* monozygotic; *DZ* dizygotic) and gender. Note: other psychiatric problems included: ASD, ADHD, LD, TD, OCD, ODD and CD

psychiatric conditions in boys, most markedly for ASD and OCD, while in girls for all psychiatric conditions except TD and OCD, with most marked elevations in ASD and ODD. The odds ratio of constipation and lactose intolerance was elevated in girls with REP compared to controls. Concordance for REP was higher in MZ than in DZ co-twins. Co-twin girls were more often concordant for REP itself, while co-twin boys more often had other comorbid psychiatric problems.

Restrictive eating problems in a nationwide general population of pre-pubertal children

The prevalence of restrictive eating problems in this sample was 0.6%. This prevalence is higher than previously reported, with one large British study quoting a prevalence of formal eating disorders of 0.15% among 11–12 year olds [17]. The higher prevalence in our study is a result of A-TAC not being a diagnostic instrument for formal eating disorders. Instead it recognizes children at risk: those whose parents report restrictive eating behaviors that potentially could lead to serious disorders. The prevalence figures in the current study of a non-clinical population may also reflect the fact that many youths with eating problems do not access treatment or receive a diagnosis, and that a high burden of disorders is likely to exist at a non-clinical sample level [10].

Table 3 Prevalence of somatic problems in co-twins of probands with restrictive eating problems (REP)

	% of co-twins with somatic problems	% of co-twins with only somatic problems[a]	% of co-twin without somatic or psychiatric problems[b]
Boys *n* = 35	24.3	5.3	39.3
Girls *n* = 50	26.3	6.7	43.3

[a]Only somatic problem but no REP or any other psychiatric problems
[b]Those without any somatic problems or REP or psychiatric problem

In this young study population, there was 1.4 times more girls than boys with REP. The higher proportion of REP cases in girls compared to boys is in agreement with findings of previous studies (for a review see [18]). Formal eating disorders have previously been described as far more common in female adolescents and adults than in males, with a rate ratio of lifetime prevalence of anorexia nervosa and bulimia nervosa in males versus females reported to be equal to or less than 1 to 10 [19]. However more recent studies utilizing DSM-5 criteria have shown a more equal sex distribution. A study of a Canadian adolescent community sample [20] showed that 2.2% of males and 4.5% of females met formal DSM-5 criteria for an eating disorder, and a further 1.1% of males and 5.1% of females met subthreshold criteria for eating disorders. Adolescent boys are also more likely to present with eating disorders other than formal AN or BN, such as atypical AN [21]. It has been suggested that gender differences in presentations, as well as gender specific differences in social constructions around weight ideals and eating habits, contribute to fewer clinically diagnosed cases of eating disorders in young males [21].

The present study assesses for eating disorders that include fear of gaining weight and weight loss/lack of weight gain for at least a year, conditions that put the individual at risk of developing AN or BN. It does not investigate eating problems without weight concerns, e.g. ARFID, or for binge eating disorder. Should these conditions have been investigated in this study it is likely that a more equal gender distribution would have been seen in this young age group. Fisher et al. [9] have established that ARFID occurs at an earlier age than AN or BN (12.9 years vs. 15.6 years vs 16.5 years) and that ARFID is more common in males than AN or BN, though female cases still dominate the ARFID category.

Co-existing psychiatric problems in probands

The findings of the present study emphasize that psychiatric problems should be considered in children with REP and vice versa. One in three boys and one in four girls with REP screened positive for ADHD in our general population sample. Evidence is gathering that ADHD is common among children with eating problems [22], more markedly in boys than in girls, and especially if ADHD and ASD symptoms coexist [6] which they commonly do. One in six boys and girls with REP screened positive for ASD. Feeding problems are overrepresented in children with ASD [23] and consequential extreme low and high BMIs have been observed in ASD, potentially as an effect of stereotyped or repetitive behaviors [24].

Our study indicates a strong trend towards boys with REP having a higher prevalence of psychiatric comorbidities than girls with REP (mean composite number of psychiatric comorbid psychiatric diagnoses 1.90 in boys, 1.09 in girls, $p = 0.051$). This overrepresentation is consistent with previous findings regarding gender differences in eating disorders [19]. The increased risk of REP and comorbid learning difficulties also mirrors previous findings. Some degree of problematic eating is evident in nearly all children with intellectual disability whether mild, moderate or severe [25] and eating disorders seem to be overrepresented in adult institutionalized patients with intellectual disability and to a lesser degree in adult individuals with intellectual disability living at home [26, 27].

There was an eleven-fold increased odds ratio of OCD in boys with REP in our study, while the twofold increased odds ratio for girls did not reach statistical significance. Eating disorders are known to be associated with OCD [28, 29] and in adult populations one third of patients with AN or BN have a lifetime diagnosis of OCD which more often than not precedes the debut of AN [30]. There are significant gender differences in the lifetime prevalence of AN and BN among patients with OCD [31] with marked female overrepresentation, while in this study boys with REP had more OCD than girls. The earlier debut of OCD in boys than in girls overall [31] could be a possible explanation for the gender difference on display in this sample.

Our sample displayed markedly increased odds of ODD and CD in both boys and girls with REP. There is a relative scarcity of research of links between REP and ODD or CD. One study showed that in a lifetime perspective, adults with BN and binge eating disorder, but not AN, had an increased risk of a lifetime diagnosis of ODD and CD [22] and a more recent study showed that children with restrictive or selective eating had higher rates of externalizing and oppositional behaviors [32]. ODD and CD often co-exists with other neurodevelopmental problems, most notably ADHD. Whether ODD or CD in isolation would increase risk of REP was not assessed in the present study.

Co-existing gastrointestinal problems in probands

Gastrointestinal complaints are common in pre-pubertal children in general and more so in children who have formal eating disorders [9]. It is well established that there is a strong overlap between gastrointestinal symptoms and psychiatric disorders (for a review see e.g. Korterink et al. [33]). Furthermore, before pubertal age, psychiatric problems often present with somatic symptoms. In general, girls are known to have more functional complaints including functional abdominal pain [33] than boys. Pain is a common symptom in gastrointestinal disorders including lactose intolerance and constipation, and both sex-determined biological differences in pain thresholds and a gender-influenced greater willingness to report somatic experiences e.g. pain can be at play [34].

Constipation is a common problem in childhood (0.7–29%, median 8.9 (5.3–17.4)) [35]. It is typically characterized by infrequent bowel evacuations, large stools, and difficult or painful defecation [36]. In this study, we found increased odds of constipation for girls but not boys with REP. Evidence regarding gender differences in prevalence of childhood constipation in the general population is conflicting, with five of seven studies in a systematic review showing no difference and two studies showing overrepresentation in girls [35]. Constipation has previously been identified as a risk factor for disordered eating in an Israeli study of female adolescents [37]. Constipation in patients with AN is associated with slowed colonic transit time and this delay in transit may contribute to bloating, thus further exacerbating patients' fear of fatness [38]. Consequent rectal distension could also reflexively inhibit gastric emptying, thus slowing down transit times further [38]. Constipation in children could be a consequence of reduced food intake generally. It is worsened by dehydration [39], and diet poor in fiber and nutrients [40], conditions for which children with REP may be at risk. Further, in AN poor muscle strength as a consequence of atrophy may contribute to constipation [41].

Lactose intolerance is a clinical syndrome where ingestion of lactose or lactose-containing food substances gives one or more of the following symptoms: abdominal pain, diarrhea, nausea, flatulence, and bloating [42]. Girls with REP had a twice increased risk of lactose intolerance and to our knowledge such a link has not previously been reported.

Prolonged problems with diarrhea are common complaints in pediatric practice. It is a symptom with several potential causes including infections and antibiotics treatment, irritable bowel syndrome, lactose intolerance and celiac disease for older children [43]. Chronic diarrhea refers to the persistence of loose stools (generally with increase in stool frequency) for at least 14 days [43]. The risk of diarrhea is known to be increased in children with developmental problems e.g. ASD [44]. We did not see any increased odds for diarrhea in children with REP which may seem surprising, given that problems with diarrhea are frequent in certain types of adolescent eating disorders e.g. AN purging subtype [45] and have been reported as a presenting complaint in children with ARFID presenting to pediatric services [46]. However, it is likely that restrictive eating behaviors in this population predispose more to constipation than to diarrhea. Overall, gastrointestinal symptoms are more common in patients with ARFID compared to cases of AN and BN [9]. If cases of ARFID were also screened for in this study, it is likely that the frequencies of gastrointestinal comorbidity would have been higher.

The high frequencies of gastrointestinal comorbidities in cases of REP should be viewed in the light of comorbidity figures for other psychiatric conditions, amongst which anxiety disorders are the most prevalent in younger age groups. In one study of 42 pediatric patients with functional chronic abdominal pain, 43% met criteria for depression and 79% for at least one anxiety disorder at the time of assessment [47], though it should be considered when interpreting these results that several anxiety disorder criteria according to DSM-IV-R [13] include somatic symptoms [48]. Another prospective study [49] of 332 pre-adolescent cases with functional abdominal pain compared to controls found elevated odds ratios of lifetime anxiety disorder (OR = 4.9) and anxiety disorder at time of follow up (OR = 3.6) in early adulthood. This study also showed that anxiety problems often persisted at follow up, even when gastrointestinal complaints had resolved. Egger, Costello, Erkanli and Angold [50] found in their population study of 9–16-year-old children that somatic complaints were strongly associated with emotional disorders in girls and with disruptive behaviors in boys. Specifically, boys with stomach aches had an increased OR of comorbid ODD (3.6) and ADHD (3.5). Interestingly, for girls an elevated OR for stomach aches comorbid to anxiety disorder was only seen in combination with another somatic complaint (headaches or musculoskeletal pain) in that study.

Description of co-twins of probands with restrictive eating problems

Eating disorders are known to be at least moderately heritable. The heritability of AN was reported at 56% in a large genetic review [51] while Thornton, Mazzeo, & Bulik [52] quote heritability estimates for BN at 54–83% and binge eating disorder at 41–57%. Our findings that concordant REP is more often found in MZ than in DZ twins seems to strengthen previous findings about the importance of genetic background factors. There was a higher concordance rate found for REP in girls than in boys. These findings suggest a gender difference in the heritability pattern of REP and support the hypothesis formulated by Strober et al. [53] that eating disorders in men are more serious and require a greater loading of genes or adverse familial environmental factors for its expression compared to that in females.

Eating disorders have been suggested to be neurodevelopmental conditions [54]. In our study, there was a considerable overlap between REP probands and their co-twins with regards to either concordant REP, or co-occurring REP and neurodevelopmental problems. These findings suggest that REP potentially should be covered under the broad, thorough and holistic multidisciplinary assessments of Early Symptomatic Syndromes Eliciting Neurodevelopmental Clinical Examinations (ESSENCE) as suggested by Gillberg [55].

Comorbidity - clinical and public health implications

There is not one single given definition of comorbidity generally [56] or in the area of child neurodevelopmental problems specifically [55], but comorbidity is here, as often, defined as co-existence of at least two separate diagnosed disorders whether or not they share a common pathophysiology. In the clinic, there is significant overlap in symptoms between different disorders, in the somatic as well as the psychiatric field, and at least in the neurodevelopmental field, children often move across diagnostic categories over time [55].

In general terms and for a range of conditions, the presence of comorbidities has been associated with multiple negative outcomes, including worse psychological and somatic health outcomes per se, and reduced quality of life and impaired overall function [48, 56].

For health care practitioners challenges include more complex clinical management [56], with increasing demands on interface with other agencies, and an increased risk of complications e.g. polypharmacy. The presence of comorbidities is also associated with costs that increase exponentially as the number of chronic conditions increases [56].

The challenges of comorbidity and their persistence thus call for well worked out and integrated pathways between family doctors, pediatricians and child psychiatrists and consideration of establishing multidisciplinary teams branching these specialties for children with significant eating problems.

Limitations

This study has some important limitations. As previously described [57], the screening diagnosis of REP in the current version of A-TAC has not been formally validated. However, the criteria in the interview to get a screening diagnosis of REP are strict: a combination of weight loss/lack of weight gain for a whole year and having expressed fear of gaining weight or growing fat is required, making screening cases likely not only to be clinically significant but also indicating individuals at risk for developing formal eating disorders if they do not already have them [11].

An obvious limitation is that this is not a clinical sample, and individuals were identified as having gastrointestinal problems with parental report rather than by physician diagnosis. Parents generally have a fairly good knowledge about existence of children's gastrointestinal symptoms but not necessarily the exact nature of the problem [58, 59].

As a cross-sectional study, this research establishes association between REP and somatic / psychiatric symptoms. It does not however examine causality of symptoms. Further research is warranted to examine symptom development and the pathological processes at play.

Further, the study population utilized was twins and this means that absolute prevalence numbers should be interpreted with some caution.

Finally, despite drawing on a large number of study participants, REPs are relatively uncommon in prepubertal children. This has a limiting effect of the power to detect significant differences between REP cases and controls.

Conclusions

Restrictive eating problems increased the odds of comorbidities for all psychiatric problems studied, in particular for autism spectrum disorders. Girls with restrictive eating problems had increased odds of having lactose intolerance and constipation. The heterogeneous eating problems are often resistant to treatment, especially if underlying neurodevelopmental problems are neglected. A transdiagnostic approach will be useful to the development of characterisation, diagnostic formulation, and targeted intervention in eating disorders.

The study shows the importance of considering comorbidities in clinical assessment of children with restrictive eating problems.

Abbreviations

ADHD: Attention deficit / hyperactivity disorder; AN: Anorexia nervosa; ARFID: Avoidant/restrictive food intake disorder; ASD: Autism spectrum disorder; A-TAC: The Autism-Tics, AD/HD and other Comorbidities inventory; BN: Bulimia nervosa; CATSS: Child and adolescent twin study in Sweden; CD: Conduct disorder; ds: Different sex; DSM-5: Diagnostic and Statistical Manual of Mental Disorders, 5th ed; DSM-IV-R: Diagnostic and Statistical Manual of Mental Disorders, 4th ed. revised; DZ: Dizygotic; LD: Learning disorder; MZ: Monozygotic; OCD: Obsessive-compulsive disorder; ODD: Oppositional defiant disorder; OR: Odds ratio; REP: Restrictive eating problems; ss: Same sex; TD: Tics disorder

Acknowledgements

The authors would like to acknowledge the families who participated in this study.

Funding

This research was supported, in parts, by grants from ALF i Skåne - Agreement concerning research and education of doctors; and Dr. Sten Theander's foundation for research in Anorexia Nervosa. The funding agencies had no roles in the preparation or the content of the paper.

Authors' contributions

JT, MR and NK jointly identified the research question and designed the study. PL, MR and HA gained ethical approval and supplied the raw data which NK extracted. JT and NK performed all data analysis. All authors provided interpretation of data. JT, MR and NK wrote the draft manuscript. PL and HA critically reviewed the manuscript and suggested revisions. All authors read and approved the final manuscript.

Competing interests

The authors declare that they have no competing interests.

Author details

[1]Lund University, Medical Faculty, Department of Clinical Sciences Lund, Child and Adolescent Psychiatry, Baravägen 1, S-221 85 Lund, Sweden. [2]Gillberg Neuropsychiatry Centre, University of Gothenburg, Gothenburg, Sweden. [3]Department of Medical Epidemiology and Biostatistics, Karolinska

Institutet, Stockholm, Sweden. [4]CELAM (Centre for Ethics, Law and Mental Health), Institute of Neuroscience and Physiology, University of Gothenburg, Gothenburg, Sweden. [5]Department of Health Sciences, University West, Trollhättan, Sweden.

References

1. Le Grange D, O'Connor M, Hughes EK, Macdonald J, Little K, Olsson CA. Developmental antecedents of abnormal eating attitudes and behaviors in adolescence. Int J Eat Disord. 2014;447:813–24. doi:10.1002/eat.22331.
2. Kelly NR, Shank LM, Bakalar JL, Tanofsky-Kraff M. Pediatric feeding and eating disorders: current state of diagnosis and treatment. Curr Psychiatry Rep. 2014;16:446. doi:10.1007/s11920-014-0446-z.
3. American Psychiatric Association. Diagnostic and statistical manual of mental disorders. 5th ed. Washington, DC: Author; 2013.
4. Nicholls DE, Viner RM. Childhood risk factors for lifetime anorexia nervosa by age 30 years in a national birth cohort. J Am Acad Child Adolesc Psychiatry. 2009;48:791–9. doi:10.1097/CHI.0b013e3181ab8b75.
5. Kotler LA, Cohen P, Davies M, Pine DS, Walsh BT. Longitudinal relationships between childhood, adolescent and adult eating disorders. J Am Acad Child Adolesc Psychiatry. 2001;40:1434–40. doi:10.1097/00004583-200112000-00014.
6. Råstam M, Täljemark J, Tajnia A, Lundström S, Gustafsson P, et al. Eating problems and overlap with ADHD and autism spectrum disorders in a nationwide twin study of 9- and 12-year old children. Scientific World J. 2013; doi:10.1155/2013/315429.
7. Salbach-Andrae H, Lenz K, Simmendinger N, Klindowski N, Lehmkuhl U, Pfeiffer E. Psychiatric comorbidities among female adolescents with anorexia nervosa. Child Psychiatry Hum Dev. 2008;39:261–72. doi:10.1007/s10578-007-0086-1.
8. Rosen DS. American Academy of Pediatrics Committee on Adolescence. Identification and management of eating disorders in children and adolescents. Pediatrics. 2010;126:1240–53. doi:10.1542/peds.2010-2821.
9. Fisher MM, Rosen DS, Ornstein RM, Mammel KA, Katzman DK, et al. Characteristics of avoidant/restrictive food intake disorder in children and adolescents: a "new disorder" in DSM-5. J Adolesc Health. 2014;55:49–52. doi:10.1016/j.jadohealth.2013.11.013.
10. Anckarsäter H, Lundström S, Kollberg L, Kerekes N, Palm C, et al. The Child and Adolescent Twin Study in Sweden (CATSS). Twin Res Hum Genet. 2011; 14:495–508. doi:10.1375/twin.14.16.495.
11. Hannelius U, Gherman L, Mäkelä W, Lindstedt A, Zucchelli M, et al. Large-scale zygosity testing using single nucleotide polymorphisms. Twin Res Hum Genet. 2007;10:604–25. doi:10.1375/twin.10.4.604.
12. Larson T, Anckarsäter H, Gillberg C, Ståhlberg O, Carlström E, et al. The Autism-Tics, AD/HD and other Comorbidities inventory (A-TAC): further validation of a telephone interview for epidemiological research. BMC Psychiatry. 2010;10:1. doi:10.1186/1471-244X-10-1.
13. American Psychiatric Association. Diagnostic and statistical manual of mental disorders. 4th ed. Washington, DC: Author; 2000. text rev
14. Kerekes N, Lundström S, Chang Z, Tajnia A, Jern P, et al. Oppositional defiant- and conduct disorder-like problems: neurodevelopmental predictors and genetic background in boys and girls, in a nationwide twin study. PeerJ. 2014;2e:359. doi:10.7717/peerj.359.
15. Larson T, Kerekes N, Selinus EN, Lichtenstein P, Gumpert CH, et al. Reliability of Autism-Tics, AD/HD, and other Comorbidities (A-TAC) inventory in a test-retest design. Psychol Rep. 2014;114:93–103. doi:10.1186/1471-244X-10-1.
16. Lundström S, Reichenberg A, Melke J, Råstam M, Kerekes N, et al. Autism spectrum disorders and coexisting disorders in a nationwide Swedish twin study. J Am Acad Child Adolesc Psychiatry. 2015;56:702–10. doi:10.1111/jcpp.12329.
17. Ford T, Goodman R, Meltzer H. The British child and adolescent mental health survey 1999: the prevalence of DSM-IV disorders. J Am Acad Child Adolesc Psychiatry. 2003;42:1203–11. doi:10.1097/00004583-200310000-00011.
18. Muise AM, Stein DG, Arbess G. Eating disorders in adolescent boys: a review of the adolescent and young adult literature. J Adolesc Health. 2003;33:427–35. doi:10.1016/S1054-139X(03)00060-0.
19. Raevuori A, Keski-Rahkonen A, Hoek HW. A review of eating disorders in males. Curr Opin Psychiatry. 2014;27:426–30. doi:10.1097/YCO.0000000000000113.
20. Kinasz K, Accurso EC, Kass AE, Le Grange D. Does sex matter in the clinical presentation of eating disorders in youth? J Adolesc Health. 2016;58:410–6. doi:10.1016/j.jadohealth.2015.11.005.
21. Flament MF, Henderson K, Buchholz A, Obeid N, Nguyen NH, et al. Weight Status and DSM-5 eating disorders of eating disorders in adolescents from the community. J Am Acad Child Adolesc Psychiatry. 2015;54:403–11. doi:10.1016/j.jaac.2015.01.020.
22. Hudson JI, Hiripi E, Pope HG Jr, Kessler RC. The prevalence and correlates of eating disorders in the national comorbidity survey replication. Biol Psychiatry. 2007;61:348–58. doi:10.1016/j.biopsych.2006.03.040.
23. Sharp WG, Berry RC, McCracken C, Nuhu NN, Marvel E, et al. Feeding problems and nutrient intake in children with autism spectrum disorders: a meta-analysis and comprehensive review of the literature. J Autism Dev Disord. 2013;43:2159–73. doi:10.1007/s10803-013-1771-5.
24. Kerekes N, Tajnia A, Lichtenstein P, Lundström S, Anckarsäter H, et al. Neurodevelopmental problems and extremes in BMI. PeerJ. 2015;3e:1024. doi:10.7717/peerj.1024.
25. Gal E, Hardal-Nasser R, Engel-Yeger B. The relationship between the severity of eating problems and intellectual development deficit level. Res Dev Disabil. 2011;32:1464–9. doi:10.1016/j.ridd.2010.12.003.
26. Hove O. Prevalence of eating disorders in adults with mental retardation living in the community. Am J Ment Retard. 2004;109:501–6. doi:10.1352/0895-8017(2004)109<501:POEDIA>2.0.CO;2.
27. Gravestock S. Eating disorders in adults with intellectual disability. J Intellect Disabil Res. 2000;44:625–37. doi:10.1111/j.1365-2788.2000.00308.x.
28. Godart NT, Flament MF, Perdereau F, Jeammet P. Comorbidity between eating disorders and anxiety disorders: a review. Int J Eat Disord. 2002;32: 253–70. doi:10.1002/eat.10096.
29. Wentz E, Gillberg IC, Anckarsäter H, Gillberg C, Råstam M. Adolescent-onset anorexia nervosa: 18-year outcome. Br J Psychiatry. 2009;194:168–74. doi:10.1192/bjp.bp.107.048686.
30. Kaye WH, Bulik CM, Thornton L, Barbarich N, Masters K. Comorbidity of anxiety disorders with anorexia nervosa and bulimia nervosa. Am J Psychiat. 2004;161:2215–21. doi:10.1176/appi.ajp.161.12.2215.
31. Torresan RC, Ramos-Cerqueira AT, Shavitt RG, do Rosário MC, de Mathis MA, et al. Symptom dimensions, clinical course and comorbidity in men and women with obsessive-compulsive disorder. Psychiatry Res. 2013;209:186–95. doi:10.1016/j.psychres.2012.12.006.
32. Equit M, Pälmke M, Becker N, Moritz AM, Becker S, von Gontard A. Eating problems in young children – a population-based study. Acta Paediatr. 2013;102:149–55. doi:10.1111/apa.12078.
33. Korterink JJ, Diederen K, Benninga MA, Tabbers MM. Epidemiology of pediatric functional abdominal pain disorders: a meta-analysis. PLoS One. 2015;10:e0126982. doi:10.1371/journal.pone.0126982.
34. Wise EA, Price DD, Myers CD, Heft MW, Robinson ME. Gender role expectations of pain: relationship to experimental pain perception. Pain. 2002;96:335–42. doi:10.1016/j.pain.2009.06.028.
35. van den Berg MM, Benninga MA, Di Lorenzo C. Epidemiology of childhood constipation: a systematic review. Am J Gastroenterol. 2006;101:2401–9. doi:10.1111/j.1572-0241.2006.00771.x.
36. Rubin G, Dale A. Chronic constipation in children. Br Med J. 2006;333:1051–5. doi:10.1136/bmj.39007.760174.47.
37. Kaluski DN, Natamba BK, Goldsmith R, Shimony T, Berry EM. Determinants of disordered eating behaviors among Israeli adolescent girls. Eat Disord. 2008; 16:146–59. doi:10.1080/10640260801887303.
38. Kamal N, Chami T, Andersen A, Rosell FA, Schuster MM, Whitehead WE. Delayed gastrointestinal transit times in anorexia nervosa and bulimia nervosa. Gastroenterology. 1991;101:1320–4. http://dx.doi.org/10.1016/0016-5058(91)90083-W
39. Arnaud MJ. Mild dehydration: a risk factor for constipation? Eur J Clin Nutr. 2003;57(Suppl 2):S88–95. doi:10.1038/sj.ecn.16019007.
40. Roma E, Adamidis D, Nikolara R, Constantopoulus A, Messaritakis J. Diet and chronic constipation in children: the role of fiber. J Pediatr Gastroenterol Nutr. 1999;28:169–74. doi:10.1097/00005176-199902000-00015.
41. Sileri P, Franceschilli L, De Lorenzo A, Mezzani B, Todisco P, et al. Defecatory disorders in anorexia nervosa: a clinical study. Tech Coloproctol. 2014;18: 439–44. doi:10.1007/s10151-013-1068-x.
42. Heyman MB. Lactose intolerance in infants, children and adolescents. Pediatrics. 2006;118:1279–86. doi:10.1542/peds.2006-1721.
43. Guarino A, Lo Vecchio A, Berni CR. Chronic diarrhoea in children. Best Pract Res Clin Gastroenterol. 2012;26:649–61. doi:10.1016/j.bpg.2012.11.004.

44. McElhanon BO, McCracken C, Karpen S, Sharp WG. Gastrointestinal symptoms in autism spectrum disorders: a meta-analysis. Pediatrics. 2014; 133:872–83. doi:10.1542/peds.2013-3995.
45. Silber TJ. Anorexia nervosa among children and adolescents. Adv Paediatr. 2005;52:49–76. doi:10.1016/j.yapd.2005.03.003.
46. Eddy KT, Thomas JJ, Hastings E, Edkins K, Lamont E, et al. Prevalence of DSM-5 avoidant/restrictive food intake disorder in a pediatric gastroenterology healthcare network. Int J Eat Disord. 2015;48:464–70. doi: 10.1002/eat.22350.
47. Campo JV, Bridge J, Ehmann M, Altman S, Lucas A, et al. Recurrent abdominal pain, anxiety, and depression in primary care. Pediatrics. 2004; 113:817–24. doi:10.1111/j.1365-2214.2004.00456_1.x.
48. Ramsawh HJ, Chavira DA, Stein MB. The burden of anxiety disorders in pediatric medical settings: prevalence, phenomenology and a research agend. Arch Paediatr Adolesc Med. 2010;164:956–72. doi:10.1001/ archpediatrics.2010.170.
49. Shelby GD, Shirkey KC, Sherman AL, Beck JE, Haman K, et al. Functional abdominal pain in childhood and long-term vulnerability to anxiety disorders. Pediatrics. 2013;132:475–82. doi:10.1542/peds.2012-2191.
50. Egger HL, Costello EJ, Erkanli A, Angold A. Somatic complaints and psychopathology in children and adolescents: stomach aches, musculoskeletal pains, and headaches. J Am Acad Child Adolesc Psychiatry. 1999;38:852–60. http://dx.doi.org/10.1097/00004583-199907000-00015
51. Sullivan PF, Daly MJ, O'Donovan M. Genetic architecture of psychiatric disorders: the emerging picture and its implications. Nat Rev Genet. 2012;13: 537–51. doi:10.1038/nrg3240.
52. Thornton LM, Mazzeo SE, Bulik CM. The heritability of eating disorders: methods and current findings. Curr Top Behav Neurosci. 2011;6:141–56. doi: 10.1007/7854_2010_91.
53. Strober M, Freeman R, Lampert C, Diamond J, Kaye W. Males with anorexia nervosa: a controlled study of eating disorders in first-degree relatives. Int J Eat Disord. 2001;29:263–9. doi:10.1002/eat.1017.
54. Connan F, Campbell IC, Katzman M, Lightman SL, Treasure J. A neurodevelopmental model for anorexia nervosa. Physiol Behav. 2003;79: 13–24. doi:10.1016/S0031-9384(03)00101-X.
55. Gillberg C. The ESSENCE in child psychiatry: Early Symptomatic Syndromes Eliciting Neurodevelopmental Clinical Examinations. Res Dev Disabil. 2010; 31:1543–51. doi:10.1016/j.ridd.2010.06.002.
56. Valderas JM, Starfield B, Sibbald B, Salisbury C, Roland M. Defining comorbidity: implications for understanding health and health services. Ann Fam Med. 2009;7:357–63. doi:10.1370/afm.983.
57. Anckarsäter H, Larson T, Hansson SL, Carlström E, Ståhlberg O, et al. Child neurodevelopmental and behavioural problems are intercorrelated and dimensionally distributed in the general population. Open Psychiatry J. 2008;2:5–11. doi:10.2174/1874354400802010005.
58. Gorrindo P, Williams KC, Lee EB, Walker LS, McGrew SG, Levitt P. Gastrointestinal dysfunction in autism: parental report, clinical evaluation, and associated factors. Autism Res. 2012;5:101–8. doi:10.1002/aur.237.
59. van Tillburg MA, Squires M, Blos-Martin N, Leiby A, Langseder A. Test of the child/adolescent Rome III criteria: agreement with physician diagnosis and daily function. Neurogastroenterol Motil. 2013;25:302–e246. doi:10.1111/ nmo.12056.

2

Specialized group intervention for compulsive exercise in inpatients with eating disorders: feasibility and preliminary outcomes

Nina Dittmer[1,2*], Ulrich Voderholzer[1,3], Mareike von der Mühlen[1], Michael Marwitz[1], Markus Fumi[1], Claudia Mönch[1], Katharina Alexandridis[1], Ulrich Cuntz[1,4], Corinna Jacobi[2] and Sandra Schlegl[5]

Abstract

Background: Patients with eating disorders (ED) often suffer from compulsive exercise behavior, which is associated with lower short-term response to treatment and poorer long-term outcome. Evidence-based interventions specifically targeting compulsive exercise behavior have been scarce so far. We developed a manualized group therapeutic approach integrating cognitive-behavioral therapy, exercise therapy and exposure with response management to promote healthy exercise behavior. Our objective was to examine the feasibility and acceptance of this new approach as add-on to regular inpatient treatment in a pilot study. Additionally, we wanted to estimate preliminary effect sizes.

Methods: Thirty-two female, adolescent and adult eating disordered inpatients were recruited. According to the 4th ed. of the Diagnostic and Statistical Manual of Mental Disorders (DSM-IV), twenty-six patients met criteria for Anorexia nervosa (AN), two for Bulimia nervosa and four for eating disorder not otherwise specified. Semi-structured interviews were conducted for qualitative evaluation of feasibility and acceptance of the new intervention. Patients completed the Commitment to Exercise Scale (CES) and the Compulsive Exercise Test (CET) for assessment of compulsive exercise, the Eating Disorder Inventory-2 for assessment of eating disorder pathology, the Beck Depression Inventory-II and Brief Symptom Inventory for assessment of depressive and general psychopathology and the Emotion Regulation Skills Questionnaire for assessment of emotion regulation before the beginning and at the end of the group intervention. Additionally, weight gain was monitored.

Results: Feasibility of our approach was confirmed. All patients reported a high satisfaction with both structure and content of the group. Between pre- and post-intervention, patients showed significant reductions in compulsive exercise (effect size CES: 1.44; effect size CET total: 0.93), drive for thinness (effect size: 0.48), depressive symptoms (effect size: 0.36), general psychopathology (effect size: 0.29) and acceptance of emotions (effect size: − 0.62). Patients with AN also showed significant mean weight gain during the intervention (effect size: − 0.44).

Conclusions: Results of our pilot study indicate that our integrative approach to compulsive exercise in ED patients might represent a promising new therapeutic option. Feasibility and acceptance of the intervention were confirmed. Preliminary effect sizes on most outcomes were promising. As improvements in Body-mass-index, eating disorder and general psychopathology are also to be expected by routine inpatient treatment, a large randomized trial is currently underway to evaluate the efficacy of this new intervention.

Keywords: Eating disorders, Compulsive exercise, Inpatient treatment, Specialized group intervention, Feasibility

* Correspondence: NDittmer@schoen-kliniken.de
[1]Schoen Clinic Roseneck, Am Roseneck 6, Prien am Chiemsee, Germany
[2]Department of Clinical Psychology and E-Mental-Health, Technische Universität Dresden, Dresden, Germany
Full list of author information is available at the end of the article

Plain English summary

Patients with eating disorders often suffer from compulsive exercise behavior, which is associated with lower short-term treatment success and poorer long-term outcome. Interventions specifically targeting compulsive exercise behavior are scarce. We developed a structured group therapy to promote healthy exercise behavior by reducing both the compulsive nature and excessive amount of the patients' exercise behavior. We evaluated our new approach in inpatients with eating disorders in a first small study: All patients reported a high satisfaction with both structure and content of the group. During participation in the group therapy, patients showed strong reductions in compulsive exercise behavior, eating disorder and depressive symptoms. Underweight patients also showed a relevant weight gain. Due to these promising results we are currently evaluating this new therapeutic approach in a large clinical trial.

Background

Eating disorders (ED) are serious psychiatric disorders often associated with a chronic course and significantly elevated mortality rates [1–3]. A common and distinctive symptom of Anorexia nervosa (AN) known for over 100 years is excessive physical activity despite severe emaciation [4]. Compulsive exercise behavior is observed in 31% to 81% of adolescent and adult patients with AN depending on assessment method, sample and measure used to assess compulsive exercise [4–7].

Several studies have shown compulsive exercise to be associated with longer hospital stays and higher rates of suicidal behavior. It also represents a significant predictor for relapse and chronic course of the eating disorder [8–11]. A review of the existing literature found higher levels of dietary restraint [5, 12], anxiety [13–15] and depression [12, 15] to be consistently associated with compulsive exercise in AN. A high level of physical activity, retrospectively assessed before the onset of the ED during adolescence can also be regarded as potential risk factor for AN [6, 16, 17]. Furthermore, obsessive-compulsive symptoms and AN-subtype may be risk factors for compulsive exercise [12, 15, 18]. In the past years, it has been suggested that hypoleptinemia may represent an underlying endocrinological factor driving hyperactivity in AN [19, 20].

Although examined less frequently compared with AN, between 20% and 57% of patients with Bulimia nervosa (BN) are reported to show compulsive exercise behavior [6, 15, 21]. For BN, "excessive exercise" at a frequency of at least twice per week for three months was explicitly listed as one of several inappropriate compensatory behaviors in the 4th ed. of the Diagnostic and Statistical Manual of Mental Disorders (DSM-IV) [22]. In the 5th ed. of the Diagnostic and Statistical Manual of Mental Disorders (DSM-5) [23], the frequency of "excessive exercise" as a compensatory behavior was reduced to once per week for three months. In both DSM-IV and DSM-5, only the quantitative dimension of this behavior was taken into account.

Despite the importance of the phenomenon, there has so far been no consensus concerning terminology and definition of compulsive exercise: Several studies defined "excessive exercise" based on quantitative features such as exercise frequency, intensity and duration [12, 14, 24, 25]. Other studies specifically emphasized the compulsive, ritualized and uncontrollable quality of "compulsive exercise" [26–28] or even regarded it as culturally rooted variant of Obsessive-compulsive disorder (OCD) [25]. However, a recent Delphi Study by Noetel and colleagues [29] found "compulsive exercise" to be the preferred term for describing the phenomenon. Consensus was reached among the international group of experts that a definition of compulsive exercise should consider both quantitative and qualitative dimensions [29]. Recent studies indicate that compulsive exercise is maintained by a complex interplay of different factors - compulsivity, difficulties in emotion regulation, weight and shape concerns and rigid and perfectionistic personality traits [15, 18, 30, 31].

In our opinion, a comprehensive treatment rationale targeting several of these factors is called for to address the complexity of the behavior including the following:

1. Elements of Cognitive-behavioral therapy (CBT) like psychoeducation and cognitive restructuring are essential in challenging dysfunctional beliefs about exercise, weight and shape [29, 32].
2. Exposure and response prevention strategies are needed to target the compulsive quality of the exercise behavior, as they are considered the first-choice intervention for OCD [32]. Recent recommendations for ED interventions put a special focus on exposure treatment [33, 34], further validating the integration of exposure in a treatment protocol for compulsive exercise.
3. ED patients experience higher levels of emotion intensity, have more difficulties in acceptance of emotions and in emotion regulation and show increased use of dysfunctional emotion regulation strategies compared to healthy controls [35]. Compulsive exercise may serve as emotion regulation strategy similar to food restriction or bulimic behaviors [14, 24, 31, 36]. Training affected patients in new and functional long-term emotion regulation strategies seems paramount.
4. Supporting the normalization of eating behavior by supervised meals is considered a central element of general ED treatment [34, 37, 38]. In analogy, a

therapeutic approach for compulsive exercise should include exercise-based elements directly supporting normalization of exercise behavior.

In the 1980s and 1990s, first treatment approaches applied response prevention techniques including one hour of supervised bed rest after meals to reduce compulsive exercise behavior [39]. A 2005 review by Hechler and colleagues [40] showed that unstructured psycho-education, self-monitoring of daily physical activity and cognitive restructuring were the most frequently used treatment approaches.

Recently, two new treatment approaches were developed: Hay and colleagues [41] recently conducted a multicenter randomized controlled trial (RCT) in an outpatient setting evaluating a new CBT-based treatment approach. Schlegel and colleagues [42] developed an exercise-based program for outpatients which is currently being evaluated in an RCT.

According to the rationale outlined above, we consider it essential for a leap forward in the management of compulsive exercise to address several of the maintaining factors like compulsivity, emotion regulation or distorted cognitions as well as the establishment of a healthy exercise behavior simultaneously. A therapeutic approach that corresponds to this demand by comprising CBT-based and exercise-based elements is still missing.

Our team aimed to fill this gap to further improve treatment options for affected patients:

We developed an innovative therapeutic approach for compulsive exercise behavior integrating CBT, exposure and response prevention, emotion regulation techniques and exercise-based elements in one manualized group therapeutic approach. The current study aimed to examine feasibility and acceptance of this new specific approach as add-on to regular inpatient treatment in a pilot study. Additionally we aimed at obtaining pre-post data to estimate preliminary effect sizes of the intervention.

Methods

Sample

Our sample consisted of $N = 32$ female adolescent and adult ED inpatients admitted to a large hospital for behavioral medicine in Germany (Schoen Clinic Roseneck; Prien am Chiemsee) between November 2012 and January 2013.

Inclusion criteria were: (1) DSM-IV diagnosis of AN (307.1), BN (307.51) and atypical AN or BN/Eating disorder not otherwise specified (EDNOS) (307.50), (2) presence of compulsive exercise, which was defined based on modified DSM-IV criteria for OCD, thereby taking into account qualitative and quantitative dimensions (Table 1), (3) age: 14–45 years, (4) informed written consent and, in case of minors, additional informed written consent by legal guardians.

Table 1 Working definition of compulsive exercise

Compulsive exercise
A. Compulsive exercise as defined by (1) and (2): 1) Repetitive exercise that the person feels driven to perform in response to an obsession or according to rules that must be applied rigidly 2) The exercise is aimed at preventing or reducing distress or at preventing some dreaded event or situation; however the compulsive exercise is clearly excessive
B. At some point during the course of the disorder the person has recognized that the compulsive exercising is excessive or unreasonable
C. The compulsive exercise causes marked distress, is time-consuming (takes more than one hour a day), significantly interferes with the person's normal routine, occupational functioning, usual social activities or relationships or is continued despite medical injury or illness
Criteria A. + C. are considered obligatory, whereas criterion B. is optional

Exclusion criteria were: (1) body-mass-index (BMI) < 13 kg/m^2 at the beginning of the intervention, (2) drug, alcohol or other substance abuse, (3) presence of additional severe psychiatric (i.e. psychotic and bipolar disorders) or neurological diseases (i.e. multiple sclerosis) and suicidality, (4) concurrent treatment for OCD, (5) severe somatic complications prohibiting light to moderate supervised exercise, and (6) marked cognitive impairment due to underweight severe enough to preclude attending and following a 100 min group session. The clinical assessment of cognitive impairment was based on the Association for Methodology and Documentation in Psychiatry (AMDP) System [43]: Patients had to report moderate or severe deficits in comprehension, attention span and short- or long-term memory or these deficits had to be observable by the clinician during the screening procedure.

The intervention

The intervention represents a combination of routine inpatient treatment and a specific intervention for the promotion of healthy exercise behavior as add-on intervention.

Routine treatment

The specialized inpatient treatment for patients with ED consists of a multimodal cognitive-behavioral approach and intense psychiatric and internist treatment. All patients receive individual treatment twice per week, a non-specific problem-solving group treatment three times per week and take part in a manualized, symptom-oriented group intervention for ED patients. Furthermore, all ED patients participate in supervised meals three times per day, meal preparation classes, social skills training and art therapy. Patients can also take part in exercise therapy depending on their weight and physical condition. All underweight patients are required to gain at least 700 g per week, which is monitored by bi-weekly weight checks and visualized on individual weight charts. If no sufficient weight gain is reached, further steps include an increase of food intake, administration of high caloric fluids or – in very severe cases – nasal tube feeding.

"Healthy exercise behavior" intervention

In addition to routine treatment, all ED patients who participated in the present study took part in a specific manualized group intervention called "Healthy exercise behavior (HEB)" which specifically targets compulsive exercise behavior. The overarching goal of this intervention is threefold: First, to reduce the excessive quantity of the exercise behavior and reestablish "healthy" exercise behavior, taking into account each patient's current weight and general health condition. Second, to reduce the compulsive quality of the exercise behavior and establish a more flexible exercise regimen. Third, to re-experience joy, social interaction and relaxation when exercising.

The HEB intervention is manual-based, comprises eight sessions (of 100 min), takes place twice a week and is delivered by a clinical psychologist and a sports therapist. It is conceptualized as closed group for eight to ten patients with sequential sessions. During each session, cognitive-behavioral as well as exercise-based treatment elements complement each other. Between the sessions, patients are required to complete homework tasks (e.g. behavioral analyses or interviews with peers). Group sessions are supplemented by individual graded exposure and response prevention tasks concerning exercise behavior guided by one of the therapists. Table 2 summarizes the content of each group session.

Procedure

Patients were recruited consecutively during inpatient treatment. Eligible participants answered a number of screening questions covering inclusion and exclusion criteria. Subsequently, they received detailed information on the study and gave informed written consent to participate. For minors, an additional briefing of their legal guardians was provided via telephone. Informed consent forms were sent out to the legal guardians and had to be signed and returned. Outcome measures were compulsive exercise, BMI, ED psychopathology and general psychopathology assessed within three days before the beginning and after termination of HEB group.

Following the intervention, semi-structured interviews were conducted by an independent clinician, where patients were given the opportunity for detailed feedback concerning general set-up, therapeutic value and content of the group therapy.

The study protocol was approved by the ethics committee of the University Hospital of Ludwig Maximilian University Munich (project number: 060–13).

Measures

Measures for assessment of eligibility

Structured Interview for Anorexic and Bulimic Disorders for DSM-IV and ICD-10 (SIAB-EX): The SIAB-EX is a semi-standardized expert rating for the assessment of ED symptoms and frequent additional symptoms. For the current study, the diagnostically relevant questions of the SIAB-EX [44] were employed.

Assessment of compulsive exercise: Compulsive exercise was assessed by modified questions of The Structured Clinical Interview for DSM-IV Axis I Disorders (SCID-I) [45, 46] for OCD (section F: anxiety disorders). The questions of this clinical interview can be found in the Appendix.

Feasibility and intervention acceptance

For assessment of feasibility and intervention acceptance, we assessed recruitment and retention rates, number of sessions attended, difficulties in integrating the study into routine inpatient treatment and conducted semi-structured interviews. In these interviews patients first rated their satisfaction with the structure of HEB on a 5-point Likert scale from 1 (= very satisfied) to 5 (= not at all satisfied). They also rated whether they would recommend the group to other affected patients (1 = full recommendation to 5 = no recommendation). Following that, they rated the overall helpfulness of HEB as well as which therapeutic topics they considered to be most helpful (1 = very helpful to 5 = not at all helpful). Patients were also asked what they especially liked about the respective therapeutic element and whether they had suggestions for improvement. Answers to these open questions were recorded and transcribed.

Outcome measures for pre-post assessment

Commitment to Exercise Scale (CES) The CES [47, 48] is an eight-item self-report measure frequently used for the assessment of compulsive exercise in patients with ED. It reflects obligatory and pathological aspects of exercise. Cronbach's α for the overall scale was calculated as 0.82 [48], indicating a good internal consistency. In accordance with Thome and colleagues [49], we used a 4-point Likert scale instead of the original answering format. Cronbach's α in our sample was 0.88, implying a good internal consistency. Convergent and divergent validity of the measure were shown [48].

Table 2 Content of "Healthy exercise behavior (HEB)" intervention

Symptom-oriented group intervention "Healthy exercise behavior (HEB)"			
Session	Content		
	CBT	Exercise therapy	Self-set goals for the next session
1	Introduction: structure, content and goals of HEB	Trying out different kinds of movement, playful[a] getting to know each other	
	Reflection of individual compulsive exercise behavior		
2	Risk situations for compulsive exercise	Life-kinetic exercise[b]	
	Behavioral analysis of compulsive exercise	Yoga	
3	Group: exposure rationale and preparation Individually: actual exposures		
	Norms concerning "healthy exercise": differentiation between healthy and compulsive exercise behavior	Partner exercise "walking"	
4	Norms concerning "healthy exercise": differentiation between healthy and compulsive exercise behavior	Playful[a] movement	
5	"Myths and facts": psychoeducation	Instructed exercise on body perception concerning different body structures	
6	Alternatives for coping with high stress	Trying out short, intense movement intervals for releasing high stress	
	Preparation: "One week with healthy leisure and exercise behavior"		
7	Alternative emotion regulation: emotions as guides for needs	Expressing basic emotions	
8	Review: "One week with healthy leisure and exercise behavior"	Trying out various kinds of exercise focusing on joyful, cooperative activities	
	Conclusion		

CBT Cognitive-behavioral therapy; [a] Playful: Exploration of movement that focuses on fun and social interaction instead of competition and energy consumption; [b] Life-kinetics: Mental training that increases physical and cognitive performance by exercises that impose both physical and cognitive demands

Compulsive Exercise Test (CET) The CET ([50]; Schlegl S, Dittmer N, Vierl L, Rauh E, Huber T, Voderholzer U: Validation of the German version of the Compulsive Exercise Test in patients with Eat Disord in preparation) is a self-report inventory that assesses additional aspects of compulsive exercise with five subscales: 1. Avoidance and Rule-driven behavior, 2. Weight Control Exercise, 3. Mood Improvement, 4. Lack of Exercise Enjoyment, and 5. Exercise Rigidity. The inventory consists of 24 items that are answered on a six-point Likert scale ranging from 0 ("never true") to 5 ("always true"). Cronbach's α for the overall scale was calculated as 0.85 [50], showing the good internal consistency of the CET.

Cronbach's α in our sample was 0.87, indicating a good internal consistency. Concurrent and divergent validity of the instrument were shown [50].

Eating Disorder Inventory-2 (EDI-2) The EDI-2 [51–53] is a 91-item multidimensional self-report questionnaire considered as gold standard for the assessment of core dimensions of disordered eating and related symptomatology. It consists of 11 subscales and can be applied for adolescents from age 13 onwards and adults. Cronbach's α for the overall scale was calculated as 0.96 [52], indicating an excellent internal consistency. In our sample Cronbach's α was 0.84, showing a good internal consistency. Convergent and divergent validity of the measure were shown [52, 53]. Beyond the three main subscales *Drive for Thinness, Bulimia* and *Body Dissatisfaction* of the EDI-2, we used the subscale *Perfectionism*, as perfectionism is considered an important personality characteristic for maintaining compulsive exercise behavior [31].

Beck Depression Inventory-II (BDI-II) The BDI-II [54, 55] is a self-report inventory that consists of 21 items and is widely used as a screening instrument for the presence and severity of depressive symptoms during the past two weeks. It may be used for adolescents and adults from age 13 onwards. Cronbach's α for the overall scale was between $0.89 \leq \alpha \leq 0.93$ in psychiatric samples [55], showing an excellent internal consistency. Cronbach's α in our sample was 0.90, indicating again an excellent internal consistency. Convergent and divergent validity of the measure were shown [55].

Brief Symptom Inventory (BSI) The BSI [56, 57] represents a 53-item self-report inventory that assesses subjective impairment by nine physical and psychological symptom groups. It can be used for adolescents and adults from age 13 onwards. Cronbach's α for the overall scale was calculated as 0.92 for adults [56], showing an excellent internal consistency. In our sample Cronbach's α was 0.96, indicating an excellent internal consistency. Validity of the instrument was shown [56].

Emotion Regulation Skills Questionnaire (ERSQ) The ERSQ [58] represents a 27-item self-report instrument that assesses the situation-adapted interplay of different emotion regulation abilities based on the Adaptive Coping with Emotions Model proposed by Berking [59]. It may be used for adolescents and adults from age 12 onwards [60]. Cronbach's α for the overall scale was calculated as 0.90, showing an excellent internal consistency [58]. In our sample Cronbach's α was 0.89, indicating again an excellent internal consistency. Validity of the instrument was shown [58]. Based on the findings of Svaldi and colleagues [35], we were especially interested in changes concerning acceptance of emotions and emotion regulation strategies, so we only used the subscales *Acceptance of Emotions* and *Emotion Regulation* of ERSQ.

Statistical procedures

Data were analyzed using Statistical Package of Social Science (SPSS) software (Version 20.0) [61]. For all outcomes, paired t-tests were used to assess pre-post changes. Effect sizes (ES) were calculated using the formula: $ES = \frac{M_{pre}-M_{post}}{SD_{pre}}$ as recommended for single group pre-post study designs [62]. Here, *Mpre* represents the sample mean of the respective variable before the intervention, *Mpost* the mean of the same variable after the intervention and *SDpre* the standard deviation of *Mpre*. An alpha level of $p \leq 0.05$ was applied to all statistical analyses.

Results

Participants

Of the 59 consecutively screened patients, 32 adolescent and adult female ED patients (adolescents: $n = 9$; adults: $n = 23$) were eligible: 26 patients met DSM-IV criteria for AN, two for BN and four for EDNOS. Concerning non-eligible patients, 17 patients did not meet inclusion criteria, three patients denied participation and seven patients were not eligible for other reasons. Clinical and demographic characteristics of the sample are presented in Table 3. Of the enrolled 32 patients, nine dropped out over the course of the study, 23 patients completed the study.

Feasibility and intervention acceptance

Recruitment rate was 54.2%, drop-out rate was 28.1%. However, only two patients (6.2%) specifically withdrew from HEB study while continuing inpatient treatment, the remaining seven patients dropped out of the entire inpatient treatment. All patients who completed the study attended seven to eight HEB sessions. The only difficulty in conducting the study in our inpatient setting was to find time slots where overlap with other treatment elements was minimized. Patients' satisfaction with the structure of HEB is summarized in Fig. 1.

Table 3 Clinical and demographic characteristics of the sample

Subtype of eating disorder, n (%)	
AN restrictive	19 (59.4%)
AN binge/purge	7 (21.9%)
BN non-purging	1 (3.1%)
BN purging	1 (3.1%)
Atypical AN and atypical BN/EDNOS	4 (12.5%)
Comorbid diagnoses, n (%)	
OCD	2 (6.3%)
MDD	29 (90.6%)
Age, years	
M (SD)	22.66 (8.25)
BMI at admission, kg/m^2	
M (SD)	15.41 (2.54)
Previous inpatient treatment, n	
M (SD)	1.44 (1.89)
Length current treatment, weeks	
M (SD)	15.69 (6.49)
Time from admission to participation in HEB, days	
M (SD)	42.03 (31.28)
Time spent with compulsive exercise, hours/day	
M (SD)	4.14 (2.74)

AN Anorexia nervosa, *BN* Bulimia nervosa, *EDNOS* Eating disorder not otherwise specified, *HEB* "Healthy exercise behavior" intervention, *OCD* Obsessive-compulsive disorder, *MDD* Major depressive Disorder, *BMI* Body-mass-index, *M* Mean, *SD* Standard deviation

Regarding recommendation of the intervention to other affected patients, 85% of the patients stated that they "fully recommend" participation in HEB, 15% stated that they would "strongly recommend" participation.-Concerning overall helpfulness of the intervention, 40% of the patients indicated that they regarded HEB as "very helpful", 45% as "pretty helpful" and 15% as "partially helpful". One patient stated after her participation that *"I made a lot of progress. Of course, I am not completely free of it, but that compulsion is much less. I have to go for a walk, I have to go running - those urges are gone."*

Figure 2 shows in detail, how the different therapeutic topics covered in HEB were evaluated. Patients especially appreciated the differentiation between healthy and compulsive exercise and the establishment of a healthy norm concerning exercise, psychoeducation and graded exposures. One patient described her astonishment *"that she [her healthy interview partner] does not exercise as much as I thought a normal person would to*

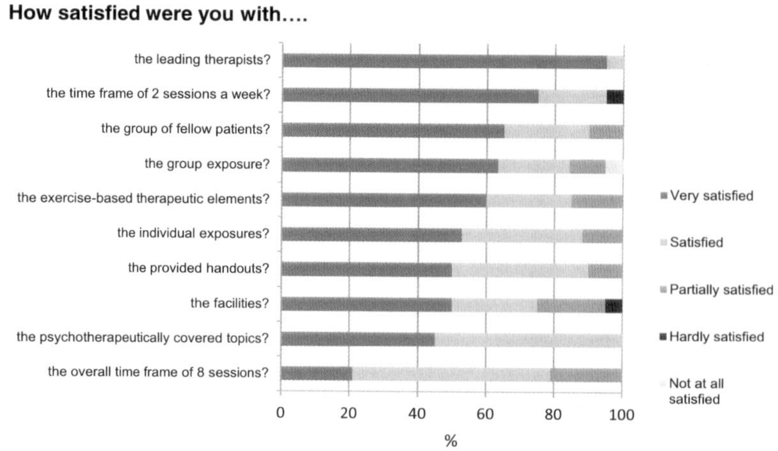

Fig. 1 Satisfaction with structure of HEB

stay slim.", followed by the insight *"And yeah, I really, extremely overdo it."*

Concerning graded exposures one patient pointedly described *"Yes, to really face my fears in this moment: fears of insane weight gain, fears of what is going to happen if I stop running. And to deal with the topics that arise if I do not run away all the time, literally run away...."*

Pre-post data

Pre-post changes in compulsive exercise behavior, weight and BMI, ED symptomatology, depressive symptoms, general psychopathology and emotion regulation as well as estimated ES are summarized in Table 4. Patients showed significant reductions in compulsive exercise behavior (effect size CES: 1.44; effect size CET total: 0.93), Drive for Thinness (effect size: 0.48), depressive symptoms (effect size: 0.36), general psychopathology (effect size: 0.29) and Acceptance of emotions (effect size: 0.62). Patients with AN also showed significant mean weight gain during the intervention (effect size: – 0.44).

Discussion

The aim of the present pilot study was to examine feasibility and acceptance of a newly developed, add-on intervention to inpatient treatment for compulsive exercise behavior in patients with ED. Additionally we aimed at obtaining preliminary pre-post data to estimate effect sizes of the intervention in preparation for a larger RCT to test the efficacy of the intervention. Our comprehensive approach integrating cognitive-behavioral, exercise-based and exposure and response prevention elements shows promising results:

Implementation of the HEB study proved to be feasible, recruitment and retention rates were comparable to large studies [63], and patients reported good satisfaction with both structure and therapeutic topics of the HEB intervention in qualitative interviews. All patients

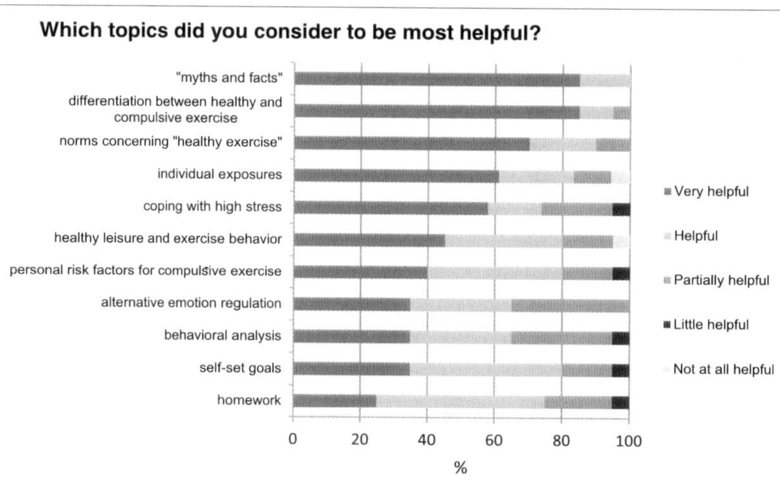

Fig. 2 Helpfulness of HEB topics

Table 4 Results of quantitative measures

Measure	Pre-Intervention Mean (SD)	Post-Intervention Mean (SD)	t	*p*	Effect size
Commitment to Exercise Scale	3.23 (0.55)	2.45 (0.56)	8.00	< 0.001	1.44
Compulsive Exercise Test					
Avoidance and Rule-driven Behavior	3.75 (1.06)	2.64 (0.98)	6.76	< 0.001	1.04
Weight Control Exercise	3.29 (1.24)	2.65 (1.07)	4.17	< 0.001	0.52
Mood Improvement	4.29 (0.78)	3.33 (1.09)	5.17	< 0.001	1.23
Lack of Exercise Enjoyment	1.71 (1.27)	1.92 (1.12)	−1.25	n.s.	
Exercise Rigidity	3.83 (1.06)	2.82 (1.03)	4.26	< 0.001	0.95
Total score	16.98 (3.88)	13.39 (3.43)	5.70	< 0.001	0.93
BMI (kg/m^2) of AN patients	15.67 (1.54)	16.35 (1.50)	−5.91	< 0.001	−0.44
Eating Disorder Inventory-2					
Drive for Thinness	12.81 (6.52)	9.67 (6.36)	5.62	< 0.001	0.48
Bulimia	0.98 (1.71)	0.54 (1.44)	1.65	n.s.	
Body Dissatisfaction	16.83 (7.16)	15.96 (7.18)	1.94	n.s.	
Perfectionism	8.23 (4.44)	6.83 (3.07)	2.37	0.027	0.26
Beck Depression Inventory-II	1.36 (0.55)	1.16 (0.55)	3.42	0.002	0.36
Brief Symptom Inventory (General Severity Index)	1.37 (0.65)	1.18 (0.61)	2.42	0.024	0.29
Emotion Regulation Skills Questionnaire					
Acceptance of Emotions	1.71 (0.89)	2.26 (0.79)	−3.47	0.002	−0.62
Regulation of Emotions	1.40 (0.82)	1.49 (0.79)	−0.68	n.s.	

BMI Body-mass-index, *M* Mean, *SD* Standard deviation

stated that they would recommend participation in the intervention to other affected patients, indicating a very high acceptance of the treatment protocol.

Patients showed significant reductions on the CES reflecting obligatory and pathological aspects of exercise. We found significant reductions with mostly high effect sizes on most CET subscales. Reductions were especially marked on those subscales which best reflect the compulsive nature of the exercise behavior (CET subscales *Avoidance and Rule-driven Behavior* and *Exercise Rigidity*). Additionally, we observed a significant reduction on the subscale *Mood Improvement,* implying that compulsive exercise was perceived as less enjoyable at the end of the intervention. This might be explained by confrontation with the negative consequences of the compulsive exercise during the HEB intervention. In addition to changes in compulsive exercise behavior, AN patients in our study achieved a significant weight gain. However, weight gain is considered one of the major goals of inpatient treatment, and in the absence of a control group it is unclear which part of the comprehensive intervention primarily drove the weight gain. Scores on patients' EDI-2 subscales *Drive for Thinness and Perfectionism* were reduced. The significant reductions in these two subscales are of particular importance, as eating pathology and perfectionism are considered key correlates of compulsive exercise in the maintenance model of compulsive exercise behavior proposed by Meyer and colleagues [31]. Over the four weeks of participation in the HEB intervention, patients' ability to *accept* unpleasant *emotions* when necessary increased. According to the Adaptive Coping with Emotions Model, the ability to accept undesired emotions represents one of the most relevant factors for mental health [59, 64], which highlights the importance of improvement during treatment. Since patients participated in a multimodal therapeutic approach in our hospital, their improved emotion regulation strategies could be attributed to their participation in the HEB intervention directly or possibly to other elements of our approach.

Discussing our results in the light of current research on the topic, the scarcity of the same has to be kept in mind. Schlegel et al. [42] conducted a pilot study to evaluate their exercise-based program and reported high reductions in CES total score together with a dropout rate of 34%. A direct comparison of results seems difficult due to different therapeutic settings (inpatient vs. outpatient) and samples (adults + adolescents with a minimum BMI of 13 kg/m^2 vs. adults only with a minimum BMI of 17 kg/m^2). At present, they conduct an RCT for evaluation of the efficacy of their approach. To our knowledge, results of the RCT of Hay and colleagues [41] have not been published yet.

Our concept of HEB seems very much in line with the results of the Delphi study conducted by Noetel and colleagues [29]: Experts recommended to gradually reintroduce healthy exercise under supervision rather than to completely prohibit exercise. Consensus was also reached regarding the importance of psychoeducation on exercise as well as patients learning emotion regulation strategies, identifying risk situations and conducting behavioral analyses for compulsive exercise behavior - all core elements of HEB. For future research, is seems crucial to develop and validate a comprehensive clinical interview for assessing compulsive exercise - which does not exist so far - based on the items where consensus was achieved in the Delphi Study. Due to its pilot character there are several limitations to our study: First, the sample size of our pilot study was small. Second, generalization of our results to the general ED population might be limited by the following two factors: Admission to inpatient treatment implies a considerable severity of eating disorder symptomatology, a BMI < 15 kg/m^2, somatic complications or continuous weight loss. In addition, ED patients choosing to participate in our study were possibly more motivated and less anxious and rigid concerning the modification of their exercise behavior. Third, as no control group was implemented in our study, our results, especially those concerning BMI increase, have to be interpreted carefully, as all AN patients, irrespective of their participation in our study, were expected to gain at least 0.7 kg per week as part of routine inpatient treatment. Comparable uncontrolled repeated measures study designs were however used in inpatient ED studies by Gale and colleagues [65] as well as Tchanturia and colleagues [66, 67]. Fourth, we did not measure actual levels of exercise by accelerometry. However, we consider measures of actual levels of exercise (as assessed by accelerometry) and of cognitions and emotions around exercise (as assessed by CES and CET) equally important: We assume that changes in dysfunctional exercise cognitions and the development of adequate emotion regulation strategies (e.g. "non-exercise" based emotion-regulation) provide the basis for changes in actual levels of exercise. Additionally, levels of exercise are usually restricted during inpatient treatment, so changes in cognitions and emotions around exercise might even better track "real changes" than changes in exercise levels. Of course, we integrated accelerometry in our subsequent RCT.

Conclusions

Zipfel and colleagues [68] recognized treatment of compulsive exercise as one of the key unmet challenges in the treatment of ED. Our results indicate that our integrative approach to compulsive exercise in ED patients might represent a promising new therapeutic option. This pilot study confirmed the feasibility and acceptance of the intervention. Preliminary effect sizes on most outcomes were promising.

However, to determine the efficacy of the HEB intervention, a larger dismantling trial is needed, comparing the multimodal routine inpatient treatment (treatment as usual (TAU)) with the additional participation in HEB as add-on module (TAU + HEB) and comprising a sufficiently large sample size. Currently, our research group conducts a large randomized trial to evaluate the efficacy of this treatment approach as add-on element to regular inpatient treatment number (ISRCTN14208852). The development of three new and different approaches in the treatment of compulsive exercise in ED – one CBT-based [41], one exercise-based [42], and one integrative approach – offers fresh opportunities for this so far neglected phenomenon [69]. Each is currently being evaluated in large RCTs by the respective work groups. Comprehensive, evidence-based therapeutic options for compulsive exercise behavior becoming available will represent a milestone for overall optimization of ED treatment.

Appendix

Clinical interview for assessment of compulsive exercise (preliminary version)

A1: Do you have to exercise over and over again and can't resist doing so? What do you have to do?

A2: Why do you have to exercise? What would happen if you did not exercise?

B: Do you exercise more than you should or that makes sense?

C1: What effect does your exercise behavior have on your life?

C2: Does your exercise behavior bother you a lot?

C3: How much time do you spend exercising?

C4: Do you continue exercising when sick or injured?

Abbreviations

AN: Anorexia nervosa; BDI-II: Beck Depression Inventory-II; BMI: Body-mass-index; BN: Bulimia nervosa; BSI: Brief Symptom Inventory; CBT: Cognitive-behavioral therapy; CES: Commitment to Exercise Scale; CET: Compulsive Exercise Test; DSM-5: 5th ed. of the Diagnostic and Statistical Manual of Mental Disorders; DSM-IV: 4th ed. of the Diagnostic and Statistical Manual of Mental Disorders; ED: Eating disorders; EDI-2: Eating Disorder Inventory-2; EDNOS: Eating disorder not otherwise specified; ES: Effect size; ERSQ: Emotion Regulation Skills Questionnaire; HEB: "Healthy exercise behavior" intervention; M: Mean; MDD: Major depressive disorder; OCD: Obsessive-compulsive disorder; RCT: Randomized controlled trial; SCID-I: The Structured Clinical Interview for DSM-IV Axis I Disorders; SD: Standard deviation; SIAB-EX: Structured Interview for Anorexic and Bulimic Disorders for DSM-IV and ICD-10; SPSS: Statistical Package of Social Science; TAU: Treatment as usual

Acknowledgements

We sincerely thank all patients for their participation in our study. We gratefully acknowledge the support of all colleagues at Schoen Clinic Roseneck who contributed to this study. We especially thank Veronika Bauer, Carolina Bürger, Christina Neumayr, Barbara Barton and Kerstin Hupe for their assistance with data collection, data entry and data management.

Authors' contributions

The HEB manual was developed by KA, UC, ND, MF, CM, MvM,and the manual development headed by MM. HEB groups for the study were led by KA, ND, MF, CM, MvM. Study design was developed by ND, UV, SS. ND was responsible for patient recruitment and data collection. Data analysis was completed by ND, CJ, SS. ND wrote the manuscript draft. UV, CJ, SS revised the manuscript draft. All authors read and approved the final manuscript.

Competing interests

The authors declare that they have no competing interests.

Author details

[1]Schoen Clinic Roseneck, Am Roseneck 6, Prien am Chiemsee, Germany. [2]Department of Clinical Psychology and E-Mental-Health, Technische Universität Dresden, Dresden, Germany. [3]Department of Psychiatry and Psychotherapy, University Hospital of Freiburg, Freiburg, Germany. [4]Paracelsus Medical University, Salzburg, Austria. [5]Department of Psychiatry and Psychotherapy, University Hospital of Munich (LMU), Munich, Germany.

References

1. Arcelus J, Mitchell AJ, Wales J, Nielsen S. Mortality rates in patients with anorexia nervosa and other eating disorders: a meta-analysis of 36 studies. Arch Gen Psychiatry. 2011;68:724–31.
2. Fichter MM, Quadflieg N, Hedlund S. Twelve-year course and outcome predictors of anorexia nervosa. Int J Eat Disord. 2006;39:87–100.
3. Steinhausen H-C. The outcome of anorexia nervosa in the 20th century. Am J Psychiatry. 2002;159:1284–93.
4. Hebebrand J, Exner C, Hebebrand K, Holtkamp C, Casper RC, Remschmidt H, Herpertz-Dahlmann B, Klingenspor M. Hyperactivity in patients with anorexia nervosa and in semistarved rats: evidence for a pivotal role of hypoleptinemia. Physiol Behav. 2003;79:25–37.
5. Dalle Grave R, Calugi S, Marchesini G. Compulsive exercise to control shape or weight in eating disorders: prevalence, associated features, and treatment outcome. Compr Psychiatry. 2008;49:346–52.
6. Davis C, Katzman DK, Kaptein S, Kirsh C, Brewer H, Kalmbach K, Olmsted MP, Woodside DB, Kaplan AS. The prevalence of high-level exercise in the eating disorders: etiological implications. Compr Psychiatry. 1997;38:321–6.
7. Favaro A, Caregaro L, Burlina AB, Santonastaso P. Tryptophan levels, excessive exercise, and nutritional status in anorexia nervosa. Psychosom Med. 2000;62:535–8.
8. Carter JC, Blackmore E, Sutandar-Pinnock K, Woodside DB. Relapse in anorexia nervosa: a survival analysis. Psychol Med. 2004;34:671–9.
9. Smith AR, Fink EL, Anestis MD, Ribeiro JD, Gordon KH, Davis H, Keel PK, Bardone-Cone AM, Peterson CB, Klein MH, et al. Exercise caution: over-exercise is associated with suicidality among individuals with disordered eating. Psychiatry Res. 2013;206:246–55.
10. Solenberger SE. Exercise and eating disorders: a 3-year inpatient hospital record analysis. Eat Behav. 2001;2:151–68.
11. Strober M, Freeman R, Morrell W. The long-term course of severe anorexia nervosa in adolescents: survival analysis of recovery, relapse, and outcome predictors over 10–15 years in a prospective study. Int J Eat Disord. 1997;22:339–60.
12. Bewell-Weiss CV, Carter JC. Predictors of excessive exercise in anorexia nervosa. Compr Psychiatry. 2010;51:566–71.
13. Holtkamp K, Hebebrand J, Herpertz-Dahlmann B. The contribution of anxiety and food restriction on physical activity levels in acute anorexia nervosa. Int J Eat Disord. 2004;36:163–71.
14. Penas-Lledo E, Vaz Leal FJ, Waller G. Excessive exercise in anorexia nervosa and bulimia nervosa: relation to eating characteristics and general psychopathology. Int J Eat Disord. 2002;31:370–5.
15. Shroff H, Reba L, Thornton LM, Tozzi F, Klump KL, Berrettini WH, Brandt H, Crawford S, Crow S, Fichter MM, et al. Features associated with excessive exercise in women with eating disorders. Int J Eat Disord. 2006;39:454–61.
16. Davis C, Katzman MA. Perfection as acculturation: psychological correlates of eating problems in Chinese male and female students living in the United States. Int J Eat Disord. 1999;25:65–70.
17. Jacobi C, Hayward C, De Zwaan M, Kraemer H, Agras W. Coming to terms with risk factors for eating disorders: application of risk terminology and suggestions for a general taxonomy. Psychol Bull. 2004;130:19–65.
18. Naylor H, Mountford V, Brown G. Beliefs about excessive exercise in eating disorders: the role of obsessions and compulsions. Eur Eat Disord Rev. 2011;19:226–36.
19. Holtkamp K, Herpertz-Dahlmann B, Hebebrand K, Mika C, Kratzsch J, Hebebrand J. Physical activity and restlessness correlate with leptin levels in patients with adolescent anorexia nervosa. Biol Psychiatry. 2006;60:311–3.
20. Holtkamp K, Herpertz-Dahlmann B, Mika C, Heer M, Heussen N, Fichter MM, Herpertz S, Senf W, Blum WF, Schweiger U, et al. Elevated physical activity and low leptin levels co-occur in patients with anorexia nervosa. Journal of Clinical Endocrinology & Metabolism. 2003;88:5169–74.
21. Brewerton TD, Stellefson EJ, Hibbs N, Hodges EL, Cochrane CE. Comparison of eating disorder patients with and without compulsive exercising. Int J Eat Disord. 1995;17:413–6.
22. American Psychiatric Association. *Diagnostic and statistical manual of mental disorders* 4. Edn. Washington, DC: American Psychiatric Association; 1994.
23. American Psychiatric Association: *Diagnostic and statistical manual of mental disorders*. 5. Edn. Washington, DC: Author; 2013.
24. Bratland-Sanda S, Sundgot-Borgen J, Rø Ø, Rosenvinge JH, Hoffart A, Martinsen EW. Physical activity and exercise dependence during inpatient treatment of longstanding eating disorders: an exploratory study of excessive and non-excessive exercisers. Int J Eat Disord. 2010;43:266–73.
25. Davis C, Kaptein S. Anorexia nervosa with excessive exercise: a phenotype with close links to obsessive-compulsive disorder. Psychiatry Res. 2006;142:209–17.
26. Adkins EC, Keel PK. Does "excessive" or "compulsive" best describe exercise as a symptom of bulimia nervosa? Int J Eat Disord. 2005;38:24–9.
27. Mond JM, Hay PJ, Rodgers B, Owen C. An update on the definition of "excessive exercise" in eating disorders research. Int J Eat Disord. 2006;39:147–53.
28. Meyer C, Taranis L. Exercise in the eating disorders: terms and definitions. Eur Eat Disord Rev. 2011;19:169–73.
29. Noetel M, Dawson L, Hay P, Touyz S. The assessment and treatment of unhealthy exercise in adolescents with anorexia nervosa: a Delphi study to synthesize clinical knowledge. The International Journal of Eating Disorders. 2017;50:378–88.
30. Goodwin H, Haycraft E, Willis AM, Meyer C. Compulsive exercise: the role of personality, psychological morbidity, and disordered eating. Int J Eat Disord. 2011;44:655–60.
31. Meyer C, Taranis L, Goodwin H, Haycraft E. Compulsive exercise and eating disorders. Eur Eat Disord Rev. 2011;19:174–89.
32. March J, Frances A, Carpenter D. The expert consensus guideline series: the treatment of obsessive-compulsive disorder. J Clin Psychiatry. 1997;58
33. Steinglass JE, Sysko R, Glasofer D, Albano AM, Simpson HB, Walsh BT. Rationale for the application of exposure and response prevention to the treatment of anorexia nervosa. Int J Eat Disord. 2011;44:134–41.
34. Treasure J, Cardi V, Kan C. Eating in eating disorders. Eur Eat Disord Rev. 2012;20:e42–9.
35. Svaldi J, Griepenstroh J, Tuschen-Caffier B, Ehring T. Emotion regulation deficits in eating disorders: a marker of eating pathology or general psychopathology? Psychiatry Res. 2012;197:103–11.
36. Fairburn CG, Cooper Z, Shafran R. Cognitive behaviour therapy for eating disorders: a "transdiagnostic" theory and treatment. Behav Res Ther. 2003;41:509–28.
37. Long S, Wallis DJ, Leung N, Arcelus J, Meyer C. Mealtimes on eating disorder wards: a two-study investigation. Int J Eat Disord. 2012;45:241–6.
38. Herpertz S, Herpertz-Dahlmann B, Fichter M, Tuschen-Caffier B, Zeeck A. S3-Leitlinie Diagnostik und Behandlung der Essstörungen. Berlin: Springer; 2011.
39. Touyz SW, Beumont PJ, Glaun D, Phillips T, Cowie I. A comparison of lenient and strict operant conditioning programmes in refeeding patients with anorexia nervosa. Br J Psychiatry. 1984;144:517–20.
40. Hechler T, Beumont P, Touyz S, Marks P, Vocks S. Die Bedeutung körperlicher Aktivität bei Anorexia nervosa: Dimensionen, Erfassung und Behandlungsstrategien aus Expertensicht. Verhaltenstherapie. 2005;15:140–7.
41. Moving forward in anorexia nervosa treatment. A randomised controlled trial of the Loughborough Eat Disord Activity therapy versus general cognitive Behav Ther efficacy in reducing pathological exercise behaviours

and cognitions. https://www.anzctr.org.au/Trial/Registration/TrialReview.aspx?id=320881&isReview=true.
42. Schlegel S, Hartmann A, Fuchs R, Zeeck A. The Freiburg sport therapy program for eating disordered outpatients: a pilot study. Eating and Weight Disorders - Studies on Anorexia, Bulimia and Obesity. 2015;20:319–27.
43. Stieglitz RD, Haug A, Fahndrich E, Rosler M, Trabert W. Comprehensive psychopathological assessment based on the Association for Methodology and Documentation in psychiatry (AMDP) system: development, methodological foundation, application in clinical routine, and research. Front Psychiatry. 2017;8:45.
44. Fichter MM, Quadflieg N. Strukturiertes Inventar für Anorektische und Bulimische Essstörungen (SIAB). Göttingen: Hogrefe; 1999.
45. Wittchen HU, Zaudig M, Fydrich T. SKID. Strukturiertes Klinisches Interview für DSM-IV. Achse I und Achse II (Handanweisung). Göttingen: Hogrefe; 1997.
46. First MB, Spitzer RL, Gibbon M, JBW W. Structured clinical interview for DSM-IV Axis I disorders, clinician version (SCID-CV). Washington, D.C.: American Psychiatric Press, Inc.; 1996.
47. Davis C, Brewer H, Ratusny D. Behavioral frequency and psychological commitment: necessary concepts in the study of excessive exercising. J Behav Med. 1993;16:611–28.
48. Zeeck A, Schlegel S, Giel KE, Junne F, Kopp C, Joos A, Davis C, Hartmann A. Validation of the German version of the commitment to exercise scale. Psychopathology. 2017;50:146–56.
49. Thome JL, Espelage DL. Obligatory exercise and eating pathology in college females: replication and development of a structural model. Eat Behav. 2007;8:334–49.
50. Taranis L, Touyz S, Meyer C. Disordered eating and exercise: development and preliminary validation of the compulsive exercise test (CET). Eur Eat Disord Rev. 2011;19:256–68.
51. Garner DM. *Eating disorder inventory-2: Professional manual.* Odessa: psychological assessment. Resources. 1991;
52. Paul T, Thiel A. Eating Disorder Inventory-2 (EDI-2): Deutsche Version. Göttingen: Hogrefe; 2005.
53. Salbach-Andrae H, Schneider N, Bürger A, Pfeiffer E, Lehmkuhl U, Holzhausen M. Psychometrische Gütekriterien des Eating Disorder Inventory (EDI-2) bei Jugendlichen. Zeitschrift für Kinder- und Jugendpsychiatrie und Psychotherapie. 2010;38:219–28.
54. Beck AT, Steer RA, Brown GK. Manual for the Beck depression inventory-II. San Antonio: Psychological Corporation; 1996.
55. Hautzinger M, Keller F, Kühner C. BDI-II. Beck-depressions-Inventar. Revision. Pearson Assessment: Frankfurt; 2009.
56. Franke G, Brief Symptom BSI, Inventory v LR. *Derogatis (Kurzform der SCL-90-R) - Deutsche Version.* Göttingen: Beltz. Test. 2000;
57. Derogatis LR. Brief Symptom Inventory (BSI): Administration, scoring, and procedures manual. Minneapolis: NCS: Pearson; 1993.
58. Berking M, Znoj H. Entwicklung und Validierung eines Fragebogens zur standardisierten Selbsteinschätzung emotionaler Kompetenzen (SEK-27). Z Psychiatr Psychol Psychother. 2008;56:141–53.
59. Berking M. Training emotionaler Kompetenzen. In: Berlin. Heidelberg: Springer; 2010.
60. SEK-27 - Fragebogen zur standardisierten Selbsteinschätzung emotionaler Kompetenzen (PSYNDEX Tests Abstract). http://www.zpid.de/retrieval/PSYNDEXTests.php?id=9005957.
61. IBM Corp. IBM SPSS Statistics for Windows, Version 20.0. Armonk: IBM Corp; 2011.
62. Maier-Riehle B, Zwingmann C. Effektstärkevarianten beim Eingruppen-Prä-Post-Design: Eine kritische Betrachtung. Die Rehabilitation. 2000;39:189–99.
63. Zipfel S, Wild B, Gross G, Friederich HC, Teufel M, Schellberg D, Giel K, de Zwaan M, Dinkel A, Herpertz S, et al. Focal psychodynamic therapy, cognitive behaviour therapy, and optimised treatment as usual in outpatients with anorexia nervosa (ANTOP study): randomised controlled trial. Lancet. 2014;383:127–37.
64. Berking M, Ebert D, Cuijpers P, Hofmann SG. Emotion regulation skills training enhances the efficacy of inpatient cognitive behavioral therapy for major depressive disorder: a randomized controlled trial. Psychother Psychosom. 2013;82:234–45.
65. Gale C, Gilbert P, Read N, Goss K. An evaluation of the impact of introducing compassion focused therapy to a standard treatment programme for people with eating disorders. Clinical Psychology Psychotherapy. 2014;21:1–12.
66. Tchanturia K, Doris E, Fleming C. Effectiveness of cognitive remediation and emotion skills training (CREST) for anorexia nervosa in group format: a naturalistic pilot study. Eur Eat Disord Rev. 2014;22:200–5.
67. Tchanturia K, Larsson E, Adamson J. Brief group intervention targeting perfectionism in adults with anorexia nervosa: empirically informed protocol. Eur Eat Disord Rev. 2016;24:489–93.
68. Zipfel S, Giel K, Bulik CM, Hay P, Schmidt U: Anorexia nervosa: aetiology, assessment, and treatment. Lancet Psychiatry 2015.
69. Touyz S, Hay P, Noetel M: Is the neglect of exercise in anorexia nervosa research a case of "running out" of ideas or do we need to take a "LEAP" of faith into the future? J Eat Disord. 2017;5:35. https://doi.org/10.1186/s40337-017-0157-z.

Development and validation of makeup and sexualized clothing questionnaires

Haylie Smith[1], Marisol Perez[1*], Michael R. Sladek[1], Carolyn Black Becker[2], Tara K. Ohrt[1] and Amanda B. Bruening[1]

Abstract

Background: Body acceptance programs on college campuses indicated that collegiate women often report feeling pressure to dress in a sexualized manner, and use makeup to enhance beauty. Currently, no quantitative measures exist to assess attitudes and daily behaviors that may arise in response to perceived pressure to wear makeup or dress in a provocative manner. The goal of the current studies was to develop brief self-report questionnaires aimed at assessing makeup and sexualized clothing use and attitudes in young women.

Methods: An exploratory factor analysis in a sample of 403 undergraduate women was used in Study 1 to create items to measure the pressure women feel to wear makeup and sexualized clothing. A confirmatory factor analysis ($N = 153$) was used in Study 2 to confirm the factor structure found in Study 1. An incremental validity analysis was also conducted in Study 2. Across both studies, participants completed online questionnaires.

Results: In Study 1, items were developed for two questionnaires to assess perceived pressure to wear makeup and discomfort when not wearing makeup, and perceived pressure to wear sexualized clothing, and body image concerns with regards to sexualized clothing. The exploratory factor analyses revealed Unconfident and Unease scales for the Makeup Questionnaire (MUQ) and Body Dissatisfaction and Pressure scales for the Sexualized Clothing Questionnaire (SCQ). In Study 2, the confirmatory factor analyses confirmed the factor structure for the MUQ and SCQ. The incremental validity analysis revealed that these measures can be used to predict self-objectification and shape and weight concern in women.

Conclusion: These studies provide preliminary support for the factor structure of two novel questionnaires aimed at assessing perceived pressure to wear makeup and sexualized clothing.

Keywords: Makeup, Sexualized clothing, Self-objectification, Pressure, College women

Plain English summary

Women are increasingly promoted as objects in today's society, especially in the media. As a result of this objectification of women, women feel the need to engage in daily behaviors, such as putting on makeup and sexualized clothing, to meet societies' standards of beauty. Therefore, this study created scales to measure the pressure women feel to wear makeup and sexualized clothing. The scales for makeup assess women's confidence without makeup, as well as their pressure to wear makeup all the time, even when running errands. The scales for sexualized clothing assess whether women avoid wearing sexualized clothing due to body image concerns, as well as the pressure they feel from society to wear revealing clothes. Then, we found that these scales can be used to predict harmful behaviors in women, such as seeing themselves as an object and being preoccupied with their shape and weight.

* Correspondence: marisol.perez@asu.edu
[1]Psychology Department Arizona State University, 950 South McAllister Avenue Room 237, Tempe, AZ 85287-1104, USA
Full list of author information is available at the end of the article

Background

Development and validation of makeup and sexualized clothing questionnaires

Since the 1980s, researchers note that certain environments within Western society treat women as sexual objects, with a focus on beauty and appearance [1–3]. Furthermore, Grauf, Murnen, & Krause note the increasingly sexualized depiction of girls in magazines over time demonstrates Western society's escalating view of girls and women as sexual objects [4]. Self-objectification theory, which has been used to examine the consequences of treating women and girls as sexual objects (e.g., eating disorders, low self-esteem, and depression), proposes that a woman views herself as an object from a third-person perspective so as to be able to anticipate societal responses to her [5–7]. Research suggests that self-objectification can be associated with increased body monitoring, body shame, and appearance anxiety [5, 8]. Additionally, increased self-objectification is correlated with eating disorder pathology, body dissatisfaction, thin-ideal internalization, depression, and overall decreases in life satisfaction [9, 10]. In addition to its impact on mental health, self-objectification has been found to hinder performance on cognitive tasks [11, 12]. It is important to note, however, that the majority of research on self-objectification has focused on trait-level constructs (i.e., habitual patterns of behavior, attitudes and emotion); to date limited research has examined the daily impact of objectification.

As noted above, self-objectification may serve an adaptive function by allowing women to predict how others in an objectifying society will respond to them [5]. Taking a third party gaze, however, also may motivate women to engage in behaviors that allow them to conform with societal ideals, thereby increasing societal approval. For instance, the media, which commonly objectifies women, typically presents the ideal woman as wearing both makeup and sexualized clothing [13]. Theoretically, women who are higher in self-objectification should experience greater pressure to conform to societal appearance standards, which promote the use of sexualized clothing and makeup [5, 10].

Media campaigns promote makeup as a means to increase female beauty and attractiveness by enhancing some facial features and hiding others. As a result of successful media campaigns, U.S. consumers (mostly female consumers) spend billions of dollars on cosmetics each year [14, 15]. Self-objectification has been shown to predict momentary changes in women's behaviors and performance (e.g., cognitive performance on the Stroop task), as well as more chronic changes in mood and behavior (e.g., depression, anxiety, eating disorders) [5]. Self-objectification also can be used to provide a framework for understanding women's makeup use. For example, it is possible that women experience appearance anxiety due to the flaws they perceive on their faces. To reduce such appearance anxiety, women may wear makeup in an attempt to cover up their flaws or enhance their self-perceived attributes. To date, most makeup research focuses on how other people view women wearing makeup; for instance, one study found that men and women associate more implicit, positive attributes towards women wearing makeup [16]. More specifically, women wearing makeup were more likely to be viewed as high status professionals and as having positive personality traits compared to women not wearing facial makeup [16]. However, this study on makeup did not assess how women themselves felt about wearing makeup.

Images of women and girls in the media also link beauty with sexuality [4]. The sexualization of women permeates multiple facets of entertainment including television, billboards, magazines, video games, Facebook, and clothing stores [6, 13, 17, 18]. For example, stiletto heels were originally almost exclusively worn by porn stars and mainly depicted in pornography, but now they are a common accessory for women [19]. Based on the idea that society views women as sexual objects, pressure to dress in a sexualized manner may also be a daily manifestation of self-objectification.

To date, no quantitative survey measures have been developed to assist researchers in assessing the pressure women feel to use makeup and wear sexualized clothing. Thus, the purpose of the current set of studies was to create two questionnaires examining behaviors and attitudes associated with makeup and sexualized clothing use. In Study 1, the goal was to create measures assessing the pressure women feel to wear makeup and sexualized clothing; the goal of Study 2 was to confirm the factor structures from Study 1 and assess the incremental validity of the scales.

Study 1

In Study 1, we developed items designed to assess beliefs and practices related to wearing makeup and sexualized clothing. We used an exploratory factor analysis (EFA) to examine the factor structure of the items. To further investigate the construct validity of the developed questionnaires, we hypothesized that the scales for makeup and sexualized clothing would be positively associated with self-objectification. Previous research indicates that self-objectification is concurrently associated with body dissatisfaction, eating disorder pathology, and thin-ideal internalization [20, 21]; thus, we hypothesized that these variables would be positively associated with scores on the makeup and sexualized clothing scales. Specifically, we expected that both a) greater discomfort when not wearing makeup and b) greater pressure to dress in sexualized clothing would be associated with greater body dissatisfaction, thin-ideal internalization, and preoccupations with shape and weight. Support for these hypotheses would corroborate the construct validity of the new questionnaires.

Method

Participants and procedure

All first-year undergraduate women residing on all campuses of a large, public university in the southwestern U.S. received an email asking them to fill out an online health behavior survey (N = 5284). In the email, women

18 years of age or older were invited to participate. This study was approved by the University's Institutional Review Board and women completed an online consent form prior to completing the study. The online consent form, further re-affirmed that participants had to be 18 years of age. For this study, a total of 403 first-year college women (8%) participated in the online survey. Participants received $15 for their participation. Participants ranged in age from 18 to 32 years old (M_{age} = 18.79; *SD* = 1.14). The ethnic breakdown of the sample was Hispanic (22%), Non-Hispanic (71%), and missing data (8%). The majority of participants identified as Caucasian (65%) with the remaining identifying as Asian (14%), African American (8%), Pacific Islander/Hawaiian (2%), Native American/Alaskan (3%), and Other (3%). Participants were able to endorse more than one race. In addition to completing the newly created Makeup and Sexualized Clothing Questionnaires, participants completed validated measures of body satisfaction, eating disorder symptoms, self-objectification, and thin-ideal internalization.

Item development

Body image experts collaborating at two universities in the southwestern U.S. (Trinity University and Arizona State University) created items based on direct experience running the Body Project, a body acceptance program, as well as comments from college women who participated in the program. Consistently, authors MP and CB noted women participating in the Body Project groups would discuss the use of makeup and sexualized clothing as daily costs to the ultra-thin ideal of beauty within the U.S. Initially, the authors created a total of 24 items to assess how frequently women did not wear makeup in work/academic settings, around the home, and while running errands such as grocery shopping. Also, items were developed concerning how attractive and competent women felt without makeup. Additionally, researchers developed items designed to measure the pressure women felt to dress in a sexualized way and how body image concerns impacted this pressure. The 24 items were discussed by 3 focus groups with a total of 27 undergraduate women who had previously participated in the Body Project. They discussed each item, the importance of the construct, and the wording of each item. Based on the focus group feedback, 13 items were retained and extensively edited. Then, items were reviewed by Dr. Eric Stice, the original creator of the Body Project.

The final items for the Makeup Questionnaire and the Sexualized Clothing Questionnaire assess women's beliefs and attitudes regarding their attractiveness and confidence without makeup, their willingness to not wear makeup, and the pressure they perceive to wear sexualized clothing in light of how body image may impact this choice. To fill out the questionnaires, women responded to different statements assessed on a Likert scale ranging from 1 (*strongly disagree*) to 5 (*strongly agree*). For a complete list of the 13 items selected see Tables 1 and 2. Items 1 and 4 of the MUQ were reverse scored. Then, total scores were calculated for each scale by summing responses to the items, where higher scores indicate a greater discomfort without makeup and more pressure to wear sexualized clothing.

Body dissatisfaction

The Body Parts Satisfaction Scale-Revised (BPSS-R) assessed satisfaction with eleven body parts including the arms and stomach, as well as satisfaction with height, weight, and overall muscle tone [22]. Responses were recorded using a 6-point Likert scale ranging from 1 (*extremely dissatisfied*) to 6 (*extremely satisfied*), with an additional item assessing overall body satisfaction. For this measure, item scores were averaged, and higher scores indicated less pathology such that women with higher scores were more satisfied with their bodies [22]. For the current study, Cronbach's alpha was .92.

Shape and weight concern

Participants also completed the Eating Disorders Examination-Questionnaire (EDE-Q) Shape and Weight Concern subscales because these constructs are viewed as core psychopathology in bulimia nervosa [23]. These 13 items assessed how preoccupied women are with their current weight, as well as the shape of their body. The scores were averaged, and higher scores indicated

Table 1 Summary of Exploratory Factor Analysis Results for Makeup Questionnaire using Maximum Likelihood Estimation

	Factor Loadings	
Item	MUQ Unconfident	MUQ Unease
MUQ3. If I do not have makeup on, I feel less attractive.	**.87**	.03
MUQ6. Makeup makes me more attractive.	**.87**	−.18
MUQ5. If I do not have makeup on, I feel less competent.	**.54**	.31
MUQ4. I feel comfortable not wearing makeup to run errands (e.g., grocery store).	.23	**−.85**
MUQ1. I feel comfortable not wearing makeup to school.	−.11	**−.74**
MUQ2. I do not leave the house without any makeup on.	.25	**.54**
MUQ7. I believe women who are not wearing makeup are less attractive.	.21	.24
Eigenvalues	3.49	1.15
% of variance	49.85	16.45

Promax rotation was applied. Factor loadings in bold reflect items retained. *N* = 403

Table 2 Summary of Exploratory Factor Analysis Results for Sexualized Clothing Questionnaire using Maximum Likelihood Estimation

	Factor Loadings	
Item	SCQ Body Discomfort	SCQ Pressure
SCQ2: I do not wear revealing clothing because of body image concerns.	**1.00**	−.08
SCQ1: I purposely wear clothing that is less sexualized because of body image concerns.	**.80**	−.01
SCQ3: I feel pressure by society to dress in a sexualized manner.	.01	**.83**
SCQ4: On campus, I feel added pressure to dress in a sexualized manner.	.14	**.79**
SCQ5: Over time, I have noticed that my attire is becoming less conservative.	−.11	**.59**
SCQ6: The way women dress on campus bothers me.	.38	.11
Eigenvalues	2.85	1.36
% of variance	47.48	22.58

Promax rotation was applied. Factor loadings in bold reflect items retained. *N* = 403

greater pathology. Past research documents the internal consistency of the Shape Concern subscale; Cronbach's alpha was .93 at a baseline assessment and .92 at the 12 to 16-week follow-up, with a strong test-retest reliability coefficient of .94. Scores on the Weight Concern subscale also display strong internal consistency with a Cronbach's alpha was .89 at a baseline assessment and .89 at the 12 to 16-week follow-up, as with a strong test-retest reliability of .92 [23]. For this study, Cronbach's alphas were .90 and .83 for Shape Concern and Weight Concern, respectively.

Self-objectification

The Objectified Body Consciousness Scale (OBCS) Body Surveillance subscale comprises 8 items that assessed women's preoccupation with their bodies, as well as how often they compared themselves to other women (e.g., "I often worry about whether the clothes I am wearing make me look good") [24]. Participants responded using a 5-point Likert scale ranging from 1 (*strongly agree*) to 5 (*strongly disagree*). These scores were averaged, and a higher score indicated a high level of body surveillance. Cronbach's alpha of Body Surveillance was .74.

Thin-ideal internalization

Internalization of the idealized female body type (i.e., believing that thinner woman are more successful and happier in life) was assessed using two measures [25]. The first measure, Ideal-Body Stereotype Scale-Revised (IBSS-R), is a 10-item scale that asks women to report what they view as attractive, with responses recorded on a 5-point Likert scale ranging from 1 (*strongly disagree*) to 5 (*strongly agree*). Example item: "Slim women are more attractive" [25]. The scores were averaged, and greater scores indicated more thin-ideal internalization. Scores on the IBSS-R have demonstrated internal consistency with a Cronbach's alpha of .91, test-retest reliability coefficient of .80, as well as predictive validity [25]. For the current study, Cronbach's alpha of the IBSS-R was .90. The second measure used, the Body Image Culture Survey (BICS), includes 12 items assessing the extent to which a person believes that achieving the thin ideal would improve life [26]. Example item: "Being thinner than I am now would increase my sense of worth" [26]. Items were scored on a 5-point Likert scale ranging from 1 (*no chance*) to 5 (*certain to happen*), then scores were averaged with greater scores indicating more thin-ideal internalization. Cronbach's alpha of the BICS was .97.

Results

Exploratory factor analysis of makeup questionnaire

Using SPSS 23, an exploratory factor analysis was conducted using maximum likelihood estimation. The Kiaser-Meyer-Olkin measure of sampling adequacy, which is the degree of common variance among the items, was .82, well above the recommended .70 [27]. The Bartlett's Test of Sphericity was significant, χ^2 (21) = 1090.08, $p < .01$. Using Kaiser's [28] eigenvalue rule of thumb, two factors had eigenvalues greater than 1.0, which was confirmed further by visual inspection of a scree plot [29]. Based on the results of the factor analysis, two factors were retained. A promax rotation was applied because it was assumed the latent factors would be correlated. After rotation, the two factors accounted for 66.30% of the variance. Both factors were moderately correlated (r = .56). Out the 7 items, 3 loaded onto the first factor, and 3 loaded onto the second factor. See Table 1 for a summary of the factor loadings. Items loading highly on the first factor to emerge referred to feelings of unattractiveness and lack of competence that women felt when not wearing makeup and was labeled "Unconfident." Items loading highly on the second factor to emerge referred to lack of comfort when not wearing makeup in daily situations and thus was labeled "Unease." As item 7 failed to load onto any factor, it was eliminated from the final measure. Internal consistency for the scales was .82 for MUQ Unconfident, and .77 for MUQ Unease.

Exploratory factor analysis of sexualized clothing questionnaire

A second exploratory factor analysis was conducted using maximum likelihood estimation to assess the items of the Sexualized Clothing Questionnaire (SCQ). The Kiaser-Meyer-Olkin Measure was .69 [27]. The Bartlett's

Test of Sphericity was significant, χ^2 (15) = 938.66, p < .01. Using Kaiser's [28] eigenvalue rule of thumb, two factors had eigenvalues greater than 1.0, which was further confirmed by visual inspection of a scree plot [29]. A factor analysis was repeated, and two factors were retained. A promax rotation was applied as it was theorized the latent factors would be correlated. After rotation, the two factors accounted for 70.06% of the variance, and the factors were moderately correlated (r = .44). Out of the 6 items, 2 loaded onto the first factor, and 3 loaded onto the second factor. Table 2 provides a summary of the factor loadings. Items loading highly on the first factor related to not dressing in a sexualized fashion due to body image concerns, labeled "Body Discomfort." Items loading highly on the second factor related to societal pressure to wear sexualized clothing; as such, it was labeled "Pressure." Item 6 was deleted due to low factor loadings and because the question focused on perceptions of others, while all the other questions on the questionnaire were focused on the self. Spearman-Brown analysis for SCQ Body Discomfort was .77, and internal consistency for SCQ Pressure was .78.

Correlational analyses

Pearson correlations tested the associations between MUQ Unconfident, MUQ Unease, SCQ Body Discomfort, SCQ Pressure, and self-objectification and other hypothesized correlates including body satisfaction, shape and weight concerns, and thin-ideal internalization. All correlations were in the expected direction (see Table 3). Higher thin-ideal internalization and self-objectification scores were associated with higher scores on the MUQ and SCQ scales. Similarly, higher body satisfaction scores were associated with lower scores on the MUQ and SCQ scales. MUQ Unconfident, MUQ Unease, and SCQ Pressure were all significantly correlated with body satisfaction (i.e., BPSS-R), self-objectification (i.e., Body Surveillance), Shape Concern, Weight Concern, and both thin-ideal internalization scales (i.e., IBSS-R, BICS). Additionally, the Body Discomfort scale on the SCQ was significantly correlated with all measures except Body Surveillance. Overall, the newly created Makeup Questionnaire scales and the Sexualized Clothing Questionnaire scales were significantly correlated with measures commonly used to assess self-objectification and its consequences.

Discussion

This first study aimed to extend the current literature through the creation of measures assessing makeup use and pressure to wear sexualized clothing. Overall, results provided evidence for two scales for each new questionnaire. The Makeup Questionnaire (MUQ) comprised a 3-item scale labeled Unconfident (i.e., women's feelings of attractiveness and competency not wearing makeup) and a 3-item scale labeled Unease (i.e., women's willingness and comfort with not wearing makeup to school, the store, or out of the house in general). The Sexualized Clothing Questionnaire (SCQ) comprised a 2-item scale labeled Body Discomfort (i.e., the extent to which body image concerns impact women's clothing selection) and a 3-item scale labeled Pressure (i.e., the perceived pressure women feel to dress in a sexualized way).

To provide support for the construct validity of scores on these new scales, it was hypothesized that the scales would be correlated with self-objectification and other known correlates, such as thin-ideal internalization and body dissatisfaction. Results revealed that MUQ Unconfident, MUQ Unease, and SCQ Pressure were significantly

Table 3 Bivariate correlations between measures and descriptive statistics for study 1

	1	2	3	4	5	6	7	8	9	10
1. MUQ Unconfident										
2. MUQ Unease	.536^{b}									
3. SCQ Body Discomfort	.234^{b}	.151^{b}								
4. SCQ Pressure	.256^{b}	.067	.349^{b}							
5. Thin-ideal Stereotype	.333^{b}	.131^{b}	.167^{b}	.245^{b}						
6. Body Image Culture	.322^{b}	.148^{b}	.456^{b}	.267^{b}	.352^{b}					
7. Shape Concern	.237^{b}	.129^{a}	.448^{b}	.236^{b}	.323^{b}	.539^{b}				
8. Weight Concern	.258^{b}	.142^{b}	.384^{b}	.214^{b}	.288^{b}	.527^{b}	.770^{b}			
9. Body Part Satisfaction	−.245^{b}	−.155^{b}	−.421^{b}	−.232^{b}	−.185^{b}	−.461^{b}	−.561^{b}	−.499^{b}		
10. Body Surveillance	.140^{b}	.229^{b}	.095	.134^{b}	.157^{b}	.103^{a}	.159^{b}	.146^{b}	.179^{b}	
Mean	9.244	6.821	5.133	8.216	3.734	32.77	2.420	2.248	60.104	24.839
Standard Deviation	3.247	3.270	2.292	2.950	0.775	13.202	0.967	0.983	16.002	3.759

N = 403. ^{a}Correlation is significant at the 0.05 level (2-tailed). ^{b}Correlation is significant at the 0.01 level (2-tailed). IBSSR – thin ideal internalization; BICS – belief that attaining thin ideal will improve life; Shape Concern – dissatisfaction with body shape; Weight Concern – dissatisfaction with weight; BPSSR – body part satisfaction; Body Surveillance – self-objectification

correlated with self-objectification and its consequences in the expected direction (the IBSS-R, BICS, Shape Concern, Weight Concern, BPSS-R, and Body Surveillance). That is, higher self-objectification scores were associated with more discomfort without makeup, less confidence without makeup, and more pressure to dress in a sexualized manner. This supports self-objectification theory [5], which suggests that women who are more prone to self-objectify are more likely to experience appearance anxiety, manifested in the current study as less confidence without makeup and more pressure to dress sexually to fit a societal ideal. Interestingly, SCQ Body Discomfort was not significantly correlated with self-objectification, but was significantly correlated with thin-ideal internalization and all of the body dissatisfaction measures, suggesting that body discomfort regarding sexualized clothing may be more strongly related to body dissatisfaction.

The significant correlations within Table 3 range from .10 to .56. The lowest correlations tended to be with the Body Surveillance scale, a measure of self-objectification; however the correlations are consistent with the existing literature using the same measures [30, 31]. In addition, correlations among thin-ideal internalization, body parts satisfaction, shape concerns and weight concerns are representative of the existing literature [31, 32]. This suggests are sample was consistent with the literature on known questionnaires [30–32].

Study 2

In Study 2, we aimed to replicate the results of Study 1, demonstrating that the items selected from Study 1 and factor structures replicate using a confirmatory factor analysis (CFA). Similar to Study 1, the scales were examined using correlational analyses with self-objectification and its consequences (e.g., body dissatisfaction, thin-ideal internalization, etc.). This study also examined the test-retest reliability of the scales. Additionally, we assessed the incremental validity of the created scales for each questionnaire using hierarchical multiple regression models. Incremental validity is important because the analysis reveals whether our created measures uniquely predict disordered behaviors of women, specifically self-objectification and shape and weight concerns, over and above the influence of known predictors. Previous research documents that thin-ideal internalization predicts self-objectification and body dissatisfaction, and self-objectification has been found to predict body dissatisfaction [21, 32]. Additionally, thin-ideal internalization and body dissatisfaction predict eating disorder pathology using longitudinal data [21, 32, 33]. Given that thin-ideal internalization and body dissatisfaction are closely intertwined with predicting self-objectification and eating disorder pathology, such as shape and weight concerns, we adjusted for thin-ideal internalization and body dissatisfaction in our analysis of incremental validity. Using longitudinal data, we hypothesized that our scales would uniquely predict changes in self-objectification and shape and weight concerns 12–16 weeks later (T2), while adjusting for thin-ideal internalization and body dissatisfaction at Time 1 (T1). Body Mass Index (BMI) was included as a covariate in these analyses because past research has found body dissatisfaction and body surveillance to be higher among overweight/obese women [30, 34].

Method

Participants and procedure

All first-year undergraduate women residing on all campuses of a large, public university in the southwestern U.S. received an email asking them to fill out an online health behavior survey. For this study, a total of 174 first-year college women participated in the online survey. These participants were different from the women who participated in Study 1. Participants ranged in age from 18 to 23 years old ($M_{age} = 18.46$; $SD = .76$). The ethnic breakdown of the sample was Hispanic (27%), Non-Hispanic (71%), and missing data (2%). The majority of participants identified as Caucasian (76%) with the remaining 24% comprised of Asian (15%), African American (9%), Pacific Islander/Hawaiian (3%), Native American/Alaskan (1%), and Other (3%). Participants were able to endorse more than one race. This study was approved by the University's Institutional Review Board and women completed an online consent form prior to completing the study. Participants received $15 for their participation. Inclusion criteria consisted of being an undergraduate woman residing on campus and a minimum of 18 years of age. Women agreed to fill out a baseline online survey (T1) and a follow-up online survey 12 to 16 weeks later (T2).

Measures

Makeup use

The MUQ developed in Study 1 was found to have two scales: Unconfident, which assessed how wearing makeup impacts women's feelings of competency and attractiveness, and Unease, which assessed how willing women are to not wear makeup in public places. Each scale consisted of 3 items rated on a Likert scale from 1 (*strongly disagree*) to 5 (*strongly agree*), where higher scores indicated less confidence and comfort while wearing makeup. Cronbach's alpha of MUQ Unconfident was .77 for baseline and .76 for T2. Cronbach's alpha of MUQ Unease was .80 for baseline and .82 for T2.

Use of sexualized clothing

The SCQ developed in Study 1 was found to have two scales: Body Discomfort, consisting of 2 items that assessed how body image concerns impact what women wear, and Pressure, consisting of 3 items that assessed how pressured women feel to dress in a sexualized way. Each item was rated on a Likert scale from 1 (*strongly disagree*) to 5 (*strongly agree*), where higher scores indicated more body discomfort and pressure with regards to wearing sexualized clothing. Internal consistency of the SCQ Body Discomfort was assessed using a Spearman-Brown analysis and was .83 for baseline and .78 for T2. Cronbach's alpha of SCQ Pressure was .79 for baseline and .82 for T2. For more detailed information on additional measures, see the descriptions in Study 1.

Body image scales

Similar to Study 1, a number of well-known body image self-report questionnaires were used at both time points. Cronbach's alpha of the BPSS-R [22]was .88 for baseline and .92 for T2. Cronbach's alpha of Shape Concern [23] was .87 for baseline and .90 for T2. Cronbach's alpha of Weight Concern [23] was .79 for baseline and .78 for T2. Cronbach's alpha of Body Surveillance [24] was .78 for baseline and .73 for T2. Cronbach's alpha of the IBSS-R [25] was .83 for baseline and .88 for T2. Cronbach's alpha of the BICS [26] was .97 for baseline and .97 for T2.

Body mass index (BMI)

Participants self-reported their height and weight. BMI was calculated using the United States Centers for Disease Control's gender- and age-based charts for adults [35]. BMI was included as a covariate for the incremental validity analyses.

Results

After deletion of participants with incomplete data, the remaining 153 participants provided complete data on the questionnaires across both time points.

Confirmatory factor analysis of makeup questionnaire

Using Mplus [36], confirmatory factor analysis was conducted using baseline scores. For the Makeup Questionnaire, fit of a two-factor model was evaluated following the EFA findings in Study 1. We used maximum likelihood estimation and allowed Factors 1 and 2 to covary [37]. According to several fit indices, the two-factor model was an adequate fit, χ^2 (8) = 15.48, $p > .05$ [38] CFI was .98 and above the recommended .95 [39], AGFI was .91 and above the recommended .80 [40], RMSEA was .08, which is considered moderate fit [41], and PClose was .19 and above the recommended .05 [40].

Confirmatory factor analysis of sexualized clothing questionnaire

A second CFA was conducted using only baseline data for the Sexualized Clothing Questionnaire. Using a similar strategy as above, the model was an adequate fit, χ^2 (4) = 5.93, $p > .05$ [38], CFI was .99 and above the recommended .95 [39], AGFI was .94 and above the recommended .80 [40], RMSEA was .06, which is considered good fit [41], and PClose was .37 and above the recommended .05 [40]. Upon closer analysis, Item 5 was conceptually different than the rest of the items on the measure. All the other items in the SCQ measure current feelings, while Item 5 assesses a retrospective inspection of attire over time. In addition, based on the standardized estimates of the item loadings, item 5 had a low loading of .37. For these reasons, it was deleted from the model. After the item was deleted, a two-factor model provided an excellent fit, χ^2 (1) = .03, $p > .05$ [38], CFI was 1.00 [39], AGFI was .99 [40], RMSEA was .00 [41], and PClose was .89 [40].

Test-retest reliability

MUQ Unconfident scale scores had strong temporal stability across 12–16 weeks, $r(151) = .68$, $p < .01$ [39]. MUQ Unease scores also displayed strong temporal stability, $r(151) = .72$, $p < .01$ [39]. Similarly, SCQ Body Discomfort scores had strong temporal stability, $r(151) = .69$, $p < .01$ [39]. SCQ Pressure scores displayed moderate stability, $r(151) = .51$, $p < .01$ [39].

Correlational analyses

Pearson correlations were used to test associations between MUQ Unconfident, MUQ Unease, SCQ Body Discomfort, SCQ Pressure, and the Objectified Body Consciousness Scale, as well as measures examining the consequences of self-objectification at T1 and T2. The cross-sectional correlations for MUQ Unconfident at T1 were similar to the results from Study 1. MUQ Unconfident was significantly correlated with self-objectification, body dissatisfaction, shape and weight concerns, and thin-ideal internalization. MUQ Unease was previously significantly correlated with body dissatisfaction, eating pathology, self-objectification, thin-ideal internalization in the expected direction in Study 1. When tested with the current sample at T1, the cross-sectional correlations between the MUQ Unease scale and all the other variables were significant and in the expected direction, except the correlations with weight and shape concerns were not significant (see Table 4). In other words, as MUQ Unease increased, scores on thin-ideal internalization and self-objectification increased, where scores on body satisfaction decreased. SCQ Pressure was previously correlated with self-objectification, thin-ideal internalization, and body dissatisfaction in the expected direction in Study 1,

Table 4 Study 2 Cross-sectional, Bivariate Correlations between Measures for Time 1 and Time 2

		1	2	3	4	5	6	7	8	9	10
Time 1											
1. MUQ Unconfident		–	.551[b]	.202[a]	.128	.283[b]	.312[b]	.186[a]	.186[a]	–.306[b]	.374[b]
2. MUQ Unease		.510[b]	–	.217[b]	.084	.220[b]	.220[b]	.152	.130	–.193[a]	.398[b]
3. SCQ Body Discomfort		.220[b]	.144	–	.256[b]	.203[a]	.388[b]	.506[b]	.498[b]	–.417[b]	.332[b]
4. SCQ Pressure		.045	–.052	.257[b]	–	.374[b]	.212[b]	.173[a]	.230[b]	–.088	.257[b]
5. Thin-ideal Stereotype		.335[b]	.092	.223[b]	.211[b]	–	.385[b]	.260[b]	.274[b]	–.117	.382[b]
6. Body Image Culture		.403[b]	.159[a]	.529[b]	.132	.389[b]	–	.645[b]	.699[b]	–.416[b]	.394[b]
7. Shape Concern		.249[b]	.037	.620[b]	.271[b]	.380[b]	.649[b]	–	.847[b]	–.608[b]	.503[b]
8. Weight Concern		.300[b]	.081	.591[b]	.243[b]	.390[b]	.746[b]	.833[b]	–	–.555[b]	.391[b]
9. Body Part Satisfaction		–.289[b]	–.153	–.500[b]	–.180[a]	–.311[b]	–.538[b]	–.592[b]	–.609[b]	–	–.405[b]
10. Body Surveillance		.412[b]	.425[b]	.297[b]	.185[a]	.397[b]	.435[b]	.453[b]	.471[b]	–.460[b]	–
Time 2											
Mean	Time 1	9.961	7.255	5.307	5.516	3.727	32.536	2.426	2.230	59.665	27.654
	Time 2	9.915	7.196	5.477	5.647	3.738	34.314	2.431	2.173	59.158	27.608
Standard Deviation	Time 1	2.967	3.176	2.396	2.081	0.610	12.541	0.885	0.864	14.650	4.772
	Time 2	2.707	3.169	2.227	2.150	0.662	13.599	0.904	0.881	17.054	4.487

[a]Correlation is significant at the 0.05 level (2-tailed). [b]Correlation is significant at the 0.01 level (2-tailed). $N = 153$
Bivariate correlations for time 1 are presented above the diagonal and bivariate correlations for time 2 are presented below the diagonal

but in the present sample this scale was not correlated with body dissatisfaction. The cross-sectional correlations between SCQ Body Discomfort with self-objectification, body dissatisfaction, thin-ideal internalization, and shape and weight concerns were significant, while in Study 1 SCQ Body Discomfort was not correlated with self-objectification. All cross-sectional correlations at T2 were in the expected direction: women who scored higher on thin-ideal internalization and self-objectification tended to score higher on MUQ and SCQ scales, and women who scored lower on body satisfaction tended to score higher on the MUQ and SCQ scales.

MUQ Unease was not significantly correlated with body dissatisfaction, shape and weight concerns, and one measure of thin-ideal internalization (IBSS-R; see Table 4). In contrast, scores on the SCQ Pressure scale were not significantly associated with scores on the BICS. Overall, MUQ Unconfident and SCQ Body Discomfort supported the hypothesis for Study 2 because they were both significantly correlated with the measures assessing body dissatisfaction, shape and weight concerns, self-objectification, and thin-ideal internalization at two different points in time. SCQ Pressure was significantly correlated with the majority of these measures. However, MUQ Unease only correlated with one scale measuring thin-ideal internalization and another scale measuring self-objectification at T2 (BICS and Body Surveillance), which differed from what was found at T1, and at Study 1.

Incremental validity analyses

The incremental validity of the scales from the MUQ and the SCQ was assessed using a series of hierarchical multiple regression models to predict changes in self-objectification, shape concern, and weight concern after adjusting for known predictors of these outcomes. This was done to assess whether daily consequences of self-objectification (e.g., wearing makeup and sexualized clothing) could predict changes in self-objectification as well as shape and weight concerns (i.e., core psychopathology for bulimia nervosa). Therefore, it was hypothesized that these scales would uniquely predict changes in self-objectification and shape and weight concerns, while adjusting for common predictors of self-objectification and eating disorder pathology (e.g., thin-ideal internalization, body dissatisfaction).

Step 1 was a two-occasion autoregressive model, in which scores on the outcome measure (e.g., self-objectification) at T1 were added to predict the same outcome at T2. Then, in Step 2, scale scores from the MUQ and SCQ at T1 were added (in separate models). In Step 3, scale scores at T2 were added to assess whether *changes* in the new measures of interest were associated with changes in each of the three outcomes. Lastly, in Step 4, common predictors of the outcomes (e.g., thin ideal internalization, body dissatisfaction) were added to the models to assess whether the new measures contributed unique variance in predicting the outcomes (see Table 5). These analyses were conducted in SAS 9.3.

Table 5 Summary of significant hierarchical multiple regression models predicting self-objectification, shape concern, and weight concern

	B	*SE* B	β	*t*	R^2	*F*
Predicting T2 self-objectification						
T1 self-objectification	0.61	0.06	0.65	9.48**		
T1 MUQ Unease	−0.26	0.12	−0.19	−2.25*		
T2 MUQ Unease	0.48	0.11	0.34	4.28**		
Thin-ideal internalization	−0.26	0.43	−0.04	−0.61		
Body dissatisfaction	−0.03	0.02	−0.10	−1.68	0.56	37.83**
Predicting T2 shape concern						
Model 1						
T1 Shape Concern	0.47	0.08	0.46	6.18**		
T1 SCQ Body Discomfort	0.0004	0.03	0.001	0.01		
T2 SCQ Body Discomfort	0.13	0.03	0.33	4.19**		
Thin-ideal internalization	0.06	0.08	0.04	0.68		
Body dissatisfaction	−0.01	0.004	−0.10	−1.45	0.57	38.71**
Model 2						
T1 Shape Concern	0.60	0.08	0.58	7.87**		
T1 SCQ Pressure	−0.03	0.03	−0.08	−1.12		
T2 SCQ Pressure	0.08	0.03	0.19	2.83**		
Thin-ideal internalization	0.07	0.09	0.05	0.80		
Body dissatisfaction	−0.01	0.005	−0.15	−2.10*	0.51	31.50**
Predicting T2 weight concern						
Model 1						
T1 Weight Concern	0.47	0.07	0.46	6.73**		
T1 SCQ Body Discomfort	0.01	0.03	0.03	0.34		
T2 SCQ Body Discomfort	0.11	0.03	0.28	3.70**		
Thin-ideal internalization	0.07	0.08	0.05	0.85		
Body dissatisfaction	−0.01	0.004	−0.17	−2.59*	0.60	44.03**
Model 2						
T1 Weight Concern	0.57	0.07	0.57	8.20**		
T1 SCQ Pressure	−0.03	0.03	−0.08	−1.10		
T2 SCQ Pressure	0.06	0.03	0.14	2.22*		
Thin-ideal internalization	0.09	0.09	0.07	1.06		
Body dissatisfaction	−0.01	0.004	−0.23	−3.44**	0.55	36.25**

N = 157. Thin-ideal internalization and body dissatisfaction were measured at T1. B = unstandardized partial regression coefficient. *SE* B = standard error of the unstandardized estimate. β = standardized beta weight. Values for R^2 are adjusted. Scale scores not presented here were not significant predictors of any of these three outcomes (*ps* > .08). Models were highly similarly when also controlling for BMI. **p* < .05. ***p* < .01

Self-objectification In the first set of models, MUQ Unconfident, MUQ Unease, SCQ Body Discomfort, and SCQ Pressure were used to predict self-objectification. Changes in MUQ Unconfident from T1 to T2 did not significantly predict changes in self-objectification ($B = .23$, $p = .10$) above and beyond thin-ideal internalization and body dissatisfaction. However, as displayed in Table 5, increases in MUQ Unease from T1 to T2 were significantly associated with increases in self-objectification ($p < .05$). Changes in scores on MUQ Unease accounted for approximately 5% of the variance in self-objectification at T2 ($\Delta R^2 = .05$) over and above other predictors, including the autoregressive component of the model (i.e., self-objectification predicting itself over time). Changes in SCQ Body Discomfort and SCQ Pressure did not significantly predict changes in self-objectification (*ps* > .10) above and beyond thin-ideal internalization and body dissatisfaction. Model results were highly similar when also adjusting for BMI.

Shape and weight concern In the second set of models, Shape Concern and Weight Concern were the outcomes; MUQ Unconfident, MUQ Unease, SCQ Body Discomfort, and SCQ Pressure were used as the predictors. Changes in MUQ Unconfident and MUQ Unease did not significantly predict changes in Shape and Weight Concern (*ps* > .08) above and beyond thin-ideal internalization and body dissatisfaction. However, as displayed in Table 5, increases in SCQ Body Discomfort from T1 to T2 significantly predicted increases in Shape Concern and Weight Concern, while controlling for thin-ideal internalization and body dissatisfaction. Changes in scores on SCQ Body Discomfort accounted for approximately 7% and 6% of the variances in shape and weight concern, respectively, over and above other predictors. Additionally, as displayed in Table 5, increases in SCQ Pressure from T1 to T2 significantly predicted increases in Shape Concern and Weight Concern, while adjusting for thin-ideal internalization and body dissatisfaction. Changes in scores on SCQ Pressure accounted for approximately 2% and 1% of the variances in Shape and Weight Concern, respectively, over and above other predictors. Model results were highly similar when also adjusting for BMI.

Discussion

The aim of Study 2 was to replicate the initial factor structure of the MUQ and SCQ found in Study 1. In addition, Study 2 aimed to explore and establish the psychometric properties of these scales. Overall, results from this study replicated the initial factor structure and items of the MUQ and SCQ found in Study 1. The correlational analyses of the MUQ Unease, SCQ Body Discomfort, and SCQ Pressure scales provided different results from Study 1, but the correlational analyses of MUQ Unconfident were similar to the results from Study 1. MUQ Unconfident and SCQ Body Discomfort supported the hypothesis that the makeup and sexualized clothing scales would be correlated with self-objectification and its consequences across both time points.

These results suggest the daily consequences of confidence regarding makeup use and body discomfort regarding wearing sexualized clothing are related to self-objectification, thin-ideal internalization, body dissatisfaction, and shape and weight concerns. SCQ Pressure was significantly correlated with the majority of the scales assessing self-objectification and its consequences. However, MUQ Unease only correlated with thin-ideal internalization and self-objectification at T2. In total, there were only 5 significant correlations from Study 1 that did not replicate in Time 1 of Study 2. The different correlational results in Study 2 might suggest that wearing makeup and sexualized clothing are impacted by changes over time and/or across different groups of college women. More specifically, one group of college women may have lost interest in trying to achieve the unrealistic beauty expectation of society over time, where another group may have felt an increase in pressure to wear makeup and sexualized clothing.

Results from hierarchical multiple regression analyses indicated that changes in scores on the MUQ were associated with changes in self-objectification, whereas changes in scores on the SCQ were related more to changes in shape concern and weight concern. These results support our hypothesis. Specifically, changes in MUQ Unease significantly predicted changes in self-objectification, even when controlling for initial scores on thin-ideal internalization and body dissatisfaction. On the other hand, changes in SCQ Body Discomfort and SCQ Pressure significantly predicted changes in shape concern and weight concern, while adjusting for thin-ideal internalization and body dissatisfaction. However, it is important to note that the SCQ scales uniquely predicted a small amount of variance in shape and weight concerns. Overall, the incremental validity analysis revealed that our scales offer unique prediction of self-objectification and eating disorder symptoms over and above commonly used measures. Specifically, the daily action of wearing makeup can predict changes in levels of self-objectification while controlling for common predictors of self-objectification (i.e., thin-ideal internalization and body dissatisfaction). These results relate to self-objectification theory in that wearing makeup could be an indication of women viewing themselves as an object. Additionally, the daily action of wearing sexualized clothing can predict changes in shape and weight concerns while controlling for common predictors of eating disorder pathology (i.e., thin-ideal internalization and body dissatisfaction).

Despite the longitudinal design, it is possible that changes in self-objectification or shape and weight concerns prompt changes in makeup or sexualized clothing use. As such, cause and effect should not be inferred from the present analyses. It is also possible that these processes are reciprocally linked over time, or a third variable could be producing change in scores on both the new measures and the outcomes of interest.

General discussion

The overall goal of these studies was to create a valid and reliable measure assessing women's comfort level wearing or not wearing makeup and the pressure women feel to dress in a sexualized way. These measures were created in Study 1, and an EFA was used to better understand whether there are underlying components of these constructs. Two scales emerged from the EFA of the Makeup Questionnaire. Factor 1 was labeled Unconfident because items assessed how confident women feel wearing or not wearing makeup, and Factor 2 was labeled Unease because items assessed how comfortable women feel wearing or not wearing makeup to the store, school, or out of the house in general. Two scales emerged from the EFA of the Sexualized Clothing Questionnaire. Factor 1 was labeled Body Discomfort because items assessed if body image concerns prevent women from wearing sexualized clothing, and Factor 2 was labeled Pressure because items assessed the pressure women feel to dress in a sexualized way. Pearson correlations between MUQ Unconfident, MUQ Unease, SCQ Body Discomfort, SCQ Pressure, and self-objectification and other correlates revealed that the MUQ and SCQ scales significantly correlate with self-objectification, thin-ideal internalization, body dissatisfaction, and eating disorder symptoms. All correlations were in the expected direction: women who scored higher on thin-ideal internalization and self-objectification tended to score higher on MUQ and SCQ scales, and women who scored lower on body satisfaction tended to score higher on the MUQ and SCQ scales.

A second study confirmed the factor structure from Study 1 using a CFA of each scale and indicated that these scales were relatively stable over time. The CFA of SCQ Body Discomfort confirmed the factor structure found in Study 1, and this scale was found to be stable over time. However, the CFA of SCQ Pressure deleted an item from the original scale, and this scale had the potential to change over time. After the CFA conducted in Study 2, the final scales were: the 3-item Unconfident scale, the 3-item Unease scale, the 2-item Body Discomfort scale, and the 2-item Pressure scale. Overall, confidence, comfort, and body discomfort were stable over time according to the test-retest reliability scores. Correlational analyses revealed differences from Study 1, suggesting that wearing makeup and sexualized clothing may be impacted by changes over time across different groups of people. Additionally, the incremental validity of the scales was assessed using a series of hierarchical multiple regression models to predict changes in self-objectification, shape concern, and weight concern after adjusting for known predictors of these outcomes. Results supported the hypotheses that MUQ Unconfident and MUQ Unease would predict changes in self-objectification. While SCQ Body Discomfort and SCQ Pressure predicted changes in shape concern and weight concern, the amount of unique variance accounted for was rather small and potentially not clinically meaningful.

This study contributes to the current research on makeup use and sexualized clothing, as it provides researchers and clinicians a way to measure the pressure women feel to wear makeup and dress in a sexualized way. It is important to note that across the three assessment occasions women reported moderate levels of makeup and sexualized clothing use, with approximately 25% of the women across all occasions reporting high levels of appearance anxiety and pressure. This suggests that makeup wearing and pressure to dress in a sexualized manner are salient in their daily lives, and thus important constructs to assess in women. Given that MUQ significantly predicted changes in self-objectification, the MUQ may measure daily behavior women engage in that encourages self-objectification (or possibly results from self-objectification). This is a unique contribution to self-objectification theory; previous studies have focused on trait levels of appearance anxiety and body dissatisfaction, whereas MUQ is an assessment of a daily behavior.

This study also contributes to the study of body dissatisfaction. Body dissatisfaction is most frequently measured in the literature using trait-level measures [42]. The SCQ was designed as a more daily consequence of thin ideal internalization and body dissatisfaction. Our results across Study 1 and 2 support this. SCQ was consistently associated with body dissatisfaction. In addition, SCQ at baseline predicted increases in Shape and Weight Concerns scales at T2. The sexualized clothing scales allow researchers to measure a part of this sexual objectification theory because the scales assessed how pressured women felt to dress in a sexualized way, as well as if the weight and shape of their body prevented them from wearing sexualized clothing. Therefore, the sexualized clothing scales help determine the degree to which a woman is separating her clothing from who she is as a person.

There are also a few limitations of this study. The first limitation is the sample comprising exclusively college women, perhaps limiting whether these results generalize to older women or young adult women not attending college. Secondly, self-report measures, like the questionnaires, are prone to certain types of biases that could impact the results. Although self-report measures allow women to admit to feelings and behaviors that they may be reluctant to reveal in an interview setting, participants are unable to expand on and explain their feelings about makeup and sexualized clothing in greater depth. Another limitation to this present study is time, as this study was conducted under a limited time frame of three to four months between time 1 and time 2; more assessment time points across a longer time frame would have allowed for more sophisticated analysis of how makeup and sexualized clothing related to self-objectification.

Conclusions

Despite these limitations, this study calls attention to the pressure women feel to wear makeup and sexualized clothing. Additionally, this study reveals a need for our society to develop more sensitive measures to assess this pressure, so that we can develop better ways to help women resist this pressure to wear makeup and sexualized clothing. The MUQ scales give researchers a way to measure and record the pressure women feel to conform to society's ideal image of beauty through wearing facial makeup. Additionally, the SCQ scales provide researchers with a tool to assess the impact of society's views regarding sexualization and sexualized clothing on young women. These new measures assessing the pressure women feel to wear makeup and sexualized clothing make people aware of this pressure, which is the first step toward addressing this pressure.

Acknowledgements
None.

Funding
We would like to thank the College of Liberal Arts and Sciences at Arizona State University for providing the funds for participants.

Authors' contributions
HS: conducted the literature review, analyses, wrote the introduction, methods, and discussion, assisted in the interpretation of analyses and writing results, and edited the manuscript; MP: assisted with idea development, conducted analyses, wrote results, provided extensive edits and feedback on the manuscript; MRS: conducted hierarchical regression and edited the manuscript; CBB: assisted with initial idea development of manuscript and edited the manuscript; TKO: collected data and edited the manuscript; ABB: collected data and edited the manuscript. All authors read and approved the final manuscript.

Competing interests
The authors declare that they no have competing interests.

Author details
[1]Psychology Department Arizona State University, 950 South McAllister Avenue Room 237, Tempe, AZ 85287-1104, USA. [2]Department of Psychology, Trinity University, Center for the Sciences and Innovation room 253, One Trinity Place, San Antonio, TX 78212, USA.

References

1. Williams JE, Bennett SM. The definition of sex stereotypes via the adjective check list. Sex Roles. 1975;1(4):327–37.
2. Williams JE, Best, DL. (1982, 1990a). Measuring sex stereotypes: A multination study. Newbury Park, CA: Sage.
3. Williams JE, Best DL. Measuring sex stereotypes: A multination study. Newbury Park, CA: Sage; 1990a.
4. Graff KA, Murnen SK, Krause AK. Low-cut shirts and high-heeled shoes: Increased sexualization across time in magazine depictions of girls. Sex Roles. 2013;69(11-12):571–82. https://doi.org/10.1007/s11199-013-0321-0.
5. Fredrickson BL, Roberts T. Objectification theory: Toward understanding women's lived experiences and mental health risks. Psychology of Women Quarterly. 1997;21(2):173–206.
6. American Psychological Association, Task Force on the Sexualization of Girls. Report of the APA task force on the sexualization of girls. Washington, DC: American Psychological Association; 2007.
7. McKenney SJ, Bigler RS. High heels, low grades: Internalized sexualization and academic orientations among adolescent girls. Journal of Research on Adolescence. 2014;26:30–6.
8. Tiggemann M, Kuring JK. The role of body objectification in disordered eating and depressed mood. British Journal of Clinical Psychology. 2004; 43(3):299–311.
9. Calogero RM, Davis WN, Thompson JK. The role of self-objectification in the experience of women with eating disorders. Sex Roles. 2005;52(1-2):43–50.
10. Mercurio AE, Landry LJ. Self-objectification and well-being: The impact of self-objectification on women's overall sense of self-worth and life satisfaction. Sex Roles. 2008;58(7-8):458–66.
11. Quinn DM, Kallen RW, Twenge JM, Fredrickson BL. The disruptive effect of self-objectification on performance. Psychology of Women Quarterly. 2006; 30(1):59–64.
12. Fredrickson BL, Roberts T, Noll SM, Quinn DM, Twenge JM. That swimsuit becomes you: Sex differences in self-objectification, restrained eating, and math performance. Journal of Personality and Social Psychology. 1998;75(1): 269–84.
13. Kilbourne J. Mass media: Shaping the self-concept: Beauty and the beast of advertising. New York, NY: Free Press; 2003.
14. Cash TF, Cash DW. Women's use of cosmetics: psychological correlates and consequences. International Journal of Cosmetic Science. 1982;4(1):16–4.
15. Featherstone M. The body in consumer culture. In: Featherstone M, Hepworth M, Turner BS, editors. The body: Social process and cultural theory. Inc, Thousand Oaks, CA: Sage Publications; 1991. p. 170–96.
16. Richetin J, Croizet J-C, Huguet P. Facial makeup elicits positive attitudes at the implicit level: Evidence from the implicit association test. Current Research in Social Psychology. 2004;9(11):145–65.
17. Lynch T, Tompkins JE, van Driel II, Fritz N. Sexy, strong, and secondary: A content analysis of female characters in video games across 31 years. Journal of Communication. 2016;6(4):564–84.
18. Daniels EA, Zurbriggen EL. "It's not the right way to do stuff on facebook:" an investigation of adolescent girls' and young women's attitudes toward sexualized photos on social media. Sexuality Culture: An Interdisciplinary Quarterly. 2016;20(4):936–64.
19. Paul P. Pornified: How pornography is damaging our lives, our relationships, and our families. New York, NY: Times Books; 2005.
20. Noll SM, Fredrickson BL. A mediational model linking self- objectification, body shame, and disordered eating. Psychology of Women Quarterly. 1998;22:623–36.
21. Stice E. Review of the evidence for a sociocultural model of bulimia nervosa and an exploration of the mechanisms of action. Clinical Psychology Review. 1994;14:633–61.
22. Petrie TA, Tripp MM, Harvey P. Factorial and construct validity of the Body Parts Satisfaction Scale-Revised: An examination of minority and nonminority women. Psychology of Women Quarterly. 2002;26:213–21.
23. Luce KH, Crowther JH. The reliability of the eating disorder Examination—Self-report questionnaire version (EDE-Q). International Journal of Eating Disorders. 1999;25(3):349–51.
24. McKinley NM, Hyde JS. The Objectified Body Consciousness Scale: Development and validation. Psychology of Women Quarterly. 1996;20:181–215.
25. Stice E, Ziemba C, Margolis J, Flick P. The dual pathway model differentiates bulimics, subclinical bulimics, and controls: Testing the continuity hypothesis. Behavior Therapy. 1996;27(4):531–49.
26. Mazina V, Zhang A, Trockel M, Weisman H, Taylor CB, Jones M. An internet-based culture change focused program to reduce thinness-ideal internalization in college students. Submitted manuscript.
27. Cerny CA, Kaiser HF. A study of a measure of sampling adequacy for factor-analytic correlation matrices. Multivariate Behavioral Research. 1977;12(1):43–7.
28. Kaiser HF. The application of electronic computers to factor analysis. Educational and Psychological Measurement. 1960;20:141–51.
29. Cattell RB. The scree test for the number of factors. Multivariate Behavioral Research. 1966;1:245–76.
30. Frederick DA, Forbes GB, Grigorian KE, Jarcho JM. The UCLA body project I: Gender and ethnic differences in self-objectification and body satisfaction among 2,206 undergraduates. Sex Roles. 2007;57(5-6):317–27.
31. Fitzsimmons-Craft EE, Bardone-Cone AM, Bulik CM, Wonderlich SA, Crosby RD, Engel SG. Examining an elaborated sociocultural model of disordered eating among college women: The roles of social comparison and body surveillance. Body Image. 2014;11:488–500.
32. Diest V, Kroon AM, Perez M. Exploring the integration of thin-ideal internalization

and self-objectification in the prevention of eating disorders. Body Image. 2013;10(1):16–25.
33. Stice E. Risk and maintenance factors for eating pathology: A meta-analytic review. Psychological Bulletin. 2002;128:825–48.
34. Fuller-Tyszkiewicz M, Skouteris H, Mccabe M. A re-examination of the benefits of exercise for state body satisfaction: Consideration of individual difference factors. Journal of Sports Sciences 2013;31(7):706–13.
35. Centers for Disease Control. (2015, May 15). About Adult BMI. Retrieved March 28, 2017, from https://www.cdc.gov/healthyweight/assessing/bmi/adult_bmi/index.html
36. Muthén LK, Muthén. B. O. (1998). Mplus user's guide (3rd ed.). Los Angeles: Muthén & Muthén.
37. Enders CK, Bandalos DL. The relative performance of full information maximum likelihood estimation for missing data in structural equation models. Structural Equation Modeling. 2001;8(3):430–57.
38. Bollen KA. Latent variables in structural equation modeling. New York, NY: Guilford Press; 1989.
39. Bentler PM. Comparative fit indexes in structural models. Psychological Bulletin. 1990;107(2):238–46.
40. Browne MW, Cudeck R. Alternative ways of assessing model fit. In: Bollen KA, Long JS, editors. Testing Structural Equation Models. Newbury Park, CA: Sage; 1993. p. 136–62.
41. Steiger JH. Structural model evaluation and modification: An interval estimation approach. Multivariate Behavioral Research. 1990;25(2):173–80.
42. Fitzsimmons-Craft E, Bardone-Cone A, Wonderlich SA, Crosby RD, Engel SG, Bulik CM. The relationships among social comparisons, body surveillance, and body dissatisfaction in the natural environment. Behavior Therapy. 2015;46(2):257–71.

Exploring the effects of a family admissions program for adolescents with anorexia nervosa

Keren Fink[1*], Paul Rhodes[1], Jane Miskovic-Wheatley[2], Andrew Wallis[2], Stephen Touyz[1], Julian Baudinet[2] and Sloane Madden[2]

Abstract

Background: This study investigated patient experience in a Family Admissions Program (FAP) – a pilot treatment program for adolescents with Anorexia Nervosa at the Children's Hospital, Westmead. Based on Maudsley Family Based Treatment (FBT), the FAP involves an adolescent and his/her family undergoing a two-week family-based hospital admission at the outset of treatment. The program aims to increase intensity and support to a level needed by some families struggling to engage with or access FBT.

Method: Narrative Inquiry and Interpretative Phenomenological Analysis were used as a dual methodological approach to explore the prospective expectations and retrospective experiences of participants partaking in the program.

Results: Results indicated that in cases where the family unit has been particularly fractured as a result of the eating disorder, the FAP offers an opportunity for relational strengthening and reunification. Combined with the program's intensive support and proximity to hospital services, this serves to provide struggling families with enhanced skills and a stronger foundation for outpatient FBT.

Conclusions: For families deemed at risk of unsuccessful outcomes with FBT, the FAP can be considered as an appropriate treatment adjunct to place alongside or before the commencement of FBT.

Keywords: Anorexia nervosa, Maudsley family based treatment, Adolescent, Qualitative research, Eating disorders

Plain English summary

This paper looked at a novel adaptation of family based treatment (FBT) for adolescents with Anorexia Nervosa – the Family Admissions Program (FAP). The FAP involves a two-week stay in a residential hospital for the whole family of a patient who is struggling to get well with typical FBT.

Our research showed that the FAP was helpful for families who required more intensity and professional support in treatment. Being close to hospital services and supports during the FAP allowed members of these families to better develop skills to fight the illness.

A considerable number of individuals are expected to experience unsuccessful outcomes with typical FBT. This research offers important insights into how to develop more suitable adaptations of FBT for these patients and their families. This paper should be important to readers interested the areas of family therapy and eating disorders, particularly those hoping to learn about new avenues of clinical treatment in this field.

Background

Research from the past three decades has shown that family-based treatment (FBT) for childhood and adolescent Anorexia Nervosa (AN) can often lead to positive outcomes at the end of treatment [1]. Clinical trials, systematic reviews and follow-up studies of FBT for adolescent anorexia nervosa (AN) [2] have demonstrated rates of remission between 31% and 49% 12 months after

* Correspondence: kerenfink@gmail.com
[1]Clinical Psychology Unit, the University of Sydney, Sydney, NSW 2006, Australia
Full list of author information is available at the end of the article

treatment, with improving rates of remission continuing to be seen for over five years following treatment [3–7]. Despite these findings, FBT does not yield favourable outcomes in a significant minority of cases. Studies examining moderating factors of treatment in clinical populations undergoing FBT found that complex family structures and characteristics, such as high parental criticism and high expressed emotion led to lower remission rates, early dropout and continuing symptoms post-treatment at follow-up assessment points [8–11]. Having a non-intact family unit was also shown to require longer and more supportive courses of therapy in these studies. Studies investigating the optimal length and frequency of FBT sessions [2, 12, 13] have also highlighted an association between more severe psychiatric psychopathology (such as higher rates of eating disorder symptomatology, as well as comorbidity) and worse treatment outcomes. In these cases, longer and more intensive administrations of FBT were required, with the researchers suggesting that more intractable presentations of AN are more challenging for parents to contain because behavioural and psychological change takes longer to be achieved.

To account for the treatment challenges posed by the above factors, a number of different adaptations to FBT have been developed over the past years [11, 14–16]. A central idea in many proposed adaptations for FBT has been to more directly address the aforementioned factors that may be maintaining AN symptoms within the family context, as well as focus on the possible need for higher levels of intensity and support in treatment that are often needed to drive important early therapeutic change for patients and families [17, 18]. Having early therapeutic change is especially important for families who exhibit the complex structures and characteristics previously described as leading to worse treatment outcomes, as well as for patients whose more complex illness psychopathology is likely to complicate the straightforward administration of FBT. Additionally, families who come from rural or remote areas with limited or no access to ongoing and regular specialised eating disorder services are likely to need more intensive doses of FBT in order for their treatment delivery to be commensurate with how manualised FBT is meant to be administered [2, 17].

In light of the existing limitations in treatment outcomes for particular individuals with AN, a FBT-based family residential program (Family Admission Program – FAP) has been piloted at the Eating Disorder Service (EDS) at the Children's Hospital at Westmead, Australia (CHW), with the aim of targeting individuals and families who have struggled with FBT due to the aforementioned risk factors associated with poorer treatment. The FAP's objective is to create a more intensive form of FBT, which involves the adolescent patient and his/her family living in a self-contained apartment within a hospital ward for a two-week period of daily treatment, often following a short inpatient admission for refeeding and medical stabilisation [17]. During this time, the family participate in a modified and condensed form of the first phase of FBT, but with additional interventions tailored to the family's needs, such as managing distress or supporting meal time re-feeding skills. This occurs with multiple individual, sibling and family therapy sessions each week, and also multiple family meals. A comprehensive multi-disciplinary team is used to provide a higher level of medical and/or psychological support, providing the safety and containment necessary for parents to learn the skills to re-feed their child (see [17] for a detailed description of the structure, referral process and implementation of the FAP).

Despite the increasing use of the FAP at the CHW, no research exists evaluating its efficacy for the populations to which it targets. In light of this, the present study was largely exploratory in nature, aiming to investigate patients' and families' experiences during the FAP, and ask the question of what role participants felt the FAP had in their overall treatment for AN. Given the small number of participants available, a qualitative methodological approach was undertaken. This allowed for an open-ended and in-depth exploration of the phenomena in question, and also enabled richer, contextualised and more meaningful data regarding subjective experience to be elicited [19]. A secondary aim was to gain an understanding of how to improve the ongoing implementation of the FAP, and to guide future research evaluating the program's intended treatment effects.

Methods

The study comprised of two components: a Narrative Inquiry conducted with 10 families after they had completed the FAP; and an Interpretative Phenomenological Analysis (IPA) with 4 families and their clinicians, conducted both before and after they completed the FAP. This dual-methodological approach allowed for triangulation of the data, wherein phenomena in question could be studied via more than one methodology, and thus strengthen the validity of observed results [20]. These two components also complemented each other, since their combination offered the ability to have a dual set of data collection that could give a more comprehensive picture of participants' experiences of the FAP at different time points in their overall treatment for AN [20, 21]. As a methodological tool, Narrative Inquiry provides a temporal framework for phenomena in question [22]. IPA, on the other hand, is concerned with personal interpretation of events and thus helpful in gaining an understanding of the subjective experience of the participant being studied [23]. For the current study, the Narrative Inquiry was thus expected to help place the effects of the FAP within participants' overall treatment trajectories, whilst the IPA was used to capture a more detailed picture of specific and nuanced mechanisms of therapeutic change in the program. It was thus hoped that the IPA would complement the findings of the narrative inquiry by zooming in on how the features of the FAP actually worked to achieve change for participants.

A specific constructionist framework [24] was taken for the paradigms of inquiry, as it underscores the notion that meaning generated from research is inevitably a product of co-constructed knowledge between the researcher and participant. This paradigmatic approach thus allowed for the theoretical influences of the researchers to be acknowledged and incorporated into the collection and analysis of data. These influences predominantly included the core philosophical tenets of FBT, in which all the authors had clinical experience.

Narrative inquiry.

A Narrative Inquiry [22, 24, 25] was first conducted to assess and explore the role that the FAP played in the history of AN in the family, as well as the meaning that the family ascribed to the program in the recovery process. Narrative inquiry involves the construction of narratives of personal experience by participants, wherein interviews between researcher and subject typically serve as the primary means of data collection. These are then transcribed and written as the narrative, which is then analysed for overarching themes of meaning. Narrative Inquiry provides a temporal context for investigation [22], allowing participants to assign meaning to past personal events [25]. It thus seemed an appropriate methodological tool for eliciting participants' reflection on the meaning of the FAP within their overall journey through the illness.

Participants

In order to recruit as large a sample size as possible, non-purposive sampling was used, in which all families who had completed the FAP by the time that data collection commenced for the Narrative Inquiry were eligible for recruitment. Inclusion and exclusion criteria for participation in the study followed the same criteria used for participation in the FAP [17]: the participant was under 18 years of age with a primary diagnosis of an eating disorder; the participant had been medically stable (pulse 50 bpm, temperature > 35.5 °C, blood pressure > 80/40) for at least 72 h prior to admission to the FAP; the participant was eating a minimally sufficient intake for continuing medical stability.

A total of 14 families were contacted and sent information about the study. Three families declined to respond to the researchers after being sent the initial information, and so were not included in the study. One family declined to participate after being contacted by researchers. See Table 1 for details.

Table 1 Participant Demographics for Narrative Inquiry

Participant	Age	Family structure	Location	Complex presentation/ Comorbidity	Participating family members in interview	Phone/Face-to-face interview
1 (female)	12	Intact	Rural	No	Parents, adolescent, all siblings	Phone
2 (female)	12	Intact	Inner metropolitan area	No	Parents and adolescent (no siblings in family)	Face-to-face
3 (male)	13	Intact	Outer metropolitan area	No	Parents, adolescent, all siblings	Phone
4 (female)	13	Intact	Inner metropolitan area	Yes: self-harm	Parents, adolescent, all siblings	Face-to-face
5 (female)	14	Non-intact	Inner metropolitan area	No	Parents, adolescent, all siblings	Face-to-face
6 (female)	14	Intact	Rural	No	Mother, adolescent, one out of two siblings	Phone
7 (female)	15	Intact	Interstate	Yes: self-harm; OCD	Parents, adolescent, all siblings	Phone
8 (female)	15	Non-intact	Inner metropolitan area	Yes: self-harm; complex trauma	Parents, adolescent (siblings not present)	Face-to-face
9 (female)	16	Intact	Outer metropolitan area	Yes: OCD	Mother, adolescent (siblings not present)	Face-to-face
10 (female)	16	Non-intact	Inner metropolitan area	Yes: self-harm; complex trauma	Parents, adolescent, all siblings	Face-to-face

Procedure

In-depth, semi-structured interviews were developed by the authors, in line with the research question. They were then conducted either by phone or face-to-face with each family with the first author. The interview questions asked the family to recount the story of their journey with AN to date, specifically focusing on their experiences during the FAP (interview schedules can be sought from authors upon request). Interviews lasted between 60 and 90 min and were audio-recorded and transcribed verbatim. The interview transcripts were then used to create an overarching narrative by the first author, which aimed to tell the story of how and where the FAP fit within each family's experience responding to the challenges of AN. Narratives were created by first organising the data from each transcript temporally, beginning with the onset and course of AN, up to the present day, and then ending with family members' reflections on the FAP [25]. Once the data was organised in this way, it was then written into a story that flowed coherently and contained a distinct beginning, middle and end. Upon completion of the narrative, it was reviewed by the family so that any revisions they deemed necessary could be incorporated into the story to ensure that their voices and experiences were authentically reflected [26]. Families were interviewed between 6 and 10 months following their completion of the FAP. At the time of their interview, four families were still undergoing the final phases of FBT and had largely achieved weight, eating and exercise behavioural containment. All participating families had thus reached similar stages in their trajectory of treatment.

Data analysis

Data analysis first involved an in-depth, line-by-line analysis of each completed narrative, where regularly occurring words and themes could be identified [22]. From this, provisional thematic categories were developed, which reflected the main themes and subthemes running through each story. These were then compared and contrasted across cases, so that any themes or phenomena common to the participant sample could be identified. To maintain validity and rigour in the interpretation and analysis of data, cross-coding by the second author was performed with four out of the ten cases both at the beginning and end of analysis. This involved the second author going through the same analytic process, so that the final analysis yielded themes that had a reliable degree of agreement between coders.

Interpretative phenomenological analysis (IPA)

The aim of the second component of the study was to achieve a more detailed analysis of families' real-time experiences whilst they were currently undergoing the FAP, and then compare their real-time reflection of events to the clinical observations and thoughts of their treating clinicians. Since primary focus was on exploring factors within participants' experiences, and the group comprised only a small number of cases, Interpretative Phenomenological Analysis (IPA) was used. IPA has been reported useful for such sample sizes [27] and is particularly committed to obtaining a detailed and rich interpretative understanding of personal experience of a phenomenon or event [23].

Each family's treating pair of clinicians was also interviewed. The clinicians were either clinical psychologists or clinical social workers, who had been trained and practised extensively in FBT and family therapy.

Participants

Any families participating in the FAP at the time of data collection (during the year of 2014) were eligible for participation. A total of six families who underwent the FAP during 2014 were sent information about the study. The aforementioned inclusion/exclusion criteria for participation in the FAP were again used for participation in the IPA (see 'Participants' section of Narrative Inquiry). Two families who commenced but did not complete the FAP during this time were excluded from the study, so that a total of four families took part. For each of the four families, their two treating clinicians were also interviewed together as a pair. See Table 2 for details on participating families.

Table 2 Participant Demographics for IPA

Participant	Age	Family Structure	Location	Complex presentation/ Comorbidity	Participating family members in interviews	Phone/Face-to-face
1 (male)	15	Non-intact	Interstate	No	Both parents, adolescent, all siblings	Face-to-face
2 (female)	15	Non-intact	Rural	Yes: self-harm; ASD	Both parents, adolescent, all siblings	Face-to-face
3 (female)	15	Intact	Inner metropolitan area	No	Both parents, adolescent, all siblings	Face-to-face
4 (female)	12	Intact	Outer metropolitan area	No	Both parents, adolescent, all siblings	Face-to-face

Procedure

Semi-structured interviews were conducted by the first author at the hospital, with the family alone and then with their treating pair of clinicians. Interviews were conducted at two time points: once on the first day of the FAP (pre-treatment) and once on the last day of the program (post-treatment). Pre-treatment interviews asked participants to discuss the reasons behind the family's admission into the program, as well as any expectations of change. In the post-treatment interviews, participants were asked to reflect upon the family's experiences of the program and any outcomes they witnessed in light of their initial expectations (questions in both sets of interviews were appropriately phrased to suit whether it was the family or clinicians being interviewed). Both sets of interviews involved a series of open-ended questions, which encouraged participants to talk in detail about their experiences. Each interview lasted for approximately 45–60 min. The interviews were then audio-recorded and transcribed verbatim, and the transcripts coded and analysed for themes that emerged both within and between cases.

Data analysis

Data analysis was performed by the first author and began with an iterative, in-depth analysis of each set of interview transcripts [27]. Detailed codes of meaning were generated from the data, which aimed to interpret and capture the meaning that participants made from their experiences in the FAP. Recurring codes were then catalogued and connected together, so that a pattern of themes of experience of the FAP could be developed and compared across cases. The final set of themes and super-ordinate themes were formulated into a table, where evidential instances of each theme could be located in the transcript [27]. Again, rigour and validity in the interpretation and analysis of data was attained by the second author cross-coding two out of the four cases.

Table 3 Narrative Synthesis: From onset to recovery

Theme	Experience
Progressive Intensification of AN	Quick escalation of symptoms
	Series of failed treatment attempts and/ or hospital inpatient admissions
	Unsuccessful engagement with FBT
Fracturing of the family unit	Parents differing in opinion on severity, nature and appropriate treatment of illness
	Family members each feel isolated
	Family unit disconnected
Crisis point reached	AN reaches extreme level
	Family unit disconnected
	Family at 'rock-bottom'
	FAP accepted as last-resort option
Participation in FAP	Re-integration of family unit
	Positive experience overcoming AN
	Insight and motivation to fight AN
Ongoing process of recovery	Re-engagement with FBT
	Ongoing process of improvement from AN, with periods of relapses and remissions

Results

Narrative inquiry

Family members' reflections on the role of the FAP highlighted a common set of experiences that could be conceptualised into five predominant themes, from onset to recovery: 1) a progressive intensification of AN; 2) fracturing of the family unit; 3) reaching a crisis point; 4) participation in the FAP; and 5) ongoing process of recovery. See Table 3.

Progressive intensification of AN

For the majority of families, parents reported being taken aback by the seriousness and rapid escalation of their child's eating disorder symptoms –[Mother]: *"I didn't see the beginnings of the anorexia for a while... We just didn't understand what it was"*. Nearly all of the families reported a long period of trying to resolve the disorder themselves, with little success. The inability to contain the growing intensity of the AN symptoms led parents to eventually seek out more specialised assistance; however, factors such as remote living locations and severe symptomatology prevented a lot of families from accessing adequate services when needed, leaving them to feel particularly hopeless and isolated from effective supports.

No family reported successful engagement with FBT, despite being linked in with CHW by this time. Families were either unable to access services which offered eating disorder treatment (often because of their remote living location), or they struggled to engage in the therapy effectively. This was a result of a number of issues including family members being unable to agree to FBT treatment structure as planned, or because an unexpected inpatient admission meant family sessions had to be suspended.

Fracturing of the family unit

All participants reported increasing disconnection within the family unit as family members struggled with the rising intensity of the AN. Within the parental subsystem, there was often a split between parents regarding the seriousness of their child's AN, causing them to feel increasingly divided and alienated from each other, particularly in their approach on how to address and treat the disorder – [Mother]: *"my husband just did not really understand what was needed...so we would end up fighting...he'd say, 'You're making this a bigger issue. I don't see any issue,' and I'm thinking, 'Are you seeing anything!'"* Siblings similarly reported feeling distanced from the family unit, largely because of their desire to avoid the growing household strain and conflict.

Crisis point reached. Eventually, the effect of the family's sense of disconnection and despair, combined with the extreme presentation of AN, resulted in them reaching a crisis point. By this point, families felt that they had exhausted all feasible treatment options. Some of them had been offered the opportunity to participate in the FAP at previous points, but turned it down due to how disruptive they expected it would be. In other cases, it had not yet been considered a necessary step to be offered by the treating team at CHW. Nonetheless, the sense of peril experienced at the time of crisis prompted all families to agree to participate in the FAP, which they viewed it as their last remaining option – [father]: *"but then eventually... when we hit that big low, we all just decided, 'Okay, this is pretty much our last option, otherwise we've got no idea what else we can do".*

Experiences during the FAP

All families described the two-week period of the FAP as highly intensive. They attributed this to the number of therapy sessions, family meals and activities each day, as well as the experience of everyone living together in the small self-contained apartment for the whole program. A 'hothouse' effect of therapeutic change was produced, in which families described being unable to avoid confronting issues that had been previously sidelined – [adolescent]: *"When you're doing it every day, you can be directly asked questions about all the issues that you probably knew were there, but were too hard to discuss".* Coming face to face with the full extent of behaviours associated with the AN also meant that family members saw the severity of the disorder in the same way for the first time. Not only did this unify an understanding of what AN was and how it had affected their family, but it also gave them a shared experience of dealing with the disorder that could begin to bridge the gaps that had developed in different family relationships –[Mother]: *"It made [father] understand a little bit more about the illness, about what I had been dealing with, and it helped me understand about him feeling left out, shut out. So I think our relationship particularly benefited".* In addition to these relational changes, experiencing even a minor triumph or positive experience in overcoming the AN seemed to give parents motivation and confidence in continuing the principles learned during the FAP once back at home – [Father] *"and in the end...after succeeding on that food penalty plan* [a behavioural contingency management system]*...there was a breakthrough... and that changed stuff for us at home".*

Ongoing process of recovery

The time following participation in the FAP was characterised by a gradual movement away from the AN. During this period, there was also a re-engagement with FBT from eight out of the ten families, either at CHW or at a service closer to their home. Families described recovery as an ongoing process that they were still working towards (one which included the management of both mental health and AN-related issues), rather than a discrete stage at which they had arrived – [Mother] *"There's always stuff that's happening with her and [the AN] is still continual. It's still ongoing...you can't not turn on for a day".*

Interpretative phenomenological analysis

The IPA highlighted six major themes of participant experience during the FAP, which summarised both the family and clinical aims of participating in the program, as well as their final evaluations of the program's effects and outcomes. See Table 4.

Pre-treatment

Complexity requiring FAP

Prior to commencing the program, families and clinicians both spoke of complexity in the adolescent's illness presentation and family context (such as a remote living location and/or non-intact family structure) as being primary reasons prompting the family's consideration for the FAP, particularly because such factors were expected to limit the family's ability to effectively engage in FBT long-term – [clinician]: *"She wasn't eating or drinking anything in the week prior to admission, and when she was [an inpatient] she was actually trying to keep the NG tube in as much as possible, saying things like I don't want to go home... which is different to typical presentations".*

Family's hope for broad change

Families' reasons for participating in the program reflected their hopes for bettering their chances of change, not just in regard to the eating disorder symptoms, but also in terms of a wider change in the adolescent and family unit. They looked at it as a transitional step that could help them feel more skilled and prepared

Table 4 Themes of experience in IPA

Pre-treatment	Post-treatment
Complexity requiring FAP	*Changes towards the AN*
Family's hope for broad change	*Changes in the family*
Clinicians' need for further assessment	*Changes in the adolescent*

at challenging illness behaviours prior to returning home – [mother]: *"I think we were a little bit anxious about going straight into outpatient treatment... that we all weren't ready for that. So we can now be in a setting where...we are given the reign, but also given some help if we need it".*

Clinicians' need for further assessment

For the clinicians, the need for further assessment of the family unit, prior to commencing weekly outpatient treatment, was seen as important for a positive treatment experience, and thus made them the view the FAP a necessary treatment step in better consolidating ongoing FBT for these families.

Post-treatment

Changes toward the AN

For the majority of participants, their reflections following the FAP seemed to satisfy their initial expectations and desires for change. Importantly, the outcomes described by participants suggested an overall shift in the way that the family approached the AN and their situation, rather than a change in the illness itself. Whilst there was a reduction in eating disorder symptoms reported in all four families, this was not necessarily the primary point of improvement reflected upon by participants.

Changes in the family

Both clinicians and families observed changes in the way that family members viewed and related to the disorder, particularly in terms of parents feeling more confidence and effectively skilled in their capacity to manage eating disorder behaviours, as well as having a better understanding of the reality of what ongoing FBT would entail. Changes in family functioning and interactional dynamics were also noted by both clinicians and family members, predominately in regard to the way that family members related to and communicated with each other, as well as in the way that the family reorganized itself against the AN – [mother] *"we devoted a lot of the time to getting our, sort of system, working properly so we don't drop things through the cracks".*

Changes in the adolescent

Finally, for three out of the four families, some sort of wider shift within the adolescent and his/her demeanour and personality was seen. This was observed either in the way that the adolescent related to and engaged with the rest of the family, or in their behaviour and level of distress in regard to eating – [sibling]: *"she talked about wanting to get a babysitting job...and it means that she's thinking about a more positive life... she has meaning."*

Key factors of the FAP connected with post-treatment outcomes.

The IPA importantly highlighted two factors that were consistently noted across all four cases as being especially necessary in leading to the observed outcomes at the end of the FAP: a) intensity, and b) proximity to supports.

Intensity

The high frequency of sessions and self-contained family living arrangement was seen to enhance treatment intensity in a positive way. Participants explained that the increased number of sessions over the short two-week period allowed for more opportunities than normal to discuss and work through family issues that would have otherwise been put aside in the process of re-feeding – [father]: *"if you're coming in here for weekly sessions this would take months and months and months... because if you're having problems one day and it was going to be another few days until your appointment, you might not have been able to recover quite as well or work through it".* The clinicians elaborated on this point, adding that the increased face-to-face time with the family not only allowed for further assessment (which could then feed back into the direction of sessions), but it also sped up the structural change within the family unit that they were trying to achieve. The family's intensive living arrangement during the program similarly created more opportunities for change, in which there was a sense of 'induced bonding and interaction' as a result of having to live together for two weeks without any of the typical distractions and responsibilities of daily life – [father]: *"All the other distractions of work and school and the things that need to get done at home, just haven't been here".*

Proximity to supports

The close proximity to hospital supports including after-hours support and the hospital emergency department also allowed parents to have a more comprehensive idea about the full array of strategies and resources which existed and could be used if needed, particularly in extreme cases. Parents noted that this proximity also made them feel confident enough to implement and persist with these strategies, that they would have otherwise felt were too risky or extreme at home, such as calling the police or an ambulance in response to food refusal or dangerous behaviour. In addition to having access to the whole team, this created a sense of containment and safety, which seemed to further enable processes of therapeutic change to take place more easily – [father]: *"we then really clearly understood how far we could push and what resources were around us to enable [her eating] to happen".*

Discussion

The objectives of this study were twofold: first, to explore participants' experiences and processes of change during their time in the FAP; and second, to use these insights to establish possible areas of improvements of further implementations of the program, as well as to inform paths for future research of treatment effects. The two methods identified a number of common themes in the families' experiences during the FAP. Illness complexity and a desire to remediate negative impacts on family functioning were identified as reasons that families first sought to engage in the FAP, whilst structural changes in the family unit and its enhanced response to managing the AN, were seen as key positive outcomes at completion of the program. Importantly, these factors of change were also endorsed by clinicians. The confluence of themes from the two methods of qualitative analysis thus added to the strength of findings in addressing the study's objectives. Taken together, these findings highlighted four overall factors that led to change for participating patients and families.

First, the family unit appeared to reconnect and restructure itself in a way that was more effective at meeting treatment goals during the FAP. This was largely due to the adoption of more clearly delineated family roles, as well as relational styles that no longer avoided conflict. It thus seemed that the program allowed for the development of more positive family relationships, which had a protective quality that helped the family start to change longstanding unhelpful patterns of interaction. This also reflects previous findings that these structural and relational characteristics are important in effectively containing and reducing AN behaviours [2, 28, 29]. It thus seemed that the FAP helped families in this study reunify and emerge from a point of crisis, which ultimately resulted in the re-engagement with FBT for 8 out of 10 of the families in the Narrative Inquiry. This suggests that the program could help other families at risk of poor prognoses improve their responses to treatment. A suggested mechanism of change in FBT has been to increase anxiety to mobilise action; however, here change was initiated by increasing support equal to the crisis faced [2]. This may be an important adjustment to further explore, as some families may need treatment to be organised differently in order to benefit from the initial FBT goals.

Second, the presence of even a small change to managing the AN was shown to lead to a renewed sense of motivation for ongoing treatment for nearly all of the families. Such successes allowed families to challenge feelings of inadequacy and hopelessness about their child's illness. Focusing on how to initiate these types of changes appears to be a key aspect in helping families become unstuck. It is likely that the FAP creates an important type of supportive environment – one that allows families to practically do something different, but also to recognise that an exception to their previous approach is occurring. This then reduces the negative impact of their previous failures, whilst also amplifying feelings of hopefulness [30, 31].

Third, the environmental context of the FAP was important in mobilising parents' efforts at change at the same time as making them feel supported. This was largely through the immediate and proximal access to hospital-based services, which seemed to provide families with a sense of containment and reassurance. For example, the closeness to services such as the emergency department and after-hours psychological and psychiatric interventions helped parents feel confident about resorting to more extreme, but ultimately necessary, measures much earlier than would have normally been the case. This suggests potential benefits from having the family reside within the hospital, rather than at a separate location. The intensive design of the FAP was a similarly key environmental factor for participants, namely the presence of multiple daily therapy sessions, as well as the family residing together in the hospital for the duration of the program. Indeed, the benefits of intensive therapeutic engagement such as this have been historically noted in a number of other therapeutic disciplines, where the more intensive frequency of sessions has been shown to prevent opportunities for avoidance and other defences to emerge and derail treatment progress [32, 33].

Finally, the fact that families and clinicians had analogous expectations and evaluations of the FAP suggests that the two groups understood the treatment needs in a similar way. It seems that this mutual understanding could help to create a stronger therapeutic alliance between parents and clinicians which could then also add to parents' sense of support and efficacy [34]. Indeed, previous research has highlighted that there are therapeutic benefits of commonly shared treatment goals and alignment between therapists and families [35–38].

Conclusions

In light of the growing research showing that a considerable number of families will struggle with FBT [3, 18, 39] the results of this study offer potential insights into how to administer a program such as the FAP. The current results suggest that for families who are coming to treatment resource-poor, under relational strain and at an acute point of crisis, a program like the FAP can provide a higher level of therapeutic intensity and proximity to professional support, which is needed to help families feel more contained and supported in challenging the AN to a more extreme, but necessary, level than would otherwise be possible in typical outpatient administration of FBT.

Whilst this study has provided the first empirical explorations of the FAP that can highlight components of treatment important to a family admission for AN, it nonetheless possesses limitations that have implications for the utility of these findings. First, the sample size was small, particularly for the IPA. Whilst this size has been deemed empirically sufficient in previous IPA studies [27], a larger number of participants could have enabled more depth and breadth to the range of thematic categories identified. Second, all the authors had practise in FBT. Whilst the knowledge-base generated by this clinical experience likely helped to enable a deeper understanding of the treatment components and experiences that participants described in interviews, it also had the potential to influence the way in which data was analysed and interpreted. Precautions were adopted to try to accommodate for this limitation, including adopting a philosophical stance of inquiry that acknowledged the position and influences of the researchers as an active part of the empirical process [22, 24]; however, there nonetheless remained the likelihood that biases existed in the way that meaning was made from the analytical process. Notwithstanding these issues, the current study nonetheless offers important insights into the nature of the FAP, and can thus inform how future quantitative research regarding family-based hospital admission programs could be carried out to more directly investigate specific mechanisms of therapeutic change. In doing so, the avenues for treatment for individuals and families unlikely to respond successfully to FBT can continue to grow and be enhanced.

Abbreviations

AN: Anorexia Nervosa; CHW: Children's Hospital at Westmead; FAP: Family Admissions Program; FBT: Family Based Treatment; IPA: Interpretative Phenomenological Analysis

Acknowledgements

Not applicable.

Funding

Funding was not sought for the present research as it was completed as part of a thesis submitted in fulfilment of the requirements for the degree Doctor of Clinical Psychology/Master of Science at the University of Sydney.

Authors' contributions

All of the listed authors were involved in designing the work, interpreting the data and drafting and revising the final manuscript. KF, JM-W and PR were also responsible for acquiring and analysing the data. All listed authors are accountable for all aspects of the work, including any issues related to accuracy and integrity. All authors read and approved the final manuscript.

Competing interests

The authors declare that they have no competing interests.

Author details

[1]Clinical Psychology Unit, the University of Sydney, Sydney, NSW 2006, Australia. [2]Department of Psychological Medicine, Department of Adolescent Medicine, Eating Disorder Service, The Children's Hospital at Westmead, Sydney, NSW 2145, Australia.

References

1. Lock J. An update on evidence-based psychosocial treatments for eating disorders in children and adolescents. J Clin Child Adolesc Psychol. 2015;44: 702–21.
2. Lock J, Le Grange D. Treatment manual for anorexia nervosa: a family-based approach. 2nd ed. New York, NY: Guilford Press; 2012.
3. Madden S, Miskovic-Wheatley J, Wallis A, Kohn M, Lock J, Le Grange D, Touyz SA. Randomized controlled trial of in-patient treatment for anorexia nervosa in medically unstable adolescents. Psychol Med. 2015;45:415–27.
4. Watson HJ, Bulik CM. Update on the treatment of anorexia nervosa: review of clinical trials, practice guidelines and emerging interventions. Psychol Med. 2013;43:2477–500.
5. Le Grange D, Eisler I. Family interventions in adolescent anorexia nervosa. Child Adolesc Psychiatr Clin N Am. 2009;18:159–73.
6. Keel PK, Haedt A. Evidence-based psychosocial treatments for eating problems and eating disorders. Journal of Clinical Child and Adolescent Psychology. 2008;37:39–61.
7. Bulik CM, Berkman ND, Brownley KA, Sedway JA. Lohr. Anorexia nervosa treatment: a systematic review of randomised control trials. Int J Eat Disord. 2007;40:310–20.
8. Eisler I, Simic M, Russell GFM, Dare CA. Randomised controlled treatment trial of two forms of family therapy in adolescent anorexia nervosa: a five-year follow-up. J Child Psychol Psychiatry. 2007;48:552–60.
9. Le Grange D, Eisler I, Dare C, Russell GFM. Evaluation of family treatments in adolescent anorexia nervosa: a pilot study. Int J Eat Disord. 1992;12:347–57.
10. Szmukler G, Eisler I, Russell GFM, Dare C. Anorexia nervosa, parental 'expressed emotion' and dropping out of treatment. Br J Psychiatry. 1985; 147:265–71.
11. Eisler I, Dare C, Hodes M, Russell GFM, Dodge E, Le Grange D. Family therapy for anorexia nervosa: the results of a controlled comparison of two family interventions. J Child Psychol Psychiatry. 2000;41:727–36.
12. Lock J, Agras S, Bryson S, Kraemer HA. Comparison of short and long term family therapy for adolescent anorexia nervosa. Journal of American academic child and. Adolesc Psychiatry. 2005;44:253–61.
13. Lock J, Couturier J, Bryson S, Agras S. Predictors of drop-out and remission in family therapy for adolescent anorexia nervosa in a randomised control trial. Int J Eat Disord. 2006;39:639–47.
14. Jewell T, Blessitt E, Stewart C, Simic M, Eisler I. Family therapy for child and adolescent eating disorders: a critical review. Fam Process. 2016;55:1–18.
15. Girz L, Robinson AL, Foroughe M, Jasper K, Boachie A. Adapting family-based therapy to a day hospital programme for adolescents with eating disorders: preliminary outcomes and trajectories of change. J Fam Ther. 2013;35:102–20.
16. Hoste R. Incorporating family-based therapy principles into a partial hospitalization programme for adolescents with anorexia nervosa: challenges and considerations. J Fam Ther. 2015;37:41–60.
17. Wallis A, Alford C, Hanson A, Titterton J, Madden S, Kohn M. Innovations in Maudsley family-based treatment for anorexia nervosa at the Children's Hospital at Westmead: a family admission programme. J Fam Ther. 2013;35:68–81.
18. Lock J, Le Grange D, Agras WS, Fitzpatrick KK, Jo B, Accurso E, Stainer M. Can adaptive treatment improve outcomes in family-based therapy for adolescents with anorexia nervosa? Feasibility and treatment effects of a multi-site treatment study. Behav Res Ther. 2015;73:90–5.
19. Ridgeway P. ReStorying psychiatric disability. Learning from first person recovery narratives. Psychiatric Rehabilitation Journal. 2001;24:335–43.
20. Denzin NK. Sociological methods. New York: McGraw-Hill; 1978.
21. Bekhet AK, Zauszniewski JA. Methodological triangulation: an approach to understanding data. Nurse Researcher. 2012;2:40–3.

22. Clandinin DJ, Connelly FM. Narrative inquiry: experience and story in qualitative research. San Francisco: Jossey Bass; 2000.
23. Pietkiewicz I, Smith JAA. Practical guide to using interpretative phenomenological analysis in qualitative research psychology. Psychological Journal. 2014;20:7–14.
24. Gergen M, Gergen K. Narratives in action. Narrat Inq. 2006;16:112–21.
25. Polkinghorne D. Narrative configuration in qualitative analysis. Qualitative Studies in Education. 1995;8:5–23.
26. Kirkpatrick H, Byrne CA. Narrative inquiry: moving on from homelessness for individuals with a major mental illness. J Psychiatr Ment Health Nurs. 2009; 16:68–75.
27. Smith JA, Osborn M. Interpretative phenomenological analysis. In: Smith J, editor. Qualitative psychology: a practical guide to research methods. London: Sage; 2008. p. 53–80.
28. Ellison R, Rhodes P, Madden S, Miskovic J, Wallis A, Baillie A, Touyz S. Do the components of manualized family-based treatment for anorexia nervosa predict weight gain? Int J Eat Disord. 2012;45:609–14.
29. Dare C, Eisler I, Colahan M, Crowther C, Senior R, Asen E. The listening heart and the chi square: clinical and empirical perceptions in the family therapy of anorexia nervosa. J Fam Ther. 1995;17:31–57.
30. Whitney J, Eisler I. Theoretical and empirical models around caring for someone with an eating disorder: the reorganisation of family life and inter-personal maintenance factors. J Ment Health. 2005;14:575–85.
31. White M, Epston D. Narrative means to therapeutic ends. New York: W. W. Norton; 1990.
32. Gedo PM, Cohler BJ. Session frequency, regressive intensity, and the psychoanalytic process. Psychoanal Psychol. 1992;9:245–9.
33. Freedman N, Hoffenber JD, Vorus N, Frosch A. The effectiveness of psychoanalytic psychotherapy: the role of treatment duration, frequency of sessions, and the therapeutic relationship. Journal of the American Psychonalytic Association. 1999;47:741–72.
34. Rhodes P, Baillie A, Brown J, Madden S. Parental efficacy in the family-based treatment of anorexia: preliminary development of the parents versus anorexia scale (PVA). Eur Eat Disord Rev. 2005;13:399–405.
35. Heatherington L, Friedlander ML, Diamond GM, Escudero V, Pinsof WM. 25 years of systemic therapies research: progress and promise. Psychother Res. 2015;25:348–64.
36. Sly R, Morgan JF, Mountford VA, Lacey JH. Predicting premature termination of hospitalised treatment for anorexia nervosa: the roles of therapeutic alliance, motivation and behaviour change. Eating Behaviours. 2013;14:119–23.
37. Forsberg S, LoTempio E, Bryson S, Fitzpatrick KK, Le Grange D, Lock J. Int J Eat Disord. 2013;46:34–8.
38. Pereira T, Lock J, Oggins J. Role of therapeutic alliance in family therapy for adolescent anorexia nervosa. Int J Eat Disord. 2006;39:677–84.
39. Le Grange D, Lock J, Agras WS, Moye A, Bryson SW, Jo B, et al. Moderators and mediators of remission in family-based treatment and adolescent focused therapy for anorexia nervosa. Behav Res Ther. 2012;50:85–92.

5

Disordered eating behaviour in young adults with type 1 diabetes mellitus

S. Keane[1*], M. Clarke[1], M. Murphy[1], D. McGrath[2], D. Smith[3], N. Farrelly[2] and S. MacHale[1]

Abstract

Background: The combination of eating disorders and diabetes is associated with increased risk of morbidity and mortality. The aim of this study is to compare the prevalence of disordered eating behaviour (DEB) in young adults with type 1 diabetes mellitus to a sample of non-diabetic controls, and to examine the relationship of DEB to glycaemic control.

Methods: The Eating Disorder Examination Questionnaire (EDE-Q) was administered to 51 individuals aged 18–30 years attending an outpatient diabetic clinic in a large university teaching hospital. Glycaemic control was assessed by the glycosylated haemoglobin (HbA1c). The control group comprised a consecutive sample of 236 male and female students aged 18–30 years attending a university primary health care service.

Results: The mean global EDE-Q score for the diabetes group was 0.82 ± 1.1 (mean ± SD) and the mean for the control group was 1.4 ± 1.3 (mean ± SD). The diabetes group was significantly more likely to have a lower global EDE-Q score compared to the control group. There was no association between the global EDE-Q score of the diabetes group and HbA1c level.

Conclusions: We did not find increased levels of disordered eating behavior (DEB) in young adults with type 1 diabetes mellitus compared to a non-diabetic control sample.

Keywords: Eating disorders, Primary health care, Eating disorder examination questionnaire (EDE-Q), Disordered eating behaviour (DEB), diabetes mellitus

Plain English Summary

Eating disorders in individuals with diabetes results in acceleration of disease related complications. There is conflicting information in the literature regarding the prevalence of disordered eating behaviour in diabetes. In this study we examined the rates of disordered eating behaviour in a young adult sample with an established diagnosis of type 1 diabetes and compared them to a young adult control sample without diabetes. We also examined the association between the level of blood sugar control and the level of disordered eating in the diabetic sample. 274 participants were included in this study, 49 of whom had a diagnosis of type 1 diabetes. We did not find increased rates of disordered eating behaviour in our diabetic sample. Our findings highlight the importance of all clinicians, in both primary and secondary care settings, being aware of the presentation of eating disorders in young adults.

Background

The treatment of young adults with type 1 diabetes mellitus (T1DM) is often complicated by comorbid eating disorders (ED) and disordered eating behaviour (DEB). To date studies have shown varying prevalence rates of eating disorders in individuals with T1DM [1]. A 2005 meta-analysis found no significant difference in prevalence of Anorexia Nervosa in T1DM compared to controls [2]. DEB comprises a wide range of eating disorder pathology including dietary restriction, binge eating, and compensatory behaviours for the purpose of weight control, ranging from subclinical to clinical eating disorders. Compensatory behaviours include self-induced vomiting, laxative misuse and excessive exercise. The combination of diabetes with DEB is of particular concern due to its association with poor glucose control and accelerated

* Correspondence: sarahkeane5@gmail.com
[1]Department of Psychiatry, Beaumont Hospital, Beaumont Road, Dublin 9, Ireland
Full list of author information is available at the end of the article

onset of diabetes related complications [3, 4]. Retinopathy has been reported in 86% of young women, with a 7±4 year duration of diabetes, who had highly disordered eating at baseline on 4-year follow-up [3]. Moreover the coexistence of eating disorders and diabetes is frequently associated with non-compliance with treatment for diabetes and the abuse of insulin to promote weight reduction [5]. "Diabulimia" is a term increasingly used to refer to this intentional restriction or omission of insulin for weight control [6, 7]. Deliberate insulin omission is a long recognized cause of recurrent diabetic ketoacidosis in adolescents with T1DM [8]. Approximately one-third of people with T1DM intentionally omit insulin [9].

It has been hypothesized that features of T1DM may predispose vulnerable individuals to eating disorders [4]. These features include the dietary restraint necessary for management of diabetes, the cycle of weight loss at disease onset and subsequent weight gain with initiation of insulin, the trend towards higher body mass index (BMI) , and the option of misuse of insulin to influence body weight. Negative coping strategies and mood disturbances may increase the risk of developing co-morbid eating disorders in individuals with T1DM [10].

Studies to date in this area have produced conflicting results in large part due to major variations in study design. Some studies show an increased risk of DEB/ED in patients with diabetes compared with the general population [4, 11] while other studies do not report an increased risk [12–14]. Studies comparing the frequency of DEB/ED in males with and without diabetes are scarce [15]. A systematic review and meta-analysis found DEB and ED to be significantly more common in type 1 diabetic adolescents than in their peers [16]. However this difference was found to be no longer significant when restricting the analysis to studies using diabetes adapted assessment tools. Diabetes adapted tools identify eating disorder behaviours that are unique to T1DM, such as the underuse or omission of insulin for the purpose of weight loss.

Eating disorders in individuals with T1DM are significant and are associated with serious morbidity [3] and worse treatment outcomes [7]. We aimed to further explore this comorbidity by comparing the prevalence of disordered eating behaviour in a young adult sample with T1DM to a control sample in an Irish student population using the EDE-Q, a detailed questionnaire used to identify probable cases of eating disorders.

Method

The Eating Disorder Examination Questionnaire (EDE-Q) version 6.0 was used in this study. The EDE-Q is a 28 item instrument which focuses on the previous 28 days and measures core eating disorder behaviours. The EDE-Q produces a global score and four subscale scores: restraint, shape concern, weight concern and eating concern.

The global score is the average of the four subscale scores. Responses are rated on a seven-point Likert scale, and higher scores indicate greater disordered eating pathology. A cut-off score of ≥4 is commonly used to indicate clinical significance [17–20].

The frequency of key eating and compensatory behaviours such as objective binge episodes, self-induced vomiting, laxative misuse and excessive exercise are also recorded. Regular occurrence of excessive exercise was defined as exercising "in a driven or compulsive way as a means of controlling your weight, shape or amount of fat, or to burn off calories" (EDE-Q 6.0, item 18) for ≥20 times over the past 28 days. For regular occurrence, dietary restraint was defined as going "for long periods of time (8 waking hours or more) without eating anything at all in order to influence your shape or weight" (EDE-Q 6.0, item 2) for more than three times per week (≥13 times) over the past 28 days. For all other behaviours regular occurrence was defined as four or more occurrences over the past 28 days.

Participants

Patients were recruited while attending an outpatient diabetic clinic for young adults in Beaumont Hospital, a large university teaching hospital in North Dublin. Inclusion criteria were individuals aged between 18 and 30 years with a diagnosis of T1DM. A non-consecutive sample of 51 individuals (females $n = 20$, males $n = 31$) with diabetes were recruited. One male individual was excluded as he did not complete the consent form and another male because he failed to respond to over half of the items, leaving a total of 49 participants (females $n = 20$, males $n = 29$). The EDE-Q was used to assess eating disorder psychopathology. Glycaemic control in the diabetic sample was assessed by the glycosylated haemoglobin (HbA1c) measurement nearest to the date of assessment. [All, bar three, HbA1c measurements were taken within one month of the assessment. Of the HbA1c assessments that were not taken within one month, one was taken five months prior to the assessment, one four months prior and one three months prior]. None of our diabetic sample were on mixed insulin, 15% were on insulin pump therapy and the remainder were on a basal bolus regime.

For the control group the EDE-Q was administered to a consecutive sample of 236 male and female students attending a university primary health care service over a one month period. Students with T1DM or known history of chronic illness were excluded. Ten students did not consent to the study and one student did not complete the questionnaire leaving a total of 225 participants (females $n = 190$, males $n = 35$). Written informed consent was obtained from all participants. The study was reviewed and approved by the Ethics Committees of Beaumont Hospital and of Trinity College, Dublin.

Statistical analysis

The scoring methods advised by Fairburn and coauthors [21] were used for the calculation of EDE-Q subscale and global scores. With respect to the diabetic group, one participant failed to respond to over half of the items and so was excluded from the analysis. There were no other participants with more than one missing item.

With respect to missing data for the control group, 0. 3% of the items required to score the EDE-Q subscales were missing. One participant failed to respond to three of the five eating concern questions and so their eating concern subscale was excluded from the analysis. Another participant failed to respond to two items but, otherwise, there were no other participants with more than one missing item. Any missing responses were replaced with the mean item score as done in previous studies using this instrument. Differences between groups were initially examined using chi-square tests for categorical variables and t-tests for continuous variables. Univariate analyses for binary outcomes were then carried out using logistic regression with 95% confidence intervals. Confounders were adjusted for in multivariate logistic regression models. Univariate and multivariate linear regression models were used for continuous outcomes. In the univariate model (unadjusted) the outcome or dependent variable was diabetes and the independent or risk factor was eating behavior. In the multivariate models BMI and gender were added as additional independent variables. All analyses were carried out using STATA, version 13.

Results

There were 49 participants with diabetes and 225 control participants without diabetes. There were significantly more females in the control group compared to the diabetes group (x^2 (1, $N = 274) = 42.8$, $p < .0001$). 84.4% of controls were female and 40.8% of the diabetes group were female. There was no difference in age between both groups ($t(259) = 0.98$, p = =0.32) The mean age of those with diabetes was 21.4 ± 2.5 (mean ± SD) years (range: 26–18 years) and the mean age for the controls was 22 ± 4.1 (mean ± SD) years (range: 58–18 years). The mean BMI for the diabetes group was 23.5 ± 3.8 (mean ± SD) kg/m2 (range: 17.6–34.1) and the mean BMI for controls was 22.3 ± 3.5 (mean ± SD) kg/m2 (range: 15.4–39.9). Within the diabetes group 28.9% had a BMI >25 kg/m2 compared to 14.5% of the control group. However there was no significant difference in BMI between the groups when adjusted for gender (OR = 1.06, 95%CI: 0.9–1.1, $p = 0.18$).

EDE-Q scores

The diabetes group was significantly more likely to have a lower global EDE-Q score compared to the control group (OR = 0.6, 95%CI: 0.4–0.8, $p < 0.00$). The mean global EDE-Q score for the diabetes group was 0.82 ± 1.1 (mean ± SD) and the mean for the control group was 1.4 ± 1.3 (mean ± SD). The difference was still significant when adjusted for gender and BMI (OR = 0.6, 95%CI: 0.4–0.9, $p < 0.05$). There were no significant changes in the odds ratios when adjusting BMI and gender either together or individually (adjusting for gender only OR = 0.7, 95% CI: 0.5–1.1, $p < 0.05$) (adjusting for BMI only OR = 0.5, 95% CI: 0.3–0.9, $p < 0.05$). This pattern was similar for the subscales of the EDE-Q. The diabetes group had significantly lower scores on weight concern (OR = 0.7, 95%CI: 0.5–0.9, $p < 0.05$) and shape concern (OR = 0.7, 95%CI: 0.6–0.9, $p < 0.05$); both adjusted for gender and BMI. There was also a trend for lower scores for the diabetes compared to the control group on the restraint and eating-concern subscales (OR = 0.7, 95%CI: 0.5–0.8, $p = 0.07$, OR = 0.6, 95%CI: 0.4–1.1, $p = 0.08$, respectively; both adjusted for gender and BMI). See Table 1.

5.3% of controls had an EDE-Q score in the clinical range; no individuals in the diabetes group had a score in this range. 4.8% of the female controls engaged in purging behaviour with 2.1% of the sample engaging in regular self-induced vomiting. 2.1% of the female control group admitted to laxative misuse with 1.6% of the sample admitting to regular laxative misuse. None of the diabetic females engaged in any purging or laxative misuse behaviours. Both female diabetic and control groups engaged in similar amounts of objective binge episodes. Overall, when combining for gender, 14.3% of the diabetic group and 16% of the control group engaged in regular binging behavior. 5% of the female diabetic group admitted to regular excessive exercise compared to 1.1% of the female control group. See Table 2.

2.9% of the male controls engaged in purging behaviour, which was comparable to 3.4% of the male diabetics. None of the male controls or diabetics engaged in any regular self-induced vomiting. Table 3 shows the proportion of men engaging in any or regular

Table 1 Eating Disorder Examination Questionaire (EDE-Q) global and subscale scores

EDE-Q	Diabetic Group (*n* = 49)	Control Group (*n* = 225)
	Means (S.D)	*Means (S.D)*
Global Score	0.82 (1.1)	1.4 (1.3)
Restraint	0.7 (1.1)	1.2 (1.3)
Eating Concern	0.4 (0.6)	0.8 (1.1)
Shape Concern	1.2 (1.6)	2.1 (1.6)
Weight Concern	0.9 (1.2)	1.7 (1.6)

Table 2 Proportion of women engaging in any or regular occurrence of key eating and compensatory behaviours

Key Behaviour	Any Occurrence (%)		Regular Occurrence (%)	
	Diabetic N = 20	Control N = 190	Diabetic N = 20	Control N = 190
Objective Binge Episodes (OBE)	40	31.5 $p = 0.441$	20	15.8 $p = 0.410$
Self-induced Vomiting	0	4.8 $p = 0.395$	0	2.1 $p = 0.665$
Laxative Misuse	0	2.1 $p = 0.665$	0	1.6 $p = 0.737$
Excessive Exercise	30	30.5 $p = 0.965$	5	1.1 $p = 0.264$

occurrence of key eating and compensatory behaviours. There were no statistically significant differences in the key behaviors, whether any occurrence or regular. Statistical testing was done with a chi-square test in cases where the number of variables in each cell exceeded five, and with a Fisher's Exact test when it did not.

HbA1c level

The mean HbA1c level for the diabetes group was 76 ± 23.3 (mean ± SD) mmol/mol (9.1%). 14.9% of the sample had a HbA1c of < 53 mmol/mol (7.0%). 6.4% had a reading of between 53 mmol/mol < 58 mmol/mol (7.0 < 7.5%). 6.4% had a reading of between 58 mmol/mol < 64 mmol/mol (7.5 < 8.0%). 27.7% had a reading of between 64 mmol/mol < 75 mmol/mol (8.0 < 9.0%). 12.8% had a reading of between 75 mmol/mol < 86 mmol/mol (9 < 10%) and 31.9% of the sample had a reading of ≥ 86 mmol/mol (10%). There was no association between the global EDE-Q score of the diabetes group and HbA1c level; there was also no association between any of the EDE-Q subscale scores and HbA1c level. Individuals with diabetes who had a BMI of < 18.5 ($N = 18$) had a significantly lower HbA1c level compared to those with a healthy BMI between 18.5 and 25 ($\beta = 39.1$, $t(42) = 2.3$, $p = 0.05$; adjusted for gender). There was no difference in HbA1c level between those with a BMI of over 25 and those with a healthy BMI. There was also no difference in HbA1c level across ages in the diabetes group.

Discussion

The EDE-Q results of our study did not show an increased prevalence of DEB in a young adult sample with T1DM compared to a student control sample. The diabetic group had significantly lower global EDE-Q scores compared to the control sample, which was still significant when adjusted for gender and BMI. This pattern was similar for each of the individual subscales of the EDE-Q, also adjusted for gender and BMI. Although methodologically different, our results concur with the lower adjusted prevalence of DEB in patients with diabetes compared with a comparison group of other studies [13, 14].

Interestingly, none of the female diabetics engaged in any serious compensatory behaviours such as self-induced vomiting or laxative misuse. A potential confounder to consider is that having the option of insulin restriction for the purpose of weight control could result in reduction of other purging behaviours in individuals with diabetes. This may have biased our results as we did not adapt the EDE-Q for individuals with diabetes and we did not assess the diabetic specific DEB of insulin purging. The Diabetes Eating Problem Survey (DEPS-R) is a 16 item, self-report, screening measure for assessing disordered eating in diabetes which has demonstrated internal consistency and construct validity and may be a useful screening tool in this population [22]. Also, our diabetic sample consisted of a young adult group attending a secondary care endocrine outpatient clinic with access to multidisciplinary support, including dietician input.

The mean HbA1c level for the diabetic group was 76 mmol/mol (9.1%). There was no association between the global EDE-Q score of the diabetes group and the HbA1c level. There was also no association between any of the EDE-Q subscale scores and HbA1c level. However, as none of the diabetic group scored within the clinical range on EDE-Q this result should be interpreted with caution.

Research in this area has been conflicting due to huge variation in methodological approaches used to date and the lack of standardised, universally accepted assessment

Table 3 Proportion of men engaging in any or regular occurrence of key eating and compensatory behaviours

Key Behaviour	Any Occurrence (%)		Regular Occurrence (%)	
	Diabetic N = 29	Control N = 35	Diabetic N = 29	Control N = 35
Objective Binge Episodes (OBE)	20.7	22.9 $p = 0.835$	10.3	17.1 $p = 0.342$
Self-induced Vomiting	3.4	2.9 $p = 0.705$	0	0
Laxative Misuse	3.4	0 $p = 0.453$	0	0
Excessive Exercise	31	14.3 $p = 0.107$	0	2.9 $p = 0.547$

tools for the detection of DEB. We used a detailed questionnaire, the EDE-Q, which has shown good psychometric properties and can be used to identify probable cases of eating disorders [20]. The EDE-Q is the self-report version of the Eating Disorder Examination (EDE) , which is widely considered the instrument of choice for the assessment and diagnosis of DSM eating disorders [23]. Studies have shown a high level of agreement between the EDE-Q and the EDE interview in the assessment of attitudinal features of eating disorder psychopathology [20].

This study has a number of limitations. First, the relatively small sample of young adults with diabetes recruited limited power to identify differences between the samples. We acknowledge the possibility of type II error in our findings. It is important to consider that our methods of recruitment (i.e: a non-consecutive diabetic sample and a consecutive control sample) may have also influenced our findings as individuals with eating disorders have a tendency to conceal their illness and avoid professional help [24, 25].

A further limitation is that, as the control group was taken from a third level university sample, it is likely to contain a greater prevalence of high achieving perfectionistic individuals of a different sociodemographic background and hence is not generalizable to the general young adult population. Additionally, the control sample was recruited from individuals attending a primary care service for non-eating disorder related difficulties and, as such, may represent a false high prevalence compared to those who do not access health care services. However, it is worth noting that the mean global EDE-Q score for the female component of our control group (1.51) was comparable to mean global scores obtained in previous studies of an English community based sample (1.55) as well as a Swedish (1.56) and an Australian (1.52) general population sample [26]. Also, the EDE-Q is a self-report measure which is not a diabetic specific assessment tool and does not ask about the manipulation or omission of insulin to influence weight.

Conclusions

We did not find increased levels of disordered eating in a non-consecutive outpatient sample of young adults with T1DM compared to a non-diabetic control group. A limitation of our study is that we did not use a screening tool that was adapted for individuals with T1DM. Studies are needed to determine risk factors for disordered eating in people with diabetes over and above the presence of diabetes. Early identification and intervention is crucial given the risk of increased morbidity and mortality associated with the combination of eating disorders and diabetes [1]. Future studies should focus on the identification of patients with comorbid DEB and T1DM using diabetic specific screening instruments, the development of preventative and treatment interventions, and the integration of these interventions into mainstream diabetic care.

Abbreviations

BMI: Body mass index; CI: Confidence interval; DEB: Disordered eating behavior; ED: Eating disorders; EDE: Eating Disorder Examination.; EDE-Q: Eating Disorder Examination Questionnaire; HbA1c: Glycosylated haemoglobin; OR: Odds ratio; SD: standard deviation; STATA: syllabic abbreviation of the words statistics and data (the name of a statistical software package); T1DM: Type 1 diabetes mellitus

Funding

The author(s) received no financial support for the research, authorship, and/or publication of this article.

Authors' contributions

SK, MM, DM, DS, NF and SM all made contributions to study design and acquisition of data. SK, MC and SM analysed and interpreted the data. All listed authors contributed to drafting of manuscript. All authors read and approved the final manuscript.

Competing interests

The authors declare that they have no competing interests.

Author details

[1]Department of Psychiatry, Beaumont Hospital, Beaumont Road, Dublin 9, Ireland. [2]Trinity College Health Service, Dublin, Ireland. [3]Department of Endocrinology, Beaumont Hospital, Beaumont Road, Dublin 9, Ireland.

References

1. Pinhas-Hamiel O, Levy-Shraga Y. Eating disorders in adolescents with type 2 and type 1 diabetes. Curr Diab Rep. 2013;13:289–97.
2. Mannucci E, Rotella F, Ricca V, Moretti S, Placidi GF, Rotella CM. Eating disorders in patients with type 1 diabetes: a meta-analysis. J Endocrinol Investig. 2005;28:417–9.
3. Rydall AC, Rodin GM, Olmsted MP, Devenyi RG, Daneman D. Disordered eating behavior and microvascular complications in young women with insulin-dependent diabetes mellitus. N Engl J Med. 1997;336:1849–54.
4. Jones JM, Lawson ML, Daneman D, Olmsted MP, Rodin G. Eating disorders in adolescent females with and without type 1 diabetes: cross sectional study. BMJ. 2000;320:1563–6.
5. Biggs MM, Basco MR, Patterson G, Raskin P. Insulin withholding for weight control in women with diabetes. Diabetes Care. 1994;17:1186–9.
6. Larranaga A, Docet MF, Garcia-Mayor RV. Disordered eating behaviors in type 1 diabetic patients. World J Diabetes. 2011;2(11):189–95.
7. Custal N, Arcelus J, Aguera Z, Bove FI, Wales J, et al. Treatment outcome of patients with comorbid type 1 diabetes and eating disorders. BMC Psychiatry. 2014;14:140.
8. Golden MP, Herrold AJ, Orr DP. An approach to prevention of recurrent diabetic ketoacidosis in the pediatric population. J Pediatr. 1985;107(2):195–200.

9. Pinhas-Hamiel O, Hamiel U, Levy-Shraga Y. Eating disorders in adolescents with type 1 diabetes: challenges in diagnosis and treatment. World J Diabetes. 2015;6(3):517–26.
10. Gagnon C, Aime A, Belanger C. Predictors of comorbid eating disorders and diabetes in people with type 1 and type 2 diabetes. Can J Diabetes. 2017; 41(1):52–7.
11. Engstrom I, Kroon M, Arvidsson CG, Segnestam K, Snellman K, Aman J. Eating disorders in adolescent girls with insulin-dependent diabetes mellitus: a population-based case-control study. Acta Paediatr. 1999;88:175–80.
12. Meltzer LJ, Johnson SB, Prine JM, Banks RA, Desrosiers PM, Silverstein JH. Disordered eating, body mass, and glycaemic control in adolescents with type 1 diabetes. Diabetes Care. 2001;24:678–82.
13. Baechle C, Castillo K, Strasburger K, Stahl-Pehe A, Meissner T, et al. Is disordered eating behavior more prevalent in adolescents with early-onset type 1 diabetes than in their representative peers? Int J Eat Disord. 2014;47: 342–52.
14. Ackard DM, Vik N, Neumark-Sztainer D, Schmitz KH, Hannan P, Jacobs DR. Disordered eating and body dissatisfaction in adolescents with type 1 diabetes and a population-based comparison sample: comparative prevalence and clinical implications. Pediatr Diabetes. 2008;9:312–9.
15. Svensson M, Engstrom I, Aman J. Higher drive for thinness in adolescent males with insulin-dependent diabetes mellitus compared with healthy controls. Acta Paediatr. 2003;92:114–7.
16. Young V, Eiser C, Johnson B, Brierley S, Epton T, Elliott J, Heller S. Eating problems in adolescents with type 1 diabetes: a systematic review with meta-analysis. Diabet Med. 2013;30:189–98.
17. Carter JC, Stewart DA, Fairburn CG. Eating disorder examination questionnaire: norms for young adolescent girls. Behav Res Ther. 2001;39(5): 625–32.
18. Lavender JM, De Young KP, Anderson DA. Eating disorder examination questionnaire (EDE-Q): norms for undergraduate men. Eat Behav. 2010;11(2): 119–21.
19. Luce KH, Crowther JH, Pole M. Eating disorder examination questionnaire (EDE-Q): norms for undergraduate women. Int J Eat Disord. 2008;41:273–6.
20. Mond JM, Hay PJ, Rodgers B, Owen C. Eating disorder examination questionnaire (EDE-Q): norms for young adult women. Behav Res Ther. 2006;44(1):53–62.
21. Fairburn CG, Cooper Z, O'Connor ME. Appendix A, Eating Disorder Examination. In: Fairburn CG Cognitive Behaviour Therapy and eating disorders. New York: Guilford Press; 2008. p. p269.
22. Markowitz JT, Butler DA, Volkening LK, Antisdel JE, Anderson BJ, Laffel L. Brief screening tool for disordered eating in diabetes: internal consistency and external validity in a contemporary sample of pediatric patients with type 1 diabetes. Diabetes Care. 2010;33:495–500.
23. Mond JM, Hay PJ, Rodgers B, Owen C, Beumont PJ. Validity of the eating disorder examination questionnaire (EDE-Q) in screening for eating disorders in community samples. Behav Res Ther. 2004;42(5):551–67.
24. Hsu LK. Epidemiology of the eating disorders. The Psychiatric Clinics of North America. 1996;19:681–700.
25. Treasure J, Schmidt U, Van Furth E. The handbook of eating disorders. 2nd ed. England: John Wiley & Sons; 2003.
26. Keane S, Clarke M, McGrath D, Farrelly N, MacHale S. Eating disorder examination questionnaire (EDE-Q): norms for female university students attending a university primary health care service in Ireland. Ir J Psychol Med. 2017;34(1):7–11.

6

Sport practice, physical structure, and body image among university students

Stefania Toselli and Federico Spiga*

Abstract

Background: The aim of this study was to estimate body image perception in undergraduate students, and to investigate its associations with weight status, abdominal obesity, muscularity, gender and sport.

Methods: The sample consisted of 231 Italian students (174 males and 57 females); anthropometric measurements, taken by trained technicians, were: height, weight, arm-circumference, waist and hip circumferences. BMI, WHR and Δ arm-circumference were calculated. Body image was assessed using body silhouette charts. Information about sport (currently practiced sport, starting age, and weekly hours of sport) was acquired with questionnaires.

Results: Females perceived themselves as slightly overweight, while males identified themselves as normal weight. Females had a tendency to desire to be thinner in all weight status categories; in males, normal weight subjects had a tendency to desire to be larger, while overweight wished to be thinner. Sport practice was significantly higher in males. Individuals who were overweight and did less sport were significantly more likely to have higher body dissatisfaction.

Conclusions: The present study highlights a positive relationship between sport practice, corpulence and body image perception.

Keywords: Body image, Body dissatisfaction, Sport practice, Weight status

Plain English summary

The aim of this study is to research associations between body image, obesity, muscularity, gender and sport among university students. The sample consisted of 231 subjects; anthropometric measurements, body image and information about sport were acquired by trained technicians. Females perceive themselves as slightly overweight and wished to be thinner, normal weight males wished to be larger, while people who were overweight wished to be thinner. Sport practice was significantly higher in males. People who were overweight and did less sport were significantly more likely to have higher body dissatisfaction.

The present study highlighted the importance of sport in improving self-consciousness, well-being, and health. Encouraging sport practice may improve self-determination, self-acceptance, and pursuing these positive effects may motivate individuals to initiate and maintain regular exercise routines.

* Correspondence: federico.spiga2@unibo.it
Universita degli Studi di Bologna, Bologna, Italy

Background

Body self-esteem is multidimensional and consists of self-evaluation, as well as others' perception of body weight and general appearance [1]. Body self-esteem is strongly related to overall self-esteem [1, 2], which is not surprising because the media in Western societies presents images of the ideal body and wields pressure for women to have a very thin body and men to have a big and muscular body [3–5].

Self-confidence is strongly influenced by body image in youth populations [6]. While this aspect has been widely studied in women, it is also an important predictor of psychological well-being in young men [7]. Furthermore, gender is often identified with characteristics and traits considered optimal for males and females that constitute masculinity and femininity, respectively [3, 8]. Previous research suggests that gender influences the perception of healthy lifestyles and health-related decisions [9–11].

It is moreover important to consider that the media's representation of males and females is changing. In particular, "drive for muscularity", the extent to which an individual wish to increase his muscularity, is a growing issue, and it brings its own set of associated health problems, such as increased level of eating pathology [12].

The media displays women's bodies as not only thin, but also athletic and toned, and the drive for muscularity in Western women could be due to the emphasis the society gives to physical exercise as part of an ideal lifestyle [13]. So, an intervention aimed to treating and preventing body image concerns may well include a focus on not just thin ideals but also on thinness linked with toned muscles, to critically evaluate unrealistic ideals that the individuals are striving to attain [14]. Contemporary Western culture has also become increasingly focused on male bodies and male body image has changed along with cultural and societal values. Young men feel a social expectation to be more muscular, and this may be associated with social power and self-confidence [15–17]. It is not surprising that men are joining their female peers in the experience of body dissatisfaction [18]. Thus, the body prototypes for both men and women have changed suggesting goals not always easy to achieve [18, 19] and this has had a negative impact on self-esteem, body dissatisfaction and drive for muscularity in both men and women [13, 14]. In addition to gender differences, physical activity plays an important role in body self-esteem in Western society and culture, and a toned body is desirable for the presentation of oneself to others [20–24]. Positive body image perception leads to a sense of efficacy, self-determination, personal acceptance and self-acceptance, which are all closely linked to the development of self-esteem.

Misperception of weight, defined as the difference between the individual's perceived weight status and his/her actual weight status, can influence health behaviors [25].

Studies show that overweight misperception varies by gender, as females perceive themselves as overweight more frequently than males of the same body mass index (BMI) do [9, 26]. Misperception of overweight/obesity among adolescents of normal weight can have negative consequences as body dissatisfaction, may influence diet and consequently trigger the development of eating disorders [26]. In addition, adolescents who undergo dietary restriction and unhealthy or "do-it-yourself" weight control are at an increased risk of weight gain over time [27]. In recent years there has been an increasing prevalence of eating disorders in young men, probably also because of the negative influences of the mass media mentioned above. It was found that 10%–20% of the cases of anorexia nervosa and bulimia nervosa, and up to 40% of cases of binge eating disorders, occur in men [28]. The role that weight status has on body dissatisfaction in men requires hence further investigation.

With regard to the aims of the present study it is important to note that using BMI alone, the most used indicator to define weight status, has numerous limitations. It does not consider differences in fat mass and fat free mass/muscle mass, leading to incorrectly classifications [28]; in addition, it does not consider body fat distribution that has important health risks implications. Furthermore, body fat distribution is a mediating factor for body size estimation accuracy. In their study on obese women, Rhodes & O'Neil [29] reported that those with lower body fat distribution tended to underestimate their body size and professed to feel thinner than they actually are, while those with upper and mixed-type body fat distributions tended to overestimate their body size and feel heavier than they actually are. Since their results concerned obese women, the reliability of these findings also on non-obese subjects of both sexes deserves to be evaluated, considering other measurements, such as circumferences, muscularity and fat distribution.

Thus, our study goals were to evaluate body image perception, main health-related anthropometric characteristics (considering in addition to weight status, also muscularity and fat distribution) and sport practice in second-year undergraduate male and female students attending university, as well as to explore the impact of gender on these variables and to study the associations between them. In the literature female students generally present a lower BMI and a higher dissatisfaction than males and engage in less physical exercise. However, given the changes in body image perception to which people, particularly youth, are subject to, we wanted to investigate associations between weight status and body image perception in both sexes.

Furthermore, since using BMI alone to define weight status has limitations, and since muscularity and fat distribution are informative indicators another aim was to examine their role as possible mediating factors in body image perception and dissatisfaction.

Methods

A cross-sectional study of 231 university students aged 21.4 ± 2.0 years was conducted during the 2013–2014 academic year. The subjects (174 males and 57 females) were attending the School of Pharmacy, Biotechnology and Sports Sciences at the University of Bologna (Italy) and assessed during the laboratory lessons for the Anthropometry and Ergonomics course in the second year of the degree program.

The study was approved by the Bioethics Committee of the University of Bologna; all participants gave their consent for the study and had the right not to participate and/or withdraw from the study at any time.

A self-administered questionnaire obtained demographic (gender, age) and sport participation information (sport practice - considered as club sports, namely planned sports activities led by staff - and sport hours per week). Anthropometric measurements were taken in private by trained technicians in the University laboratory using standardized procedures [30, 31]. Height was recorded to the nearest 0.1 cm with a stadiometer, and weight was measured to the nearest 0.1 kg with a high-precision mechanical scale. Body mass index (BMI) was calculated as weight (kg) divided by height squared (m2). Students were classified as underweight, normal-weight, overweight, and obese based on the World Health Organization (WHO) cutoffs [32]. As there was only one obese subject (one male), he was included in the overweight group for further data analysis. For measurement of body circumferences, relaxed arm circumference was measured at the midpoint between the acromion and the olecranon using a non-stretch tape.

Contracted arm circumference was assessed by the same method but with the arm flexed at 90° and the biceps muscle fully contracted. Delta arm circumference (Δ arm circumference) was calculated by subtracting relaxed arm circumference from contracted arm circumference. Waist circumference was measured at the midpoint between the lower border of the rib cage and the iliac crest using a flexible inch tape. Hip circumference was measured at the widest portion of the buttocks. Circumferences were measured over the naked skin and recorded to the nearest 0.1 cm. Waist-Hip Ratio (WHR) was calculated as waist circumference divided by hip circumference.

Body image perception was assessed using body silhouette charts [33]. Subjects were shown nine male or female silhouettes (marked F.1, F.2, F.3, F.4, F.5, F.6, F.7, F.8, and F.9), ordered in morphology from emaciation to obesity. Subjects were asked to select the silhouette that they believed was most similar to their own ('actual' figure), as well as the silhouette that they most desired ('ideal' figure). Using the classification recommended by Sánchez-Villegas et al. 2001, the silhouette series were divided into four categories (underweight, normal weight, overweight, and obese): Figs. 1, 2 and 3 correspond to "underweight" status, Figs. 4 and 5 correspond to "normal weight" status, Figs. 6 and 7 correspond to "overweight" status, and Figs. 8 and 9 correspond to "obese" status. A body dissatisfaction score (BDS) was calculated by subtracting the "ideal figure" from the "actual figure" score. A positive BDS score indicated the actual figure was larger than the ideal figure and a negative score indicated the actual figure was thinner than the ideal figure A BDS score of 0 indicated no discrepancy (same figure chosen as actual and ideal) [34].

Physical activity frequency of each subject was determined by the hours of sport training during a typical week as declared by the subject.

Data analysis was performed using Statistica for Windows, version 7.1 (StatSoft Italia srl, Vigonza, Padua, Italy). Data were expressed as mean and standard deviation. Comparisons between the genders and between subjects who do or do not engage in sport were performed using Student's t-test and non-parametric Mann-Whitney U tests for normal and non-normally distributed variables, respectively.

Comparisons among weight status and sport practice frequencies were performed using chi-square (and Fisher's exact tests when appropriate). Body image perception in relation to weight status category was analyzed using analysis of variance (ANOVA).

Pearson's correlation analysis were computed between actual self, ideal self, and BDS and anthropometric characters (BMI, muscularity and fat distribution). Multiple linear regression models were performed. Actual self, ideal self, and BDS were considered to be dependent variables. Gender, BMI, Δ arm circumference, WHR, sport practice, sport hours per week were considered to be independent variables, using a three-step model.

In the first model we included gender. In the second model, we also included the anthropometric characteristics (BMI, Δ arm circumference, WHR) of the participants. In the third model sport practice and sport hours per week were finally included. Significance was set at $p < 0.05$.

Results

Mean values for anthropometric characteristics and body image perception according to gender are reported in Table 1.

In females mean BMI and WHR values did not exceed the cut-off [32, 35]. The majority of females were normal weight (91.2%), while the prevalence of underweight and overweight was low (5.3% and 3.5% respectively) (Table 1). Only the 3.5% of subjects exceeded the WHR cut-off.

Considering weight status and fat distribution together, the females that present higher values than WHR cut-off belonged to a normal weight category.

A little more than half of females practiced sport, but the weekly sport hours were high (Table 1).

With regard to body image perception, females perceived themselves as slightly overweight (5.2) on an average, and chose an ideal figure in the normal weight category. As consequence, the BDS was positive, denoting dissatisfaction (1.7) (Table 1). In females actual and ideal figures, as well as BDS, were higher with increasing of weight status. Females in all of the weight categories tended to desire a thinner figure (Table 2), although actual figure was the only significant difference in females tested with ANOVA (df1, df2 = 53,2; F = 5.80; $p < 0.00$).

Table 1 Sample characteristics, weight status and sport practice by gender

	Males	Females	*p* value	*t* value	t (df)	chi-square
Sample characteristics*	Mean (SD)	Mean (SD)				
Height (cm)	177.6 (7.0)	165.3 (6.5)	<.001	11.77	229	
Weight (kg)	73.6 (9.5)	59.2 (6.6)	<.001	10.62	229	
Body Mass Index (BMI)	23.3 (2.4)	21.6 (2.1)	<.001	4.60	229	
Relaxed Arm Circumference (cm)	29.1 (2.9)	26.2 (2.6)	<.001	6.87	229	
Contracted Arm Circumference (cm)	31.5 (3.0)	27.6 (2.4)	<.001	9.00	229	
Δ Arm Circumferences (cm)	2.4 (1.1)	1.4 (0.9)	<.001	6.10	229	
Waist Circumference (cm)	78.6 (5.8)	70.0 (5.0)	<.001	9.99	229	
Hip Circumference (cm)	96.5 (6.8)	95.5 (7.2)	0.166	1.40	228	
WHR	0.8 (0.1)	0.7 (0.0)	<.001	9.89	228	
Sport Hours per Week	6.9 (3.3)	6.5 (4.1)	0.016	2.43	229	
[a]Actual Figure	3.8 (1.6)	5.2 (1.3)	<.001	−5.79	224	
[b]Ideal Figure	3.7 (0.9)	3.5 (1.0)	0.108	1.61	224	
[c]Body Dissatisfaction Score (BDS)	0.1 (1.4)	1.7 (1.3)	<.001	−7.63	224	
Weight Status[#]	%	%	<.001			19.2
Underweight	0.0	5.3				
Normal Weight	77.0	91.2				
Overweight	23.0	3.5				
Sport practice[#]	%	%				
Practice	77.6	57.9	0.004			8.3

[a]Subjects were shown nine silhouettes ordered from 1 to 9, from emaciation to obesity, and they selected the silhouette that they believed was most similar to their own (Actual Figure)
[b]Subjects were shown nine silhouettes ordered from 1 to 9, from emaciation to obesity, and they selected the silhouette that they most desired (Ideal Figure)
[c]BDS was calculated by subtracting the "ideal figure" from the "actual figure" score
*Comparisons were performed using Student's t-test
[#]Comparisons were performed using chi-square

Tukey's post-hoc comparisons showed a statistical difference in actual figure between underweight and overweight subjects.

Considering the difference in actual figures, ideal figures, and BDS between females who practice or not sport, a significant difference emerged for actual figure (df = 54, $T = 2147$, $p = 0.036$). Even if the BMI of two groups did not differ (sport = 21.7 vs. no sport = 21.5; df = 55, F = 1.07, $p = 0.877$), females that were not practicing sport perceived themselves larger (5.6 vs. 4.8). Males presented mean BMI and WHR values below the cut-off [32, 35]. As regards weight status, the majority of the sample was of normal weight (77.0%), only one subject was obese and the rest of the sample was overweight. The one subject in the obese category was grouped under the overweight category for further

Table 2 Body image assessment by weight status

	Underweight Mean (SD)	Normalweight Mean (SD)	Overweight Mean (SD)	F (df1, df2)	*p* value
Females					
Actual Figure	3.0 (0.0)	5.2 (1.2)	6.5 (2.1)	5.80 (53,2)	0.005
Ideal Figure	2.7 (0.6)	3.5 (1.0)	4.5 (0.7)	2.15 (53,2)	0.126
BDS	0.3 (0.6)	1.8 (1.3)	2.0 (1.4)	1.94 (53,2)	0.154
Males					
Actual Figure	-	3.3 (1.4)	5.4 (1.1)	68.98 (168, 1)	<.001
Ideal Figure	-	3.6 (0.9)	4.1 (1.0)	7.42 (168, 1)	0.007
BDS	-	−0.3 (1.3)	1.3 (1.1)	49.31 (168, 1)	<.001

Statistical analyses were performed using ANOVA and Tukey's post hoc test
df degree of freedom. *F* F values

analyses. (Table 1). The frequency of subjects exceeding the WHR cut-off was 5.7%.

Considering weight status and fat distribution together, the males that presented higher values than WHR cut-off were normal weight (70%) or overweight (30%). 77.6% of males participated in sport and time spent participating in sport was an average of 6.9 h for week (Table 1).

As regards body image perception, males identified themselves as normal weight (3.8) and perceived themselves (ideal figure) in the same category (3.7); as consequence, the BDS was low (0.1). Analogously to females, actual and ideal figures, as well as BDS, were higher with increasing weight status. In males the differences between actual and ideal figures and BDS were always significant (Table 2), as the normal weight males desired a larger figure whereas the overweight males desired a thinner figure.

Considering fat distribution, no significant differences were noticed in the choice of actual and ideal figures and BDS between subjects of the same weight status category but exceeding or not cut-off for WHR. No statistical differences in actual figures, ideal figures, and BDS are detected between males who are engaged or not in sport (df = 168, $p > 0.05$).

Males did not present a correct perception of their weight status (chi-square = 49.60, $p < 0.001$) and they tended to categorize themselves in lower weight categories than those they actually belonged to (Table 3). Females misperceived their weight status as well (chi-square = 19.17, $p < 0.001$) (Table 3).

To get a more accurate assessment of the relationship between body image perception and anthropometric characteristics we performed a correlation analysis considering, in addition to BMI, also muscularity and fat distribution (Table 4). A significant correlation emerged only with BMI: in particular in males actual figure, ideal figure and BDS were significantly correlated with BMI, while in females only actual figure and BDS were correlated with BMI (Table 4).

To investigate the most informative predictors and their effects on actual figure, ideal figure and BDS, a hierarchical regression analysis was performed. According to the first model, being male was significantly associated with a lower self-perception score and BDS (Table 5).

Table 4 Correlation between actual figure, ideal figure, BDS and anthropometric indexes

	BMI	Δ Arm Circumference	WHR
Females			
Actual Figure	0.61	−0.08	−0.01
	p = <.001	p = 0.534	p = 0.958
Ideal Figure	0.20	0.01	0.08
	p = 0.132	p = 0.930	p = 0.537
BDS	0.49	−0.01	−0.07
	p = <.001	p = 0.465	p = 0.589
Males			
Actual Figure	0.65	−0.05	0.09
	p = <.001	p = 0.514	p = 0.226
Ideal Figure	0.24	0.03	0.01
	p = 0.002	p = 0.731	p = 0.873
BDS	0.58	−0.07	0.01
	p = <.001	p = 0.329	p = 0.203

Adding anthropometric characteristics to the model led to a significant increase of R2 in the second model. In addition to gender, higher BMI was significantly associated with higher actual figure values and body image dissatisfaction. BMI was the only significant predictor of ideal figure. When the third model is considered, including sport practice and sport hours per week, in addition to gender and BMI, the interaction between gender and sport practice proved to be a significant predictor of actual figure values. BMI remains the only significant predictor for ideal figure status. With regards to BDS, increasing BMI and lack of sport practice were significantly associated with higher body image dissatisfaction, whereas male gender, in general, was associated with a lower BDS.

Discussion

Males in the present study had higher BMI values, a more centripetal fat distribution, and greater arm muscularity. The higher BMI value in males were in

Table 3 Perceived body images of participants by their actual body weight status

	Weight status categories					
	Males %			Females %		
	Underweight	Normalweight	Overweight	Underweight	Normalweight	Overweight
Perceived Body Image:						
Underweight	-	60.3	0.0	100.0	9.8	0.0
Normalweight	-	32.1	57.9	0.0	43.1	50.0
Overweight	-	6.9	42.1	0.0	45.1	0.0
Obese	-	0.8	2.6	0.0	2.0	50.0

Table 5 Hierarchical regression model to examine predictors for actual figure, ideal figure, and BDS

	Model 1				Model 2				Model 3			
Predictor Variables	β	T	CI	*p*	β	T	CI	*p*	β	T	CI	*p*
Actual Figure												
Gender (M)	−0.36	−5.79	(−0.92,-0.45)	<.001	−0.52	−8.27	(−1.23, −0.75)	<.001	−0.54	−8.44	(−1.27, −0.79)	<.001
BMI					0.63	12.47	(0.35, 0.49)	<.001	0.63	12.64	(0.36, 0.49)	<.001
Δ Arm Circumferences					−0.01	−0.13	(−0.16, 0.14)	0.895	−0.02	−0.39	(−0.18, 0.12)	0.698
WHR					−0.03	−0.47	(−3.78, 2.34)	0.641	−0.03	−0.47	(−3.76, 2.32)	0.641
Sport Hours per Week									0.01	0.21	(−0.05, 0.06)	0.831
Sport Practice (NO)									0.12	1.79	(−0.02, 0.48)	0.075
Gender/Sport Interaction									−0.13	−2.34	(−0.42, −0.04)	0.020
R^2	0.13				0.49				0.51			
Adjusted R^2	0.13				0.48				0.50			
p	<.001				<.001				<.001			
Ideal Figure												
Gender (M)	0.11	1.61	(3.44, 3.73)	0.108	0.02	0.25	(−0.16, 0.21)	0.800	0.00	−0.03	(−0.19, 0.19)	0.973
BMI					0.24	3.51	(0.04, 0.15)	<.001	0.25	3.62	(0.04, 0.15)	<.001
Δ Arm Circumferences					0.05	0.64	(−0.08, 0,16)	0.526	0.02	0.30	(−0.10, 0.14)	0.767
WHR					0.00	0.00	(−2.42, 2.42)	0.998	−0.01	−0.08	(−2.52, 2.31)	0.932
Sport Hours per Week									−0.14	−1.50	(−0.07, 0.01)	0.135
Sport Practice (NO)									−0.06	−0.63	(−0.27, 0.14)	0.528
Gender/Sport Interaction									−0.13	−1.74	(−0.29, 0.02)	0.083
R^2	0.01				0.07				0.09			
Adjusted R^2	0.01				0.05				0.06			
p	0.108				0.005				0.005			
BDS												
Gender (M)	−0.45	−7.63	(−1.01, −0.59)	<.001	−0.58	−8.83	(−1.24, −0.79)	<.001	−0.58	−8.73	(−1.26, −0.79)	<.001
BMI					0.53	10.11	(0.26, 0.39)	<.001	0.53	10.14	(0.26, 0.39)	<.001
Δ Arm Circumferences					−0.04	−0.66	(−0.19, 0.10)	0.509	−0.04	−0.65	(−0.19, 0.10)	0.518
WHR					−0.03	−0.49	(−3.67, 2.22)	0.628	−0.02	−0.41	(−3.54, 2.31)	0.679
Sport Hours per Week									0.10	1.46	(−0.01, 0.08)	0.147
Sport Practice (NO)									0.17	2.38	(0.05, 0.54)	0.018
Gender/Sport Interaction									−0.06	−1.00	(−0.28, 0.09)	0.318
R^2	0.21				0.46				0.48			
Adjusted R^2	0.20				0.45				0.46			
p	<.001				<.001				<.001			

accordance with the results of other authors and therefore confirm the data from literature and does not point out any trend toward a reduction of BMI values in our sample [11, 36–38]. Some Authors reported an increasing incidence of eating disorders in young men in recent years and an increased social pressure on men to have low body fat and high muscularity [28, 39]. The findings of the present study indicated a high proportion of normal weight subjects among the sample and a prevalence of overweight, as reported in accordance other studies regarding Western and Southern European males, while lower for females [40].

Also regarding body image perception males confirm their tendency to perceive themselves slender. This observation was further confirmed by the reduced proportion of males who had a correct self-perception of their weight status, as they tended to underestimate their body size. This underestimation may be due to a denial of their own nutritional status [28, 41]. This misperception may impede efforts to prevent chronic degenerative diseases and other problems associated with excess weight in people with severe weight disorders. In contrast, normal weight and overweight women tended to overestimate their body size. Although both sexes prefer ideals of thinness, this tendency was more marked in females. Our study confirms the difference in body image self-perception between the two sexes, indicating that men may be paying less attention to their image [10, 41, 42]. Males who want to increase muscle mass could also desire a heavier body weight, since muscle tissue weighs more than adipose tissue [43].

In women, overestimation of body size may reflect environmental factors associated with the development of eating disorders [41, 44, 45]. Social expectations and stereotypes attached to gender in relation to body image may substantially influence weight perception and body image dissatisfaction. This may be associated with the conditioning factors in society that contribute to the stresses of modern life.

The desire for underweight and normal-weight women to have a more slender appearance may be instilled by mass media that promote pathologically underweight beauty models. The ideal body has undergone a substantial, as advertising and media outlets have propagated the representation of attractiveness as a thin, fit body shape for females, and a lean, muscular physique for males [5, 18, 42]. These beauty models spread through the media and are often influencing the behavior and food habits of children and adults [46, 47]. However, current standards of beauty are pervasive and unattainable for many individuals, and the pressure to achieve the elusive ideal body often leads to a diminished body image, increased eating disorders, and unsuccessful attempts at weight control [43]. Body prototypes for both men and women are becoming more restrictive and the media's representation of males and females is changing [12, 13].

Weight status influenced actual and ideal figures as well as body dissatisfaction in our study, as they all rose with increasing weight status, in both genders. This trend was noticeable in females, as they showed a high prevalence of dissatisfaction with body weight and ideal body image. Considering sport practice, despite the BMI being similar, women who practiced sports perceived themselves slimmer than those who did not participate in sport.

In the present study men seemed not to still joining their female peers in the experience of body dissatisfaction, in contrast to Smith et al. [18]. Muscularity-oriented body image concern is becoming an increasing issue, but, contrary to expectations, the correlation between actual and ideal figures and BDS and muscularity in this study were not significant. The correlation between actual and ideal figures and BDS and fat distribution were also not significant. At this point it should be noted that the frequencies of subjects of the present study that exceeded the WHR cut-off were low in both sexes (5.7% in males and 3.5% in females), and this could have influenced the results.

On the other hand, the correlations with BMI were significant. To better understand the most informative predictors and their effects on actual figure, ideal figure and BDS, multiple regression models were carried out. These found that female gender was significantly associated with more overweight self-perception scores, thinner body ideal and consequently, higher body dissatisfaction.

Higher BMI was also significantly associated with a more overweight actual self-perception and increased body dissatisfaction. Subjects who did not involve in any sport activities presented significantly higher body dissatisfaction than those who participated in sports. A significantly greater proportion of females (almost twice as much as males) did not perform sport activities. The interaction between gender and sport activity significantly influenced the perceived actual figure status: being female and inactive increased actual figure perception. This was further confirmed by the statistically significant difference ($p < 0.05$) between active and inactive girls in terms of the actual figure perception.

In our study more active subjects (especially females) were more satisfied with their body image than their less active counterparts. This is in general agreement with other studies examining these associations in youth [21]. Our initial hypothesis that muscularity (based on the difference between the relaxed and contracted arm circumferences), distribution of body fat (as assessed by WHR), and the hours of sport activity may influence the perception of body image, was not confirmed by the results of our regression analyses. However, from the same analyses, sex, BMI and sport practice seemed to be the major correlates of body image perception and dissatisfaction.

An important strength of this study is that specialized personnel directly measured the sample of students, taking in account not only height and weight but also measures related to muscularity and fat distribution.

Limitations of this study must also be acknowledged. Due to the cross-sectional design used, although the model suggested possible directional relationships amongst variables, it is not possible to confirm causal pathways and further prospective research is needed in order to do this. The body silhouettes used to calculate body dissatisfaction differed only with respect to body fat, not muscularity, which makes the connections of body dissatisfaction with other variables in the study problematic, particularly for men.

In addition, a complete objective evaluation of physical activity was not carried out as the use of accelerometers was impracticable in this study.

Conclusion

Overall, the present study highlighted a positive relationship between sport practice and body image perception, which underscores the importance of sport in improving self-consciousness, well-being, and health. Encouraging sport practice may improve sense of efficacy, feelings of self-determination, personal acceptance, and self-acceptance, and pursuing these positive effects may motivate individuals to initiate and maintain regular exercise routines. Dedicated long-term health education programs for students should focus on changing perceptions of body size and weight, emphasizing the importance of healthy lifestyle that includes sport practice, and popularizing a realistic and healthy body shape to debunk mass-media influences, especially among females.

Acknowledgements
We would like to thank all the students who volunteered for the study.

Funding
Not applicable.

Authors' contributions
ST planned the study, ST and FS participated to the data collection and did all the statistical analysis. All authors were involved with data interpretation, critical revisions of the paper. All authors read and approved the final manuscript.

Competing interests
The authors declare that they have no competing interests.

References

1. Skorek M, Song AV, Dunham Y. Self-esteem as a mediator between personality traits and body esteem: path analyses across gender and race/ethnicity. PLoS One. 2014;9(11):e112086.
2. Shriver LH, Harrist AW, Page M, Hubbs-Tait L, Moulton M, Topham G. Differences in body esteem by weight status, gender, and physical activity among young elementary school-aged children. Body Image. 2013;10:78–84.
3. Alfano L, Hildebrandt T, Bannon K, Walker C, Walton KE. The impact of gender on the assessment of body checking behavior. Body Image. 2011;8(1):20–5.
4. Bartlett CP, Vowels CL, Saucier DA. Meta-analyses of the effects of media images on men's body-image concerns. J Soc Clin Psychol. 2008;27:279–310.
5. Cho A, Lee J. Body dissatisfaction levels and gender differences in attentional biases toward idealized bodies. Body Image. 2013;10(1):95–102.
6. Perry DG, Pauletti RE. Gender and adolescent development. J Res Adolesc. 2011;21:61–74.
7. Marcos Marcos J, Avilés NR, del Río Lozano M, Cuadros JP, García Calvente M (2013) del M. Performing masculinity, influencing health: a qualitative mixed-methods study of young Spanish men. Global Health Action 6: 21134.
8. Blashill AJ. Gender roles, eating pathology, and body dissatisfaction in men: a meta-analysis. Body Image. 2011;8(1):1–11.
9. Nolen-Hoesksema S. Possible contributors to the gender differences in alcohol use and problems. J Gen Psychol. 2006;133(4):357–74.
10. Lemon SC, Rosal MC, Zapka J, Borg A, Andersen V. Contributions of weight perceptions to weight loss attempts: differences by body mass index and gender. Body Image. 2009;6(2):90–6.
11. Maruf FA, Akinpelu AO, Nwankwo MJ. Perceived body image and weight: discrepancies and gender differences among university undergraduates. Afr Health Sci. 2012;4:464–72.
12. Bucchianeri MM, Serrano JL, Pastula A, Corning AF. Drive for muscularity is heightened in body-dissatisfied men who socially compare. Eat Disord J Treat Preven. 2014;22(3):221–32.
13. Cramblitt B, Pritchard M. Media's influence on the drive for muscularity in undergraduates. Eat Behav. 2013;14(4):441–6.
14. Benton C, Karazsia BT. The effect of thin and muscular images on women's body satisfaction. Body Image. 2015;13:22–7.
15. Griffiths S, Murray SB, Touyz S. Extending the masculinity hypothesis: an investigation of gender role conformity, body dissatisfaction, and disordered eating in young heterosexual men. Psychol Men Masculinity. 2015;16(1):108–14.
16. Kanayama G, Barry S, Hudson JI, Pope HG Jr. Body image and attitudes toward male roles in anabolic-androgenic steroid users. Am J Psychiatry. 2006;163(4):697–703.
17. Murray SB, Rieger E, Karlov L, Touyz SW. Masculinity and femininity in the divergence of male body image concerns. J Eat Disord. 2013;28:1–11.
18. Smith AR, Hawkeswood SE, Bodell LP, Joiner TE. Muscularity versus leanness: an examination of body ideals and predictors of disordered eating in heterosexual and gay college students. Body Image. 2011;8(3):232–6. doi:10.1016/j.bodyim.2011.03.005.
19. Baghurst T, Hollander DB, Nardella B, Haff GG. Change in sociocultural ideal male physique: an examination of past and present action figures. Body Image. 2006;3(1):87–91.
20. Campbell A, Hausenblas HA. Effects of exercise interventions on body image: a meta-analysis. J Health Psychol. 2011;14:780–93.
21. Kruger J, Lee CD, Ainsworth BE, Macera CA. Body size satisfaction and physical activity levels among men and women. Obesity. 2008;16(8):1976–9.
22. Coelho CG, Giatti L, Molina MD, Nunes MA, Barreto SM. Body image and nutritional status are associated with physical activity in men and women: the ELSA-Brazil study. Int J Environ Res Public Health. 2015;12(6):6179–96.
23. Schmalz DL, Deane GD, Birch LL, Davison KK. A longitudinal assessment of the links between physical activity and self-esteem in early adolescent non-Hispanic females. J Adolesc Health. 2007;41(6):559–65.
24. Korn L, Gonen E, Shaked Y, Golan M. Health perceptions, self and body image, physical activity and nutrition among undergraduate students in Israel. PLoS One. 2013;8(3):e58543. doi:10.1371/journal.pone.0058543.
25. Pash KE, Klein EG, Laska MN, Velazquez CE, Moe SG, Lytle LA. Weight misperception and health risk behaviors among early adolescents. Am J Health Behav. 2011;35:797–806.
26. Ter Bogt TF, van Dorsselaer SA, Monshouwer K, Verdurmen JE, Engels RC, Vollebergh WA. Body mass index and body weight perception as risk factors for internalizing and externalizing problem behavior among adolescents. J Adolesc Health. 2006;39:27–34.
27. Jáuregui-Lobera I, Ezquerra-Cabrera M, Carbonero-Carreño R, Ruiz-Prieto I. Weight misperception, self-reported physical fitness, dieting and some psychological variables as risk factors for eating disorders. Nutrients. 2013;5:4486–502.
28. Gardner RM. Weight status and the perception of body image in men. Psychol Res Behav Manag. 2014;25(7):175–84. doi:10.2147/PRBM.S49053.
29. Rhodes SK, O'Neil PM. Effects of body fat distribution on body size estimation accuracy among obese women. Int J Obes Relat Metab Disord. 1997;21(3):250–3.
30. Weiner JS, Lourie JA. Practical human biology. London: Academic Press; 1981.
31. Lohman TG, Roche AF, Martorell R. Anthropometric standardization reference manual. Champaign: Human Kinetics Books; 1988.
32. World Health Organization (2014) BMI classification. http://apps.who.int/bmi/index.jsp?introPage=intro_3.html. Accessed 15 Apr 2014.
33. Sánchez-Villegas A, Madrigal H, Martínez-González MA, Kearney J, Gibney MJ, de Irala J, Martínez JA. Perception of body image as indicator of weight status in the European union. J Hum Nutr Diet. 2011;14(2):93–102.

34. Mciza Z, Goedecke JH, Steyn NP, Charlton K, Puoane T, Meltzer S, Levitt NS, Labert EV. Development and validation of instruments measuring body image and body weight dissatisfaction in south African mothers and their daughters. Public Health Nutr. 2005;8:509–19.
35. World Health Organization (2008) Waist Circumference and Waist–Hip Ratio: report of a WHO expert consultation, Accessed 02/05/2016.
36. Frederick DA, Buchanan GM, Sadehgi-Azar L, Peplau LA, Haselton MG, Berezovskaya A, Lipinski RE. Desiring the muscular ideal: Men's body satisfaction in the United States, Ukraine, and Ghana. Psychol Men Masculinity. 2007;8(2):103–17.
37. Zaccagni L, Masotti S, Donati R, Mazzoni G, Gualdi-Russo E. Body image and weight perceptions in relation to actual measurements by means of a new index and level of physical activity in Italian university students. J Transl Med. 2014;11:12–42.
38. Peltzer K, Pengpid S, Samuels TA, Özcan NK, Mantilla C, Rahamefy OH, Wong ML, Gasparishvili A. Prevalence of overweight/obesity and its associated factors among university students from 22 countries. Int J Environ Res Public Health. 2014;11(7):7425–41. doi:10.3390/ijerph110707425.
39. Jones WR, Morgan JF. Obesity surgery. Psychiatric needs must be considered. BMJ. 2010;28:341–c5298.
40. Mikolajczyk RT, Maxwell AE, El Ansari W, Stock C, Petkeviciene J, Guillen-Grima F. Relationship between perceived body weight and body mass index based on self- reported height and weight among university students: a cross-sectional study in seven European countries. BMC Public Health. 2010;27:10–40.
41. Kakeshita IS, de Sousa AS. Relationship between body mass index and self-perception among university students. Revista de Saude Publica. 2006;40(3):497–504.
42. Knauss C, Paxton SJ, Alsaker FD. Body dissatisfaction in adolescent boys and girls: objectified body consciousness, internalization of the media body ideal and perceived pressure from media. Sex Roles. 2008;59:633–43.
43. Neighbors LA, Sobal J. Prevalence and magnitude of body weight and shape dissatisfaction among university students. Eat Behav. 2007;8(4):429–39.
44. Kinsaul JAE, Curtin L, Bazzini D, Martz D. Empowerment, feminism, and self-efficacy: relationships to body image and disordered eating. Body Image. 2014;11(1):63–7.
45. Drumond Andrade FC, Raffaelli M, Teran-Garcia M, Jerman JA, Aradillas Garcia C, Up Amigos 2009 Study Group (2012) Weight status misperception among Mexican young adults. Body Image 9(1):184–8. doi: 10.1016/j.bodyim.2011.10.006.
46. Duchin O, Mora-Plazas M, Marin C, de Leon CM, Lee JM, Baylin A, Villamor E. BMI and sociodemographic correlates of body image perception and attitudes in school-aged children. Public Health Nutr. 2013;4:1–10.
47. Toselli S, Brasili P, Spiga F. Body image, body dissatisfaction and weight status in children from Emilia-Romagna (Italy): comparison between immigrant and native-born. Ann Hum Biol. 2014;41(1):23–8.

7

Disordered eating attitudes in female students of An-Najah National University

Raghad N. Saleh[1], Razan A. Salameh[1], Heba H. Yhya[1] and Waleed M. Sweileh[2*]

Abstract

Background: Eating disorders (ED) are serious psychiatric disorders characterized by unhealthy eating habits. There is a limited number of studies on eating disorders among female university students in Arab countries. Therefore, the objective of this study was to examine the prevalence of disordered eating attitudes (EA) among female students at An-Najah National University, Palestine.

Methods: A survey study on 2001 female students at An-Najah National University was carried out. The Sick, Control, One Stone, Fat, Food (SCOFF) screening questionnaire and the Eating Attitudes Test (EAT-26) were used.

Results: Of the 2001 participants, 28.6% scored ≥ 20 on the EAT-26 while 38.2% scored ≥ 2 on the SCOFF scale. A significant positive correlation was found between body mass index (BMI) and EAT-26 and SCOFF scores. There was a significant difference in EAT-26 ($p < .01$) and SCOFF scores ($p = .037$) between different academic specializations. Female students in non-scientific fields (arts and humanities) obtained higher scores than female students in scientific/medical fields. Age was significantly and negatively correlated with EAT-26 scores but not with SCOFF scores. Approximately 85% of students with scores in the "high risk" category of the EAT-26 scale endorsed the item "**I am terrified about being overweight**".

Conclusion: Awareness regarding appropriate nutrition in relation to body weight is needed among female university students. A general university elective course in this regard might be helpful.

Keywords: Female students, Palestine, Eating disorder, SCOFF, EAT-26

Plain English summary

Eating disorders are common in young females. There is inadequate literature on eating disorders in university students in Arab countries in general, and in Palestinian territories, in particular. A survey of approximately 2000 female students at An-Najah National University using internationally accepted scales showed a relatively high prevalence of disordered eating attitudes. Age, academic specializations, and body weight were important factors associated with disordered eating attitude. The higher the body weight, the higher the risk of having disordered eating attitudes. Younger females had higher disordered eating attitudes than older students. Female university students in non-scientific field had higher disordered eating attitude than those in scientific fields. To combat the influence of media on female university students, educational material regarding health body weight need to be developed and distributed.

* Correspondence: waleedsweileh@yahoo.com
[2]Department of Physiology, Pharmacology, and Toxicology, College of Medicine and Health Sciences, An-Najah National University, Nablus 44839, Palestine
Full list of author information is available at the end of the article

Background

Eating disorders (EDs) are a group of mental illnesses characterized by abnormal eating habits [1]. From a clinical point of view, EDs are an important cause of morbidity and mortality in adolescent girls and young adult women due to the severe changes in their eating behaviors [2, 3]. In the Middle East and in many Arabic countries obesity is prevalent. In fact, the prevalence of overweight and obesity in the Middle East has been estimated to be the second in the world, only after North America [4]. Given that obesity is a major driving force for disordered eating attitudes [5, 6], it is expected that EDs are increasing in Arab populations. A literature search using SciVerse Scopus indicated that there are 19 published articles on eating disorders among women in Arab countries [7, 8]. However, only few were carried out in female university students [9, 10]. Studies from the USA and European countries indicated that female university students had a high prevalence of EDs [11, 12]. University students have several risk factors that increase their risk of eating disorders, such as peer pressure, academic stress, living in dormitories, close relationships, social interaction, and high life expectations [13, 14]. Studies have shown that early detection and treatment of EDs can lead to full recovery [15, 16]. Therefore, screening for EDs in university students using simple and valid scales may allow early detection and appropriate medical and psychological intervention. Examples of useful scales for detection of EDs include the Sick, Control, One stone, Fat, Food (SCOFF) [17–21] and Eating Attitudes Test-26 (EAT-26) [22, 23] which can facilitate screening and early detection of EDs among college students [17, 20].

Based on this background, we hypothesized that the prevalence of EDs in Palestinian female university students is as high as reported in other Arab and non-Arab countries. The results of the current study will add to the literature on ED among Arab female adolescents and young adults, which will allow for comparative analysis with other cultural and ethnic groups, given that cultural differences in EDs do exist [24]. Furthermore, in this study, we will investigate how variables such as body weight, residence (living with family or in student dormitories), and academic specialization might be associated with ED, which may help in tailoring intervention strategies on university campuses.

Methods

Participants

Female students in different academic disciplines at An-Najah National University were invited to participate in this study.

Instruments

The researchers reviewed several articles published among female university students in the Middle East region and developed a questionnaire to be used for the purpose of this survey study. The questionnaire included several demographic variables; such as age, place of living, and academic specialization. The questionnaire also included two commonly used scales; SCOFF and EAT-26 [2, 19, 25]. Each of them is a highly reliable and valid scale and used to assess the risk of eating disorders.

SCOFF scale

The SCOFF is a screening questionnaire developed by Morgan et al. [19], which contains five short questions regarding key aspects of eating disorders such as vomiting, concerns about losing control over how much one eats, weight loss, feeling fat and whether food dominates life. The SCOFF scale consists of five yes/no questions. The Arabic version of the SCOFF (A-SCOFF) was obtained from the author who validated this version of the scale [17]. The scoring of SCOFF was as follows: one point for every "yes" answer and 0 for every "no" answer. A total score of ≥ 2 indicates that the participant has a high possibility of having anorexia nervosa or bulimia nervosa [19]. The Arabic version of the SCOFF has a sensitivity of 80.0%, a specificity of 72.7%, and a Cronbach alpha scale reliability coefficient of 0.43 [17]. In this study, Cronbach's α of the A-SCOFF equaled 0.38.

EAT-26 scale

The EAT-26 scale has three subscales with a total of 26 questions: 1) Dieting, 2) Bulimia and Food Preoccupation and 3) Oral Control [25]. Each item (except the 25th item) has six response options ranging in value from 0 to 3 ("always" = 3, "almost always" = 2, "often" = 1, "seldom" = 0, "hardly ever" = 0 and "never" = 0). Item 25 has a reversed score ("always", "nearly always" and "often" = 0, "seldom" = 1, "almost never" = 2, "never" = 3). The total score of EAT-26 equals the sum of scores for the 26 items. A score of ≥ 20 is defined as being characteristic of a "disordered eating attitude". In this study, the Cronbach's α of EAT-26 was 0.87. The Arabic language version of this scale was validated more than two decades ago and found to be valid and reliable [26]. The Arabic version used in the current study was a translation made by the authors to suit the Palestinian Arabic accent and was generated with the help of English and medical professionals.

Behavioral scale

The EAT-26 has three criteria for determining if the participant needs to seek further evaluation of the risk of having ED. These criteria include the EAT-26 scores, low body weight compared to age-matched norms, and behavioral questions indicative of possible ED [2]. In the current study, five behavioral questions were added to the EAT-26 to determine the presence of extreme weight-control behaviors as well as providing an estimate of their frequency. These questions assess self-reported binge eating, self-induced vomiting, use of laxatives, over-exercising, and loss of more than 8 kg over the preceding 6 months. According to the guideline, individuals who endorsed any of these items have high potential of having ED and require further assessment by trained mental health specialist [27–30].

Procedure

This was a cross-sectional study carried out at An-Najah National University, the largest university in Nablus and elsewhere in the Palestinian territories. Approximately 10,000 female students are currently enrolled at An-Najah National University in various academic specializations. This study was carried out during the autumn semester of 2017 and included female students from different specialties in the two main campuses of the university.

The researchers distributed the questionnaires to female students in seven different sites in the university where students from all colleges usually spend their break time. The distribution and collection process were carried out for eight consecutive days with 300 questionnaires being distributed daily. The distribution and collection of the questionnaires were carried out by three co-authors (H.Y, R.N.S and R.A.S).

Data entry

All data collected were entered into the Statistical Package for Social Science (SPSS) 20 software. The variables included in the study were age, academic specialization (coded as "1" for those in humanities and "2" for those in other fields that included: science, engineering, and medicine), and living situation (coded as "1" for living with family and "2" for living in dormitories). Both height and weight were measured by the researchers using a standard electronic scale and stadiometer obtained from the University. Body Mass Index (BMI) was calculated by dividing body weight in kilograms by the height in meters squared. The following classification was used: BMI $\geq$ 30.00 indicates obesity, 25.00 $\leq$ BMI < 30 overweight, 18.5 $\leq$ BMI < 25 defines the normal range, BMI < 18.5 is considered as underweight [31].

Ethical approval

The questionnaire was anonymous, to ensure confidentiality. Furthermore, an approval from the institutional review board [32] at An-Najah National University was obtained to carry out the study among female university students. Since no clinical intervention or blood testing was involved in the study, verbal consent, and not a written consent, was obtained from all participants, according to IRB regulations.

Results

Characteristics of the participants

In the current study, the researchers distributed approximately 2500 questionnaire. In total, 2001 female students completed and returned the questionnaire, giving a response rate of 97.1%. More than half (1092; 54.6%) of the participants were from faculties of humanities and arts while the remaining (909; 45.4%) were from faculties of medicine or science or engineering. The majority of respondents (1676; 83.8%) were living with their families while the remaining were living in student dormitories. The mean age ± SD of the respondents was 19.5 ± 1.4 years while BMI mean ± SD was 21.7 ± 3.4 kg/m^2. Based on BMI classification, 1467 (73.3%) of the participants had a BMI in the "normal" range, 281 (14.0%) in the "underweight" range, and 253 (12.6%) in the "overweight/obese" range.

Eat-26 and SCOFF scores

Table 1 shows Cronbach α value for the scales used and the mean ± SD scores of both SCOFF and EAT-26 subscales. Internal consistency of EAT-26 and its subscales were high, but that of the SCOFF was low. According to the EAT-26 scale, the number of female students considered to be at high risk of disordered eating attitudes was 573 (28.6%), while according to the SCOFF, the number was 767 (38.3%). There was a significant and positive correlation between SCOFF scores and EAT-26 and its subscale scores (Table 2), suggesting a high degree of agreement between the two scales.

Univariate analysis of EAT-26 scores

There was a significant and negative correlation (r = − 0.058, p = .008) between age and EAT-26 scores suggestive of higher risk of ED among younger female students. There was also a significant and positive correlation between BMI and EAT-26 (Spearman correlation r = 0.173, p < 0.011) suggestive of higher risk of ED among females with higher BMI values. Females in the academic field of humanities had a mean ± SD on the EAT-26 of 16.4 ± 10.8 while females in science/engineering/medicine had a mean ± SD of 13.9 ± 9.7. The difference was significant (p < 0.01). Analysis of EAT-26 items indicated that out of the 573 high-risk individuals, 84.5% (n = 484) were "terrified of being overweight", 48.7% (n = 279) reported that "food controls their life", and 55% (n = 315) reported "cutting food into pieces". In the behavioral scale appended to the EAT-26, more than half (53.5%) did not endorse any of the items, while the remaining 930 (46.5%) endorsed at least one of the additional ED behaviours, which suggests a need for further investigation of potential EDs.

Table 1 Analysis of SOFF and EAT-26 scores

Variable	Cronbach's α	Mean ± SD and	Range of scores
SCOFF	0.38	1.25 ± 1.032	0–4
EAT – 26	0.87	15.27 ± 10.38	0–69
D subscale	0.88	8.21 ± 6.977	0–39
O subscale	0.79	4.67 ± 6.977	0–21
B subscale	0.86	2.39 ± 3.272	0–17

Table 2 Correlation between SCOFF scores and EAT-26 scores

		EAT-26	D-score	O-scale	B-score
SCOFF scores	Pearson Correlation	0.423[a]	0.404[a]	0.075[a]	0.391[a]
	Sig. (2-tailed)	0.000	0.000	0.001	0.000

[a]denotes significance with p value less than 0.01

Univariate analysis of SCOFF scores

There was no significant correlation ($p = .725$) between age and SCOFF scores. However, there was a significant correlation between BMI values and SCOFF scores ($r = .225$, $p < 0.001$) such that females with higher BMI values had higher SCOFF scores, which is consistent with results obtained on the EAT-26. Furthermore, there was a significant difference in SCOFF mean scores between humanities students (1.4 ± 1.0) and those in science/medicine/engineering faculties (1.2 ± 1.0) ($p = .037$).

Discussion

The aim of this study was to investigate the prevalence of eating disorder attitudes among a large sample of female university students using two common eating disorder scales. The two scales showed similar relationships with most variables except for age, which was significantly correlated with the EAT-26 but not the SCOFF. In the context of this study, the internal consistency of the SCOFF was low, while that of the EAT-26 was very high, suggesting that results obtained from EAT-26 were more reliable than that of the SCOFF, even though the SCOFF is simpler scale than the EAT-26.

When compared with similar studies on female university students carried out elsewhere, the rates of eating disorder attitudes/behaviours in the present study were higher than those obtained in Nigeria [33], Iran [34–36], China [37–39], France [37], USA [3, 40, 41], Spain [42], Lebanon [43], Thailand [44], Greece [45], Brazil [46] but lower than those obtained in Bangladesh [47] and Vietnam [48]. Therefore, our results show higher rates than most of those from other countries. The results reported in the current study were within the range of findings from other Arab countries, including Palestine. The reported percentage of girls and young women at risk of ED in Saudi Arabia was 24.6% [26], 29.4% in Oman [49], 23.4% in the UAE [50], and approximately 38% in Palestine 38.9% [14].

The finding of higher rates in this study could be attributed to the new evolving life of Palestinians who have had several decades of hardship. The situation in the Palestinian territories is very complex with regard to exposure to the westernized secular Israeli culture. While female Palestinian students generally have limited exposure to the Israeli community, female Palestinian students from Jerusalem and Israeli Arab students studying at An-Najah National University are exposed to Israeli culture. Such exposure could be affecting views regarding body image and body weight. Palestinian females who are not directly exposed to the Israeli community still experience exposure to Israeli media through television, social media, and other means of communication. Furthermore, recently there has been increased exposure to Turkish media. Such movies and TV shows may also influence the attitudes of Arab females, given that Turkish society is less conservative compared to that of Arab culture. Palestinian culture has been oppressed for decades, and isolated from most direct means of communication with neighboring Arab countries. However, recent communication through social media may have created a conflict in attitudes toward women, female bodies, and beauty standards. The traditional Palestinian culture gives little attention to body weight and what the female body should look like. However, partly due to the above, there has been an increased emphasis on body weight as an important aesthetic item.

The current study showed that there was a significant correlation between BMI and both EAT-26 score and SCOFF score. This was unsurprising, as similar findings have been reported in other studies [51–53]. The current study also showed that academic specialization in faculties related to humanities was significantly associated with high EAT-26 scores as well as high SCOFF score. This finding, o the authors' knowledge, has not been reported previously in the literature. One interpretation of this finding is that female humanities students tend to have more free time to watch television advertisements and use social media, as well as for activities focusing on beauty and body image than students in science- and engineering-based fields, who tend to experience higher academic pressure and less free time. Students in medicine, engineering, and science have usually obtained high grades in high school and have high academic and professional ambitions, which tend to limit their emphasis on body weight, and use of social media regarding issues pertaining to beauty and body image.

The results of the current study revealed that the most frequently endorsed item was "**I am terrified about being overweight**" which is in the EAT-26 Dieting subscale. This indicates that female students are highly conscious about their body weight. There may be several reasons for this, such as media which shows the ideal female body as being thin. Furthermore, there is peer, cultural, and family pressure on females to be accepted socially based on modern criteria. On the Bulimia and Food Preoccupation subscale, the current study revealed that the most highly endorsed item was "I find myself preoccupied with food", whereas for the Oral Control Subscale, this item was "I cut my food into small pieces". These findings suggest that the majority of female students in the high-risk category endorsed behaviours more closely aligned with bulimia nervosa than anorexia nervosa. In Middle Eastern cultures, families tend to pressure girls and young women to eat, but also expect them to maintain an appropriate body weight and body size for marriage. These societal pressures may contribute to bulimia nervosa-like behaviours in young female students at a critical age.

This study has limitations that need to be mentioned. First, the convenience sampling method is not random, however the sample size of the study was relatively large compared with other related studies carried out in the Middle East region. Second, the scales used in this study cannot provide a diagnosis, and the lack of mental health assessment by experts made our study valuable only as an initial screening method. Hence, the true prevalence of various types of eating disorders in the Palestinian community of female students needs to be further investigated. The current study should be followed up with larger numbers of students; future studies should also take into consideration religion and level of religiosity as an important variable when investigating eating disorders. Furthermore, the extent of exposure of female students in this geographical region to Israeli community values needs to be considered when designing future studies about eating disorders.

Conclusion

This study showed suggests that (1) the prevalence of disordered eating attitudes is relatively high among female Palestinian university students, (2) disordered eating attitudes were significantly associated with BMI and academic specialization, and (3) even though both the EAT-26 and the SCOFF showed similar results, the EAT-26 appears to be more reliable when studying university students. These findings suggest the need for clinical screening of eating disorders and medical treatment if needed. Future epidemiological studies that take into consideration a greater number of demographic and psychological variables such as stress, spirituality and religiosity are recommended.

Authors' contributions

WS: concept, data analysis and presentation, manuscript preparation, and manuscript submission. RS, RS, and H.Y: Data collection, manuscript writing, literature review, data interpretation, and planning and designing the method. All authors read and approved the final manuscript.

Competing interests

The authors declare that they have no competing interests.

Author details

[1]Department of Medicine, College of Medicine and Health Sciences, An-Najah National University, Nablus 44839, Palestine. [2]Department of Physiology, Pharmacology, and Toxicology, College of Medicine and Health Sciences, An-Najah National University, Nablus 44839, Palestine.

References

1. Erskine HE, Whiteford HA, Pike KM. The global burden of eating disorders. Curr Opin Psychiatry. 2016;29(6):346–53.
2. Garner DM, Olmstead MP, Polivy J. Development and validation of a multidimensional eating disorder inventory for anorexia nervosa and bulimia. Int J Eat Disord. 1983;2(2):15–34.
3. Tavolacci MP, Grigioni S, Richard L, Meyrignac G, Déchelotte P, Ladner J. Eating disorders and associated health risks among university students. J Nutr Educ Behav. 2015;47(5):412–20.
4. Yusuf S, Hawken S, Ounpuu S, Bautista L, Franzosi MG, Commerford P, Lang CC, Rumboldt Z, Onen CL, Lisheng L, et al. Obesity and the risk of myocardial infarction in 27,000 participants from 52 countries: a case-control study. Lancet. 2005;366(9497):1640–9.
5. Calzo JP, Sonneville KR, Haines J, Blood EA, Field AE, Austin SB. The development of associations among body mass index, body dissatisfaction, and weight and shape concern in adolescent boys and girls. J Adolesc Health. 2012;51(5):517–23.
6. Mond J, van den Berg P, Boutelle K, Hannan P, Neumark-Sztainer D. Obesity, body dissatisfaction, and emotional well-being in early and late adolescence: findings from the project EAT study. J Adolesc Health. 2011; 48(4):373–8.
7. Eladawi N, Helal R, Niazy NA, Abdelsalam S. Prevalence and associated factors of eating disorders in weight management centers in Tanta, Egypt. Chin Med J. 2018;131(1):50–5.
8. Thomas J, O'Hara L, Quadflieg S, Weissgerber SC. Acculturation, out-group positivity and eating disorders symptoms among Emirati women. Eat Weight Disord. 2018;23(2):241–6.
9. Manaf NA, Saravanan C, Zuhrah B. The prevalence and inter-relationship of negative body image perception, depression and susceptibility to eating disorders among female medical undergraduate students. J Clin Diagn Res. 2016;10(3):VC01–4.
10. Shaikh MA, Shaikh IA, Kamal A, Irfan S. Eating disorders detection in female university students. J Coll Physicians Surg Pak. 2011;21(10):650.
11. Kwan MY, Gordon KH, Minnich AM, Carter DL, Troop-Gordon W. Peer victimization & amp; eating disorder symptoms in college students. J Soc Clin Psychol. 2017;36(5):419–36.
12. Lipson SK, Sonneville KR. Eating disorder symptoms among undergraduate and graduate students at 12 U.S. colleges and universities. Eat Behav. 2017; 24:81–8.
13. Sanchez-Ruiz MJ, El-Jor C, Abi Kharma J, Bassil M, Zeeni N. Personality, emotion-related variables, and media pressure predict eating disorders via disordered eating in Lebanese university students. Eat Weight Disord. 2017:1–10.
14. Musaiger AO, Al-Mannai M, Tayyem R, Al-Lalla O, Ali EYA, Kalam F, Benhamed MM, Saghir S, Halahleh I, Djoudi Z, et al. Risk of disordered eating attitudes among adolescents in seven Arab countries by gender and obesity: a cross-cultural study. Appetite. 2013;60(1):162–7.
15. Becker AE, Franko DL, Nussbaum K, Herzog DB. Secondary prevention for eating disorders: the impact of education, screening, and referral in a college-based screening program. Int J Eat Disord. 2004;36(2):157–62.
16. Fichter MM, Quadflieg N, Hedlund S. Twelve-year course and outcome predictors of anorexia nervosa. Int J Eat Disord. 2006;39(2):87–100.
17. Aoun A, Azzam J, Jabbour FE, Hlais S, Daham D, Amm CE, Honein K, Dechelotte P. Validation of the Arabic version of the SCOFF questionnaire for the screening of eating disorders. East Mediterr Health J. 2015;21(5):326–31.
18. Luck AJ, Morgan JF, Reid F, O'Brien A, Brunton J, Price C, Perry L, Lacey JH. The SCOFF questionnaire and clinical interview for eating disorders in general practice: comparative study. Bmj. 2002;325(7367):755–6.
19. Morgan JF, Reid F, Lacey JH. The SCOFF questionnaire: assessment of a new screening tool for eating disorders. Bmj. 1999;319(7223):1467–8.
20. Sanchez-Armass O, Raffaelli M, Andrade FCD, Wiley AR, Noyola ANM, Arguelles AC, Aradillas-Garcia C. Validation of the SCOFF questionnaire for screening of eating disorders among Mexican university students. Eat Weight Disord. 2017;22(1):153–60.

21. Solmi F, Hatch SL, Hotopf M, Treasure J, Micali N. Validation of the SCOFF questionnaire for eating disorders in a multiethnic general population sample. Int J Eat Disord. 2015;48(3):312–6.
22. Kang Q, Chan RCK, Li X, Arcelus J, Yue L, Huang J, Gu L, Fan Q, Zhang H, Xiao Z, et al. Psychometric properties of the Chinese version of the eating attitudes test in young female patients with eating disorders in mainland China. Eur Eat Disord Rev. 2017;25(6):613–7.
23. Mitsui T, Yoshida T, Komaki G. Psychometric properties of the eating disorder examination-questionnaire in Japanese adolescents. BioPsychoSocial Med. 2017;11(1):9.
24. Pike KM, Hoek HW, Dunne PE. Cultural trends and eating disorders. Curr Opin Psychiatry. 2014;27(6):436–42.
25. Garner DM, Garfinkel PE. The eating attitudes test: an index of the symptoms of anorexia nervosa. Psychol Med. 1979;9(2):273–9.
26. al-Subaie A, al-Shammari S, Bamgboye E, al-Sabhan K, al-Shehri S, Bannah AR. Validity of the Arabic version of the eating attitude test. Int J Eat Disord. 1996;20(3):321–4.
27. Garner DM, Garfinkel PE. Socio-cultural factors in the development of anorexia nervosa. Psychol Med. 1980;10(4):647–56.
28. Garner DM, Garfinkel PE, O'Shaughnessy M. The validity of the distinction between bulimia with and without anorexia nervosa. Am J Psychiatry. 1985; 142(5):581–7.
29. Garner DM, Olmsted MP, Polivy J, Garfinkel PE. Comparison between weight-preoccupied women and anorexia nervosa. Psychosom Med. 1984; 46(3):255–66.
30. Garner DM, Olmsted MP, Bohr Y, Garfinkel PE. The eating attitudes test: psychometric features and clinical correlates. Psychol Med. 1982;12(4):871–8.
31. Consultation WHOE. Appropriate body-mass index for Asian populations and its implications for policy and intervention strategies. Lancet. 2004; 363(9403):157–63.
32. Fairburn CG, Bohn K. Eating disorder NOS (EDNOS): an example of the troublesome "not otherwise specified" (NOS) category in DSM-IV. Behav Res Ther. 2005;43(6):691–701.
33. Fadipe B, Oyelohunnu MA, Olagunju AT, Aina OF, Akinbode AA, Suleiman TF. Disordered eating attitudes: demographic and clinico-anthropometric correlates among a sample of Nigerian students. Afr Health Sci. 2017;17(2):513–23.
34. Naeimi AF, Haghighian HK, Gargari BP, Alizadeh M, Rouzitalab T. Eating disorders risk and its relation to self-esteem and body image in Iranian university students of medical sciences. Eat Weight Disord. 2016;21(4):597–605.
35. Rouzitalab T, Pourghassem Gargari B, Amirsasan R, Asghari Jafarabadi M, Farsad Naeimi A, Sanoobar M. The relationship of disordered eating attitudes with body composition and anthropometric indices in physical education students. Iran Red Crescent Med J. 2015;17(11):e20727.
36. Roshandel A, Safavi M, Ghasemi I. Prevalence of eating disorders among female students of university (Tehran-Iran). Life Sci J. 2012;9(4):2822–8.
37. Tao Z, Sun Y. Eating attitudes, weight control behaviors and risk factors for eating disorders among Chinese female dance students. Eur J Psychiatry. 2015;29(4):249–58.
38. Yu J, Lu M, Tian L, Lu W, Meng F, Chen C, Tang T, He L, Yao Y. Prevalence of disordered eating attitudes among university students in Wuhu, China. Nutr Hosp. 2015;32(4):1752–7.
39. Liao Y, Liu T, Cheng Y, Wang J, Deng Y, Hao W, Chen X, Xu Y, Wang X, Tang J. Changes in eating attitudes, eating disorders and body weight in Chinese medical university students. Int J Soc Psychiatry. 2013;59(6):578–85.
40. Phillips L, Kemppainen JK, Mechling BM, MacKain S, Kim-Godwin Y, Leopard L. Eating disorders and spirituality in college students. J Psychosoc Nurs Ment Health Serv. 2015;53(1):30–7.
41. Eisenberg D, Nicklett EJ, Roeder K, Kirz NE. Eating disorder symptoms among college students: prevalence, persistence, correlates, and treatment-seeking. J Am Coll Health. 2011;59(8):700–7.
42. Martínez-González L, Fernández TV, de la Torre Molina A, Ayán CP, Bueno AC, Capelo RÁ, Mateos RC, Martín VS. Prevalence of eating disorders in college students and associated factors: uniHcos project. Nutr Hosp. 2014; 30(4):927–34.
43. Aoun A, Garcia FD, Mounzer C, Hlais S, Grigioni S, Honein K, Déchelotte P. War stress may be another risk factor for eating disorders in civilians: a study in Lebanese University students. Gen Hosp Psychiatry. 2013;35(4):393–7.
44. Pattanathaburt P, Somrongthong R, Thianthai C. Prevalence of disordered eating behaviors, body image dissatisfaction, and associated factors among Thai female undergraduate students. Int J Health Promot Educ. 2013;51(3): 151–60.
45. Gardouni A, Karakasi A, Zagkalis T, Koulierakis G. Disordered eating attitudes within female university students in Athens: association with body image perception and socioeconomic status. Rev Clin Pharmacol Pharmacokinet Int Ed. 2013;27(3):123–9.
46. Pereira LNG, Trevisol FS, Quevedo J, Jornada LK. Eating disorders among health science students at a university in southern Brazil. Revista de Psiquiatria do Rio Grande do Sul. 2011;33(1):14–9.
47. Pengpid S, Peltzer K, Ahsan GU. Risk of eating disorders among university students in Bangladesh. Int J Adolesc Med Health. 2015;27(1):93–100.
48. Ko N, Tam DM, Viet NK, Scheib P, Wirsching M, Zeeck A. Disordered eating behaviors in university students in Hanoi, Vietnam. J Eat Disord. 2015;3(1):18.
49. Al-Adawi S, Dorvlo AS, Burke DT, Al-Bahlani S, Martin RG, Al-Ismaily S. Presence and severity of anorexia and bulimia among male and female Omani and non-Omani adolescents. J Am Acad Child Adolesc Psychiatry. 2002;41(9):1124–30.
50. Eapen V, Mabrouk AA, Bin-Othman S. Disordered eating attitudes and symptomatology among adolescent girls in the United Arab Emirates. Eat Behav. 2006;7(1):53–60.
51. Fortes LD, Filgueiras JF, Ferreira ME. Risk behaviors for eating disorders and depressive symptoms: a study of female adolescents in Juiz de fora, Minas Gerais state, Brazil. Cad Saude Publica. 2014;30(11):2443–50.
52. Memon AA, Adil SE, Siddiqui EU, Naeem SS, Ali SA, Mehmood K. Eating disorders in medical students of Karachi, Pakistan-a cross-sectional study. BMC research notes. 2012;5(1):84.
53. Wong Y-C, Lin J-S, Chang Y-J. Body satisfaction, emotional intelligence, and the development of disturbed eating: a survey of Taiwanese students. Asia Pac J Clin Nutr. 2014;23(4):651–9.

Feeding and eating disorders in the DSM-5 era: a systematic review of prevalence rates in non-clinical male and female samples

Camilla Lindvall Dahlgren[1*], Line Wisting[1] and Øyvind Rø[1,2]

Abstract

Objective: The objective of this study was to systematically review the literature on the prevalence of eating disorders (EDs) during the DSM-5 era, and to report rates of point- and lifetime prevalence.

Method: A PubMed search was conducted targeting articles on the epidemiology of EDs, in particular, reported rates of prevalence. The review was performed in accordance with PRISMA guidelines, and was limited to DSM-5 based eating disorder diagnoses published between 2012 and 2017.

Results: A total of 19 studies fulfilled inclusion criteria and were included in the study.

Discussion: Following the transition to DSM-5, it is evident that the prevalence of eating disorder not otherwise specified (EDNOS)/other specified feeding and eating disorders (OSFED) has decreased as intended, and there is preliminary evidence suggesting that rates of anorexia nervosa (AN) and bulimia nervosa (BN) and binge eating disorder (BED) have increased. Further, we observed higher rates of BED prevalence among females compared to males, with rates increasing with age. A limitation to the study was the search date, and that none of the included studies investigated the "new" DSM-5 feeding disorders avoidant restrictive food intake disorder (ARFID), pica or rumination disorder warranting attention in future studies investigating the epidemiology of feeding and eating disorders.

Keywords: Epidemiology, Prevalence, Eating disorders, DSM-5, Systematic review

Plain English summary

The aim of writing this literature review was to provide the reader with an overview of published studies using the newest version of the Diagnostic and Statistical Manual of Mental Disorders, the DSM-5, in assessing eating disorder prevalence. A literature search was performed in accordance with well established guidelines, resulting in 19 studies fulfilling inclusion criteria. As intended, rates of the residual eating disorder category "other specified feeding and eating disorders" had increased, and preliminary evidence supported increased prevalence of anorexia nervosa, bulimia nervosa and binge eating disorder. No studies assessing the prevalence of feeding disorders (i.e. Pica, Rumination Disorder and Avoidant Restrictive Food Intake Disorders) were identified.

* Correspondence: camilla.lindvall@dahlgren.no
[1]Regional Department for Eating Disorders, Division of Mental Health and Addiction, Oslo University Hospital, Ullevål HF, Postboks 4950 Nydalen, 0424 Oslo, Norway
Full list of author information is available at the end of the article

Background

In 2013, the Diagnostic and Statistical Manual of Mental Disorders, Fourth Edition (DSM-IV) [1] was replaced by its successor, the DSM-5 [2], yielding a number of adjustments in diagnostic criteria across psychiatric diagnoses. For eating disorders (ED) in specific, a main intention of the DSM-5 adjustments was to decrease the number of ED cases falling into the former diagnostic category "eating disorder not otherwise specified" (EDNOS), a poorly defined and heterogeneous residual category representing the majority of DSM-IV ED cases. This was done by removing binge eating disorder (BED) from the DSM-IV EDNOS category, and reintroducing it as an independent and specified DSM-5 diagnosis, and by expanding the boundaries of anorexia nervosa (AN) and bulimia nervosa (BN). The DSM-5 retained practically all core AN features, but clarified the weight criteria by changing the wording from "a body weight less than 85% of that expected" to "significantly low weight". Also, the amenorrhea criterion was removed. For BN, the minimum frequency of binge eating episodes and inappropriate compensatory behavior was reduced from twice a week to once a week. In addition to these changes, three disorders previously reserved for children and classified as 'Feeding and Eating Disorders of Infancy or Early Childhood' were revised and introduced in the DSM-5 as independent diagnostic categories: pica, avoidant/restrictive food intake disorder (ARFID) and rumination disorder. Finally, EDNOS was replaced by other specified feeding and eating disorders (OSFED) including atypical AN, subthreshold BN and subthreshold BED, purging disorder (PD), night eating syndrome (NES), as well as unspecified feeding and eating disorders (UFED) representing cases where behaviors cause clinically significant distress/impairment of functioning, but fail to meet full criteria for a feeding or eating disorder.

In the years to come, the new diagnostic criteria for EDs are likely to yield alterations in reported point (proportion of individuals affected by a disorder at the one specific point in time) and lifetime (proportion of individuals having been affected by a disorder at any time in life up to the measurement point) prevalence rates. Historically, ED prevalence rates reported using the DSM-IV have varied considerably across studies, with discrepancies being a result of a number of methodological issues such as inconsistent use of assessment instruments [3], variations in study designs [4] and estimates calculated using non-representative samples [5]. It is therefore important to assess trends in occurrence rates on a regular basis, taking into account changes to diagnostic criteria as well as methodological aspects influencing observed trends.

Following the transition from DSM-IV to DSM-5, it is relevant to review whether the revisions to the DSM-IV have resulted in alterations in diagnostic distribution, and to identify diagnostic categories in need of further research. Four years into the DSM-5 era, a small number of studies do, in fact, show that the new diagnostic system alters the representation and distribution of ED diagnoses with evidence of increased lifetime prevalence of BN and BED [6] and increased lifetime [7] and point prevalence [8] of AN. Further, reduced numbers of identified OSFED and UFED cases [9–11] have also been reported. However, only a limited number of studies have sought to investigate the prevalence of DSM-5 feeding disorders (i.e. pica, ARFID and rumination disorder), or the occurrence of the OSFED categories such as subclinical AN, BN and BED, as well as NES and PD. In sum, there have been important recent developments that warrant further attention. These includes the emergence of new empirical findings from studies assessing ED prevalence using DSM-5 criteria, as well as findings from retrospective studies recoding DSM-IV diagnoses into new DSM-5 ED categories. The aim of this study was to systematically review the field for studies reporting ED prevalence based on DSM-5 criteria in non-clinical female and male samples. The review was performed according to PRISMA guidelines [12] and synthesized studies published between 2012 and 2017.

Methods

Search strategy

The literature was reviewed in February 2017, using the PubMed search below. The screening process was conducted according to the criteria outlined by the PRISMA guidelines, and is presented in Fig. 1.

(((((((anorexia[All Fields] AND nervosa[All Fields]) AND DSM-5[All Fields] AND prevalence[All Fields]) OR ((bulimia[All Fields] AND nervosa[All Fields]) AND DSM-5[All Fields] AND prevalence[All Fields])) OR ((binge[All Fields] AND eating[All Fields] AND disorder[All Fields]) AND DSM-5[All Fields] AND prevalence[All Fields])) OR ((eating[All Fields] AND disorder[All Fields]) AND DSM-5[All Fields] AND prevalence[All Fields])) OR (OSFED[All Fields] AND DSM-5[All Fields] AND prevalence[All Fields])) OR (PICA[All Fields] AND DSM-5[All Fields] AND prevalence[All Fields])) OR (avoidant[All Fields] AND restrictive[All Fields] AND food[All Fields] AND intake[All Fields] AND disorder[All Fields]) AND DSM-5[All Fields] AND prevalence[All Fields]) OR (rumination[All Fields] AND disorder[All Fields]) AND DSM-5[All Fields] AND prevalence[All Fields])

Eligibility criteria

Publications were targeted that examined the epidemiology of EDs, in particular ED prevalence rates, in non--clinical samples, and were selected for review according to the criteria outlined below.

A. Articles that presented ED prevalence rates based on DSM-5 criteria (articles presenting recoded diagnostic categories (e.g. from DSM-IV to DSM-5) were also eligible)
B. Articles that were written in English or had an available published English translation
C. Articles that were published in peer reviewed journals

Exclusion criteria

All papers investigating ED prevalence in clinical samples were excluded. Editorials, commentaries, [systematic] reviews, as well as articles reporting prevalence of disordered eating without utilizing DSM-5 ED diagnoses (e.g. ED *features* or *syndromes*) were omitted. Exclusions were tracked and registered (see Fig. 1). Omitted review

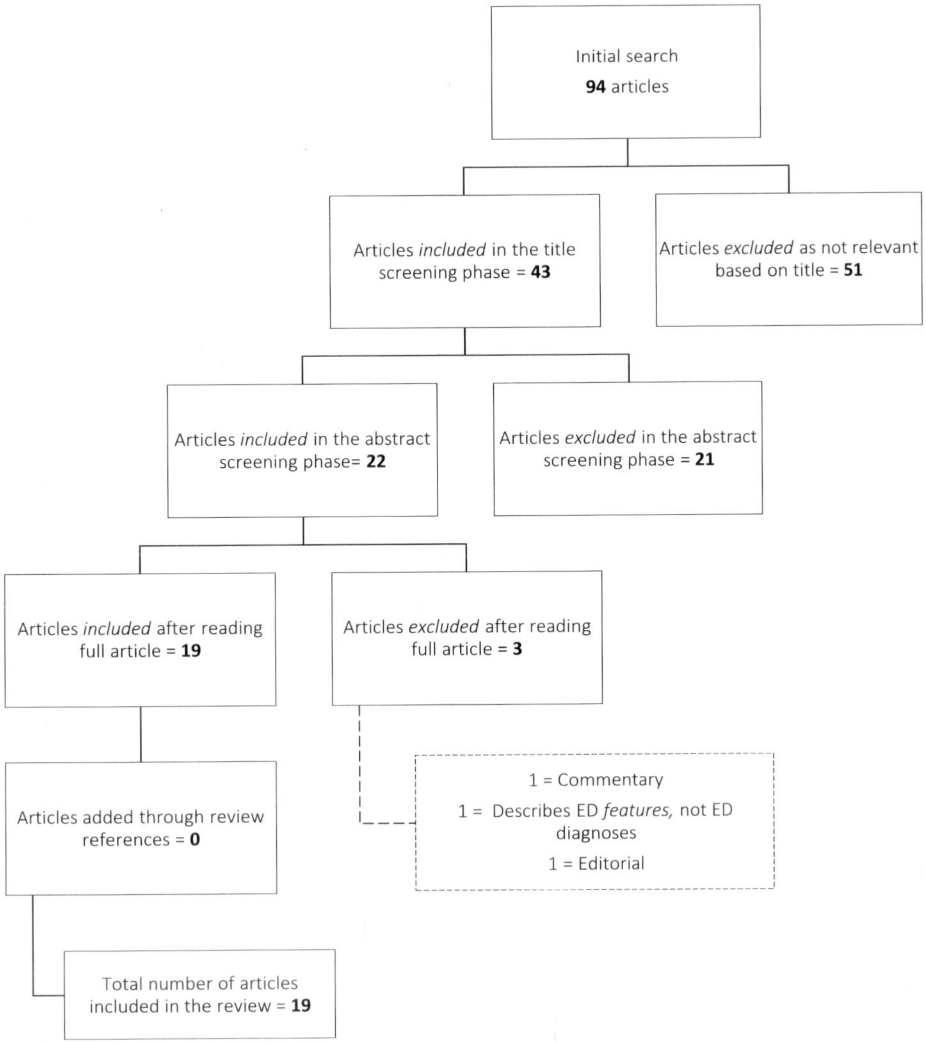

Fig. 1 The literature screening process according to PRISMA guidelines

articles were screened for additional references. No exclusions for age, gender or geographic areas were applied.

Title, abstract and article selection

Publication titles in studies obtained through the search strategy outlined earlier were reviewed by the authors CLD and LW. All titles clearly irrelevant to the aim and scope of the paper (e.g. "Food addiction – substance use disorder or behavioral addiction") were excluded during this initial screening. Publications with ambiguous titles (e.g. "Eating disorders in older women") and publication with titles clearly relevant to the aim of the paper (e.g. "Prevalence and severity of DSM-5 eating disorders in a community cohort of adolescents") were included at this stage of the screening process. Abstracts were then screened by CLD and LW using a similar strategy (i.e. screening for irrelevance, ambiguity and certainty), after which full texts were retrieved and assessed for eligibility by CLD and LW using the outlined eligibility and exclusion criteria. Agreement was reached for all included and excluded publications. None of the reviewers were blind to the authors of the texts, nor their affiliations.

Results

Search summary

The PubMed search strategy produced 94 titles, which after the initial title screen was reduced to 43. Of these 43, 21 were omitted in the abstract screening process. A total of 22 papers met eligibility criteria and were retained. Subsequently, three full-text studies were excluded based on lack of relevance, leading to a total inclusion of 19 studies. No additional studies were found through the screening of review articles. A more detailed overview of the screening process is presented in Fig. 1.

Table 1 summarizes all included studies. No studies meeting eligibility criteria were published before 2012. Assessments of the following full- and subthreshold diagnoses were reported: ED, AN, BN, BED, OSFED and UFED. OSFED included atypical AN (OSFED-AN) subthreshold BN (OSFED-BN) and subthreshold BED (OSFED-BED), as well as purging disorder (OSFED-PD) and night eating syndrome (OSFED-NES). No studies reporting ARFID, rumination disorder or Pica were identified.

The majority of included studies presented data from US samples (*N* = 5), closely followed by Australia (*N* = 3), Germany (*N* = 2), Finland (N = 2) and Canada (N = 2). Portugal, Sweden, United Kingdom, Switzerland and the Netherlands all represented one individual study. Ages ranged from 11 to 96, with eight studies reporting data from adults only (>18), nine studies reporting rates from mixed age samples (i.e. children, adolescents *and* adults) and two studies presented data collected in samples below the age of 15. Sample sizes ranged from 496 to 22,397, and approximately 25% (*N* = 5) of the included studies followed a two-stage design approach in estimating ED prevalence. Six studies used interviews alone to establish ED diagnoses, and seven studies employed self-reports. Trace et al. [6] did not specify the design of the study. Disregarding prevalence reports using data from overlapping samples [7, 10, 13, 14], all studies employing 2-stage designs had used different screening instruments.

Prevalence rates

In 2-stage design studies, lifetime AN prevalence rates in females ranged from 1.7% [15] to 3.6% [9], and point prevalence ranged from 0.67% [9] to 1.2% [15]. Only one study reported male AN prevalence and they found both point and lifetime to be 0.1% [15]. BN was most commonly assessed using point prevalence, but was only assessed in two out the five 2-stage design studies [9, 15]. These studies reported nearly identical point BN prevalence rates of 0.59% and 0.6% respectively in females. Point prevalence rates for BED were reported in three studies, and ranged from 0.62% [9] (females only) to 3.6% [16] (males and females combined). Lifetime prevalence rates for OSFED ranged from 0.3% in males [15] to 0.6% in females [10] and point prevalence from 0.0% in males [15] to 2.4% in a sample combining male and females rates. Lifetime prevalence rates of UFED in females were 0.2% [15] and 0.9% [10] respectively.

In interview based studies, lifetime prevalence of AN in females ranged from 0.8% [17] to 1.9% [4]. Lifetime BN prevalence in females of was only reported in one of these studies, with a rate of 2.6% [17]. In two out of the six interview-based studies, lifetime rates of BED were reported. BED in females were 3.0% [17] and 3.6% [18] respectively, whereas the corresponding rates for males were only assessed in one study [18] reporting a rate of 2.1%. In females prevalence of OSFED was reported in the interview based prevalence studies, with overall OSFED point prevalence rates ranging from 5% [19] to lifetime prevalence rate of 11% [17].

Point prevalence was most commonly reported in studies using the self-report design. Here, AN rates ranged from 0.06% [14] to 1.2% in females [15]. BN prevalence rates ranged from 0.45% [11] to 8.7% in females [20]. BED rates ranged from 0.0% (in males) [20] to 4.1% (in females). Two studies [21, 22] set out to investigate the occurrence of night eating syndrome (NES). In these studies, point prevalence was established using the Night Eating Questionnaire (NEQ) [23] and a brief version of the Eating Disorder Examination Questionnaire, the EDE-Q8 [24]. Rates reported for both genders were 1.1% and 4.2% respectively.

Discussion

The current study reviewed the prevalence of DSM-5 eating disorders. A total of 19 studies were identified in our literature search, with results showing substantial variability in prevalence rates. A wide range of both point- and lifetime prevalence rates were reported across included studies, with variance being dependent on, first and foremost, the methodologics applied.

As intended, a number of studies now support the decline in EDNOS/OSFED prevalence following the DSM-5 diagnostic revision intention [10, 11]. Decreased EDNOS/OSFED prevalence has also been reported in studies having recoded ED diagnoses [9, 13, 20]. However, although the introduction of the new DSM-5 criteria appears to have resolved some of the challenges associated with EDNOS, OSFED still represents a heterogeneous group in the DSM-5, including a variety of different ED conditions. For example, PD, which has been shown to be associated with significant medical complications [25], was investigated specifically in three studies in our review [11, 14, 26]. Prevalence rates ranged from 0.58% (CI 0.42-0.80) – 3.77% (CI 3.14-4.49) with results illustrating a trend towards higher rates in females compared to males, as well as higher rates in adults compared to adolescents. However, it should be noted that lifetime prevalence rates as opposed to point prevalence rates, in general, is expected to be higher, especially when assessed in older populations. Night eating syndrome (NES) was also included in the DSM-5 OSFED category, and specifically assessed in two of the reviewed studies. [21, 22] Both adopted the self-report measure Night Eating Questionnaire (NEQ) [23]. Whereas de Zwaan and colleagues [23] reported a point prevalence of 1.1% among males and females aged 14-85 years (mean age 48), Runfola et al. [24] reported a prevalence of 4.2 among males and females aged 18-26 years (mean age 21). These discrepant findings in

Table 1 Overview of included studies published 2012-2017. Studies are grouped by design and listed in chronological order

Author (Year)	N	Country	Gender (N or %)	Age range Mean (*SD*)	Sample	Assessment	Prevalence type	Prevalence (%) of ED, AN, BN (95% CI)	Prevalence (%) of BED, OSFED, UFED (95% CI)
2-STAGE DESIGN									
Mustelin et al. [10][a]	2825	Finland	♀	22-27 24.4 (0.9)	FinnTwin16 sample	*Screening:* Self-report questionnaire developed for the study and three subscales from the EDI-2 *Diagnosis:* SCID-I/NP	Lifetime	NR	OSFED + UFED: 1.5 (1.1-2.1) OSFED: 0.6 (0.3-1.0) UFED: 0.9 (0.6-1-4)
Mustelin et al. [7][b]	2825	Finland	♀	22-27 24.4 (0.9)	FinnTwin16 sample	*Screening:* Self-report questionnaire developed for the study and three subscales from the EDI-2 *Diagnosis:* SCID-I/NP	Lifetime	AN: 3.6 (2.7-4.2)	NR
Solmi et al. [16][c]	1698	UK	♀ (66%) ♂ (44%)	16-90 (mean and SD not available)	SELCoH	*Screening:* SCOFF *Diagnosis:* SCID-I-N/P	Point	ED: 7.4 (4.1-)13.0 AN: 0.0 (0) BN: 0.8 (0.4-1.9)	BED: 3.6 (1.4-9.0) OSFED: 2.4 (0.9-6.7) OSFED-PD: 0.6 (0.2-1.5%)
Smink et al. [15][d]	1597	Holland	♀ (53.9%) ♂ (56.1%)	19.1 (0.6) (age range not available)	Community cohort	*Screening*: Questionnaire on mental health and social functioning, height/weight and WHO-CIDI *Diagnosis*: SCID-I and parts of EDE	Lifetime (L) Point (P)	♀ ED (L, P): 5.7, 3.7 (4.2-7.5, 2.6-5.2) AN (L, P): 1.7, 1.2 (1.0-2.9, 0.6-2.1) BN (L, P): 0.8, 0.6 (0.3-1.7, 0.2-1.3) ♂ ED (L, P): 1.2, 0.5 (0.6-2.3, 0.1-1.4) AN (L, P): 0.1, 0.1 (0.0-0.8, 0.0-0.8) BN (L, P): 0.1, 0.1 (0.0-0.8, 0.0-0.8)	♀ BED (L, P): 2.3, 1.6 (1.4-3.6, 0.9-2.7) OSFED (L, P): 0.6, 0.3 (0.2-1.3, 0.1-1.0) UFED (L, P): 0.2, 0.0 (0.0-0.8, 0) ♂ BED (L, P): 0.7, 0.3 (0.2-1.6, 0.0-1-0) OSFED (L, P): 0.3, 0.0 (0.0-1.0, 0) UFED (L, P): 0.0, 0.0 (0,0)
Machado et al. [9]	3048	Portugal	♀	12-23 16.2 (1.3) 18-58 21.8 (4.3)	Female high-school and university students	*Screening*: EDE-Q *Diagnosis*: EDE	Point	ED: 3.87 (CI NR) AN: 0.69 (CI NR) BN: 0.59 (CI NR)	BED: 0.62 (CI NR) EDNOS: 1.97 (CI NR)
INTERVIEW									
Mohler-Kuo et al. [4][e]	10,038	Switzerland	♀ (56%) ♂ (44%)	15-60 (mean and SD not available)	Household survey	WHO-CIDI	Lifetime (L) 12-month (12-m)	♀AN (L, 12-m): 1.9, 0.07 (1.6-2-3, 0.03-0.2) AN ♂ (L, 12-m): 0.2, 0.03 (0.1-0.4, 0.004-0.2)	NR
Hay et al. [11][f]	6041	Australia	♀ (–) ♂ (–)	15-96 (mean and SD not available)	Cross sectional population sample.	Items based on diagnostic items from the EDE	Point (3-month)	Total sample (% females): ED: 16.3 (15.4-17.3) AN: 0.46 (83%) (0.32-0.67) BN: 0.66 (69%) (0.49-0.9)	Total sample (% females): BED: 5.58 (57%) (5.03-6.19) OSFED-BN: 0.70 (74%) (0.51-0.94) OSFED-BED: 6.92 (55%) (6.31-7.59) OSFED-PD: 0.58 (77%) (0.42-0.80) UFED: 1.41 (73%) (1.14-1.74)
Munn-Chernoff et al. [26][g]	3230 1790[MZ] 1440[DZ]	USA	♀	18-29 Median: 22 (mean and SD not available)	Population-based twin study	Adapted version of SSAGA	Lifetime	AN: 1.37 (1.00-1.84)	OSFED-PD: 3.77 (3.14-4.49)
Fairweather-Smith & Wade [19][h]	699	Australia	♀	12.7-19.8 (across 3 waves) (age range not available)	Adolescent female twin pairs	EDE	Calculated a total prevalence rate based on wave 1-3	ED: 10.4 (8.3-12.9) AN: 2.0 (CI NR) BN: 1.0 (CI NR)	BED: 2.4 (CI NR) OSFED: 5.0 (CI NR) OSFED-AN:1.9 (CI NR) OSFED-BN:2.6 (CI NR) OSFED-PD: 0.6 (CI NR)
Stice et al. [17][i]	496	USA	♀	Baseline: 12-15 Mean = 13 (SD not available)	Community sample	EDDI	Lifetime (L)	AN: 0.8 (± 0.6) BN: 2.6 (± 1.4)	BED: 3.0 (± 1.3) OSFED: 11.5 (± 2.8) OSFED-AN: 2.8 (±1.5) OSFED-BN: 4.4 (±1.6)

Table 1 Overview of included studies published 2012-2017. Studies are grouped by design and listed in chronological order *(Continued)*

Author (Year)	N	Country	Gender (N or %)	Age range Mean (*SD*)	Sample	Assessment	Prevalence type	Prevalence (%) of ED, AN, BN (95% CI)	Prevalence (%) of BED, OSFED, UFED (95% CI)
									OSFED-BED: 3.6 (± 1.5) OSFED-PD: 3.4 (± 1.6)
Hudson et al. [18][j]	888	USA	♀ (66.4%) ♂ (33.6%)	18-70 46.7 (17.4)	First-degree relatives of probands with or without BED	SCID	Lifetime (L) Point (P)	NR	♀ BED (L, P): 3.6, 1.7 (CI NR) ♂ BED (L, P): 2.1, 0.8 (CI NR)
SELF-REPORT									
Cossrow et al. [27][k]	22,397	USA	♀ (54.4%) ♂ (45.6%)	≥18 51.1(15.8) (age range not available)	NHWS sample	Questions assessing BED criteria through a self-administered Internet survey	Lifetime (L) 3-month (3-m) 12-month (12-m)	NR	BED ♀ + ♂ (L, 3-m, 12-m): 2.03, 1.19, 1.64 (1.83-2.26, 1.04-1.37, 1.45-1.85) BED ♀: (L, 3-m, 12-m): 2,61, 1,60, 2.00 (2.34-2.92, 1.38-1.85, 1.76-2.28) BED ♂: (L, 3-m, 12-m): 1.41, 0,76, 1,24 (1.13-1.77, 0.56-1.03, 0.97-1.59)
Hammerle et al. [36][l]	1654	Germany	♀ (*N* = 873) ♂ (*N* = 781)	13.4 (0.8) (age range not available)	National school-based cross-sectional survey	SIAB-S (as questionnaire) and EDI-2	Point	*Full syndrome* (sex ratio female-male) AN: 0.3 (5:0) (0.1-0.7) BN: 0.4 (5:1) (0.2-0.8)	BED: 0.5 (5:3) (0.2-0.9) OSFED-AN: 3.6 (45:13) (2.7-4-5) OSFED-BN:0.0 (–) (0,-) OSFED-BED: 0.0 (–) (0,-) OSFED-PD: 1.9 (22:9) (1.3-2.77)
Flament et al. [14][m]	3043	Canada	♀ (*N* = 41.2%) ♂ (*N* = 58.8%)	11-21 14.2 (1.6)	Community sample	EDDS	Point	ED (♀, ♂): 4.46, 2.21 (4.4-4.5, 1.5-3.2) AN (♀, ♂): 0.06, 0.0 (0.00-0.31, 0) BN (♀, ♂): 2.01, 1.31 (1.23-3.25, 0.80-2.13)	BED (♀, ♂): 0.68, 0.16 (0.27-1.71, 0.04-0.65) OSFED-PD (♀, ♂): 1.51, 0.74 (0.89-2.53, 0.38-1.41)
Flament et al. [13][n]	3022	Canada	♀ (*N* = 1789) ♂ (*N* = 1233)	11-20 14.2 (1.6)	Community sample	EDDS	Point	ED (♀ + ♂): 3.7 (2.8-4.7) AN (♀ + ♂): 0.1 (0.0-0.1) BN (♀ + ♂): 1.6 (1.61.1-2.5)	BED (♀ + ♂): 0.5 (0.2-1.2) OSFED-PD (♀ + ♂): 1.4 (1.0-1.9)
de Zwaan et al. [21][o]	2460	Germany	♀ (51.1%) ♂ (48.9%)	14-85 48.1 (19.0)	Population sample	NEQ and EDE-Q8	Point	NR	OSFED-NES: 1.1 (CI NR)
Runfola et al. [22]	1636	USA	♀ (59.5%) ♂ (40.5%)	18-26 20.9 (1.7)	University students	An online survey using the NEQ	Point	NR	OSFED-NES: 4.2 (CI NR)
Allen et al. [20][p]	1383	Australia	♀ (49%) ♂ (51%)	14-20 14-years: 14.0 (0.2) 17-years: 16.9 (0.2) 20-years: 20.0 (0.4)	Prospective, population-based cohort study	Items adapted from the ChEDE and the EDE-Q	Point	ED (♀, ♂) 14-yrs: 8.5, 1.2 17-yrs: 15.2, 2.6 20-yrs: 15.2, 2.9 AN (♀, ♂)	BED (♀, ♂) 14-yrs: 1.8, 0.0 17-yrs: 1.4, 1.2 20-yrs: 4.1, 0.7 OSFED (♀, ♂) 14-yrs: 3.6, 0.7 17-yrs: 4.1, 0.9 20-yrs: 2.7, 0.6

Table 1 Overview of included studies published 2012-2017. Studies are grouped by design and listed in chronological order *(Continued)*

Author (Year)	N	Country	Gender (N or %)	Age range Mean (*SD*)	Sample	Assessment	Prevalence type	Prevalence (%) of ED, AN, BN (95% CI)	Prevalence (%) of BED, OSFED, UFED (95% CI)
								14-yrs: 0.3, 0.0 17-yrs: 1.4, 0.0 20-yrs: 0.6, 0.0 BN (♀, ♂) 14-yrs: 2.7, 0.4 17-yrs: 8.7, 0.7 20-yrs: 7.9, 1.6	OSFED-PD (♀, ♂) 14-yrs: 2.7, 0.4 17-yrs: 2.1, 0.6 20-yrs: 1.6, 0.3 OSFED-AN (♀, ♂) 14-yrs: 0.9, 0.3 17-yrs: 0.0, 0.0 20-yrs: 0.1, 0.3
OTHER									
Trace et al. [6][q]	13,295	Sweden	♀	20-47 (mean and SD not available)	Twin registry subsample	An expanded SCID based instrument	Lifetime	BN: 1.6 (CI NR)	BED 0.4 (CI NR)

Note. Prevalence rates are presented exactly as reported in their respective studies. ♀ = Females; ♂ = Males
Abbreviations: *95% CI* 95% Confidence Interval, *NR* Not Reported, *ED* Eating Disorders, *AN* Anorexia Nervosa, *ARFID* Avoidant Restrictive Food Intake Disorder, *BN* Bulimia Nervosa, *BED* Binge Eating Disorder, *OSFED* Other Specified Feeding and Eating Disorders, *UFED* Unspecified Feeding and Eating Disorders, *L* Lifetime prevalence, *P* Point prevalence, *12-m* 12-month prevalence, *3-m* 3-month prevalence
[a] = Prevalence rates are based on the same sample as in Mustelin et al. [7][b]. Reported prevalence rates are based on observed cases. Finn Twin16 is a nationwide population based cohort. SCID I-N/P = Structured Clinical Interview for DSM-IV-TR Axis I Disorders, Research Version, Non-Patient Edition [37]; EDI-2 = Eating Disorder Inventory-2 [38]
[b] = Prevalence rates are based on the same sample as in Mustelin et al. [10][a]. AN diagnoses were first assessed using DSM-IV, then retrospectively recoded using DSM-5 criteria
[c] = SELCoH = South East London Community Health Study. SCOFF = Sick, Control, One stone, Fat, Food Questionnaire [39]
[c] = SCID-I = Structured Clinical Interview for DSM-IV Axis I Disorders
[d] = WHO-CIDI = World Health Organization Composite International Diagnostic Interview [40]
[e] = EDE = the Eating Disorder Examination [41]
[g] = MZ = Monozygotic twins; DZ = Dizygotic twins; SSAGA = An adaptation of the Semi-Structured Assessment on the Genetics of Alcoholism [42];
[h] = CI was not reported (NR) for separate ED diagnoses
[i] = EDDI = The Eating Disorder Diagnostic Interview [43]; The diagnostic category "Feeding or eating disorder not elsewhere classified (FEDNEC)" was renamed by the authors of the current review, to OSFED
[j] = BED diagnoses were first assessed using DSM-IV, then retrospectively recoded using DSM-5 criteria. CI was not reported (NR) for any ED diagnoses
[k] = NHWS = the National Health and Wellness Survey
[l] = SIAB-S = the Structured Interview for Anorexia and Bulimia Nervosa Self-report [44]; OSFED-AN = Atypical AN (all criteria is med except significantly low weight), OSFED-BN = Subthreshold BN (of low frequency and/or limited duration), OSFED-BED = Subthreshold BED (of low frequency and/or limited duration), OSFED-PD = Purging Disorder (Recurrent purging in the absence of binge eating)
[m] = EDDS = the Eating Disorder Diagnostic Scale [45]. NB: Prevalence rates originate from the Flament et al. [14][m] study where overall (♀ + ♂) ED rates are reported
[n] = Prevalence rates based on the same sample, stratified by gender are presented in Flament et al. [14][n]
[o] = NEQ = Night Eating Questionnaire [23]; EDE-Q8 = The Eating Disorder Examination Questionnaire 8 [24]
[p] = ChEDE = the Child Eating Disorder Examination [46]. Confidence intervals were reported visually (using error bars) in the study, but were not presented clearly enough to exclude risk of misinterpretation, and were therefore not included in the table
[q] = Prevalence rates reported represent binge eating frequency per month ≥4 times

prevalence may relate to the differences in age between the two samples, but more research is warranted to investigate this further. Additionally, the new category Unspecified Feeding or Eating Disorder (UFED) was introduced in the DSM-5. UFED is used to describe symptoms characteristic of feeding or eating disorders causing significant stress or impairments in functioning, but without meeting full criteria for an ED diagnosis. The UFED category can be used when reasons for not meeting full criteria is lacking or not further specified by clinicians. Three of the included studies [10, 11, 15] reported prevalence of UFED, with rates ranging from 0.0% to 1.41%. Further research is needed to yield more information about the prevalence of PD, NES, and UFED.

After being included as an EDNOS in DSM-IV, BED was introduced as a specified and independent diagnostic category in DSM-5. Prevalence of BED was reported in several studies included in this review, and the prevalence of BED generally increased by increasing age in the reviewed studies. For example, Allen et al. [20] assessed BED among 1383 young Australian males and females at ages 14, 17, and 20. Point prevalence increased from 1.8% to 4.1% from age 14 to 20 (increase from 0.0% to 0.7% in males). Similarly, Stice et al. [17] investigated 496 young females (mean age 13 years at baseline), and reported a cumulative incidence of 2.7% and a lifetime prevalence at 3.0% by age 20. Finally, Trace et al. [6] assessed a larger and older sample of 13,295 females aged 20-47 years, with a reported lifetime prevalence of 5.8%. Prevalence of BED was generally higher among females than males across studies. A potential explanation for variability in BED prevalence rates is the inconsistent or lack of use of the DSM-5 marked distress criterion and binge eating specifiers such as guilt after binge eating [11].

Impact of the DSM-5 on prevalence estimates

It is of interest to review whether the transition from DSM-IV to DSM-5 has yielded the intended alterations in reported prevalence, i.e. increased prevalence of AN and BN, and decreased prevalence of the residual category EDNOS/OSFED. Several of the included studies in the present review have estimated prevalence of EDs as defined by both DSM-IV and DSM-5 in the same sample. Such recoding of diagnostic categories according to DSM-IV versus DSM-5 informs us on the impact of the DSM-5 on different ED prevalence rates. One study [7] assessed prevalence of AN by first adopting DSM-IV criteria. Subsequent to recoding according to the DSM-5 criteria, the authors observed a 60% increase in lifetime prevalence of AN among the 2825 female participants (mean age 24 years), from 2.2 to 3.6%. Another study recoding from DSM-IV to DSM-5 diagnoses investigated 1383 males (49%) and females at ages 14, 17, and 20 [20]. Significantly greater ED prevalence rates were reported when using DSM-5 criteria at all ages for females, and at age 17 only for males. These findings are in line with the study of Flament et al. [13] reporting that prevalence of full-threshold EDs increased from 1.8 to 3.7% after recoding from DSM-IV to DSM-5 criteria. Decreased prevalence of the residual ED categories (EDNOS/OSFED) when adopting DSM-5 criteria have also been reported across studies having recoded ED diagnoses [9, 13, 20]. It is worth noting that although research recoding ED prevalence from DSM-IV to DSM-5 has been important in the initial evaluation of the proposed DSM-5 criteria, these studies may have missed patients who initially did not qualify for an ED diagnoses based on DSM-IV, but who would have met criteria for a DSM-5 ED. This may imply a risk of inaccurate prevalence estimates in these studies.

A main intention of the DSM-IV revisions was to minimize the use of catch-all diagnoses such as Eating Disorders Not Otherwise Specified (EDNOS), the most frequently, reported ED diagnosis in the DSM-IV. However, the revisions made may not only contribute to altered rates of AN, BN and OSFED diagnoses, but may also increase the likelihood of reaching the threshold for a formal ED diagnosis. As the new OSFED category includes disorders which lack strict diagnostic criteria (e.g. PD and NES which lacks frequency criteria), clinicians and researchers should be vigilant with regards to the characteristics, especially significant distress and impairments, separating eating *disturbances* from eating *disorders*.

Methodological aspects

Methodological aspects are likely to influence both lifetime- and point prevalence rates including assessment measures adopted and samples investigated [3]. The majority of studies in this review adopted self-report to assign ED diagnoses, followed by interviews and 2-stage designs. Although self-report assessments have its obvious advantages in terms of being cost- and time effective, only diagnostic interviews can help determine the presence (or absence) of a formal ED diagnosis as defined by the DSM. Methodological issues such as these should be considered when interpreting prevalence rates across studies. In addition to assessment measure per se, recruitment strategy and design are important aspects to consider when evaluating quality of studies and consequently reliability of results. The 2-stage design, including stage one with screening followed by stage two with clinical diagnostic interview, have been considered the preferred approach to estimate prevalence rates. In the current study, aiming to review the prevalence of diagnosable EDs as defined by the diagnostic manual DSM-5, it may therefore be timely to consider the included 2-stage design studies [7, 9, 10, 15, 16] to be among the highest ranked studies in terms of quality. However, another marker of quality in epidemiological studies is sample size. The reviewed studies with the largest sample sizes include samples of $N = 6041$ [11], 13,295 [6], 10,038 [4], and 22,397 [27]. It is worth noting that none of these latter studies are among the mentioned 2-stage design studies, demonstrating the necessity to consider multiple methodological aspects when evaluating quality. In addition to the above-mentioned aspects, sample characteristics are likely to influence reported prevalence rates, and includes both age ranges and gender distributions. One of the intentions of the DSM-5 was to better capture EDs in males than during the DSM-IV era, and was a central rationale for removing the amenorrhea criteria for AN. However, as the DSM-5 revisions have contributed to higher prevalence of full-threshold AN and BN in general, it is difficult to detect whether the DSM-5 has led to better detection of male EDs per se. Also, although the amenorrhea criterion has been removed, the core ED psychopathology outlined in the DSM-5 is still biased towards females as it focuses on drive for thinness rather than muscularity. Furthermore, assessment measures used to detect ED psychopathology are often gender biased in that they have been developed to capture "female" psychopathology and symptoms, and also, as they most commonly are validated using female samples [28, 29]. Issues such as these may complicate the detection and description of ED pathology in males. Another methodological issue subsequent to the introduction of DSM-5 is the removal of a specific weight threshold for AN. This has clear advantages, maybe in particular in terms of individual and flexible evaluations in clinical settings, but it is worth noting that in research, the lack of an explicit weight criterion may lead to larger weight variations compared to earlier. In general, it is important to strive for consistent use of DSM-5 categories, which will aid the interpretation of prevalence rates across studies.

New diagnostic categories in the DSM-5 include ARFID (problem with eating not related to weight or shape concerns, leading to inability to take in adequate nutrition), pica (recurrent consumption of "nonnutritive, nonfood" items), and rumination disorder (RD; i.e. recurrent, effortless regurgitation of food). Although none of the included studies investigated these full-threshold diagnoses, three studies which were excluded due to their sub-threshold nature, addressed features of ARFID [30], pica and RD [31], reporting frequency numbers ranging from 0 to 3.2%. More research is needed to determine the prevalence of these diagnostic categories.

Finally, this review reports the prevalence of eating disorders according DSM-5 criteria. In a historical perspective there have been important changes to the diagnostic criteria since AN and BN were introduced in the DSM-III [32] in 1980. For example, in the DSM-III, the weight loss criteria for AN was "*25% below original body weight*", which was then revised to "*body weight less than 85% of that expected*" in the DSM-IV [1], and subsequently, redefined in the DSM-5 [2] to "*significantly low body weight*". For BN there were no criteria for frequency of binge eating and compensatory behavior in the DSM-III. With the DSM-III-R update, the frequency was specified to twice a week, and in DSM-5, it was reduced to once a week. These revisions will greatly influence prevalence rates in the years to come, and are crucial to address when comparing DSM-5 based prevalence to earlier epidemiological studies in EDs.

Strengths and limitations

This is the first systematic review of DSM-5 prevalence studies in EDs, and offers the reader an early snapshot of the extant prevalence literature. The core strength of the study is the thoroughness of the systematic literature review, and the detailed screening process conducted by two of the authors. Conversely, only one database was used to search the literature and only articles that were written in English (or had an available published English translation) were reviewed representing a limitation of the current study. Further, a meta-analysis was not performed which also represents a potential weakness. In addition, our search date (February 2017) dates our paper. In this interim, three publications relevant to the scope of our paper have been published. Hay et al. [33] investigated the prevalence and burden of ARFID and other DSM-5 EDs in an Australian population, Ernst et al. [34] explored how the DSM-5 revisions affected the prevalence, sex ratio and diagnostic distribution of EDNOS/OSFED in a student sample, and Micali et al. [35] investigated lifetime and 12-month prevalence of EDs amongst women in mid-life. Their relevance to the extant literature warrant a more detailed account in future epidemiological ED studies.

Conclusions

In conclusion, prevalence rates varied significantly across the 19 studies reviewed, much likely due to variations in study design, diagnostic assessment routines, samples sizes and characteristics. None of the included studies investigated the prevalence of the DSM-5 feeding disorders pica, ARFID and RD, warranting further investigation in future epidemiological studies. As our review is limited by a small number of studies published during a limited time frame, and in addition, fails to capture the full range of DSM-5 diagnoses, reported trends should be interpreted with caution.

Abbreviations

12-m: 12-month; 3-m: 3-month; AN: Anorexia nervosa; ARFID: Avoidant restrictive food intake disorder; BED: Binge eating disorder; BN: Bulimia nervosa; CI: Confidence interval; DSM-5: Diagnostic and statistical manual of mental disorders, fifth edition; DSM-IV: Diagnostic and statistical manual of mental disorders, fourth edition; ED: Eating disorder; EDE: Eating disorder examination; EDI-2: Eating disorder inventory; EDNOS: Eating disorder not otherwise specified; L: Lifetime; NEQ: Night eating questionnaire; NES: Night eating syndrome; NR: Not reported; OSFED: Other specified feeding and eating disorders; P: Point; PD: Purging disorder; SCID I-N/P: Structured clinical interview for DSM-IV-TR axis I disorders, research version, non-patient edition; SCID-I: Structured clinical interview for DSM-IV axis I disorders; SCOFF: Sick, control, one stone, fat, food questionnaire; SELCoH: South East London Community Health Study; UFED: Unspecified feeding and eating disorder; WHO-CIDI: World Health Organization Composite International Diagnostic Interview

Acknowledgements

Not applicable.

Funding

The work on this paper was supported by the Regional Department for Eating Disorders, Division of Mental Health and Addiction, Oslo University Hospital, Ullevål HF.

Authors' contributions

CLD, LW and ØR conceived of the study and initiated the study design. CLD, LW and ØR participated in the analysis and/or interpretation of data. CLD and LW drafted the manuscript, and all three authors revised it critically for important intellectual content. All three authors, CLD, LW and ØR, approved of the version of the manuscript to be published.

Competing interests

The authors declare that they have no competing interests.

Author details

[1]Regional Department for Eating Disorders, Division of Mental Health and Addiction, Oslo University Hospital, Ullevål HF, Postboks 4950 Nydalen, 0424 Oslo, Norway. [2]Institute of Clinical Medicine, University of Oslo, P.O. Box 1171 Blindern, 0318 Oslo, Norway.

References

1. American Psychiatric Association. Diagnostic and statistical manual of mental disorders DSM-IV. 4th ed. Washington, DC: American Psychiatric Association; 1994.
2. American Psychiatric Association. Diagnostic and statistical manual of mental disorders DSM-5. 5th ed. Washington, DC: American Psychiatric Association; 2013.
3. Lindvall Dahlgren, C. And L. Wisting, Transitioning from DSM-IV to DSM-5: a systematic review of eating disorder prevalence assessment. Int J Eat Disord, 2016;49:975.
4. Mohler-Kuo M, et al. The prevalence, correlates, and help-seeking of eating disorders in Switzerland. Psychol Med. 2016;46(13):2749–58.
5. Hoek, H.W. And D. Van Hoeken, Review of the prevalence and incidence of eating disorders. Int J Eat Disord, 2003. 34:383.
6. Trace SE, et al. Effects of reducing the frequency and duration criteria for binge eating on lifetime prevalence of bulimia nervosa and binge eating disorder: implications for DSM-5. Int J Eat Disord. 2012;45(4):531–6.
7. Mustelin L, et al. The DSM-5 diagnostic criteria for anorexia nervosa may change its population prevalence and prognostic value. J Psychiatr Res. 2016;77:85–91.
8. Ornstein RM, et al. Distribution of eating disorders in children and adolescents using the proposed DSM-5 criteria for feeding and eating disorders. J Adolesc Health. 2013;53(2):303–5.
9. Machado, P.P., S. Goncalves, And H.W. Hoek, DSM-5 reduces the proportion of EDNOS cases: evidence from community samples. Int J Eat Disord, 2013. 46(1):60-65.
10. Mustelin, L., V.L. Lehtokari, And A. Keski-Rahkonen, Other specified and unspecified feeding or eating disorders among women in the community. Int J Eat Disord, 2016. 49(11):1010-1017.
11. Hay, P., F. Girosi, And J. Mond, Prevalence and sociodemographic correlates of DSM-5 eating disorders in the Australian population. J Eat Disord, 2015. 3:19.
12. Moher D, et al. Preferred reporting items for systematic review and meta-analysis protocols (PRISMA-P) 2015 statement. Syst Rev. 2015;4(1).1.
13. Flament MF, et al. Comparative distribution and validity of DSM-IV and DSM-5 diagnoses of eating disorders in adolescents from the community. Eur Eat Disord Rev. 2015;23(2):100–10.
14. Flament MF, et al. Weight status and DSM-5 diagnoses of eating disorders in adolescents from the community. J Am Acad Child Adolesc Psychiatry. 2015;54(5):403–411.E2.
15. Smink FR, et al. Prevalence and severity of DSM-5 eating disorders in a community cohort of adolescents. Int J Eat Disord. 2014;47(6):610–9.
16. Solmi F, et al. Eating disorders in a multi-ethnic inner-city UK sample: prevalence, comorbidity and service use. Soc Psychiatry Psychiatr Epidemiol. 2016;51(3):369–81.
17. Stice, E., C.N. Marti, And P. Rohde, Prevalence, incidence, impairment, and course of the proposed DSM-5 eating disorder diagnoses in an 8-year prospective community study of young women. J Abnorm Psychol, 2013. 122(2):445-457.
18. Hudson JI, et al. By how much will the proposed new DSM-5 criteria increase the prevalence of binge eating disorder? Int J Eat Disord. 2012; 45(1):139–41.
19. Fairweather-Schmidt, A.K. And T.D. Wade, DSM-5 eating disorders and other specified eating and feeding disorders: is there a meaningful differentiation? Int J Eat Disord, 2014. 47(5):524-533.
20. Allen KL, et al. DSM-IV-TR and DSM-5 eating disorders in adolescents: prevalence, stability, and psychosocial correlates in a population-based sample of male and female adolescents. J Abnorm Psychol. 2013;122(3):720–32.
21. De Zwaan M, et al. Prevalence and correlates of night eating in the German general population. PLoS One. 2014;9(5):E97667.
22. Runfola CD, et al. Prevalence and clinical significance of night eating syndrome in university students. J Adolesc Health. 2014;55(1):41–8.
23. Allison KC, et al. The night eating questionnaire (NEQ): psychometric properties of a measure of severity of the night eating syndrome. Eat Behav. 2008;9(1):62–72.
24. Kliem S, et al. The eating disorder examination-questionnaire 8: a brief measure of eating disorder psychopathology (EDE-Q8). Int J Eat Disord. 2016;49(6):613–6.
25. Forney KJ, et al. The medical complications associated with purging. Int J Eat Disord. 2016;49(3):249–59.
26. Munn-Chernoff MA, et al. Prevalence of and familial influences on purging disorder in a community sample of female twins. Int J Eat Disord. 2015; 48(6):601–6.
27. Cossrow N, et al. Estimating the prevalence of binge eating disorder in a community sample from the United States: comparing DSM-IV-TR and DSM-5 criteria. J Clin Psychiatry. 2016;77(8):E968–74.
28. Darcy AM, et al. The eating disorders examination in adolescent males with anorexia nervosa: how does it compare to adolescent females? Int. J. Eat. Disord. 2012;45(1):110–4.
29. Stanford, S.C. And R. Lemberg, Measuring eating disorders in men: development of the eating disorder assessment for men (EDAM). Eat Disord, 2012. 20(5):427-436.
30. Kurz S, et al. Early-onset restrictive eating disturbances in primary school boys and girls. Eur Child Adolesc Psychiatry. 2015;24(7):779–85.
31. Delaney CB, et al. Pica and rumination behavior among individuals seeking treatment for eating disorders or obesity. Int J Eat Disord. 2015;48(2):238–48.
32. American Psychiatric Association. Diagnostical and statistical manual of mental disorders. 3rd ed. Washington, DC: American Psychiatric Association Press; 1980.
33. Hay P, et al. Burden and health-related quality of life of eating disorders, including avoidant/restrictive food intake disorder (ARFID), in the Australian population. J Eat Disord. 2017;5:21.
34. Ernst, V., A. Burger, And F. Hammerle, Prevalence and severity of eating disorders: a comparison of DSM-IV and DSM-5 among German adolescents. Int J Eat Disord, 2017. 50(11):1255-1263.
35. Micali N, et al. Lifetime and 12-month prevalence of eating disorders amongst women in mid-life: a population-based study of diagnoses and risk factors. BMC Med. 2017;15(1):12.
36. Hammerle F, et al. Thinking dimensional: prevalence of DSM-5 early adolescent full syndrome, partial and subthreshold eating disorders in a cross-sectional survey in German schools. BMJ Open. 2016;6(5):E010843.
37. First MB, et al. Structured clinical interview for DSM-IV-TR axis I disorders, research version, non-patient edition (SCID-I/NP). New York: Biometrics Research, New York State Psychiatric Institute; 2002.
38. Garner DM. Eating disorder inventory-2 manual. Psychological assessment resources. Lutz: Psychological Assessment Resources; 1991.
39. Morgan, J.F., F. Reid, And J.H. Lacey, The SCOFF questionnaire: assessment of a new screening tool for eating disorders. BMJ, 1999. 319(7223):1467-1468.
40. Kessler, R.C. And T.B. Ustun, The World Mental Health (WMH) survey initiative version of the World Health Organization (WHO) Composite International Diagnostic Interview (CIDI). Int J Methods Psychiatr Res, 2004. 13(2):93-121.
41. Fairburn, C.G., Z. Cooper, And M. O'connor, Eating disorder examination (16. 0d), In Cognitive behavior therapy and eating disorders, C.G. Fairburn, Editor. 2008, Guilford Press: New York.
42. Bucholz KK, et al. A new, semi-structured psychiatric interview for use in genetic linkage studies: a report on the reliability of the SSAGA. J Stud Alcohol. 1994;55(2):149–58.
43. Stice E, et al. Dissonance and healthy weight eating disorder prevention programs: long-term effects from a randomized efficacy trial. J Consult Clin Psychol. 2008;76(2):329–40.
44. Fichter, M.M. And N. Quadflieg, Comparing self-and expert rating: a self-report screening version (SIAB-S) of the structured interview for anorexic and bulimic syndromes for DSM-IV and ICD-10 (SIAB-EX). Eur Arch Psychiatry Clin Neurosci, 2000. 250(4):175-185.
45. Stice, E., C.F. Telch, And S.L. Rizvi, Development and validation of the eating disorder diagnostic scale: a brief self-report measure of anorexia, bulimia, and binge-eating disorder. Psychol Assess, 2000. 12:123-131.
46. Bryant-Waugh RJ, et al. The use of the eating disorder examination with children: a pilot study. Int. J. Eat. Disord. 1996;19:391–7.

Treatment of children and adolescents with avoidant/restrictive food intake disorder: a case series examining the feasibility of family therapy and adjunctive treatments

Wendy Spettigue[1,3*], Mark L. Norris[2,3], Alexandre Santos[3] and Nicole Obeid[3]

Abstract

Background: To date, little research has examined the effectiveness of either modified Family-Based Therapy or psychopharmacological treatments for patients diagnosed with avoidant/restrictive food intake disorder (ARFID), and there is little evidence to guide clinicians treating children and adolescents with ARFID. This case series describes the clinical presentations, treatments and outcomes of six patient diagnosed with ARFID who were treated sequentially by a child psychiatrist and adolescent medicine physician in a hospital-based eating disorder program.

Case Presentations: Five out of six cases were female and median age of patients at assessment was 12.9 ($SD = 1.13$) years. On average, patients' percentage of treatment goal weight was 80.5% at initial assessment ($SD = 8.56$) and 81.9% ($SD = 7.08$) when family therapy began. Cases 1, 2 and 3 were admitted to a specialized inpatient unit at assessment due to medical instability (2) or failed outpatient treatment (1), and all six cases presented with severe co-morbid anxiety. All patients were treated using a combination of medical monitoring, family therapy, medication (including olanzapine, fluoxetine and in two cases cyproheptadine), and cognitive behavioural therapy. At treatment termination, all six patients had achieved their goal weight.

Conclusion: These cases illustrate the complex ways in which young patients with ARFID can present, the illness' effect on development and mental health, and the positive outcomes associated with weight gain and concurrent treatment for co-morbid anxiety disorders.

Keywords: Avoidant/restrictive food intake disorder, Family therapy, Pharmacotherapy, Case series

Plain English summary

To date, little research has examined the effectiveness of either family therapy or medications for patients diagnosed with avoidant/restrictive food intake disorder (ARFID), and there is little evidence to guide clinicians treating children and adolescents with this newly classified eating disorder. This case series describes six patients diagnosed with ARFID and treated by a child psychiatrist and a pediatrician in a hospital-based eating disorder program. Five out of six cases were female and average age of patients was 12.9 years, with an average percentage of goal weight at assessment of 80.5%. Three cases were admitted to a specialized inpatient unit at assessment due to medical instability or failed outpatient treatment, and all six cases presented with severe anxiety. All patients were treated using a combination of medical monitoring, family therapy, medication and cognitive behavioural therapy. At treatment termination, all six patients had achieved their goal weight. These cases illustrate the complex ways in which young patients with ARFID can present, the illness' effect on development and mental health, and the positive outcomes associated with weight gain and concurrent treatment for anxiety.

* Correspondence: wspettigue@cheo.on.ca
[1]Department of Psychiatry, Children's Hospital of Eastern Ontario, University of Ottawa, 401 Smyth Road, Ottawa, ON K1H 8L1, Canada
[3]Children's Hospital of Eastern Ontario Research Institute, 401 Smyth Road, Ottawa, ON K1H 5B2, Canada
Full list of author information is available at the end of the article

Background

Family-based therapy (FBT) is a treatment method that has been robustly used for the treatment of eating disorders (EDs) in adolescents, such as anorexia nervosa (AN) and bulimia nervosa (BN) [1–4]. Early models of FBT were first introduced in the 1970's and 80's [5, 6], providing a foundation for the modern-day Maudsley outpatient FBT model, which was manualized and popularized by Lock et al. in *Treatment manual for anorexia nervosa: a family-based approach* [7]. FBT is designed to empower family members to support the recovery of the patient in a home setting by providing parents and siblings with education on EDs, lifting blame and guilt from the family and patient, raising anxiety about the seriousness of the illness, externalizing the ED as an enemy, and encouraging parents to implement refeeding strategies [8]. Meta-analytic research has shown that FBT is more effective at increasing rates of remission when compared to treatment as usual in adolescent patients suffering from AN or BN [2, 3]. Further research has suggested that FBT is effective at promoting weight gain and improving psychological functioning in AN patients [1].

Another line of evolving research suggests that olanzapine, an atypical antipsychotic, may also have merit as an adjunctive medication for patients with AN, with reported improvements in weight gain, anxiety and body image, although few adolescent-specific studies have been conducted to date [9–13]. To a similar degree, some conflicting research has shown that the use of fluoxetine, a selective serotonin reuptake inhibitor (SSRI), may reduce co-morbid symptoms of depression, anxiety, and obsessive compulsive disorder for weight-restored adult AN patients [14–16]. SSRIs are indicated for the treatment of anxiety and depression in adolescents without eating disorders [17, 18]. Despite the evidence supporting the use of FBT as an effective treatment for AN and BN in children and adolescents, and evidence for the possible role of both olanzapine and fluoxetine in the treatment of youth with AN, to date, little research has examined the effectiveness of family therapy or psychopharmacological treatments for patients diagnosed with avoidant/restrictive food intake disorder (ARFID).

Introduced in the 5th edition of the Diagnostic and Statistical Manual of Mental Disorders (DSM-5) [19], ARFID is a type of restrictive ED characterized by a persistent failure to meet appropriate nutritional and/or energy needs, resulting in at least one of the following: significant weight loss, significant nutritional deficiency, dependence on enteral feeding or nutritional supplements, and/or a marked interference in psychosocial functioning. Further, the disturbance is not explained by a lack of food availability, cultural practices, body image concerns, or concurrent medical and/or mental conditions. Due to its recent introduction and heterogeneous nature, specialized treatments for patients diagnosed with ARFID have not yet been well established [20, 21].

A recently published review of 48 ARFID cases by Norris and colleagues [20] suggests substantial heterogeneity in terms of case presentations and contributing factors. Three specific subtypes of ARFID were identified (aligning with example presentations outlined in the DSM-5): those with weight loss and/or medical compromise as a consequence of apparent low appetite and lack of interest in eating (classified as "ARFID-limited intake" subtype), restriction arising as a result of sensory sensitivity i.e. "picky eaters" (classified as "ARFID-limited variety" subtype), and restriction based upon food avoidance and/or fear of aversive consequences of eating, such as fear of pain, nausea or choking ("ARFID-aversive" subtype). Clinical characteristics of the 48 patients varied depending on the assigned subtype; we hypothesize that recognizing and understanding these differences will have relevance as to the utility and success of specific targeted treatments for ARFID. There was some overlap of ARFID subtypes, with 13% of the sample presenting with a mixed presentation. The aim of this case series is to clinically describe and examine immediate outcomes in the treatment of six adolescent ARFID patients sequentially treated by a child psychiatrist and adolescent medicine (AM) physician in a tertiary care hospital ED setting and to comment on how each case presentation helped to influence the overall treatment plan. Of our six cases, two represent the "ARFID-aversive" subtype and the other four represent mixed subtypes: one with a combination of "ARFID-limited variety" subtype and "ARFID-aversive" subtype, and three with mixed "limited variety" and "limited intake" subtypes. All six patients received family therapy sessions that were based on the 'Maudsley' model of FBT principles for treating adolescent AN, but modified and adapted to the particular patient, diagnosis, and subtype of ARFID; these 'modified FBT' sessions will subsequently be referred to in the paper as "family therapy" sessions (though note they are referred to on the patient weight graphs below as "FBT" sessions due to limited space).

Method

A retrospective review was conducted of the medical charts of six sequential patients with ARFID referred for treatment by an Adolescent Medicine (AM) physician based at a Canadian tertiary care center to a child psychiatrist on an adolescent ED team at the same center, and information gathered was subsequently de-identified and stored in an electronic database. For confidentiality purposes, names included in this paper have been changed to protect patients' privacy. Signed consent and assent forms were obtained from patients and their primary caregivers for the study, which was approved by the hospital's Research Ethics Board.

Case presentations

Table 1 provides an overview of demographic information for the 6 patients included in this case series. On average, patients' percentage of treatment goal weight (%TGW), was 80.5% at initial assessment ($SD = 8.56$) and 81.9% ($SD = 7.08$) when family therapy began. TGW for each patient was calculated by the AM physician using established methods for ED populations (in these cases by using prior premorbid growth percentiles to establish the TGW) [22]. The median age of patients at treatment initiation was 12.9 ($SD = 1.13$) years. Three of the six patients were admitted to a specialized ED inpatient unit at initial assessment due to medical instability (2) or due to failed outpatient treatment prior to family therapy (1). At the termination of treatment with the ED team, all six patients achieved their TGW.

Case 1: Amy

Amy is a 12.5 year old girl in grade 7 with a history of mild phobias but no previous social anxiety, who lives with two working parents in a middle class home. At 11 years of age she became terrified after witnessing her dog choke on a piece of rawhide bone. Thereafter, she started to worry obsessively about choking. She started to prefer soft foods, to take tiny bites and to chew her food many times before she would swallow. She took a very long time to eat, wouldn't eat lunch or snacks at school, and became increasingly slow and restrictive in her eating. Amy was admitted to hospital at a body mass index (BMI) of 13.5 kg/m^2 (83.0% of TGW) and diagnosed with ARFID. Her case history was most in keeping with the ARFID-aversive subtype. She spent 38 days in hospital, receiving family therapy and psychoeducation and support for parents, who were very resistant to, and anxious during, passes out of the hospital environment. With inpatient family therapy sessions, parents were empowered to take control of nutrition on passes and to ensure that Amy finished everything. Her treatment was initially augmented in hospital with olanzapine 2.5 mg at bedtime, and as she approached her TGW she was started on fluoxetine 10 mg/day to help manage her severe anxiety.

Amy was discharged home at 100% of her TGW, but with an ongoing fear of choking that continued to impact her eating (e.g. still taking very small bites and a long time to eat, and avoiding foods that she feared she might choke on). Outpatient family therapy was augmented with cognitive behavioural therapy (with parents present). Amy developed and worked on a hierarchical ladder of feared foods, and was encouraged to practice eating using a timer, to take bigger bites, and to eat with peers at school. Although Amy did not describe social anxiety at school or worrying about schoolwork, she did develop a fear of going out with parents. Her fluoxetine was increased to 20 mg/day as a consequence of Amy's increased anxiety. The family described the increased dose of fluoxetine as helping significantly with Amy's fear of going out, and opted not to increase the dose further. Over the next 5 months (and nine therapy sessions), Amy recovered completely from her ED and fear of choking and was able to reach a healthy weight and to continue to grow, at which point she was discharged from care from the ED team.

Weight at start of family therapy: 30.3 kg.
%TGW at start of family therapy: 83%.
Weight at end of family therapy: 43.2 kg.
%TGW at end of family therapy: > 100% (Fig. 1).

Table 1 Demographic Information of Described ARFID Patients

	ARFID Cohort ($N = 6$)	Range (min – max)
Sex		
Male	1 (17%)	
Female	5 (83%)	
Ethnic Background		
Caucasian	6 (100%)	
Age [Mean (*SD*)]	12.73 (1.15)	10–14
Length of Self-reported Illness at Initial Assessment [Mean (*SD*)]	14.67 (10.42)	3–24

Notes. Where appropriate, data are expressed as mean (SD) or n (%). Age is expressed in years; length of illness is expressed in months

Case 2: Susan

Susan is a 10.9 year old girl who lives at home with 2 professional parents and a younger sister. She was described as a very anxious child; past medical history was notable for a history of frequent stomach pains of no known medial cause, and school refusal, though no eating or growth problems. Susan developed repeat episodes of viral gastroenteritis over a two week period which left her convinced that resuming eating had caused her gastro-intestinal symptoms. As a result, over the next few months she progressively ate less and lost weight. She underwent a full medical work-up but no pathology was identified. Her parents progressively eliminated foods that could potentially exacerbate her symptoms of abdominal pain and nausea, but with limited effect. She was admitted to the pediatric ward weighing 75.8% of TGW (BMI 11.8 kg/m^2). Given her refusal to eat, she was initially re-nourished with liquid nutrition (Ensure) via nasogastric (NG) tube, but weight gain was very slow and difficult. She refused to eat or drink, would kick and scream and become hysterical whenever food was presented, and screamed throughout the duration of her NG feeds. One month after admission there had been minimal progress, so the ED team was consulted and family therapy was initiated. Her case history was felt to be in keeping with ARFID-aversive subtype.

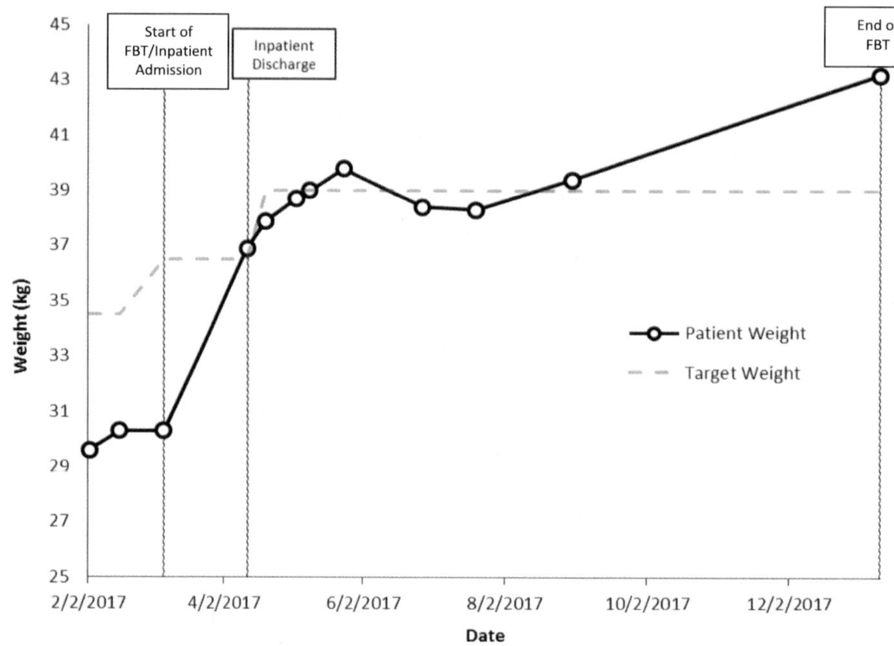

Fig. 1 Case 1 weight graph (Amy)

In addition to family therapy, Susan was treated with olanzapine over the course of her admission to help with her severe agitation and anxiety; she was started on 2.5 mg at night and the dose was gradually increased to a maximum of 2.5 mg in the morning and 5 mg at night.

Both parents were convinced that this must be a medical problem. The therapist worked to empower and educate parents, lift guilt and blame, and also to raise anxiety about the need for parents to take control of the nutrition and help their daughter to eat. The therapist explained the 'vicious cycle' of how weight loss leads to more anxiety, a 'smaller' stomach, more stomach pain, and the need for more nutrition to reach IBW. Thus, the only 'way out' is with renourishment and weight gain. Parents would try to be firm and help Susan to take the nutrition, but Susan would kick and scream hysterically and refuse, crying that her stomach hurt too much and she couldn't eat. Parents and Susan were helped to see that "not eating is not an option;" it is a mandatory part of treatment and the only way to recover. Susan was taught to use relaxation techniques and her mother was taught to support her, e.g. by providing soothing massage, empathy, and whatever helped Susan to tolerate taking the nutrition. Susan insisted that all that helped was walking. Thus, she would take her (mandatory) nutrition, crying and sobbing loudly, and then walk up and down the hospital halls. Gradually Susan's intake increased, along with her weight, and the pain and hysterical sobbing lessened. Parents were encouraged to take Susan on as many passes as possible, which she initially resisted, saying that it hurt too much to eat at home. She and her parents were helped to see that change is stressful and that unless Susan was going to live in the hospital forever, she would need help with learning to eat at home. Gradually, passes became increasingly more successful, and weight increased. Susan was discharged home two months after admission, at 100% of her initial TGW.

Following discharge, Susan continued weekly family therapy sessions. Although her weight gain continued as she grew in height, she resisted numerous foods that she was fearful of eating for fear of abdominal pain. She also exhibited separation anxiety and school avoidance. Family therapy continued, cognitive behavioural therapy was also utilized, and gradually, food variety increased. Parents opted for home schooling. Fluoxetine 10 mg in the morning was started for severe anxiety, and the dose was titrated over the following months up to 40 mg/day. Concurrently, her olanzapine was tapered and discontinued. At the end of treatment (after 6 therapy sessions but with follow up by the AM physician over a total of 3.5 months), she was able to eat all foods, she could socialize and participate in sports, and she could eat without issue at restaurants (which previously caused anxiety as well).

Weight at start of family therapy: 26.7 kg.

%TGW at start of family therapy: 79%.

Weight at end of family therapy: 41.6 kg.

%TGW at end of family therapy: > 100% (Fig. 2).

Case 3: Ethan

Ethan is a 13.1 year old boy with mild-moderate autism spectrum disorder (ASD) who lives on a farm with his

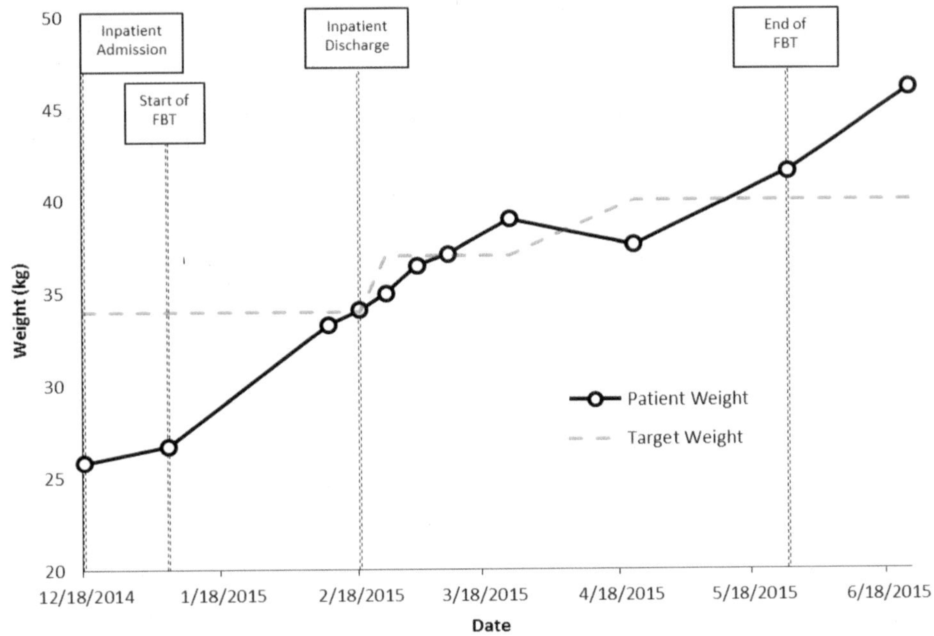

Fig. 2 Case 2 weight graph (Susan)

father and grandparents. He enjoys school, where he attends a special class because of his intellectual disability. He had a history of "picky" eating but no history of low weight or growth problems. One day while riding, Ethan fell off his horse and injured his ribs. He experienced severe rib pain with swallowing. As a result, he limited his food intake to minimize the pain. As weight decreased, his restriction intensified and he became increasingly anxious about eating. Ethan was eventually admitted to hospital where he spent one month on the pediatric ward, had a full medical work-up, and was discharged home at a slightly lower weight than at admission. His history was in keeping with a mixed ARFID presentation: ARFID-limited variety subtype plus ARFID-aversive subtype. He was readmitted to a specialized ED inpatient unit in the weeks that followed (at 72% TGW). Father needed to work on the farm, so Ethan's grandmother stayed in hospital with Ethan and worked with the family therapist.

Initially, Ethan would take very small amounts orally and then say he was too "full". He would have temper tantrums when pushed to eat more, and would often gag or vomit if made to eat. His treatment was augmented with olanzapine and titrated from 2.5 mg up to 7.5 mg/day to help with his anxiety around meals, and to facilitate weight gain. Given his longstanding food selectivity and sensory issues, the ED dietician also allowed accommodations with respect to the meals that he received in hospital. Grandmother was empowered to ensure that Ethan finished everything on his tray, and was asked by staff to tell Ethan that if he didn't finish his meal he could not have a pass off the ward. However, grandmother said she did not want to be the "bad guy" and instead chose (and was empowered to choose) to find other ways to help Ethan to finish his meals. For example, she chose to take him in a wheelchair for a walk around the hospital after he had finished half his meal, and they would then return and he would finish the rest of his meal. This worked well. Father would visit on weekends to provide meal support, and despite his anxiety about doctors and hospitals, started attending family sessions. Ethan was thrilled to be granted passes to eat at fast-food restaurants, but his weight started to drop as passes increased. He was ordering high calorie foods, but would get up and leave the restaurant before he had finished his portion. The therapist worked with both father and grandmother to help them to support Ethan to stay and finish all of his nutrition before they would leave.

Ethan's pace, intake and weight gradually improved and he was discharged after a two month stay at 88% of his TGW so that he could begin the new school year. He was discharged on olanzapine 5 mg at bedtime and fluoxetine 10 mg/day. The family continued outpatient family therapy over the next month, but weight dropped and the family was resistant to driving the long distance to the hospital for therapy sessions. The therapist followed up with grandmother by phone and empowered her to track Ethan's weight at home and to increase nutrition in keeping with his increased activity on the farm. His fluoxetine was gradually titrated up to 40 mg/day over the next three months. The fluoxetine was noted to significantly decrease his anxiety at school, and weight gain improved thereafter. At a follow-up appointment 4 months after discharge, Ethan had reached his TGW. His olanzapine was tapered and discontinued very slowly over the following months and he continued on fluoxetine with excellent effect.

Weight at start of family therapy: 31.8 kg;

%TGW at start of family therapy: 72%;

Weight at end of family therapy: 37.6 kg;

%TGW at end of family therapy: 85% (though some telephone conversations continued).

Weight at last follow up with AM physician: 44.2 kg (100% TGW) (Fig. 3).

Case 4: Jacqueline

Jacqueline is a 14.4 year old girl with a history of social and generalized anxiety disorder, obsessive compulsive disorder (OCD) and ASD traits. She presented with a 1–2 year history of increasingly restrictive intake. Parents noted: "She has always been picky, but if you gave her the foods she liked she would eat them; now she won't eat them." Parents described getting every bite into her as "a struggle." They also described her as very rigid, controlling, and more recently having huge temper tantrums, sleep problems and problems concentrating. She also looked and acted like a much younger child, and had symptoms of what appeared to be severe attention-deficit hyperactivity disorder (ADHD), as she frantically ran around the office and refused to sit still during the consultation, although she was described as a good student until this year, with no prior history of ADHD or of school or behavior problems. At initial assessment, she was on the 3rd percentile for weight; this put her at 90% of her TGW based on her growth curve, but with a history of having been underweight for a prolonged period and having always been a picky eater with very low appetite. She was in grade 9 at the time of assessment with a history of social isolation and increased anxiety at school for the past two years. There was a past history of bullying and social isolation in elementary school but no recent acute stressors or trauma. Her history was most consistent with a mixed ARFID presentation: ARFID-limited intake and ARFID-limited variety subtypes. A comprehensive medical work-up was negative.

Family therapy (with both divorced parents attending with Jacqueline) began within weeks of her initial assessment, and her treatment was augmented with olanzapine 2.5 mg at bedtime, which was later increased to 5 mg. The parents opted not to use a weight graph in sessions, as they were worried that Jacqueline would become "obsessed" with the numbers, but parents were informed weekly whether weight was up or down. Jacqueline was kept home from school and her mother stayed home from work to focus on renourishing her. After a few weeks Jacqueline's weight had improved and she became bored and expressed a desire to return to school, so attended school in the mornings in the "resource room" (where she ate a 'mandatory' morning snack) and then came home for lunch. Jacquie gained weight well as her treatment continued over the course of 6 months (13

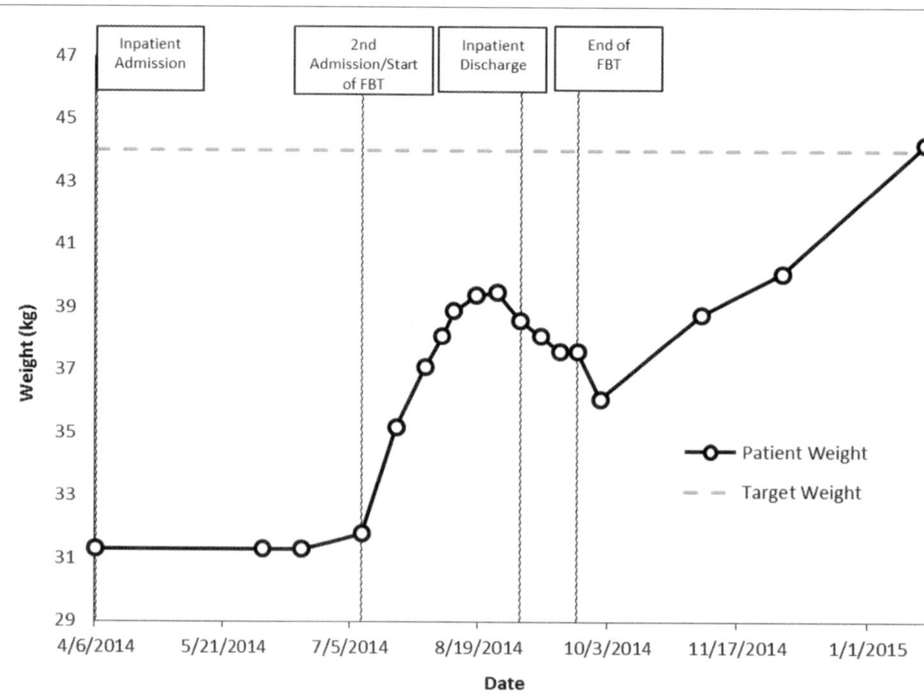

Fig. 3 Case 3 weight graph (Ethan)

family therapy sessions). Of note, as weight increased, she became less "picky" about her eating and able to eat more variety. She also became significantly less hyperactive and regressed, and began to speak more in therapy. As a result, her treatment was augmented with weekly individual therapy sessions in addition to her family therapy. She expressed very high anxiety, both about her schoolwork and about socializing with peers. She was given information about 'Asperger syndrome,' which she found helpful. She continued to gain weight and reached her TGW, ending up on the 25th percentile for weight, with a height near the 25th percentile and an overall BMI of 50% for girls her age. Once she reached her TGW, the olanzapine was tapered and stopped, and an SSRI (fluvoxamine 25 mg/day) was started to target her anxiety. The fluvoxamine was increased gradually from 50 mg to 100 mg/day, but this dose was associated with increased agitation and restlessness, including one weekend when Jacqueline spent the entire weekend in her pajamas pacing back and forth in her bedroom. The fluvoxamine was decreased back down to 50 mg/day and the agitation disappeared, although the family chose to continue the medication as they found the 50 mg dose continued to have a positive effect on her anxiety. By the end of treatment, Jacqueline could sit well throughout a one-hour therapy session with no symptoms of her initial hyperactivity or restlessness; she was also less irritable, more cheerful and affectionate with her family, and more mature and articulate.

Weight at start of family therapy: 37.4 kg.

%TGW at start of family therapy: 93%.

Weight at end of family therapy: 46.5 kg;

%TGW at end of family therapy: > 100% (new TGW: 46 kg) (Fig. 4).

Cases 5 and 6: Hannah and Emily

Hannah and Emily are non-identical twins, 12.9 years old in grade 7 at the time of assessment. Both presented at low weight: Hannah was 73.2% of TGW and Emily was 83.3% of TGW. Emily had a history of severe anxiety and OCD; Hannah was described as not anxious by parents, although her anxiety became obvious over time, once she was re-nourished. The twins were very close to each other. Both girls appeared young for age, and had separation anxiety, and both were strongly attached to their mother, who they slept with every night. Family history was notable for anxiety, bipolar disorder and schizophrenia. Both girls were described as having always been highly picky eaters with long-standing low appetites; mother described being very stressed by always having to cook a different supper for each girl. Both patients were felt to exhibit symptoms most consistent with a mixed ARFID presentation: ARFID-limited intake and ARFID-limited variety subtypes.

During family therapy sessions, which focused on food intake, weight was graphed weekly and parents were empowered to do whatever they needed to do to increase weight for both girls. Parents opted to add liquid supplements twice a day to help improve overall intake. Both girls tried hard to please, but described low appetite, difficulty eating enough food, and not liking many foods. For example, Emily described eating just macaroni salad, goldfish crackers, water and Oreo cookies all day. Weight gain was slow, so treatment was augmented with

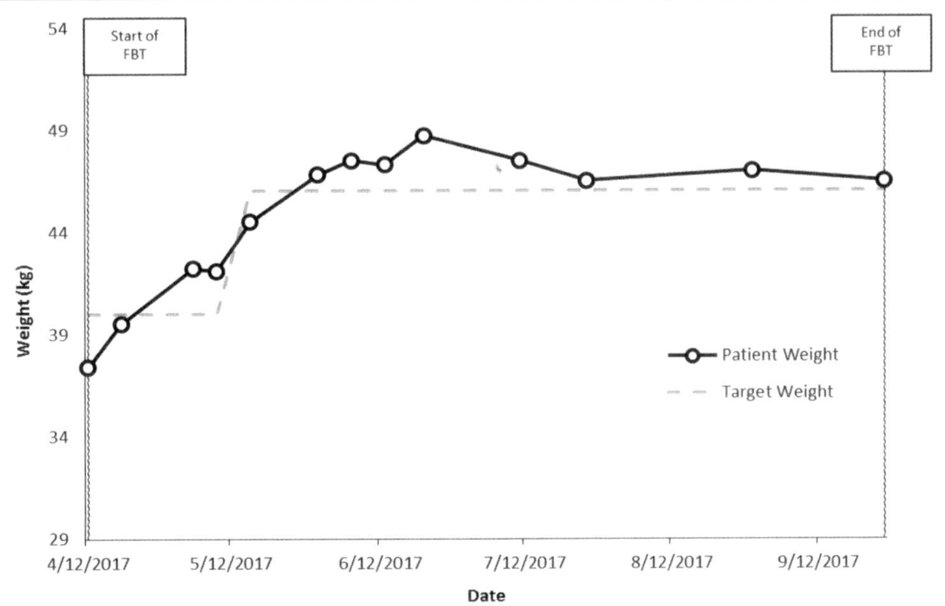

Fig. 4 Case 4 weight graph (Jacqueline)

cyproheptadine (an appetite stimulant, which was started at a dose of 2 mg twice a day and increased to 2 mg in the morning and 4 mg in the afternoon) and then subsequently olanzapine was added as well, at a dose of 2.5 mg at bedtime (the dose was not increased beyond this as their mother was worried that the girls might have trouble waking in the morning). For both girls, olanzapine helped with sleep, anxiety and weight gain. It was clear that Emily's anxiety was very high at school, which interfered with her appetite and intake and was also associated with low mood and self-harm urges, so parents elected to take her out of school. This was helpful, and as Emily's weight was increasing at a faster rate, Hannah was then also taken out of school.

As weight increased, social and generalized anxiety did not decrease for either girl, but food variety did improve. Both twins started eating and liking new foods, and by mid-Fall were back at school and able to eat the same thing for supper for the first time in their lives. In each case, as the girls approached their TGW and started to grow taller as well, fluoxetine was prescribed to help target their anxiety (starting at 10 mg/day and gradually increased to a dose of 40 mg/day) and the cyproheptadine was tapered and eventually stopped. The olanzapine 2.5 mg at bedtime was also stopped, but both girls experienced a significant increase in social and generalized anxiety after the olanzapine was discontinued, so it was restarted, and eventually the dose was increased to 3.75 mg at bedtime due to ongoing severe anxiety. Emily reached her TGW at family session 8 and Hannah at session 16 (within 3 and 6 months of treatment respectively). During treatment, Hannah's weight went from 27.1 kg at assessment to 39.9 kg at last follow up, while Emily's weight increased from 32.9 kg at assessment to 43.3 kg at follow up (Figs. 5 and 6).

Discussion

ARFID is a new diagnosis in the DSM-5 [19]. While the literature describing ARFID is increasing [20, 21, 23–27], to date, there are no randomized or open trials examining treatment outcomes for ARFID, and no treatment guidelines for clinicians to follow. Adapted FBT has been suggested as a potentially useful treatment for pediatric ARFID patients [28, 29]. Although recommended to a similar degree when compared to patients with AN in the study by Strandjorn and colleagues [29], few adolescent ARFID patients took part in the FBT sessions, thus limiting the study's conclusions on the utility of adapted FBT as an integrative treatment method for ARFID. Furthermore, no accounts of barriers and/or facilitators to implementing adapted FBT in this population have been reported.

Similarly, currently there is only one case series that explores the utility of olanzapine for ARFID treatment. In Brewerton and D'Agostino's study [30], it was demonstrated that for 9 patients, the use of low-dose olanzapine adjunctive to other treatment modalities may have improved patients' appetite and weight gain, and helped reduce symptoms of anxiety and depression. Regarding cyproheptadine, there is little published support for its use in patients with ARFID, although published reports predating ARFID's introduction in the DSM-5 have

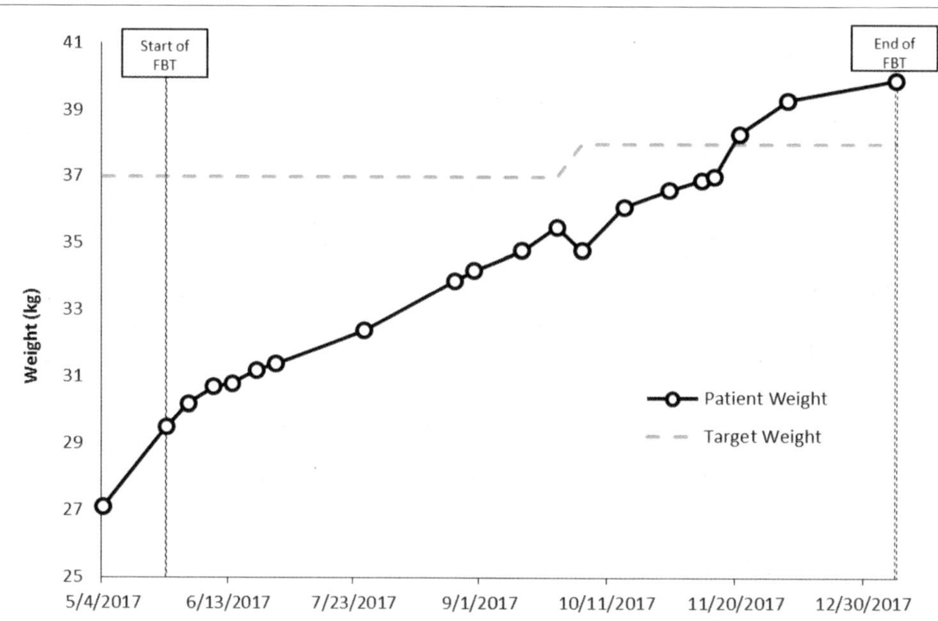

Fig. 5 Case 5 weight graph (Hannah)

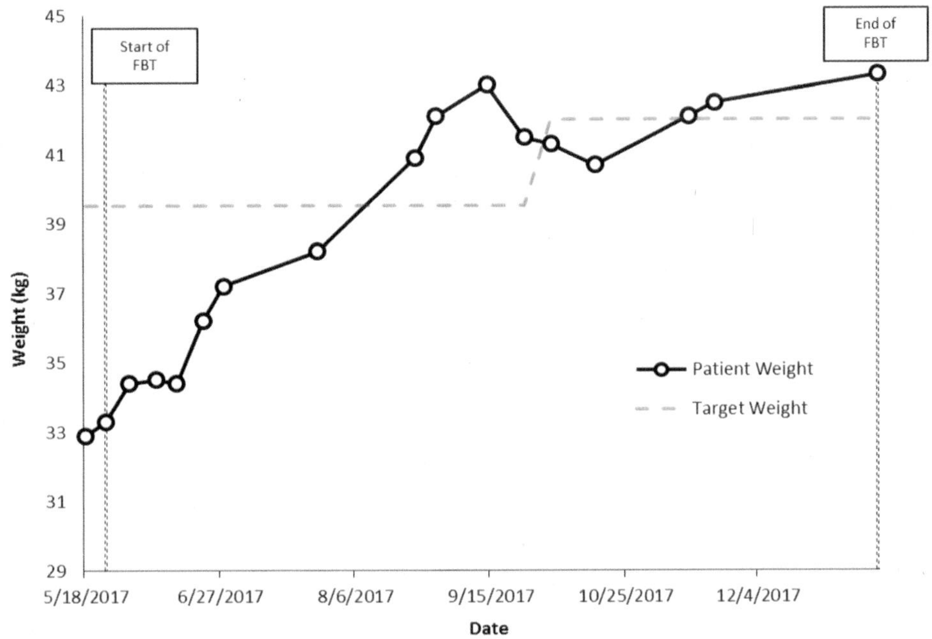

Fig. 6 Case 6 weight graph (Emily)

suggested some benefit in younger children with feeding difficulties [31, 32].

This paper describes six cases of children and adolescents with ARFID who were treated by a senior psychiatrist and AM physician at a tertiary care hospital's specialized ED program, using a combination of medical monitoring, family therapy (using FBT principles but adapted for ARFID), medication (including olanzapine, fluoxetine and in two cases cyproheptadine), and where indicated, cognitive behavioural therapy. Upon reflection, family therapy using 'Maudsley' FBT principles, in combination with pharmacotherapy, seems well suited to the treatment of underweight children and adolescents with ARFID, given that FBT for anorexia nervosa focuses on lifting blame, raising anxiety about the dangers of low weight and malnutrition in young people, and empowering parents to take charge of nutrition and to focus on the goal of weight gain. The shared elements in the family therapy sessions for these six ARFID cases include providing psychoeducation to the families about the effects and negative consequences of low weight and insufficient nutrition, raising anxiety about the seriousness of the problem and the need for weight gain, lifting guilt or blame in all family members, empowering parents/caregivers to stand up to the illness and to take charge of nutrition, providing empathy and compassion for the patient, helping the parents to empathize with their child's pain, fear or discomfort while still being firm about the need to take the nutrition, and focusing the family on issues relating to intake and weight gain, often with detailed intake inventories and the use of weight graphs. Certain other elements of therapy depended on the particular 'subtype' of ARFID or the particular details of the case. For example, a child with a severe choking phobia was given cognitive behavioural therapy including psychoeducation about anxiety and phobias, a hierarchy of feared foods, and gradual exposure therapy. Children with severe anxiety at school were taken out of school until weight was at least partially restored, and measures were taken to make the school environment less stressful. Where indicated, individual therapy was sometimes added to the family sessions. In all six of the cases, co-morbid anxiety seemed to affect intake and impair treatment progress. As a means of attenuating this severe distress, augmented treatment for anxiety using psychotherapy (for 5 of the 6 cases) and pharmacotherapy (olanzapine and/or an SSRI, for all 6 cases) was required in conjunction with family therapy to meet the needs of patients.

Further research is required to better understand which treatments or combinations of treatments are best for which illness presentations and subtypes, and how specific presentations might predict response to differing treatment modalities. Moving forward, it will be important for researchers studying treatments for pediatric ARFID to design controlled trials that investigate the effectiveness of 'Maudsley-type' family therapy, medication, or cognitive behavioural therapy when used alone and not in combination with other treatments, before studying their combinations. It will also be important for investigators to determine which types of patients (e.g. subtypes of ARFID) respond best to which treatment.

Finally, while family therapy adapted from FBT for the treatment of pediatric anorexia nervosa seems suitable for children and adolescents with ARFID, other treatment modalities should be studied for adults diagnosed with ARFID.

Limitations of the present report include the fact that multiple treatment modalities were implemented in an uncontrolled manner, and that our sample size is small without a comparator group. In addition, treatment settings were not standardized (e.g. some patients initiated treatment in hospital, while others began as outpatients). Despite these limitations, the relative absence of specific treatment descriptions in the literature highlight the need for case descriptions to provide preliminary evidence for funding of further controlled research trials.

Conclusions

This paper describes six adolescents with ARFID who were successfully treated with a combination of medication plus family therapy, and where indicated, targeted cognitive behavioural therapy. These cases illustrate the complex and various ways in which young patients with ARFID can present, the illness' effect on development and mental health, and the positive outcomes associated with weight gain and concurrent treatment for co-morbid anxiety disorders.

Abbreviations

%TGW : Percentage of Treatment Goal Weight; ADHD: Attention-Deficit Hyperactivity Disorder; AM: Adolescent Medicine; AN: Anorexia Nervosa; ARFID: Avoidant/Restrictive Food Intake Disorder; ASD: Autism Spectrum Disorder; BMI: Body Mass Index; BN: Bulimia Nervosa; DSM-5: Diagnostic and Statistical Manual of Mental Disorders – 5th Edition; ED: Eating Disorder; FBT: Family-Based Therapy; NG: Nasogastric; OCD: Obsessive Compulsive Disorder; SSRI: Selective Serotonin Reuptake Inhibitor

Authors' contributions

WS is the senior psychiatrist who conceptualized the study, designed the protocol, treated and described each case, and revised the manuscript to its final version. MLN is the adolescent medicine physician who oversaw management for eating disorder patients and helped with writing of the manuscript. AS performed the retrospective chart reviews, helped with data analysis and wrote the first draft of the manuscript. NO performed data analysis and assisted with the revision of the manuscript. All authors critically revised the manuscript, and all authors have read and approved the final manuscript.

Competing interests

The authors declare that they have no competing interests.

Author details

[1]Department of Psychiatry, Children's Hospital of Eastern Ontario, University of Ottawa, 401 Smyth Road, Ottawa, ON K1H 8L1, Canada. [2]Division of Adolescent Health, Department of Pediatrics, Children's Hospital of Eastern Ontario, 401 Smyth Road, Ottawa, ON K1H 8L1, Canada. [3]Children's Hospital of Eastern Ontario Research Institute, 401 Smyth Road, Ottawa, ON K1H 5B2, Canada.

References

1. Bulik CM, Berkman ND, Brownley KA, Sedway JA, Lohr KN. Anorexia nervosa treatment: a systematic review of randomized controlled trials. Int J Eat Disord. 2007;40(4):293–309. https://doi.org/10.1002/eat.20367.
2. Couturier J, Kimber M, Szatmari P. Efficacy of family-based treatment for adolescents with eating disorders: a systematic review and meta-analysis. Int J Eat Disord. 2013;46(1):3–11. https://doi.org/10.1002/eat.22042.
3. Fisher CA, Hetrick SE, Rushford N. Family therapy for anorexia nervosa. Cochrane Database Syst Rev. 2010;2010 https://doi.org/10.1002/14651858.CD004780.pub2.
4. Medway M, Rhodes P. (2016). Young people's experience of family therapy for anorexia nervosa: a qualitative meta-synthesis. Adv Eat Disord Theory Res Pract. 2016;4(2):189–207. https://doi.org/10.1080/21662630.2016.1164609.
5. Dare C. The family therapy of anorexia nervosa. J Psychiatr Res. 1985;19(2–3): 435–43. https://doi.org/10.1016/0022-3956(85)90050-0.
6. Minuchin S, Baker L, Rosman BL, Liebman R, Milman L, Todd TC. A conceptual model of psychosomatic illness in children: family organization and family therapy. Arch Gen Psychiatry. 1975;32(8):1031–8. https://doi.org/10.1001/archpsyc.1975.01760260095008.
7. Lock J, le Grange D, Agras S, Dare C. Treatment manual for anorexia nervosa: a family-based approach. New York: Guildford Press; 2001.
8. Lock J, le Grange D. Treatment manual for anorexia nervosa: a family-based approach. 2nd ed. New York: Guildford Press; 2012.
9. Bosanac P, Burrows G, Norman T. Olanzapine in anorexia nervosa. Aust N Z J Psychiatry. 2003;37(4):494. https://doi.org/10.1046/j.1440-1614.2003.01221.x.
10. Powers PS, Santana CA, Bannon YS. Olanzapine in the treatment of anorexia nervosa: an open label trial. Int J Eat Disord. 2002;32(2):146–54. https://doi.org/10.1002/eat.10084.
11. Bissada H, Tasca GA, Barber AM, Bradwejn J. Olanzapine in the treatment of low body weight and obsessive thinking in women with anorexia nervosa: a randomized, double-blind, placebo-controlled trial. Am J Psychiatry. 2008; 165(10):1281–8. https://doi.org/10.1176/appi.ajp.2008.07121900.
12. Couturier J, Spettigue W. Pharmacotherapy for eating disorders in children and adolescents. In: le Grange D, Lock J, editors. Eating disorders in children and adolescents: a clinical handbook. New York: Guilford Press; 2011. p. 402–20.
13. Flament M, Bissada H, Spettigue W. Evidence-based pharmacotherapy of eating disorders. Int J Neuropsychopharmacol. 2012;15(2):189–207. https://doi.org/10.1017/S1461145711000381.
14. Kim SS. Role of fluoxetine in anorexia nervosa. Ann Pharmacother. 2003; 37(6):890–2. https://doi.org/10.1345/aph.1C362.
15. Kaye WH, Nagata T, Weltzin TE, Hsu LK, Sokol MS, McConaha C, et al. Double-blind placebo-controlled administration of fluoxetine in restricting- and restricting-purging-type anorexia nervosa. Biol Psychiatry. 2001;49(7):644–52. https://doi.org/10.1016/S0006-3223(00)01013-1.
16. Sebaaly JC, Cox S, Hughes CM, Kennedy ML, Garris SS. Use of fluoxetine in anorexia nervosa before and after weight restoration. Ann Pharmacother. 2013;47(9):1201–5. https://doi.org/10.1177/1060028013503127.
17. Connolly SD, Bernstein G. AACAP work group on quality issues. Practice parameters for the assessment and treatment of children and adolescents with anxiety disorders. J Am Acad Child Adolesc Psychiatry. 2007;46(2):267–83. https://doi.org/10.1097/01.chi.0000246070.23695.06.
18. Birmaher B, Brent D. AACAP work group on quality issues. Practice parameters for the assessment and treatment of children and adolescents with depressive disorders. J Am Acad Child Adolesc Psychiatry. 2007;46(11): 1503–11526. https://doi.org/10.1097/chi.0b013e318145ae1c.
19. American Psychiatric Association. Diagnostic and statistical manual of mental disorders. 5th ed. Arlington: American Psychiatric Publishing; 2013.
20. Norris ML, Spettigue W, Hammond NG, Katzman DK, Zucker N, Yelle K, et al. Building evidence for the use of descriptive subtypes in youth with avoidant restrictive food intake disorder. Int J Eat Disord. 2018;51(2):170–3. https://doi.org/10.1002/eat.22814.
21. Ornstein RM, Essayli JH, Nicely TA, Masciulli E, Lane-Loney S. Treatment of avoidant/restrictive food intake disorder in a cohort of young patients in a partial hospitalization program for eating disorders. Int J Eat Disord. 2017; 50(9):1067–74. https://doi.org/10.1002/eat.22737.
22. Norris ML, Hiebert J, Katzman DK. Determining treatment goal weights for children and adolescents with anorexia nervosa. Paediatr Child Health. Available at: https://www.cps.ca/en/documents/position/goal-weights. Last accessed 13 Jun 2018
23. Fisher MM, Rosen DS, Ornstein RM, Mammel KA, Katzman DK, Rome ES, et al. Characteristics of avoidant/restrictive food intake disorder in children and

adolescents: a "new disorder" in DSM-5. J Adolesc Health. 2014;55(1):49–52. https://doi.org/10.1016/j.jadohealth.2013.11.013.
24. Norris ML, Robinson A, Obeid N, Harrison M, Spettigue W, Henderson K. Exploring avoidant/restrictive food intake disorder in eating disordered patients: a descriptive study. Int J Eat Disord. 2014;47(5):495–9. https://doi.org/10.1002/eat.22217.
25. Norris ML, Spettigue W, Katzman DK. Update on eating disorders: current perspectives on avoidant/restrictive food intake disorder in children and youth. Neuropsychiatr Dis Treat. 2016;12:213–8. https://doi.org/10.2147/NDT.S82538.
26. Strandjord SE, Sieke EH, Richmond M, Rome ES. Avoidant/restrictive food intake disorder: illness and hospital course in patients hospitalized for nutritional insufficiency. J Adolesc Health. 2015;57(6):673–8. https://doi.org/10.1016/j.jadohealth.2015.08.003.
27. Thomas J, Lawson E, Micali N, Misra M, Deckersbach T, Eddy K. Avoidant/restrictive food intake disorder: a three-dimensional model of neurobiology with implications for etiology and treatment. Curr Psychiatry Rep. 2017;19(8):1–9. https://doi.org/10.1007/s11920-017-0795-5.
28. Fitzpatrick KK, Forsberg SE, Colborn D. Family-based therapy for avoidant restrictive food intake disorder: families facing food neophobias. In: Loeb KL, le Grange D, Lock J, editors. Family therapy for adolescent eating and weight disorders: new applications. New York: Routledge; 2015. p. 256–76.
29. Strandjord SE, Sabik J, Nahra A, Abdulkader Z, Sieke EH, Worley S, Rome ES. Avoidant/restrictive food intake disorder: treatment choice and outcome in the outpatient setting. J Adolesc Health. 2016;58(2):S37–8. https://doi.org/10.1016/j.jadohealth.2015.10.088.
30. Brewerton TD, D'Agostino M. Adjunctive use of olanzapine in the treatment of avoidant restrictive food intake disorder in children and adolescents in an eating disorders program. J Child Adolesc Psychopharmacol. 2017;27(10):920–2. https://doi.org/10.1089/cap.2017.0133.
31. Merhar SL, Pentiuk SP, Mukkada VA, Meinzen-Derr J, Kaul A, Butler DR. A retrospective review of cyproheptadine for feeding intolerance in children less than three years of age: effects and side effects. Acta Paediatr. 2016;105(8):967–70. https://doi.org/10.1111/apa.13477.
32. Sant'Anna AM, Hammes PS, Porporino M, Martel C, Zygmuntowicz C, Ramsay M. Use of cyproheptadine in young children with feeding difficulties and poor growth in a pediatric feeding program. J Pediatr Gastroenterol Nutr. 2014;59(5):674–8. https://doi.org/10.1097/MPG.0000000000000467.

10

Eating behaviour disorders among adolescents in a middle school

Tingting Feng[1] and Dawit Shawel Abebe[2*]

Abstract

Background: Disordered eating behaviours (DEB) are significant public health challenges among adolescents. DEB are prevalent among Chinese young people and replication epidemiological studies in DEB are needed due to ongoing rapid modernization and socio-economic change. In addition, there has been no prevention or intervention programs for DEB in most of rural areas in China and research in DEB in rural China is limited. More research in DEB in rural China is needed for increased awareness of prevention strategies. The objectives of the study are to examine the prevalence and associated factors of DEB among rural Chinese adolescents.

Methods: Four hundred and sixty-six students aged 11–18 years old from a middle school in rural China were invited to complete a self-reported questionnaire that included measures on DEB and psychosocial factors. The SCOFF questionnaire was applied to measure DEB (i.e., a score of > = 2 indicates a likely case of DEB). Logistic regression models were applied for data analyses. A *p*-value <0.05 was regarded as statistically significant.

Results: There were 389 adolescents (11–18 years) included in this study with the prevalence of DEB being 28.8%. No significant differences were found between male adolescents (30.5%) and female adolescents (27.1%). Independently, perceived overweight (OR = 2.80, 95% CI = 1.05–7.48), negative affect (OR = 1.07, 95% CI = 1.03–1.12), body dissatisfaction (OR = 0.96, 95% CI = 0.93–0.99), and watching TV (OR = 2.40, 95% CI = 1.11–5.18) were significantly ($p < 0.05$) associated with DEB.

Conclusion: This study indicates a high prevalence rate of DEB among rural adolescents and associated factors of DEB from a school-based sample. Such findings imply that local public health systems should pay more attention to DEB and design prevention and intervention strategies for DEB.

Keywords: Disordered eating behaviours, Associated factors, Adolescents, China

Plain English summary

Disordered Eating Behaviours (DEB) start to appear during adolescence and bring serious consequences. Previous studies showed DEB is becoming common in China, and even more prevalent than that is in Western countries. However, limited research has been conducted among adolescents in rural China. The current study aimed to establish the prevalence of DEB and associated psychosocial factors among rural adolescents. Results from the current research showed a high prevalence rate of DEB among rural adolescents and associated psychosocial factors of DEB.

Background

Disordered Eating Behaviours (DEB) are abnormal eating attitudes and behaviours which have much in common with diagnosed eating disorders [1].These can have serious implications which relate to depression, substance abuse, suicidal behaviours, social isolation and which may develop into an eating disorder [2, 3].

DEB has long been regarded as strongly related to Western cultures but according to a review in the most recent published epidemiologic data relevant to eating disorders in Asia and the Pacific, abnormal eating

* Correspondence: dawit.s.abebe@nova.hioa.no
[2]Norwegian Social Research (NOVA), Oslo and Akershus University College of Applied Sciences, Oslo, Norway
Full list of author information is available at the end of the article

behaviours found to be highly prevalent in China [4]. Traditional Chinese culture considers plumpness as beautiful and slimness as reflecting poverty. However, China has been dramatically influenced by Western cultures for the past 39 years due to the 'open-door policy'. The thin-ideal has come to overshadow standards for beauty which contributes to body dissatisfaction and DEB among females [5]. Accordingly, a number of Chinese studies report a high prevalence of DEB [6–13]. Specifically, female adolescents living in Hong Kong have been found to have the highest prevalence of DEB (10.8%), followed by those from Shenzhen (5.2%) and from Hunan (2.5%) [6]. Two school-based studies in Taiwan revealed DEB in 17.1% and 10.4% of high school female adolescents [7, 8]. Further, a school-based study in Hong Kong revealed that DEB were present in 3.9% of adolescent males and 6.5% of adolescent females [9]. Three school-based studies in Mainland China have also reported that the prevalence of DEB varied from 2.3% to 17% among middle school and college students [10–12]. Western studies have revealed DEB in 29.4% of female adolescents, specifically 14.9% of male adolescents in Germany, and 56% of female adolescents and 28% of male adolescents in US [14, 15]. However, few studies in DEB have included male adolescents in China [9, 13]. The variations in measuring instrument, sample characteristics, methodological approaches and study areas, however, may limit the comparability of prevalence across studies. The updated epidemiologic review in 2016 suggested that fat concern and weight control behaviours are prevalent among Chinese young people and replication epidemiological studies in eating disturbances are needed due to ongoing rapid modernization and socioeconomic change [4].

Psychosocial risk factors are strongly associated with a high prevalence of DEB among adolescents [13, 16]. For instance, longitudinal studies conducted in Southern China found body dissatisfaction, negative affect, perceived sociocultural pressures, and high socioeconomic status (SES) all have significant associations with DEB. [13, 17].

A comparative study among female adolescents in three different socioeconomically communities of China documented that those in rural areas had fewer concerns about body fat and demonstrated a lower prevalence rate of DEB than those in developed cities [6]. Socioeconomic development in China is growing very fast nowadays and the rapid ongoing socioeconomic transition has influenced rural China to a large extent. Rural populations now have more opportunities to access the mass media, which may relate to a higher risk of DEB. T Jackson and H Chen have reported that Chinese middle adolescent girls reported higher levels of appearance experiences related to mass media and DEB [18], and pressure from mass media related to DEB have been observed in Chinese adolescent boys [19]. There are some studies examining the epidemiology of eating disorders in rural China [17, 20, 21], but little research has focused on epidemiology of DEB in rural China. In more than 20 years, there has been only one study which has focused on DEB among Chinese female adolescents in a rural area [6]. Further, given that little attention has been paid to DEB in both genders in rural China, it is necessary to re-investigate the situation under current influences. The present study, therefore, aimed to examine prevalence and associated psychosocial factors of DEB among male adolescents and female adolescents at a Chinese middle school in a rural area. This may contribute to the updated information in the epidemiology of DEB in China and also respond to the updated review's request for replication studies, that is this review suggested further replication epidemiological studies in eating disturbances due to ongoing rapid modernization and socio-economic change [4].

Methods

Participants and study procedure

All students from a middle school – a secondary high school – in Dongfanghong town (a less economically developed rural area), Heilongjiang province were invited to participate in the study. In 2015, the per capita annual income in our sample area was 30,977 RMB (or $4509). The school that was studied was the only middle school in this area. Four hundred and sixty-six students aged 11–18 years old were invited to complete an anonymous, self-reported questionnaire covering a wide range of topics including DEB and related psychosocial behaviours on a voluntary basis.

Before starting the research, schoolteachers were trained by researchers and schoolteachers explained the study to students and were able to answer students' questions. During the study, the confidentiality and the anonymity of participants were assured. With the assistance of schoolteachers, the questionnaires were administered in September 2015 – at the beginning of autumn semester. The class teachers decided the time when questionnaires were conducted. They usually selected self-learning class (students studied by themselves) and the time of self-learning class was different among classrooms. The students used around 1 h -2 h to finish the questionnaires. The class teachers collected the questionnaires following completion and returned them to the researcher. Of 466 questionnaires that were issued, 389 valid questionnaires were returned (a response rate of 83.5%).

Outcome variables

SCOFF: The SCOFF questionnaire is an effective tool that can screen DEB quickly [22]. It includes five items addressing the main features of DEB [22]. See the

Additional file 1: Table S1 for the descriptive statistics of each item.

One point for every "yes"; a score of > = 2 indicates a likely case of DEB. The scale has been validated and has demonstrated effective specificity in identifying DEB [23]. The Chinese version of the SCOFF questionnaire has been proved to be effective for detecting potential DEB [24].

Independent variables

Body Mass Index (BMI) was computed from self-reported measures of height and weight. Self-reported BMI has been demonstrated to be a reliable measure of BMI [25]. The classification of BMI was made according to BMI cut-offs by the Working Group on Obesity in China (WGOC) [26]: ≤ 18.49 kg/m^2 (underweight), 18.50–23.99 kg/m^2 (normal weight), 24–27.99 (overweight), ≥ 28 (obesity). We combined the overweight group and the obesity group into one category due to the small number size in the obesity group.

Participants were asked to describe their weight perceptions. Responses were ranged into three groups: underweight, average /normal, and overweight.

Compared weight perceptions with actual BMI, weight misconception was ranged into four groups: misconception of underweight, overweight, normal weight and correct weight conception. See the Additional file 2: Table S2 for the association between BMI and perceived weight categories.

Body dissatisfaction was examined using a Body Part Satisfaction Scale with each response from 1 = extremely dissatisfied to 6 = extremely satisfied [27]. The scale consists of eight items rating the individual's level of satisfaction with the following body areas: face, upper torso, middle torso, lower torso, muscle tone, weight, height and overall appearance. A high score indicates a higher level of body satisfaction. The scale has shown reliable psychometrics [27]. The Chinese version of this scale has been tested and has strong reliability [18]. The internal consistency of the scale was 0.90.

Depressive symptoms were measured by the Positive and Negative Affect Schedule [28]. This schedule is a 20-item test with 10 items for negative affect and positive affect, respectively. Participants were asked to describe the extent to which they had varying feelings and emotions in the past month from 1 = very slightly or not at all to 5 = extremely. The scale has shown good validity and acceptable psychometric properties [28]. The original scale has been tested on Chinese samples [19].

The Perceived Sociocultural Pressure Scale was used to assess pressures to be thin from family, friends, dating partners and media [18]. The questionnaire has 10 items that investigate perceived sociocultural pressures to be thin. An example of an item is: "I've noticed a strong message from my family to have a thin body". Three items are for family and friends, respectively. Two items are for dating partners and media, respectively. Responses ranged from 1 = not at all to 5 = extremely. Higher scores indicate more perceived pressure. Internal consistency ($\alpha = 0.83$), test-retest reliability ($r = 0.93$) and predictive validity of this scale have been documented [29]. The scale has been tested and used in Chinese samples [19].

Media use was assessed by a media exposure questionnaire. Participants were asked: whether they watch television and DVDs, whether they use the Internet, whether they use chat rooms and play computer games, as well as how long they spent on media. The questionnaire was developed from a Chinese study [5].

Parental socioeconomic status (SES) was determined on the adolescents' report of parents' occupation. Occupations were categorized according to the classification by the Chinese National Bureau of Statistics [30] with nine items to be selected. Four groups were created based on the salary of occupations: professional, service, labourers, and unemployed. The variables of mother's job and father's job were merged into one variable (parents' occupation), recording the higher of the two values.

Age and sex were also recorded.

Statistical analysis

Chi-square analysis was used to compare differences in prevalence of DEB and for comparing perceived weight categories to BMI categories. To examine associated factors of DEB, first, a univariate logistic regression was employed to examine the association between each of the independent variable and DEB, and then multiple logistic analysis was performed. A forward stepwise multiple logistic regression was performed to determine factors significantly associated with DEB, including independent variables based on univariate logistic regression results (cut-off point $p \leqslant 0.25$). Age and gender were controlled. The final model was built based on this forward stepwise multiple logistic regression ($p \leqslant 0.05$). The multi-collinearity among associated factors was examined with *collin* command in Stata (mean variance inflation factor (VIF) = 1.43, correlation matrix = 0.0528). Secondly, Model fit to the data (validity and reliability) was assessed by the likelihood ratio χ^2 test, Hosmer-Lemeshowgoodness-of-fit test and receiver operating characteristics (ROC) curve. $P \leqslant 0.05$ was regarded as statistically significant and odds ratio (OR) with 95% confidence intervals (95% CI) were calculated. Data analyses were conducted with the Statistical Package for the Social Sciences (SPSS) 22.0 and StataSE 14.

Ethical clearance

The study was approved by the Regional Committee for Medical Research Ethics in Norway, and the Committee for the middle school in Dongfanghong, China.

Results

Descriptive summary of the study participants

Table 1 presents the descriptive summary of study participants ($N = 389$).

Prevalence of disordered eating behaviours

Table 2 presents the prevalence of DEB according to the participants' general information by using chi-square analysis. The prevalence of DEB among adolescents was 28.8%. The prevalence of DEB among male adolescents and female adolescents was 27.1% and 30.5%, respectively; no significant differences were found based on gender. No significant differences of prevalence of DEB were found across different age groups. Significant differences in the prevalence of DEB were found in different BMI groups, χ^2 (2) = 14.896, $p = .001$. Overweight adolescents (42.9%) had a significantly higher prevalence of DEB as compared to underweight adolescents (18.6%). Significant differences in the prevalence of DEB were also found in different perceived weight groups, χ^2 (2) = 51.524, $p < .001$. Adolescents in the perceived overweight group (54.4%) had a significantly higher prevalence of DEB than those among the perceived underweight group (18.0%). Significant differences in the prevalence of DEB were found in different weight misconception groups, χ^2 (2) = 43.399, $p < .001$. Adolescents with overweight misconception (59.4%) had a significantly higher prevalence of DEB than those without overweight misconception. There were no significant differences in the prevalence of DEB among students across different SES groups. Associations between misconception of over−/under-weight and DEB by gender is shown in the Additional file 3: Table S3.

Psychosocial factors independently predicting disordered eating behaviours

Table 3 presents results from univariate and multiple logistic regression analyses reporting psychosocial associated factors of DEB. The final multiple regression model included perceived weight, body dissatisfaction, negative affect and watching TV. The risk of having DEB among the perceived overweight group was 2.8 times higher than among those in the perceived underweight group. Students with higher levels of body dissatisfaction were significantly more likely to develop DEB compared to those with lower levels of dissatisfaction. Students with a higher negative affect were significantly more likely to develop DEB compared with those with a lower negative affect. Students watching TV were almost three times more likely to report DEB than students who did not watch TV. The corresponding coefficients and standard errors in the multiple logistic regression model are shown in the Additional file 4: Table S4.

The reliability and the validity of the multiple logistic regression model was assessed by employing post-estimation statistics (likelihood ratio χ^2 test significant, $\chi^2 = 107.925$, degrees of freedom (df) = 9, $p < 0.001$; Hosmer-Lemeshow χ^2 test = 10.196, df = 8, $p = 0.252$). The Hosmer-Lemeshow test of the goodness-of-fit suggests the model is a good fit to the data (small Chi-squared values with larger p-value closer to 1). Area under the ROC curve (AUC) was 0.825 with 95% confidence interval (0.781, 0.869), which is a prediction power for the model.

Discussion

The main findings of this school-based study reveal a high prevalence rate of DEB among male adolescents (27.1%) and female adolescents (30.5%). The study also found that perceived weight, negative affect, body dissatisfaction, and watching TV were significantly associated with DEB among adolescents.

The prevalence estimates of the current study are among a wide range of previous school-based studies conducted in China (2.26%–58.3%) [10, 31–33]. The available information on DEB in rural China has been reported by Sing Lee and Antoinette M. Lee [6]. In their study, 266 school female adolescents from Grade 11 from Rural Hunan were included with a prevalence rate of 2.5%. In the present study, prevalence was much higher. This may be attributed to different screening instruments for DEB. The study by Sing Lee and Antoinette M. Lee [6] used EAT-26 as the screening instrument, while we used SCOFF. The sensitivity and the specificity between the two instruments are different and SCOFF has been reported to have a tendency toward overinclusion [34]. It is further comparable to reports from Western countries; in spite of variation in measuring instruments, study methodologies and sample compositions: for instance 29.4% of female adolescents and 14.9% of male adolescents in Germany, and 56% of female adolescents and 28% of male adolescents in US [14, 15]. Given the harmful consequences related to DEB and the high prevalence of DEB, it is vital for public health officials to increase public awareness by introducing relevant and important information about DEB at individual, school and society level. In this way, health organisations can aim at intervening and preventing harmful eating behaviours. So far, there has been no such programs for DEB in the local region.

This study did not show significant gender differences in prevalence of DEB. Most Chinese and Western studies report that prevalence of DEB was significantly higher among female adolescents than among male adolescents [9, 14, 15]. The prevalence of DEB for males is possibly rising and the incidence of DEB for males may have been underrated due to cultural stigma [35]. It may also due to changing lifestyles: increased access to TV,

Table 1 Descriptive summary of the study participants (*N* = 389)

Variables	N	Percent	M	sd
Female	190	48.8		
SCOFF total score (five tiems)			1.0	1.1
0	172	44.2		
1	105	27.0		
2	67	17.2		
3	32	8.2		
4	12	3.1		
5	1	0.3		
Age(year)			15.1	1.7
Early Adolescence [11–13]	95	24.4		
Middle Adolescence [14–16]	198	50.9		
Late Adolescence [17, 18]	96	24.7		
BMI(kg/m^2)			20.5	4.7
Underweight	140	36.0		
Normal Weight	169	43.4		
Overweight	77	19.8		
Perceived Weight				
Underweight	61	15.7		
Normal Weight	214	55.0		
Overweight	114	29.3		
Weight Misconception				
Misconception of Underweight	18	4.6		
Misconception of Normal Weight	102	26.2		
Misconception of Overweight	57	14.7		
Correct Weight Conception	207	53.2		
Parents' Occupation				
Professional	115	29.6		
Service	72	18.5		
Labourers	48	12.3		
Unemployed	154	39.6		
With DEB	112	28.8		
Pressure				
Family			1.9	1.1
Friend			1.8	1.0
Dating			1.5	1.0
Media			1.6	1.1
Watch TV	323	83.0		
Watch DVD	74	19.0		
Surfing Online	353	90.7		
Chat Online	316	81.2		
Play Online	253	65.0		
Hours on Media average - 0-4.9 h	315	81		
Hours on Media Total			14.1	9.1
Body Satisfaction			31.1	8.4

Table 1 Descriptive summary of the study participants (*N* = 389) *(Continued)*

Variables	N	Percent	M	sd
Face			4.0	1.3
Upper torso			4.0	1.3
Middle torso			4.0	1.4
Lower torso			4.0	1.4
Muscle tone			3.7	1.4
Height			3.8	1.4
Weight			3.7	1.5
Overall appearance			4.1	1.2
Positive Affect			29.6	7.5
Negative Affect			21.2	7.2

N number, *M* mean, *sd* standard deviation
Pressure perceived sociocultural pressure to thin body and weight loss
Hours on Media Total time on Internet working days + time on Internet weekends + time on TV working days + time on TV weekends
Hours on Media average Hours on Media Total ÷ 4

social media, Internet and gaming. It is possible that female adolescents and male adolescents have a similar risk for developing DEB. More attention, therefore, should be also be paid to male adolescents who are at risk of DEB.

The present study found perceived weight as a significant associated factor of DEB. Results are consistent with previous observations on perceived weight status in Chinese adolescents [6] and Western samples [36, 37]. It has been suggested that one's perceived weight has a greater influence than one's actual weight when engaging in DEB [38]. In addition, a considerable number of adolescents in this study misperception with regard to weight status, which is consistent with previous Chinese research [39]. Furthermore, separate logistical regression in this study showed that students with the misconception of being overweight were more likely to report DEB. This is in line with previous research [38] and it indicates that one possible avenue for prevention programs may be a focus upon helping students develop accurate weight perception.

Along the same lines, body dissatisfaction was a significant associated factor for DEB. Similar results have been reported in both Chinese and Western research [13, 16]. The thin-ideal image contributes to perfectionism and body dissatisfaction. Male adolescents wish to become more muscular and achieve the male-ideal of V-shaped figure. On the other hand, female adolescents wish to become thinner and achieve the female-ideal of extremely thin. They put much emphasis upon having a perfect body shape, though they have a clinically healthy weight. Perfectionism and body dissatisfaction are both highly correlated with DEB [40]. Body dissatisfaction can increase dieting behaviours [41] and negative affect [16],

Table 2 Prevalence of disordered eating behaviours across participants' general information

	With DEB % (N)	Without DEB % (N)	Chi-square Statistic
Gender			0.545
Female	30.5 (58)	69.5 (132)	
Male	27.1 (54)	72.9 (145)	
Age			4.919
Early Adolescent [11–13]	24.2 (23)	75.8 (72)	
Middle Adolescent [14–16]	26.8 (53)	73.2 (145)	
Late Adolescent [17, 18]	37.5 (36)	62.5 (60)	
BMI			14.896**
Underweight	18.6 (26)	81.4 (114)	
Normal Weight	30.8 (52)	69.2 (117)	
Overweight	42.9 (33)	57.1 (44)	
Perceived Weight			51.524***
Underweight	18.0 (11)	82.0 (50)	
Normal Weight	18.2 (39)	81.8 (175)	
Overweight	54.4 (62)	45.6 (52)	
Weight Misconception			41.521***
Misconception of Underweight	22.2 (4)	77.8 (14)	
Misconception of Normal Weight	13.7 (14)	86.3 (88)	
Misconception of Overweight	61.4 (35)	38.6 (22)	
Correct Weight Conception	27.5 (57)	72.5 (150)	
Parents' Occupation			2.218
Professional	33.9 (39)	66.1 (76)	
Service	25.0 (18)	75.0 (54)	
Labourers	27.1 (13)	72.9 (35)	
Unemployed	27.3 (42)	72.7 (112)	

N number of participants
*$p < 0.05$, **$p < 0.01$, ***$p < 0.001$

which can, in turn, lead to poor eating habits and increased eating disturbances.

Negative affect was significantly associated with DEB in this study. The result is in agreement with previous Chinese and Western research [13, 16]. One explanation is that negative urgency (i.e., the tendency to act rashly in response to negative affect) is significantly associated with disordered eating [42]. Another explanation can be derived from escape theory - people tend to escape negative emotions by abnormal eating (overeating) and they believe or have learned that overeating can relieve negative emotions [43, 44]. Moreover, negative affect and disordered eating may be interacted mutually, where the feeling of shame and guilty caused by disordered eating may result in negative self-perceptions among female adolescents [44].

In addition, this study found television access as a significant associated factor of DEB. A small number of adolescents did not have access to TV, possibly related to high academic expectations, family economic situations or personal preference. Media consumption can significantly predict female adolescents' DEB and male adolescents' interest in dieting [45]. Such an effect of media can also be found in other non-western studies. For example, research in Fiji [46], Pakistan [47], Japan [48], and Korea [49] have documented significant associations between media exposure and DEB. Becker [50] has also discussed how Western media introduced by TV has caused thin-ideal internalization among Fijian females. Garfinkel and Garner suggest: "The media have capitalized upon and promoted this image (of thinness) and through popular programming have portrayed the successful and beautiful protagonists as thin. Thinness has thus become associated with self-control and success." (p.145) [51]. Other media variables in this study did not show significant associations with DEB. It is possible that specific media exposure may contribute to thin body and eating disturbances instead of other general media variables.

Although BMI did not contribute to the multiple logistical regression model in this study, BMI was significantly positively associated with DEB from univariate logistical regression analysis. Previous research showed there may exist a U-shaped relation between DEB and BMI [52, 53]. That is, disordered eating behaviours were more problematic at the two extreme ends of BMI (underweight and obesity).

In addition, there is a non-significant trend of increasing prevalence of DEB with age in this study; late adolescents reported highest prevalence of DEB. This may be related to an increased social and emotional stress. Late adolescents, face an exceptional amount of pressure to succeed in college entrance examinations and achieve parental expectations [54] and experience peer competition, copious homework and reduced social support. These stressors may be associated with an increased risk for DEB [55].

This study adds to a growing literature on epidemiology of DEB among adolescents in China. It, therefore, provides current knowledge on the epidemiology of DEB in rural China, which helps to capture more attention to DEB in rural China. Since DEB may develop into more severe forms of DEB or eating disorders without appropriate intervention strategies, it is important to design early interventions against DEB. Secondly, this study included both male adolescents and female adolescents which has provided valuable insights into DEB in both genders. Thirdly, this study found risky behaviours associated with DEB among adolescents, which may contribute to better identification of high-risk groups and may be helpful for early prevention and intervention

Table 3 Multiple logistic regression model showing factors associated with disordered eating behaviours

	Univariate Logistic Regression Analysis per Independent Variable		Forward Multivariate Stepwise Logistic Regression Analysis	
	OR (95% CI)	*P*	OR (95% CI)	*P*
BMI				
Underweight	1		–	–
Normal Weight	1.95 (1.14–3.33)	.015**	–	–
Overweight	3.29 (1.77–6.11)	<.001****	–	–
Perceived Weight				
Underweight	1		1	
Normal Weight	1.01 (0.48–2.12)	.973	0.79 (0.34–1.86)	.589
Overweight	5.42 (2.56–11.47)	<.001****	2.80 (1.05–7.48)	.041**
Weight Misconception				
Correct Weight Conception	1		–	–
Misconception of Underweight	0.75 (0.24–2.38)	.628	–	–
Misconception of Normal Weight	0.42 (0.22–0.80)	.008***	–	–
Misconception of Overweight	4.19 (2.27–7.74)	<.001****	–	–
Pressure from family	2.17 (1.75–2.70)	<.001****	–	–
Pressure from friends	2.48 (1.93–3.18)	<.001****	–	–
Pressure from dating	1.86 (1.48–2.34)	<.001****	–	–
Pressure from media	1.90 (1.53–2.36)	<.001****	–	–
Watch TV				
No	1		1	
Yes	1.80 (0.94–3.46)	.076*	2.40 (1.11–5.18)	.026**
Watch DVD				
No	1		–	–
Yes	1.67 (0.98–2.85)	.058*	–	–
Chat Online				
No	1		–	–
Yes	2.35 (1.21–4.57)	.011**	–	–
Play Online				
No	1		–	–
Yes	1.34 (0.84–2.14)	.23*	–	–
Body Satisfaction	0.92 (0.89–0.95)	<.001****	0.96 (0.93–0.99)	.019**
Positive Affect	0.96 (0.93–0.99)	.005***	–	–
Negative Affect	1.10 (1.06–1.14)	<.001****	1.07 (1.03–1.12)	<.001****

OR odds ratio, *CI* confidence interval
Pressure perceived sociocultural pressure to thin body and weight loss
$^*p \leqslant 0.25$, $^{**}p < 0.05$, $^{***}p < 0.01$, $^{****}p < 0.001$

programs. For instance, adolescents with inaccurate weight perception and body dissatisfaction could be a targeted group for eating problems' prevention programs. A school-based program could be carried out by helping students reduce weight-related teasing, improve self-esteem and body satisfaction.

This study has some limitations, however. Firstly, the cross-sectional nature of this study could cause difficulty for examining cause-and-effect relationships between DEB and associated factors. Secondly, self-report measures in this study may lead to under- or overestimation of prevalence of DEB and associated factors. For example, self-reported BMI may overestimate measured BMI at the low end of the BMI scale and underestimate measured BMI at the high end [56]. Thirdly, unknown response bias may exist that can reduce the reliability and validity of the study. For example, students may respond untruthfully or give answers that they felt the researchers wanted to hear. Fourthly, the limitation of the SCOFF questionnaire needs to be considered. Since it has shown low sensitivity in a validation population-based study [57]. Fifthly, information on students' reading level was not available. Since low reading levels may lead to misunderstanding of the questionnaires, the lack of data on reading levels may reduce the reliability of the study. Lastly, this study was school-based and thus access to participants was limited by those who were attending school. No accurate statistical information about school dropout rate was available. According to a literature review in 2015 [58], cumulative dropout rate in rural secondary schools was as high as 63%, while dropout rate in cities was less than 10%. There have been no statistics for students attending vocational and technical schools in China. This sample may be biased towards adolescents with higher education, therefore. The results would be more representative by conducting a population- or community-based study.

Conclusion

The present study has re-examined DEB among Chinese adolescents in a rural area. It suggests that DEB among rural Chinese adolescents are prevalent. Perceived weight, negative affect, body dissatisfaction and watching TV are significant associated factors for DEB among adolescents. This may provide valuable implications for prevention and intervention strategies in DEB. Furthermore, longitudinal population-based studies are recommended to produce a more comprehensive understanding of causes and risk factors of DEB among Chinese adolescents.

Additional files

Additional file 1: Table S1. Descriptive statistics of each item of SCOFF. (DOCX 11 kb)

Additional file 2: Table S2. Cross-tabulation of BMI and perceived weight categories among adolescents. (DOCX 11 kb)

Additional file 3: Table S3. Associations between misconception of over–/under-weight and DEB by gender. (DOCX 11 kb)

Additional file 4: Table S4. Multiple logistic regression model showing factors associated with disordered eating behaviours by coefficient and standard errors. (DOCX 13 kb)

Abbreviations

AUC: Area under the ROC curve; BMI: Body Mass Index; CI: Confidence intervals; DEB: Disordered eating behaviours; df: Degrees of freedom; M: Mean; N: Number; OR: Odds ratio; ROC curve: Receiver operating characteristics curve; sd: Standard deviation; SES: Socioeconomic status; SPSS: Statistical package for the social sciences; VIF: Variance inflation factor

Acknowledgements

The authors sincerely thank Li Chunying, Zhao Yanhua and Gong Chengzhi for help during research in the first middle school. The authors thank teachers' and students' in the first middle school for their cooperation.

Funding

This was a self-financed study.

Authors' contributions

TF made substantial contributions to study design, acquisition of data, analysis and interpretation of data, and writing the manuscript. DSA made substantial contributions to study design, analysis and interpretation of data, revising the manuscript critically for important intellectual content and general supervision of the research. Both authors read and approved the final manuscript.

Competing interests

The authors declare that they have no competing interests.

Author details

[1]University of Oslo, Oslo, Norway. [2]Norwegian Social Research (NOVA), Oslo and Akershus University College of Applied Sciences, Oslo, Norway.

References

1. Association AP. Diagnostic and statistical manual of mental disorders (DSM-5®): American Psychiatric Pub; 2013.
2. Shisslak CM, Crago M, Estes LS. The spectrum of eating disturbances. Int J Eat Disord. 1995;18(3):209–19.
3. Haedt AA, Keel PK. Comparing definitions of purging disorder on point prevalence and associations with external validators. Int J Eat Disord. 2010; 43(5):433–9.
4. Thomas JJ, Lee S, Becker AE. Updates in the epidemiology of eating disorders in Asia and the Pacific. Curr Opin Psychiatry. 2016;29(6):354–62.
5. Peat CM, Von Holle A, Watson H, Huang L, Thornton LM, Zhang B, et al. The association between internet and television access and disordered eating in a Chinese sample. Int J Eat Disord. 2015;48(6):663–9.
6. Lee S, Lee AM. Disordered eating in three communities of China: A comparative study of female high school students in Hong Kong, Shenzhen, and rural Hunan. Int J Eat Disord. 2000;27(3):317–27.
7. Chang Y-J, Lin W, Wong Y. Survey on eating disorder-related thoughts, behaviors, and their relationship with food intake and nutritional status in female high school students in Taiwan. J Am Coll Nutr. 2011;30(1):39–48.
8. Tsai M-R, Chang Y-J, Lien P-J. Survey on eating disorders related thoughts, behaviors and dietary intake in female junior high school students in Taiwan. Asia Pac J Clin Nutr. 2011;20(2):196.
9. Tam CK, Ng CF, Yu CM, Young BW. Disordered eating attitudes and behaviours among adolescents in Hong Kong: prevalence and correlates. J Paediatr Child Health. 2007;43(12):811–7.
10. Lu X, Zhang N. A survey of eating behaviors among 703 female university and middle schoole students in Nanjing. Chin Sch Health. 2008;29:637–8.
11. Liao Y, Liu T, Cheng Y, Wang J, Deng Y, Hao W, et al. Changes in eating attitudes, eating disorders and body weight in Chinese medical university students. Int J Soc Psychiatry. 2013;59(6):578–85.
12. Liang XM, Guo LT, Liu KZ. A cross-sectional investigation on eating disorders in 1486 female students from universities, senior high schools and junior high schools in Chengdu. Chin J Epidemiol. 2008;29(4):321–4.
13. Jackson T, Chen H. Risk factors for disordered eating during early and middle adolescence: A two year longitudinal study of mainland Chinese boys and girls. J Abnorm Child Psychol. 2014;42(5):791–802.
14. Wille D-PN, Hölling D-PH, Vloet TD, Ravens-Sieberer U. group Bs. Disordered eating behaviour and attitudes, associated psychopathology and health-related quality of life: results of the BELLA study. Eur Child Adolesc Psychiatry. 2008;17(1):82–91.
15. Croll J, Neumark-Sztainer D, Story M, Ireland M. Prevalence and risk and protective factors related to disordered eating behaviors among adolescents: relationship to gender and ethnicity. J Adolesc Health. 2002;31(2):166–75.
16. Stice E. Risk and maintenance factors for eating pathology: a meta-analytic review. Psychol Bull. 2002;128(5):825.
17. Chen H, Jackson T. Prevalence and sociodemographic correlates of eating disorder endorsements among adolescents and young adults from China. Eur Eat Disord Rev. 2008;16(5):375–85.
18. Jackson T, Chen H. Risk factors for disordered eating during early and middle adolescence: Prospective evidence from mainland Chinese boys and girls. J Abnorm Psychol. 2011;120(2):454.

19. Jackson T, Chen H. Predicting changes in eating disorder symptoms among Chinese adolescents: A 9-month prospective study. J Psychosom Res. 2008; 64(1):87–95.
20. Zhang J, Conwell Y, Zhou L, Jiang C. Culture, risk factors and suicide in rural China: a psychological autopsy case control study. Acta Psychiatr Scand. 2004;110(6):430–7.
21. Jackson T, Chen H. Identifying the eating disorder symptomatic in China: The role of sociocultural factors and culturally defined appearance concerns. J Psychosom Res. 2007;62(2):241–9.
22. Morgan JF, Reid F, Lacey JH. The SCOFF questionnaire: a new screening tool for eating disorders. West J Med. 2000;172(3):164.
23. Hill LS, Reid F, Morgan JF, Lacey JH. SCOFF, the development of an eating disorder screening questionnaire. Int J Eat Disord. 2010;43(4):344–51.
24. Leung SF, Lee KL, Lee SM, Leung SC, Hung WS, Lee WL, et al. Psychometric properties of the SCOFF questionnaire (Chinese version) for screening eating disorders in Hong Kong secondary school students: A cross-sectional study. Int J Nurs Stud. 2009;46(2):239–47.
25. Brener ND, McManus T, Galuska DA, Lowry R, Wechsler H. Reliability and validity of self-reported height and weight among high school students. J Adolesc Health. 2003;32(4):281–7.
26. Ma GS, Li YP, Hu XQ, Cui ZH, Yang XG, Chen CM. Report on childhood obesity in China (2). Verification of BMI classification reference for overweight and obesity in Chinese children and adolescents. Biomed Environ Sci. 2006;19(1):1–7.
27. Shepeliak N. Gender and cultural differences in body dissatisfaction and self-esteem [dissertation on the Internet].[New York(America)]: Pace University; 2006 [cited 2006 Aug 3]. Available from: http://digitalcommons.pace.edu/honorscollege_theses/35.
28. Watson D, Clark LA, Tellegen A. Development and validation of brief measures of positive and negative affect: the PANAS scales. J Pers Soc Psychol. 1988;54(6):1063.
29. Stice E, Bearman SK. Body-image and eating disturbances prospectively predict increases in depressive symptoms in adolescent girls: a growth curve analysis. Dev Psychol. 2001;37(5):597.
30. China NBoSo. Average salary by type of work in China 2014 [updated 2014]. Available from: http://data.stats.gov.cn/easyquery.htm?cn=C01.
31. Fu D, Wang J, Chen W, Bi Y. Disordered eating attitudes and behaviors and related mood states among female university students in Beijing. Chin Ment Health J. 2005;19(8):525-8.
32. Qian MLX. Dieting and eating disorder of female students in colleges in Beijing. Chin Ment Health J. 2002;16(11):5.
33. Fan Y, Duan Y, Hao L, Li Y, Yang Y. Status of eating disorders of high school students in seven cities of China. Chin J Health Educ. 2009;125:657–9.
34. Luck AJ, JF ML, Reid F, O'brien A, Brunton J, Price C, et al. The SCOFF questionnaire and clinical interview for eating disorders in general practice: comparative study. BMJ. 2002;325(7367):755–6.
35. Carlat DJ, Camargo CA. Review of bulimia nervosa in males. Am J Psychiatry. 1991;148(7):831–43.
36. Forbush K, Heatherton TF, Keel PK. Relationships between perfectionism and specific disordered eating behaviors. Int J Eat Disord. 2007;40(1):37–41.
37. Jacobi C, Hayward C, de Zwaan M, Kraemer HC, Agras WS. Coming to terms with risk factors for eating disorders: application of risk terminology and suggestions for a general taxonomy. Psychol Bull. 2004;130(1):19.
38. Eichen DM, Conner BT, Daly BP, Fauber RL. Weight perception, substance use, and disordered eating behaviors: Comparing normal weight and overweight high-school students. J Youth Adolesc. 2012;41(1):1–13.
39. Xie B, Chou C-P, Spruijt-Metz D, Reynolds K, Clark F, Palmer PH, et al. Weight perception and weight-related sociocultural and behavioral factors in Chinese adolescents. Prev Med. 2006;42(3):229–34.
40. Flett GL, Hewitt PL. Perfectionism and maladjustment: An overview of theoretical, definitional, and treatment issues. Perfectionism: Theory, research, and treatment. Washington, DC: American Psychological Association; 2002. p. 5–31.
41. Stice E, Hayward C, Cameron R, Killen J. Body image and eating related factors predict onset of depression in female adolescents. J Abnorm Psychol. 2000;109:438.
42. Racine SE, Keel PK, Burt SA, Sisk CL, Neale M, Boker S, et al. Exploring the relationship between negative urgency and dysregulated eating: Etiologic associations and the role of negative affect. J Abnorm Psychol. 2013;122(2):433.
43. Heatherton TF, Baumeister RF. Binge eating as escape from self-awareness. Psychol Bull. 1991;110(1):86.
44. Spoor ST, Bekker MH, Van Strien T, van Heck GL. Relations between negative affect, coping, and emotional eating. Appetite. 2007;48(3):368–76.
45. Harrison K, Cantor J. The relationship between media consumption and eating disorders. J Commun. 1997;47(1):40–67.
46. Becker AE, Burwell RA, Herzog DB, Hamburg P, Gilman SE. Eating behaviours and attitudes following prolonged exposure to television among ethnic Fijian adolescent girls. Br J Psychiatry. 2002;180(6):509–14.
47. Khan AN, Khalid S, Khan HI, Jabeen M. Impact of today's media on university student's body image in Pakistan: a conservative, developing country's perspective. BMC Public Health. 2011;11(1):379.
48. Yamamiya Y, Shroff H, Thompson JK. The tripartite influence model of body image and eating disturbance: A replication with a Japanese sample. Int J Eat Disord. 2008;41(1):88–91.
49. RYU HR, Lyle RM, MCCABE GP. Factors associated with weight concerns and unhealthy eating patterns among young Korean females. Eat Disord. 2003; 11(2):129–41.
50. Becker AE. Television, disordered eating, and young women in Fiji: Negotiating body image and identity during rapid social change. Cult Med Psychiatry. 2004,28(4):533–59.
51. Garfinkel PE, Garner D. M. Anorexia nervosa: A multidimensional perspective. New York: Brunner/Mazel; 1982.
52. Darby A, Hay P, Mond J, Rodgers B, Owen C. Disordered eating behaviours and cognitions in young women with obesity: relationship with psychological status. Int J Obes. 2007;31(5):876–82.
53. Rø Ø, Reas DL, Rosenvinge J. The impact of age and BMI on Eating Disorder Examination Questionnaire (EDE-Q) scores in a community sample. Eat Behav. 2012;13(2):158–61.
54. Li H, Prevatt F. Fears and related anxieties in Chinese high school students. Sch Psychol Int. 2008;29(1):89–104.
55. Abebe DS, Torgersen L, Lien L, Hafstad GS. Soest Tv. Predictors of disordered eating in adolescence and young adulthood: A population-based, longitudinal study of females and males in Norway. Int J Behav Dev. 2014;38(2):128–38.
56. Stommel M, Schoenborn CA. Accuracy and usefulness of BMI measures based on self-reported weight and height: findings from the NHANES & NHIS 2001-2006. BMC Public Health. 2009;9(1):421.
57. Solmi F, Hatch SL, Hotopf M, Treasure J, Micali N. Validation of the SCOFF questionnaire for eating disorders in a multiethnic general population sample. Int J Eat Disord. 2015;48(3):312–6.
58. Shi Y, Zhang L, Ma Y, Yi H, Liu C, Johnson N, et al. Dropping out of rural China's secondary schools: A mixed-methods analysis. China Q. 2015;224:1048–69.

HAPIFED: a Healthy APproach to weIght management and Food in Eating Disorders: a case series and manual development

Felipe Q. da Luz[1,2,3], Jessica Swinbourne[1], Amanda Sainsbury[1,2], Stephen Touyz[2], Marly Palavras[4], Angelica Claudino[4] and Phillipa Hay[5*]

Abstract

Background: There is a high prevalence of overweight or obesity in people with eating disorders. However, therapies for eating disorders, namely binge eating disorder and bulimia nervosa, do not address weight management. Conversely, weight loss treatments for people with overweight or obesity do not address psychological aspects related to eating disorders. Thus we developed a new treatment for overweight or obesity with comorbid binge eating disorder or bulimia nervosa, entitled HAPIFED (a **H**ealthy **AP**proach to weIght management and **F**ood in **E**ating **D**isorders). This paper describes HAPIFED and reports a case series examining its feasibility and acceptability.

Methods: Eleven participants with overweight or obesity and binge eating disorder or bulimia nervosa were treated with HAPIFED in two separate groups (with once or twice weekly meetings). Weight, body mass index (BMI) and eating disorder symptoms, as well as depression, anxiety and stress, were assessed at baseline and at the end of the 20-session HAPIFED intervention.

Results: Eight of the 11 participants completed the intervention, with diverse results. Six of the 8 participants who completed HAPIFED reduced their weight between baseline and the end of the intervention. Median scores on the Eating Disorder Examination Questionnaire for binge eating, restraint, and concerns about eating or weight and shape, were reduced in the group overall between baseline and the end of the intervention. One participant, who at baseline was inducing vomiting and misusing laxatives in an attempt to lose weight, reduced these behaviors by the end of the intervention. Three participants at baseline were undertaking episodes of compulsive exercise, and they reduced or stopped this behavior, but one participant commenced episodes of compulsive exercise by the end of the intervention. All participants who completed the intervention rated the suitability and success of HAPIFED as 7 or more out of 10 (0 = not at all suitable/successful; 10 = extremely suitable/successful).

Conclusion: This case series supports the feasibility and acceptability of HAPIFED as a potential new treatment for overweight or obesity with comorbid binge eating disorder or bulimia nervosa. Clinical trials are necessary to examine the efficacy and effectiveness of HAPIFED.

Keywords: Binge eating disorder, Bulimia nervosa, Obesity, Overweight, Integrated treatment

* Correspondence: p.hay@westernsydney.edu.au
[5]Centre for Health Research, School of Medicine, Western Sydney University, Locked Bag 1797, Penrith, NSW 2751, Australia
Full list of author information is available at the end of the article

Plain English Summary

Obesity is a growing problem, and its co-morbidity with disorders of binge eating is growing faster than either problem on its own. Persistent binge eating helps explain why usual 'diets' often fail. We have developed a new approach that integrates the best of current behavioral weight loss therapies with the leading psychological therapy for disorders of binge eating, namely cognitive behavior therapy. This new approach, named HAPIFED (a **H**ealthy **AP**proach to we**I**ght management and **F**ood in **E**ating **D**isorders), aims to help people to achieve sustained weight loss by reducing disordered eating and enhancing psychological wellbeing. This paper presents the outcome in a small number of people treated with this new approach. We also include a treatment manual (Additional file 1) that was refined after our initial experience with this new approach. The treatment was acceptable to the participants and appeared helpful in reducing weight and binge eating. However, there was no control group. Larger studies with a control group are needed to test this new approach.

Background

The occurrence of binge eating disorder (BED) or bulimia nervosa (BN) in individuals with overweight or obesity can range from 51.6% amongst people enrolling for weight loss programs [1] to 87.8% in clinic surveys [2]. Moreover, recent epidemiological evidence shows that while the independent prevalence of eating disorder behaviors – notably binge eating and very strict dieting/fasting – and obesity have increased steadily in the past 20 years, there were even higher increases in the prevalence of eating disorder behaviors with comorbid obesity [3]. There is good evidence supporting the use of psychological therapies for the treatment of BED [4–6] and BN [4, 7, 8], however these therapies are not designed to assist with weight loss in people with comorbid overweight or obesity. On the flip side, behavioral weight loss therapies (BWLTs) can reduce body weight and binge eating in individuals with obesity. One example of a BWLT is the LEARN program (Lifestyle Exercise Attitudes Relationships Nutrition) [9], which effectively reduced both excess weight and binge eating in participants of a clinical trial involving 16 sessions over a 24-week period [10]. Nonetheless, there are three important limitations with BWLTs. Firstly, weight regain after BWLTs is common [11], as is true of any weight loss intervention [12, 13]. A second limitation is that BWLTs were not designed to treat eating disorders psychopathology. A third limitation is that to our knowledge, BWLTs have not been studied in people with BN, however this is necessary due to the increase in the prevalence of overweight and obesity in patients with BN [14]. The development of interventions that result in sustainable reductions in excess body weight while also treating BED and BN would be of benefit, because individuals with overweight or obesity and comorbid eating disorders have been shown to benefit – in terms of weight management and reduction of binge eating – as a result of diet-induced weight loss [15–17]. Experts in the field usually recommend treating the eating disorder first, and attempts to reduce weight are recommended only once the eating behavior has stabilized [4]. However, an intervention simultaneously targeting eating disorders and weight loss would likely be appealing to the target population, because individuals with obesity and co-morbid eating disorders seek weight loss treatments in preference to treatments for disordered eating [18–22]. Furthermore, continued binge eating may contribute to the high relapse rates observed in weight loss treatments [23]. Thus, in this work we developed and tested an intervention that addresses the limitations of existing approaches for individuals with overweight or obesity and co-morbid BED or BN.

The specific aim of this research was to develop and pilot test a new multi-disciplinary mutualized therapy that integrates a BWLT for obesity [24, 25] with the leading psychotherapeutic intervention for eating disorders (cognitive behavior therapy – enhanced, or CBT-E) [4]. We named this new therapy HAPIFED (a **H**ealthy **AP**proach to we**I**ght management and **F**ood in **E**ating **D**isorders). This paper details the HAPIFED manual and describes a case series of individuals with overweight or obesity and comorbid eating disorders (BED or BN) who completed a pilot HAPIFED intervention. The feasibility and acceptability of HAPIFED were specifically examined.

Methods

Description of the treatment

HAPIFED is an extension of CBT-E for eating disorders [4], via integration into the program of BWLT [24, 25] and multidisciplinary education about nutrition and exercise (see Table 1). HAPIFED departs from the focus on avoiding or reversing restrictive dieting that is part of CBT-E, and instead emphasizes eating according to bodily hunger and satiety signals [24, 25], with the aim of promoting moderate weight loss. HAPIFED also promotes active behavior change through behavioral experiments that participants engage in between sessions.

In the current study, all HAPIFED sessions were group-based and were of 90-min' duration. The HAPIFED program involved a total of 20 group sessions with a Doctoral-level clinical psychologist and a Masters-level co-therapist that were trained and supervised to conduct HAPIFED. In addition to the standard CBT-E protocol [4], HAPIFED included conjoint sessions for nutritional counseling (one session lead by a dietitian), healthy exercise (one session lead by an exercise physiologist) and

Table 1 Comparison of characteristics of CBT-E, BWLT and HAPIFED

Treatment components Included	CBT-E [4]	BWLT [9]	HAPIFED [4]
Personalised eating disorder CBT formulation	Yes, for eating disorder only	No	#Yes, for eating disorder and overweight/obesity
Psycho-education	Yes, for eating disorder only	Yes, for overweight/obesity only	Yes, for eating disorder and overweight/obesity
Nutritional counselling	Yes, not dietician led	Yes, dietician led	Yes, dietician led
Behavioural monitoring	Yes	Yes	Yes (including appetite cues)
Socratic questioning (cognitive therapy)	Yes	No	Yes
Multidisciplinary	No	Yes	Yes
Session (number)	20	16	20*
Weight loss management included	No	Yes	Yes
Behavioural activation	No	Yes	Yes
"Healthy" exercise promoted	No	Yes	Yes
Emotion regulation skills	Yes	No	Yes

This includes the role of dietary restriction in contributing to binge eating. *In the modifications made to HAPIFED subsequent to this study, the session number has been increased to 30. This table was adapted from Palavras et al. *Trials*. 2015 [41]. CBT-E = Cognitive behaviour therapy – enhanced; BWLT = Behavioral Weight Loss Therapy; HAPIFED = a **H**ealthy **AP**proach to we**I**ght management and **F**ood in **E**ating **D**isorders

BWLT (two sessions). HAPIFED incorporated approaches that included healthy lifestyle changes and appetite awareness, with the aim of reducing eating as a means of regulating emotions. Approaches were informed by an understanding of the effects of starvation [24]. Monitoring and encouragement of food intake according to levels of physical hunger and satiety, consumption of vegetables and fruits, and moderate exercise continued throughout HAPIFED. Each stage of HAPIFED is described in greater detail below and summarized in Table 2, and the current version of the full manual is appended (Additional file 1).

Stages of treatment

In Stage 1 (Sessions 1–7), participants were provided with information about eating disorders, an introduction to the transdiagnostic cognitive-behavioral model of eating disorders [4], and information on non-hungry and hungry eating. In-session weighing and monitoring of eating behavior were also commenced. Monitoring forms were provided to participants, and therapists asked participants to take note – in real-time – of food/drinks consumed, their level of hunger and satiety before and after eating/drinking, the place where they ate/drank, any eating disorder behaviors (e.g. binge eating, inducing vomiting etc.), as well as any situation that could have influenced their eating behavior. In this stage, a session outlining hunger regulation as outlined previously [24] was conducted. Specific steps were outlined to inform patients on eating according to their hunger and satiety signals in order to promote weight loss. Additionally, participants were encouraged to eat 5 or more serves of vegetables and 2 or more serves of fruit per day, and to gradually build up to a level of physical activity that is considered necessary for the prevention of weight regain after weight loss (up to 10,000–12,000 steps per day or its equivalent in other activities) [26]. Stage 1 also included information sessions on general nutrition and exercise. Exercise was addressed using the Loughborough Eating Disorders Activity Program (LEAP) [27], with the goal of incorporating "healthy" exercise, instead of insufficient or compulsive exercise that is often seen in individuals with weight and eating disorders [28]. All in all, these instructions encouraged healthy lifestyle changes that are known to bring about modest weight loss [29, 30]. Therapists also discussed with participants how their relatives and friends could potentially support them with establishing and maintaining healthy eating habits. Lastly, in Stage 1, an activity on mindful eating was conducted with participants.

Stage 2 (Sessions 8–9) included the practice of relaxation activities (namely slow breathing and progressive muscle relaxation), followed by a review of participants' progress with the treatment. Stage 2 also included a personalization of the transdiagnostic cognitive-behavioral model of eating disorders [4]. During these sessions, participants were instructed to revisit aspects of the model, such as over-evaluation of weight and shape and their control, strict dieting, as well as events and associated mood change, and the influence of these parameters on their eating behaviors. Participants' monitoring of their eating behaviors (as described in Stage 1) was revised regularly. Participants were also reminded of the steps that were described in Stage 1 and that are helpful in promoting weight loss.

In Stage 3 (Sessions 10–17), monitoring of eating and weight control behaviors (including eating according to physical hunger and satiety signals, or binge eating,

Table 2 Brief summary of the main activities/goals of each session of the HAPIFED pilot study

STAGE 1	
Session 1	Information about the treatment: real-time recording of eating behavior, weighing and treatment goals. Psychoeducation on eating disorders and the transdiagnostic cognitive-behavioral model of eating disorders.
Session 2	Assessment of participants' real-time recording of their eating behavior and assessment of their eating habits. Psychoeducation on eating disorders continues. Information on behavioral weight loss therapy.
Session 3	Psychoeducation on the importance of regular eating. Information on physical activity including discussion on healthy and excessive exercise.
Session 4	Review of participants' understanding of the behavioral weight loss therapy. Discussion on purging and its negative consequences. Nutritional education.
Session 5	Discussion of factors that can lead to and maintain binge eating. Discussion on how feelings of fullness after eating can trigger eating disorder behaviors.
Session 6	Discussion of participants' engagement in physical activity. Review of participants' understanding of the difference between healthy and excessive exercising.
Session 7	Discussions on how significant others (e.g. family and friends) can be helpful in helping participants improve their eating behaviors. Mindful eating activity and discussion.
STAGE 2	
Session 8	Slow breathing activity. Review of participants' progress with the treatment and identification of potential barriers to change. Review and personalization of the transdiagnostic cognitive-behavioral model of eating disorders.
Session 9	Progressive muscle relaxation. Review of participants' progress with the treatment and identification of potential barriers to change. Review and personalization of the transdiagnostic cognitive-behavioral model of eating disorders.
STAGE 3	
Session 10	Discussion on the negative consequences of overvaluation of the importance of body shape and weight. Activity on helping participants identify parts of their bodies that they like.
Session 11	Discussion on the importance of other domains of self-evaluation not related to body shape or weight. Activity on identifying participants' positive characteristics (not related to body shape or weight).
Session 12	Discussion on the importance of participants engaging in self-nurturing activities in order to maintain a positive mindset and how this can be beneficial for their eating behavior. Discussion on excessive body shape checking or avoidance, and their negative consequences.
Session 13	Discussion on factors that can contribute to participants' "feeling fat". Discussion on ways of increasing self-confidence and its benefits.
Session 14	Therapists focus on Socratic questioning in order to help participants identify their cognitive distortions regarding "feeling fat" and other dysfunctional thoughts related to their eating disorder. Review and discussion of the transdiagnostic cognitive-behavioral model of eating disorders.
Session 15	Discussion on black/white (dichotomous) thinking and perfectionism related to eating disorders. Activity on helping participants reflect on the origins of overvaluation of the importance of body shape and weight.
Session 16	Discussion on the "eating disorders mindset". Discussion on how participants could create and maintain social connections with people that are supportive (and not detrimental) of their recovery from the eating disorder.
Session 17	Discussion on the negative effects of strict and unhealthy dietary restraint. Discussion on the negative consequences of overvaluation of the importance of body shape and weight, and the benefits of developing other core values and engagement in healthy activities related to these new values.
STAGE 4	
Session 18	Discussion of relapse prevention strategies. Discussion on strategies to respond in a healthy manner to event-related negative changes in eating. Activity on proactive problem solving.
Session 19	Discussion on residual binges by reviewing factors that may contribute to their maintenance. Discussion on strategies to respond in a healthy manner to mood-related negative changes in eating. Discussion on unhelpful thinking styles that contribute to the maintenance of eating disorders.
Session 20	Discussion on participants' plans for healthy eating after the treatment has finished, relapse prevention and new core values. End of treatment.

excessive body checking or avoidance, exercise, and the urge to compulsively over-exercise or engage in other compensatory behaviors in response to eating, such as vomiting) continued, with an additional emphasis on behavioral experiments. The behavioral experiments occurred by asking participants to engage between sessions in individualized therapeutic activities that help to oppose eating disorder behaviors (e.g. suggesting to a participant to engage in some alternatively pleasurable activity such as going for a walk in the park when feeling tempted to binge eat). Behavioral experiments were introduced in order to decrease eating disorder symptoms, establish regular meal patterns, and promote self-control. Other components that were introduced in Stage 3 were activities that helped participants to develop awareness of parts of their bodies and their personal characteristics that they like, self-nurturing activities, as well as activities to increase participants' confidence. Challenging the beliefs and attitudes that tend to reinforce eating disorder behaviors, such as valuing oneself according to one's weight and shape, and "all or nothing" (black/white, or dichotomous) thinking, were employed. The origins and negative consequences of self-evaluation that is excessively focused on weight, shape or eating, were discussed.

Stage 4 (Sessions 18–20) involved relapse prevention strategies specially focused on residual binge eating episodes triggered by adverse events and mood. Proactive problem-solving was also incorporated at this stage, in order to help participants deal with situations that trigger eating disorder behaviors. During this last stage, there was continuing reinforcement of participants' monitoring of their eating behaviors as well as other aspects of the BWLT (consumption of 5 or more serves of vegetables and 2 or more serves of fruit per day, and aiming to undertake physical activities to the equivalent of 10,000–12,000 steps per day).

Participants

Participants were recruited through online announcements in the staff news at the University of Sydney and via advertisement in a local newspaper (mX News Media, Surry Hills, New South Wales, Australia). Inclusion criteria were body mass index (BMI) > 27 kg/m^2, age > 18 years, and primary diagnosis of BED or BN according to the criteria in the Diagnostic and Statistical Manual of Mental Disorders, fifth edition (DSM-5) [31]. Exclusion criteria were diagnosis of psychosis, bipolar disorder or a high level of suicide risk. The Mini International Neuropsychiatric Interview (MINI) [32] was used to assess eating disorders and other mental health features related to the inclusion and exclusion criteria. Assessments were performed by a research assistant who also assessed other exclusion criteria, namely current use of weight loss medication, a history of bariatric surgery, or medical conditions (e.g. Prader-Willi syndrome, Cushing's syndrome) or use of medications (e.g. insulin, hydrocortisone) that interfere with appetite control. Those who met eligibility criteria were asked to provide written informed consent prior to participation in the trial.

Post-treatment assessment occurred at the end of the last treatment session (session 20). There were 11 participants commencing the treatment (see Fig. 1): six were treated in a group with twice-weekly sessions, and five were treated in a group with once weekly sessions. Of these, five out of six and three out of five, respectively, attended Session 20 of their respective groups. Of the 11 participants who commenced treatment, 3 withdrew after the first session, with 2 of these participants citing conflicting work schedules and 1 indicating that the program was not suitable for them. Of the 8 participants that attended Session 20 (the last treatment session), 7 participants attended 14 or more sessions (70% attendance), and 1 participant attended 12 out of 20 sessions (60% attendance). All of these 8 participants were female, aged from 28 to 69 years, with BMI from 28 to 36.8 kg/m^2 at treatment commencement. Six of these 8 participants were employed and 2 were unemployed. In addition to the diagnosis of BED or BN, some participants also met criteria for other mental health disorders, namely major depressive disorder (3 participants), post-traumatic stress disorder (2 participants), social phobia (2 participants), obsessive compulsive disorder (1 participant) and generalized anxiety disorder (1participant) (see Table 3).

Measures

The following measures were made at baseline and at the end of the treatment, unless stated otherwise.

Physical measures

Participants were weighed without shoes or any heavy clothes (e.g. jackets) before treatment and once a week throughout treatment, at the group session. Participants who attended the group with sessions twice a week were also weighed only once a week. As all sessions were held in the morning, participants were always weighed in the morning. Participants' height was measured only at the baseline assessment using a stadiometer, and this was used to calculate BMI before and after treatment.

Eating Disorder Examination Questionnaire (EDE-Q)

The EDE-Q is the self-report questionnaire based on the "gold standard" Eating Disorder Examination (EDE) for the assessment of eating disorder symptoms [33, 34].

Depression Anxiety and Stress Scale (DASS-21)

The 21-item DASS [35–37] is a self-report questionnaire that was used to assess symptoms of depression, anxiety and stress.

Mini International Neuropsychiatric Interview (MINI)

The MINI [32] is a structured diagnostic interview designed to assess the existence of mental disorders. It was used at baseline only, to assess participants' eating disorders and comorbidity with other psychiatric disorders. The MINI was conducted by a research assistant with each participant individually.

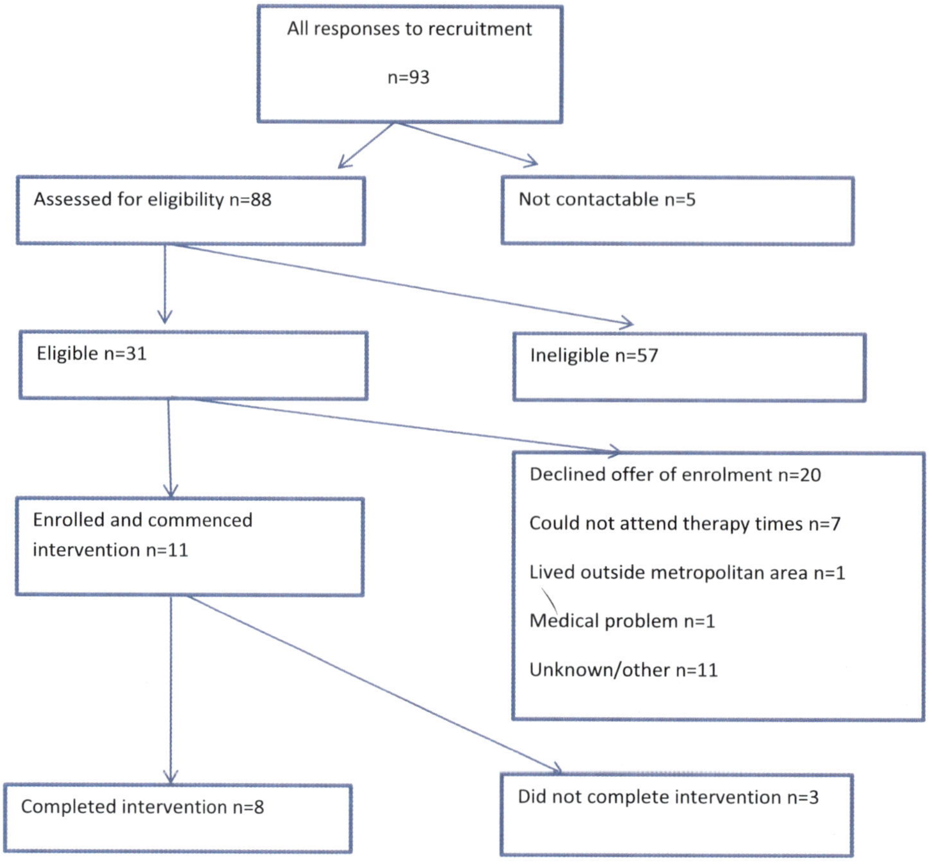

Fig. 1 Participant flow

This interview lasts for approximately 15 min and provides an accurate assessment of mental disorders as defined in the DSM-5 [31].

Participants' acceptance of the treatment

In order to examine the acceptability of the treatment, at the end of the program participants were asked to give their opinion, as a rating, on the suitability and success of the treatment. This took the form of a short questionnaire with the following two questions: How suitable do you think the treatment was for your problem? How successful do you think the treatment here has been? Participants' answers could range from 0 (not at all suitable/successful) to 10 (extremely suitable/successful). This rating occurred blinded to the therapists with participants rating this in a short questionnaire administered by a research assistant.

Statistical analysis

In order to have a quantitative analysis of the data, we chose to calculate medians and interquartile ranges rather than means and standard deviations, because means and standard deviations are subject to biasing when using small sample sizes, such as the small number of participants assessed in this study. Additionally, we reported only descriptive results and did not compute *p*-values.

Results

Weight

Participants' weight change from baseline to the end of the treatment included six participants that lost weight and two participants that gained weight (Table 3).

Eating disorder symptoms

Scores on the EDE-Q (Table 3) showed the following changes in eating disorder symptoms. Changes in restraint from baseline to end of treatment were diverse (four participants reduced restraint, one showed no change and three increased restraint). All of the eight participants reduced concerns about eating by the end of the treatment, in comparison to their baseline measures. Six and seven out of eight participants reduced concerns about weight and shape, respectively, at the end of the treatment in comparison to their baseline measures, and one participant increased concern about shape (albeit only by 0.1 points) by the end of the treatment in comparison to baseline measurement. Six

Table 3 Participants' psychiatric diagnosis, weight, BMI and eating disorder symptoms at baseline and at the end of the HAPIFED treatment

Participant ID	ED Diagnosis and comorbidities	Weight (kg)		Weight change (%)	BMI Kg/m^2		EDE-Q																			
							Restraint		Eating concerns		Weight concerns		Shape concerns		Global score		OBE		SBE		Vomit		Laxatives		Compulsive exercise	
		Pre	Post		Pre	Post	Pre	Post	Pre	Post	Pre	Post	Pre	Post	Pre	Post	Pre	Post	Pre	Post	Pre	Post	Pre	Post	Pre	Post
1	BN MDD SP OCD	110.9	111.7	+0.7%	40.7	41.0	1.4	2.2	4.6	4.4	5.4	5.2	5.7	5.4	4.2	4.3	12	6	4	5	0	0	0	0	0	0
2	BED	88.1	87.1	- 1.1%	33.5	33.1	2.0	2.6	5.2	1.6	4.6	4.6	4.9	4.0	4.2	3.2	10	10	10	08	0	0	0	0	0	0
3	BED MDD	85.1	85.8	+0.8%	32.8	33.1	3.6	2.4	1.6	0.8	2.8	1.6	3.3	2.0	2.8	1.7	4	14	0	0	0	0	0	0	0	0
4	BN	82.6	81.6	- 1.2%	28.5	28.2	3.2	0.6	4.4	1.0	4.2	2.4	5.1	3.5	4.2	1.8	18	2	8	4	20	3	28	3	4	0
5	BN	85.8	84.0	- 2.0%	31.9	31.2	1.8	1.8	3.4	2.4	5.6	3.2	5.8	4.3	4.1	2.9	5	3	10	0	0	0	0	0	15	3
6	BN MDD PTSD	106.4	104.3	- 1.9%	36.8	36.0	0.6	3.2	3.0	2.6	3.2	3.2	4.2	4.3	2.7	3.3	4	12	0	10	0	0	0	0	0	5
7	BED	106.3	105.1	- 1.1%	39.0	38.6	2.4	1.2	5.6	1.4	5.2	1.4	6.0	3.3	4.8	1.8	25	5	0	5	0	0	0	0	0	0
8	BN PTSD SP GAD	79.8	75.0	- 6%	33.2	31.2	6.0	3.6	4.2	0	4.4	2.4	5.7	2.2	5.0	2.0	15	0	10	0	0	0	0	0	15	0
Median change (IQ range)		−1.1 (−1.9 to −0.1)			−0.4 (−0.75 to 0)		−0.6 (−1.7 to 0.7)		−2.4 (−3.9 to −0.6)		−1.5 (−2.2 to −0.1)		−1.4 (−2.1 to −0.6)		−1.1 (−2.7 to −0.4)		−4.0 (−15.5 to 4.0)		−1.0 (−7.0 to 3.0)		0 (0 to 0)		0 (0 to 0)		0 (−8.0 to 0)	

HAPIFED a **H**ealthy **AP**proach to we**I**ght management and **F**ood in **E**ating **D**isorders, *ID* identification number, *ED* Eating disorder, *BMI* Body mass index, *EDE-Q* Eating Disorder Examination Questionnaire, *Pre* pre-treatment (weight at Session 1), *Post* post-treatment (weight at Session 20), *BN* Bulimia nervosa, *MDD* Major depressive disorder, *SP* Social phobia, *OCD* Obsessive-compulsive disorder, *BED* Binge eating disorder, *PTSD* Posttraumatic stress disorder, *GAD* Generalized anxiety disorder, *IQ* Interquartile, *OBE* Objective binge eating, *SBE* Subjective binge eating

participants reduced their global score on the EDE-Q, and two participants showed slightly increased scores (from 4.2 to 4.3 and from 2.7 to 3.3).

Diverse changes in frequency of binge eating episodes occurred from baseline to the end of the treatment. In regards to objective binge eating episodes (OBE), five participants showed reduced, one showed no change and two showed increased episodes at the end of treatment. In regards to subjective binge eating episodes (SBE), four showed reduced, one showed no change and three showed increased episodes from pre-treatment (baseline) to post-treatment.

Five participants met criteria for BN at baseline, however their compensatory behaviors were diverse. One participant reported inducing vomiting and using laxatives, two participants reported episodes of driven or compulsive exercise and two participants reported fasting as a means of trying to control their weight or shape. The following changes occurred in regards to compensatory behaviors (namely vomiting, use of laxatives and driven or compulsive exercise). The only participant who reported vomiting and using laxatives as a means of trying to control weight or shape reduced these behaviors from baseline to the end of the treatment. Three participants reported episodes of driven or compulsive exercise as a means of controlling weight or shape at baseline, and reduced this behavior by the end of the treatment. One participant showed onset of episodes of driven or compulsive exercise at the end of treatment. It is noteworthy that during the program, some participants appeared to have difficulty understanding the difference between healthy and driven or compulsive exercise, and this may have influenced the increase in driven or compulsive exercise seen in the participant mentioned above.

Symptoms of depression, anxiety and stress

The changes in scores of depression, anxiety and stress from baseline to the end of treatment are shown in Table 4. For symptoms of depression, six participants showed a reduction and two showed an increase from pre- to post-treatment assessments. In regards to symptoms of anxiety, five participants showed a reduction, one had no change and two showed increased symptoms from start to end of treatment. In regards to symptoms of stress, five showed reduced and three showed increased symptoms over the course of treatment.

Participants' acceptance of the treatment

All participants scored equal to or higher than seven out of ten in regards to how suitable and successful they rated the treatment (see Table 4).

Discussion

The aim of this study was to examine the feasibility and acceptability of a new treatment for eating disorders (BED or BN) with comorbid overweight or obesity, named HAPIFED, using a case series. Eight participants were assessed at baseline and at the end of treatment in regards to weight status, eating disorder symptoms, mental health status (symptoms of depression, anxiety and stress) and their perception of suitability and success of the treatment.

Overall the changes in regards to weight and eating disorder symptoms were positive. Six out of eight participants exhibited a reduction in weight and six out of eight participants showed a reduction in eating disorder symptoms (according to global EDE-Q scores) at the end of the intervention in comparison to their baseline measures. Some individuals showed increases in weight or eating disorder symptoms, namely restraint, binge

Table 4 Participants' symptoms of depression, anxiety and stress at baseline and in the end of the HAPIFED treatment, as well as participants' opinion about how suitable and successful the treatment was

Participant ID	DASS-21						Suitable treatment[a]	Successful treatment[a]
	Depression		Anxiety		Stress			
	Pre	Post	Pre	Post	Pre	Post		
1	24	20	10	14	14	18	9	8
2	22	14	16	12	20	10	7	7
3	2	10	0	0	0	6	10	8
4	16	4	2	0	12	4	10	9
5	8	0	12	4	26	4	10	8
6	28	22	16	18	24	26	7	8
7	18	14	8	4	22	16	8	8
8	38	42	18	12	28	26	10	10
Median change (IQ range)	−5.0 (−8.0 to 0)		−3.0 (−5.0 to 1.0)		−4.0 (−9.0 to 3.0)		8.5 (7.0 to 10.0)	8.0 (8.0 to 8.5)

HAPIFED a **H**ealthy **AP**proach to we**I**ght management and **F**ood in **E**ating **D**isorders, *ID* identification number, *DASS-21* Depression, Anxiety and Stress Scale (21-item), *Pre* pre-treatment (baseline), *Post* post-treatment (end of treatment), *IQ* Interquartile. [a] Scores ranged from 0 (not at all suitable/successful) to 10 (extremely suitable/successful)

eating, and compulsive exercise. In regards to the increase in restraint, it is noteworthy that while this is usually considered a symptom of eating disorders [4], for some individuals with overweight or obesity, a reasonable increase in restraint is actually positive and beneficial in assisting with weight loss [38]. During this pilot study we observed that some participants struggled to engage in healthy levels of exercise, as indicated by their engaging only in the opposite extremes of sedentary behavior or excessive exercise.

The results of this pilot study enabled further development of the therapy in order to potentially optimize it for individuals with BED or BN with comorbid overweight or obesity. Modifications to the therapy implemented in this pilot study were made and a new HAPIFED manual (Additional file 1) was developed. Modifications included the addition of a bi-weekly review of participants' progress with eating according to physical hunger and satiety signals, consumption of adequate quantities of vegetables and fruits, as well as engagement in regular physical activity, in order to promote weight loss. We also recommend in the new HAPIFED manual that in future use of the program, pedometers be provided to participants in order to facilitate monitoring and motivation for physical activity, with a clearer emphasis on healthy versus excessive or driven exercise. Moreover, 20 sessions were considered too few for effective treatment, and 30 sessions are recommended in the revised HAPIFED manual, because extended care in the context of recovery from binge eating disorders was found to predict better outcomes [39]. Participants found it onerous to attend HAPIFED sessions twice weekly during work hours. As such, once weekly and/or after work hours would likely have enabled more people to attend regularly. Additional changes to the revised HAPIFED manual involved increases in the number of nutritional education sessions and physical activity educations sessions, development of a formulation of disordered eating and weight gain, increased focus on problem solving, training in interpersonal skills, brainstorming with participants on helpful modifications to the home environment, restructuring of cognitive distortions, and an increased number of sessions on relapse prevention.

This study had some limitations. The number of cases presented is small and is thus not representative of patients with BED or BN and comorbid overweight or obesity. Participants were submitted to treatments with different frequency (once or twice a week), and this may have influenced the outcomes. Four out of eight cases presented met criteria for other comorbid psychiatric diagnoses in addition to BED or BN, and this may have influenced their response to treatment. Furthermore, this study does not provide information regarding causal effects of the treatment on weight, eating disorder symptoms or mental health due to its methodological design, not being a randomized controlled trial. Finally, symptoms were assessed with the self-report EDE-Q and not with the structured interview, namely the Eating Disorder Examination (EDE) [4]. Therefore, future randomized controlled trials to test the efficacy of HAPIFED in comparison to a control intervention are needed, along with effectiveness trials to test the effects of this new treatment in real world clinical practices. Future research examining the treatment of impulsivity in individuals with binge eating disorders [40] and comorbid overweight or obesity may also improve the understanding of additional treatment components to reduce binge eating.

Conclusion

In summary, changes in weight, eating disorder symptoms, mental health and acceptability of treatment were examined in a case series of participants with BED or BN with comorbid overweight or obesity treated with HAPIFED. This research showed that most participants in the case series had lower weight, reduced eating disorder symptoms and improved mental health status at the end of treatment in comparison to baseline. At the end of the intervention, all participants reported that HAPIFED was a suitable and successful treatment. This study supports the feasibility and acceptability of treating BED or BN with comorbid overweight or obesity. This study also enabled the development of an improved HAPIFED manual that requires evaluation in future clinical trials.

Abbreviations

BED: Binge eating disorder; BN: Bulimia nervosa; BWLT: Behavioral weight loss therapy; CAPES: Coordenação de aperfeiçoamento de pessoal de nível superior; CBT-E: Cognitive behavior therapy – enhanced; DASS-21: Depression anxiety and stress scale; DSM-5: Diagnostic and statistical manual of mental disorders, fifth edition; EDE: Eating disorder examination; EDE-Q: Eating disorder examination questionnaire; HAPIFED: Healthy APproach to weIght management and Food in Eating Disorders; LEAP: Loughborough eating disorders activity program; LEARN: Lifestyle exercise attitudes relationships nutrition; MINI: Mini international neuropsychiatric interview; NHMRC: National health and medical research council; OBE: Objective binge eating; SBE: Subjective binge eating

Acknowledgements

We thank Nasim Foroughi for assisting with the data collection.

Funding

This work was supported by the CAPES Foundation, Ministry of Education of Brazil, via scholarships to FQL, MAP and PH, and via the National Health and

Medical Research Council (NHMRC) of Australia via a Project Grant and Senior Research Fellowship to AS.

Authors' contributions
PH, ST, AS, JS and FQL participated in the design of the study. FQL, JS and AS were the therapists of the study. FQL, JS, PH and AS were lead authors of the HAPIFED manul (Attachmetn 1). MP and AC together with all the other authors analyzed data and were involved in writing the manuscript. All authors read and approved the final manuscript.

Competing interests
AS has received payment from Eli Lilly, the Pharmacy Guild of Australia, Novo Nordisk and the Dietitians Association of Australia for seminar presentation at conferences, and from Nestlé Nutrition for consulting services. She is also the author of The Don't Go Hungry Diet (Bantam, Australia and New Zealand, 2007) and Don't Go Hungry For Life (Bantam, Australia and New Zealand, 2011). SWT receives royalties from Hogrefe and Huber and McGraw-Hill Publishers, and has also been the recipient of an honorarium from Shire Pharmaceuticals. PH receives royalties from Hogrefe and Huber, McGraw-Hill and BioMedCentral publishers. PH and ST are co-Editors-in-Chief of Journal of Eating Disorders.

Author details
[1]The University of Sydney, The Boden Institute of Obesity, Nutrition, Exercise & Eating Disorders, Sydney Medical School, Charles Perkins Centre, Camperdown, NSW 2006, Australia. [2]The University of Sydney, School of Psychology, Faculty of Science, Camperdown, NSW 2006, Australia. [3]CAPES Foundation, Ministry of Education of Brazil, Brasília, DF 70040-020, Brazil. [4]Program of Orientation and Attention of Eating Disorders, Federal University of São Paulo, São Paulo, Brazil. [5]Centre for Health Research, School of Medicine, Western Sydney University, Locked Bag 1797, Penrith, NSW 2751, Australia.

References
1. Palavras MA, Kaio GH, Mari JJ, Claudino AM. A review of Latin American studies on binge eating disorder. Rev Bras Psiquiatr. 2011;33:s81–94.
2. Villarejo C, Fernandez-Aranda F, Jimenez-Murcia S, Penas-Lledo E, Granero R, Penelo E, et al. Lifetime obesity in patients with eating disorders: increasing prevalence, clinical and personality correlates. Eur Eat Disord Rev. 2012;20(3):250–4.
3. da Luz FQ, Sainsbury A, Mannan H, Touyz S, Mitchison D, Hay P. Prevalence of obesity and comorbid eating disorder behaviors in South Australia from 1995 to 2015. Int J Obes. 2017. doi:10.1038/ijo.2017.79.
4. Fairburn C. Cognitive behavior therapy and eating disorders. New York: Guilford; 2008.
5. Telch CF, Agras WS, Linehan MM. Dialectical behavior therapy for binge eating disorder. J Consult Clin Psychol. 2001;69(6):1061–5.
6. Robinson A. Integrative Response Therapy for Binge Eating Disorder. Cogn Behav Pract. 2013;20(1):93–105.
7. Safer DL, Telch CF, Agras WS. Dialectical behavior therapy for bulimia nervosa. Am J Psychiatry. 2001;158(4):632–4.
8. Glasofer DR, Devlin MJ. Cognitive Behavioral Therapy for Bulimia Nervosa. Psychotherapy. 2013;50(4):537–42.
9. Brownell KD. The LEARN program for weight management. American Health: Dallas, TX; 2000.
10. Grilo CM, Masheb RM, Wilson GT, Gueorguieva R, White MA. Cognitive-behavioral therapy, behavioral weight loss, and sequential treatment for obese patients with binge-eating disorder: a randomized controlled trial. J Consult Clin Psychol. 2011;79(5):675–85.
11. Smith CF, Wing RR. New directions in behavioral weight-loss programs. Diabetes Spectr. 2000;13(3):142.
12. Franz MJ, VanWormer JJ, Crain AL, Boucher JL, Histon T, Caplan W, et al. Weight-loss outcomes: a systematic review and meta-analysis of weight-loss clinical trials with a minimum 1-year follow-up. J Am Diet Assoc. 2007;107(10):1755–67.
13. Kushner RF, Sorensen KW. Prevention of Weight Regain Following Bariatric Surgery. Curr Obes Rep. 2015;4(2):198–206.
14. Bulik CM, Marcus MD, Zerwas S, Levine MD, La Via M. The Changing "Weightscape" of Bulimia Nervosa. Am J Psychiatry. 2012;169(10):1031–6.
15. Burton E, Stice E. Evaluation of a healthy-weight treatment program for bulimia nervosa: A preliminary randomized trial. Behav Res Ther. 2006;44(12):1727–38.
16. da Luz FQ, Hay P, Gibson AA, Touyz SW, Swinbourne JM, Roekenes JA, et al. Does severe dietary energy restriction increase binge eating in overweight or obese individuals? A systematic review. Obes Rev. 2015;16(8):652–65.
17. Ariel AH, Perri MG. Effect of dose of behavioral treatment for obesity on binge eating severity. Eat Behav. 2016;22:55–61.
18. Hay P, Claudino A. Evidence Based Tretment for the Eating Disorders. In: Agras S, editor. Oxford Handbook of Eating Disorders. New York: Oxford University Press; 2010. p. 252–79.
19. Evans EJ, Hay PJ, Mond J, Paxton SJ, Quirk F, Rodgers B, et al. Barriers to help-seeking in young women with eating disorders: a qualitative exploration in a longitudinal community survey. Eat Disord. 2011;19(3):270–85.
20. Mond J, Myers T, Crosby R, Hay P, Mitchell J. Bulimic Eating Disorders in Primary Care: Hidden Morbidity Still? J Clin Psychol Med Settings. 2010;17(1):56 63.
21. Hart LM, Granillo MT, Jorm AF, Paxton SJ. Unmet need for treatment in the eating disorders: a systematic review of eating disorder specific treatment seeking among community cases. Clin Psychol Rev. 2011;31(5):727–35.
22. Niego SH, Kofman MD, Weiss JJ, Geliebter A. Binge eating in the bariatric surgery population: A review of the literature. Int J Eat Disord. 2007;40(4):349–59.
23. Agras WS, Telch CF, Arnow B, Eldredge K, Marnell M. One-year follow-up of cognitive-behavioral therapy for obese individuals with binge eating disorder. J Consult Clin Psychol. 1997;65(2):343–7.
24. Sainsbury-Salis A. The don't go hungry diet. Bantam: Australia; 2007.
25. Sainsbury-Salis A. Don't go hungry for life. Bantam: Australia; 2011.
26. Donnelly JE, Blair SN, Jakicic JM, Manore MM, Rankin JW, Smith BK. American College of Sports Medicine Position Stand. Appropriate physical activity intervention strategies for weight loss and prevention of weight regain for adults. Med Sci Sports Exerc. 2009;41(2):459–71.
27. Young S, Rhodes P, Touyz S, Arcelus J, Meyer C, Pike K, et al. "Exercising hard or hardly exercising?" Objective and subjective measures of physical activity in patients with anorexia nervosa. J Eat Disord. 2015;3(Suppl 1):O55.
28. Holland LA, Brown TA, Keel PK. Defining features of unhealthy exercise associated with disordered eating and eating disorder diagnoses. Psychol Sport Exerc. 2014;15(1):116–23.
29. Dietitians Association of Australia. Best practice guidelines for the treatment of overweight and obesity in adults. Canberra: DAA; 2012.
30. National Health and Medical Research Council. Australian Dietary Guidelines. Canberra: National Health and Medical Research Council; 2013.
31. American Psychiatric Association. Diagnostic and statistical manual of mental disorders: fifth edition. 5th ed; 2013.
32. Sheehan DV, Lecrubier Y, Sheehan KH, Amorim P, Janavs J, Weiller E, et al. The Mini-International Neuropsychiatric Interview (M.I.N.I.): the development and validation of a structured diagnostic psychiatric interview for DSM-IV and ICD-10. J Clin Psychiatry. 1998;59(Suppl 20):22–33. quiz 4-57
33. Beglin SJ, Fairburn CG. Evaluation of a new instrument for the detection of eating disorders in community samples. Psychiatry Res. 1992;44(3):191–201.
34. Mond JM, Hay PJ, Rodgers B, Owen C, Beumont PJ. Validity of the Eating Disorder Examination Questionnaire (EDE-Q) in screening for eating disorders in community samples. Behav Res Ther. 2004;42(5):551–67.
35. Lovibond SH, Lovibond PF. Manual for the depression anxiety stress scales. 2 ed. Sydney: Psychology Foundation of Australia; 1995. ISBN 7334-1423-0.
36. Henry JD, Crawford JR. The short-form version of the Depression Anxiety Stress Scales (DASS-21): construct validity and normative data in a large non-clinical sample. Br J Clin Psychol/Br Psychol Soc. 2005;44(Pt 2):227–39.
37. Antony MM, Bieling PJ, Cox BJ, Enns MW, Swinson RP. Psychometric properties of the 42-item and 21-item versions of the Depression Anxiety Stress Scales in clinical groups and a community sample. Psychol Assess. 1998;10(2):176–81.
38. McGuire MT, Jeffery RW, French SA, Hannan PJ. The relationship between restraint and weight and weight-related behaviors among individuals in a community weight gain prevention trial. Int J Obes Relat Metab Disord. 2001;25(4):574.
39. Brauhardt A, de Zwaan M, Hilbert A. The therapeutic process in psychological treatments for eating disorders: A systematic review. Int J Eat Disord. 2014;47(6):565 84.

Role of gender in the treatment experiences of people with an eating disorder

Priyanka Thapliyal[1*], Phillipa Hay[1] and Janet Conti[2]

Abstract

Background: Traditionally perceived as a disorder of women, Eating Disorders (EDs) are known to have impacts on people irrespective of their gender. This study is designed to synthesise the available qualitative research studies to more broadly understand the diverse experiences of ED and their treatment, specifically in relationship to issues of gender.

Methods: The methodology involved a systematic search and quality appraisal of the literature published after 1980 using terms that aimed to represent the primary concepts of "role of gender" and "treatment experiences" and "eating disorders". Nine qualitative studies met the inclusion criteria. Meta-themes were inductively generated through a synthesis of data across themes from the relevant included papers.

Results: Analysis of data was constructed around three meta-themes, each with subthemes. The first meta-theme "Out of sight, out of mind" depicted the experience of gender issues that were marginalised in treatment. More specifically for transgender people, when gender issues were ignored by treatment providers, this frequently led to non-disclosure of their gender identity. Furthermore, men were less likely to be assessed for an eating disorder and within this context; diagnosis of an ED and referral to specialist treatment was frequently hindered. The second meta-theme "Lack of literacy among health care providers" focused on issues related to misdiagnosis of EDs, and the question of whether this was related to a lack of health literacy amongst health professionals. The final theme "Pathways into treatment that address stigma and other barriers" highlighted the need for the development of future treatment interventions address the complex social reality of the experiencing person, including questions of gender.

Conclusion: Gender issues impact upon the ED experience and require broader consideration in the development and evaluation of ED treatment interventions, including the further development of gender-informed interventions.

Keywords: Eating disorders, Gender, Treatment, Experiences

Plain English summary

This meta-synthesis aims to more richly understand issues related to gender in EDs and their treatment across relevant qualitative research studies. For the purpose, 9 qualitative research studies that represented concepts of "role of gender", "treatment experiences" and "eating disorders" were analysed and meta-themes across the studies were constructed.

Results are presented in the form of three meta-themes that consist of a number of subthemes. The first meta-theme highlighted the significance of gender issues in the ED experience and some of the impacts of this on the ED treatment experience, particularly for transgender people and men, The second meta-theme constructed the gap in addressing gender issues in treatments as a lack of health literacy amongst health providers in the assessment and treatment for an ED. Consistent with the perspectives

* Correspondence: p.thapliyal@westernsydney.edu.au
[1]Translational Health Research Institute (THRI), School of Medicine, Western Sydney University, Sydney, NSW, Australia
Full list of author information is available at the end of the article

of the experiencing person, the final meta-theme emphasised the need for a gender-informed and gender-specific treatment for eating disorders; this focus may ultimately result in better treatment outcomes.

Background

Eating disorders (EDs) are long known to be much more frequent in women than men and thus have been typically constructed as a woman's disorder. A meta-analysis [1] of community surveys reported the lifetime, 12-month, and 4-week prevalence of EDs among females as 4.2-, 2.6-, and 3.2- fold the corresponding prevalence in males. ED presentations differ across gender as men are more likely to report overeating whereas women are more likely to endorse loss of control while eating [2]. Women have been found to have higher scores for ED behaviours such as drive for thinness, bulimia and body dissatisfaction compared to men [3]. Results from a comparative study [4] have also suggested that men were more likely to present with less severe ED pathology (weight, shape and eating concerns and dietary restraint) than women. However, it is unclear whether this was due to a true difference in symptomatology or to biases inherent in the measures towards thinness rather than muscular/larger bodies, which are more favoured by men [5]. Cross-sectional studies also have found that men with EDs exhibit high rates of psychiatric co-morbidity [6–8], a later age of onset [9] and a history of premorbid overweight [10] compared to women with EDs.

Gender and the under identification of experiences as ED

Men are less likely to seek ED treatment services and are also less likely to be diagnosed with an ED if they do seek help for psychological difficulties. In Australia, only 13.6% of men with EDs have ever sought ED treatment [11]. Men have reported greater difficulty in disclosing ED problems as the admission of being a male with an ED does not fit with the societal perceptions of EDs as occurring only in women [12]. Other barriers identified for seeking professional treatment for an ED for both men and women have included stigma and feelings of shame and fear [13].One study found the main sex difference in the experience of stigma being the extent to which sufferers are made to feel "less of a women" versus 'less of a man' [14]. In addition to the findings that men are reluctant to seek help [15] there exists a lack of awareness among clinicians and under diagnosis of EDs in men [12, 16]. This is despite similar symptomatology [17, 18] similar treatment responses [19–21] and similar outcomes [17] among men and women with EDs.

There nevertheless exists a paucity of research comparing treatment outcomes between men and women. One of the few published studies that has compared men and women's responses to a day hospital treatment program reported no significant differences [22]. On the other hand, a study that compared the response rate to cognitive behavioural therapy between a group of 131 men and 131 women between 1998 and 2015 found that male ED patients who completed treatment (specifically BN and OSFED) were more likely to achieve full remission than women with the same diagnosis [23]. In contrast, men who engage in treatment with significantly low body weight, co-morbidity and little family support, like women, have been found to experience greater difficulty in achieving a positive treatment outcome [24].

A greater understanding of factors that contribute to difficulties in engaging in care for EDs is needed. Some have argued that interventions need to focus on male specific issues such as weight history, gender orientation, compulsive exercise, body image and dynamics of depression and shame [25]. Whilst there seems to is an argument for the provision of tailored treatment interventions for men [21], or "male-friendly" services [26], there is no substantive research or recommendations for other groups, such as transgender people. The perspectives and experiences of the person have also tended to be obscured by treatment outcome studies that focus on researcher selected variables including weight restoration and ED symptomatology. Additionally, there are notably few studies that have focussed on the treatment experiences of men [21] and even fewer that focus on the experiences of ED and their treatment for transgender individuals.

Furthermore, there is lack of consensus about relevance of gender per se in treatment [27]. This is despite the push for more of a focus on feminist issues in ED treatments by women [28] and the development of feminist therapies [29].

Current review

Despite a number of literature reviews [12, 26, 30, 31] on gender and EDs, there currently exists no meta-syntheses of qualitative research studies in this area. Additionally, there has been limited consideration within these reviews of the potentially diverse treatment experiences of people who identify as Lesbian, Gay, Bisexual, Transgender and Intersex (LGBTI). This paper is designed to address this gap through synthesising the available qualitative research on gender issues in EDs and their treatment and, through a richer understanding of the diversity of ED, inform future treatment interventions.

Methods

The present study employed meta-ethnography methodology [32] and followed ENTREQ statement (Enhancing Transparency in Reporting the synthesis of Qualitative research) [33]. ENTREQ consists of 21 items grouped into five main domains: introduction, methods and methodology, literature search and selection, appraisal, and synthesis of findings.

Databases and search methodology

A pre-planned systematic search of the literature was conducted in October and November, 2017 using the Electronic Database (Scopus), Psych Info, Pub Med (Medline), grey literature database (digital thesis) and generic web searches (Google Scholar). Subsequently, a hand-search of the reference lists from the selected papers was followed. The search terms are presented in Additional file 1: Search terms "Eating disorders" OR "Anorexia" OR "Bulimia" OR "Binge eating" AND "Treatment" OR "Therapy" AND "Gender" OR "Men" OR "Male" OR "Women" OR "Female" AND "Qualitative". These terms aimed to represent the primary concepts of "role of gender" and "treatment experiences" and "eating disorders" with PUBYEAR> 1980.

Study selection

The initial database search returned 45 abstracts after removing duplicates. This included studies that were located through hand-searching the reference lists in the potential papers and provided further key papers and so on iteratively to achieve a comprehensive range of articles. The primary researcher (PT) then screened the abstracts and excluded studies that did not address the research aim. The second stage of the study selection process involved examining each of the 45 articles and considering those that satisfied the following inclusion criteria:

1. Journal peer reviewed article, thesis and Pro Quest;
2. Articles published from1980–2017;
3. Participants had an ED according to current diagnostic schemes (Diagnostic & Statistical Manual of Mental Disorders (DSM) or International Statistical Classification of Disease and Related Health Problems (ICD));
4. The study addressed treatment experience and included any gender (male, female or transgender);
5. Used a qualitative study methodology;
6. The study addressed some aspects of the role of gender or sexual orientation in the treatment for people with an ED.

The increase in number of ED cases and publications occurred in early to mid-eighties and this coincided with establishment of the *International Journal of Eating Disorders* in 1982 and development of contemporary treatments. Therefore, articles published from 1980 were included.

Forty-five studies met these criteria 1–4 and included for further review by two researchers (PT and PH). Studies were excluded that were not qualitative and/or excluded gender issues in treatment (details are provided in the Additional file 2: Table S2). A summary of the excluded studies grouped by the primary reason of exclusion is provided in additional file 2: List of studies excluded from the review with exclusion reason. This process resulted in a total of 9 studies that met inclusion criteria into the metasynthesis. Figure 1 is the PRISMA flow diagram.

Coding of studies

Each of the 9 included studies were coded using a rating sheet according to the following characteristics: Author name, year published, country (location of study), age of participants (age range or mean), and sample size, gender (male, female, and transgender).

Analysis strategy

The studies employed a qualitative methodology to examine gender issues as relevant to the ED experience and its treatment. Studies were excluded if they were not published in English, not about EDs and were not a study of treatment experience. All the included studies were assessed for quality by all authors based on the Relevance, Appropriateness, Transparency and Soundness (RATS) [34] and Critical Appraisal Skills Programme (CASP) [35] criteria namely: 1) relevance, where the research question was explicit and linked to the existing knowledge base, 2) methods were described and justified, 3) there was transparency in regards to selection, recruitment, data collection, role of researchers/investigators, and ethics, and 4) there was rigor of analysis and reporting.

Meta-themes were inductively generated through a synthesis of data across themes from the included papers. We followed the method described in Shaw [36] where all three authors:

1) Read and coded the papers separately with the intention of generating diverse codes through these multiple perspectives with the aim of generating "thick description" ([37], pg.6) of the data and enhance the validity of data interpretation and analysis.
2) These diverse codes were collaboratively constructed, through group discussion and consensus on interpretative understanding [38] into a table of themes as reported in the primary paper (first-order constructs);
3) Together authors translated first-order constructs, that located the subjective experiences of participants across studies, into second order constructs or meta-themes that interpreted collective experiences within the context of a larger structure [39] and provided a comparison of concepts between studies; and

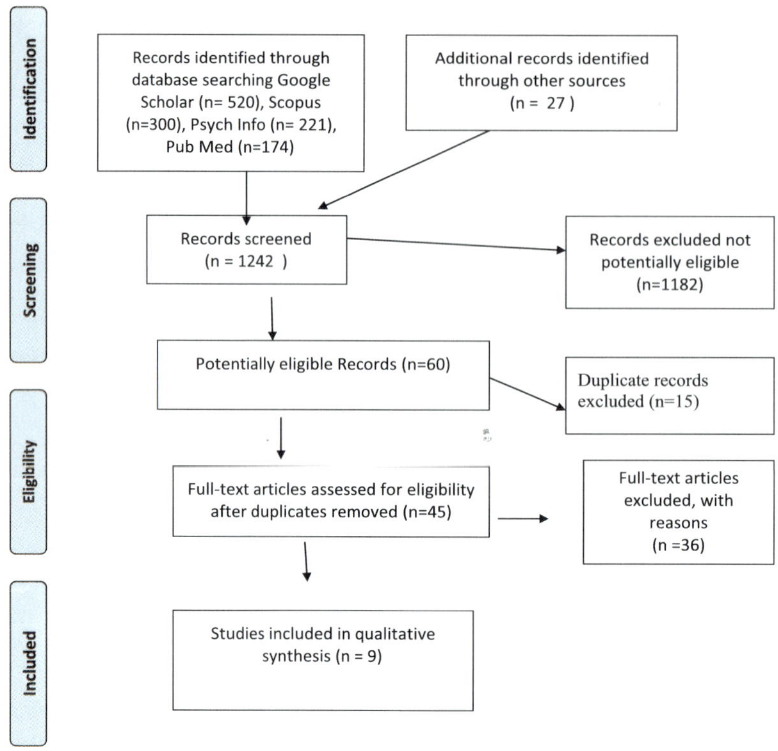

Fig. 1 Prisma Flow Diagram

4) Presented findings as a series of meta-themes supported by quotes from the original papers.

Results

Study characteristics

The characteristics of the qualitative studies about role of gender in the treatment experiences of ED are detailed in Table 1.

Methodologies employed

All the studies were conducted using known qualitative methods with the qualitative data being generated by interview (seven studies), self-written report (one study) and online questionnaire (one study).

Year and location of studies

The studies that met selection criteria were published between the years 1999 and 2017 with the majority conducted in the United Kingdom ($n = 5$) followed by Australia ($n = 2$) and United States ($n = 2$).

Sample and participant characteristics

Sample size

Apart from the online survey study [40] that had a larger sample size ($n = 84$), all the other qualitative studies had sample sizes between 5 to 15 participants.

Participant age

In all but one study [41], the age of participants were documented, with participants reported to be between 16 to 58 years.

Gender

In the studies included in the metasynthesis, 5 had only male participants [12, 26, 41–43], 3 had only female participants and focused on gender issues in treatment [28, 29, 44] and one study [40] explored the treatment experiences of transgender that had female, male and non-binary (not categorically either gender) participants.

Type of eating disorder

The studies comprised of participants diagnosed with AN ($n = 2$), AN, BN, BED and EDNOS ($n = 2$), AN, BN and BED ($n = 1$), only AN and BN ($n = 4$), and two studies did not specify participants' ED diagnosis.

Sexuality

The studies included people who identified as heterosexual, bisexual, Bi/pansexual female ($n = 2$), only female where sexual orientation was unknown ($n = 1$), only heterosexual male ($n = 2$), hetero and gay males ($n = 3$), and female, male and non-binary participants ($n = 1$).

Table 1 Characteristics of included studies

S.N	Author, Year, Country	Participants	Eating Disorder diagnoses	Study question	Study design and transparency	Rigor of analysis and reporting
1	Dearden &Mulgrew (2013), Australia	1) representatives of organizations, 2) practitioners, and 3) 5 men clients aged 22–58 years, long-standing ED issues of 4–19 years	Two with formal diagnosis of AN and BED	Research question clear based on systematic review	Purposive sampling, followed by snowballing, males were self-selected by invitation form health care organization, general-inductive approach, open-ended written self-report single author thematic analysis	Quality mixed, unclear role of researchers and ethics, analytic approach described, quotes used and triangulation (3 sources), saturation not reported, limitations discussed (small sample and use written survey)
2	Raisanen& Hunt (2014), UK	Men (*n* = 10) age 17-25 years 7-Heterosexual, 3- gay	AN, BN& EDNOS	Research question clear	Qualitative interviews.	Qualitative interpretative approach, use of quotes. Themes and subtheme discussed in detail.
3	Duffy et al. (2016), USA	Transgender (*n* = 84)	AN, BN, BED & EDNOS	Clear research question.	Online questionnaire	Inductive thematic analysis
4	Robinson et al. (2013), UK	Men (*n* = 8)	AN, BN & EDNOS	Research question clear.	Semi structured interviews.	Interpretative phenomenological analysis
5	Beer and Wren (2012) UK- England Specialist services	Men (*n* = 9), aged 21–42 years	All but most AN	Research question clear and based on systematic review	Interviews, interpretive phenomenological analysis, secondary report of unpublished thesis thus transparency unclear	Quality unclear, design and analytic approach not reported in publication (book chapter)
6	Drummond & Murray (2002), Australia	Men (*n* = 8) age unclear	AN& BN	Research question clear and based on systematic review	In-depth qualitative interview, provided for flexibility.	Inductive approach, repeated examination of the data to identify common themes in relation to the phenomenon being researched.
7	Su Holmes (2016) UK	Women (*n* = 15), age 19–45 years, 13-heterosexual, 1-bisexual, 1- bi/pansexual	AN, BN, BED	Clear research question	One-to-one interview	Thematic discourse analysis,
8	Holmes et al. (2017), UK	Women (*n* = 7), age 19–51 years	AN	Clear research question	Semi-structured individual interview	Thematic Discourse analysis
9	Crenshaw (1998) Thesis	Women (*N* = 10) aged 27–59 years of 40 participants in a feminist therapy	AN = 2, BN purging = 2, BN non purging = 6	Clear research question	Purposive sampling; Semi-structured individual interview	Constant comparative method of data analysis

AN anorexia nervosa, *BN* bulimia nervosa,*BED* Binge eating disorder

Table 2 Translation of themes related to gender issues in treatment for an ED across the primary papers

THEMES	SUB-THEMES	PAPER-ORIGIN
1. Out of sight out of mind	a) So bloomin' obvious: Gender issues "erased" or undervalued in treatment	Duffy et al., 2017 [40],Holmes, 2016 [28], Holmes, 2017 [44], Robinson et al., 2013 [12].
	b) Decision to not disclose gender identity (Transgender group)	Duffy et al., 2016 [40].
2. Health literacy regarding gender issues amongst health care providers	a) Under or misdiagnosed in men.	Dearden &Mulgrew, 2013 [26], Drummond, 2002 [41], Raisanen& Hunt, 2014 [43].
	b) Health literacy specific to gender	Duffy et al., 2017 [40], Holmes, 2016 [28], Robinson et al., 2013 [12]
	c) Does gender really matter in treatment?	Crenshaw [29], Drummond, 2002 [41], Holmes, 2017 [44], Holmes, 2016 [28], Robinson et al., 2013 [12]
3. Creating Pathways into treatment that address stigma and other barriers	a) A women's problem? Addressing stigma for men	De Beer & Wren [42], Holmes 2016 [28], Raisanen & Hunt, 2014 [43]
	b) Gender informed treatment	Crenshaw [29], Dearden & Mulgrew, 2013 [26], Duffy et al., 2016 [40], Holmes 2016 [28], Raisanen & Hunt, 2014 [43].

Synthesis of themes

The identified themes related to gender issues in treatments were translated and presented in Table 2. This metasynthesis generated a series of interconnected meta-themes that highlighted the interrelationship between gender and ED treatment experiences (Fig. 2). The implications for clinical practice are then discussed.

Theme 1: Out of sight out of mind

Questions of gender identity were consistently, although likely to be unintentionally, marginalised by treatment service providers for women [28], men [12] and transgender people [40]. These issues were argued, by those who identified them, as relevant and significant to the ED experience and their frequent omission in treatment was highlighted across the studies.

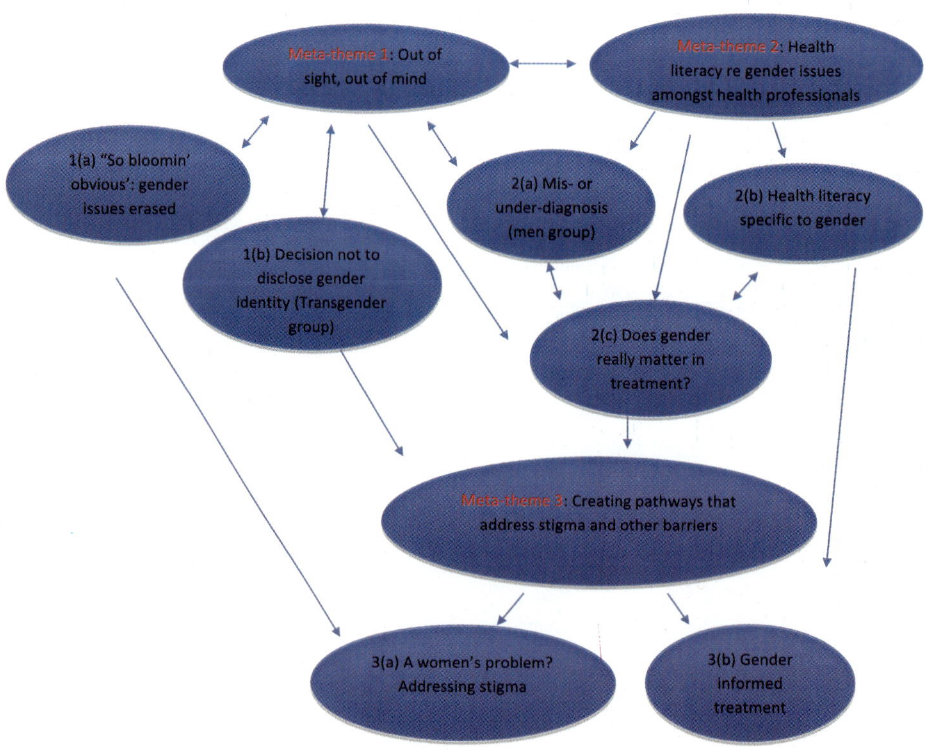

Fig. 2 Meta-themes of the experience of gender in eating disorder treatment

a) "So bloomin' obvious": Gender issues "erased" or undervalued in treatment

Of the two studies that explored gender issues for women [28, 44], the majority of women experienced gender as not specifically addressed in their treatment.

EXTRACT 1

> *"It would have been a whole lot easier if these [feminist] perspectives] were used in my treatment.... It always felt like me against the system which is really isolating...I would have seen that it wasn't just me being crazy.... The idea of eating disorders being a problem of society I actually found really reassuring.... rather than just you've gotta sort yourself out and fit back into the society structure that we've got."* (P8) [28].

For participant 8 [28] the lack of focus on gender issues in treatment was not neutral in its effects and contributed to a sense of isolation. Additionally, the absence of focus on the societal context within which EDs develop recruited her into the idea of herself as "just me being crazy" and an individualistic perspective of having to "sort yourself out".

Gender issues were positioned by the women as integral to their experience and they struggled to understand this omission in ED treatments, with one participant arguing that their inclusion should be *"so bloomin' obvious"* (P8) [28]. When addressed in therapy, however, there was a tendency in one study [45] to accommodate gender onto pre-existing treatment interventions and rendered these issues as only superficially addressed: *"I was just told, um, to try and not notice images of bodies. .. It's a bit ridiculous really."* (P9) [28].

In the only study with transgender people [40], around 60% ($n = 50$) of the participants disclosed their gender identity to their clinicians.

EXTRACT 2a

> *"Every primary care provider that I have interacted with simply sidesteps or ignores my articulation of a trans identity. It's as if the gesture never happened"* (P) [40].

EXTRACT 2b

> "Since *coming out, my identity has been erased in treatment because clinicians and therapists aren't comfortable with a transgender individual who does not identify as male or female*" (P) [40].

Participants who disclosed their gender identity to therapists were most frequently concerned by the experience of their gender identity being ignored by practitioners (for example, Extract 2a). The power of this therapist response was highlighted by another participant for whom an important dimension of their selfhood was erased (Extract 2b). An overarching theme in this study highlighted a parallel process between the struggle to "come out" as transgender and the struggle for health professionals to engage with this dimension of their selfhood. This ran counter to their yearning for acceptance of their gender identity from the health professionals who treated them.

One study into men's experiences of treatment found that being a solitary male in a group therapy intervention was experienced and interpreted as purposeful exclusion, even if this may not have been the intention of the facilitator or group members.

EXTRACT 3

> *"[As the only male] you become aware of people holding back or you being purposely excluded, or people saying 'maybe it's best if you're not in this group"* (Bill) [12].

Within this stretch of text, the impacts of being the solitary male was a sense of himself as an outsider to the group with his exclusion being understood as what's in the "best" interest of the group. This indicates the power of being marginalised through gender difference and that there are real effects of gender being ignored in ED treatment interventions.

b) Decision to not disclose gender identity (transgender group)

In the one study into transgender people's experience of ED treatment, 40% ($n = 28$) of the participants reported that they decided not to disclose their gender identity to treatment providers [40].

EXTRACT 4a

> *"I have stopped telling therapists, doctors, and groups that I don't identify as a woman. It makes them uncomfortable and alienates me. Lying is easier"* (P) [40].

EXTRACT 4b

> *"I did not discuss my issues around gender identity when I was in the treatment program, and I was treated as though I were a male patient"* (P) [40].

Centred on this "choice" not to disclose their gender identity was an effort to avoid stigma and discrimination that they had previously experienced through specific past negative experiences with health care providers, including that their disclosure "makes them [health professionals] feel uncomfortable" (P) [40], or simple logistics (e.g., treatment centre that treated only women). Furthermore, this concealment of their gender identity contributed to further marginalisation ("alienates me") [40], the sense of themselves as "lying" (Extract 4a) and their identity being assumed to be that of the gender with which they did not identify (Extract 4b).

Theme 2: Health literacy regarding gender issues amongst health care providers

Implicit in the frequent absence of gender issues being addressed in therapeutic contexts was the question of the health literacy. This meta-theme encompasses the varied contexts within which when the participants across these studies experienced gender issues as marginalised in their treatment.

a) Mis- or under diagnosis in men

Men's experiences of help-seeking indicated that to qualify for treatment and/or their struggles to be taken seriously, they needed to disclose and present with more serious patterns of ED symptomatology. Two of the 5 studies that researched men's treatment experiences, found that 30% [43] to40% [26] of men were misdiagnosed with either all the men [26],or a proportion of them [43], being given other mental health diagnoses that included mood disorders and anxiety.

EXTRACT 5a

"The one GP I went to, back when it was first starting and I was a somewhat healthy weight still, dismissed my concerns as" "just stress" (P) [26].

EXTRACT 5b

"You haven't got bulimia, you're just depressed, I'm probably quite confident in saying that was probably because you know I was male, you know I didn't live up to the stereotype of being young and female" (P3) [43].

These men argued that their distress was minimised and "dismissed" by the health professionals who treated them. Two of the 5 men in Dearden & Mulgrew's study [26] highlighted how their distress was measured by the extent of their weight loss (Extract 5a) and one man's experience of minimisation was signified through his use of quotation marks as "just stress".

Another participant's (Extract 5b) [43] experience of minimisation of their symptoms by a health professional was understood as him not fitting the gendered "stereotype" of the sort of person diagnosed with an ED. Instead his experience was positioned and minimised as "just depressed", which ruled out a more complex formulation that took into consideration the interrelationship between ED symptoms, under nutrition and low mood [46].

The issue of being under diagnosed contributed to further distress in 4 of 16 men across 2 studies [41, 43] through a heightening of ED symptomatology and associated health risks.

EXTRACT 6a

"I didn't like drinking too much overnight. [However,] I did start to restrict how much water I was having and stuff like that. Actually that idea came into my head from one of the psychiatrists down at the clinic. He asked me if I was restricting my fluid intake. And up until then, I wasn't restricting my fluid intake. I didn't really figure water was going to do too much. He basically told me straight out, "We can't do too much for you here at our clinic. I don't know why you were sent here...because you're not at the critical level." So I figured if I'm going to get to this critical level I may as well start restricting my water intake" (P) [41].

EXTRACT 6b

"I didn't say anything. I was dumbfounded, like I couldn't believe a physician would say something like that, because I just thought, you know, if there's nothing physically wrong but something's happening surely that means there's something psychological. And if it's to the extent where I've lost three stone at this point, you know, shouldn't I be getting referred. ... basically I walked outside and punched a wall and broke my knuckle because I was so angry. That he'd sat there and called me weak and blah blahblah [Precisely] to" "man up" and "Not be weak but be strong and deal with the problem" (P5) [43].

The perceived response of being denied treatment because of not being at a "critical level" (Extract 6a) was for one man an incitement to compete for the diagnosis and treatment through an escalation of ED behaviours that included restriction of fluids. The interaction between gender and the social practice of competitiveness may have profound implications for how men engage or do not engage in ED treatments. This may become increasingly dangerous in contexts where health care resources are scarce and health professionals inadvertently do not consider the possibility or extent of men's ED symptoms and distress. In extract 6a, the participant's negotiation of social power and status was to engage more intensively in ED practices to prove that he had an ED and qualified for treatment. On the other hand, participant 5's [43] response of anger signified an identity violation [47] that was built on a masculine discourse where ED behaviours in a man were assumed to be a sign of weakness rather than distress ("he called me weak"; Extract 6b).

The gendering of the ED experience builds further the assumption that the experience of an eating disorder, like gendered constructions of women [48], is a sign of weakness in men.

b) Health literacy specific to gender

The lack of health literacy amongst health care practitioners was reported across the diverse ED experiences of transgender [40] people, men [12] and women [28]. This sub-theme encapsulated the emotional distress experienced by the participants in these studies when gendered issues were ignored.

EXTRACT 7a

"I have been regularly misgendered over the course of my treatment. It's kind of par for the course by now, but it's still really upsetting. Even my therapist doesn't really understand how to use my pronouns and has referred me to as "girl" and "daughter", despite the fact that I've come out to her" (P) [40].

EXTRACT 7b

"I can't help but ...wonder how my life might have been different ...if anyone who saw me in the course of my treatment had been able to recognize my gender dysphoria and inform me that there were ways of addressing my extreme discomfort with my post-pubertal body other than starving myself " (P) [40].

EXTRACT 7d

"My therapist is excellent in her work, but it seems she does not understand non-binary genders" (P) [40].

In the only study that explored the experiences of transgender people [40], 11% ($n = 9$) described the experience of being misgendered by the clinicians who treated them, that was after disclosing their gender identity and 17% ($n = 14$) of participants argued that clinicians need to be more informed about gender-specific issues. This experience of being misgendered was not neutral in its effects and contributed to further distress (for example, extract 7a). The marginalisation of their transgender experiences and how these were inextricably intertwined with a range of other experiences, including the ED, was experienced as central in their struggles to progress in treatment (Extracts 7b). Even when a therapist was experienced as "excellent" (Extract 7c), there was evidence of an unexamined world view that was underpinned by the dominance of both heterosexual [49] and dualistic gender norms. The absence of scope to focus on their gender identity meant that an important aspect of their embodied subjectivity and lived experience (including their experience of an ED) was (inadvertently) obscured by therapeutic processes.

The difficulty in finding ED treatment services that had scope to tailor services to their needs and preferences, appeared to be a crucial problem for transgender participants in this study [40]. In addition, the lack of comprehensive ED treatment services ameliorated the efforts to seek holistic treatment for a trans, rape survivor (Extract 7c). Within this extract, this participant challenged and criticized the present health care system as having failed them.

Likewise, studies into women's ED experiences highlighted the implications of a lack of focus on gender issues on these women's sense of identity.

EXTRACT 8

"When I was reading [Orbach's Hunger Strike] . . . I tried bringing it up with the psychiatrist . . . She would just look at me like I was barmy – like that was more madness coming from me" . . . I was quite confused about it but it was like "OK let's put [the book] . . . away again: that's just [name removed] being crazy again . . ."(P5) [28]

The understanding of her ED experience within its societal context enabled participant 5 [28] to resist the pathologisation of herself as "crazy" and assisted her navigating her identity within a society that prizes the thin female body [50]. On the other hand, the dominance of an individualistic disorder discourse over a feminist perspective on EDs meant that when she raised feminist issues in treatment, she interpreted her therapist's response as confirming her identity "crazy" person.

Although the experience of body image issues and their relationship to the EDs maybe divergent across genders, a consistent theme across these experiences was a lack of recognition of gender issues in therapies that "pigeonhole" people into the dominant construction of an ED as a woman's disorder. This was identified as particularly problematic in the non-dominant groups of men and transgender people.

EXTRACT 9a

"The groups I'd be sitting in on ... on the ward with all the women ... body image things, they really didn't bear any relation to ... the issues that I had" (Bill) [12].

EXTRACT 9b

"In spite of my identification, "professionals" tend to fall back on essentialist notions: "you are a man." I am simply not interested in educating professionals about my gender or identity; it's the one space where I do not have the energy left to do so" (P) [40]

Despite these diverse experiences of one man (Extract 9a) and a transgender woman (Extract 9b), both these people faced a sense of alienation in their respective treatment interventions. Being the only male in a treatment program, Bill experienced himself as an outsider whose issues as a man were left unaddressed. The transgender participant (Extract 9b) who no longer identified as a man felt frustrated and abandoned by health professionals due to repetitive assumption of his identity as "a man".

c)Does gender really matter in treatment?

All the eight studies highlighted the diverse views of participants on whether gender issues mattered in treatment and there was a lack of consensus about its relevance for inclusion in the understanding of EDs and their treatment. For example, in one of the 5 studies on men [12], there were contradictory views both within and between the men's narratives about whether to raise the questions of gender in treatment or not.

EXTRACT 10a

"I think it's pretty much gender-excluding as a disorder. The reasons why you get there are probably slightly different but in the end all roads lead to Rome [...] the gender part is not significant but no ... too many people with like mind and that mind are deranged" (Bill) [12].

EXTRACT 10b

"Everyone is different, and ultimately every case is different, and although people suffering from bulimia have got the same thing, it's probably for a number of different reasons" (Greg) [12].

EXTRACT 10c

"Perpetuation of maintenance of their disorders as a feminized illness" (P) [41].

Bill [12] struggled between his experience as an outsider in a program focused on women's issues (extract 9a) and his position that "gender part is not significant" (extract 10a). In taking up an individualistic discourse to understand the ED experience ("the mind is deranged" (Bill, extract 10a) and "everyone is different" (Greg, extract 10b)), the men's accounts were troubled on the question of whether gender was relevant in the ED experience and its treatment. On the other hand, one out of 6 men in Drummond & Murray study's [41] critiqued ED treatments as being built on the construction of EDs as a "feminized illness" (extract 10c).

Underpinning these diverse perspectives is the tension between addressing the unique issues faced by an individual, yet also understanding an individual and their ED experience within their social context. Likewise, the women in these studies also expressed diverse opinions on whether gender was relevant or not to their experience of an ED and its treatment.

EXTRACT 11a

"People that aren't female get eating disorders as well... I think that men are also held to quite high standards when it comes to exercise and things like that so...I don't know; I don't think eating disorders really are a feminist issue" (P4) [44].

EXTRACT 11b

"Feminism.... I like the idea of women having rights... but then I think it can also go borderline, you know, women are great, men aren't... When we ask for more and more and more through feminism, I think it's borderline sexist" (P2) [44].

These women were also troubled by the question of whether EDs are appropriately understood and treated as a feminist issue (Extract 11a) or whether by arguing for their inclusion in treatment, they were being "sexist" themselves (Extracts11b). Although gendered constructions structure reality in ways that are frequently outside a person's conscious awareness, one woman positioned therapy that addressed these complex issues as tapping into "deeper... more subtle" dimensions of her lived experience, including *"expectations of men and women around food... and weight loss"* (Extract 11c) (P7) [44]. Although women in one study [33] experienced a notable absence of gender issues being addressed in their ED treatment, another study found women's experiences of a feminist group ED intervention to be beneficial [29] (see below Theme 3b for further detail). This intervention focused on consciousness raising [29] thereby drawing on feminist perspectives as transformative to the intervention, rather than merely accommodative of gender [45] as an "add on" to treatment as usual.

Theme 3: Creating pathways into treatment that address stigma and other barriers

a) A women's problem? Addressing stigma

The construction of eating disorders as a "women's disorder" presented a challenge to men's masculine identity, particularly as the feminising of a disorder is frequently associated with weakness (see subtheme 2a). Therefore, the application of this diagnostic category to men was troubled, particularly in one study [42] where the men reported feeling emasculated through stigma associated with an eating disorder diagnosis.

EXTRACT 12a

"It can feel like an admission of being less than male" (P) [42].

EXTRACT 12b

"I didn't like being pushed around." (P) [42].

The men's responses to an ED diagnosis and its treatment were diverse. Assumed in a masculine discourse area sense of authority, competitiveness and physical strength [51]. Therefore within this context it was hardly surprising that these men struggled to initiate help-seeking for an ED. Help-seeking may be understood as a fear of losing autonomy through giving up control and a mistrust of giving over control over to others [44]. An ED diagnosis was also associated with self-stigma of having a "female illness" as one of the men associated an ED with being *"less than male"* (Extract 12a) and, in the context of an inpatient admission, another man associated care with control and being "pushed around" in treatment (extract 12b). The experience of being "pushed around" in treatment sat in contrast to one woman's experiences of being "pushed" to talk about her experiences in the context of a feminist-informed intervention.

EXTRACT 13

"Right we need to talk about this, and [she] really pushed me...It...was then that somebody actually clicked that there was more going on than people had picked up on" (P3) [28].

This woman recounted how being "pushed" by her psychologist after a near successful suicide attempt was a helpful therapeutic intervention for her at that time. This juxtaposition between this man and woman's experiences highlights how gender is intertwined with power and the ways this is negotiated within the therapeutic relationship and the treatment intervention.

EXTRACT 14

"I did make contact with my doctor...I just said that what I had done and what had happened...he talked through the whole process [er] with me and explained that, the very serious side effects to doing that to myself. [Um]Obviously encouraging me you know for it not to continue doing what I can. [Er] He was happy to refer me [um] to someone, but you know that was my choice" (P7) [43].

Although the recurrent issues for men across the studies were either misdiagnosis or a lack of gender specific treatment, in the above extract one man talked about what was helpful in his treatment experience was clear communication and a sense of personal agency in choosing his treatment pathways.

b) Gender informed treatment

A recurrent theme across women's inpatient treatment experiences was the extent by which they experienced themselves as having voice in their treatment.

EXTRACT 15

"It is only once you learnt that kind of submissive femininity where you don't protest and you don't seek "excessive" independence or your own views that you'd be kind of granted the right to speak again, although on, like, really limited terms" (P12) [28].

This woman highlighted how although she was "granted the right to speak" (extract 15), this was on the terms of a submissive voice that was unquestioning of their treatment [28]. Implicit in this woman's experience is the power of the health professionals to confine the terms of speaking to the dominant treatment discourse. Experienced as authoritarian and harsh, one participant recounted how she was withheld one-to-one therapy until she reached a baseline weight [28].

In contrast, the study of a therapeutic intervention that aimed to raise a feminist consciousness was experienced as supportive with the 7 participants describing an initial anxiety which progressed to 'acceptance' and an enhanced sense of self-worth, empowerment and increased confidence.

EXTRACT 16a

"It's impacted my self-confidence as a woman. In fact, a lot of my life, I would say earlier in my life I would say to people, "don't respond to me as a woman, respond to me as a person." I'm responding to you not as a man but as a person. To try to neutralize the playing field. But the point is, I am a woman. And so coming to grips with that—and now I make no excuses for it. I claim it. And it takes two people to fight. It takes two people to really engage in an energetic disagreement, so I just don't engage. I state my point of view and . . .off we go. It's been—it really has helped me claim my space with pride. Not with fear, but pride". (Mary) [29].

EXTRACT 16b

"Well, I guess that the biggest thing that I learned in this program about feminist consciousness that I'm using is knowing that I can explore all possibilities of sexuality. That's the biggest thing that I have learned" (Katie) [29].

The women in this study described greater acceptance and ownership of both their gender and sexual orientation (extract 16a) as well as a sense of personal agency to choose their sexual orientation, which for Katie was experienced as a sense of expansiveness of her experiences of her sexuality (extract 16b). Leila spoke of choosing to have lesbian friends for the first time *"who've told me that I am attractive, sensual, and I don't feel put off or frightened by that."* [29] and Mary spoke of choosing to hold a friend's hand who happened to be a woman and not being afraid to do so.

The need for a gender-inclusive treatment was also argued by studies focused on men's ED treatment experiences, with a number of men arguing that the available information was either gender-blind or gender inappropriate.

EXTRACT 17a

"Like you hear the side effects of having an eating disorder on like women. Like they can become infertile and stuff like that, but I've never seen any for men." So I like went and was like, "look well what are they for men? 'Cos like that I could like have a side effect and wouldn't know" (P1) [43].

EXTRACT 17b

"The only information I got was [er] a scare sheet basically. It was this was going to happen if you keep going. Basically the big one that they circled was, 'Oh you won't be able to be sexually active' for men. And that was the biggest thing" (P5) [43].

EXTRACT 17c

"If we had more male friendly health care system more men might talk about eating issues" (P) [26].

For the 9 men in Raisanen & Hunt 's study [43], the lack of male-specific information had a range of impacts including the obscuring of information related to the physical effects of an ED for men (Extract 17a)or the antithesis of this, where this information was perceived by one man as a 'a scare sheet' that highlighted the possibility of impotence or lack of sex drive (extract 17b). The concerns regarding gender specific treatment for men ran across these studies with one respondent in the Dearden & Mulgrew study [26] who believed that having a more *"male friendly"* health care system might provide a context for men to voice their experiences (extract 17c) .

EXTRACT 18

"It would be reassuring to see programs which include some sort of reference to their inclusivity of transgender/gender-diverse people" (P) [44].

The lack of appropriate ED treatments led to a reluctance for some participants who identified as transgender to reach out for fear of receiving inadequate or inappropriate care. For others who sought help, the process of trying to identify an appropriate treatment centre was experienced as stressful. Nevertheless, there was still sense of optimism among the transgender participants to have inclusive treatment centres in future.

Discussion

The present study synthesised qualitative research studies in order to understand the experience of gender in the experience of an ED and its treatment across diverse groups of people. Meta-themes captured the consistent and diverse experiences across these studies where gender issues were experienced as marginalised by therapists, treatment teams and treatment interventions for women, transgender and men. When gender issues were addressed in ED treatments, participant experiences indicated that the dominant therapeutic response was to accommodate these issues onto pre-existing individualistic formulations and treatment models that construct the ED as a disorder that exists within [52]. That was, rather than gender issues being addressed in ways that transformed these approaches [53].

For the women, this was experienced as their voice being filtered and constrained within the treatment context where they were permitted to speak, but mainly within the terms of the dominant individualistic disorder discourse [45] thereby leaving intact this discourse intact [53]. Within these contexts, interventions were reported to only superficially address the real issues that these women faced that were intertwined with their gender. One study, however, found that when gender was directly addressed in a group context that the women experienced greater ownership and acceptance of their gender and sexuality and understood their experience in the context of a broader socio cultural perspective.

Men repeatedly spoke of under diagnosis and/or requiring severe ED symptom patterns to qualify for specialised ED treatments. Although this issue of symptom severity as a gateway to ED treatment services is not unique to men [51], there continues to exist a question as to whether men's ED symptoms and distress need to be more severe and of greater risk before they are noticed by health professionals as eligible for an ED diagnosis and its treatment [54]. This issue of requiring more intense levels of ED symptomatology for men with an EDs to be taken seriously for treatment, echoed the prevalent notion that EDs are a "female illness" [12, 17, 55]. Furthermore, the use of physical diagnostics, including BMI and body weight as central criteria for ED diagnosis and assessment of ED severity were perceived by a number of men as questionable. In addition to under diagnosis, when men's distress was located within the ED discourse, they frequently reported a lack of access to tailored treatment interventions that addressed the unique issues faced by men.

For transgender people, the lack of health literacy and tailored interventions that acknowledged their gender identity and how this interrelated with their ED experience was a substantive finding, albeit from the only research study in this population that met criteria for inclusion in this metasynthesis. Transgender participants faced presumptions and bewilderment from clinicians about how to respond to their gender identity and provide a holistic treatment intervention that could handle the complexity of the interrelationship between the ED experience and their identity as transgender. These experiences of transgender people that questioned the mental health professionals 'competence in treating individuals identifying as transgender was of major concern and resonated with previous studies [56, 57]. Participant's sought acknowledgement and acceptance of their gender identity by the therapist and reportedly felt ignored and marginalised. The predominance of negative responses is striking and participants' experiences indicated that this added to their distress. The non-disclosure of gender-identity could have influenced the treatment efficacy as concealment of one's identity impedes necessary aspects (for e.g., trust, mutual respect, and therapeutic alliance) of treatment [58].

Implicit in the marginalisation of gender issues in ED treatments was the meta-theme of an inadequacy of health literacy in relation to gender issues for women, men and transgender people. Across these studies there was consistent evidence that ignoring gender in therapeutic interventions was not neutral in its effects. However, the question of whether or not therapists should raise and address gender in treatments was also troubled as a number of participants across these studies also argued that treatments should not focus on EDs as a feminist issue [59]. There was only one woman who expressed a preference for a specific feminist approach and one (supportive) study of a therapy that was transformed by feminist issues in ED. This is likely to reflect deficiencies in the availability of and the evidence for, feminist therapies for ED [60]. Furthermore, it was noteworthy that for some women, being recruited into a submissive position during ED treatment acted to reinforce their perceptions that this is normal and appropriate for their gender.

The unique needs and preferences for men in ED treatments were highlighted where men talked of their isolation in programs that were tailored to predominantly treat women, lacked ED health information specific to EDs in men and frequently failed to focus on the unique issues of what it means for a man to be diagnosed with a problem that is predominantly associated with women. For example, in light of the conflicted assumptions embedded in a sense of masculine identity that contributes to gender role conflict and emasculation in men [55, 61] the ED experience may contribute to a flawed sense of identity that a man who experiences an ED is "less than a male" [42]. Studies reported [41, 62, 63] that men expressed a wish for their *maleness* to be recognised in treatment. Engagement is ED treatment was experienced as difficult for these men because of the unique challenges faced by them, particularly around societal gender norms and masculinity that are associated with control and physical strength [64]. Thus there is the risk of a dissonance in the therapeutic relationship where men are ambivalent about losing autonomy and the therapist's view of them as a patient in need of treatment. It is therefore, important to train practitioners in the identification of EDs in men, including in interventions that give men therapeutic opportunities to examine and question gender norms rather than inadvertently applying them to themselves (for example, through the practice of narrative therapy [65]). It is pertinent to know where and how men position themselves on masculine discourses related to strength, power and control because this has implications for whether and how they engage in ED treatment services. Providing room for men to have a voice in therapy and context to challenge some of these masculine norms around strength control and power that act as restraints to help-seeking may assist them to engage earlier and more meaningfully in treatment interventions for ED.

A concerning finding is that few of the participants in the studies reported having had a positive experience in relation to the ways gender was addressed in ED treatments. This gap in treatment services is likely to be a significant barrier to care and has significant implications for clinical practice and future research.

Implications for clinical practice and future research

The present metasynthesis raises a number of issues that are of clinical importance in the implementation of gender issues in ED treatments. A notable finding relates to the importance of increasing health literacy amongst health professionals, which resonates with other research that has identified the need to address the skills of health professionals in ED assessment and treatment interventions [66, 67]. There also exists a need to address some of the assumptions, biases and negative stereotypes, particularly in relation to people who identify as transgender. The significant absence of health professional literacy related to the unique issues faced by those who identify as transgender risked in heightening these peoples' distress. There exists a clear need for health professionals to address their often unintentional biases and negative assumptions about people who identify as transgender; for example, through reflective practice in supervision [68].

The interaction between gender and the social practice of competitiveness may have profound implications for how men engage or do not engage in ED treatments. This may become increasingly dangerous in contexts where health care resources are scarce and health professionals inadvertently do not understand the extent of men's symptoms and distress. Courtenay [69] has argued that "social practices that undermine men's health are often signifiers of masculinity and instruments that men use in the negotiation of social power and status" (p.1385). A proportion of the men across these studies negotiated social power and status through more intensively engaging in ED practices to prove to those who treated them, that they had an ED and to qualify for treatment. Previous studies in gender and ED have argued [55, 70, 71] that women have been the focus of information around EDs epidemiology, symptoms, assessment and treatment, leaving a paucity of relevant knowledge for other populations (males and transgender) to inform and tailor treatment interventions. One example is the use of physical diagnostics (e.g. body weight and Body Mass Index-BMI) for assessment and weight as the important criteria for ED diagnosis needs to be amended because of the risk this poses to the under-identification and diagnosis of EDs in men who typically lie on the elevated side because of body musculature.

Though the relationship between gender and ED is not a linear, causal relationship, the experience places an individual in certain sociocultural niche, where he/she may be more prone to specific risk factors such as media influences [72]. Therefore, recognition and tailored treatments of EDs that are transformed by gendered perspectives, including those of the non-dominant and vulnerable groups (men and transgender) needs more detailed consideration.

Limitations and strengths

A strength of this metasynthesis is the rigorous qualitative search for papers and with coding by 3 authors before deriving themes from the relevant studies. As metasynthesis do not have access to the original data, sources of bias in the original primary studies (for example misinterpretation of participants' voice) can introduce bias in the synthesis [73]. The reasonably smaller number of studies included in the review could be considered a limitation; however, this has allowed exploration and analysis of interview data in these papers in greater detail to enrich understanding. That there was only one study on ED experiences of transgender people highlights the extent of marginalisation of this group. Additionally, all the studies included were in English, leading to a possibility of missing other relevant articles published in non-English language.

Conclusion

This metasynthesis highlights the inadequacies in ED treatments in addressing issues related to gender amongst diverse gender populations. How identity is negotiated in the context of the lived experience of an ED is embodied and this metasynthesis provides evidence that gender plays a significant role in this embodiment. Therefore, the conscious or inadvertent ignoring or marginalising of questions and issues related to gender in ED treatments has and will continue to have inevitable implications for the processes and extent by which people engage in ED treatments. Greater consideration and inclusion of gendered perspectives in ED identification and the transformation of ED treatments holds scope for more significant and meaningful positive outcomes for those with lived experience.

Abbreviations

AN: Anorexia Nervosa; BED: Binge Eating Disorder; BMI: Body Mass Index; BN: Bulimia Nervosa; CASP: Critical Appraisal Skills Programme; DSM: Diagnostic and Statistical Manual of Mental Disorders; EDNOS: Eating Disorders Not Otherwise Specified; EDs: Eating Disorders; ENTREQ: Enhancing Transparency in Reporting the synthesis of Qualitative research; ICD: International Statistical Classification of Diseases and Related Health Problems; LGBTI: Lesbian, Gay, Bisexual, Transgender and Intersex; OS/UFED: Other Specified or Unspecified Eating Disorders; RATS: Relevance, Appropriateness, Transparency and Soundness

Funding

Financial support was provided to PT from Western Sydney University doctoral scholarship.

Authors' contributions

PT and PH drafted the search strategy and inclusion/exclusion criteria. The database search for final included papers was done by PT. All the 3 authors coded the articles separately and then analysis and interpretation was done together by the authors. The draft of the article is prepared by PT and critically revised by PH and JC. All the authors (PT, PH and JC) gave their approval to publish this article.

Competing interests

PH receives/has received sessional fees and lecture fees from the Australian Medical Council, Therapeutic Guidelines publication, and New South Wales Institute of Psychiatry and royalties/honoraria from Hogrefe and Huber, McGraw Hill Education, and Blackwell Scientific Publications, Biomed Central and PlosMedicine and she has received research grants from the NHMRC and ARC. She is Deputy Chair of the National Eating Disorders Collaboration

Steering Committee in Australia (2012-) and Member of the ICD-11 Working Group for Eating Disorders (2012-) and was Chair Clinical Practice Guidelines Project Working Group (Eating Disorders) of RANZCP (2012–2015). She has prepared a report under contract for Shire Pharmaceuticals in regard to Binge Eating Disorder (July 2017). All views in this paper are her own. She is Editor-in-Chief of this Journal.

Author details

[1]Translational Health Research Institute (THRI), School of Medicine, Western Sydney University, Sydney, NSW, Australia. [2]School of Social Sciences and Psychology, Western Sydney University, Sydney, NSW, Australia.

References

1. Qian J, Hu Q, Wan Y, Li T, Wu M, Ren Z, et al. Prevalence of eating disorders in the general population: a systematic review. Shanghai Arch Psychiatry. 2013;25:212.
2. Striegel-Moore RH, Rosselli F, Perrin N, DeBar L, Wilson GT, May A, Kraemer HC. Gender difference in the prevalence of eating disorder symptoms. Int J Eat Disord. 2009;42:471–4.
3. Garaigordobil M, Maganto C. Sexism and eating disorders: gender differences, changes with age, and relations between both constructs. Revista de Psicopatología y PsicologíaClínica. 2013;18:183–92.
4. Kinasz K, Accurso EC, Kass AE, Le Grange D. Does sex matter in the clinical presentation of eating disorders in youth? J Adolesc Health. 2016;58:410–6.
5. Smith KE, Mason TB, Murray SB, Griffiths S, Leonard RC, Wetterneck CT, Lavender JM. Male clinical norms and sex differences on the eating disorder inventory (EDI) and eating disorder examination questionnaire (EDE-Q). Int J Eat Disord. 2017;50:769–75.
6. Carlat DJ, Camargo CA Jr, Herzog DB. Eating disorders in males: a report on 135 patients. Am J Psychiatry. 1997;154:1127.
7. Striegel-Moore RH, Garvin V, Dohm FA, Rosenheck RA. Eating disorders in a national sample of hospitalized female and male veterans: detection rates and psychiatric comorbidity. Int J Eat Disord. 1999;25:405–14.
8. Raevuori A, Hoek HW, Susser E, Kaprio J, Rissanen A, Keski-Rahkonen A. Epidemiology of anorexia nervosa in men: a nationwide study of Finnish twins. PLoS One. 2009;4:e4402.
9. Mitchison D, Mond J. Epidemiology of eating disorders, eating disordered behaviour, and body image disturbance in males: a narrative review. Journal of Eating Disorders. 2015;3:20.
10. Gueguen J, Godart N, Chambry J, Brun-Eberentz A, Foulon C, Snezana M, Guelfi JD, Rouillon F, Falissard B, Huas C. Severe anorexia nervosa in men: comparison with severe AN in women and analysis of mortality. InternationalJournal of Eating Disorders. 2012;45:537–45.
11. Thapliyal P, Mitchison D, Miller C, Bowden J, Alejandro González-Chica D, Stocks N, Touyz S, Hay P. Comparison of mental health treatment status and use of antidepressants in men and women with eating disorders. Eating disorders. 2017;19:1–15.
12. Robinson KJ, Mountford VA, Sperlinger DJ. Being men with eating disorders: perspectives of male eating disorder service-users. J Health Psychol. 2013;18: 176–86.
13. Regan P, Cachelin FM, Minnick AM. Initial treatment seeking from professional health care providers for eating disorders: a review and synthesis of potential barriers to and facilitators of "first contact". Int J Eat Disord. 2017;50:190–209.
14. Griffiths S, Mond JM, Murray SB, Touyz S. The prevalence and adverse associations of stigmatization in people with eating disorders. Int J Eat Disord. 2015;48:767–74.
15. Ming TS, Lin Miao Shan P, Kuek Shu Cen A, Lian LE, Boon Swee Kim E. Men do get it: Eating disorders in males from an Asian perspective. ASEAN Journal of Psychiatry. 2014;15:1.
16. Thapliyal P, Mitchison D, Hay P. Insights into the experiences of treatment for an eating disorder in men: a qualitative study of autobiographies. Behav Sci. 2017;7(2):38.
17. Woodside DB, Garfinkel PE, Lin E, Goering P, Kaplan AS, Goldbloom DS, Kennedy SH. Comparisons of men with full or partial eating disorders, men without eating disorders, and women with eating disorders in the community. Am J Psychiatr. 2001;158:570–4.
18. Fairburn CG, Harrison PJ. Eating disorders. Lancet. 2003;361:407–16.
19. Fernández-Aranda F, Krug I, Jiménez-Murcia S, Granero R, Núñez A, Penelo E, Solano R, Treasure J. Male eating disorders and therapy: a controlled pilot study with one year follow-up. J Behav Ther Exp Psychiatry. 2009;40: 479–86.
20. Björk T, Wallin K, Pettersen G. Male experiences of life after recovery from an eating disorder. Eat Disord. 2012;20:460–8.
21. Weltzin TE, Cornella-Carlson T, Fitzpatrick ME, Kennington B, Bean P, Jefferies C. Treatment issues and outcomes for males with eating disorders. Eat Disord. 2012;20:444–59.
22. Woodside DB, Kaplan AS. Day hospital treatment in males with eating disorders—response and comparison to females. J Psychosom Res. 1994;38:471–5.
23. Agüera Z, Sánchez I, Granero R, Riesco N, Steward T, Martín-Romera V, Jiménez-Murcia S, Romero X, Caroleo M, Segura-García C, Menchon JM. Short-term treatment outcomes and dropout risk in men and women with eating disorders. Eur Eat Disord Rev. 2017;25:293–301.
24. Andersen A. Analysis of treatment experience and outcome from the Johns Hopkins eating disorders program 1975–1990. In: Halmi KA, editor. Psychobiology and treatment of anorexia nervosa and bulimia nervosa. Washington, D.C.: American psychiatric press; 1992. p. 93–124.
25. Strother E, Lemberg R, Stanford SC, Turberville D. Eating disorders in men: underdiagnosed, undertreated, and misunderstood. Eat Disord. 2012;20:346–55.
26. Dearden A, Mulgrew KE. Service provision for men with eating issues in Australia: an analysis of Organisations', Practitioners', and Men's experiences. Aust Soc Work. 2013;66:590–606.
27. Thapliyal P, Hay PJ. Treatment experiences of males with an eating disorder: a systematic review of qualitative studies. Translational Dev Psychiatry. 2014; 2(1):25552.
28. Holmes S. 'Blindness to the obvious'? Treatment experiences and feminist approaches to eating disorders. Feminism & Psychology. 2016;26:464–86.
29. Crenshaw CR. The experience of women who participated in an eating disorder treatment program designed to develop a feminist consciousness. Thesis 1998. Georgia State University (USA).
30. Olivardia R, Pope HG Jr, Mangweth B, Hudson JI. Eating disorders in college men. Am J Psychiatry. 1995;152:1279.
31. Lewinsohn PM, Seeley JR, Moerk KC, Striegel-Moore RH. Gender differences in eating disorder symptoms in young adults. InternationalJournalofEating Disorders. 2002;32:426–40.
32. Noblit GW, Hare RD. Meta-ethnography: Synthesizing qualitative studies: Sage; 1988.
33. Tong A, Flemming K, McInnes E, Oliver S, Craig J. Enhancing transparency in reporting the synthesis of qualitative research: ENTREQ. BMC Med Res Methodol. 2012;12:181.
34. Clark J. How to peer review a qualitative manuscript. Peer review in health sciences. 2003;2:219–35.
35. Singh J. Critical appraisal skills programme. Journal of pharmacology and Pharmacotherapeutics. 2013;4:76. Downloaded 20 November, 2017. http:// www.casp-uk.net//.
36. Shaw RL. Identifying and synthesizing qualitative literature. In: Harper D, Thompson AR, editors. Qualitative research methods in mental health and psychotherapy: A guide for students and practitioners. NY: John Wiley & Sons, Ltd; 2012. p. 9–22.
37. Geertz C. The interpretation of cultures. New York: Basic Books; 1973.
38. Saldana J. The coding manual for qualitative researchers. London: Sage; 2009.
39. Charmaz C. Grounded theory methods in social justice research. In: Denzin NK, Lincoln Y, editors. Handbook of qualitative research. 4th ed. Thousand oaks, CA: Sage; 2011. p. 359–80.
40. Duffy ME, Henkel KE, Earnshaw VA. Transgender clients' experiences of eating disorder treatment. Journal of LGBT Issues in Counseling. 2016;10(3): 136–49.
41. Drummond MJ. Men, body image, and eating disorders. International Journal of Men's Health. 2002;1:89.
42. de Beer Z, Wren B. Eating disorders in males. In: Fox J, Goss K, editors. Wiley series in clinical psychology. Eating and its disorders. New Jersey: Wiley-Blackwell; 2012. p. 427–41.

43. Räisänen U, Hunt K. The role of gendered constructions of eating disorders in delayed help-seeking in men: a qualitative interview study. BMJ Open. 2014;4:e004342.
44. Holmes S, Drake S, Odgers K, Wilson J. Feminist approaches to anorexia nervosa: a qualitative study of a treatment group. Journal of Eating Disorders. 2017;5:36.
45. Sampson EE. Identity politics: challenges to psychology's understanding. Am Psychol. 1993;48:1219–30.
46. Gamer DM, Rockert W, Olmsted MP, Johnson C, Coscina DV. Psychoeducational principles in the treatment of bulimia and anorexia nervosa. In: Handbook of psychotherapy for anorexia nervosa and bulimia; 1985. p. 513–72.
47. Phillips A. A stab at hinting. In: The Beast in the Nursery; 1998. p. 63–91.
48. Olivardia R, Pope HG Jr, Borowiecki JJ III, Cohane GH. Biceps and body image: the relationship between muscularity and self-esteem, depression, and eating disorder symptoms. Psychol Men Masculinity. 2004;5:112.
49. Hewson D. Heterosexual dominance in the world of therapy? Adelaide: Dulwich Centre Publications; 2002.
50. Steiner-Adair C, Purcell A. Approaches to mainstreaming eating disorders prevention. Eat Disord. 1996;4:294–309.
51. Rance N, Moller NP, Clarke V. 'Eating disorders are not about food, they're about life': client perspectives on anorexia nervosa treatment. J Health Psychol. 2017;22:582–94.
52. Neimeyer RA, Raskin J. Constructions of disorder. Washington, DC: American Psychological Association; 2000.
53. Sampson EE. Celebrating the other: a dialogic account of human nature. Boulder: Westview Press; 1993.
54. Cibralic S, Conti JE. "I'm more acknowledged": a qualitative exploration of Men's positioning of their body image, eating, and exercise concerns. J Constr Psychol. 2017;31(2):186-205.
55. Greenberg ST, Schoen EG. Males and eating disorders: gender-based therapy for eating disorder recovery. Prof Psychol Res Pract. 2008;39:464.
56. Carroll L, Gilroy PJ, Ryan J. Counseling transgendered, transsexual, and gender-variant clients. Journal of Counseling& Development. 2002;80:131–9.
57. Shipherd JC, Green KE, Abramovitz S. Transgender clients: identifying and minimizing barriers to mental health treatment. Journal of Gay & Lesbian Mental Health. 2010;14:94–108.
58. Williams M, Haverkamp BE. Identifying critical competencies for psychotherapeutic practice with eating disordered clients: a Delphi study. Eat Disord. 2010;18:91–109.
59. Rich E, editor Young women, feminist identities and neo-liberalism. Women's Studies International Forum; 2005: Pergamon: Elsevier.
60. Hay PJ, Claudino AM, Touyz S, Abd Elbaky G. Individual psychological therapy in the outpatient treatment of adults with anorexia nervosa. Cochrane Libr. 2015. CD003909-CD003909.
61. Gillberg IC, Råstam M, Gillberg C. Anorexia nervosa outcome: six-year controlled longitudinal study of 51 cases including a population cohort. J Am Acad Child Adolesc Psychiatry. 1994;33:729–39.
62. Copperman J. Eating disorders in the United Kingdom: review of the provision of health care services for men with eating disorders: eating disorders association Norwich; 2000.
63. White M. Maps of narrative practice. New York: WW Norton & Company; 2007.
64. Day K, Stump C, Carreon D. Confrontation and loss of control: masculinity and men's fear in public space. J Environ Psychol. 2003;23:311–22.
65. Drummond M. Life as a male'anorexic'. Australian Journal of Primary Health. 1999;5:80–9.
66. Diana E, Polimeni-Walker I. Treating individuals with eating disorders in family practice: a needs assessment. Eat Disord. 2004;12:293–301.
67. Hay P, Darby A, Mond J. Knowledge and beliefs about bulimia nervosa and its treatment: a comparative study of three disciplines. J Clin Psychol Med Settings. 2007;14:59–68.
68. Hewson D, Carroll, M. Reflective practice in Supervision 2016.
69. Courtenay WH. Constructions of masculinity and their influence on men's well-being: a theory of gender and health. Soc Sci Med. 2000;50:1385–401.
70. National Institute for Health and Clinical Excellence. Core Interventions in the Treatment and Management of Anorexia Nervosa, Bulimia Nervosa and Related Eating Disorders, CG9. London: National Institute for Health and Clinical Excellence.2004.
71. Malson H. The thin woman: feminism, post-structuralism and the social psychology of anorexia nervosa. New York: Routledge; 2003.
72. Kuna J, Sobow T. Sexual orientation and eating disorders: exploring the possible link. Psychiatria I Psychologia Kliniczna-journal of psychiatry and clinical. Psychology. 2017;17:189–94.
73. Bondas T, Hall EO. Challenges in approaching metasynthesis research. Qual Health Res. 2007;17:113–21.

13

The role of personality in body image dissatisfaction and disordered eating: discrepancies between men and women

L. P. MacNeill, L. A. Best* and L. L. Davis

Abstract

Background: Body image and disordered eating research has focused mostly on the female experience. The present study examined gender differences in the relationship between personality, disordered eating, and body image dissatisfaction.

Methods: Participants were 238 female and 85 male undergraduates (M_{age} = 20.52 years, SD = 4.22) at a Canadian university. Materials included a battery of self-report questionnaires pertaining to personality, body image, and disordered eating.

Results: As expected, females reported more body dissatisfaction and disordered eating than males. Personality factors were found to be significantly related to the experience of body dissatisfaction in both genders. Further, several personality traits significantly contributed to the prediction of male (high Neuroticism, low Conscientiousness) and female (high Neuroticism) body dissatisfaction beyond the influence of body mass index (BMI). Interestingly, and contrary to findings with female participants, personality traits were not significantly related to disordered eating scores in men. Among women, disordered eating scores were significantly predicted by high Neuroticism and Extraversion, and low Conscientiousness.

Conclusions: Although the relationship between disordered eating, body image dissatisfaction, and personality is well-documented in females, this relation may differ for males. The focus on male body image has been increasing in Western society; exploring how males view their bodies may be beneficial to researchers and clinicians alike.

Keywords: Gender differences, Big five personality factors, Disordered eating, Body image dissatisfaction

Plain English summary

Body image concerns do not discriminate; body dissatisfaction and its consequences are relevant to men and women of all ages. Traditionally, disordered eating and body image research has been conducted with populations of young females; therefore, more studies that concentrate on both male and female experiences of body dissatisfaction and disordered eating attitudes and behaviours are needed. Our study examined associations between body dissatisfaction, disordered eating, and personality in both genders. Several of our findings were consistent with those reported in previous studies: women reported higher levels of body dissatisfaction and disordered eating behaviours compared to men; and, personality traits were related to the experience of body dissatisfaction in both genders. Interestingly, the association between disordered eating and personality traits differed for men and women such that personality was associated with disordered eating in women, but not in men. These findings suggest that male and female experiences of body dissatisfaction and disordered eating may differ in important, clinically relevant ways. A further exploration of these differences could be beneficial in informing the prevention and treatment of body image concerns and disordered eating attitudes and behaviours in both genders.

Background

In the past, body image research had primarily investigated body dissatisfaction and disordered eating in

* Correspondence: lbest@unb.ca
Deparment of Psychology, University of New Brunswick, Saint John, 100 Tucker Park Road, P.O. Box 5050, Saint John, NB E2L 4L5, Canada

women; however, the focus on the study of men has been increasing. Perceptions of the ideal female body may be altered by frequent media exposure to thin female bodies [1–3], which may lead women to experience more body dissatisfaction and body focus than men [2–8]. Moreover, body dissatisfaction in women has been consistently associated with disordered eating behaviours and the development of eating disorders [9–12].

For women in particular, disordered eating behaviours have become so common in Western society that dieting is widely considered *normal* [13]. Given their pervasiveness in Western society, researchers have investigated various psychological correlates of body dissatisfaction and disordered eating in an attempt to elucidate their etiology. Gender differences have received less attention; however, gender differences among these relationships may indicate that male and female experiences of body dissatisfaction and disordered eating differ in important, clinically relevant ways. Previous literature suggests that significant variance in the development, onset, and maintenance of eating disorders can be attributed to personality factors [14, 15]. Therefore, the current study aimed to elucidate potential gender differences in the relationship between body dissatisfaction, disordered eating, and the five factor model (FFM) of personality in a sample of Canadian undergraduate students. One purpose of this study was to determine whether specific predictors of body dissatisfaction and disordered eating were similar for males and females. Although there is a growing body of research on body dissatisfaction and disordered eating attitudes among males, very little research has included examinations of how personality affects these outcomes. To our knowledge, this study is one of the few that examines the influence of personality after controlling for body mass index (BMI) in a sample of male participants.

Gender differences in body dissatisfaction and disordered eating

The importance of physical appearance is more emphasized for women, and appearance norms are especially pervasive in Western society where they are conveyed through a variety of social agents, most notably the mass media [16–18]. As a result, women often experience greater body focus and body dissatisfaction than men [3, 5, 8, 19]. Women consistently choose ideal figures that are smaller than their perceived current size [2, 3, 6–8], whereas males choose ideal body sizes that are similar to, or larger than, their perceived current size [8, 20, 21]. In a study by Grieve, Newton, Kelley, Miller, and Kerr [22], men chose an ideal male body that was more muscular than their current body and thought that women would prefer a more muscular male body than was actually preferred by females.

Further, it has been found that a participant's BMI category is related to gender differences in body dissatisfaction. The relationship between BMI and body dissatisfaction is linear for women, meaning women become more dissatisfied with their bodies as their BMI increases [23]. This relationship for men, however, is more complex; men with either a low BMI or a high BMI are typically more dissatisfied with their bodies than men who fall in a middle range of the BMI [2, 23]. Very thin women approach the thin societal ideal for women and would therefore be more satisfied with their appearance, whereas very thin men, would deviate farther from the muscular male ideal of Western society and would therefore show more dissatisfaction.

It is believed that gender differences in disordered eating are also influenced by the idealization of thinness for women in Western Society [24–26]. Anorexia Nervosa and Bulimia Nervosa are characterized by abnormal eating behaviours, weight regulation, and distorted attitudes and perceptions about body weight and shape, and both disorders are more common in women [10, 27, 28]. In a recent review of studies assessing eating disorder prevalence [29], results indicated that in two-stage design studies, point prevalence was most frequently described with overall eating disorder rates for females ranging from 0.5% [30] to 5.3% [31], and those for males ranging from 0.62% [32] to 0.64% [31]. Data reveals that females are more likely than males to respond to their weight concerns by engaging in dieting behaviours, binge eating, and purging behaviours [11, 33, 34]. In contrast, men are more likely to use other activities such as exercise for weight control and these are not captured or discussed in men's assessments [11, 33, 35–37].

In recent decades, the media focus on male bodies has been increasing, which may lead to a shift in male body perceptions (i.e., the muscular ideal) [7, 22, 38, 39]. With the increasing pressure on men to attain certain societal ideals, disordered eating in men could increase and this muscular ideal could minimize the gap in body image concerns and disordered eating among men and women [7].

Personality correlates of body dissatisfaction and disordered eating

Many researchers agree that five basic dimensions explain individual differences in personality [40, 41]. This model includes the personality traits Neuroticism, Extraversion, Openness to experience, Agreeableness, and Conscientiousness [42, 43]. Using the FFM, research with women has demonstrated that body image dissatisfaction and disordered eating are consistently related to higher levels of neuroticism and lower levels of extraversion [44–49].

For example, Dalley et al. [44] investigated the relationship between body image dissatisfaction and neuroticism, and found that neuroticism is a salient factor in the development of body dissatisfaction in women. Neuroticism has also been shown to intensify the negative effects of other variables, such as BMI [50, 51]. Likewise, Swami et al. [52] used the FFM to investigate the relationship between personality and body dissatisfaction and found that neuroticism was positively related to level of body dissatisfaction, while extraversion was negatively related to level of body dissatisfaction.

The FFM has also been applied to disordered eating attitudes and behaviours in women [45, 46]. For instance, Miller et al. [46] examined the relationship between neuroticism, extraversion, and eating attitudes in women and found that neuroticism was positively related to disordered eating, and extraversion was negatively related to disordered eating. Similarly, MacLaren and Best [45] investigated the relationship between personality and eating attitudes in female university students and found that disordered eating attitudes were related to high neuroticism and low extraversion. Although researchers have explored these personality correlates of eating attitudes and behaviours in women, to date, little research has been done examining these correlates in men who have similar levels of body dissatisfaction and disordered eating attitudes.

The current study

The current paper focuses on the examination of potential gender differences in the relationship between body dissatisfaction, eating attitudes, and the FFM of personality. Males have not been the typical focus of body image and disordered eating research and, to date, no published studies have investigated these factors in both genders. Although clinical samples are optimal, given the relatively low prevalence of ED in males and females, obtaining a sample with sufficient power would be very difficult. We feel this research is an important first step that can elucidate important correlates and inform future clinical research. Further, even in non-clinical populations, negative attitudes about body image and eating can lead to adverse mental and physical health outcomes and prevalence rates for disordered eating and body dissatisfaction are high in university samples.

Hypotheses:

1. Women would report greater levels of body dissatisfaction and disordered eating than men.
2. Personality scores would predict levels of disordered eating in women. Given the lack of literature, no specific prediction was made for men.
3. Personality scores would predict levels of body dissatisfaction in women. Given the lack of literature, no specific prediction was made for men.

Although our results are preliminary, the current report provides a broader and more dynamic picture of gender differences in body image and eating behaviours.

Methods

Participants

Participants ($N = 323$) were undergraduate students at a small Atlantic Canadian university enrolled in introductory-level psychology courses. Participants were recruited over a two-year time period through poster advertisements on campus, and were offered course credit for their participation. Participants took part in the study in small groups ranging in size from 2 to 20 individuals, depending on participant availability. During the data collection session, participants completed a battery of self-report questionnaires in random order, where a demographics sheet always appeared first. Written informed consent was given by all participants and all study procedures were approved by the University's Research Ethics Board.

Measures

Disordered eating

The Eating Attitudes Test-26 (EAT-26) [53] contains 26 self-report items and measures atypical behaviours and attitudes about eating (e.g., "Find myself preoccupied with food"; "Avoid eating when I am hungry"). These thoughts, feelings, and behaviours are scored on a 6-point Likert scale ranging from 1 (*always*) to 6 (*never*). Scores were reverse coded such that higher EAT-26 scores are indicative of higher levels of disordered eating. The EAT-26 has demonstrated good reliability and validity in males and females and is an adequate screening tool in non-clinical settings [53, 54]. In the current study, the internal reliability ranged from $\alpha = .88$ for females and $\alpha = .83$ for males.

Body image dissatisfaction

The Body Image Ideals Questionnaire (BIQ) [55] is a 22-item self-report questionnaire that measures the self-perceived discrepancy between internalized ideals and current body condition in regards to 11 physical characteristics: height; skin complexion; hair texture and thickness; facial features; muscle tone and definition; body proportions; weight; chest (or breast) size; physical strength; physical coordination; and, overall appearance (e.g., "My ideal muscle tone and definition is:"). In Part A, each physical characteristic is rated on a 4 point Likert scale ranging from 0 (*exactly as I am*) to 3 (*very unlike me*). In Part B, each physical characteristic is again rated in terms of importance (e.g., "How important to you is your ideal physical coordination?"). Each item is rated on a 4 point Likert scale ranging from 0 (*not important*) to 3 (*very important*). The mean of the item-by-item cross-products of discrepancy by importance ratings is then calculated for each participant. The BIQ has demonstrated good reliability and validity for women and men respectively [23, 55]. Further, in a study comparing several popular body dissatisfaction inventories, Davis, Lilly, Proctor, and Best [56] found that the BIQ correlated highly with other body dissatisfaction measures that are gender specific and, when used as a criterion variable in regression models, this scale accounted for the highest level of variability for males and females. The internal reliability of this scale was α = .80 for females and α = .82 for males in the current study.

Personality

Data sets from two samples were combined for the current purposes. The studies used one of two measures of personality; however, both measures reflect the FFM of personality and result in congruent factor scores. In the first study, the Neuroticism, Extraversion and Openness Personality Inventory-Revised (NEO-PI-R) [42, 43] was used. This measure is a 240-item self-report questionnaire that measures five factors of personality: Neuroticism; Extraversion; Openness to experience; Agreeableness; and, Conscientiousness. Each item is scored on a 5-point Likert scale ranging from 1 (*strongly disagree*) to 5 (*strongly agree*). This personality inventory is a reliable and valid self-report instrument used for assessing the personality domains of the Five-Factor Model in males and females [43]. In the second study, the NEO Five-Factor Inventory-3 (NEO-FFI-3) was administered. This measure is a 60-item self-report questionnaire that provides FFM Factor Scores [57]. The 60 FFI items are a sample of the 240 NEO-PI-R items but the instrument provides only summary factor scores rather than more specific facet level scores. There is a high correlation between the factor scores on these scales ($r > .75$) [43]. Each item is scored on a 5-point Likert scale ranging from 0 (*strongly agree*) to 4 (*strongly disagree*). The Adult version of this personality inventory is a reliable and valid self-report instrument for males and females [57]. For females in the current study, the internal reliabilities of the subscales were: α = .82 (Neuroticism); α = .80 (Extraversion); α = .64 (Openness to experiences); α = .78 (Agreeableness); and, α = .81 (Conscientiousness). The lower reliability of the Openness subscale is somewhat concerning but this factor was not a variable of interest in the regression analyses (this scale has consistently lower internal reliability than other factors). For males in the current study, the internal reliabilities of the subscales were: α = .87 (Neuroticism); α = .82 (Extraversion); α = .74 (Openness to experiences); α = .78 (Agreeableness); and, α = .84 (Conscientiousness).

Results

Sample characteristics

After screening the data set and removing univariate and multivariate outliers, the sample consisted of 323 university students (73.7% female), and the age of participants ranged from 17 to 47 years ($M = 20.52$, $SD = 4.22$). Among female participants, self-reported height ranged from 58 in. to 74 in. ($M = 65.06$, $SD = 2.86$) and self-reported weight ranged from 81 lb to 350 lb ($M = 144.66$, $SD = 33.01$), resulting in an average self-reported BMI of 24.02 kg/m^2 ($SD = 4.97$). The self-reported height of male participants ranged from 59 in. to 80 in. ($M = 71.14$, $SD = 3.31$) and self-reported weight ranged from 110 lb to 320 lb ($M = 177.79$, $SD = 33.85$), resulting in an average self-reported BMI of 24.66 kg/m^2 ($SD = 4.21$). The difference between the self-reported BMIs of women and men was not statistically significant. In addition, the correlation between age and BMI was not statistically significant, $r(321) = .11$, $p = .07$. Although previous researchers have reported that the relation between BMI and body dissatisfaction was nonlinear for male participants, in the current study a linear model best described the associations between BMI and dissatisfaction for both genders.

As expected, women reported greater levels of body dissatisfaction and disordered eating than men, with women scoring higher on the EAT-26, $t(319) = 2.95$, $p = .003$, $d = 0.38$, and BIQ, $t(321) = 3.45$, $p = .001$, $d = 0.44$. Gender differences were further explored by examining differences in personality traits. With regard to personality traits, women reported higher levels of both Neuroticism, $t(321) = 5.34$, $p < .001$, $d = 0.68$, and Agreeableness, $t(321) = 3.86$, $p < .001$, $d = 0.49$. See Table 1 for means and standard deviations for all measures.

Table 1 Means and standard deviations for all measures

	Females		Males	
	M	*SD*	*M*	*SD*
BMI	24.02	4.97	24.66	4.21
EAT-Total	14.87	12.05	10.69	8.13
BIQ	2.19	1.44	1.57	1.37
Neuroticism	2.25	0.56	1.87	0.58
Extraversion	2.36	0.54	2.45	0.52
Openness	2.48	0.47	2.47	0.45
Agreeableness	2.58	0.48	2.35	0.45
Conscientiousness	2.37	0.49	2.36	0.46

Correlational relationships

Correlational relationships were examined first to determine which personality factors were most strongly related to body dissatisfaction and disordered eating in women and men. As suggested by previous research, among women, there was a statistically significant positive correlation between total EAT-26 scores and Neuroticism scores as well as statistically significant negative correlations between total EAT-26 scores and Agreeableness and Conscientiousness scores. Interestingly and contrary to consistent findings with women, levels of Neuroticism were not significantly related to total EAT-26 scores in men. In fact, none of the personality factors were significantly correlated with total EAT-26 scores in men (see Table 2).

Further, among women, there was a statistically significant positive correlation between BIQ and Neuroticism scores as well as statistically significant negative correlations between BIQ and Agreeableness and Conscientiousness scores. In men, there was a statistically significant positive correlation between BIQ scores and Neuroticism scores as well as negative correlations between BIQ scores and Extraversion and Conscientiousness scores. Interestingly, for women, BIQ scores were significantly positively correlated with EAT-26 scores but among men, BIQ scores were not significantly correlated with total EAT-26 scores (see Table 2).

Prediction of body dissatisfaction

In order to determine if the sample size was adequate, we conducted a power analysis (using G-Power). Assuming a small effect size, power analysis results indicated that 84 participants would be necessary to achieve a power of .80, suggesting that analyses could be conducted separately for males and females. Prior to analysis, the dataset was screened for model assumptions and no violations were detected. Given that a nonlinear relation between BMI and body dissatisfaction has been reported, we examined linearity statistics as well as scatterplots between predictor and criterion variables with loess curves fitted for males and females. Overall, in assessing both BIQ and EAT-26 scores, any departures from linearity were quite small. Further, linear transformations did not improve the predictability of the models and, as such, for ease of interpretation and comparison, we used hierarchical linear regressions to compare gender differences in dissatisfaction and eating behaviours.

A series of four hierarchical multiple regression analyses were performed to assess the role of personality in the prediction of body dissatisfaction and disordered eating in women and men, separately. For both men and women, BIQ scores were entered as the criterion variable in the first analysis. BMI was entered on the first step to control for reported current body size. The five NEO factor scores were entered on the second step. Although many researchers choose to include gender as a Block 1 variable or as a moderating variable, we chose not to because we wanted to examine unique processes that are at work in male and female dissatisfaction. If added as a Block 1 variable, the overall model would be statistically significant, with gender adding statistically significant predictability to the model. As such, the effects of gender would be controlled in subsequent blocks. Although this is a valid way of considering the data, running separate analyses allows us to discern specific differences in the predictors of dissatisfaction in males and females.

Among female participants, the overall model was statistically significant, R^2 = .23, F(6, 226) = 11.53, p < .001. On the first step, BMI emerged as a statistically significant predictor of body dissatisfaction, R^2 = .07, F(1, 231) = 17.31, p < .001, and after controlling for BMI, Neuroticism scores accounted for the most unique variance, β = .40, t(228) = 6.48, p < .001 (see Table 3). For males, the overall model was also statistically significant, R^2 = .42 F(6, 77) = 9.18, p = .001. On the first step, BMI emerged as a statistically significant predictor of body dissatisfaction, R^2 = .13, F(1, 82) = 13.15, p < .001, and after controlling for BMI, Neuroticism scores accounted for the most unique variance, β = .35, t(82) = 3.53, p = .001, followed by Conscientiousness scores, β = −.19, t(82) = −2.15, p = .035 (see Table 3).

To examine specific differences in eating attitudes, similar analyses were conducted. Total EAT scores were entered as the criterion variable in the second analysis. BMI was entered on the first step to control for reported current body size. NEO factor scores were entered on the second step. For female participants, the overall model was significant, R^2 = .11, F(6, 225) = 4.56, p = .001. Although BMI was not a statistically significant predictor of disordered eating in this model, Neuroticism scores accounted for the most unique variance, β = .22, t(225) = 2.29, p = .001, followed by Extraversion, β = .17, t(225) = 2.52, p = .012 and Conscientiousness

Table 2 Correlations between BMI, NEO factor scores, EAT scores, BIQ scores

	EAT females	EAT males	BIQ females	BIQ males
BMI	.03	.01	.26**	.37**
Neuroticism	.20**	.21	.41**	.41**
Extraversion	.07	−.17	−.12	−.22*
Openness	−.12	−.14	−.09	−.21
Agreeableness	−.18**	−.15	−.14*	−.17
Conscientiousness	−.18**	.01	−.13*	−.31**
EAT			.42**	.19

Note. *p < 0.05, ** p < 0.01

Table 3 Summary of regression analyses for the prediction of body dissatisfaction in females and males

	B	SE(*B*)	*β*
Female participants			
Step 1			
BMI	.08	.02	.26**
Step 2			
Neuroticism	.10	.16	.40**
Extraversion	.12	.17	.05
Openness to experience	−.04	.19	−.01
Agreeableness	−.13	.19	−.04
Conscientiousness	−.19	.18	−.07
Male participants			
Step 1			
BMI	.12	.03	.37**
Step 2			
Neuroticism	.83	.24	.35**
Extraversion	−.15	.26	−.06
Openness to Experience	−.40	.28	−.13
Agreeableness	−.41	.28	−.14
Conscientiousness	−.58	.27	−.19*

Note. * $p < .05$, ** $p < .01$

Table 4 Summary of regression analyses for the prediction of disordered eating in females and males

	B	SE(*B*)	*β*
Female participants			
Step 1			
BMI	.07	.16	.027
Step 2			
Neuroticism	4.79	1.46	.22**
Extraversion	3.86	1.52	.17**
Openness to experience	−2.34	1.71	−.09
Agreeableness	−2.79	1.70	−.11
Conscientiousness	−3.73	1.62	−.15**
Male participants			
Step 1			
BMI	.03	.22	.01
Step 2			
Neuroticism	2.80	1.76	.20
Extraversion	−.942	1.97	−.06
Openness to Experience	−1.43	2.1	−.08
Agreeableness	−2.06	2.06	−.12
Conscientiousness	1.26	2.02	.07

Note. * $p < .05$, ** $p < .01$

scores, $\beta = -.15$, $t(225) = -2.31$, $p = .024$ (see Table 4). For male participants, the overall model was not significant, indicating that BMI and NEO factor scores did not predict EAT scores in males (see Table 4).

Discussion

Much research has explored personality correlates of body dissatisfaction and disordered eating in women, and a high level of neuroticism is most consistently associated with these variables [44–47, 50–52, 58–60]. It was hypothesized that personality factor scores would predict body dissatisfaction for women, and this was supported in the current study. Specifically, higher levels of neuroticism predicted higher levels of body image dissatisfaction, which replicates previous findings in women [44, 47, 58, 60]. The current research extends this relation to men, as higher levels of neuroticism and lower levels of conscientiousness predicted higher levels of body image dissatisfaction in male participants. Generally, women report higher levels of neuroticism than men, and this was supported in the current study; therefore, neuroticism could act as a mediating factor in the relationship between gender and body dissatisfaction, such that women have higher levels of neuroticism, and thereby exhibit higher levels of body image dissatisfaction [61].

It was also hypothesized that personality factor scores would predict levels of disordered eating in women, and this was supported in the current study. Specifically, higher levels of neuroticism and lower levels of conscientiousness predicted higher levels of disordered eating, which is in line with previous findings with women [44, 47, 58, 60]. This relationship was not extended to men in the current study, as personality factor scores did not predict levels of disordered eating in men. These results suggest that women with disordered eating attitudes and behaviours may be more prototypical with regard to previous conceptualizations of disordered eating, compared to men. In line with conclusions made by Farstad and colleagues [15], we suggest that the consideration of personality traits in the treatment of body image and eating concerns may contribute to a better understanding of their etiology and maintenance as well as inform the development and selection of interventions that are sensitized to individual variation. Indeed, previous research has demonstrated that questionnaires assessing the Big Five traits (e.g., NEO-PI-R) have demonstrated predictive utility for treatment results and symptom variation among individuals with an Eating Disorder [15, 62].

Aside from observed dissimilarities relating to personality and disordered eating variables, gender differences were evident with regard to contributions of BMI in the prediction of body image dissatisfaction. Specifically, for females, BMI did not predict a large amount variance in body dissatisfaction (7%) compared to males (14%). These results suggest that a men's weight-to-height ratio is a stronger predictor of body dissatisfaction than in women. Generally, males who were bigger in size (i.e., larger BMI) were more dissatisfied with their appearance. On the other hand, although statistically significant, BMI was not as substantial a predictor of body dissatisfaction in women. This could be because many women, regardless of shape or size, are dissatisfied with their bodies [63].

Men may experience body dissatisfaction and/or disordered eating for different or more variable reasons than females. It is interesting to note that among male participants, the relation between body dissatisfaction and disordered eating was not statistically significant. These results warrant further examination as it appears that the processes underlying the etiology of specific eating disorders may be different for males and females. Although body dissatisfaction can serve as a warning sign for problems with eating among females, it same may not be true for males. These results highlight the importance of well-validated assessment tools that take gender specific body image and disordered eating concerns into account. For instance, although there are several male specific body image measures including: Male Body Attitudes Scale [64]; Drive for Muscularity Scale [65]; Muscle Appearance Satisfaction Scale [66]; Male Body Checking Questionnaire [67]; and, the Male Body Dissatisfaction Scale [68], these measures are designed explicitly for males, making it difficult to explore gender differences. To illustrate, in a comparison of five scales that assess body image dissatisfaction, the Body Image Ideals Questionnaire was found to account for the most variability in female body image dissatisfaction, whereas the Male Body Dissatisfaction scale accounted for the most variability in male body dissatisfaction [56]. Further, measures of disordered eating do not consist of questions relating to excessive exercise, or alternative weight control strategies that could be utilized by males. Findings such as these emphasize the need for scales that accurately measure dissatisfaction and disordered eating behaviours in both males and females.

Results of the current study should be considered in light of several limitations. First, the current sample was nonclinical and consisted mostly of young Caucasian university students. Therefore, these data should be extrapolated to other groups of individuals with caution. Second, although a power analysis indicated adequate power for all analyses, the current sample contained a low number of male participants in comparison to female participants. Although this gender distribution is common in psychological research, the power of the results would be strengthened if a higher proportion of male participants were included. Third, our predictor variables were selected because they are salient factors associated with body dissatisfaction and disordered eating. In spite of the fact that each of our regression models led to statistically significant R^2 values, effect sizes for males and females were small and there was a large proportion of unaccounted variability in these outcome variables.

Aside from the Big Five personality traits, other personality factors have been associated with eating disorders and associated concerns (e.g., body dissatisfaction) in males and females. Examples include perfectionism, impulsiveness, and approach and avoidance motivation [15]. Future research should continue to explore relations between disordered eating, body image, and diverse personality constructs. Although the present study focused on the FFM of personality, other models of personality could be explored by administering alternative measures of personality such as the Eysenck Personality Questionnaire [69] or the Temperament Character Inventory [70].

Despite these above limitations, the current study was able to compare and contrast factors associated with body image and disordered eating in women and men in the same study. Upon examination of our results, it is evident that important gender differences exist in the experience of disordered eating and body dissatisfaction in a nonclinical university population. More studies investigating factors related to body image and eating concerns in males and females are needed to corroborate these findings.

Conclusions

Consistent associations between personality factors, disordered eating, and body dissatisfaction have been drawn largely from female samples and the current research highlights the importance of considering male participants. A key finding is the lack of relationship between disordered eating and personality in men, which is a well-established association in women. Although previous studies have estimated that males account for somewhere between 5 and 15% of patients with eating disorders [10, 28], in the current study men accounted for over 18% of participants reporting symptoms of disordered eating. If the number of men with disordered eating is increasing, it is imperative to investigate factors which predict this symptomology in men. Furthermore, among men, one of the best predictors of body dissatisfaction is current body size, with larger bodies predicting more body dissatisfaction. Therefore, weight management strategies, for example, may be more appropriate for targeting these issues in men than in women. Overall, these gender differences could have potential clinical relevance, which warrant further investigation.

Acknowledgements
Not Applicable.

Funding
The author(s) received no financial support for the research, authorship, and/or publication of this article.

Authors' contributions
The current research was based on a Master of Arts graduate thesis (Lillian MacNeill) and Bachelor of Science undergraduate thesis (Leanne Davis) thesis. Lisa Best supervised both projects. Thus, the work was equally distributed among the three authors who are all members of the same laboratory. All authors read and approved the final manuscript.

Competing interests
The author(s) declared no potential conflicts of interest with respect to the research, authorship, and/or publication of this article.

References

1. Catikkas F. Physical correlates of college students' body image satisfaction levels. J Soc Behav Person. 2011;39(4):497–502.
2. Frederick DA, Forbes GB, Grigorian KE, Jarcho JM. The UCLA body project I: gender and ethnic differences in self-objectification and body satisfaction among 2,206 undergraduates. Sex Roles. 2007;57(5):317–27.
3. Hoyt WD, Kogan LR. Satisfaction with body image and peer relationships for males and females in a college environment. Sex Roles. 2002;45(3):199–215.
4. Beebe DW. The attention to body shape scale: a new measure of body focus. J Pers Assess. 1995;65(3):486–501.
5. Lokken K, Ferraro FR, Kirchner T, Bowling M. Gender differences in body size dissatisfaction among individuals with low, medium, or high levels of body focus. J Gen Psychol. 2003;130(3):305–10.
6. McDonald K, Thompson JK. Eating disturbance, body image dissatisfaction, and reasons for exercising: gender differences and correlational findings. Int J Eat Disord. 1992;11(3):289–92.
7. Mellor D, Fuller-Tyszkiewicz M, McCabe M, Ricciardelli L. Body image and self-esteem across age and gender: a short-term longitudinal study. Sex Roles. 2010;63(9):672–81.
8. Stanford JN, McCabe MP. Body image ideal among males and females: sociocultural influences and focus on different body parts. J Health Psychol. 2002;7(6):675–84.
9. Cash TF, Deagle EA. The nature and extent of body-image disturbances in anorexia nervosa and bulimia nervosa: a meta-analysis. Int J Eat Disord. 1997;22:107–25.
10. Fernandez-Arando F, Aitken A, Badia A, Gimenez L, Solano R, Collier D, et al. Personality and psychopathological traits of males with an eating disorder. Eur Eat Disord Rev. 2004;12(6):367–74.
11. Lewinsohn PM, Seeley JR, Moerk KC, Striegel-Moore R. Gender differences in eating disorder symptoms in young adults. Int J Eat Disord. 2002;32(4):426–40.
12. Stice E, Shaw HE. Role of body dissatisfaction in the onset and maintenance of eating pathology: a synthesis of research findings. J Psychosom Res. 2002;53:985–93.
13. Polivy J, Herman P. Causes of eating disorders. Annu Rev Psychol. 2002;53:187–213.
14. Cassin SE, von Ranson KM. Personality and eating disorders: a decade in review. Clin Psychol Rev. 2005;25:895–916.
15. Farstad SM, McGeown LM, Eating v RKM. Disorders and personality, 2004-2016: a systematic review and meta-analysis. Clin Psychol Rev. 2016;46:91–105.
16. Fredrickson BL, Roberts TA. Objectification theory: toward understanding women's lived experiences and mental health risks. Psychol Women Q. 1997;21:273 306.
17. López-Guimera G, Levine MP, Sánchez-Carracedo D, Fauquet J. Influence of mass media on body image and eating disordered attitudes and behaviours in females: a review of effects and processes. Media Psychol. 2010;13:387–416.
18. Thompson JK, Heinberg LJ, Altabe M, Tantleff-Dunn S. Exacting beauty: theory, assessment, and treatment of body image disturbance. Washington, DC: American Psychological Association; 1999.
19. Brechan I, Kvalem IL. Relationship between body dissatisfaction and disordered eating: mediating role of self-esteem and depression. Eat Behav. 2015;17:49–58.
20. Fallon AE, Rozin P. Sex differences in perceptions of desirable body shape. J Abnorm Psychol. 1998;94:102–5.
21. Lamb CS, Jackson LA, Cassiday PB, Priest DJ. Body figure preferences of men and women: a comparison of two generations. Sex Roles. 1993;28:345–56.
22. Grieve FG, Newton CC, Kelley L, Miller RC Jr, Kerr NA. The preferred male body shapes of college men and women. Individ Differ Res. 2005;3(3):188–92.
23. Muth JL, Cash TF. Body image attitudes: what difference does gender make? J Appl Soc Psychol. 1997;27:1438–52.
24. Hesse-Biber S, Clayton-Matthews A, Downey JA. The differential importance of weight and body-image among women and men. Genet Soc Gen Psychol Monogr. 1987;11:509–28.
25. Kashubeck-West S, Mintz LB, Weigold I. Separating the effects of gender and weight-loss desire on body satisfaction and disordered eating behavior. Sex Roles. 2005;53(7):505–18.
26. Ousley L, Cordero ED, White S. Eating disorders and body image of undergraduate men. J Am Coll Heal. 2008;56(6):617–22.
27. American Psychiatric Association. Diagnostic and statistical manual of mental disorders. 5th ed. Washington, DC: American Psychiatric Association; 2013.
28. Stoving RK, Andries A, Brixen K, Bilenberg N, Horder K. Gender differences in outcome of eating disorders: a retrospective cohort study. Psychiatry Res. 2011;186(2):362–6.
29. Lindvall DC, Wisting L. Transitioning from DSM-IV to DSM-5: a systematic review of eating disorder prevalence assessment. Int J Eat Disord. 2016;49(11):975–97.
30. Mancilla-Diaz JM, Franco-Paredes K, Vazquez-Arevalo R, Lopez-Aguilar X, Alvarez-Rayon GL, Tellez-Giron MTA. Two-stage epidemiologic study on prevalence of eating disorders in female university students in Mexico. Eur Eat Disord Rev. 2007;15:463–70.
31. Pelaez Fernandez MA, Labrador FJ, Raich RM. Prevalence of eating disorders among adolescent and young adult scholastic population in the region of Madrid (Spain). J Psychosom Res. 2007;62:681–90.
32. Vardar E, Erzengin M. The prevalence of eating disorders (EDs) and comorbid psychiatric disorders in adolescents: a two-stage community-based study. Turk Psikiyatri Derg. 2011;22:205–12.
33. Anderson C, Bulik CM. Gender differences in compensatory behaviors, weight and shape salience, and drive for thinness. Eat Behav. 2004;5(1):1–11.
34. Striegel-Moore RH, Rosselli F, Perrin N, DeBar L, Wilson GT, May A, Kraemer HC. Gender difference in the prevalence of eating disorder symptoms. Int J Eat Disord. 2009;42(5):471–4.
35. Jones WR, Morgan JF. Eating disorders in men: a review of the literature. J Public Ment Health. 2010;9:23–31.
36. Ricciardelli LA. Eating disorders in boys and men. In: Wade T, editor. Encyclopedia of feeding and eating disorders. Singapore: Springer Nature; 2017. p. 305–8.
37. Weltzin TE, Weisensel N, Franczyk D, Burnett K, Klitz C, Bean P. Eating disorders in men: Update. J Mens Health Gend. 2005;2:186–93.
38. Farquhar JC, Wasylkiw L. Media images of men: trends and consequences of body conceptualization. Psychol Men Masc. 2007;8:145–60.
39. Thompson JK, Cafri G. The muscular ideal: an introduction. In: Thompson JK, Cafri G, editors. The muscular ideal. Washington, DC: American Psychological Association; 2007. p. 3–12.
40. Digman JM. Personality structure: emergence of the five-factor model. Annu Rev Psychol. 1990;41:417–40.
41. Norman WX. Toward an adequate taxonomy of personality attributes: replicated factor structure in peer nomination personality ratings. J Abnorm Soc Psychol. 1963;66:574–83.
42. Costa PT Jr, McCrae RR. The NEO personality inventory manual. Odessa, FL: Psychological Assessment Resources; 1985.
43. Costa PT Jr, McCrae RR. Normal personality assessment in clinical practice: the NEO personality inventory. Psychol Assess. 1992;4(1):5–13.

44. Dalley SE, Buunk AP, Umit T. Female body dissatisfaction after exposure to overweight and thin media images: the role of body mass index and neuroticism. Pers Individ Dif. 2009;47:47–51.
45. MacLaren W, Best LA. Female students' disordered eating and the big five personality facets. Eat Behav. 2009;10(3):192–5.
46. Miller JL, Schmidt LA, Louis A, Vaillancourt T, McDougall P, Laliberte M. Neuroticism and introversion: a risky combination for disordered eating among a non-clinical sample of undergraduate students. Eat Behav. 2006;7(1):69–78.
47. Roberts A, Good E. Media images and female body dissatisfaction: the moderating effects of the five-factor traits. Eat Behav. 2010;11:211–6.
48. Swami V, Buchanan T, Furnham A, Tovee MJ. Five-factor personality correlates of perceptions of women's body sizes. Person Individ Dif. 2008;45(7):697–9.
49. Swami V, Hurnham A, Chamorro-Premuzic T, Akbar K, Gordon N, Harris T, et al. More than just skin deep? Personality information influences men's ratings of the attractiveness of women's body sizes. J Soc Psychol. 2010;150(6):628–47.
50. Claridge G, Davis C. What's the use of neuroticism? Person Individ Dif. 2001;31:383–400.
51. Tylka TL. The relation between body dissatisfaction and eating disorder symptomatology: an analysis of moderating variables. J Couns Psychol. 2004;52:178–91.
52. Swami V, Taylor R, Carvalho C. Body dissatisfaction assessed by the photographic figure rating scale is associated with sociocultural, personality, and media influences. Scand J Psychol. 2011;52:57–63.
53. Garner DM, Olmsted MP, Bohr Y, Garfinkel PE. The eating attitudes test: psychometric features and clinical correlates. Psychol Med. 1982;12:871–8.
54. Garfinkel PE, Newman A. The eating attitudes test: twenty-five years later. Eat Weight Disord. 2001;6:1–21.
55. Cash TF. Body ideals questionnaire. 2000. http://www.body-images.com/.
56. Davis L, Proctor C, Lilly S, Best LA. Body dissatisfaction: effects of gender, exercise, personality, and disordered eating. In: Pracana C, editor. Proceedings of the international psychological applications conference and trends. Lisbon: World Institute for Advanced Research and Science; 2016. 978-989-99389-6-0.
57. McCrae RR, Costa PT Jr. NEO inventories professional manual for the NEO personality Inventory-3, NEO five-factor Inventory-3, and NEO personality inventory revised. Lutz, FL: PAR; 2010.
58. Bergstrom RL, Neighbors C, Malheim J. Media comparisons and threats to body image: seeking evidence of self-affirmation. J Soc Clin Psychol. 2009;28:264–80.
59. Davis C, Dionne M, Lazarus L. Gender-role orientation and body image in women and men: the moderating influence of neuroticism. Sex Roles. 1996;34:493–505.
60. Groesz LM, Levine MP, Murnen SK. The effect of experimental presentation of thin images on body satisfaction: a meta-analytic review. Int J Eat Disord. 2002;31:1–16.
61. Guo S. Sex differences in personality: a meta-analysis based on "big five" factors. San Francisco, CA: Paper presented at the Annual Meeting of the American Educational Research Association; 1995.
62. Deumens RA, Noorthoorn EO, Verbraak MJ. Predictors for treatment outcome of binge eating with obesity: a naturalistic study. Eat Disord. 2012;20:276–87.
63. Tiggemann M. Sociocultural perspectives on human appearance and body image. In: Cash TF, Smolak L, editors. Body image: a handbook of theory, research, and clinical practice. 2nd ed. New York, NY: Guilford Press; 2011. p. 12–9.
64. Tylka TL, Bergeron D, Schwartz JP. Development and psychometric evaluation of the male body attitudes scale (MBAS). Body Image. 2005;2:161–75.
65. McCreary DR, Sasse DK. An exploration of the drive for muscularity in adolescent boys and girls. J Am Coll Heal. 2000;48:297–304.
66. Mayville SB, Williamson DA, White MA, Netemeyer RG, Drab DL. Development of the muscle appearance satisfaction scale: a self-report measure for the assessment of muscle dysmorphia symptoms. Assessment. 2002;9:351–60.
67. Hildebrandt T, Walker DC, Alfano L, Delinsky S, Bannon K. Development and validation of a male specific body checking questionnaire. Int J Eat Disord. 2010;43(1):77–87.
68. Ochner N, Gray JA, Brickner K. The development and initial validation of a new measure of male body dissatisfaction. Eat Behav. 2009;10:197–201.
69. Eysenck JJ, Eysenck SBG. Eysenck personality questionnaire-revised (EPQ-R). London: Hodder & Stoughton; 1991.
70. Cloninger RC. The temperament and character inventory (TCI): a guide to its development and use. Center for Psychobiology of Personality: St. Louis; 1994.

14

Identifying fundamental criteria for eating disorder recovery

Jan Alexander de Vos[1,2*], Andrea LaMarre[3], Mirjam Radstaak[1], Charlotte Ariane Bijkerk[2], Ernst T. Bohlmeijer[1,4] and Gerben J. Westerhof[1]

Abstract

Background: Outcome studies for eating disorders regularly measure pathology change or remission as the only outcome. Researchers, patients and recovered individuals highlight the importance of using additional criteria for measuring eating disorder recovery. There is no clear consensus on which additional criteria are most fundamental. Studies focusing on the perspectives of recovered patients show criteria which are closely related to dimensions of positive functioning as conceptualized in the complete mental health model. The aim of this study was to identify fundamental criteria for eating disorder recovery according to recovered individuals.

Methods: A systematic review and a qualitative meta-analytic approach were used. Eighteen studies with recovered individuals and meeting various quality criteria were included. The result sections of the included papers were searched for themes that were stated as criteria for recovery or 'being recovered'. All themes were analyzed using a meta-summary technique. Themes were labeled into criteria for recovery and the frequency of the found criteria was examined.

Results: In addition to the remission of eating disorder pathology, dimensions of psychological well-being and self-adaptability/resilience were found to be fundamental criteria for eating disorder recovery. The most frequently mentioned criteria were: self-acceptance, positive relationships, personal growth, decrease in eating disorder behavior/cognitions, self-adaptability/resilience and autonomy.

Conclusions: People who have recovered rate psychological well-being as a central criterion for ED recovery in addition to the remission of eating disorder symptoms. Supplementary criteria, besides symptom remission, are needed to measure recovery. We recommend including measurements of psychological well-being and self-adaptability/resilience in future research, such as outcome studies and in routine outcome measurement.

Keywords: Eating disorders, Recovery, Psychopathology, Psychological well-being, Positive mental health, Meta-analysis, Qualitative research, Systematic review, Positive psychology

Plain English summary

In this study, we examined the perspective on criteria for eating disorder recovery among recovered patients. We searched in scientific databases for all published qualitative studies on eating disorder recovery. Eighteen studies were included after meeting rigorous inclusion criteria. The results sections of these studies were analyzed by extracting relevant themes for eating disorder recovery. After calculating effect sizes for the criteria, we found high effect sizes for: self-acceptance, positive relations with others, personal growth, eating disorder remission, self-adaptability, and autonomy, indicating that these are important criteria according to recovered individuals. In addition to the remission of the eating disorder symptoms, dimensions of psychological well-being and self-adaptability/resilience are found as important criteria for eating disorder recovery. This study, among others, shows relevant criteria for eating

* Correspondence: s.devos@humanconcern.nl
[1]Centre for eHealth and Well-being Research, University of Twente, Psychology, Health, & Technology, Enschede, The Netherlands
[2]Human Concern Foundation, center for Eating Disorders, Amsterdam, The Netherlands
Full list of author information is available at the end of the article

disorder recovery in addition to the remission of eating disorder symptoms.

Background

Eating disorders (EDs) are serious mental disorders that impact all facets of people's lives, including quality of life at home and work, personal functioning, and social life [1–3]. Anorexia Nervosa (AN) has the highest mortality rate of all mental illnesses [4, 5]. Eating disorders are often chronic and refractory [6].

In the last decade, clinical guidelines have been established with treatment options based on evidence (evidence-based care) [7–9]. These treatment options, however, work only for a percentage of patients; for AN in particular, there is no single superior treatment option [10–12]. Effectiveness and efficacy studies, herein called outcome studies, are critical for establishing guidelines for evidence-based care. Outcome studies use measures to examine which treatments are effective, based on the degree of recovery from an ED on certain criteria. There is significant disagreement in the field around the definition of ED recovery, and the relevant criteria that must be present in order to claim "recovery"; see for instance McGilley & Szablewski for an overview [13–18]. As a result, rates of recovery within outcome studies vary widely, ranging from 3% to 96% depending on the criteria used [19]. Recovery is usually measured as the remission of ED symptoms [20]. In a systematic review of 119 patient outcome studies on AN, Steinhausen [20] concluded that remission from all essential clinical symptoms could be considered as recovery; however, he also noted substantial variation in outcome criteria between studies. In a systematic review of predictors of ED outcomes by Vall and Wade [21], over 80% of the 126 included studies reported outcomes based solely on symptom remission [21]. Commonly-used measures were: frequency or absence of binging/purging, change or reaching cut off scores on a questionnaire/interview for measuring ED symptoms (Fairburn & Beglin [22]), changes or remission from overall ED symptoms, or change in BMI or reaching a specific cut off point [21]. In sum, outcome studies generally frame recovery around clinically relevant changes in ED symptoms, or remission.

Simultaneously, a growing body of literature in the ED field highlights that ED symptom change (remission) is not sufficient for understanding, capturing and measuring ED recovery and emphasizes the importance of additional criteria, related to (mental) health, such as quality of life, well-being, psychological, social and emotional functioning [16, 23–26]. This study aims to identify fundamental criteria for recovery from eating disorders focusing on criteria related to clinical symptoms and additional criteria, related to mental health and well-being.

Mental health: the important role of well-being

Psychologists have lobbied for decades to convey that health is not merely the absence of disease (i.e. symptoms), but also the presence of something positive [27–34]. The emergence of positive psychology, for example, is based on re-focusing the exclusive attention on absence of pathology as a marker for health only, to positive aspects of mental and social functioning as markers for well-being as well [30]. This is in line with the declaration of the World Health Organization (WHO) on mental health: 'a state of well-being in which the individual realizes his or her own abilities, can cope with the normal stresses of life, can work productively and fruitfully, and is able to make a contribution to his or her community' (p. 12 [35]). Keyes [36] proposed the 'complete mental health model', based on this definition, taking both the absence of psychopathology and the presence of well-being as two related but different aspects of health into account. He did not define health and well-being as a fixed state, but operationalized it as a syndrome consisting of several criteria, where upon people can develop, meeting certain thresholds for optimal well-being [37].

Well-being is theoretically divided into psychological, emotional and social well-being [31, 37, 38]. Psychological well-being (PWB) was conceptualized by Ryff [38] and consists of six key dimensions: self-acceptance, autonomy, environmental mastery, purpose and meaning in life, personal growth and positive relationships with others [34, 38]. This is the model used when we refer to PWB throughout this article. Emotional well-being includes happiness, positive affect and avowed life satisfaction. Social well-being encompasses social contribution, integration, actualization, acceptance and coherence [36]; see for instance [38–40] for an overview of well-being and its theoretical and philosophical background. Recent studies show that psychopathology and well-being are separate but complementary aspects of mental health and reflect two related continua, instead of being opposites on one continuum [29, 37, 40]. In addition, a bi-directional relationship between psychopathology and positive mental health over time is found [41].

The complete mental health model emphasizes the importance of positive functioning for mental health, however, this is widely neglected in research on eating disorders [42]. While several studies have focused on positive mental health in terms of quality of life or subjective well-being, only one study examined all PWB dimensions among eating disorder patients [1, 3, 23, 42–44]. In the study that examined PWB, the authors found that ED patients had impaired PWB compared to a control group [42]. Also, these studies examined the presence of PWB among eating disorder patients, it has not been examined as a criterion for recovery.

In qualitative research examining recovery criteria from eating disorders, there are many recovery themes that are related to the dimensions for well-being. Bowlby and Anderson [45], for instance, found several themes for recovery in a sample of therapists who were recovered from an eating disorder. Most of these themes matched the descriptions of the well-being dimensions. For example, the themes 'learning to understand and value the self' matches with the well-being dimensions "personal growth" and "self-acceptance", the theme "finding purpose and meaning in life" matches with the dimension "purpose" and the theme "developing healthy and meaningful relationships" matches with "positive relationships with others". In a survey examining criteria for recovery from eating disorders, Noordenbos and Seubring [25] found high consensus between ex-patients and clinicians on all of the proposed 52 statements, divided into five themes: eating behavior, physical, psychological, emotional, and social functioning. However, patients labeled self-esteem, a positive body attitude and expressing emotions as more important, while therapists accentuated eating behavior and physical recovery [25]. Emanuelli and colleagues [26] replicated this study in a sample of patients and clinicians, and concluded that recovery included general criteria (e.g. social, psychological, and emotional) and specific eating disorder criteria (e.g. weight controlling behaviors and evaluation of one's appearance) [26]. Patients and clinicians agreed on the ranking of importance of most criteria, but patients considered "psychological, emotional, social" and "evaluation of one's own appearance" criteria as more important for recovery than did clinicians. The researchers did not find weight and weight gain as central criteria for defining recovery [26]. Dawson, Rhodes and Touyz [24] used a different approach, and conducted an extensive Delphi study with ED professionals to determine criteria for recovery from Anorexia Nervosa (AN). They also concluded that, in addition to the minimal criteria (i.e., weight restoration and symptom reduction), psychological and quality of life measures should be part of the definition for AN recovery.

While these studies show the importance of additional criteria, they have several limitations, making it difficult to understand which criteria are most fundamental besides the ED pathology based criteria (remission). Noordenbos and Seubring [25] and Emmanuelli and colleagues [26] used a pre-fixed set of statements, making their study susceptible to missing criteria which might have been endorsed by ex-patients or clinicians had they been articulated in the design of the study. Several qualitative studies show criteria for recovery that were not present in the consensus studies with the pre-fixed statements [25, 26], such as improved self-acceptance, identity development, feelings of purpose and meaning in life, self-management and empowerment [45–47]. Other studies only focused on AN or did not take the perspective of recovered individuals into account. The importance of exploring the perspectives of those with lived experience on their recovery cannot be understated in this regard. Studies have shown that the orientation of patients towards recovery can change over time and during treatment [48, 49].

In conclusion, outcome studies tend to follow criteria for recovery that are based on changes in ED symptoms (remission), rather than aiming to ascertain health and well-being. It remains inconclusive which recovery criteria should be considered as fundamental. We argue that knowledge from individuals who have recovered from an ED should be leading and incorporated into the establishment of fundamental criteria for recovery. Qualitative studies examining the personal experience from recovered individuals highlight the importance of taking additional recovery criteria into account, which are closely related to the dimensions of well-being. However, the results of these qualitative studies have never been systematically reviewed. Responding to this knowledge gap, we carried out a systematic review and meta-analysis of existing qualitative studies of ED recovery.

The aim of this study is to identify fundamental criteria for recovery according to recovered individuals by performing a qualitative meta-analysis. Qualitative meta-analysis can be explained as the aggregation of studies to discover the essential elements of a phenomenon, and translating these results into a more comprehensive description or clear end-product [50, 51]. An integrative interpretation of findings from multiple qualitative studies is therefore more substantive than those resulting from individual investigations [50, 52]. To our knowledge, this is the first study to use a qualitative meta-analysis to further identify fundamental criteria for ED recovery over all ED types, among people who were considered recovered.

Method

Search strategy and selection of studies

Guidelines from the PRISMA statement for reporting systematic reviews were used for the search strategy [53]. The first step was to perform a systematic search in two electronic databases, Medline and PsycInfo (final search date 04–02-2016). Terms were searched within all fields. There was no limitation for the year in which the study was published. The main search terms were (Recovery OR Recovered) AND (Eating Disorders OR Anorexia Nervosa OR Bulimia Nervosa OR Binge Eating Disorder) AND (Qualitative), resulting in 238 hits from PubMed and 403 hits from PsycInfo (with a subselection "qualitative studies").The second step was an additional search in which the reference list of two comprehensive qualitative studies of eating disorder recovery [45, 46] were screened. The third step was to screen all articles in the Google Scholar search engine that had cited [45, 46] (search date: 06–02-2016). Duplicates were removed as follows: 103 duplicates between PsycInfo and PubMed, 5 duplicates between study [45] and [46] and 49 duplicates between the first (PsycInfo and PubMed) and the additional search. In total 630 unique studies remained for screening.

The inclusion criteria were studies that 1) reported on the processes or criteria for eating disorder recovery, 2) included recovered individuals, either because they considered themselves to be recovered, and/or the study used a rigorous system to assess recovery, 3) used a qualitative study design, 4) were published in a peer-reviewed journal or edited academic book, and 5) had a rigorous system for ensuring the credibility of data-analysis (i.e. meeting the CASP protocol, see Procedure and analysis). All ED types as defined in the DSM5 [54] were included, since we were interested in overall criteria for recovery for ED patients. Studies which only or primarily included patients who were not considered recovered were excluded, as we were interested in understanding the markers or criteria for recovery, as opposed to future perspectives on recovery from those actively experiencing eating disorders. Unpublished reports and dissertations were not included to avoid studies that have not been peer-reviewed for quality and also to ensure that studies were not duplicating results [55].

The first and second author screened all eligible studies separately in two phases. In the first phase, selection was based on title and abstract. In the second phase, all selected articles were independently screened by the first two authors based on full text. Inter-rater agreement (kappa coefficient) between authors in the second round of screening was 0.81 (95% CI .68–.91). When there was no agreement, the first two authors discussed decisions to include or exclude studies until agreement was reached. Finally, the reference lists of the included studies were cross-checked on eligible studies. This did not result in extra studies. In total 18 studies were included in the meta-analysis (see Fig. 1).

Procedure and analysis

A qualitative meta-analysis requires both 1) an assessment of the quality of the studies (i.e. the influence of the method of investigation on the findings) and, 2) results of a more comprehensive explanation of a phenomenon, including its ambiguities and differences found in the primary studies [50].

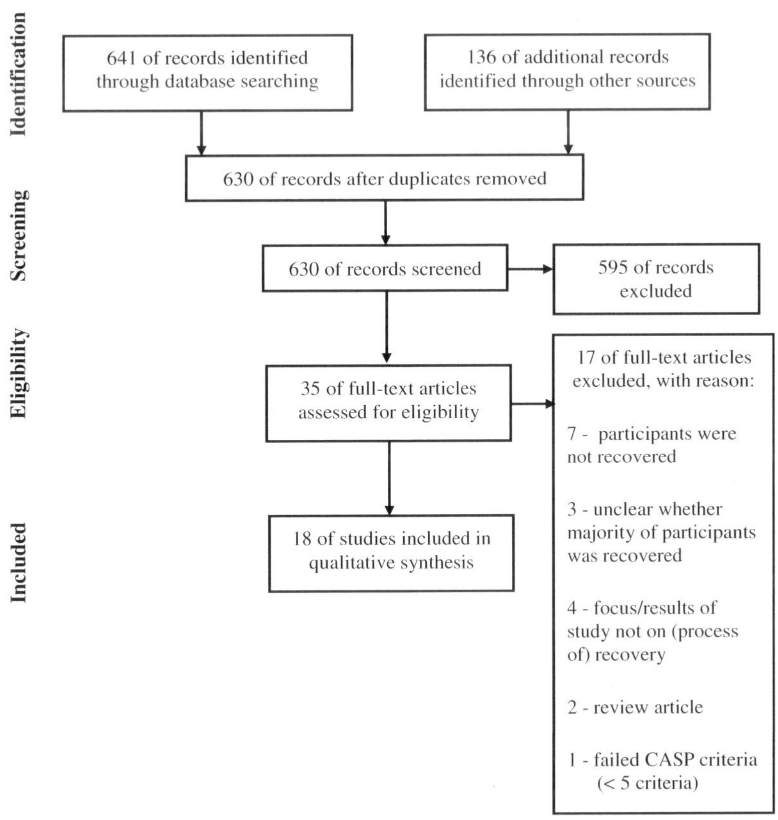

Fig. 1 Prisma diagram of study selection

Assessment of the quality of the studies

For the first requirement the Critical Appraisal Skills Programme (CASP) [56] in addition to a complementary rating, was used. The CASP method is a standardized tool to help researchers to systematically examine qualitative studies. CASP is a commonly used method within qualitative meta-analysis, or -synthesis studies to assess credibility, value and relevance of the selected studies [47, 57–59]. In accordance with the CASP method and study [47], the quality of the studies was assessed on 10 themes, and classified as "A", low risk of bias (studies meeting 9 or 10 of the questions) or "B" moderate risk of bias (studies meeting at least 5 of the questions, but not more then 8). CASP method applies the following 10 criteria: 1) a clear statement of the aims, 2) methodological design is adequate to aims, 3) research design is appropriate to address aims, 4) recruitment strategy is appropriate to aims, 5) data collection in a way that addresses research issue, 6) relationship between researcher and participant is considered, 7) ethical issues are considered, 8) sufficiently rigorous analysis, 9) clear statement of findings, 10) importance of research. Besides the CASP method, a complementary rating for checking credibility was used by dividing studies in "A", low risk of bias (participants were recovered/in recovery for at least 2 years and recovery was at least self-reported), and "B" moderate risk of bias (participants were recovered/in recovery for less than 2 years, or it was unclear how long participants were recovered and/or it was unclear whether recovery was self-reported). Combining both ratings resulted in 4 possible categories: 1) "A/A", low risk of bias, 2) "A/B" and, 3) "B/A", moderate risk of bias, and 4) "B/B" substantial risk of bias.

Analysis of criteria for recovery

For the second requirement, a meta summary technique described by Sandelowski & Barroso [60] was used. In contrast to meta-synthesis analysis, this method allows for extracting themes and an evaluation of their frequencies [50, 60]. The following strategy was used: 1) extract relevant themes from each study, 2) reduce these themes into abstract findings and 3) calculate effect sizes. First, the result sections of the included papers were searched for themes that were stated as criteria for recovery or "being recovered". Themes that were included were: themes that were stated by all participants and themes endorsed by an unknown number of participants, but wherein the theme was part of a main category. For instance, in one study [46], it was unclear how many respondents endorsed on the theme "sense of self-worth", this theme was, however, part of a main category in the results, "discovering and reclaiming self as good enough" and therefore included. Themes that specifically addressed aspects of the process of recovery (i.e. how long it took, development, stages) were excluded, as were themes that were part of the first or initial phases of a recovery process, since we were interested in criteria which are present when people are fully recovered. The themes were identified independently by the first and second author and stored in their original content. To obtain one dataset for the second step (abstract findings), results were first discussed per study for half of the included articles. For the other half of the studies, the data set of the first author was used by the second author to look for further differences in themes. Differences in found statements were discussed until agreement was reached. This resulted in a dataset with 346 statements which was audited by the third and fourth author.In the second step, the reduction into abstract findings, the labels were established. Eating disorder pathology was divided in three sub labels (behavior/cognitions, body evaluation and physical functions). For the additional themes, the well-being dimensions were used since they seem to relate closely to the themes that are described in qualitative research on eating disorder recovery. The following additional labels were used; emotional, psychological and social well-being with their underlying dimensions as stated in earlier work [31, 36, 38]. Also, a "miscellaneous" label was used for criteria that did not fit into one of the other labels. All themes were read carefully by the first two authors to examine whether they could be labeled corresponding the concept labels. Some of the well-being dimensions were very strictly or narrowly described in the literature [31, 37, 38], A minor adjustment in the description of three labels was necessary for the purpose of labeling the themes (see Table 1 for the adjustments). Then, all 346 original themes were labeled separately by the first and fourth author. Inter-rater agreement (kappa coefficient) for the labeling process between the authors was .81 (95% CI .77–.86) before discussion.

Interpretation of results

During the discussion, the miscellaneous label could be split into two sub labels (self-management/resilience and spiritual integration). Themes that were part of the discussion were "social contribution" versus "purpose and meaning in life". The theme "Helping others", for instance was sometimes explained as a new purpose for participants, but it is also a form of social contribution. Other things that were discussed were; "Identity integration" as part of "personal growth" or as a separate label, and "self-adaptability/resilience" as a part of "autonomy" or as a separate label. See Table 1 for an overview of the final list regarding the labels and descriptives.In the third step, frequency and intensity effect sizes were calculated for all labels. The frequency effect size shows how frequent labels are mentioned across studies and is

Table 1 Labels

Health criteria	Description
1. Eating disorder pathology	
ED behavior/cognitions	Improvement/absence of ED related behavior (bingeing/purging, slimming,) and cognitions (more relaxed/normal thoughts/affect regarding food/weight/exercising).
ED body evaluation	More relaxed regarding body/weight (satisfaction/evaluation).
ED physical functions	Improvement in BMI and/or other physical functions.
2. Emotional well-being	
Avowed happiness	Feeling happy, feeling joy, enjoyment.
Positive affect	Feeling cheerful, in good spirits, calm, and peaceful, satisfied, and full of life.
Avowed life satisfaction	Feeling satisfied with life in general or specific areas of one's life.
3. Psychological well-being	
Self-acceptance	Holding positive attitudes towards oneself and past life and conceding and accepting varied aspects of self, holding a compassionate attitude towards self. [a] *Having self-respect. Having feelings of self-worth or self-esteem/confidence. Taking self-care.*
Environmental mastery	Exhibiting the capability to manage a complex environment, and the ability to choose or manage and mould environments to one's needs.
Positive relationships with others	Having warm, satisfying, trusting personal relationships and being capable of empathy and intimacy and being open and personal to others.
Personal growth	Showing insight into one's own self and potential, having a sense of development, and being open to new and challenging experiences. [a] *Identity formation/integration: Having a sense of integration of several/all aspects of self and or formation of (healthy/autonomous) aspects of self.*
Autonomy	Exhibiting a self-direction that is often guided by one's own socially accepted and conventional internal standards and resisting unsavory social pressures. [a] *Self-determination, independence, and the regulation of behavior from within* [81]. *Autonomy as used in self-determination theory means acting with the experience of choice* [39].
Purpose in life	Holding goals and beliefs that affirm one's sense of direction in life and feeling that life had a purpose and meaning.
4. Social well-being	
Social contribution	Feeling that one's own life is useful to society and that the output of one's activities is valued by or valuable to others.
Social integration	Having a sense of belonging to a community and deriving comfort and support from that community.
Social actualization	Believing that people, social groups, and society have potential and can evolve or grow positively.
Social acceptance	Having a positive attitude towards others while acknowledging and accepting people's differences and their complexity.
Social coherence	Being interested in society or social life, and feeling that society and culture are intelligible, somewhat logical, predictable, and meaningful.
5. Miscellaneous labels	
Self-adaptability/resilience	Copingstrategies/resilience/empowerment/willpower/persistance/emotion-regulation, (Healthy) strategies to cope with emotions and difficult life situations.
Spiritual integration	Having a sense of being part of, or in contact with a higher power (Universe, God, Jesus, other) and deriving comfort and support from that. Exercises/activities that promote this: meditation, going to Church, praying etc.

Note: well-being descriptions are published earlier in [29, 31], [a] = added descriptions to the original labels

calculated by dividing the number of studies containing the same finding by the total number of studies [60]. Labels were indicated as strong evidence for ED recovery criteria, when they were reported by at least 75% of the primary studies, as substantial evidence when they were reported by 50% to 75% of the primary studies, as moderate evidence when they were reported by 25% to 50% of the primary studies, and as insufficient evidence if less than 25% of the studies reported on a dimension. Although these cut-off points are rather arbitrary, we decided to use quartiles as cut off for ease of interpretation and pragmatic value for those seeking evidence on recovery criteria.

The intensity effect size gives a clear measure for how fundamental recovery criteria are compared to each other. The intensity effect size is calculated as the number of findings for a criteria produced in all studies, divided by all findings [60]. To examine possible effects of the methodological quality of the studies on the results, differences in outcomes on the intensity effect size between low risk of bias studies (A/A) and substantial risk for bias studies (B/B) were tested using a proportion significance test (χ^2 test for homogeneity).

Results

Descriptives

See Table 2 for an overview of the included studies and quality rating. The 18 included studies covered 286 participants (269 women and 17 men), with an average age of 30.2 years (SD = 7.3 years). One hundred-sixty-three participants had been diagnosed with AN, 25 participants had been diagnosed with Bulimia Nervosa (BN), 18 participants had a history of both AN and BN diagnosis over their life course, 8 participants had been diagnosed with Binge Eating Disorders (BED) and 13 participants had been diagnosed with an Eating Disorder Not Otherwise Specified (EDNOS). The average duration of the eating disorder was 8.2 years (*SD* = 5.1, study number: 1,3,6,11,16) with a minimum length of 1.5 years and a maximum length of 44 years (study number: 1,6,11,16,17). The average length of recovery was 9.1 years (SD = 6.1 years, study number: 1,3,6,11), with a range of 1 year to 35 years (study number: 1,2,6,7,8,11,13,17). However, for many studies this was unknown.

Criteria for eating disorder recovery

See Table 3 for the intensity and frequency effect sizes of the criteria for recovery. The frequency effect sizes show strong evidence for positive relationships with others (100%), self-acceptance (88.9%), autonomy (83.3%), personal growth (77.8%), improved ED behavior/cognitions (77.8%), self-adaptability/resilience (77.8%). Substantial to moderate evidence was found for improved body evaluation (55.6%), social contribution (50%), purpose and meaning in life (38.9%), spiritual integration (33.3%), improved (ED) physical functioning (27.8%) and positive affect (27.8%). Insufficient evidence was found for happiness (22.2%), avowed life satisfaction (22.2%), environmental mastery (11.1%), social acceptance (11.1%), social integration (11.1%), social actualization (0%) and social coherence (0%).

Examining the effect sizes of the overall mental health dimensions; psychological well-being accounted for 52.3% of all recovery criteria, eating disorder pathology for 20.8%, self-adaptability/resilience and spiritual integration for 13.8%, social well-being for 8.6% and emotional well-being for 4.6%. Examining the intensity effect sizes of the underlying eating disorder pathology criteria; improved ED behavior/cognitions accounted for 12.4% of the whole sample, improved body evaluation for 5.8% and physical improvement for 2.6%. Improved behavior/cognitions were described in the original studies in several ways. Recurring themes were; returning to a normal eating pattern, no weight phobia, or ending the obsession with weight/food. Physical improvement was primarily about weight recovery and improvement of physical complications.

Testing risk of bias

Eight studies had an "AA" status and 8 studies a "BB" status. Except for the criteria "personal growth" and "spiritual integration", no differences in proportions of the intensity effect sizes were found between "AA" and "BB" studies (see Table 3). Only two studies had a moderate indication for bias (A/B, or B/A) status and could not be used for testing significance because of the low sample size (Fig. 2).

Discussion

Criteria for recovery were examined using a qualitative meta-analytic approach. Studies were selected that examined the personal experiences of recovered individuals.

Fundamental recovery criteria

The aim of this study was to identify fundamental criteria for ED recovery according to recovered individuals. Several health dimensions besides symptom remission were found that should be considered as fundamental criteria of eating disorder (ED) recovery. Large frequency effect sizes, indicating strong evidence, were found for the following six criteria: positive relationships with others, self-acceptance, autonomy, personal growth, improved ED behavior/cognitions and self-adaptability/resilience. Further, substantial to moderate evidence was found for the following six criteria: improved body evaluation, social contribution, purpose and meaning in life, spiritual integration, improved physical functioning and positive affect. At last, insufficient evidence was found for the following seven criteria: happiness, avowed life satisfaction, environmental mastery, social acceptance, social integration, social actualization and social coherence. These results show a clear perspective of the relevant criteria from the perspective of people who have experienced recovery. While remission of ED pathology is considered important, many criteria were about psychological well-being (PWB). Moreover, PWB was

Table 2 Summary of included studies

Nr	Study	Country	Diagnosis	N of Participants	Study focus	Ethics approval	Data collection	Data analysis	Credibility	Recovery criteria	Minimalrecovery length	Quality rating
1	[74]	Australia	AN	8	Process of recovery chronic AN	Yes	Open ended interviews (face to face)	Narrative inquiry	Member-check with each participant, cross-check by two authors	Self-reported, Bardone-Cone criteria (2010)	5 years	A/A
2	[46]	Canada	AN	9	Recovery from AN	Unknown	In depth open ended interviews	Grounded theory approach	Review process by 3 individuals	Self-report	3 years	A/A
3	[85]	U.S.	AN, BNEDNOS	17	Athletes' ED recovery experiences	Yes	Semi structured interviews	Content analysis procedure	Reviewing of coding structure by two colleagues, discussion until agreement	DSM-IV-TR criteria	3 months	B/B
4	[75]	Several	AN	3	Influences on the process of recovery from AN	No	Purposive/ extreme sampling to identify published narratives	Framework approach to qualitative analysis	Coding by two authors, discussion until agreement	As described by the personal account	Unknown	B/B
5	[86]	Sweden	BN	5	Experiences of recovery from AN	Yes	Open ended interviews (semi-structured)	Narrative interviews with qualitative content analysis	Added quotations from participants to results	Self-reported (being healthy)	2 years	A/A
6	[87]	U.K.	AN	15	Views of recovering from AN	Yes	Semi structured interviews (in-depth, by phone)	Interpretative phenomenological analysis	Discussion between authors	Self defined recovery/ recovered	No requirement	B/B
7	[88]	U.S.	AN	22	Perspectives of recovered individuals on ED, recovery and social support	Yes	Interviews	Generic qualitative description analysis	Separately coded by two authors, comparing initial codes and consensus seeking. Member checking with participants	Measured: eating screen	1 year	A/B
8	[89]	Brazil	AN	15	Factors involved in the outcome of AN	Yes	Ethnographic Face to face interviews (semi-structured)	Grounded theory approach	Analyzing separately, calculating inter-rater agreement	Reported by self, family member and assistant MD	5 years	A/A
9	[90]	Norway Sweden	AN, BNEDNOS	15	Experiences of life after recovery	Yes	Open ended interviews (semi-structured)	Phenomenological approach	Analyzed by three different teams and discussion until consensus	Self-report (experienced recovery or marked improvement)	Unknown	A/B
10	[91]	Sweden	AN	58	Patient perspectives of AN recovery	Yes	Interview	Content analysis procedure	Separate analysis by three researchers, calculating inter-rater agreement	Clinical assessment (DSM-III-R)	Unknown	B/B
11	[45]	U.S.	AN, BN	13	Exploring ED recovery	Yes	Semi structured interviews	Phenomenological approach	Addressing researcher bias, authors independently reading transcripts, and	Self-report	6 years	A/A

Table 2 Summary of included studies *(Continued)*

								discussing emergent themes, included extended quotations			
12	[79]	Israel	AN	18	Patients perspective of recovery from AN	Yes	In depth semi-structured interviews	Phenomenological approach	Adding quotes to results	DSM-IV	5 years	A/A
13	[92]	Canada	BED	6	Recovery from binge eating disorder	Unknown	Two interviews (unstructured and structured)	Grounded theory approach	Audit by second author	Self-reported, DSM-IV (objective measure)	6 months	A/B
14	[93]	U.K.	AN	6	The patients perspective of recovery from AN	Unknown	Interview	Case descriptions	Unknown	Assessment	Unknown	B/B
15	[94]	U.S.	AN, BN	3	Rethinking recovery	Yes	Semi structured interview	Interpretative biographical method	Working with performance texts	Self-identified as recovered	Unclear (well into process of recovery)	B/B
16	[95]	Sweden	AN, BNEDNOS	14	Patients perception having recovered from an ED	Yes	Semi structured interviews	Phenomenological approach	second author scrutinized statements in relation to conceptions and categories	Self-identified as recovered at 1 year follow-up	Unclear	A/B
17	[96]	Australia	AN, BN	20	Experiences of developing and recovering from ED	Yes	Open ended interviews (semi-structured)	Live history interviews	two researchers reading and making margin notes	Self-reported	3 years	A/A
18	[80]	Canada	AN	12	Understanding journey of recovery from AN	Yes	Interviews	Feminist grounded theory	confirm/refine explication of emerging theory by participants	Self-identified as recovered	Unknown	B/B

Table 3 Meta-analysis: Intensity and frequency effect sizes of ED recovery criteria

Recovery Criteria			All (N = 18)	A/A (N = 8)	B/B (N = 8)		
	Evidence for recovery	Frequency effect size	Intensity effect size	Intensity effect size	Intensity effect size	χ^2	P (2-sided)
Self-acceptance	Strong	88.9%	15.3%	17.6%	13.8%	.679	.486
Positive relationsships with others	Strong	100%	12.7%	13.4%	14.6%	.070	.791
Personal growth	Strong	77.8%	12.7%	18.5%	8.5%	**5.432**	**.020**
Decrease in ED behavior/cognitions	Strong	77.8%	12.4%	9.2%	12.3%	.603	.437
Self-adaptability/resilience	Strong	77.8%	9.2%	9.2%	7.7%	.082	.774
Autonomy	Strong	83.3%	7.8%	8.4%	9.2%	-	.791*
Social contribution	Substantial	50%	6.9%	6.7%	6.9%	.004	.950
Improved (ED) body evaluation	Substantial	55.6%	5.8%	1.7%	6.2%		
Spiritual integration	Moderate	33.3%	2.9%	.8%	6.2%	-	**.037***
Purpose & meaning	Moderate	38.9%	2.9%	3.4%	3.1%	.016	.899
Improved (ED) physical functioning	Moderate	27.8%	2.6%	4.2%	1.5%	-	.264*
Happiness	Insufficient	22.2%	1.7%	.8%	1.5%	-	1.000*
Positive affect	Moderate	27.8%	1.7%	2.5%	.8%	-	.351*
Other	-	33.3%	1.7%	.8%	2.3%	-	.623*
Avowed life satisfaction	Insufficient	22.2%	1.2%	.8%	.8%	-	1.000*
Environmental mastery	Insufficient	11.1%	.9%	.8%	1.5%	-	1.000*
Social acceptance	Insufficient	11.1%	.9%	-	2.3%		.247*
Social integration	Insufficient	11.1%	.9%	.8%	.8%		1.000*
Social actualization	Insufficient	- -	-	-	-	-	-
Social coherence	Insufficient	- -	-	-	-	-	-

Note: Frequency effect size: Total N of studies divided by N of studies containing a criteria * 100, Intensity effect size: N of found criteria produced in all studies, divided by all found criteria in all studies * 100, χ^2 test of homogeneity (differences in two proportions), * p was calculated by Fisher's Exact test for violation of the minimal sample size of the χ^2 test

mentioned more (52.3% of all criteria) than the remission of ED pathology (20.8% of all criteria) as a marker for recovery.

These results underscore the conclusions of earlier work about the importance of including psychological dimensions in definitions of ED recovery [17, 26, 61]. PWB is not about happiness or positive affect, but explained as living a good life, with purpose and meaning, growing towards optimal functioning and self-realization [39, 62]. The philosophical roots of PWB lead back to Aristotle's formulation about the virtues life. The essence of this Greek philosophy is to know yourself and to become what you are [62]. Many themes in the studies were about finding a new or 'healthy' identity and developing self-insight and self-acceptance. Our results suggest that the underlying dimensions of PWB should be considered as fundamental aspects of ED recovery, perhaps even important to focus on during treatment than the abatement of symptoms. A focus on well-being in treatment has been suggested earlier for other psychiatric disorders by Fava and others [32, 41]. It is noted that Parloff and colleagues already suggested in 1954 that the goals of psychotherapy were not necessarily the reduction of symptoms, but increased personal effectiveness [32]. Several therapies have been developed focusing on PWB [63–68]. PWB is further related to work productivity, physical and overall mental health, and care consumption, even when controlling for symptoms of mental illness [37, 69, 70]. It can also improve the quality of life for psychiatric patients, and the change to recover on symptoms and decrease the risk of relapse [69, 71].

Environmental mastery was the only PWB dimension that showed insufficient evidence. However, environmental mastery could be considered to be an aspect of self-adaptability. Self-adaptability is defined broader, taking social and emotional adaptability into account. If the description of environmental mastery was described more broadly, taking all aspects of self-adaptability into account, this probably would have been found as evidence for a criterion for ED recovery. Limitations in the first WHO definition of health have recently led to a new definition of health, described as the ability to adapt and to self-manage, in the face of social, physical and emotional challenges [72, 73]. The importance of self-

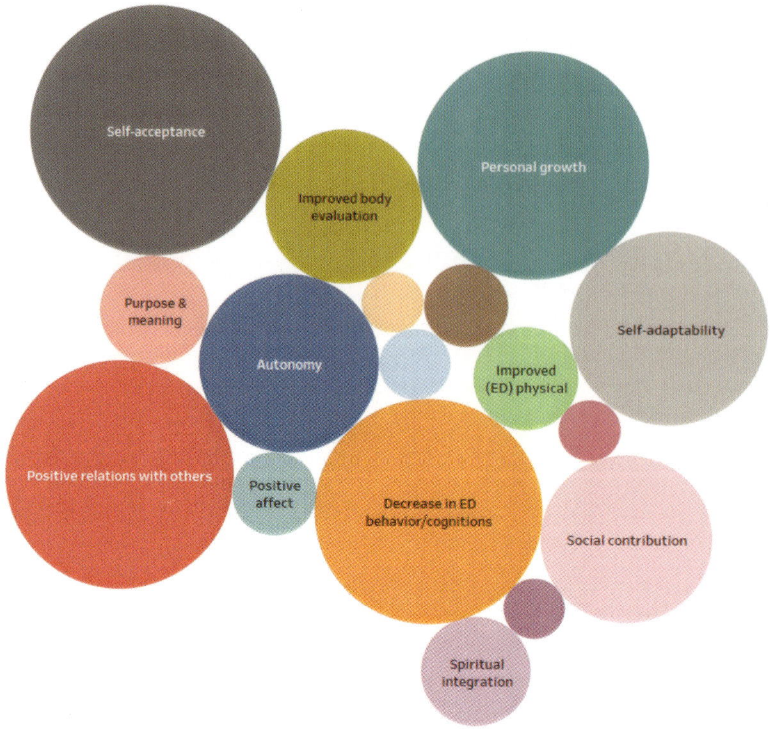

Fig. 2 Intensity effect sizes of criteria for recovery. Circles represent criteria for recovery and are based on the intensity effectsizes. The larger the circle, the larger the intensity effectsize. Circles that are labeled with a text have moderate, substantial or strong evidence for a recovery criteria. Circles that are not labeled with a text are the remaining criteria

adaptability/resilience as a criterion for ED recovery, fits this recently proposed definition of health [73]. In addition, Ryff stated that PWB is fundamentally anchored in how individuals face the challenges of life [62]. It is noted that "being recovered" is certainly not achieving a perfect state on the found criteria. It is explained as a unique and self-determined process by recovered individuals, without a clear endpoint [46, 74–79]. A new definition for ED recovery based on the latest definition of health and the results of this study could be: recovery from an ED is the ability to adapt and to self-manage in the face of social, physical and emotional challenges with an overall tendency towards growth in psychological well-being and adequate symptom remission (for instance as operationalized by Bardone-Cone et al. [18]). ED patients reported an overall impairment in PWB in a controlled study, which was not necessarily dependent on the presence of high levels of symptom severity, suggesting that PWB does not simply correspond to the absence of pathology [42]. Well-being and pathology as two different but related aspects of health has been well validated in several samples of the normal population and in patients [31, 36, 41].

"Recovery" may also indicate both a process and a state [32]. For eating disorder recovery, criteria also occupy a tenuous place between facilitators of recovery and criteria for demonstrating recovery in the literature. It is not always clear whether these themes are offered as requirements for ascertaining the degree to which someone is recovered or as facilitators to achieve recovery. In outcome studies, most themes, from changes in BMI to improvement in self-esteem, are used both as predictor variables and outcome variables; see for instance Vall and Wade [21]. One of the conclusions of a recent meta-synthesis was that the presence of supportive relationships is an important facilitator for recovery [47]. Recovery in the qualitative sense is often described as a process or journey [74, 75, 80]; and yet, what we need in a clinical sense is criteria to gauge and compare outcomes (see also Rosenvinge and Pettersen [17], p. 1). We argue that recovery dimensions that remain important aspects for individuals' health, such as positive relationships, are operationalized as criteria for recovery, in accordance with health and well-being definitions [37, 81]. It is likely that these criteria, related to well-being, are also important as criteria for recovery for other pychiatric disorders, such as depression. In a sample of patients with depressive symptoms, it was found that not only psychopathology improves, but also that PWB increases during treatment [82]. In another outcome study it was found that many patients with depressive symptoms improved either on psychopathology, or on the well-being dimensions and not on both, suggesting that both are important to measure in outcome studies and should be considered as criteria for recovery for psychiatric disorders [83].

Limitations

Although a qualitative meta-analytic approach allows for a more comprehensive explanation of a phenomenon than the individual qualitative studies explain, there are several limitations concerning this study. First, the presented methods and results were influenced by the methodology of the primary studies and their findings. Some of the primary studies failed to provide sufficient details about the background of the participants, used methods and/or results. It is also unclear how different systems of data analysis have formed the results in the primary studies. By examining differences in outcomes between low risk of bias studies and risk of bias studies we tried to minimize the risk of bias. Second, that some hypothesized dimensions were or were not supported does not necessarily depend only on the studies and participants, but also may be a flaw in inadequate thematic analysis or misclassification of themes. We tried to address possible classification bias by independent analysis and calculating an interrater agreement. Third, this study shows frequencies, constituting the importance of recovery criteria, but fails to show the contradictions between studies, including, but not least, that to claim that those in the study were recovered, they had to determine provisional criteria for recovery, which differed significantly between studies. The method of this study did not allow to examine differences in criteria between type of eating disorder. Most primary studies focused on either, AN, or all eating disorder types, which makes it difficult to divide results into ED type groups. Further research could focus on differences in well-being criteria between ED types. In a study examining the dimensions of psychological well-being among ED patients, differences in severity were found [42]. Compared with a control group, patients with BN had greater impairment on all psychological well-being scales, whereas patients with BED showed greater impairment on only three scales and patients with AN on only two scales. It is possible that improvement on the several well-being dimensions has a different priority depending on the ED type [42]. Also, the search strategy was quite narrow, with a lack of synonyms for "recovery" or "recovered", such as "remission", "rehabilitation", "restoration". However, we argue that these synonyms are not used regularly in qualitative ED recovery studies examining the view of patients or recovered individuals. In fact, in the reference-check, no suitable other studies were found using these synonyms. At last, this study examined criteria for being recovered among people who were considered recovered. Further research should examine how these recovery criteria develop and influence each other during the recovery process.

Conclusions

We conclude that psychological well-being and self-adaptability are core aspects of recovery in addition to remission of ED symptoms. A focus in treatment on these health dimensions seems therefore important to achieve recovery. Whether someone is recovered or not remains a question primarily to be answered by the patient her/himself. However, to find best treatment options, researchers and clinicians need to measure the most fundamental criteria for recovery. This study, among other studies [16, 17, 25, 26, 47, 84], provides a further direction to understand which criteria are most important to measure. Developing and validating instruments that measure recovery on these fundamental criteria is warranted. It is also advised to establish an international standard or guideline on how to measure ED recovery outcomes and which instruments to use, so that we might be able to compare treatment outcomes in the near future.

Abbreviations

AN: Anorexia Nervosa; BED: Binge Eating Disorder; BN: Bulimia Nervosa; ED: Eating Disorder; EDNOS: Eating Disorder Not Otherwise Specified; PWB: Psychological Well-being

Acknowledgements

The authors would like to thank Beth McGilley for her excellent comments on the manuscript.

Funding

The authors do not have any funds available for this study.

Authors' contributions

The contributions of the authors were as follows: ETB rewrote the introduction, results and discussion and commented on all versions of the manuscript. GJW, wrote several parts of the introduction, audited the analysis, and commented on all versions of the manuscript. MR wrote parts in the introduction and discussion, improved the procedure of the analysis, audited the analysis, and commented on all versions of the manuscript. CAB analysed the data by labeling the original themes and commented on one version of the manuscript. ALM wrote several parts of the introduction, searched for eligible studies, helped with the analysis, and commented on several versions of the manuscript. JAV selected the articles from the databases, searched for eligible studies, analysed the data by labeling the original themes, did the significance tests, and wrote most parts of the manuscript and tables. All authors read and approved the final manuscript.

Competing interests

The authors declare that they have no competing interests.

Author details
[1]Centre for eHealth and Well-being Research, University of Twente, Psychology, Health, & Technology, Enschede, The Netherlands. [2]Human Concern Foundation, center for Eating Disorders, Amsterdam, The Netherlands. [3]University of Guelph, Department of Family Relations and Applied Nutrition, Ontario, Canada. [4]Optentia Research Focus Area, North-West University (VTC), Vanderbijlpark, South Africa.

References

1. Jenkins HRR, Meyer C, Blissett JM. Eating disorders and quality of life: a review of the literature. Clin Psychol Rev. 2011;31:113–21.
2. Mitchison D, Hay PJ, Slewa-Younan S, Mond J. Time trends in population prevalence of eating disorder behaviors and their relationship to quality of life. PLoS One. 2012;7:e48450.
3. Mond J, Hay PJ, Rodgers B, Owen C. Quality of life impairment in a community sample of women with eating disorders. Aust N Z J Psychiatry. 2012;46:561–8.
4. Hoek HW. Incidence, prevalence and mortality of anorexia nervosa and other eating disorders. Curr Opin Psychiatry. 2006;19:389–94.
5. Harris EC, Barraclough B. Excess mortality of mental disorder. Br J Psychiatry. 1998;173:11–53.
6. Löwe B, Zipfel S, Buchholz C, Dupont Y, Reas DL, Herzog W. Long-term outcome of anorexia nervosa in a prospective 21-year follow-up study. Psychol Med. 2001;31:881–90.
7. Hay PJ, Chinn D, Forbes D, Madden S, Newton R, Sugenor L, et al. Royal Australian and new Zealand College of Psychiatrists clinical practice guidelines for the treatment of eating disorders. Aust New Zeal J Psychiatry. 2014;48:1–62.
8. Trimbos: Multidisciplinaire richtlijn eetstoornissen: richtlijn voor de diagnostiek en behandeling van eetstoornissen [Multidisciplinary quideline for diagnostics and treatment of eating disorders] [Internet]. Utrecht: Trimbos Instituut; 2006. Available from: www.ggzrichtlijnen.nl/eetstoornissen.
9. Yager J, Devlin MJ, Halmi KA, Herzog DB, Iii JEM, Powers P, et al. Treatment of patients with eating disorders, third edition work group on eating disorders guide to using this practice guideline introduction 2006;
10. Bulik CM, Berkman ND, Brownley KA, Sedway JA, Lohr KN. Anorexia nervosa treatment: a systematic review of randomized controlled trials. Int J Eat Disord. 2007;40:310–20.
11. Hay PJ. A systematic review of evidence for psychological treatments in eating disorders: 2005-2012. Int J Eat Disord. 2013;46:462–9.
12. Zipfel S, Giel KE, Bulik CM, Hay P, Schmidt U. Anorexia nervosa: aetiology, assessment, and treatment. The lancet Psychiatry. 2015;2:1099–111.
13. Berkman ND, Lohr KN, Bulik CM. Outcomes of eating disorders: a systematic review of the literature. Int J Eat Disord. 2007;40:293–309.
14. Noordenbos G. When have eating disordered patients recovered and what do the DSM-IV criteria tell about recovery? Eat Disord J Treat Prev. 2011;19:234–45.
15. McGilley BH, Szablewski JK. Chapter 12 - recipe for recovery: necessary ingredients for the Client's and Clinician's success. In: Maine M, McGilley BH, Bunnell DW, editors. Treatment of eating disorders. San Diego: Academic Press; 2010. p. 197–213.
16. Jarman M, Walsh S. Evaluating recovery from anorexia nervosa and bulimia nervosa: integrating lessons learned from research and clinical practice. Clin Psychol Rev. 1999;19:773–88.
17. Rosenvinge JH, Pettersen G: Relevant topics in eating disorders; in Lobera IJ (ed). InTech, 2012.
18. Bardone-Cone AM, Harney MB, Maldonado CR, Lawson MA, Robinson P, Smith R, et al. Defining recovery from an eating disorder: conceptualization, validation, and examination of psychosocial functioning and psychiatric comorbidity. Behav Res Ther. 2010;48:194–202.
19. Couturier J, Lock J. What is recovery in adolescents anorexia nervosa? Int J Eat Disord. 2006;39:550–5.
20. Steinhausen HC. The outcome of anorexia nervosa in the 20th century. Am J Psychiatry. 2002;159:1284–93.
21. Vall E, Wade TD. Predictors of treatment outcome in individuals with eating disorders: a systematic review and meta-analysis. Int J Eat Disord. 2015;48:946–71.
22. Fairburn CG, Beglin S. Assessment of eating disorders: interview or self-report questionnaire? Int J Eat Disord. 1994;16:363–70.
23. de la Rie SM, Noordenbos G, van Furth EF. Quality of life and eating disorders. Qual Life Res. 2005;14:1511–22.
24. Dawson L, Rhodes P, Touyz S. Defining recovery from anorexia nervosa: a Delphi study to explore practitioners' views. J Eat Disord. 2015; doi:10.1080/21662630.2015.1009145.
25. Noordenbos G, Seubring A. Criteria for recovery from eating disorders according to patients and therapists. Eat Disord. 2006;14:41–54.
26. Emanuelli P, Waller G, Jones-Chester M, Ostuzzi R. Recovery from disordered eating: sufferers' and clinicians' perspectives. Eur Eat Disord Rev. 2012;20:363–72.
27. Keyes CLM. The mental health continuum: from languishing to flourishing in life. J Health Soc Behav. 2002;43:207–22.
28. Jahoda M. Current concepts of positive mental health. Joint commission on mental health and illness monograph series. Vol 1. New York, US: Basic Books; 1958. p. xxi.
29. Westerhof GJ, Keyes CLM. Mental illness and mental health: the two continua model across the lifespan. J Adult Dev. 2010;17:110–9.
30. Seligman M, Csikszentmihalyi M. Positive psychology: an introduction. Am Psychol. 2000;55:5–14.
31. Lamers SMA. Positive mental health : measurement, relevance and implications; 2012. doi:10.3990/1.9789036533706.
32. Fava GA. The concept of recovery in affective disorders. Psychother Psychosom. 1996;65:2–13.
33. Fava GA, Ruini C. Development and characteristics of a well-being enhancing psychotherapeutic strategy: well-being therapy. J Behav Ther Exp Psychiatry. 2003;34:45–63.
34. Ryff CD, Singer B. Psychological well-being: meaning, measurement, and implications for psychotherapy research. Psychother Psychosom. 1996;65:14–23.
35. World Health Organization. Promoting mental health: concepts, emerging evidence, practice. Geneva: WHO; 2005.
36. Keyes CLM. Mental illness and/or mental health? Investigating axioms of the complete state model of health. J Consult Clin Psychol. 2005;73
37. Keyes CLM. Mental illness and/or mental health? Investigating axioms of the complete state model of health. J Consult Clin Psychol. 2005;73:539–48.
38. Ryff C. Happiness is everything, or is it? Explorations on the meaning of psychological well-being. J Pers Soc Psychol. 1989;57:1069–81.
39. Deci EL, Ryan RM. Hedonia, eudaimonia, and well-being: an introduction. [Internet]. J Happiness Stud. 2008;9:1–11.
40. Lamers SMA, Westerhof GJ, Bohlmeijer ET, CLM K. Mental health and illness in relation to physical health across the lifespan. New York: Springer; 2013.
41. Lamers SMA, Westerhof GJ, Glas C a. W, Bohlmeijer ET: the bidirectional relation between positive mental health and psychopathology in a longitudinal representative panel study. J Posit Psychol 2015;9760:1–8.
42. Tomba E, Offidani E, Tecuta L, Schumann R, Ballardini D. Psychological well-being in out-patients with eating disorders: a controlled study. Int J Eat Disord. 2014;47:252–8.
43. Doll HA, Petersen SE, Stewart-brown SL. Eating disorders and emotional and physical well-being: associations between student self-reports of eating disorders and quality of life as measured by the SF-36. Qual Life Res. 2005;14:705–17.
44. de la Rie SM, Noordenbos G, Donker M, van Furth E. The patient's view on quality of life and eating disorders. Int J Eat Disord. 2007;40:13–20.
45. Bowlby CCG, Anderson TTL, Hall MEL, Willingham MMM, Lewis Hall M, Willingham MMM. Recovered professionals exploring eating disorder recovery: a qualitative investigation of meaning. Clin Soc Work J. 2012;43:1–10.
46. Lamoureux MMH, Bottorff JL. "Becoming the real me": recovering from anorexia nervosa. Health Care Women Int. 2005;26:170–88.
47. Duncan TK, Sebar B, Lee J. Reclamation of power and self: a meta-synthesis exploring the process of recovery from anorexia nervosa. Adv Eat Disord Theory Res Pract. 2015;3:177–90.
48. Leslie J: Understanding the changing landscape of client perspectives of recovery from anorexia nervosa. 2014.
49. Shohet M. Narrating anorexia: "full" and "struggling" genres of recovery. Ethos. 2007;35:344–82.
50. Timulak L. Meta-analysis of qualitative studies : a tool for reviewing qualitative research findings in psychotherapy. Psychother Res. 2009;19:591–600.

51. Schreiber R, Crooks D, Stern PN. Qualitative meta-analysis. In: Morse JM, editor. Completing a qualitative project: details and dialogue. CA, Sage: Thousand Oaks; 1997. p. 311–26.
52. Finfgeld DL. Metasynthesis: the state of the art—so far. Qual Health Res. 2003;13:893–904.
53. Liberati A, Altman DG, Tetzlaff J, Mulrow C, JPA I, Clarke M, et al. Annals of internal medicine academia and clinic the PRISMA statement for reporting systematic reviews and meta-analyses of studies that evaluate health care Interventions. Ann Intern Med. 2009;151:W65–94.
54. American Psychiatric Association: Diagnostics and statistical manual of mental disorders (5th ed.). Washington DC: APA; 2013.
55. Barroso J, Powell-Cope GM. Metasynthesis of qualitative research on living with HIV infection. Qual Health Res. 2000;10:340–53.
56. Critical Appraisal Skills Programme (CASP): Qualitative Research Checklist: 10 questions to help you make sense of qualitative research [Internet]. Oxford: Better Value Healthcare; 2013. Available from: www.casp-uk.net.
57. Espindola CR, Blay SL. Anorexia nervosa treatment from the patient perspective: a metasynthesis of qualitative studies. Ann Clin Psychiatry. 2009;21:38–48.
58. Feder GS, Hutson M, Ramsay J, Taket AR. Women exposed to intimate partner violence: expectations and experiences when they encounter health care professionals: a meta-analysis of qualitative studies. Arch Intern Med. 2006;166:22–37.
59. Campbell R, Pound P, Pope C, Britten N, Pill R, Morgan M, et al. Evaluating meta- ethnography: a synthesis of qualitative research on lay experiences of diabetes and diabetes care. Soc Sci Med. 2003;54:671–84.
60. Sandelowski M, Barroso J. Creating metasummaries of qualitative findings. Nurs Res. 2003;52:226–33.
61. Noordenbos G. Which criteria for recovery are relevant according to eating disorder patients and therapists? Eat Disord J Treat Prev. 2011;19:441–51.
62. Ryff CD. Psychological well-being revisited: advances in the science and practice of Eudaimonia. Psychother Psychosom. 2014;83:10–28.
63. Fava GA, Rafanelli C, Cazzaro M, Conti S, Grandi S. Well-being therapy. A novel psychotherapeutic approach for residual symptoms of affective disorders. Psychol Med. 1998;28:475–80.
64. Weiss LA, Westerhof GJ, Bohlmeijer ET. Can we increase psychological well-being? The effects of interventions on psychological well-being: a meta-analysis of randomized controlled trials. PLoS One. 2016;11:1–16.
65. Weiss LA, Westerhof GJ, Bohlmeijer ET. Nudging socially isolated people towards well-being with the "happiness route": design of a randomized controlled trial for the evaluation of a happiness-based intervention. Health Qual Life Outcomes. 2013;11:159.
66. Fava GA, Ruini C, Rafanelli C, Finos L, Salmaso L, Mangelli L, et al. Well-being therapy of generalized anxiety disorder. Psychother Psychosom. 2005;74:26–30.
67. Gander F, Proyer RT, Ruch W. Positive psychology interventions addressing pleasure, engagement, meaning, positive relationships, and accomplishment increase well-being and ameliorate depressive symptoms: a randomized, placebo-controlled online study. Front Psychol. 2016;7 doi:10.3389/fpsyg.2016.00686.
68. Fava GA, Tomba E. Increasing psychological well-being and resilience by psychotherapeutic methods. J Pers. 2009;77:1903–34.
69. Weiss LA. Direction: happiness. Improving well-being of vulnerable groups. Enschede, the Netherlands: University of Twente; 2016.
70. Chida Y, Steptoe A. Positive psychological well-being and mortality: a quantitative review of prospective observational studies. Psychosom Med. 2008;70(7):741–56.
71. Sin N, Della Porta M, Lyubomirsky S. Tailoring positive psychology interventions to treat depressed individuals. In: Donaldson S, Csikszentmihalyi M, Nakamura J, editors. Applied positive psychology: improving everyday life, health, schools, work, and society; 2011. p. 79–96.
72. Huber M, van Vliet M, Giezenberg M, Winkens B, Heerkens Y, Dagnelie PC, et al. Towards a "patient-centred" operationalisation of the new dynamic concept of health: a mixed methods study. BMJ Open. 2016;6:e010091.
73. Huber M, Knottnerus JA, Green L, Horst HVD, Jadad AR, Kromhout D, et al. How should we define health? Br Med J. 2011;343:1–3.
74. Dawson L, Rhodes P, Touyz S. "doing the impossible": the process of recovery from chronic anorexia nervosa. Qual Health Res. 2014;24:494–505.
75. Hay PJ, Cho K. A qualitative exploration of influences on the process of recovery from personal written accounts of people with anorexia nervosa. Women Health. 2013;53:730–40.
76. Lindgren B-M, Enmark A, Bohman A, Lundstrom M. A qualitative study of young women's experiences of recovery from bulimia nervosa. J Adv Nurs. 2015;71:860–9.
77. Jenkins J, Ogden J. Becoming "whole" again: a qualitative study of women's views of recovering from anorexia nervosa; 2012. p. 1–25.
78. Nilsson K, Hägglöf B. Patient perspectives of recovery in adolescent onset anorexia nervosa. Eat Disord. 2006;14:305–11.
79. Shahar M, Latzer Y, Buchbinder E. Recovery from anorexia nervosa: the patient's perspective. In: Stein D, Latzer Y, Stein D, editors. Latzer Y (Ed) (eds): treatment and recovery of eating disorders. Shahar: Meirav, Nova Science Publishers; 2012. p. 171–85.
80. Weaver K, Wuest J, Ciliska D. Understanding Women's journey of recovering from anorexia nervosa. Qual Health Res. 2005 Feb;15:188–206.
81. Ryff C, Keyes CLM. The structure of psychological well-being revisited. J Pers Soc Psychol. 1995;69(4):719–27.
82. Bohlmeijer ET, Lamers SMA, Fledderus M. Flourishing in people with depressive symptomatology increases withacceptance and commitment therapy. Post-hoc analyses of a randomized controlled trial. Behav Res Ther. 2015;65:101–6.
83. Trompetter HR, Lamers SMA, Westerhof GJ, Fledderus M, Bohlmeijer ET. Both positive mental health and psychopathology should be monitored in psychotherapy: confirmation for the dual-factor model in acceptance and commitment therapy. Behav Res Ther. 2017;91:58–63.
84. Dawson L, Rhodes P, Touyz S. Defining recovery from anorexia nervosa: a Delphi study to determine expert practitioners' views. Adv Eat Disord Theory Res Pract. 2015; doi:10.1080/21662630.2015.1009145.
85. Arthur-Cameselle JNJ. Quatromoni P a: eating disorders in collegiate female athletes: Factors that assist recovery. Eat Disord. 2014;22:50–61.
86. Lindgren B-M, Enmark A, Bohman A, Lundström M. A qualitative study of young women's experiences of recovery from bulimia nervosa. J Adv Nurs. 2015;71:860–9.
87. Jenkins J, Ogden J. Becoming "whole" again: a qualitative study of women's views of recovering from anorexia nervosa. Eur Eat Disord Rev. 2012;20:e23–31.
88. Linville D, Brown T, Sturm K, McDougal T. Eating disorders and social support: perspectives of recovered individuals. Eat Disord. 2012;20:216–31.
89. Espíndola CR, Blay SL. Long term remission of anorexia nervosa: Factors involved in the outcome of female patients. PLoS One. 2013;8:e56275.
90. Björk T, Wallin K, Pettersen G. Male experiences of life after recovery from an eating disorder. Eat Disord. 2012;20:460–8.
91. Nilsson K, Hagglof B. Patient perspectives of recovery in adolescent onset anorexia nervosa. Eat Disord. 2006;14:305–11.
92. Krentz A, Chew J, Arthur N. Recovery from binge eating disorder. Can J Couns. 2005;39:118–35.
93. Hsu GLK, Crisp AH, Callender JS. Recovery in anorexia nervosa — the Patient's perspective. Int J. 1992;11:341–50.
94. Matusek JA, Knudson RM. Rethinking recovery from eating disorders: spiritual and political dimensions. Qual Health Res. 2009;19:697–707.
95. Björk T, Ahlström G. The patient's perception of having recovered from an eating disorder. Health Care Women Int. 2008;29:926–44.
96. Patching J, Lawler J. Understanding women's experiences of developing an eating disorder and recovering: a life-history approach. Nurs Inq. 2009;16(1):10–21.

15

Family-based treatment for transition age youth: parental self-efficacy and caregiver accommodation

Gina Dimitropoulos[1,8*], Ashley L. Landers[2], Victoria E. Freeman[3], Jason Novick[4], Olivia Cullen[1], Marla Engelberg[5], Cathleen Steinegger[6] and Daniel Le Grange[7]

Abstract

Background: Family-Based Treatment (FBT) is the first line of care in paediatric treatment while adult programs focus on individualized models of care. Transition age youth (TAY) with Anorexia Nervosa (AN) are in a unique life stage and between systems of care. As such, they and their caregivers may benefit from specialized, developmentally tailored models of treatment.

Methods: The primary purpose of this study was to assess if parental self-efficacy and caregiver accommodation changed in caregivers during the course of FBT-TAY for AN. The secondary aim was to determine if changes in parental self-efficacy and caregiver accommodation contributed to improvements in eating disorder behaviour and weight restoration in the transition age youth with AN. Twenty-six participants (ages 16–22) and 39 caregivers were recruited. Caregivers completed the Parents versus Anorexia Scale and Accommodation and Enabling Scale for Eating Disorders at baseline, end-of-treatment (EOT), and 3 months follow-up.

Results: Unbalanced repeated measures designs for parental self-efficacy and caregiver accommodation towards illness behaviours were conducted using generalized estimation equations. Parental self-efficacy increased from baseline to EOT, although not significantly (p = .398). Parental self-efficacy significantly increased from baseline to 3 months post-treatment (p = .002). Caregiver accommodation towards the illness significantly decreased from baseline to EOT (p = 0.0001), but not from baseline to 3 months post-treatment (p = 1.000). Stepwise ordinary least squares regression estimates of eating disorder behaviour and weight restoration did not show that changes in parental-self efficacy and caregiver accommodation predict eating disorder behaviour or weight restoration at EOT or 3 months post-treatment.

Conclusions: Our findings demonstrate, albeit preliminary at this stage, that FBT-TAY promotes positive increases in parental self-efficacy and assists caregivers in decreasing their accommodation to illness behaviours for transition age youth with AN. However, changes in the parental factors did not influence changes in eating and weight in the transition age youth.

Keywords: Family-based treatment, Family therapy, Anorexia nervosa, Eating disorders, Transition age youth, Caregivers

* Correspondence: gdimit@ucalgary.ca
[1]Faculty of Social Work, Matheson Centre for Mental Health Research, University of Calgary, 4212-2800 University Way N.W., Calgary, Alberta, Canada
[8]Hotchkiss Brain Institute, University of Calgary, 4212-2800 University Way N.W., Calgary, Alberta, Canada
Full list of author information is available at the end of the article

Plain English summary

Family-Based Treatment for Transition Age Youth were delivered to 26 participants with Anorexia Nervosa (ages 16–22) and their families. This study evaluated how family members responded to eating disorder (ED) behaviours throughout the course of this treatment. This study also evaluated how confident family members felt about their ability to help their loved one with ED behaviours throughout the course of treatment. The impact of changes in parental responses and confidence in helping with eating disorder symptoms and weight gain was examined. Throughout the course of treatment caregiver accommodation to eating disorder behaviour decreased and feelings of parental self-efficacy increased. However, changes in parental self-efficacy and accommodation did not predict changes in eating disorder behaviour and weight restoration in transition age youth with AN.

Background

Anorexia Nervosa (AN) is a life threatening mental health condition [1] with severe consequences such as cardiac failure, osteoporosis [2], increased risk for suicide [3, 4] and significant comorbidities such as anxiety, depression and substance use disorders [5]. To prevent severe and enduring presentations of AN it is important that effective early interventions be provided to promote the best outcomes [6]. There is evidence for the use of family therapies (FT) with adolescents with AN [7], including Family-Based Treatment (FBT). However, there is limited evidence-based practice models for transition age youth between the ages of 18 to 24 [8–10]. Researching effective treatments for this age group is a necessary next step in the treatment of AN.

Family-based treatment for adolescent anorexia nervosa

There are a variety of family therapy approaches developed for the treatment of AN such as Family Therapies for AN (FT-AN) and Multi-Family Therapy for AN (MFT-AN) [11]. The current study has focused on treatment using manualized FBT. At this time, FTs for AN are the most efficacious treatment for medically stable adolescents with AN [12, 13], and FT-AN is considered an appropriate treatment for this population [14]. The current study focuses on a manualized form of FT-AN: Family-Based Treatment (FBT). This treatment is guided by five fundamental principles: an agnostic view of the illness, externalization of the illness as something separate from the adolescent, emphasis on increasing parental empowerment, a focus on restoring healthy eating, and the therapist as a consultant to the family [15]. When compared to other treatments for AN, FBT has been found to reduce the need for hospital admissions during treatment [16], and has superior treatment outcomes on eating disorder symptomatology at end of treatment when compared to individual treatment and full remission at 6- and 12-month follow-up [17].

Family-based treatments for transition age youth with anorexia nervosa

Althought studies of FBT indicate that it is an effective treatment [18] and that for participants ages 9 to 19 years, there are not significant differences in treatment outcomes based on age [19], FBT is not commonly used in specialized adult eating disorder programs (EDPs). This is possibly becausefamilies are not intrinsically present in adult ED treatment, whereas families often accompany youth to assessments and treatment in the pediatric system. However, there may be special considerations for transition age youth (ages 16 to approximately 25) that may necessitate unique family involvement, vital to the treatment of their illness in both pediatric and adult care.

Transition age youth experience many transitions that define their developmental stage, such as post-secondary education, increased fiscal responsibility, changing geographic location, and increased personal responsibility and autonomy [20]. For transition age youth with AN, these markers of young adulthood are present despite the limitations of their illness. Dimitropoulos et al., [21] found that eating disorder clinicians identified that many transition age youth express a desire for age appropriate support from their caregivers, including negotiating levels of involvement and support for their growing independence and confidence to overcome their ED. Due to a better understanding of these concerns for young adult development, experts in the field have begun exploring how to adapt FBT for transition age youth [8, 9].

An open trial of FBT for transition age youth (FBT-TAY) that encouraged negotiation between supportive caregivers and the independence of the youth has recently shown promising outcomes for individuals with AN [9]. FBT-TAY was designed for those between the ages of 16 to 25 and is an adaptation of FBT, which emphasises a collaboration between the transition age youth and his/her family, while maintaining their age-appropriate autonomy. Another pilot study of FBT for Young Adults (FBT-Y), where a similar collaborative approach to treatment was used, also showed promise with 59% of participants who completed treatment retaining weight restoration at 12 months post-treatment [8]. These adaptations of FBT are important for those ages 16 to 25 who are going through major life transitions [22], as well as moving from the pediatric to adult health care system [23].

Caregivers' impact on family-based treatment

Parental self-efficacy has been identified as a potential mechanism of change that promotes positive treatment outcome in FBT [24, 25]. Parental self-efficacy, as measured by the Parents versus Anorexia scale (PvA), is the ability for caregivers to be empowered in terms of supporting weight gain in their child [26]. Behavioural support around weight gain is required as in FBT parents are responsible for the re-nourishment of their child through consistent meal support as well as halting ED behaviours such as purging or excessive exercise. When parents achieve confidence in the re-nourishment process during the first four sessions of FBT, the adolescent is more likely to be weight restored at the end of treatment, as well as greater reductions in symptoms of depression and anxiety [26, 27]. Further, Robinson et al. [26] found that parents undergoing FBT with their adolescent had significant increases in parental self-efficacy throughout treatment which was predictive of reductions in ED psychopathology as well. Taken together, parental self-efficacy seems an important factor for positive treatment outcomes for adolescents in FBT. However, there were no studies that directly assessed caregiver self-efficacy in FBT for transition age youth with AN.

Caregivers may also engage in behaviours that inadvertently exacerbate ED symptoms [27, 28]. Eating disorders often lead families to 're-organize' such that monitoring and managing symptoms become the primary concern. When this occurs, family functioning can decline and caregivers can feel helpless [28]. When caregivers inadvertantly accommodate the illness, they are engaging in maladaptive behaviours such as avoiding social situations, allowing meal restrictions, or enabling their loved one to continue a strenuous exercise regimen [29]. In a recent study by Stillar et al. [30], caregivers that experienced more fear and self-blame were also more likely to allow recovery-interfering behaviours in their loved one. It is important to note that the longer a loved one has had an ED, the more accommodating caregivers become to the illness' symptoms as measured by the Accommodation and Enabling Scale of Eating Disorders (AESED) [29]. It is clear that accommodation and enabling behaviors seen in caregivers can negatively influence parental self-efficacy and thus negatively impact treatment outcomes. To date, there are no studies directly assessing caregiver accommodation and enabling behaviours in FBT for transition age youth with AN.

Aims

The primary aim of the study was to determine if parental self-efficacy and caregiver accommodation changed in a course of FBT-TAY from baseline to the end-of-treatment (EOT), and 3 months post-treatment. The second aim of the study was to determine if changes in parental self-efficacy and caregiver accommodation influenced changes in eating disorder behaviour and weight restoration at EOT and 3 months post-treatment in transition age youth with AN.

Method

Data collection

An open trial of FBT-TAY was conducted across one adult and two pediatric hospital sites in Ontario, Canada between August 2014 and September 2016. The acceptability, feasibility, and impact of FBT-TAY on eating disorder behaviors and weight restoration is described by Dimitropoulos et al. [9]. Three hospital sites were selected to ensure a diverse sample of adolescents and young adults from pediatric and adult speciality ED clinics was obtained. Each hospital contained a specialized EDP and participants were recruited at the point of assessment for admittance into the EDP, as well as through community advertising. During initial assessment or a the time of self-referral from the community, confirmation of diagnosis was made by a psychologist or psychiatrist and if a potential participant was still interested in the study, they then met with the study coordinator and participated in informed consent. For an in depth description of the treatment please see Dimitropoulos et al., 2017 [9].

All potential participants were offered treatment as usual (TAU) or FBT-TAY. FBT was the TAU in both pediatric hospital sites (ages 12–18). In the pediatric hospitals, potential participants were offered either traditional FBT or FBT-TAY. At the adult hospital site, TAU was an intensive cognitive behavioral therapy (CBT) based group program within an inpatient (average stay of 5 months) or day hospital (average stay of 5 weeks) setting. In the adult hospital, family therapy was an optional component of treatment. At the point of assessment, if a potential participant met eligibility criteria (described below) for the FBT-TAY open trial, they were referred to the study coordinator. Potential participants were asked to identify at least one caregiver to participate in treatment. To support the autonomy of the transition age youth, caregiver selection was entirely left to their discretion and was defined broadly to include parents, guardians, siblings, partners, extended family and/or friends. All caregivers and participants with an eating disorder gave informed consent and were then assigned to a FBT-TAY study therapist. Further details about the methodology and participants are described by Dimitropolous et al. [9].

Family-based treatment for transition age youth

FBT-TAY includes 25 sessions over the course of three phases [31]. These phases and their goals are briefly outlined in Fig. 1. Caregivers were integrally involved in each phase in the treatment. During phase one, the therapist worked collaboratively with the transition age youth to identify ways that their caregivers could specifically support them with meal support and symptom management. Explicitly, the caregivers were asked to support the transition age youth during mealtimes and monitor symptoms. The transition age youths were asked to be responsible for communicating to their families what type of support they required to assist with recovery from the eating disorder. In this way, the transition age youth had input in how their treatment was delivered. In phase two of treatment, the entire family was encouraged to allow the transition age youth more independent eating in a variety of normal situations (e.g., on a university campus, at work, with friends). Finally, in phase three, the transition age youth was asked to develop a plan for maintained recovery and shared this plan with their caregivers. The caregivers were tasked with being the first point of contact should a struggle with the eating disorder behaviours re-emerge.

Participant and caregiver characteristics

A total of 26 young people participated in this study (*M* = 18.15 years, *SD* = 2.11). The majority of participants were female (96.2%), Caucasian (61.5%), single (88.5%), living with family or relatives (92.3%), unemployed (53.9%), and had completed some high school education (46.2%). A total of 39 caregivers (23 mothers, 16 fathers) (*M* = 50.59 years old, *SD* = 6.80) were included in the analysis. Two parents did not complete the questionnaires required for inclusion in the analysis. The majority of caregivers were Caucasian (66.7%), married/partnered (79.5%), employed full-time (74.4%), and had an undergraduate university degree or higher (61.5%). See Table 1 for information regarding caregiver demographics.

Measures

To assess the impacts of FBT-TAY on caregiver accommodation to the illness, parental self-efficacy, participant eating disorder behaviour, and weight restoration, analyses

FBT-TAY

Phase 1: Session 1	20 to 30-minutes with patient: review weight, non-negotiables of treatment, thoughts about family involvement.
	50 minutes with family: Greet the family and take a history of AN including treatments and impacts on each family member.
	Create a crisis for the parents and patient
	Charge the parents and the patient with the task of re-nourishment and ask the parents to prepare and bring a meal to the next session.
Phase 1: Family Meal	Ask each family member about eating habits at home. Discuss how family meals have changed as a result of the TAY's development and the illness. Empower the family to help loved-one take one more bite.
Phase 1: Remainder	Meet with the patient for 20 to 30 minutes, with family for 50 minutes
8-10 sessions	As the family's consultant, empower the family and the young adult to collaborate on how they can relentlessly focus on food and eating behaviours.
Phase 2	Meet with the patient for 20 to 30 minutes, with family for 50 minutes
10-12 sessions	Gradually return control of age-appropriate meals to the young adult.
	Young adult practices eating in a variety of independent settings (school, work, with partner, etc.)
Phase 3	3-5 sessions, 2 individual sessions with young adult; 2-3 family sessions
3-5 sessions	In individual meetings, create a plan with young-adult on how to stay well moving forward. Discuss the warning signs for relapse and how future struggles will be dealt with.
	In family meetings, encourage young adult to share their plan with family members.
	Review progress of therapy with the entire family and say goodbye.

Fig. 1 Summary of Family-Based Treatment for Transition Age Youth

Table 1 Caregiver Characteristics ($n = 39$)

	n	Percent or Mean	*SD*
Age		50.59	6.80
Gender			
Female	23	58.97	
Male	16	41.03	
Race			
Caucasian	26	66.67	
Non-Caucasian	13	33.33	
Marital Status			
Single	8	20.51	
Partnered/Married	31	79.49	
Living Situation			
With family, relatives, friends or partner	36	92.31	
Alone	3	7.69	
Education			
High school diploma	3	7.69	
Undergraduate university degree	24	61.54	
Some graduate education	1	2.56	
Graduate degree or higher	11	28.21	
Employment			
Part time	5	12.82	
Unemployed	2	5.13	
Employed full-time	29	74.36	
Homemaker	2	5.13	
Disabled	1	2.56	
Religion			
Christian	21	53.85	
None	8	20.51	
Jewish	6	15.38	
Hindi	3	7.69	
Muslim	1	2.56	

were performed across three timepoints: pre-treatment, post-treatment, and 3 months post-treatment.

Instruments administered to transition age youth

Eating disorder behaviour

The Eating Disorder Examination Questionnaire (EDE-Q) is a 33-item, self-report measure which comprises four subscales (Restraint, Weight Concern, Shape Concern and Eating Concern) [32]. Each subscale has demonstrated excellent reliability and validity [33]. The EDE-Q global score is calculated by averaging all subscale scores.

Weight restoration

For each participant aged 16–20, the weight restoration goal was comprised their median BMI (kg/m^2) according to age and sex [34]. For each participant aged 20.1–22, the weight restoration goal was a BMI of 20.0. At baseline, each participant's height and weight was measured by the intake nurse. Subsequently, each participant's weight was measured at the end of treatment and was self-reported for the EDE-Q three-month follow-up questionnaire. The BMI achieved by each participant aged 16–20 was divided by the median BMI for their age and sex to calculate weight restoration at baseline, end of treatment, and 3 months post-treatment. The BMI achieved by each participant aged 20.1–22 was divided by 20.0 to calculate weight restoration at each timepoint.

Caregiver instruments

Parental self-efficacy

The Parents versus Anorexia (PvA) scale was developed to assess parental self-efficacy in the role of re-nourishing a child back to health [35]. This instrument has seven items rated on a five-point Likert Scale ranging from strongly disagree to strongly agree. Scores range from seven to 35. Higher scores indicate greater self-efficacy [35]. Parental self-efficacy was measured at baseline, end of treatment, and at 3 months post-treatment for mothers and fathers.

Caregiver accommodation

The Accommodation and Enabling Scale for Eating Disorders (AESED) is a 33-item self-report scale which is used to assess the degree to which caregivers accommodate and enable illness behaviours in their loved one [29]. Responses are measured on a five-point Likert Scale ranging from zero (never) to four (every day). The total scores range from zero (0) to 132 with higher scores indicating greater enabling and tolerating of ED behaviours. This scale is made up of five subscales which have Cronbach's alpha values between .77 and .90. For the purpose of this study, we only used the total score of the AESED. Caregiver accommodation was measured at baseline, end of treatment, and 3 months post-treatment for mothers and fathers.

Missing data

Missing data was addressed using multiple imputation [36] The process of multiple imputation involves multiple copies of a dataset being created and the missing values being replaced by imputed values. These imputed values are "sampled from a predictive distribution based on the observed data" [Pg. 2, 37]. This procedure takes into consideration the uncertainty associated with the prediction of missing values by including appropriate variability within the multiply imputed values [37]. The data of every caregiver who provided data at baseline was analyzed, regardless of their completion or withdrawal. Multiple imputation is superior to other approaches to address missing data, such as mean substitution or listwise deletion [38].

Data analyses

Analyses were performed in IBM SPSS Statistics Version 24. The primary objective of this study was to investigate changes in parental self-efficacy and caregiver accommodation from baseline to end of treatment and from baseline to 3 months post-treatment. Due to the unbalanced and correlated nature of the data, unbalanced repeated measures designs for parental self-efficacy and caregiver accommodation were conducted using generalized estimation equations (GEEs) to determine the time effect while controlling for each participant. Separate analyses were undertaken for each of the predictors (the PvA total score and the AESED total score) due to concerns with multicollinearity. Bonferroni adjusted *p* values are reported for each GEE that was performed.

The second objective of this study was to investigate the impact of parental self-efficacy and caregiver accommodation to the illness on eating disorder behaviour and weight restoration in the transition age youth with AN. Ordinary Least Square (OLS) regression estimates of eating disorder behaviour and weight restoration were conducted at end of treatment and 3 months post-treatment. Separate regression analyses were undertaken for each of the predictors (changes in PvA and changes in AESED) due to concerns with multicollinearity. First, we examined whether the changes in parental self-efficacy from baseline to end of treatment predicted eating disorder behaviour and weight restoration at the end of treatment. Second, we examined whether the changes in parental self-efficacy from baseline to 3 months post-treatment predicted eating disorder behaviour and weight restoration at 3 months post-treatment. Third, we examined whether changes in caregiver accommodation from baseline to end of treatment predicted eating disorder behaviour and weight restoration at end of treatment. Finally, we examined whether changes in caregiver accommodation from baseline to 3 months post-treatment predicted t eating disorder behaviour and weight restoration at 3 months post-treatment. Z-scores were created for each variable in order to standardize measurement. This process is imperative when performing OLS regressions from multiply imputed data [39].

Results

Changes in parental self-efficacy

Table 2 presents the unbalanced repeated measures designs of parental self-efficacy by treatment time-point showing a statistically significant time effect ($\chi^2 = 11.95$, $p = .003$). Pairwise comparisons revealed that the total mean score of parental self-efficacy did not significantly increase from baseline ($M = 18.91$, $SE = 0.62$) to EOT ($M = 19.82$, $SE = 0.69$; $p = .398$), but did increase significantly increased from baseline ($M = 18.91$, $SE = 0.62$) to 3 months post-treatment ($M = 21.59$, $SE = 0.50$; $p = .002$).

Changes in caregiver accommodation

Table 2 also presents the unbalanced repeated measures designs of caregiver accommodation by treatment time-point showing a statistically significant time effect ($\chi^2 = 37.45$, $p = .0001$). Pairwise comparisons revealed that the total mean score of caregiver accommodation significantly decreased from baseline ($M = 46.31$, $SE = 3.62$) to EOT ($M = 37.75$, $SE = 3.13$; $p = 0.0001$), but not from baseline ($M = 46.31$, $SE = 3.62$) to 3 months post-treatment ($M = 45.16$, $SE = 3.17$; $p = 1.000$).

Effects of parental self-efficacy on eating disorder behaviour and weight restoration

Table 3 presents the OLS regression estimates for the effects of changes in parental self-efficacy on participant eating disorder behaviour and weight restoration at EOT and 3 months post-treatment. Changes in parental self-efficacy from baseline to EOT, or from baseline to 3 months post-treatment did not significantly predict eating disorder behaviour or weight restoration in the transition age youth.

Effects of caregiver accommodation to the illness on the transition age youth participant eating disorder behaviour and weight restoration

Table 4 presents the OLS regression estimates for the effects of changes in caregiver accommodation on eating

Table 2 Parental Self-Efficacy and Accommodation

	Baseline		End of Treatment		Three Month Follow-Up	
	n	Mean (SE)	n	Mean (SE)	n	Mean (SE)
Parental Self-Efficacy						
PvA Total Score	39	18.91 (0.61)	39	19.82 (0.69)	39	21.59 (0.50)
Significance	.003					
Caregiver Accommodation						
AESED Total Score	37	46.31 (3.62)	37	37.75 (3.13)	37	45.16 (3.17)
Significance	0.0001					

PvA Parents versus Anorexia scale, *AESED* Accommodation and Enabling Scale

Table 3 OLS Regressions for the Effects of Parental Self-Efficacy on Patient Eating Behaviours and Weight Restoration ($n = 39$)

	EDE Globa Score	Weight Restoration
	B	*B*
Parental Self-Efficacy		
Change in PvA total score from time 1 to time 2	0.09	−0.33
Significance	0.591	0.223
Parental Self-Efficacy		
Change in PvA total score from time 1 to time 3	−0.09	0.01
Significance	0.735	0.985

PvA Parents versus Anorexia scale, *EDE Global* Eating Disorder Examination Global score

disorder behaviour and weight restoration at EOT and 3 months post-treatment. Changes in caregiver accommodation from baseline to EOT, or at 3 months post-treatment, did not significantly predict eating disorder behaviour.

Discussion

The current study of FBT for transition age youth with AN aimed to explore how parental self-efficacy and caregiver accommodation to the illness changed over the course of treatment. We further sought to identify whether such changes in parental self-efficacy and caregiver accommodation were predictive of changes in eating disorder behaviour and weight in the transition age youth at EOT and/or three-months post-treatment. We found that parental self-efficacy increased, but not significantly, from baseline to EOT. However, parental self-efficacy increased significantly from baseline to 3 months post-treatment. The results further revealed that accommodation to the illness decreased significantly from baseline to EOT, but not from baseline to 3 months post-treatment. Neither parental self-efficacy nor caregiver accommodation predicted change in ED symptoms and weight in the transition age youth at EOT or 3 months post-treatment. Overall, this study demonstrated that caregivers became increasingly more confident in their ability to support their loved one with AN, and perceived themselves as engaging less with/or permitting fewer ED symptoms throughout treatment. However, these changes did not predict change in the transition age youth's eating disorder symptoms or weight.

Change in parental self efficacy and Accomodation Behaviours

Transition age youth are between pediatric and adult systems of care, which requires special treatment attention to their unique developmental challenges. The experience of both wanting the support of family and friends while also negotiating boundaries for increased autonomy and independence can complicate how caregivers and transition age youth work together to diminish AN behaviours. Previous research on adolescent FBT found decreased parental self-efficacy and fear was linked with higher accommodation to the illness [30]. When families participate in FBT, caregiver mood and anxiety improve which correlates with increased self-efficacy [26].

It is important to note that the tool used to assess parental self-efficacy, the PvA, was developed for and is primarily used to assess empowerment in the context of child and adolescent treatment of EDs using FT [35]. Items on the PvA scale include: "I feel equipped with the specific practical strategies for the task of bringing about the complete recovery of my child in the home setting", "while parents are important, children with anorexia will never get better until they receive some sort of individual therapy themselves", and "It is more my responsibility than my child's to bring him/her to a healthy weight"

Table 4 OLS Regressions for the Effects of Parental Accommodation to Eating Disorders on Patient Eating Behaviours and Weight Restoration ($n = 37$)

	EDE Global Score	Weight Restoration
	B	*B*
Accommodation		
Change in AESED total score from time 1 to time 2	0.03	−0.12
Significance	0.865	0.582
Accommodation		
Change in AESED total score from time 1 to time 3	0.05	0.19
Significance	0.873	0.579

AESED Accommodation and Enabling Scale for Eating Disorders, *EDE Global* Eating Disorder Examination Global score

[35]. These items indicate a scale used to understand parental empowerment in the context of child and adolescent EDs treated with FTs where parents are an integral part of the support young people need as they are working to make behavioural changes [12, 13]. The items on the scale may not be applicable to transition age youth or a FBT-TAY model given the treatment goals: creating a collaborative approach between transition age youth and their families, individual therapy with the transition age youth, and individual development of recovery and maintenance plans in the final phase of treatment.

Interestingly, despite the limitations of the scale and the collaborative focus of FBT for TAY, caregivers still experienced a significant increase in parental self-efficacy from baseline to EOT. Working to empower parents and reduce fear and self-blame is a focus of FBT and other family therapies for AN (ex: FT-AN) [40]. Therefore, empowerment was prioritized in the development of FBT-TAY despite the increased autonomy in the transition age youth, which may explain the increased sense of self-efficacy throughout treatment and at 3 month follow-up. The majority of the transition age youth in the study sample were living at home (92.3%) and were struggling with AN-R or AN-BP. Within the FBTTAY model, parents were purposefully supported to feel empowered in helping their young adult with eating and recovery. The young adult was purposefully supported to develop acceptance of this parental support. This was achieved by the therapist acting as consultant to both the transition age youth and their caregivers. For example, therapists provided psychoeducation of the potential benefits of family involvement in meal support, particularly in the early phase of treatment; given the severity of complications that can develop when an individual is suffering with an ED [1–5], transition age youth may benefit from time limited support from their caregivers that would not typically be considered age appropriate.

The collaborative approach outlined above may be counter intuitive to families at this life stage where it is developmentally appropriate for young adults and parents to begin separating financially, geographically, and shifting their relationship from one of dependence to interdependence [20, 22]. However, FBT-TAY therapists collaborated with families to help them understand that short-term parental support may help transition age youth eventually achieve independent, age-appropriate, levels of autonomy around food and eating. FBT-TAY progressively focused on the development of healthy eating behaviours in a wide variety of settings such as at home, school and with persons outside the family. In phase 1 of treatment parents provided significant support for eating in a variety of situations while in phase 2, control of eating across various situations was gradually shifted entirely back to the transition age youth. This was focused upon so that transition age youth could practice and gain confidence eating and maintaining their recovery while also successfully engaging in the transitions inherent to emerging adulthood such as changes in school, work, finances and relationships [20, 22]. The use of FBT TAY is different from FBT for adolescents as young adults were asked to grant permission to their parents to take control of the provision of food preparation, serving and support during meals. It was also different from adult models of care where those over the age 18 are viewed as the most primarily responsible for their own recovery.

The result of increased parental self-efficacy over the course of FBT-TAY provides context for the caregiver's significant decrease in accommodation behaviours over the course of treatment. Despite the unique features of transition age youth, caregivers in our sample were comparable to other adolescent and adult caregiver samples in terms of baseline accommodation and enabling scores [41–44]. The behavioural focus on FBT for transition age youth supports the identified caregivers, in every session, to collaborate with their transition age youth to support a reduction of eating disorder symptoms and facilitate weight gain. This treatment focus may explain why caregivers experienced a significant decrease in accommodation behaviours, however, the effects of this change were not maintained at 3 months post-treatment, indicating that this change may have been treatment dependent.

Change in caregivers associated with change in transition age youth ED outcomes

In the current study, neither parental self-efficacy nor accommodation predicted change in eating disorder symptoms. This differs from past literature in the treatment of adolescent AN has found that parental self-efficacy increases during treatment with FBT [45]. In a study of 121 adolescents with AN, Byrne et al. (2015) found that families randomized to FBT had significantly greater increases in parental self-efficacy which was predictive of greater weight gain by EOT [24]. Most recently, parental self-efficacy has been found to be a significant mediator for increased weight gain in the adolescent by session 10 of FBT [46]. The transition age youth in the current sample differed from previously studied adolescents, and there was no predictive effect of change in parental self efficacy for FBT-TAY.

FBT-TAY differs from standard manualized FBT [15]. It begins with a very close collaboration with the transition age youth and parents and then an important goal of the therapy is to promote autonomous and independent eating in the transition age youth as well as age appropriate life re-integration (e.g..: return to College/University, living independelty and/or with peers or partner, etc.). This heightened focus on the transition age youth's autonomy may account for why changes in caregiver's self efficacy was not predictive of ED outcomes for the transition age youth. In the treatment of pediatric AN with standard FBT, it has been found that while parental self-efficacy is a significant predictor of weight gain, adolescent's own self-efficacy is not [24] which again reinforces that the age appropriate nature of behavioural control by a caregiver may be different in adolescent vs transition age youth with AN.

Therapies that swiftly target caregiver beliefs about their ability to support a loved one are very important in facilitating their efforts to address disordered eating particularly during meal times. A caregiver's ability to cope and provide support is impacted over time by feelings of fear and self-blame which erode a caregiver's efficacy (e.g., accommodating to symptoms of restriction, purging, or over-exercise) [27, 28, 42, 47, 48]. The erosion of previously held caregiving skills can quickly spark a cyclical relationship between those with AN and their caregivers that makes the illness harder to overcome and increases the degree and duration of burden on caregivers [49]. Caregivers often experience social isolation, stigma, psychological distress [50, 51].

Clinical implications and future directions

It is possible that FBT-TAY can be effective in halting or reversing caregiver disempowerment as well as decreasing accommodation behaviours in caregivers during the course of treatment. This is an important advancement in terms of our knowledge of the role of caregivers in the treatment of EDs in transition age youth. Currently, care for transition age youth receiving treatment in adult systems do not routinely involve caregivers, but instead prioritize individual or group-based models. Therefore, caregivers who are still intimately involved in the daily life of transition age youth are typically excluded from treatment of those over the age of 18. This is a problematic systemic issue that the current study proposes can be amended by introducing a developmentally appropriate model of treatment that recognizes the role that parents can play in supporting their adult child while also empowering the individual with the illness. Programs should begin to identify the unique needs of transition age youth and their caregivers to better serve this population. Future research should establish the efficacy of FBT-TAY via a randomized controlled trial. We also recommend furture research evaluating FBT-TAY to other family based treatment modalities like FT-AN or MFT-AN [11].

Strengths and limitations

FBT-TAY was manualized and all study therapists were provided initial training followed by weekly supervision throughout the study. Even though the study used a novel model of treatment, it was developed using direct feedback from clinicians focused on working with transition age youth with AN [21]. Finally, the study sample and setting included both pediatric and adult programs which increases the real-world applicability of study findings to transition age youth accessing eating disorder treatment. The present study was not without limitations. We recruited a diverse range of caregivers in terms of age (range of 40–71 years), and gender (58.54% mothers), however, most were Caucasian (65.98%), held a college education or higher (90.25%), and were within an hour's drive from a major city centre, limiting the generalizability of our findings. The study recruited a modest number of individuals with AN and their caregivers, and was only able to follow participants for 3 months post-treatment which is not sufficient to ascertain the long-term impacts of the FBT-TAY on caregivers.

Conclusion

The current study is the first to describe the impact of FBT-TAY on caregivers of transition age youth with AN Acknowledging the unique needs of transition age youth who are between pediatric and adult systems of care is an important line of inquiry given the limited involvement of family members in treatment for older adolescents and young adults. The current study aimed to identify if involving family in the treatment of transition age youth using FBT-TAY would elicit benefits in the caregivers. This study demonstrates that FBT-TAY has promise and may lead to changes in caregivers of transition age youth with AN presenting for treatment in both pediatric and adult programs. Future studies should assess the impact of treatments on caregivers given the mental health impacts (e.g. depression, anxiety, burden) of caregiving (e.g. meal support, attending appointments, monitoring symptoms), and the positive treatment impacts for those with an ED (e.g. reduced hospital stays, decreased ED psychopathology, and increased quality of life).

Abbreviations

AESED: Accomodation and enabling scale for eating disorders; AN: Anorexia nervosa; AN-BP: Anorexia nervosa binge purge sub-type; AN-R: Anorexia nervosa restrictive sub-type; CBT: Cognitive behavioral therapy; EDPs: Eating disorder programs; EDs: Eating disorders; EOT: End of treatment; FBT: Family-based treatment; FBT-TAY: Family-based treatment for transition age youth; FT: Family therapy; MFT: Multi-family therapy; PvA: Parents versus anorexia scale; RCT: Randomized controlled trial; TAU: Treatment as usual; TAY: Transition age youth

Acknowledgements

The study authors would like to thank all of the participating young adults and caregivers in this study, without whom the research would not have been possible. We would also like to thank all participating hospital sites and FBT-TAY clinicians who conducted therapy.

Funding

The current study was partically funded by the Ontario Mental Health Foundation (OMHF).

Authors' contributions

GD with collaboration from DLG developed and manualized the FBT-TAY model. ME and CS maintained data sets at their respective hospital sites before all data was transferred for analysis. VF and GD collected and maintained the full data set which was fully analyzed by AL and JN under the supervision of GD. GD, VF, AL, JN, OC, ME, CS and DLG were major contributors in writing the manuscript. All authors read and approved the final manuscript.

Competing interests

Dr. Le Grange receives Royalties from Guilford Press and Routledge, and is Co-Director of the Training Institute for Child and Adolescent Eating Disorders, LLC. All other study authors have no competing interests to declare.

Author details

[1]Faculty of Social Work, Matheson Centre for Mental Health Research, University of Calgary, 4212-2800 University Way N.W., Calgary, Alberta, Canada. [2]Department of Human Development and Family Science, Virginia Polytechnic Institute and State University, Falls Church, VA, USA. [3]University Health Network, Toronto General Hospital, Toronto, Ontario, Canada. [4]Department of Sociology, Mount Royal University, Calgary, Alberta, Canada. [5]Adolescent Eating Disorder Program, North York General Hospital, Toronto, Ontario, Canada. [6]Division of Adolescent Medicine, The Hospital for Sick Children and the University of Toronto, Toronto, Ontario, Canada. [7]Department of Psychiatry, University of California, San Francisco, CA, USA. [8]Hotchkiss Brain Institute, University of Calgary, 4212-2800 University Way N.W., Calgary, Alberta, Canada.

References

1. Arcelus J, Mitchell AJ, Wales J, Nielsen S. Mortality rates in patients with anorexia nervosa and other eating disorders: a meta-analysis of 36 studies. Arch Gen Psychiatry. 2011;68:724–31.
2. Meczekalski B, Podfigurna-Stopa A, Katulski K. Long-term consequences of anorexia nervosa. Maturitas. 2013;75:215–20.
3. Specker S, Peterson CB, Eckert ED, Swanson SA, Crow SJ, Mitchell JE, Raymond NC. Increased mortality in bulimia nervosa and other eating disorders. Am J Psychiatry. 2009;166:1342–6.
4. Bühren K, Schwarte R, Fluck F, Timmesfeld N, Krei M, Egberts K, Pfeiffer E, Fleischhaker C, Wewetzer C, Herpertz-Dahlmann B. Comorbid psychiatric disorders in female adolescents with first-onset anorexia nervosa. Eur Eat Disord Rev. 2014;22:39–44.
5. Vardar E, Erzengin M. The prevalence of eating disorders (EDs) and comorbid psychiatric disorders in adolescents: a two-stage community-based study. Turkish J Psychiatry. 2011;22:205–12.
6. Treasure J, Russell G. The case for early intervention in anorexia nervosa: theoretical exploration of maintaining factors. Br J Psychiatry. 2011;199:5–7.
7. Fisher CA, Hetrick SE, Rushford N. Family therapy for anorexia nervosa. Cochrane Database Syst Rev. 2010;4:CD004780.
8. Chen EY, Weissman JA, Zeffiro TA, Yiu A, Eneva KT, Arlt JM, Swantek MJ. Family-based therapy for young adults with anorexia nervosa restores weight. Int J Eat Disord. 2016;49(7):701.
9. Dimitropoulos G, Landers A, Freeman VE, Novick J, Garber A, Le Grange D: Open trial for family-based treatment of anorexia nervosa for tansition age youth. J Can Acad Child Adolesc Psychiatry in press.
10. Hay PJ, Claudino AM, Touyz S, Abd Elbaky G. Individual psychological therapy in the outpatient treatment of adults with anorexia nervosa. Cochrane Database Syst Rev. 2015;7:CD003909.
11. Eisler I, Simic M, Hodsoll J, Asen E, Berelowitz M, Connan F, Ellis G, Hugo P, Schmidt U, Treasure J, Yi I. A pragmatic randomised multi-Centre trial of multifamily and single family therapy for adolescent anorexia nervosa. BMC psychiatry. 2016;16(1):422.
12. Jewell T, Blessitt E, Stewart C, Simic M, Eisler I. Family therapy for child and adolescent eating disorders: a critical review. Fam Process. 2016;
13. Watson HJ, Bulik CM. Update on the treatment of anorexia nervosa: review of clinical trials, practice guidelines and emerging interventions. Psychol Med. 2012;
14. National Institute for Health and Care Excellence (UK). Eating Disorders: Regonigition and treatment. London. 2017. Retrieved at: https://www.nice.org.uk/guidance/ng69.
15. Lock J, le Grange D. Family-based treatment of eating disorders. Int J Eat Disord. 2005;
16. Lock J, Agras WS, Bryson SW, Brandt H, Halmi KA, Kaye W, Wilfley D, Woodside B, Pajarito S, Jo B. Does family-based treatment reduce the need for hospitalization in adolescent anorexia nervosa? 2016. 49(9): 891–894.
17. Lock J, Le Grange D, Agras WS, Moye A, Bryson SW, Jo B. Randomized clinical trial comparing family-based treatment with adolescent-focused individual therapy for adolescents with anorexia nervosa. Arch Gen Psychiatry. 2010.Oct 4;67(1):1025–32.
18. Couturier J, Kimber M, Szatmari P. Efficacy of family-based treatment for adolescents with eating disorders: a systematic review and meta-analysis. Int J Eat Disord. 2013;
19. Loeb KL, LeGrange D. Family-based treatment for adolescent eating disorders: current status, new applications and future directions. Int J Child Adolesc health. 2009;2(2):243–54.
20. Arnett JJ. The oxford handbook of emerging adulthood. New York, NY: Oxford University Press; 2015.
21. Dimitropoulos G, Freeman VE, Allemang B, Couturier J, McVey G, Lock J, Le Grange D. Family-based treatment with transition age youth with anorexia nervosa: a qualitative summary of application in clinical practice. J Eat Disord. 2015;3:1–1.
22. Arnett JJ. Emerging adulthood: a theory of development from the late teens through the twenties. Am Psychol. 2000;55:469–80.
23. Dimitropoulos G, Toulany A, Herschman J, Kovacs A, Steinegger C, Bardsley J, Sandhu S, Gregory C, Colton P, Anderson J, Kaufman M. A qualitative study on the experiences of young adults with eating disorders transferring from pediatric to adult care. Eat Disord. 2015;23:144–62.
24. Byrne CE, Accurso EC, Arnow KD, Lock J, Le Grange D. An exploratory examination of patient and parental self-efficacy as predictors of weight gain in adolescents with anorexia nervosa. Int J Eat Disord. 2015;48:883–8.
25. Ellison R, Rhodes P, Madden S, Miskovic J, Wallis A, Bailie A, Kohn M, Touyz S. Do the components of manualized family-based treatment for anorexia nervosa predict weight gain? Int J Eat Disord. 2012;45:609–14.
26. Robinson AL, Strahan E, Girz L, Wilson A, Boachie A. 'I know i can help you': parental self-efficacy predicts adolescent outcomes in family-based therapy for eating disorders. Eur Eat Disord Rev. 2013;21:108–14.
27. Fox JR, Dean M, Whittlesea A. The experience of caring for or living with an individual with an eating disorder: a meta-synthesis of qualitative studies. Clin Psychol Psychother. 2017;24:103–25.
28. Whitney J, Eisler I. Theoretical and empirical models around caring for someone with an eating disorder: the reorganization of family life and inter-personal maintenance factors. J Ment Health. 2005;14:575–85.
29. Sepulveda AR, Kyriacou O, Treasure J. Development and validation of the accommodation and enabling scale for eating disorders (AESED) for caregivers in eating disorders. BMC Health Serv Res. 2009;9:171.
30. Stillar A, Strahan E, Nash P, Files N, Scarborough J, Mayman S, Henderson K, Gusella J, Connors L, Orr ES, et al. The influence of carer fear and self-blame when supporting a loved one with an eating disorder. Eat Disord. 2016;24:173–85.
31. Dimitropoulos G, Anderson K, Lock J, Le Grange D. Family-based treatments with transition age youth iwth eatings disorders. In: Loeb K, Lock J, Le Grange D, editors. Family therapy for adolescent eating and weight disorders: new applications. New York. NY: Routledge; 2014. p. 230–55.
32. Fairburn CG, Beglin SJ. Assessment of eating disorder psychopathology: interview or self-report questionnaire? Int J Eat Disord. 1994;

33. Luce KH, Crowther JH. The reliability of the eating disorder examination—self-report questionnaire version (EDE-Q). Int J Eat Disord. 1999;
34. Centres for Disease Control. 2009. http://www.cdc.gov/growthcharts/clinical_charts.htm.
35. Rhodes P, Baillie A, Brown J, Madden S. Parental efficacy in the family-based treatment of anorexia: preliminary development of the parents versus anorexia scale (PVA). Eur Eat Disord Rev. 2005;13:399–405.
36. Rubin DB. Multiple imputation for nonresponse in surveys. New York, NY: Wiley; 1987.
37. Sterne JA, White IR, Carlin JB, Spratt M, Royston P, Kenward MG, Wood AM, Carpenter JR. Multiple imputation for missing data in epidemiological and clinical research: potential and pitfalls. BMJ. 2009;338:1–5.
38. Croy CD, Novins DK. Methods for addressing missing data in psychiatricand developmental research. J Am Acad Adolesc Child Psychiatry. 2005;44(12):1230–40.
39. Tak Fung, PhD, written communication, February 2018.
40. Eisler I, Simic M, Blessitt E, Dodge L, et al. Maudsley Service Manual, 2016.
41. Anastasiadou D, Medina-Pradas C, Sepulveda AR, Treasure J. A systematic review of family caregiving in eating disorders. Eat Behav. 2014;
42. Goddard E, Macdonald P, Sepulveda AR, Naumann U, Landau S, Schmidt U, Treasure J. Cognitive interpersonal maintenance model of eating disorders: intervention for carers. Br J Psychiatry. 2011;199:225–31.
43. Grover M, Naumann U, Mohammad-Dar L, Glennon D, Ringwood S, Eisler I, Williams C, Treasure J, Schmidt U. A randomized controlled trial of an internet-based cognitive-behavioural skills package for carers of people with anorexia nervosa. Psychol Med. 2011;
44. Sepulveda AR, Todd G, Whitaker W, Grover M, Stahl D, Treasure J. Expressed emotion in relatives of patients with eating disorders following skills training program. Int J Eat Disord. 2010 Nov 1;43(7):603–10.
45. Le Grange D, Lock J, Agras WS, Moye A, Bryson SW, Jo B, Kraemer HC. Moderators and mediators of remission in family-based treatment and adolescent focused therapy for anorexia nervosa. Behav Res Ther. 2012;
46. Sadeh-Sharvit S, Arnow KD, Osipov L, Lock JD, Jo B, Pajarito S, Brandt H, Dodge E, Halmi KA, Johnson C, Kaye W. Are parental self-efficacy and family flexibility mediators of treatment for anorexia nervosa? Int J Eat Disord. 2018;
47. Schmidt U, Treasure J. Anorexia nervosa: valued and visible. A cognitive-interpersonal maintenance model and its implications for research and practice. Br J Clin Psychol. 2006;45:343–66.
48. Treasure J, Nazar BP. Interventions for the carers of patients with eating disorders. Curr Psychiatry Rep. 2016;18:1–7.
49. Anastasiadou D, Medina-Pradas C, Sepulveda AR, Treasure J. A systematic review of family caregiving in eating disorders. Eat Behav. 2014;15:464–77.
50. Dimitropoulos G, Carter J, Schachter R, Woodside DB. Predictors of family functioning in carers of individuals with anorexia nervosa. Int J Eat Disord. 2008;41:739–47.
51. Highet N, Thompson M, King RM. The experience of living with a person with an eating disorder: the impact on the carers. Eat Disord. 2005;

16

A content analysis of thinspiration, fitspiration, and bonespiration imagery on social media

Catherine Victoria Talbot[1,3*], Jeffrey Gavin[1], Tommy van Steen[1,2] and Yvette Morey[2]

Abstract

Background: On social media, images such as thinspiration, fitspiration, and bonespiration, are shared to inspire certain body ideals. Previous research has demonstrated that exposure to these groups of content is associated with increased body dissatisfaction and decreased self-esteem. It is therefore important that the bodies featured within these groups of content are more fully understood so that effective interventions and preventative measures can be informed, developed, and implemented.

Method: A content analysis was conducted on a sample of body-focussed images with the hashtags thinspiration, fitspiration, and bonespiration from three social media platforms.

Results: The analyses showed that thinspiration and bonespiration content contained more thin and objectified bodies, compared to fitspiration which featured a greater prevalence of muscles and muscular bodies. In addition, bonespiration content contained more bone protrusions and fewer muscles than thinspiration content.

Conclusions: The findings suggest fitspiration may be a less unhealthy type of content; however, a subgroup of imagery was identified which idealised the extremely thin body type and as such this content should also be approached with caution. Future research should utilise qualitative methods to further develop understandings of the body ideals that are constructed within these groups of content and the motivations behind posting this content.

Keywords: Thinspiration, Fitspiration, Bonespiration, Social media, Body image, Content analysis

Plain English summary

Thinspiration refers to imagery commonly shared on social media that encourages a user to be thin. Likewise, fitspiration and bonespiration are imagery that inspire a user to be fit and extremely thin, respectively. There has been limited research that has analysed and compared the physical attributes of thinspiration and fitspiration content, and no research has analysed bonespiration. This study aimed to (i) examine the features of bonespiration content in relation to thinspiration and fitspiration; and (ii) explore how fitspiration compared to thinspiration and bonespiration.

The researchers conducted a content analysis on 734 images with hashtags thinspiration, fitspiration, and bonespiration, shared on the social media platforms Twitter, Instagram, and WeHeartit. Similarities were generally observed between thinspiration and bonespiration; however, bonespiration content contained fewer muscles and more bone protrusions, indicating that bonespiration may represent an exaggerated form of thinspiration. Thinspiration and bonespiration contained more thin, objectified bodies when compared to fitspiration, which contained more muscles and muscular bodies. This indicates that fitspiration may represent a less unhealthy form of content when compared to thinspiration and bonespiration. Fitspiration should still be approached with caution, however, as a small group of fitspiration content was identified that was similar to thinspiration with regards to the presence of extremely thin bodies.

* Correspondence: ct500@exeter.ac.uk
[1]University of Bath, Claverton Down Road, Bath BA2 7AY, UK
[3]University of Exeter Medical School, College House 1.23, St Luke's Campus, Heavitree Road, Exeter EX1 2LU, UK
Full list of author information is available at the end of the article

Background

It has been well established that the mass media has played an important role in communicating beauty ideals [1], namely the thin beauty ideal commonly assigned to femininity. The mass communication of this body ideal may result an unattainable and unrealistic construction of feminine beauty [2, 3]. Exposure to these thin ideals can result in decreased body satisfaction [4–7]. Decreased body satisfaction is a cause for serious concern, especially for adolescent girls as this group commonly experience body dissatisfaction [8]. Indeed, decreased body satisfaction has been associated with unhealthy weight control behaviours and binge eating [9], eating disorder symptomatology [10, 11], depressive symptoms and low self-esteem [12].

Until recently, studies have focussed upon the effects of exposure to conventional mass media, such as newspapers, magazines and television; however, a growing emphasis is now being placed upon the role of social media and the effect it can have upon young people who are consuming and interacting with it [1]. Perloff [1] has discussed the how social media technologies differ from mass media communication, where social media can provide users with a personal outlet, interactivity, a feeling of presence, and a community of like-minded individuals. On social media, users are both sources and receivers of information, who can actively shape online interaction that enhance autonomy, self-efficacy, and personal agency [13].

When social media users go online they are exposed to a multitude of thin-idealised female bodies on their news feed of celebrities, people within their social network, and bodies of people they do not know. It could therefore be argued that social media, with its constant availability for interaction and content creation, has increased the exposure that young women have to certain body ideals [1].

'Inspirational' imagery is often shared on social media with the aim of inspiring a user to achieve a certain, often unachievable, body type. Thinspiration refers to content posted on social media that inspires a user to be thin, and this is typically achieved through the presentation of images that contain thin bodies, as well as weight loss quotes and techniques [14]. Thinspiration has received considerable attention within the public eye, where this content has been accused of being dangerous and a contributor towards the onset of eating disorders [15, 16]. This may be because thinspiration has traditionally been associated with the pro-eating disorder (proED) community [17], a community that has identified eating disorders as a lifestyle choice, rather than an illness [18]. More recently, thinspiration content has moved away from its typical association with the proED community and has been shared by everyday social media users [19].

In a content analysis of thinspiration, Ghaznavi and Taylor [19] found that these images tended be sexually suggestive and objectifying, and featured extremely thin, bony, scantily-clad women. Thinspiration, with its emphasis upon the thin body ideal, could therefore be damaging to the body satisfaction of social media users. This is a serious cause for concern, especially if thinspiration content has become part of the everyday social media user's experience.

After searching the hashtag 'thinspiration' on various social media platforms, a user will quickly find co-occurring hashtags that are associated with the proED community, such as '#proana'. 'Bonespiration' is another commonly featured hashtag and refers to content that idealises the extremely thin body through the presentation of protruding bones [19]. A search for the hashtag 'bonespo' on Instagram results in over 130,000 posts, which are being updated daily. Bonespiration has received some antagonism within the public eye [20], but it is generally less well known which could be because this content is still firmly engrained within the pro-ED community. Bonespiration has, therefore, received no attention within the academic literature and as such its relation to thinspiration and the physical characteristics of the bodies featured within this content remains unknown.

By contrast, 'fitspiration' has been coined by the fitness community as an allegedly-healthy alternative to thinspiration and bonespiration. Fitspiration encourages a user to achieve a supposedly fit body through images that encourage exercise and healthy nutrition [21]. Fitspiration has been largely used within the public eye to encourage *healthy* bodies [22] and was generally considered to be a positive type of content.

More recently, there has been increasing disdain towards fitspiration, where various studies have suggested that fitspiration may result in increased negative mood, body dissatisfaction and decreased state appearance and self-esteem [23]. The physical characteristics of fitspiration could explain this, as it has been identified that most images contained only one body type: thin and toned [23]. Images were also found to contain some objectifying elements. In an analysis of fitspiration content on Instagram, nearly 90% of the bodies were coded as having low body fat and 55% were coded as muscular [24]. Whilst fitspiration presents itself as a healthy alternative it may, however, contain some negative elements typically found within thinspiration content.

To the authors' knowledge, only one study to date has directly compared these groups of content. Boepple and Thompson [25] compared thinspiration and fitspiration content, and found similarities with regards to messages that concerned body weight, thinness, eating guild and restriction, stigmatisation of fat, and objectification of the female form. Although these risky messages dominated the thinspiration content, they were also prevalent within the fitspiration group.

Whilst these findings provide great insight, Boepple and Thompson [25] analysed content featured on websites, rather than social media. Websites lack the interactivity provided by social media, where users can receive, construct, and communicate their ideas, instead of passively receiving content via a website. It is therefore likely that thinspiration and fitspiration content are presented differently on social media. Additionally, the researchers focussed upon the messages that the content conveyed, and did not specifically analyse and compare the bodies featured within this content.

There is a sparsity of research that has analysed and compared the physical attributes of thinspiration and fitspiration content, and to date there has been no research which has analysed bonespiration content. The present study will compare the bodies featured within thinspiration, bonespiration, and fitspiration to (i) examine the features of bonespiration content in relation to thinspiration and (ii) explore how fitspiration shared on social media compares to thinspiration and bonespiration. This research is important because previous studies have already associated exposure to this content with increased body dissatisfaction and decreased self-esteem, and it is therefore essential that the bodies featured within this content are more fully understood so that effective interventions and preventative measures can be developed.

Method

Sample

Images with the relevant hashtags for thinspiration, fitspiration, and bonespiration content were sampled from three social media platforms – Instagram, Twitter, and WeHeartIt. These platforms were chosen due to their popularity and their use of hashtag systems that facilitate photo-sharing [26]. Initially, 999 images were captured from 505 different social media profiles across the three platforms; however, whilst the authors appreciate there has been a female bias within research concerning body image, thinspiration and bonespiration appeared to feature more female bodies and so a decision was made to focus on images that contained only female bodies. After removing the images containing male bodies or no bodies at all, 734 images were analysed.

Codebook

Prior to this study, no single unified codebook had been utilised across studies to analyse the bodies featured within the 'inspirational' content posted on social media. The codebook was derived from the previous codebooks employed by Ghaznavi and Taylor [19] in an analysis of thinspiration content, Deighton-Smith and Bell [24] in an analysis of fitspiration content, and Boepple and Thompson's [25] comparison of thinspiration and fitspiration websites. The codes for content were also developed by the first and last author after an initial scoping review of the images which determined what codes were relevant for the analysis.

The bodies in the images were coded for body type and objectification. Body type was coded for to determine which body ideals were featured within the different types of content, codes for body type included: thin body, muscular body, bone protrusions, and presence of muscles. A thin body was operationalised as a body that was low in body fat, and a muscular body was defined as a toned body, bodies could be both thin and muscular [24]. Whilst there are many different types of bodies, the authors only coded for thin and muscular bodies as only these body types were observed in the initial scoping review of the images. In addition, these groups of content are supposed to be aspirational in nature and so it was likely that only these body types would feature in the imagery. Codes for bone protrusions included protruding ribs, collarbones, spines, and hips. These bone protrusions indicated the presence of an extremely thin body. The presence of muscles included codes for abdominal muscles and other muscles, which also informed the coding decision regarding the overall presence of a muscular body within the image.

The proportion of the body featured within the image was coded as an indicator of objectification of the body, which has been previously used as a code in other content analyses [19, 24]. An image that featured more than 50% of the body was coded as a full body, whilst an image that featured less than 50% of the body was coded as a half body. For this code, a decreased representation of the body indicated increased objectification, this is because decreased visibility of the body reduces the body to an object where it is seen in relation to its individual parts, and is not viewed in its entirety.

Procedure

The images were sampled by inputting the hashtags '#thinspiration,' '#fitpiration,' and '#bonespiration' into the search engines of Twitter, Instagram, and WeHeartit; however, as Instagram had banned all thinspiration content, adaptations were made to the hashtag language in order to locate this content. The website 'Websta.me' was used to identify alternative hashtags associated with the hashtags thinspiration, fitspiration, and bonespiration. Although bonespiration and fitspiration content were not restricted by blocking algorithms at the time of this study, alternative hashtags were also identified for these groups of content to maintain consistency, examples of these alternative hashtags included but were not limited to: '#thynspo,'#thynspiration,'#fitspo,'#-bonespooo,' etc. The top five alternative hashtags for each group were used each week to locate the sample and these hashtags were used across all three social media platforms to maintain consistency.

The sample of images was collected and archived using the data-archiving software Evernote across a period of six months between February 2015 and August 2015. The sample was then analysed using the codebook. During the analysis, the images were randomised so that the coding process was not impacted by exposure to the imagery, e.g. if the coder was exposed to only extremely thin bodies at one time, it was possible that they may view a thin body as larger than it appeared by comparison. A second coder analysed 10% of the sample to determine inter-rater reliability.

Ethical approval was acquired from the University of Bath Psychology ethics committee (Ethics Committee reference number = 15-017).

Results

Sample

The sample consisted of 734 images, 189 images with fitspiration tags, 269 images with thinspiration tags and 276 images with bonespiration tags. Chi-square tests were used to compare the prevalence of content between the thinspiration, fitspiration, and bonespiration groups.

Interrater reliability

Cohen's kappa was used to examine the interrater reliability of the codes. The Cohen's kappa scores for the codes of content ranged from .724-.920, and thus exceeded the threshold score of .70 which is considered to be indicative of good reliability (Neuendorf, 2002). See Table 1 for a complete list of the kappa scores per variable.

Body type

To understand what bodies are constructed and idealised within fitspiration, thinspiration, and bonespiration content, different body types were coded for. For this part of the analysis, a thin body was operationalized as a body that was low in body fat, and a muscular body was identified as body which was toned and featured muscles (Deighton-Smith & Bell, 2014). A body could be coded as both thin and muscular.

There was a significant effect of type of content on number of images containing a thin body, $\chi^2(2) = 32.05$, $p < .001$. Pairwise comparisons showed that while thinspiration and bonespiration did not differ in terms of depicting thin bodies, $\chi^2(1) = 0.38$, $p = .54$, thinspiration content did result in significant higher number of images containing thin bodies compared to the fitspiration content, $\chi^2(1) = 23.15$, $p < .001$. A similar significant difference was found between bonespiration and fitspiration content, $\chi^2(1) = 19.13$, $p < .001$.

In relation to the presence of muscular bodies, there was a significant effect of type of content on number of images containing a muscular body $\chi^2(2) = 156.39$, $p < .001$. Fitspiration content featured a significantly greater proportion of muscular bodies, when compared to thinspiration content, $\chi^2(1) - 78.90$, $p < .001$. In turn, the thinspiration content featured a significantly greater proportion of muscular bodies compared to the content of bonespiration images, $\chi^2(1) = 6.46$, $p = .011$. This suggests that, compared to thinspiration and bonespiration content, fitspiration content may have less of a focus upon the thin ideal, and instead by comparison places a greater emphasis upon muscular physique than thinspiration and bonespiration.

Table 1 Percentages of images depicting body image attributes for each of the three different hashtags (fitspiration, thinspiration and bonespiration) and the overall chi square test and Cohen's Kappa for each attribute

	Fitspiration	Thinspiration	Bonespiration	χ2	p	Cohen's Kappa
Body type						
Thin body	81.1%[a]	95.4%[b]	94.2%[b]	43.6	<.001	0.844
Muscular body	46.2%[a]	9.4%[b]	4.0%[c]	165	<.001	0.857
Muscles						
Abdomen muscles	30.9%[a]	11.5%[b]	4.7%[c]	65.8	<.001	0.827
Other muscles	28.2%[a]	3.7%[b]	0.0%[c]	126	<.001	0.724
Bone protrusions						
Hip bones	9.0%[a]	22.8%[b]	26.4%[b]	22.1	<.001	0.920
Ribs	11.6%[a]	15.6%[a]	22.8%[b]	10.7	0.005	0.869
Collarbones	15.9%[a]	16.0%[a]	21.7%[a]	3.91	0.14	0.779
Spine	1.1%[a]	2.2%[a]	5.8%[b]	9.42	0.009	0.794
Objectification						
< 50% of the body shown	33.9%[a]	49.8%[b]	53.6%[b]	18.80	<.001	0.881
Full body shown	63.5%[a]	48.7%[b]	42.8%[b]	19.7	<.001	0.905

In each row, different letters indicate significant differences between these categories

In total, 7.94% of the fitspiration images, 5.43% of bonespiration images, and 4.09% thinspiration images were not coded as both thin and muscular. This indicates that the vast proportion of all three groups of content featured thin and muscular bodies.

Muscles

The notion that fitspiration places a greater focus upon muscular bodies than thinspiration and bonespiration content was further supported when abdominal muscles and other muscles were considered. Fitspiration content contained significantly more abdomen muscles than the thinspiration content $\chi^2(1) = 26.36, p < .001$. Likewise, the fitspiration content also featured a significantly greater amount of other muscles than the thinspiration content $\chi^2(1) = 55.27, p < .001$. These differences were also found between the thinspiration and bonespiration content for the presence of abdominal muscles, $\chi^2(1) = 8.52$ $p = .004$, and other muscles, $\chi^2(1) = 10.53, p = .001$. Overall, fitspiration shows the highest level of muscles in the images, followed by thinspiration content, while bonespiration content had the lowest level of muscles visible in the analysed images.

Bone protrusions

For this analysis, bone protrusions indicated the presence of an extremely thin body. A set of χ^2-tests showed significant differences across content groups for hip bones, $\chi^2(2) = 22.14, p < .001$, ribs, $\chi^2(2) = 10.66, p = .005$, and spines, $\chi^2(2) = 9.42, p = .009$, but not for collarbones, $\chi^2(2) = 3.91, p = .14$. When the presence of protruding bones was coded for across the groups of content, the previously observed difference between the thinspiration and fitspiration groups disappeared. As demonstrated in Table 1, the thinspiration and fitspiration group did not significantly differ across codes for protruding ribs, collarbones, and spines. A significant difference was only found between these groups on hip bone coding, with thinspiration content showing higher levels of hip bone visibility compared to the fitspiration content $\chi^2(1) = 14.98, p < .001$. However, differences were found between the bonespiration and fitspiration groups in relation to bone protrusions, whereby the bonespiration group showed significantly larger prevalence of protruding hipbones, $\chi^2(1) = 21.90, p < .001$, ribs, $\chi^2(1) = 9.40, p = .002$ and spines, $\chi^2(1) = 6.77, p = .009$. Compared to thinspiration, the bonespiration content showed significant higher visibility of ribs ($\chi^2(1) = 4.56, p = .03$) and spines ($\chi^2(1) = 4.47, p = .03$), but this was not the case for hip bones and collarbones.

This observed similarity between the thinspiration and fitspiration groups suggests that there might be a subgroup of fitspiration content, which is alike to thinspiration content, in relation to the idealisation of the extremely thin body; however, the prevalence of the extremely thin body within the fitspiration group did not equal the prevalence of this type of content featured within the bonespiration group.

Objectification

In previous studies (e.g. Boepple & Thompson, 2015, Deighton-Smith & Bell, 2016), decreased visibility of the whole body has been associated with increased objectification of the body. In the present study, bodies were coded as either a half body (less than 50% of the body was visible) or a full body (more than 50% of the body was visible). It was therefore assumed that a greater prevalence of half bodies reflected an increased objectification of the body.

The analysis showed that the thinspiration group contained significantly more half bodies than the fitspiration group $\chi^2(1) = 11.51, p = .001$. A similar difference was found when the bonespiration and fitspiration group were compared, whereby the bonespiration group featured a significantly greater proportion of half bodies than the fitspiration group $\chi^2(1) = 17.66, p < .001$. The thinspiration and bonespiration groups did not differ significantly on this factor $\chi^2(1) = 0.79, p < .37$. These findings suggest that fitspiration groups differed significantly from bonespiration and thinspiration content with regards to the objectification of the female body, whereby the thinspiration and bonespiration groups had a greater focus upon the objectification of the female form. Table 1 presents an overview of the findings.

Discussion

The results from this study indicate that there are consistent differences between fitspiration content, when compared to thinspiration and bonespiration. Thinspiration and bonespiration content featured more thin objectified bodies; however, fitspiration content was similar to thinspiration content across codes for bone protrusions and, therefore, showed similarities with regards to the idealisation of the extremely thin body.

Similarities were generally observed between thinspiration and bonespiration content, yet bonespiration content contained fewer muscles and more bone protrusions which indicates that bonespiration may be a more extreme form of thinspiration that idealises the extremely thin body type.

The observed similarities between thinspiration and fitspiration content with regards to the presence of bone protrusions suggests that there is a subgroup of fitspiration content which is akin to thinspiration with regards to the idealisation of the extremely thin body type. This subsample of fitspiration content could be potentially dangerous due to the popularity and greater acceptance of this content. The everyday user could, therefore, be at risk of viewing this potentially harmful content that idealises the extremely thin female body.

The findings from this study should not be used to suggest that fitspiration is a healthy form of content or that the bodies featured within this content are 'normal' bodies. For example, when analysed in isolation, over 80% of the fitspiration imagery contained thin bodies and this figure only reached significance when compared to the other two groups of content. Also, almost one third of the fitspiration content featured abdominal muscles, which is not representative of the general population, and therefore suggests that there is an overrepresentation of abdominal musculature within fitspiration content. This can also be discussed in relation to thin body type idealised by thinspiration as a female would need to have low body weight for her abdominal muscles to be visible. So, whilst fitspiration contains less thin, extremely thin, and objectified bodies, the bodies featured within this content should not be seen as normal and it should still be approached with caution.

The present study adds to the current body of literature by further developing understandings of what body ideals are constructed on social media. This study has provided insight by utilising an observational method in a naturalistic setting, and due to the pictorial nature of the research offers visual insight into what female body types are idealised by users.

This study has replicated the findings of Ghaznavi and Taylor [19] as a large proportion of thin objectified bodies were identified within the thinspiration group. Although a less pronounced effect was found for bone protrusions within the thinspiration group, this could have been a product of the different platforms utilised for analysis. Likewise, the present study reflects Deighton-Smith and Bell's [24] findings where a large proportion of the fitspiration content was coded as thin body (i.e. low in body fat) and muscular.

The present study adds to this body of literature by further developing these studies and conducting a direct comparison between the groups of content to highlight that fitspiration content does not as greatly impose thin and objectified bodies upon users, compared to thinspiration and bonespiration content.

The present study is the first to date to include bonespiration as a group for analysis. This adds to the understanding of what body types are constructed within the proED community on social media through the sharing of imagery, in which bonespiration content idealised a more extremely thin body type through the presentation of various bone protrusions. The bonespiration content also featured more objectified bodies compared to fitspiration content. This study, therefore, marks a baseline for further research to investigate bonespiration content.

Since the thinspiration and bonespiration groups contained such large proportions of thin and objectified female bodies, it raises important policy making questions about whether this content should be removed and blocked on social media, especially since this content is so easy to locate. This is a particular concern for the bonespiration content, which idealised extremely thin and more unhealthy body types. Despite this, as evidenced by the methodology utilised for this study, blocking this content would be an unrealistic and ineffective strategy for tackling this phenomenon. This is because social media users are easily able to manipulate the language of hashtags to sustain content and avoid the blocking algorithms. So, simply blocking content like thinspiration and bonespiration will not stop it from existing.

Instead of focusing on removing thinspiration and bonespiration, a more sustainable solution would involve developing interventions to minimise the impact of exposure to this content. One method could be to develop young people's resilience towards this type of content using media-literacy programs [27]. By further investigating and developing understandings of thinspiration, fitspiration, and bonespiration, effective interventions and preventative measures can be informed, established, and implemented.

The present study also has implications for clinical practice particularly with regards to the treatment of individuals with eating disorders, such as anorexia or bulimia. Clinicians and parents need to be made aware of how easily bonespiration and thinspiration can be accessed on social media, and how actively engaging with this content could have negative consequences for an individual's body image.

Limitations

As this study was a content analysis, it could be argued that it was merely descriptive; however, descriptive studies of content hold a key place within communication research [28] and the present study marks a necessary step towards understanding the physical attributes of thinspiration, fitspiration, and bonespiration.

Furthermore, as the method incorporated adaptations of language to locate the thinspiration content, it is possible that the thinspiration sample represented an extreme form of thinspiration, whereby users actively used these alternative hashtags to ensure that the content was seen and sustained. Further research could explore this idea by investigating whether there are differences between content with similar hashtags such as '#thynspiration' and '#thynspo'. This might explain some of the observed similarities between thinspiration and bonespiration content.

Future research

To investigate these groups of content further, future research could adopt qualitative methods to gain a deeper insight into meanings that users construct by posting this content on social media. For example, future research could analyse the text that accompanies the imagery as well as the comments from other users.

Future research should also examine content that directly opposes the traditional thin ideal. For example, hashtags such as '#curvespo' and '#thick' are associated with a more voluptuous female body ideal and could be analysed and compared to the bodies featured within thinspiration, fitspiration, and bonespiration content.

Finally, future research could involve other social media platforms. Different platforms may attract different groups of users as shown by the diverse age demographics of Twitter, Instagram, and We Heart It [29]. A similar study by Ghaznavi and Taylor[19] found that thinspiration content on Pinterest was less objectifying and placed a greater emphasis upon the muscular body, when compared to Twitter. Future research should account for this by segmenting the analysis by social media platform.

Conclusion

In conclusion, fitspiration contained less thin and objectified bodies when compared to thinspiration and bonespiration. Similarities were found between thinspiration and bonespiration content, but bonespiration contained fewer muscles and more bone protrustions which indicates that bonespiration may represent an exaggerated form of thinspiration. The findings suggest that fitspiration content generally offers a less unhealthy body ideal alternative to thinspiration and bonespiration; however, there was a subgroup of the fitspiration sample which was alike to thinspiration with regards to the idealisation of the extremely thin body type, and as such users should still approach this content with caution. Future research should utilise qualitative methods to further develop understandings of the body ideals constructed within these groups of content and the motivations behind posting this content.

Acknowledgements
Not applicable

Funding
Not Applicable

Author's contributions
CT collected and interpreted the data. JG supervised the project. TvS conducted the data analysis. YM assisted with the design of the study and the revision of the manuscript. All authors read and approved the final manuscript.

Competing interests
The authors declare that they have no competing interests.

Author details
[1]University of Bath, Claverton Down Road, Bath BA2 7AY, UK. [2]University of the West of England, Coldharbour Lane, Frenchay, Bristol BS16 1QY, UK. [3]University of Exeter Medical School, College House 1.23, St Luke's Campus, Heavitree Road, Exeter EX1 2LU, UK.

References
1. Perloff RM. Social media effects on young Women's body image concerns: theoretical perspectives and an agenda for research. Sex Roles. 2014;71(11-12):363–77. doi: 10.1007/s11199-014-0384-6.
2. Thompson JK, Heinberg LJ, Altabe M, Tantleff-Dunn S. Exacting Beauty: Theory, Assessment, and Treatment of Body Image Disturbance. American Psychological Association; 1999.
3. Tiggemann M. Sociocultural perspectives on human appearance and body image. In: Cash TF, Smolak L, editors. Body image: a handbook of Sicence, practice, and prevention. 2nd ed. New York: Guilford Press; 2011. p. 12–9.
4. Bell BT, Lawton R, Dittmar H. The impact of thin models in music videos on adolescent girls' body dissatisfaction. Body Image. 2007;4(2):137–45. doi: 10.1016/j.bodyim.2007.02.003.
5. Groesz LM, Levine MP, Murnen SK. The effect of experimental presentation of thin media images on body satisfaction: a meta-analytic review. Int J Eat Disord. 2002;31(1):1–16. doi: 10.1002/eat.10005.
6. Tiggemann M, McGill B. The role of social comparison in the effect of magazine advertisements on women's mood and body dissatisfaction. J Soc Clin Psychol. 2004;23(1):23–44. doi: 10.1521/jscp.23.1.23.26991.
7. Tiggemann M, Slater A. Thin ideals in music television: a source of social comparison and body dissatisfaction. Int J Eat Disord. 2004;35(1):48–58. doi: 10.1002/eat.10214.
8. Micali N, Ploubidis G, De Stavola B, Simonoff E, Treasure J. Frequency and patterns of eating disorder symptoms in early adolescence. J Adolesc Health. 2014;54(5):574–81. doi: 10.1016/j.jadohealth.2013.10.200.
9. Neumark-Sztainer D, Paxton SJ, Hannan PJ, Haines J, Story M. Does body satisfaction matter? Five-year longitudinal associations between body satisfaction and health behaviors in adolescent females and males. J Adolesc Health. 2006;39(2):244–51. doi: 10.1016/j.jadohealth.2005.12.001.
10. Ackard DM, Croll JK, Kearney-Cooke A. Dieting frequency among college females: association with disordered eating, body image, and related psychological problems. J Psychosom Res. 2002;52(3):129–36. doi: 10.1016/S0022-3999(01)00269-0.
11. Allen KL, Byrne SM, Crosby RD. Distinguishing between risk factors for bulimia nervosa, binge eating disorder, and purging disorder. J Youth Adolesc. 2015;44(8):1580–91. doi: 10.1007/s10964-014-0186-8.
12. Paxton SJ, Neumark-Sztainer D, Hannan PJ, Eisenberg ME. Body dissatisfaction prospectively predicts depressive mood and low self-esteem in adolescent girls and boys and low self-esteem in adolescent girls and boys. J Clin Child Adolesc Psychol. 2006;35(4):539–49. doi: 10.1207/s15374424jccp3504.
13. Sundar SS, Oh J, Kang H, Sreenivasan A. How does technology persuade? Theoretical mechanisms for persuasive technologies. In: The sage handbook of persuasion: developments in theory and practice. 2nd ed. Thousand Oaks: Sage; 2013. p. 388–404.
14. Boero N, Pascoe CJ. Pro-anorexia communities and online interaction: bringing the pro-ana body online. Body Soc. 2012;18(2):27–57. doi: 10.1177/1357034X12440827.
15. Francis E. Mother, Daughter warns others about dangers of "thinspiration." *Fox 17*. http://fox17online.com/2016/06/15/mother-daughter-warn-others-about-dangers-of-thinspiration/. Published June 2016. Accessed March 27, 2017.
16. Zolfagharifard E. #thinspiration should be BANNED: Researchers say tag can harm women, even if they don't search for it. *Daily Mail*. http://www.dailymail.co.uk/sciencetech/article-3078871/thinspiration-BANNED-Researchers-say-tag-harm-women-don-t-search-it.html. Published May 2015. Accessed 27 Mar 2017.
17. Lapinski MK. StarvingforPerfect.Com: a theoretically based content analysis of pro-eating disorder web sites. Health Commun. 2009;20(3):243–51. doi: 10.1207/s15327027hc2003.

18. Crowe N, Watts M. "We"re just like Gok, but in reverse': Ana girls – empowerment and resistance in digital communities. Int J Adolesc Youth. 2014;3843(March 2016):1–12. doi: 10.1080/02673843.2013.856802.
19. Ghaznavi J, Taylor LD. Bones, body parts, and sex appeal: an analysis of #thinspiration images on popular social media. Body Image. 2015;14:54–61. doi: 10.1016/j.bodyim.2015.03.006.
20. Seselja E. Instagram Launches Tool to help users at risk of self-harm. *ABC*. http://www.abc.net.au/news/2016-10-21/instagram-introduce-self-harm-precention-tool/7950218. Published October 21, 2016. Accessed 27 Mar 2017.
21. Tiggemann M, Zaccardo M. Strong is the new skinny: a content analysis of fitspiration websites. J Health Psychol. 2016;17:1–9. doi: 10.1016/j.bodyim.2016.03.001.
22. Marie Claire. Why Army Woman are the Ultimate #Fitspiration. Marie Claire. March 2016. http://www.marieclaire.co.uk/uncategorised/why-army-women-are-the-ultimate-fitspiration-15688. Accessed 27 Mar 2017.
23. Tiggemann M, Zaccardo M. "Exercise to be fit, not skinny": the effect of fitspiration imagery on women's body image. Body Image. 2015;15:61–7. doi: 10.1016/j.bodyim.2015.06.003.
24. Deighton-Smith N, Bell BT. Objectifying fitness: a content and thematic analysis of #Fitspiration images on social media. Psychol Pop Media Cult. 2017;6(1):1–41.
25. Boepple L, Thompson JK. A content analytic comparison of fitspiration and thinspiration websites. Int J Eat Disord. 2016;49(1):98–101. doi: 10.1002/eat.22403.
26. Ebizmba. Top 15 Most Popular Photo Sharing Sites. http://www.ebizmba.com/articles/photo-sharing-sites. Published 2016. Accessed March 27, 2017.
27. Yager Z, Diedrichs PC, Ricciardelli LA, Halliwell E. What works in secondary schools? A systematic review of classroom-based body image programs. Body Image. 2013;10(3):271–81. doi: 10.1016/j.bodyim.2013.04.001.
28. Riffe D, Lacy S, Fico F. Analysing media messages: using quantitative content analysis in research. 3rd ed. New York: Routledge; 2014.
29. Duggan M, Ellison NB, Lampe C, Lenhart A, Madden M. Social media update 2014. *Pew Res Cent*. 2015;(January):18. doi:https://doi.org/10.1111/j.1083 6101.2007.00393.x.

Prevalence of disturbed eating behavior and associated symptoms of anxiety and depression among adult males and females with type 1 diabetes

Line Wisting[1,2*], Torild Skrivarhaug[2,3,4,5], Knut Dahl-Jørgensen[2,3,4,5] and Øyvind Rø[1,6]

Abstract

Background: The increased prevalence of disturbed eating behaviors (DEB), depression, and anxiety in type 1 diabetes (T1D) is generally well established; however the majority of existing research to date has focused on female adolescents and young adults. Data on males and older females is scarce. The aim of this study was to assess prevalence of DEB and symptoms of depression and anxiety among adult males and females with type 1 diabetes, to investigate differences between individuals scoring below and above the cut-off on psychopathology, and to examine patterns of eating disorder psychopathology by age and weight.

Methods: A total of 282 adults with type 1 diabetes aged 18–79 years participated in the study. Measures included the Diabetes Eating Problem Survey – Revised (DEPS-R), the Hospital Anxiety and Depression Scale (HADS), and clinical data from the Norwegian Quality Improvement of Laboratory Examinations (NOKLUS) system.

Results: A total of 20.3% of the whole sample (13.3% among males and 24.8% among females) scored above the DEPS-R cut-off score for DEB. As for depression and anxiety, the prevalence in the whole sample was 6.2% and 19.0%, respectively. The prevalence was generally higher in females than males across all psychopathology measures. HbA1c was significantly associated with the DEPS-R total score ($p < .01$) among females, but not with depression and anxiety. Mean DEPS-R score decreased with increasing age, and when our previous reported data from children and adolescents are included, a peak prevalence in DEB in adolescence and young adult age is demonstrated.

Conclusions: The results of this study point to the need for increased awareness of psychological comorbidity among adults with type 1 diabetes, in particular young adult females. Screening is recommended to secure early detection and subsequent intervention for these individuals.

Plain English summary

Although increased rates of disturbed eating behaviors (DEB), depression, and anxiety in type 1 diabetes (T1D) are generally reported, data on males and older females is lacking. This study examined frequency of DEB, depression, and anxiety among 282 adult males and females with T1D across a wide age span. Approximately one-fifth of the participants (and a quarter of all females) scored above cut-off for DEB, 6.2% scored above cut-off for depression, and 19.0% for anxiety. The prevalence was generally higher in females than males across all psychopathology. HbA1c (a measure of long term blood glucose levels) was significantly associated with DEB, but not with depression and anxiety. Symptoms of DEB decreased with increasing age, and when our previous reported data from children and adolescents are included, a peak in levels of DEB during late adolescence and young adulthood was observed. Therefore, increased awareness of psychological comorbidity among adults with T1D is warranted, especially among young adult females.

* Correspondence: line.wisting@ous-hf.no
[1]Regional Department for Eating Disorders, Division of Mental Health and Addiction, Oslo University Hospital, P.O. Box 4956 Nydalen, N-0424 Oslo, Norway
[2]Oslo Diabetes Research Centre, P.O. Box 4956 Nydalen, N-0424 Oslo, Norway
Full list of author information is available at the end of the article

Background

Eating disorders are characterized by a restricted or chaotic food intake, a morbid preoccupation with food, weight, and shape and a distorted body image (1). The Diagnostic and Statistical Manual of Mental Disorders (DSM-5) defines the eating disorders anorexia nervosa, bulimia nervosa, binge eating disorder, other specified feeding and eating disorders and unspecified feeding and eating disorders [1]. Additionally, there are reports of some lower degree eating disturbances which do not meet frequency- or severity criteria for a formal eating disorder diagnosis as defined by diagnostic manuals such as the DSM-5. These disturbances have been defined as disturbed eating behaviors (DEB) [2], a term which will be used to describe all eating disorder psychopathology in this study.

Individuals with type T1D have been found to be at risk of developing DEB, with prevalence rates in T1D reported to be 2–3 times higher in individuals with T1D compared to healthy controls [3–5]. Possible contributing factors include the weight loss accompanied with T1D onset, the weight gain subsequent to diagnosis and initiation of intensive insulin therapy [6], and the required monitoring of food intake in order to plan insulin dosing. Finally, the availability of insulin omission as a unique, T1D-specific compensatory behavior, reported in up to 37% of females with T1D [7], is considered a potential risk factor for developing DEB in T1D. This comorbidity is associated with accelerated onset of T1D complications and increased rates of mortality compared with individuals with T1D without disturbed eating [7, 8].

The eating disorder literature has generally focused the most on adolescent and young adult populations, but increased attention has acknowledged the presence of eating disorder psychopathology also in older samples [9]. It is likely that this will be reflected in adult T1D samples as well. Although the increased prevalence of DEB in T1D is generally well established, a majority of existing research to date has focused on female adolescents and young adults [10, 11]. There is a lack of knowledge about levels of DEB among males and older females with T1D. It is known that risk of DEB varies with age and weight in the general population and among children and adolescents with T1D. It is unclear whether this is true for adults with T1D.

Mood and anxiety disorders have been found to be the most common psychiatric comorbidity in eating disorder populations [12]. Similarly, an array of research has documented increased prevalence of depression and anxiety in individuals with T1D compared to healthy controls [10, 13, 14]. Furthermore, although a majority of the literature reports positive correlations between psychopathology and poor metabolic control [15–19], other studies have yielded mixed support for these associations [20–23].

This study aimed to **i)** assess the prevalence of DEB and associated symptoms of depression and anxiety among adult males and females with T1D; **ii)** investigate differences between individuals scoring below and above the cut-off on psychopathology, with a specific focus on metabolic control; and **iii)** examine patterns of eating disorder psychopathology by age and weight.

Methods

Design

This is a cross-sectional design study.

Procedure

Patients with T1D were recruited from the Norwegian Diabetic Centre (NDC) between February 2016 and October 2017. The NDC is an outpatient clinic for adults (approximately 1300) with T1D, located in Oslo. Patients from Oslo and surrounding areas are referred to the NDC by both general practitioners and hospitals. The NDC is a multidisciplinary clinic organized under the Norwegian Health South-East Authority. Questionnaires were completed as part of a routine T1D consultation at the outpatient clinic. The regional ethics committee approved the study, and written consent was obtained from all participants.

Measures

The Diabetes Eating Problem Survey – Revised (DEPS-R) [24] is a diabetes-specific screening tool for disturbed eating and consists of 16 items. Responses are scored on a 6-point Likert scale and higher scores indicate greater pathology. A recommended cut-off score of > = 20 has been empirically established as a threshold indicating the need for further clinical assessment of eating pathology [24]. The DEPS-R has been translated and validated in a Norwegian adolescent sample aged 11–19 years [25].

The Hospital Anxiety and Depression Scale (HADS) [26] was developed to map symptoms of anxiety and depression in patients in treatment of somatic diseases. Somatic symptoms on anxiety and depression are therefore avoided in HADS in order to prevent that somatic illnesses would be misinterpreted as symptoms of anxiety and depression. HADS consists of two subscales, measuring anxiety (HADS-A) and depression (HADS-D), in addition to the total score. The Norwegian version of HADS has previously demonstrated satisfactory psychometric properties [27]. A cut-off score of ≥8 is often used for the two subscales to indicate symptoms of anxiety and/or depression need for further evaluation, whereas a cut-off score of ≥11 is used to indicate a case (i.e. moderate to severe symptoms). T1D is often associated with fear of hypoglycemia, fear of complications, and diabetes distress [10, 17], which may lead to elevated scores on the HADS. To minimize the risk of over pathologizing due to such diabetes-specific aspects, the current study therefore adopts the cut-off score of 11 to report prevalence of symptoms of depression and anxiety. However, as control data has been carried out using a cut-off of 8, rates based on this cut-off score will also be briefly reported for comparative purposes.

BMI was calculated based on self-reported weight and height (kg/m^2), and further categorized into the following four groups according to the World Health Organization classification scheme [28]: underweight (BMI < 18.5), normal weight (BMI ≥ 18.5–24.9), overweight (BMI ≥ 25–29.9), and obese (BMI ≥ 30).

Age was categorized based on the Center for Disease Control and Prevention (CDC) age groupings [29]: 15–24 years (youngest person was 18 in the current study), 25–34 years, 35–44 years, 45–54 years, 55–64 years, and ≥ 65 years. These age groups are used in previous ED research [30]. Given the relatively low number of participants > 55 years, the two latter groups were collapsed, yielding a total of five age groups (18–24 years, 25–34 years, 35–44 years, 45–54 years, and 55 years and above).

Clinical data was assessed via the Norwegian Quality Improvement of Laboratory Examinations (NOKLUS) system, and was conducted as part of standard clinical T1D assessment at the Norwegian Diabetic Centre. T1D clinical data include HbA1c, T1D onset, and treatment mode. HbA1c is a measure of long term blood glucose levels and reflects average blood glucose the preceding 8–12 weeks. HbA1c is used here as a measure of metabolic control. A reasonable HbA1c target for many nonpregnant adults is < 7.0% (53 mmol/mol). The providers might reasonably suggest a more stringent HbA1c goals such as 6.5% (48 mmol/mol) for selected individual patients if this can be achieved without significant hypoglycemia or other adverse effects of treatment (i.e., polypharmacy) [31].

Data analyses

Pearson correlations were conducted to investigate associations between variables. In line with Cohen [32], correlations of .10 to .29 were interpreted as small, .30 to .49 as medium and .50 to 1.0 as large. Independent samples t-tests were carried out to investigate group differences. Pearson chi-squares were used for categorical variables. Alpha level was set to $p < .05$. Effect sizes were calculated by means of Cohen's *d*. Following the guidelines by Cohen [32], effect sizes > 0.2 were interpreted as small, > 0.5 as medium and > 0.8 as large. Statistical analyses were conducted using SPSS version 23 (SPSS IBM, NY, USA) [33].

Results

Participant characteristics

A total of 282 males and females aged 18–79 years (60% females) participated in the study (mean age 42.11; SD: 15.19). Table 1 illustrates sample characteristics. Mean age of T1D onset was 15.14 (SD: 11.18), mean HbA1c was 7.75% (SD: .91), and mean BMI was 25.96 (SD: 4.13). A total of 56.3% administered insulin with an insulin pen and 43.3% with a pump. All patients used basal/bolus insulin treatment, none fixed premixed regimens.

Prevalence of disturbed eating behavior, depression, and anxiety

A total of 20.3% of the whole sample scored above the established DEPS-R cut-off score for DEB (Table 2). When split by gender, 13.3% of the males and 24.8% of the females scored above the cut-off score. As for depression and anxiety, when using the cut-off score of 11, the prevalence in the whole sample was 6.2% and 19.0%, respectively. In males only, the prevalence was 3.6% for depression and 8.1% for anxiety. The prevalence was generally higher in females than males across all psychopathology scores, with rates of depression and anxiety at 7.8 and 26.4%.

Prevalence rates for depression and anxiety when using a cut-off score of 8 was also assessed, yielding prevalence rates of 13.8% and 35.4% for depression and anxiety for the whole sample. When split by gender, the prevalence of depression and anxiety was 11.8% and 24.3% among males and 15.1% and 42.9% among females.

The frequency of participants scoring above the cut-off score one more than one of the psychopathology measures (disturbed eating, depression, and anxiety) was

Table 1 Participant characteristics

	All *N* = 282	Males *N* = 112 (40%)	Females *N* = 170 (60%)	Sig. level	Effect size
Age	42.11 (15.19)	44.57 (15.92)	40.47 (14.49)	.05	.27
Diabetes onset (years)	15.14 (11.18)	15.43 (10.92)	14.94 (11.38)	ns	–
HbA1c (%)	7.75 (.91)	7.61 (.89)	7.85 (.91)	ns	–
Diabetes duration (years)	27.09 (14.44)	29.14 (14.82)	25.71 (14.05)	ns	–
BMI self-report	25.96 (4.13)	26.47 (3.82)	25.63 (4.30)	ns	–
Mode of insulin treatment	56.3% pen 43.3% pump	60.9% pen 38.0% pump	53.4% pen 46.6% pump		

Data are mean (SD). Significance level ($p < .001$, .01, and .05) and effect size (ES) estimation (Cohen's *d*) is calculated when differences are significant. *Ns* not statistical significant differences

Table 2 Prevalence rates of DEB, anxiety, and depression, in adult males and females with T1D, based on a cut-off score for DEB of 20 or more on the DEPS-R, and 11 or more on the HADS subscales anxiety and depression

	All	Males	Females	*P*-value
DEB	20.3%	13.3%	24.8%	.05
Depression	6.2%	3.6%	7.8%	ns
Anxiety	19%	8.1%	26.4%	.001

The Chi-square test for independence was used to investigate whether the proportion of individuals scoring above the cut-off scores on the DEPS-R as well as the HAD anxiety and depression subscales, was significant different for males and females

also examined. In the whole sample, a total of 8.5% (4.8% of males and 11.0% of females) had two positive screens (i.e. scored above cut-off for either two of the three measures of psychopathology), whereas 5.4% (2.9% males and 7.1% females) had three positive screens (i.e. scored above the cut-off score for all three measures of psychopathology).

As shown in Table 3, there were no significant differences in metabolic control between patients with versus without DEB, depression, or anxiety. As for age, BMI, and T1D duration, the results were mixed. There were no significant differences between individuals with no psychopathology (zero positive screens) and two positive screens. When comparing individuals with no positive screens versus three positive screens, a statistical significant difference found was in age, demonstrating that individuals with three positive screens were significantly younger than individuals with no positive screens (31.9 years (10.8) versus 43.9 years (15.9), $p < 01$).

Mean DEPS-R score was 13.83 (9.16) for the total population, 11.18 (7.80) for males, and 15.57 (9.59) for females ($p < .001$, effect size −.50), indicating higher levels of eating disorder psychopathology among females. Table 4 shows the DEPS-R mean scores among males and females according to different categories of age and weight. Figures 1 and 2 further illustrate the distribution of eating disorder psychopathology by the different age and weight groups. The DEPS-R mean score decreased steadily by age among females, whereas the trend for males were more mixed. As for weight, the DEPS-R mean score increased by increasing weight category for both males and females. Mean score for the HADS depression subscale in the total sample, males, and females was 3.75 (3.61), 3.53 (3.35), and 3.90 (3.77), respectively, with no significant difference between males and females. For anxiety, the mean scores for the whole sample was 6.39 (4.27), and 5.12 (3.67) and 7.26 (4.44) for males and females, respectively.

Associations

Table 5 demonstrates associations between eating disorder psychopathology, depression, anxiety, age, BMI, and HbA1c. Significant associations were found between symptoms of eating disorder psychopathology, depression, and anxiety, with correlation coefficients ranging from .39 ($p < .001$) to .61 ($p < .001$) among males, and .47 ($p < .001$) to .68 ($p < .001$) among females. Furthermore, HbA1c was significantly associated with the DEPS-R total score among females (.27, $p < .01$), but not among males. However, HbA1c was not significantly correlated with the subscale scores of depression and anxiety in neither males nor females. BMI was significantly and positively correlated with eating the DEPS-R total score (.33, $p < .001$) and depression (.30, $p < .001$) among females, but not with anxiety. Among males, BMI was only significantly associated with the DEPS-R total score (.35, $p < .001$), but not with scores of depression or anxiety. Finally, age was significantly and negatively associated with both the DEPS-R and HADS anxiety total scores among females (−.32, $p < .001$ and − .24, $p < .01$, respectively), with lower levels of anxiety and eating disorder psychopathology with higher age (age was not significantly associated with depression). Age was not significantly associated with any of the psychopathology scores among males.

Discussion

This study reported the prevalence of DEB among adult males (13.3%) and females (24.8%) with T1D. Level of eating disorder psychopathology decreased with increasing age among females. Furthermore, symptoms of

Table 3 Comparison of participants with and without disturbed eating behavior (below/above the DEPS-R cut-off of ≥20), depression (below/above the HAD depression cut-off score ≥ 11), and anxiety (below/above the HAD anxiety cut-off score ≥ 11)

	DEB -	DEB +	Sig. level	ES	Depr -	Depr +	Sig. level	ES	Anx -	Anx +	Sig. level	ES	No pos screens	2 pos screens	Sig.level	ES	No pos screens	3 pos screens	Sig. level	ES
HbA1c (%)	7.7 (.9)	8.0 (.9)	ns	–	7.7 (.9)	8.0 (.8)	ns	–	7.7 (.9)	7.8 (.8)	ns	–	7.7 (.9)	7.9 (.8)	ns	–	7.7 (.9)	7.9 (.8)	ns	–
BMI	25.5 (3.7)	27.7 (4.9)	.01	0.5	25.8 (3.8)	29.2 (7.1)	ns	–	25.9 (3.8)	26.6 (5.4)	ns	–	25.5 (3.5)	26.9 (5.6)	ns	–	25.5 (3.5)	29.1 (6.5)	ns	–
T1D duration	28.4 (14.8)	24.0 (12.7)	.05	−0.3	27.2 (14.6)	27.5 (12.6)	ns	–	27.8 (14.8)	24.8 (13.1)	ns	–	28.3 (15.2)	31.5 (13.5)	ns	–	28.3 (15.2)	21.3 (11.0)	ns	–
Age (years)	44.1 (15.3)	35.4 (12.4)	.001	−0.6	42.3 (15.4)	39.9 (11.3)	ns	–	43.1 (15.5)	38.3 (13.1)	.05	.3	43.9 (15.9)	43.0 (14.6)	ns	–	43.9 (15.9)	31.9 (10.8)	.01	.9

Data are mean (SD), significance level ($p < .001$, .01, and .05) and effect size (ES) estimation (Cohen's *d*)

Table 4 DEPS-R mean scores in males and females with T1D according to different categories of age and weight

	All	Males	Females	Sig. level
Age				
18–24 years	16.39 (10.4)	10.36 (8.8)	19.92 (9.7)	.01
25–34 years	16.11 (10.5)	11.75 (6.7)	17.95 (11.4)	.05
35–44 years	15.46 (9.9)	14.17 (10.3)	16.32 (9.7)	ns
45–54 years	12.48 (7.1)	9.6 (5.5)	14.33 (7.5)	.05
55–64 years	10.06 (6.9)	10.71 (8.5)	9.6 (5.5)	ns
≥ 65 years	10.00 (6.0)	9.7 (5.2)	10.42 (7.3)	ns
BMI				
Underweight	4.50 (5.0)	–	4.50 (5.0)	–
Normal weight	11.89 (8.6)	9.55 (7.3)	13.20 (9.0)	.05
Overweight	13.89 (8.3)	10.48 (7.1)	16.46 (8.3)	.001
Obese	19.94 (10.5)	17.53 (8.6)	21.84 (11.6)	ns

data are means (standard deviations)

depression and anxiety were reported, with one fourth of females scoring above cut-off for anxiety. Females had generally higher scores on measures of psychopathology in terms of DEB, depression, and anxiety, than males.

Prevalence of DEB

The observed gender difference in prevalence of DEB supports previous studies of eating disorder psychopathology, both in diabetes [34, 35] and non-diabetes [36] samples. Furthermore, the prevalence increased by increasing weight, which is comparable to pediatric T1D samples [25, 37–39] as well as the ED literature in general [40]. However, it should be noted that BMI generally increases with age, and the current sample is relatively old compared to many studies of comorbid DEB and T1D. In line with previous research [40], the prevalence of DEB was highest among the young adult females, with decreasing eating disorder psychopathology with older age. This is the opposite trend to what has been reported in child and adolescent samples, where rates of disturbed eating have been found to increase by increasing age [39]. This most likely reflects the peak age of eating disorder onset during late adolescence and early adulthood among females [36]. This peak in DEB during late adolescence and early adulthood is also evident in Fig. 1, illustrating levels of DEB according to different age groups in our previous adolescent sample [39] and the current adult sample. Older adolescents and young adults with T1D is generally found to be in a vulnerable phase as they are in the process of transferring from pediatric to adult health care, indicating lower levels of care and support. Additionally, individuals at this point in life typically move away from their home for the first time [41–43].

Prevalence symptoms of anxiety

This study found that 8.1% of males and 26.4% of females scored above the cut-off score for anxiety at 11 or above (HADS-A). These rates are comparable to those reported by Lloyd et al. [44] among their mixed sample of patients with both T1D and type 2 diabetes (T2D). Using the same cut-off as the current study, a total of 25% scored above cut-off for moderate to severe symptoms of anxiety. Females tended to report more moderate-severe anxiety than males. There were no significant differences between types of diabetes. Another study used the 8 or above cut-off score on the HADS-A, and found that 22.4% of the males and 37.2% of the females had mild symptoms of anxiety. Furthermore, a systematic review of diabetes and anxiety [14] reported prevalence rates ranging from 15 to 27.5% when using the cut-off score 8 on the HADS-A. As can be expected with the use of a lower cut-off, these rates are somewhat higher than those reported in our study, and in the study by Lloyd et al. [44].

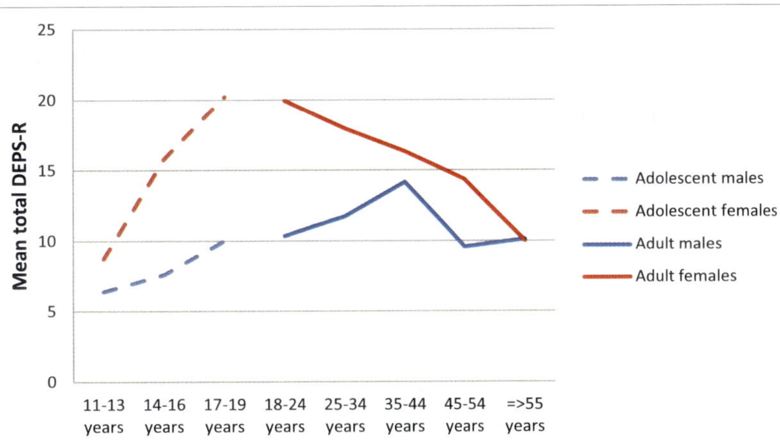

Fig. 1 Mean DEPS-R total score according to age group in the current sample of adult males and females with T1D, as depicted by a solid lineNote: Mean DEPS-R total score according to age group in our previous sample of adolescent males and females with T1D [25] is indicated by a dashed line

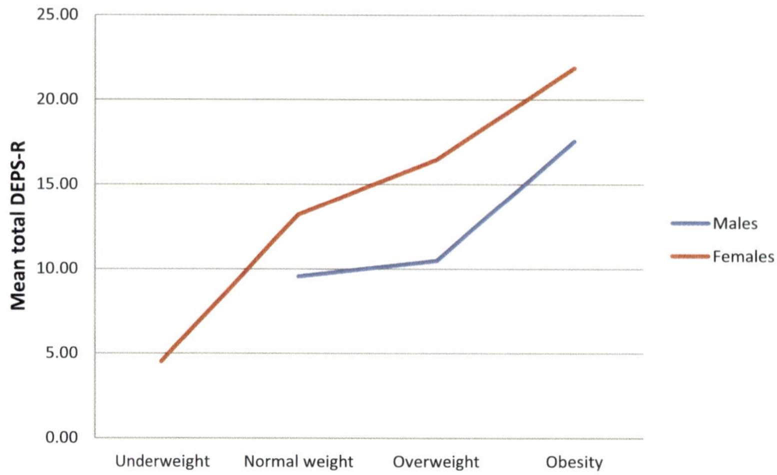

Fig. 2 Mean DEPS-R total score in males and females with T1D by BMI categoryNote: BMI was categorized into the following four groups according to the World Health Organization classification scheme (28): underweight (BMI < 18.5), normal weight (BMI ≥ 18.5–24.9), overweight (BMI ≥ 25–29.9), and obese (BMI ≥ 30)

The current study did not include a control group to compare rates of anxiety in this T1D population to those of non-diabetes controls. However, a large Norwegian population study (the HUNT 2 study) has been conducted, reporting levels of anxiety in the general population, aged 20–89 years ($N = 60.869$). Bjelland et al. [45] reported that 9.6% scored above the cut-off score of 8 for anxiety. When using the same cut-off score in our sample of both males and females with T1D, a prevalence of 35.4% was reported for anxiety. This is much higher than the prevalence reported in the HUNT study, suggesting that levels of anxiety are higher among patients with T1D than non-diabetes controls.

As the HADS is a generic measure, it should be noted that reported symptoms of anxiety in the current study may be driven by diabetes-specific distress. Previously reported diabetes-specific features of anxiety include fear of complications, fear of hypoglycemia, and invasive self-care behaviors such as fear of injections, self-monitoring of blood glucose, and insertion of subcutaneous insulin infusion devices such as an insulin pump [10]. Such illness-specific aspects may contribute to higher rates of anxiety among patients with diabetes.

Prevalence symptoms of depression

A total of 11.8% of the males and 7.8% of the females scored above the cut-off score for depression (HADS-D) in the present study, indicating moderate to severe symptoms of depression, or "caseness". Lloyd et al. [44], using the same cut-off, found that 8% of the patients with diabetes scored above the cut-off for depression, thus in line with our study. Knychala et al. [46] used the cut-off score of 8, and reported prevalence rates of 4.7% among males and 17.6% of females with diabetes. Given the lower cut-off, the higher prevalence rates compared to the previous two studies, can be expected. The meta-analysis by Anderson et al. [13], however, reported higher prevalence rates, with rates for elevated depressive symptoms being 21.3% for adults with T1D. Rates of depressive disorders, as assessed by a diagnostic

Table 5 Associations between psychopathology (disturbed eating, depression, and anxiety), age, BMI, and HbA1c, in adult males (left diagonal) and females (bold, right diagonal) with T1D

Males	Females					
	DEPS-R total	HAD depression	HAD anxiety	Age	BMI	HbA1c
DEPS-R total	–	**.47*** **	**.48*** **	**–.32*** **	**.33*** **	**.27** **
HAD depression	.39***	–	**.68*** **	**ns**	**.30*** **	**ns**
HAD anxiety	.50***	.61***	–	**–.24** **	**ns**	**ns**
Age	ns	ns	ns	–	**ns**	**ns**
BMI	.35***	ns	ns	ns	–	**.19***
HbA1c	ns	ns	ns	–.24*	ns	–

data are Pearson correlation coefficients, and significance levels are indicated by *s ($p < .001$***; $p < .01$**; $p < .05$*). *Ns* not significant associations
entries in the right diagonale are marked in bold to indicate that they refer to the females of our sample

interview, ranged from 8 to 15% in adults with T1D and T2D (no studies investigated rates in samples with T1D only). A systematic review by Roy et al. [47] reported a three-fold increase in prevalence of depression among individuals with T1D compared to those without, with prevalence rates ranging from 5.8 to 43.3% (range among individuals without diabetes was 2.7% to 11.4%).

As for comparison with Norwegian control data, the prevalence of depression when using the cut-off score of 8 was 4.9% in the HUNT 2 study [45]. When using the same cut-off in the current study, we found a prevalence of depression at 13.8%, indicating that levels of depression are higher among individuals with T1D than individuals without.

The varying prevalence rates across studies underlines the importance of considering methodological aspects when interpreting reported prevalence rates. It is important to note that reported prevalence rates are highly dependent on the adopted cut-off score, and there are variations in the literature as to which cut-off score is utilized. We chose to adopt the more conservative cut-off 11 to minimize the risk of over pathologizing. The adopted cut-off score is important to take into account when interpreting prevalence rates across studies. Finally, it should be noted that screening measures cannot be used to establish a diagnosis as defined by diagnostic manuals. This can only be done with clinical diagnostic interviews. Screening measures of psychopathology may yield inaccurate estimates, but they are a simple and quick method. Therefore, it is recommended to validate positive screens with an interview.

Above versus below cut-off on psychopathology

There was no significant difference in HbA1c among patients scoring above versus below the DEPS-R or the HADS depression or anxiety cut-off scores. Eating disorder psychopathology (mean DEPS-R total score) was, however, significantly and positively associated with metabolic control in females, but this was not the case for depression or anxiety. It is not clear why there was no significant difference in HbA1c between individuals scoring above versus below cut-off on the DEPS-R when the association between the DEPS-R total score and HbA1c is significant. One potential reason is that the analysis is less sensitive when the data are dichotomous rather than dimensional. It should also be mentioned that despite the presence of DEB, depression, and anxiety, the HbA1c in the current sample is relatively good. Further, the percentage of patients using an insulin pump is relatively high. These factors might indicate that the patients receive good T1D care within a multidisciplinary team, including psychological health care personnel. The lack of associations between depression/anxiety and metabolic control is in contrast to several other studies [15–18], although not all [23, 48]. The discrepancies in this regard across studies may be explained by various factors. For example, it has been argued that it has been suggested that distinct profiles of depression exist, which may impact outcome differently [49]. Also, it has been shown that diabetes-specific emotional distress, not depression, is associated with metabolic control [23]. These two concepts are commonly being used interchangeably, despite the fact that they are not overlapping constructs [49, 50]. An underlying construct of diabetes-specific emotional distress be considered as a core structure to link diabetes-related distress, subclinical depression, elevated depression symptoms, and major depressive disorder [50]. Targeting illness-specific cognitions may be more productive than treatment of general dysphoria in T1D [22].

Although studies have found significant relationships between the HADS scales and metabolic control [44], the lack of significant relationship between anxiety/depression and metabolic control in our study may also be explained by the use of this measure, which was specifically designed for patients within a hospital setting. To avoid false positives, i.e. avoid symptoms of somatic illness to be falsely interpreted as psychopathology, somatic symptoms of depression and anxiety are omitted in the HADS. As some of the symptoms of anxiety and depression in diagnostic manuals are indeed of somatic character, this may have influenced the expected association between these variables and metabolic control in the current study. In fact, Bot et al. [16] reported that somatic symptoms of depression were some of the symptoms of depression most strongly associated with metabolic control, which may explain the lack of significant association between depression and metabolic control in this study. This assumption may be supported by another Norwegian study, which also used the HADS, and did not find a significant association between depression and HbA1c [23]. However, they did find a significant association between diabetes-related distress and metabolic control, supporting the suggested distinction between depression and diabetes-related distress as discussed above. Taken together, this suggests that various related correlates may play a role in explaining the relationship, or lack thereof, between depression/anxiety and metabolic control, and that illness-specific distress could be taken into account.

Participants scoring above cut-off for DEB and anxiety were significantly younger than participants scoring below cut-off. Similarly, patients with three positive screens (i.e. scored above cut-off for DEB, depression, and anxiety) were significantly younger than patients scoring below cut-off on all three measures of psychopathology. Decreasing eating disorder psychopathology by increasing age among adults is in line with previous eating disorder literature among individuals without T1D [40]. Similar to the negative correlation between eating disorder psychopathology and age, patients scoring above cut-off for anxiety were significantly younger than those scoring below. Previous literature has shown evidence of decreased susceptibility to both depression and anxiety with increasing age [10, 47]. This is only partially in conjunction to the current study, since the negative correlation between depression and age was not statistically significant.

The significant associations between age and measures of psychopathology are also evident in the correlation analyses (Table 4). Furthermore, and as expected, symptoms of DEB, depression, and anxiety were significantly associated with each other, with medium to large correlations. Finally, this study specifically aimed to inspect the relationships between eating disorder psychopathology with age and weight. As illustrated by Fig. 1, DEPS-R mean scores decreased by increasing age among females. This is in line with findings from the eating disorder literature among adults [40]. In contrast, eating disorder psychopathology has been found to increase by increasing age among adolescent samples [39]. These different age patterns most likely reflect the peak onset of eating disorders during the late adolescence [51]. Further, as demonstrated in Fig. 2, eating disorder psychopathology in the current study increased by increasing weight. This is consistent to previous research among adults in the eating disorder literature [40], as well as with adolescents with T1D [39].

The inclusion of males and older females represents a strength of this study as the majority of existing literature is focused on adolescent and young adult females only. Also, the use of the diabetes-specific measure DEPS-R is a strength and in line with current recommendations [5] to yield more accurate estimates of prevalence rates. However, the cross-sectional design is a weakness as we cannot infer causality. More studies are needed to elaborate on the directions of the relationships between diabetes and psychopathology. Also, data was collected from only one diabetes clinic, and we can therefore not be sure whether the results of this study are representative for the entire adult T1D population. Furthermore, the glycemic control was not measured at the same time as the psychological assessment. Finally, the data gathered in this study was self-reports only, and we can therefore not establish formal eating disorder diagnoses as defined by diagnostic manuals such as the DSM-5.

Conclusion

In conclusion, the present study points to the need for awareness of psychological comorbidity among patients with T1D. One fourth of females suffer from symptoms of anxiety and DEB, which is likely to negatively impact quality of life, a prioritized aim for diabetes treatment, regardless of metabolic control. Screening can be recommended to secure early detection and subsequent intervention, in particular among young adult females. Finally, the effects of age should be recognized, as older adolescent [39] and young adult females with T1D appear to be in particular risk of developing eating disorder psychopathology and symptoms of anxiety. This coincides with age of transitioning from pediatric to adult health care, which is generally described to be a vulnerable phase as discussed above. Such aspects point to the need for clinicians to be particularly aware of this age group in terms of eating disturbances.

Abbreviations

BMI: Body mass index; CDC: The center for disease control and prevention; DEB: Disturbed eating behavior; DEPS-R: The diabetes eating problem survey – revised; DSM: The diagnostic and statistical manual of mental disorders; HADS: The hospital anxiety and depression scale; HADS-A: The hospital anxiety and depression scale; anxiety subscale; HADS-D: The hospital anxiety and depression scale; depression subscale; HbA1c: Hemoglobin A1c; HUNT: The Nord-Trøndelag health study; NDC: The Norwegian diabetic center; NOKLUS: The Norwegian quality improvement of laboratory examination; SPSS: The statistical package for the social sciences; T1D: Type 1 diabetes; T2D: Type 2 diabetes

Acknowledgements

The authors would like to thank the staff at the Norwegian Diabetic Centre for their valuable contributions to the recruitment and data collection for this study. Also, we would like to thank the patients for their willingness to contribute to this study.

Funding

This study is funded by the Norwegian Health South-East Authority.

Authors' contributions

LW conceived the study, was responsible for recruitment of participants and data collection, analyzed the data, and wrote the manuscript. TS and KDJ contributed to the planning of the study, contributed with clinical data collection, and to the manuscript. ØR contributed to the planning of the study and to the manuscript. All authors read and approved the final manuscript.

Competing interests

The authors declare that they have no competing interests.

Author details

[1]Regional Department for Eating Disorders, Division of Mental Health and Addiction, Oslo University Hospital, P.O. Box 4956 Nydalen, N-0424 Oslo, Norway. [2]Oslo Diabetes Research Centre, P.O. Box 4956 Nydalen, N-0424 Oslo, Norway. [3]Department of Paediatric and Adolescent Medicine, Oslo University Hospital, P.O. Box 4956 Nydalen, N-0424 Oslo, Norway. [4]Institute of Clinical Medicine, Faculty of Medicine, University of Oslo, Problemveien 7, N-0315 Oslo, Norway. [5]The Norwegian Diabetic Centre, Sponhoggveien 19,

N-0284 Oslo, Norway. [6]Institute of Clinical Medicine, Mental Health and Addiction, University of Oslo, Problemveien 7, N-0315 Oslo, Norway.

References

1. American Psychiatric Association. The Diagnostic and Statistical Manual of Mental Disorders: DSM-5. Fifth ed. Washington DC: American Psychiatric Association; 2013.
2. Olmsted MP, Colton PA, Daneman D, Rydall AC, Rodin GM. Prediction of the onset of disturbed eating behavior in adolescent girls with type 1 diabetes. Diabetes Care. 2008;31(10):1978–82.
3. Mannucci E, Rotella F, Ricca V, Moretti S, Placidi GF, Rotella CM. Eating disorders in patients with type 1 diabetes: a meta-analysis. J Endocrinol Invest. 2005;28(5):417–9.
4. Nielsen S. Eating disorders in females with type 1 diabetes: an update of a meta-analysis. Eur Eat Disord Rev. 2002;10(4):241–54.
5. Young V, Eiser C, Johnson B, Brierley S, Epton T, Elliott J, et al. Eating problems in adolescents with type 1 diabetes: a systematic review with meta-analysis. Diabet Med. 2012;30(2):189–98.
6. Weight gain associated with intensive therapy in the diabetes control and complications trial. The DCCT Research Group. Diabetes Care. 1988;11(7):567–73.
7. Goebel-Fabbri AE, Fikkan J, Franko DL, Pearson K, Anderson BJ, Weinger K. Insulin restriction and associated morbidity and mortality in women with type 1 diabetes. Diabetes Care. 2008;31(3):415–9.
8. Nielsen S, Emborg C, Molbak AG. Mortality in concurrent type 1 diabetes and anorexia nervosa. Diabetes Care. 2002;25(2):309–12.
9. Mangweth-Matzek B, Hoek HW. Epidemiology and treatment of eating disorders in men and women of middle and older age. Curr Opin Psychiatry. 2017;30(6):446–51.
10. de Groot M, Golden SH, Wagner J. Psychological conditions in adults with diabetes. Am Psychol. 2016;71(7):552–62.
11. Young-Hyman DL, Davis CL. Disordered eating behavior in individuals with diabetes: importance of context, evaluation, and classification. Diabetes Care. 2010;33(3):683–9.
12. Hudson JI, Hiripi E, Pope HG Jr, Kessler RC. The prevalence and correlates of eating disorders in the National Comorbidity Survey Replication. Biol Psychiatry. 2007;61(3):348–58.
13. Anderson RJ, Freedland KE, Clouse RE, Lustman PJ. The prevalence of comorbid depression in adults with diabetes: a meta-analysis. Diabetes Care. 2001;24(6):1069–78.
14. Smith KJ, Beland M, Clyde M, Gariepy G, Page V, Badawi G, et al. Association of diabetes with anxiety: a systematic review and meta-analysis. J Psychosom Res. 2013;74(2):89–99.
15. Bernstein CM, Stockwell MS, Gallagher MP, Rosenthal SL, Soren K. Mental health issues in adolescents and young adults with type 1 diabetes: prevalence and impact on glycemic control. ClinPediatr(Phila). 2013;52(1):10–5.
16. Bot M, Pouwer F, de Jonge P, Tack CJ, Geelhoed-Duijvestijn PH, Snoek FJ. Differential associations between depressive symptoms and glycaemic control in outpatients with diabetes. Diabet Med. 2013;30(3):e115–22.
17. Hislop AL, Fegan PG, Schlaeppi MJ, Duck M, Yeap BB. Prevalence and associations of psychological distress in young adults with type 1 diabetes. Diabet Med. 2008;25(1):91–6.
18. Lustman PJ, Anderson RJ, Freedland KE, de Groot M, Carney RM, Clouse RE. Depression and poor glycemic control: a meta-analytic review of the literature. Diabetes Care. 2000;23(7):934–42.
19. van Bastelaar KM, Pouwer F, Geelhoed-Duijvestijn PH, Tack CJ, Bazelmans E, Beekman AT, et al. Diabetes-specific emotional distress mediates the association between depressive symptoms and glycaemic control in type 1 and type 2 diabetes. Diabet Med. 2010;27(7):798–803.
20. Hessler DM, Fisher L, Polonsky WH, Masharani U, Strycker LA, Peters AL, et al. Diabetes distress is linked with worsening diabetes management over time in adults with type 1 diabetes. Diabet Med. 2017;34(9):1228–34.
21. Schmitt A, Reimer A, Kulzer B, Haak T, Gahr A, Hermanns N. Negative association between depression and diabetes control only when accompanied by diabetes-specific distress. J Behav Med. 2015;38(3):556–64.
22. Shaban C, Fosbury JA, Cavan DA, Kerr D, Skinner TC. The relationship between generic and diabetes specific psychological factors and glycaemic control in adults with type 1 diabetes. Diabetes Res Clin Pract. 2009;85(3):e26–9.
23. Strandberg RB, Graue M, Wentzel-Larsen T, Peyrot M, Rokne B. Relationships of diabetes-specific emotional distress, depression, anxiety, and overall well-being with HbA1c in adult persons with type 1 diabetes. J Psychosom Res. 2014;77(3):174–9.
24. Markowitz JT, Butler DA, Volkening LK, Antisdel JE, Anderson BJ, Laffel LM. Brief screening tool for disordered eating in diabetes: internal consistency and external validity in a contemporary sample of pediatric patients with type 1 diabetes. Diabetes Care. 2010;33(3):495–500.
25. Wisting L, Froisland DH, Skrivarhaug T, Dahl-Jorgensen K, Ro O. Psychometric properties, norms, and factor structure of the diabetes eating problem survey-revised in a large sample of children and adolescents with type 1 diabetes. Diabetes Care. 2013;36(8):2198–202.
26. Zigmond AS, Snaith RP. The hospital anxiety and depression scale. Acta Psychiatr Scand. 1983;67(6):361–70.
27. Leiknes KA, Dalsbø TK, Siqveland J. Måleegenskaper ved den norske versjonen av Hospital Anxiety and Depression Scale (HADS). 2016.
28. World Health Organization. BMI classification 2012.
29. Centers for Disease Control and Prevention (CDC). Web-based Injury Statistics Query and Reporting System (WISQARS).http://www.cdc.gov/injury/wisqars/index.html [.
30. Ballard J, Crane DR. Eating disorders treatment patterns by age. Eat Disord. 2015;23(3):262–74.
31. American Diabetes A. Standards of medical Care in Diabetes—2017 abridged for primary care providers. Clin Diabetes. 2017;35(1):5–26.
32. Cohen J. Statistical Power Analysis for the Behavioural Sciences. 2 Ed. Hillsdale; 1988.
33. IBM SPSS Statistics for Windows, Version 23. Version 23 ed: Armonk, NY: IBM Corp; 2015.
34. Bachle C, Stahl-Pehe A, Rosenbauer J. Disordered eating and insulin restriction in youths receiving intensified insulin treatment: results from a nationwide population-based study. Int J Eat Disord. 2016;49(2):191–6.
35. d'Emden H, McDermott B, D'Silva N, Dover T, Ewais T, Gibbons K, et al. Psychosocial screening and management of young people aged 18-25 years with diabetes. Intern Med J. 2017;47(4):415–23.
36. Jacobi C, Hayward C, de Zwaan M, Kraemer HC, Agras WS. Coming to terms with risk factors for eating disorders: application of risk terminology and suggestions for a general taxonomy. Psychol Bull. 2004;130(1):19–65.
37. Atik Altinok Y, Ozgur S, Meseri R, Ozen S, Darcan S, Goksen D. Reliaability and validity of the diabetes eating problem survey-revised on Turkish children and adolescents with type 1 diabetes mellitus. J Clin Res Pediatr Endocrinol. 2017;9(4):323–328.
38. Markowitz JT, Alleyn CA, Phillips R, Muir A, Young-Hyman D, Laffel LM. Disordered eating behaviors in youth with type 1 diabetes: prospective pilot assessment following initiation of insulin pump therapy. Diabetes Technol Ther. 2013;15(5):428–33.
39. Wisting L, Froisland DH, Skrivarhaug T, Dahl-Jorgensen K, Ro O. Disturbed eating behavior and omission of insulin in adolescents receiving intensified insulin treatment: a nationwide population-based study. Diabetes Care. 2013;36(11):3382–7.
40. Ro O, Reas DL, Rosenvinge J. The impact of age and BMI on eating disorder examination questionnaire (EDE-Q) scores in a community sample. Eat Behav. 2012;13(2):158–61.
41. Hilliard ME, Perlus JG, Clark LM, Haynie DL, Plotnick LP, Guttmann-Bauman I, et al. Perspectives from before and after the pediatric to adult care transition: a mixed-methods study in type 1 diabetes. Diabetes Care. 2014; 37(2):346–54.
42. Lotstein DS, Seid M, Klingensmith G, Case D, Lawrence JM, Pihoker C, et al. Transition from pediatric to adult care for youth diagnosed with type 1 diabetes in adolescence. Pediatrics. 2013;131(4):e1062–70.
43. Lyons SK, Becker DJ, Helgeson VS. Transfer from pediatric to adult health care: effects on diabetes outcomes. Pediatr Diabetes. 2014;15(1):10–7.
44. Lloyd CE, Dyer PH, Barnett AH. Prevalence of symptoms of depression and anxiety in a diabetes clinic population. Diabet Med. 2000;17(3):198–202.
45. Bjelland I, Lie SA, Dahl AA, Mykletun A, Stordal E, Kraemer HC. A dimensional versus a categorical approach to diagnosis: anxiety and depression in the HUNT 2 study. Int J Methods Psychiatr Res. 2009;18(2):128–37.
46. Knychala MA, Jorge ML, Muniz CK, Faria PN, Jorge PT. High-risk alcohol use and anxiety and depression symptoms in adolescents and adults with type 1 diabetes mellitus: a cross-sectional study. Diabetol Metab Syndr. 2015;7:24.

47. Roy T, Lloyd CE. Epidemiology of depression and diabetes: a systematic review. J Affect Disord 2012;142 Suppl:S8–21.
48. Bachle C, Lange K, Stahl-Pehe A, Castillo K, Scheuing N, Holl RW, et al. Symptoms of eating disorders and depression in emerging adults with early-onset, long-duration type 1 diabetes and their association with metabolic control. PLoS One. 2015;10(6):e0131027.
49. Snoek FJ, Bremmer MA, Hermanns N. Constructs of depression and distress in diabetes: time for an appraisal. Lancet Diabetes Endocrinol. 2015;3(6):450–60.
50. Fisher L, Gonzalez JS, Polonsky WH. The confusing tale of depression and distress in patients with diabetes: a call for greater clarity and precision. Diabet Med. 2014;31(7):764–72.
51. Bryant-Waugh R, Lask B. Overview of the eating disorders. In: Lask B, Bryant-Waugh R, editors. Eating disorders in childhood and adolescence. 3rd ed. London and New York: Routledge; 2007. p. 35–50.

18

Psychometric properties of the Iranian version of mindful eating questionnaire in women who seeking weight reduction

Zahra Abbaspoor[1], Nahid Javadifar[2], Mahsa Miryan[3] and Parvin Abedi[4*]

Abstract

Background: The aim of the present study was to test the validity, reliability and factor structure of the original Mindful Eating Questionnaire (MEQ) for use in an Iranian population.

Methods: This was a cross-sectional study conducted on 150 women who attended four athletic gyms and met the inclusion criteria in Ahvaz city in July of 2015. After linguistic validation of the Iranian version of the MEQ, the content validity ratio (CVR) and content validity index (CVI) were assessed by an expert panel. Then, exploratory factor analysis (EFA) was performed on the scale constructs and scale reliability (internal consistency and test-retest reliability) was assessed with respect to the psychometric properties of the scale.

Results: The CVR and CVI scores for the MEQ were 0.89 and 0.93, respectively. EFA loaded all 28-items with a 5-factor solution ('awareness', 'distraction', 'disinhibition', 'emotional response' and 'external cues') that jointly accounted for 53.78% of the observed variance. The results of the EFA supported the item 'When a restaurant portion is too large, I stop eating when I'm full' being placed in the external cues rather than the disinhibition subscale. This displacement improved the reliability coefficient for this subscale.
The results of internal consistency analysis, including Cronbach's alpha (ranging from 0.73 to 0.81) and intraclass correlation coefficients (ranging from 0.73 to 0.91) were satisfactory.

Conclusions: The Persian version of the MEQ appears to be valid and reliable; therefore, it can be an effective tool in designing mindfulness-based interventions for the treatment of individuals with eating disorders, overweight and obesity in an Iranian population.

Keywords: Mindfulness eating, Questionnaires, Reliability, Validity

Plain English summary

The prevalence of obesity has increased worldwide over the past decade and according to the World Health Organization, more than 650 million (13%) individuals over the age 18 years are obese. The prevalence of obesity also has increased in Iran in the recent years and reached to 21.3% in population with age > 18 years. Some disordered eating behaviours may be important factors in the prevalence of obesity.

Mindfulness is described as a non-judgmental awareness of the present moment and is effective in decreasing psychological symptoms including depression and anxiety in individuals with obesity. Several scales specifically measure mindfulness and are widely used in applied settings, but there are limited specific scales to measure mindfulness with respect to eating behaviors. The mindful eating questionnaire (MEQ) is the first scale measures mindful eating. Because of a high prevalence of overweight and obesity in Iran, this study aimed to evaluate the Mindful Eating Questionnaire (MEQ) for use in an Iranian population.

* Correspondence: parvinabedi@ymail.com
[4]Menopause, Andropause Research Center, Ahvaz Jundishapur University of Medical Sciences, Ahvaz, Iran
Full list of author information is available at the end of the article

Background

The prevalence of obesity has increased worldwide over the past decade and according to the World Health Organization, more than 650 million (13%) individuals over the age 18 years are obese [1]. The prevalence of obesity also has increased in Iran in the recent years and reached to 21.3% in population with age > 18 years [2]. Some disordered eating behaviors, such as binge eating (uncontrolled eating of a large amount of food in short periods of time) may be important factors in the prevalence of obesity [3, 4]. Psychological distress plays a role in this type of eating behavior [5]. Mindfulness approaches, such as non-judgmental awareness of the present moment, are described extensively in the scientific literature as effective interventions in decreasing psychological symptoms, including depression and anxiety [6] and also in reducing binge-type eating in individuals with obesity [7]. Several scales specifically measure mindfulness [8–11] and are widely used in applied settings, but there are limited specific scales to measure mindfulness with respect to eating behaviours. The mindful eating questionnaire (MEQ) as the first scale with good reliability and validity, measures mindful eating [12].

The MEQ is a 28 item questionnaire with five domains namely; awareness (7 questions), distraction (3 questions), disinhibition (8 questions), emotional response (4 questions) and external cue (4 questions). The total possible scores for subscales are in range of 7–28, 3–12, 8–32, 4–16 and 4–16, respectively (13).

Pintado-Cucarella et al., in their study on 216 participants used MEQ and assessed the relationship of mindful eating and body mass index. Their results showed that low score of mindful eating was significantly contributed to overweight, anxiety and binge eating [14].

Taylor et al., in their study used MEQ questionnaire and found that self-compassion is significantly related to mindful eating and body mass index [15] Also Clementi et al., assessed the abbreviated form of MEQ (including 20 questions) on 1067 samples in Italy and found that this version is a valid and reliable means to use by clinicians and researchers [16]. Framson et al., in their study found that the lower score of MEQ was significantly related to body mass index> 30 kg/m^2 in women (13).

The prevalence of obesity in Iran is relatively high (21.3%) [2], and investigation into healthful dietary behavior and related health outcomes in this population is important.

To the best of our knowledge, no study on mindfulness and eating topic have been conducted in Iran, therefore this study aimed to evaluate the psychometric properties of the Iranian version of Mindful Eating Questionnaire. We believe that this research will contribute to the existing knowledge on the topic and will provide an instrument for use by nutritionists in clinical settings as well as by researchers to evaluate the effects of mindful eating skills on healthier eating behavior in Iran.

Methods

The questionnaires

The MEQ is a 28-item questionnaire that contains five subscales: awareness (7 items), distraction (3 items), disinhibition (8 items), emotional response (4 items) and external cues (6 items). Response categories are rated on a four-point Likert scale, where a score of 1 suggests an eating behavior that is performed never/rarely and 4 indicates a behavior that is performed usually/always. The scores on questions 1, 2, 6, 7, 9, 11, 13, 17, 18, 19, 27 and 28 should be reversed. The total possible scores for awareness (7 items), distraction (3 items), disinhibition (8 items), emotional response (4 items) and external cues (4 items) subscales are in the ranges of 7–28, 3–12, 8–32, 4–16 and 4–16, respectively [13].

Translation and cultural adaptation

A forward-backward procedure was applied to translate the English version of the MEQ into the Persian language. Initially, two forward and conceptual translations were produced by two independent translators who were not aware that the tool would be subsequently translated back into English. The researchers then compared the two translations and produced the first draft of the Persian version of the questionnaire. Two other translators, who were unaware of the questionnaire, back translated the Persian questionnaire into the English language. Subsequently, in the synthesis step, the research team evaluated the final English version against the original version and, together with a specialist in psychometrics, reviewed the entire translation processes. Consequently, a test of face validity was performed to provide a pre-final version of the questionnaire. Finally, an agreement in terms of semantic, idiomatic, conceptual and cultural equivalence was reached and the final version of the questionnaire was provided. In the new questionnaire compared with original version, there were only minor modifications to the wording and additional descriptions in parentheses to improve understanding by the target group.

Design and data collection

Participants and procedure

This was a cross-sectional study conducted on 150 women who attended four gyms to perform exercise in Ahvaz city during July 2015. This group was selected because behavioral eating disorders, obesity and higher intake of food are more common in women especially in those who seeking weight loss [17, 18].

In the gyms, at the end of an exercise program and after the study aims were explained and written consent to participate was obtained, women were asked to complete the MEQ questionnaire.

Women were eligible if they met each of the following criteria: participation in any recreational exercise in the gym, functional literacy and a willingness to commit to this research study. Exclusion criteria were: professional athletes, being on diets under the supervision of a nutritionist, using any kind of pharmaceutical weight control, having any severe mood disorder controlled by pharmaceuticals and current known substance abuse. Research questionnaires were completed by participants at a separate location in the gym following the conclusion of exercise.

Statistical analysis

Face validity

The establishment of qualitative and quantitative face validity can improve the assistance of respondents in completing a questionnaire, identify any ambiguities in the wording of items and identify any inappropriate items [19–21]. To establish the qualitative face validity and to determine how long the questionnaire takes to complete, the MEQ was completed through interview with 10 women to ensure the linguistic and conceptual equivalence of the translations. On the basis of the results of the pilot study and research team opinions, necessary changes were made, the MEQ was modified as appropriate and the final questionnaire was obtained. In addition to the determination of item importance, a quantitative face validity test was conducted to measure the impact scores of items using a formula.

Content validity

To calculate the qualitative content validity, 10 experts in the fields of nutrition, psychology and reproductive health who were familiar with the psychometric process were asked to provide their views on the accuracy of item content in written form. They also checked item position, grammar and the use of appropriate words in phrases.

Furthermore, in quantitative content validity collected from a panel of 10 experts, item importance and accuracy using a three-point rating scale was examined using the content validity ratio (CVR) and evaluating the design of the items, including relevance, clarity and simplicity, by content validity index (CVI). CVR can measure between − 1.0 and 1.0. The closer to 1.0 the CVR is, the more essential the object is considered to be. In this study the content evaluation panel was composed of 10 experts and a minimum CVR of .62 is required based on Lawshe table. Only those items with CVR meeting this minimum are retained in the questionnaire [22]. The CVI was calculated according to the Lawshe table on the basis of the ratings by the experts who rated each item [23]. Judgment on each item is made as follows: if I-CVI is less than 70%, the item is not acceptable and will be omitted, the I-CVI between 70 and 79% is questionable and the item needs to revise and the I-CVI higher than 79% is appropriate [24, 25].

Construct validity

Factor analysis Factor analysis is a statistical method that enables the underlying subscales of a questionnaire to be determined [20]. Exploratory factor analysis have recommended in order to establish equivalence. This technique has been widely used specially in validation of the factor structure of the frequently translated questionnaires in a different sample or to perform adaptation of a questionnaire to another language [26]. In the present study the factor structure of the MEQ was determined by exploratory factor analysis (EFA), utilizing principal component analysis with varimax rotation [27]. Varimax is the most popular rotation method and usually produces simpler solution and easier to interpret. Varimax maximizes the sum of the variances of the squared loadings correlation between variables and factors [28]. To determine the best structure, an eigenvalue greater than 1.2 and a factor loading equal to or greater than 0.4 and scree plot were applied [29, 30] (Fig. 1).

Concurrent validity

The focus of the current available instruments used to screen eating disorders is on behaviors and diagnostic criteria but some of them such as Eating disorders belief questionnaire (EDBQ) and Three Factor Eating Questionnaire (TFEQ) are based on the drive from thinness and the fear of fatness [31]. The Eating Disorder Belief Questionnaire (EDBQ) is a relatively brief questionnaire intended for use within the eating disorder population. It is a multi-dimensional and self-report measure with 32 items and four subscales as follows: [1] negative self-beliefs, [3] weight and shape as a means to acceptance by others, [4] weight and shape as a means to self-acceptance and [5] control over eating. The negative self-beliefs subscale appears to measure generic beliefs associated with depression. The other three subscales appear to measure beliefs specific to eating disorders [32]. The EDBQ's ability to distinguish assumptions about weight and shape from assumptions about eating is important, as it has been proposed that the core psychopathology of eating disorders lies in the personal meaning attached to weight and shape [33]. This questionnaire has been validated in the Persian language [34].

Reliability

The reliability of a questionnaire is measured as the variance in a score that reflects the true score, rather than random error; that is, the extent to which measures give

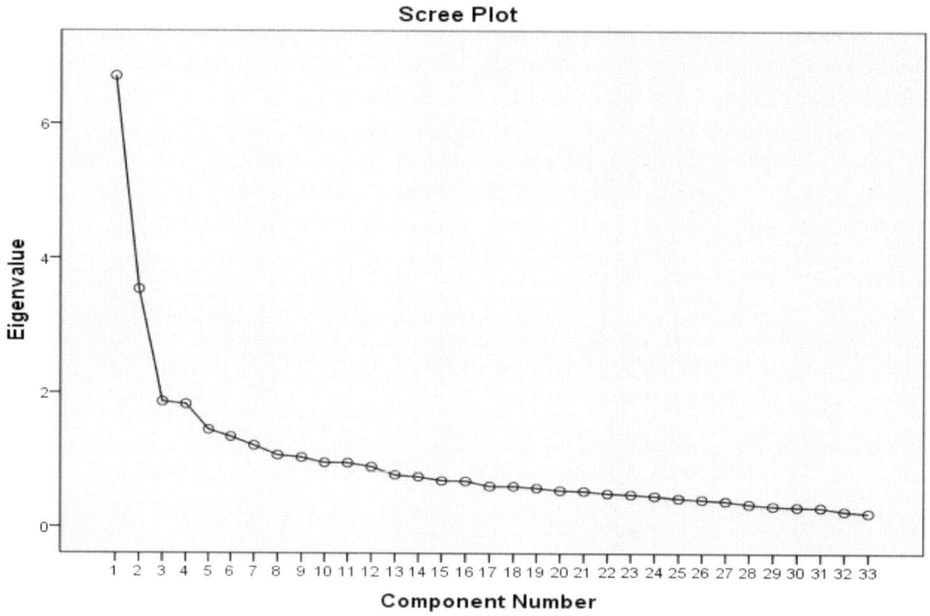

Fig. 1 Scree plot of eigenvalues for principal components analysis of MEQ

consistent or accurate results. Reliability has two common forms: internal consistency or homogeneity and test-retest reliability methods. Test-retest and internal consistency were used to assess the reliability of the MEQ. The internal consistency was assessed using the coefficient Cronbach's alpha, which ranges from 0 to 1, and values equal to or >0.70 for a scale indicate a satisfactory internal consistency [35]. Test-retest reliability measures stability over time, by administering the same test to the same subjects at two points in time. To evaluate the test-retest reliability, a total of 30 participants, randomly selected using convenience sampling, in the same manner as the initial subject recruitment, completed the Persian MEQ again four weeks later. The test-retest reliability of the scale was estimated using the intraclass correlation coefficient (ICC). The following category was selected for the interpretation of agreement levels: 00–0.2 as small, 0.21–0.40 as fair, 0.41–0.60 as moderate, 0.61–0.80 as substantial and 0.81–1 as almost perfect [36]. Statistical analysis was performed using Statistical Package for the Social Sciences 21.0 (SPSS, Inc., Chicago, IL, USA). *P* values < 0.05 were considered to indicate significant results.

Results

Participants

In all, 150 women (5 times the number of items) were included in the study [37, 38]. The mean age of the women was 27.99 (SD ± 10.83) (13–59) years. The correlation between BMI and MEQ total score was not significant, but there was an inverse significant correlation between BMI and awareness dimension of MEQ questionnaire ($p = 0.01$).

Socio-demographic and clinical characteristic of the women are presented in Table 1.

Face validity

Almost all participants indicated that the questionnaire was easy to read and understand, but minor changes

Table 1 Characteristics of the study population, $n = 150$

Age (years), mean ± SD	27.99 ± 10.83
BMI (kg/m2) mean ± SD	24.57 ± 6.05
Education, *n* (%)	
Primary school or less	3 (2)
Secondary school	4 (2.7)
Diploma	31 (20.7)
University	95 (63.3)
BMI (kg/m2)), *n* %)	
< 19	6 (4)
19–24.9	76 (50.7)
25–30	35 (23.3)
>30	24 (16)
OCP users, *n* (%)	
Yes	19 (12.7)
No	123 (82)
Menopause, *n* (%)	
Yes	7 (4.7)
No	135 (90)

were suggested to improve upon clarity. The completion time was less than 5 min. The results of the impact factor test showed that all items had an item impact score ≥ 1.5, identifying them as important in the target group.

Content validity

The CVR in this study for the total scale was 0.89 and for all items was greater than 0.62 according to 10 experts, based on the Lawshe Table [23], indicating the necessity and importance of the presence of relevant items in the scale. In measuring CVI, the scores of 26 items (92.8%) were ≥ 0.79 and for the total scale, 0.93, indicating a satisfactory content validity. On the basis of expert suggestions, some items were modified slightly.

The scores of two items, "if it doesn't cost much more, I get the larger sized food or drink regardless of how hungry I feel" and "I notice when I'm eating from a dish of candy just because it's there" were between 0.70 and 0.78. The CVI was evaluated once more using 10 experts. The I-CVI between 70 and 79% is questionable and the item needs to be revised (24).

Factor analysis

The MEQ was analysed by principal component factor analysis with varimax rotation. The overall Kaiser-Meyer-Olkin measure of sampling adequacy was 0.79. The Bartlett's test for sphericity produced a significant result ($p < 0.001$), indicating that the variables were correlated with one another. Hence, our preliminary analyses confirmed the appropriateness of principal component factor analysis for the data. The MEQ was found to have five factors. The percentage variances explained by rotated factor matrices ranged from to 8–12% per factor, with five factors explaining 53.78% of the overall variance. Percentages refer to the variance explained by each factor as follows: awareness 12.77%, disinhibition 11.75%, emotional 10.58%, external 9.81% and distraction 8.86%. Factor loading after rotation of each item is shown in Table 2.

Concurrent validity

The concurrent validity of the MEQ was calculated using Pearson's product-moment correlations with EDBQ as another relevant measure of acceptance. The results of correlational analysis between MEQ and EDBQ subscales indicated a significant correlation ($p \leq 0.001$) (Table 3). All of the MEQ subscales correlated negatively with all of the EDBQ factors, except for awareness and external cues. The mindfulness eating scale that showed the highest correlations with EDBQ measures was the emotional response factor.

Reliability

Cronbach's alpha ranged from 0.73 to 0.81 and for the scale as a whole was 0.66, indicating a reasonable reliability. The ICC for the MEQ subscales was satisfactory (ICC ranged from 0.73 to 0.91; $P < 0.05$) for each subscale, the data are presented in Table 4. Among the mindfulness eating subscales, correlational analyses showed significant positive relationships, unless the correlation between the external cues and disinhibition and emotional response subscales ($p \leq 0.001$) and the correlation between the distraction and awareness ($p < 0.008$) and external cues subscales ($p < 0.002$). There was no significant correlation between the disinhibition and awareness subscales. The strongest positive relationships were between the factors emotional response and disinhibiting ($p < 0.001$) (Table 3).

Discussion

The purpose of this study was to analyze the psychometric properties of the MEQ in an Iranian sample. This paper reports the translation procedure, structure, validity and reliability of the MEQ in Iran. The transfer of instruments that are conceptually and functionally appropriate into another language is a complex process that requires broad research [39]; therefore, in the psychometric process, we followed the guidelines for cross-cultural adjustment of psychometric measurement and obtained cultural and conceptual equivalence. Thus, like the original version, the Iranian translation of the MEQ was culturally applicable to the Iranian people.

For measures of content validity, we used both quantitative and qualitative methods to assess face and content validity in order to take advantage of this combination in evaluating construct validity [40]. According to estimates of face validity, there were no substantial changes made to the original version and only minor changes in wording or additional descriptions of some items were made to improve upon the participants' understanding. The CVI score for most items was ≥0.80 and for two items with inappropriate scores, the items were measured again after revision and corrected. CVR results revealed the necessity and importance of the presence of all items. In addition,

EFA results supported the factorial structure with the five constructs reported by Framson et al. (2009) [16]. The discrepancy was 'when a restaurant portion is too large, I stop eating when I'm full', which was originally assigned by the developers to the disinhibition factor, but was loaded on the external cues factor with an improved alpha reliability coefficient in the present study. The results reflected that the MEQ had adequate reliability indicators and internal consistency of all subscales was high (alpha from 0.73 to 0.81), similar to the values of alpha reported by Framson et al. (2009) (range,

Table 2 Factor loadings from the MEQ principal component analysis

[a]Item	Factor				
	1	2	3	4	5
A[b]21. Before I eat I take a moment to appreciate	**.829**	.110	.103	.054	.017
A 20. I notice when foods and drinks are too sweet	**.783**	.084	.180	.065	.040
A 22. I taste every bite of food that I eat.	**.762**	.085	.047	.088	.203
A 16. I appreciate the way my food looks on my plate.	**.733**	.266	.018	.076	.009
A 12. When eating a pleasant meal, I notice if …	**.596**	.315	.117	.020	.246
A 26. I notice when the food I eat affects my emotional…	**.582**	.015	.335	.025	.138
A 10. I notice when there are subtle flavors	**.467**	.136	.048	.087	.104
DI 11. If there are leftovers that I like, I take	.101	**.694**	.116	.238	.255
DI 2. When I eat at "all you can eat" buffets	.048	**.654**	.335	.092	.083
DI 15. I stop eating when I'm full even	.121	**.653**	.078	.135	.279
DI 7. When I'm eating one of my favorite .	.052	**.647**	.161	.136	.016
DI 9. If it doesn't cost much more, I get…	.056	**.542**	.123	.216	.301
DI 18. If there's good food at a party, I'll continue…	.038	**.506**	.447	.265	.161
DI 25. When I'm at a restaurant, I can tell…	.314	**.502**	.063	.042	.041
ER 27. I have trouble not eating ice cream…	.098	.016	**.777**	.071	.184
ER 13. I snack without noticing that I am eating.	.044	.058	**.640**	.308	.370
ER17. When I'm feeling stressed at work,	.107	.291	**.634**	.309	.144
ER 19. When I'm sad, I eat to feel better.	.135	.234	**.617**	.306	.185
EC 24. I notice when I'm eating from a dish	.036	.319	**.453**	.246	.189
EC 5. When a restaurant portion is too large,	.048	.011	**.406**	.144	.291
EC 8. I notice when just going into a movie.	.058	.150	.033	**.746**	.041
EC14. When I eat a big meal, I notice…	.069	.074	.203	**.717**	.194
EC 4. I recognize when food advertisements make…	.004	.201	.118	**.684**	.084
EC 23. I recognize when I'm eating and not hungry.	.211	.102	.159	**.607**	.159
EC 3. At a party where there is a lot of good food,	.053	.258	.223	**.461**	**.461**
DT 6. My thoughts tend to wander while I am eating	.039	.229	.120	.066	**.804**
DT 28. I think about things I need to do while I am eating.	.101	.140	.029	.049	**.741**
DT 1. I eat so quickly that I don't taste what I'm eating.	.014	.242	.316	.018	**.664**

[a]Items: *A* Awareness, *DI* Disinhibition, *ER* Emotional Response, *EC* External Cues, *DT* Distraction
[b]Question numbers

Table 3 Correlations between mindfulness eating and eating disorder belief factors

	Awareness	disinhibition	emotional response	external cues	distraction
EDBQ					
Negative self-beliefs	.024	−.140	−.211[b]	.141	−.161
Weight acceptance by others	.015	−.310[a]	−.319[a]	.205[b]	−.246[b]
Weight to self-acceptance	.138	−.377[a]	−.344[a]	.248[b]	−.229[b]
Control over eating	.032	−.298[a]	−.348[a]	.182	−.290[a]
Awareness		.030	−.301[a]	−.178[b]	.216[a]
Disinhibition			.518[a]	−.536[a]	.399[a]
Emotional response				−.523[a]	.513[a]
External cues					−.250[a]

[a]Correlation is significant at the 0.01 level (2-tailed)
[b]Correlation is significant at the 0.05 level (2-tailed)

0.64–0.83) [16]. The reliability of the MEQ summary scale was 0.66, similar to that reported by Framson (0.64). In general, a satisfactory level of internal consistency is considered a Cronbach's $\alpha \geq 0.7$ [41]. The test-retest reliability of the MEQ with a four-week interval was found to be high. Using the intraclass correlation coefficients test, all subscales achieved a high correlation (≥ 0.7), indicating that in a stable health state over time, the MEQ produces constant results from participants. In studies by Framson et al. (2009) and Gebolla et al. (2012), the test-retest reliability was not measured [16, 42]. In correlations with other scales, the MEQ correlated negatively with all of the EDBQ factors, except awareness and external cues. As mentioned by Framson et al., the awareness domain was taken from

Table 4 Descriptive statistics, Cronbach's alpha and ICC of the MEQ subscales

Subscales	Cronbach's alpha			
	Alpha of subscales in English version	Alpha of subscales with one item Exchanged[a]	Mean ± SD	ICC (95% confidence interval)
Awareness	(0.74)7 items	0.81	7 3.10 ± 0.32	0.73*
Disinhibition	(0.83)8 items	0.751 (7 items)	2.64 ± 0.54	0.77*
Emotional response	(0.71)4 items	0.818	3.27 ± 0.32	0.82*
External cues	(0.70)6 items	0.732 (7 items)	3.57 ± 0.56	0.91*
Distraction	(0.64)3 items	0.769	2.39 ± 0.45	0.88*

[a]When a restaurant portion is too large, I stop eating when I'm full
*P-value < 0.05

the affective sensitivity domain, which involves awareness of internal states, and external cues subscale. In the original study, there was a combination of some items loaded in this domain [16].

Limitations of the study

Since this study was conducted on women who attending gyms and participated in a physical activity program, this limits the generalizability of the results to all women and also to men. Further since athletic women have more mindful eating and these women mostly have higher education, we could not use these results for women with lower education that may have more eating and weight disorders. In the present study we benefited from EDBQ to test the concurrent validity of MEQ but it is recommended that further research conduct to include other measures of mindfulness such as Mindful Attention Awareness Scale (MAAS) to provide stronger support for concurrent validity [43].

Conclusions

Psychometric properties of the Iranian version of the MEQ with five-factor structure were approved through qualitative and quantitative face and content validity, reliability and acceptability for the target group. Using the Persian version of MEQ should be done with caution, because it was only tested among women with physical activity. So first we suggest subsequent studies in both genders of Iranian population and also in women without physical activity. Using this questionnaire will be useful in for improvements of eating behaviors and stress reduction as well as nutrition research and it can also be used in mindfulness-based interventions for dietary behavioral disorders and obesity.

Abbreviations

CVI: Content validity index; CVR: Content validity ratio; EDBQ: Eating disorder belief questionnaire; EFA: Exploratory factor analysis; ICC: Intraclass correlation coefficient; MEQ: Mindful eating questionnaire

Acknowledgments

This study was one part of the research project, and financial support was provided by the Deputy vice-chancellor for research affairs of Ahvaz Jundishapur University of Medical Sciences. We would like to thank all the participants.

Funding

The authors received no financial support for the research, authorship and publication of this article.

Authors' contributions

ZA was involved in designing of the study, collection and analysis of data and preparation of the Manuscript. PA and NJ were involved in designing and monitoring of the study and MM contributed to collection of data and helped to preparation of the manuscript. All authors read and approved the final manuscript for publication.

Competing interests

The authors declares that they have no competing interest.

Author details

[1]Midwifery Department, Reproductive Health Promotion Research Center, Ahvaz Jundishapur University of Medical Sciences, Ahvaz, Iran. [2]Reproductive Health Promotion Research Center, Ahvaz Jundishapur University of Medical Sciences, Ahvaz, Iran. [3]student of nutrition, Faculty of paramedicine, Ahvaz Jundishapur University of Medical sciences, Ahvaz, Iran. [4]Menopause, Andropause Research Center, Ahvaz Jundishapur University of Medical Sciences, Ahvaz, Iran.

References

1. World Health Organization, Fact Sheet on Obesity and Overweight. Available at: http://www.who.int/news-room/fact-sheets/detail/obesity-and-overweight. Accessed Feb 2018.
2. Rahmani A, Sayehmiri K, Asadollahi K, Sarokhani D, Islami F, Sarokhani M. Investigation of the prevalence of obesity in Iran: a systematic review and meta-analysis study. Acta Med Iran. 2015;53(10):596–607.

3. Hays NP, Bathalon GP, McCrory MA, Roubenoff R, Lipman R, Roberts SB. Eating behavior correlates of adult weight gain and obesity in healthy women aged 55–65 y. Am J Clin Nutr. 2002;75(3):476–83.
4. Gormally J, Black S, Daston S, Rardin D. The assessment of binge eating severity among obese persons. Addict Behav. 1982;7(1):47–55.
5. Colles SL, Dixon JB, O'brien PE. Loss of control is central to psychological disturbance associated with binge eating disorder. Obesity. 2008;16(3):608–14.
6. Grossman P, Niemann L, Schmidt S, Walach H. Mindfulness-based stress reduction and health benefits: a meta-analysis. J Psychosom Res. 2004;57(1):35–43.
7. Smith BW, Shelley BM, Leahigh L, Vanleit B. A preliminary study of the effects of a modified mindfulness intervention on binge eating. Complement Health Pract Rev. 2006;11(3):133–43.
8. Baer RA, Smith GT, Hopkins J, Krietemeyer J, Toney L. Using self-report assessment methods to explore facets of mindfulness. Assessment. 2006;13(1):27–45.
9. Lau MA, Bishop SR, Segal ZV, Buis T, Anderson ND, Carlson L, Shapiro S, Carmody J, Abbey S, Devins G. The Toronto mindfulness scale: development and validation. J Clin Psychol. 2006;62(12):1445–67.
10. MacKillop J, Anderson EJ. Further psychometric validation of the mindful attention awareness scale (MAAS). J Psychopathol Behav Assess. 2007;29(4):289–93.
11. Carlson LE, Brown KW. Validation of the mindful attention awareness scale in a cancer population. J Psychosom Res. 2005;58(1):29–33.
12. Organization. WHO: obesity and overweight. Accessed January 2015.
13. Framson C, Kristal AR, Schenk JM, Littman AJ, Zeliadt S, Benitez D. Development and validation of the mindful eating questionnaire. J Am Diet Assoc. 2009;109(8):1439–44.
14. Pintado-Cucarella S, Rodríguez-Salgado P. Mindful eating and its relationship with body mass index, binge eating, anxiety and negative affect. J Behav, Health Soc Issues. 2016;8(2):19–24.
15. Taylor MB, Daiss S, Krietsch K. Associations among self-compassion, mindful eating, eating disorder symptomatology, and body mass index in college students. Translational Issues in Psychological Science. 2015;1(3):229–38.
16. Clementi C, Casu G, Gremigni P. An Abbreviated Version of the Mindful Eating Questionnaire. J Nutri Educ Behav. 2017;49(4):352–356.e1.
17. Harden CJ, Corfe BM, Richardson JC, Dettmar PW, Paxman JR. Body mass index and age affect three-factor eating questionnaire scores in male subjects. Nutr Res. 2009;29:379–82.
18. American Psychiatric Association. Binge Eating Disorder, DSM-5 Diagnostic Criteria. In: Diagnostic and statistical manual of mental disorders. 5th ed. (DSM-5) Washington DC: APA; 2013.
19. Jenkinson C, McGee HM: Health status measurement: a brief but critical introduction: Radcliffe publishing; 1998.
20. Kline P: A psychometrics primer: free Assn books; 2000.
21. Lacasse Y, Godbout C, Sériès F. Health-related quality of life in obstructive sleep apnoea. Eur Respir J. 2002;19(3):499–503. https://doi.org/10.1183/09031936. 02.00216902.
22. Ayre C, Scally AJ. Critical values for Lawshe's content validity ratio: revisiting the original methods of calculation. Meas Eval Couns Dev. 2014;47(1):79–86.
23. Lawshe CH. A quantitative approach to content validity1. Pers Psychol. 1975;28(4):563–75.
24. Lynn MR. Determination and quantification of content validity. Nurs Res. 1986;35(6):382–5.
25. Polit DF, Beck CT: Nursing research: principles and methods: Lippincott Williams & Wilkins; 2004.
26. Geisinger KF, McCormick C. Testing and Assessment in Cross-Cultural Psychology. In: Graham JR, Naglieri JA, editors. Handbook of assessment psychology, vol. 10. New York: Wiley; 2003. p. 109–10.
27. Bentler PM, Bonett DG. Significance tests and goodness of fit in the analysis of covariance structures. Psychol Bull. 1980;88(3):588.
28. Hayton JC, Allen DG, Scarpello V. Factor retention decisions in exploratory factor analysis: a tutorial on parallel analysis. Organ Res Methods. 2004;7:191–205.
29. Nunnally J. Psychometric theory. New York: McGraw-Hill; 1978.
30. Sharma S. Applied multivariate techniques. USA: John Wiley & son; 1996.
31. Burton AL, Hay P, Kleitman S, Smith E, Raman J, Swinbourne J, Touyz SW, Abbott MJ. Confirmatory factor analysis and examination of the psychometric properties of the eating beliefs questionnaire. BMC Psychiatry. 2017;17(1):237. https://doi.org/10.1186/s12888-017-1394-z.
32. Cooper M, Cohen-Tovée E, Todd G, Wells A, Tovée M. The eating disorder belief questionnaire: preliminary development. Behav Res Ther. 1997;35(4):381–8.
33. Vitousek KB, Hollon SD. The investigation of schematic content and processing in eating disorders. Cogn Ther Res. 1990;14(2):191–214.
34. Shayeghian Z, Vafae M. The evaluation of psychometric properties of eating disorder beliefs questionnaire (EDBQ). Advan Cogn Sci. 2009;11(2):38–46.
35. Cronbach LJ. Coefficient alpha and the internal structure of tests. Psychometrika. 1951;16(3):297–334.
36. Landis JR, Koch GG. The measurement of observer agreement for categorical data. Biometrics. 1977;159:–174.
37. Munro BH. Statistical methods for health care research. Lippincott Williams & Wilkins. 2005;1.
38. Watson R, Stimpson A, Topping A, Porock D. Clinical competence assessment in nursing: a systematic review of the literature. J Adv Nurs. 2002;39(5):421–31.
39. Jones PS, Lee JW, Phillips LR, Zhang XE, Jaceldo KB. An adaptation of Brislin's translation model for cross-cultural research. Nurs Res. 2001;50(5):300–4.
40. Hyrkäs K, Appelqvist-Schmidlechner K, Oksa L. Validating an instrument for clinical supervision using an expert panel. Int J Nurs Stud. 2003;40(6):619–25.
41. DeVon HA, Block ME, Moyle-Wright P, Ernst DM, Hayden SJ, Lazzara DJ, Savoy SM, Kostas-Polston E. A psychometric toolbox for testing validity and reliability. J Nurs Scholarsh. 2007;39(2):155–64.
42. Cebolla A, Garcia-Palacios A, Soler J, Guillen V, Baños R, Botella C. Psychometric properties of the Spanish validation of the five facets of mindfulness questionnaire (FFMQ). Europ J Psychiatry. 2012;26(2):118–26.
43. Brown KW, Ryan RM. The benefits of being present: mindfulness and its role in psychological well-being. J Pers Soc Psychol. 2003;84:822–48.

Inhibition of return for body images in individuals with shape/weight based self-worth

Alexandra Cobb[1*], Elizabeth Rieger[2] and Jason Bell[3]

Abstract

Background: Attentional biases for body shape and weight information have been found in people with eating disorders, indicating disorder-specific changes in the way this information is processed. To date, the literature has focused on the initial capture of attention, with little research on the maintenance of attention to shape/weight-related information. The current study aims to investigate the occurrence of attentional maintenance through the use of an Inhibition of Return task to shape and weight stimuli in those with and without an eating disorder.

Method: Three groups of female participants between the ages of 16–30 years undertook an Inhibition of Return task with target images of female bodies and control images of animals. The groups were an eating disorder group ($n = 20$), a High shape/weight based self-worth group ($n = 23$), and a Low shape/weight based self-worth group ($n = 26$).

Results: The results indicated differential patterns of Inhibition of Return between the High and Low shape/weight based self-worth groups. The High group displayed increased inhibition of return for the shape/weight stimuli relative to control stimuli, while the Low group displayed reduced inhibition of return for the shape/weight stimuli compared to control stimuli. The ED group displayed a similar pattern of results to the High group, but this did not reach significance.

Conclusion: The current findings indicate that young women without an eating disorder who base their self-worth on shape/weight display a pattern of avoidance of shape/weight stimuli that is in direct contrast to those at low risk of developing eating disorders. The possible implications of these specific patterns of inhibition of return across those at varying levels of risk for an eating disorder are discussed along with their implications for intervention approaches.

Keywords: Eating disorder, Attention, Inhibition of return, IOR, Shape/weight concerns

Plain English summary

Research has indicated differences in the way body shape and weight information captures the attention of those with an eating disorder versus those without an eating disorder. Despite this, it is unclear whether attentional differences persist after this initial capture. The current research aims to answer this question by comparing the later stages of attention in a control group, a group at high risk of an eating disorder and a clinical eating disorder group. All three groups performed an attentional inhibition of return task. Results indicate that those at risk of an eating disorder avoid maintaining their attention on body shape and weight information.

* Correspondence: Alexandra.Cobb@anu.edu.au
[1]Research School of Psychology, Australian National University, Canberra, ACT 2601, Australia
Full list of author information is available at the end of the article

Background

Eating disorders are complex mental and physical illnesses that centre on disturbances in how body shape and weight are experienced and evaluated [1]. Several models posit that these disorders entail maladaptive knowledge structures that are involved in the allocation of attention [2, 3]. Vitousek and Hollon's cognitive model [4] proposes that those with eating disorders develop extensive and inaccurate schemas regarding their body shape and weight. These faulty schemas lead to automatic thoughts and systematic errors in thinking, such as selective attention and confirmation biases towards weight/shape information [5]. Aspen et al. [5]

extended this approach and posited that attentional biases are a strong contributor to the development and maintenance of eating disorders.

Supporting this conceptualisation, a large body of research has indicated that those with eating disorders exhibit attentional biases regarding disorder-salient information. Attentional biases can be conceptualised to include three components of attention: facilitated attentional capture, difficulty in disengagement, and attentional avoidance [6]. In the context of clinical disorders, facilitated attention refers to the finding that disorder salient information is often detected faster than non-salient information. Difficulty in disengagement refers to disorder salient information being harder to disengage from relative to non-salient information. Attentional avoidance refers to attention being directed away from disorder salient information. Each of these three components of attentional biases can be investigated using various attention tasks.

A large body of research has investigated the occurrence of facilitated attention and disengagement in eating disorders. Meta-analyses on the cognitive paradigms of the Stroop task and dot probe paradigm have consistently shown attentional biases regarding eating disorder-salient stimuli, such as shape/weight related words, in women diagnosed with an eating disorder [5, 7, 8]. While the Stroop task has been widely used to investigate attentional biases in eating disorders, it has a number of limitations that restrict its utility, including an inability to differentiate between the allocation of attention towards or away from target stimuli [9].

Accordingly, researchers have employed alternative paradigms such as a modified dot-probe procedure and eye tracking. Aspen et al. [5] conducted a meta-analysis on the dot-probe paradigm and concluded that those with eating disorders display an attentional bias towards stimuli connoting a larger physique, and away from stimuli connoting a thin physique. However, some research demonstrates the reverse, with vulnerable individuals (defined as those with a high level of shape/weight dissatisfaction or those endorsing eating disorder symptomatology) displaying an attentional bias towards thin stimuli and away from non-thin stimuli [10–14]. Eye tracking studies have also shown inconsistent findings, with some research indicating an attentional bias towards negatively perceived body parts [13, 15, 16] and others indicating an avoidance response [17]. While the conditions specifying the occurrence of facilitation versus avoidance of shape and weight information remain to be specified, their occurrence in individuals with eating disorder symptoms has been established.

One limitation of this research is its predominant focus on the initial stages of attention [18]. However, attention is enduring, and difficulty in disengaging attention or ongoing attentional avoidance may therefore have a role in the continuation of many disorders. For eating disorders, understanding difficulties in attentional disengagement is important, given the high level of preoccupation with shape and weight concerns [19, 20].

One way to investigate attentional disengagement is through the Inhibition of Return (IOR) phenomenon, measured using an attentional cuing task [21]. IOR has traditionally been defined as a mechanism of the visual system that encourages attention towards novel locations by inhibiting attention from returning to previously attended locations [22]. More recent work (particularly within clinical fields of research) has compared the magnitude of IOR to different types of stimuli in order to examine differences in attentional disengagement. The critical comparisons then become: 1) does IOR occur for that stimulus type, and 2) does IOR magnitude differ by stimulus type. The disengagement hypothesis of attention suggests that the process of attending includes initial capture, followed by attentional disengagement [6, 23]. A reduced IOR to one type of image but not another indicates a reduced ability to disengage attention from certain information (e.g., shape/weight stimuli). In contrast, an increased IOR to a specific image type indicates increased ability to disengage from that stimulus or a potential avoidance response.

Attentional cueing tasks have been used to research the occurrence of attentional disengagement in depressed and anxious populations [23, 24]. Results of these studies not only show attentional facilitation biases, but also increased difficulty in attentional disengagement from threatening and negative stimuli. Thus, it may be the combination of attentional capture and attentional disengagement difficulties that influences the occurrence and maintenance of these disorders.

An important consideration in the investigation of attentional disengagement is any change in the time course of disengagement, which may vary across participant groups [23]. As depicted in Fig. 1, one way to investigate disengagement is through the use of differing times between the cue (e.g. a shape/weight image) and the target (e.g., a valid or invalid located cross) onset times, known as the stimulus onset asynchrony (SOA). As outlined by Klein [22], at short SOA times, facilitation occurs, indicated by faster response times to valid target than an invalid target. However, as the SOA times increase, facilitation transitions into an inhibition effect as indicated by faster response times to invalid target than a valid target. The inhibition mechanism typically occurs from 300 ms to 1500 ms [22].

To date, only one study has investigated attentional disengagement in the context of body dissatisfaction [11]. Using an undergraduate female Chinese sample, this study found that those who experienced higher

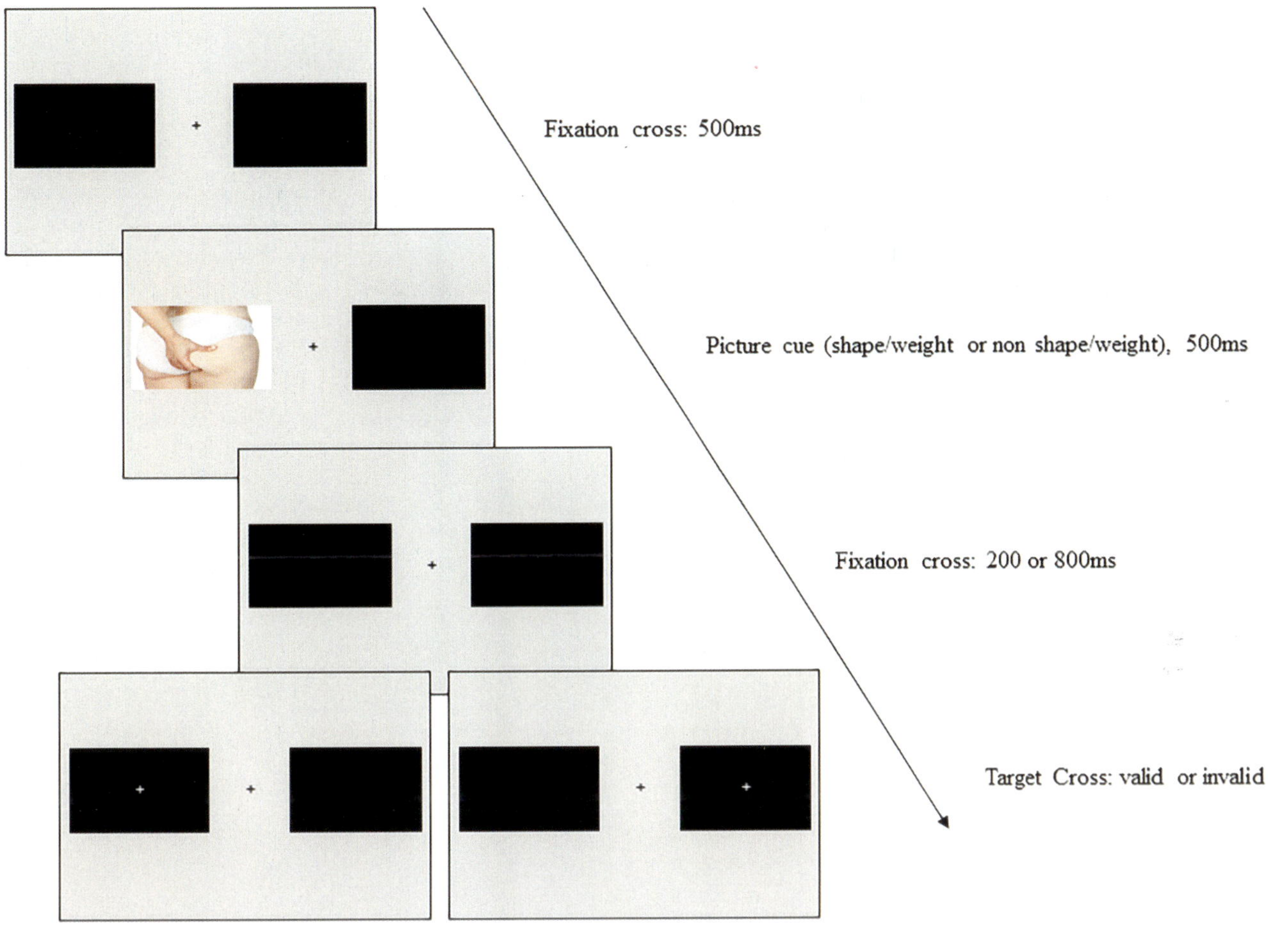

Fig. 1 IOR trial sequence

levels of body weight dissatisfaction had greater difficulty disengaging their attention from shape and weight images (i.e., a smaller IOR effect relative to the control group). Another study investigated attentional maintenance in a sample of people in the obese and normal-weight ranges and found that individuals with obesity had greater difficulty disengaging their attention from food stimuli (i.e., a smaller IOR effect relative to the control group) [25]. These studies indicate the potential for food and shape information to not only capture attention, but to also lead to greater difficulty in attentional disengagement. Further, an eye-tracking study within a non-clinical population found that those with higher body dissatisfaction had difficulty disengaging their attention from their most dissatisfying body regions when compared with controls [26]. However, while eye-tracking studies provide information as to where eye gaze is directed, they do not provide a clear index regarding which stimuli are being processed (as, for example, IOR tasks provide). Despite its strengths, no research on attentional disengagement using an IOR paradigm has been conducted within an eating disorder population.

In addition to determining whether individuals with eating disorders display distorted attentional disengagement, it is also of interest to determine whether those processes extend to individuals at risk of eating disorders, such as those with high levels of shape and/or weight-based self-worth. Cognitive models postulate that a central feature of the cognitive dysfunction characterising eating disorders is the unification of shape and weight concerns with a person's self-evaluation [19, 27, 28]. This shape/weight-based self-worth is thought to drive eating disorder behaviours to improve self-worth and is required for a *DSM-5* eating disorder diagnosis [1]. While no research has investigated the relationship between shape/weight-based self-worth and attentional disengagement, it is possible that shape/weight stimuli would have particular salience in those for whom shape/weight-related information has implications for self-worth, and therefore may result in altered attentional disengagement.

Using an attentional cueing task, the current study aims to investigate the occurrence and time course of attentional disengagement to shape/weight stimuli in the eating disorder context (including those with eating disorders and those at risk of an eating disorder due to elevated levels of shape/weight-based self-worth) at two differing SOA times. Given empirical and theoretical work suggesting that those with eating disorder symptoms experience biases in the initial stages of attention, and evidence of difficulties with attentional disengagement in other clinical populations, it is expected that those with an eating disorder and those with high shape/weight-based self-worth will experience greater difficulty disengaging their attention from shape/weight stimuli, relative to individuals with low shape/weight based self-worth, at the longer SOA time (i.e., when inhibited processing, or disengagement of attention, is typically expected to occur).

Methods

Participants

Fifty-eight female undergraduate university students aged between 16 and 30 years were recruited via the Australian National University's online recruiting system. Twenty-one females between the ages of 16–30 years who were currently seeking treatment from a public outpatient eating disorders program were recruited via flyers. All participants provided informed consent prior to participating in the study. Those aged between 16 and 18 years also provided parental consent. Ethical approval was granted by the ACT Health Human Research Ethics Committee (ETH.5.14.110) and the Australian National University Human Research Ethics Committee (2014/448).

The current study included three groups of participants: an eating disorder (ED) group, a high shape/weight concern (High) group, and a low shape/weight concern (Low) group. All participants were required to be female, given that images of females were used in the attentional task. All participants were also required to have a BMI below 25 kg/m^2, as research has indicated that the experience of being overweight or obese can have significant effects on attentional biases [29], including attentional maintenance [25]. Ten participants were excluded on this basis. Participants' BMIs ranged from (16.38–25.00).

To be included in the ED group, participants were required to have a current *DSM-5* [1] eating disorder as diagnosed by a clinician experienced in eating disorders. In line with a transdiagnostic model [19], no distinction was made between those with differing eating disorder diagnoses. The ED group was comprised of seven participants with a diagnosis of anorexia nervosa, six with a diagnosis of bulimia nervosa, and seven with a diagnosis of other specified feeding or eating disorder (OSFED).

Participants were excluded from the two non-eating disorder groups if they had symptoms suggestive of an eating disorder, as indicated by a BMI below 17.0 and/or endorsement of the eating disorder behaviours (items 13–18) assessed by the Eating Disorders Examination Questionnaire (EDE-Q) [30] at a level that may indicate a *DSM-5* eating disorder diagnosis. One participant was excluded on this basis. To be included in the High group, participants were required to score 4 or above on item 22 ('Has your weight influenced how you think about [judge] yourself as a person?') or item 23 ('Has your shape influenced how you think about [judge] yourself as a person?') of the EDE-Q, indicating moderate or greater than moderate investment in their shape/weight as a basis for self-worth. Those who scored three or below on items 22 and 23 were included in the Low group, indicating below moderate investment in their shape/weight as a basis for self-worth.

The final sample consisted of 20 participants in the ED group, 23 participants in the High group, and 26 participants in the Low group. The sample primarily consisted of Caucasian females born in Australia who had obtained senior secondary education. Table 1 depicts the ethnic and educational characteristics of the sample.

Table 1 Country of origin and educational attainment across groups

	Low	High	ED
Country of Origin	Percentage		
Australia	30.8	33.3	80.0
New Zealand	3.8	0	0
China	15.4	37.5	0
Malaysia	15.4	4.2	5.0
Singapore	3.8	0	0
Other Asian Country	26.9	16.7	5.0
Other English Speaking Country	0	8.3	5.0
Other non-English Speaking Country	3.8	0	5.0
Educational Attainment	Percentage		
Pre-Primary	0	0	0
Primary	0	0	0
Junior Secondary	0	0	25
Senior Secondary	65.4	75.0	50
Certificate Level	7.7	0	0
Advanced Diploma and Diploma Level	0	4.2	0
Bachelor Degree	19.2	20.8	10
Graduate Diploma/Graduate Certificate	3.8	0	0
Postgraduate Degree	3.8	0	5

Junior Secondary = Year 10 or equivalent, Senior Secondary = Year 12, senior secondary certificate or equivalent. Low = Low shape/weight based self-worth group, High = High shape/weight based self-worth group, ED = Eating Disorder group

Materials and measures

IOR task

The attentional cueing IOR task was administered on a laptop computer using Matlab R2012b software. It contained 22 shape/weight images and 22 animal images, which were sourced from photographic libraries or non-copyrighted images on the internet. A pilot study (unpublished) was conducted using a large pool of target (shape/weight) and control (animal) images. The target image set was designed to contain images of female body parts within the normal to overweight BMI range (consistent with the normative BMI range for Australian women) [31] with a focus on body parts associated with shape/weight concerns (i.e., stomach, thighs, and buttocks). Consistent with the method employed by the International Affective Picture System [32], the initial pool of shape and animal images was rated for valence (i.e. "how happy or unhappy the images make you feel") and arousal (i.e. "how exciting or calm the images make you feel") on 9-point Likert Self-Assessment Manikins scale, by a separate sample of female undergraduate university students ($n = 42$). Twenty two shape/weight and 22 animal images were selected from this pool based on matched ratings on valence and arousal to ensure that any differences in attention were not the result of differences in the valence or arousal of the image sets. Pilot data indicated no significant difference in the ratings of valence, $t(22) = -1.11$, $p = .276$, between the shape/weight image set ($M = 4.01$, $SD = .70$) and animal image set ($M = 4.31$, $SD = 1.06$), or arousal, $t(22) = -1.17$, $p = .25$, between the shape/weight image set ($M = 4.38$, $SD = 0.31$) and animal image set ($M = 4.65$, $SD = 1.04$).

The IOR task was a spatial cueing task based on previous designs [21, 22]. Figure 1 depicts the sequence of a single trial, which consisted of a 500 ms presentation of a central grey fixation cross, which remained on the screen throughout the trial. Following this, a picture cue, either a shape/weight image or an animal image, was presented for 500 ms in a lateral position, either 3 degrees left or 3 degrees right of the fixation cross. This was followed by a change in brightness of the central fixation cross to cue participants' attention back to the centre of the screen. Following this, a white target cross appeared in either the same location as the picture cue (valid trial) or in the opposite location (invalid trial). The time between cue picture onset and target cross appearance, the SOA time, was either 700 ms or 1300 ms [22]. Participants were instructed to respond using the left and right arrow keys on the laptop keyboard to indicate, as quickly and accurately as possible, on which side of the screen the target appeared. The next trial began after the participants' response, or after 2000 ms.

To ensure the participants' understanding, six practice trials were undertaken at the beginning of the task. Following this, participants undertook two blocks of 80 repetitions, comprising 10 repetitions of each of the eight conditions: 2 x picture type, 2 x picture location, and 2 x SOA. Twenty trials containing no target were randomly interspersed amongst the trials to ensure participant engagement and to prevent response rhythms. In total, participants completed 186 trials.

Eating disorder examination questionnaire 6.0 (EDE-Q) [33]

In order to assess the severity and frequency of eating disorder psychopathology, aid in the allocation to either the High and Low groups, screen for possible eating disorder diagnoses within the control groups, and ensure the validity of the eating disorder diagnoses in the clinical group, the EDE-Q was administered to all participants. The EDE-Q is a 28-item self-report version of the semi-structured interview based Eating Disorder Examination [34]. The EDE-Q contains four subscales of specific eating disorder psychopathology including Dietary Restraint (e.g., "Have you been deliberately trying to limit the amount of food you eat to.influence your shape or weight?"), Eating Concern (e.g., "Have you been afraid of losing control over eating?"), Weight Concern (e.g., "Have you had a strong desire to lose weight?"), and Shape Concern (e.g., "Have you felt fat?"), as well as a global eating disorder score.

The EDE-Q is widely used as it has sound psychometric properties, with research indicating high levels of convergent validity with the EDE interview [35], accuracy in differentiating those with and without eating disorders [36], and test-retest reliability [37, 38] and good internal consistency [36, 39]. In the current study, an acceptable level of internal consistency for the global EDE-Q scale was evidenced by the Cronbach's alphas for the ED group ($\alpha = .90$), the High group ($\alpha = .82$), and the Low group ($\alpha = .86$). The four subscales also indicated acceptable levels of internal consistency (given the small number of items in each scale), with a Cronbach's alpha of .873 for the Restraint subscale, .859 for the Eating Concern subscale, .917 for the Shape Concern subscale, and .890 for the Weight Concern subscale.

Body mass index

Participants' weight was recorded to the closest 0.1 kg and height measured to the closest centimetre for the calculation of BMI. The World Health Organization BMI classifications were used to classify groups as overweight (25 to 29.99) or obese (30 or greater) for screening purposes.

Procedure

Testing sessions lasted approximately 45 min and were conducted in a quiet, private, and well-lit room. Upon arrival, participants completed a written consent form.

They then undertook the IOR task and another IOR cognitive task for a separate study, in random order. Between these tasks, participants completed a distraction task aimed at reducing the risk of picture exposure in one task affecting the completion of the other task. The distraction task comprised watching 186 s of music film clips, obtained from the Database for Emotion Analysis [40]. The clips had been previously rated as neutral for valence and arousal, so were unlikely to induce any mood effects; further, they did not contain any eating disorder salient information (i.e., food or bodies) [40]. Following the IOR task, participants were administered the EDE-Q. At the completion of the session, participants in the Low and High groups had their height and weight measured using calibrated scales and a wall mounted tape measure (this information was obtained from the outpatient treatment facility for the ED group) and remuneration was provided.

Statistical analysis

All data were analysed using IBM SPSS version 23. Prior to conducting the main analyses, data underwent a screening and cleaning process aimed at assessing the occurrence of missing data, outliers, and violations of statistical assumptions. The screening and cleaning process for the IOR data was conducted at both the individual and group levels. At the individual level, one case of missing data was identified and excluded listwise. Further, reaction times less than 200 ms or greater than 2.5 standard deviations above the mean were removed, as these scores were likely to indicate disengagement from the task, which is typical in tasks of this nature [11, 25, 41]. Accuracy data was screened, with all participants obtaining accuracy scores above 75%, indicating a high level of task compliance and engagement. IOR index scores were then calculated by subtracting the mean reaction time of the invalid trials from the mean reaction time of the valid trials. Positive IOR index scores indicated IOR, or a reluctance to return attention to a previously attended location. In contrast, negative IOR index scores indicated a facilitation effect or the absence of an IOR effect. A mixed between-within analysis of variance (ANOVA) was undertaken to analyse the IOR data. The dependant variable was the IOR indices, the between-subjects factor was group (Low, High, ED) and the within-subjects factors were picture type (shape/weight, animal) and SOA (1300 ms, 1700 ms). A two-tailed p-level of < 0.05 was used for determining statistical significance.

Results

Descriptive characteristics

To assess age and education across groups, a one-way between groups ANOVA was conducted. This indicated no significant difference in age, $F(2, 67) = 2.31$, $p = .107$, or years of education, $F(2, 67) = .283$, $p = .755$, between the groups. As expected, there were significant differences in eating disorder symptomatology between the three groups. Results indicated significant differences in the EDE-Q Dietary Restraint, ($F(2, 47.80) = 17.62$, $p < .001$, Eating Concern, $F(2, 49.75) = 64.03$, $p < .001$ (using the Brown-Forsyth adjustment), Shape Concern, $F(2, 67) = 55.82$, $p < .001$, Weight Concern, $F(2, 67) = 49.80$, $p < .001$ sub scales and Global scale, $F(2, 67) = 65.01$, $p < .001$. Post hoc comparisons using the Tukey HSD test indicated that all comparisons between the means of the ED, High, and Low groups were significantly different. The ED group displayed the highest global and subscale scores, followed by the High group endorsing a moderate level of ED pathology, and the low group endorsing the lowest global and subscale scores. The EDE-Q data thus supported the conceptualisation of the groups. Table 2 presents the mean age, BMI, and EDE-Q scale scores for each of the groups.

Main analyses

Table 3 displays the mean reaction time data used to calculate the IOR index. A three-way, 2 (SOA: 700 ms and 1300 ms) × 2 (Image: Shape/Weight and Animal) × 3 (Group: ED, High, and Low), mixed design ANOVA revealed no significant main effect for image, Wilks' Lambda = .974, $F(1, 66) = 1.75$, $p = .191$, $\eta_p^2 = .026$, SOA, Wilks' Lambda = 1.00, $F(1, 66) = .003$, $p = .955$, $\eta_p^2 < .001$, or group, $F(2, 66) = .439$, $p = .646$, $\eta_p^2 = .013$. Further, there were no significant two-way interactions for image x group, Wilks' Lambda = .985, $F(2, 66) = .508$, $p = .604$, $\eta_p^2 = .015$, SOA x group, Wilks' Lambda = .985, $F(2, 66) = .499$, $p = .610$, $\eta_p^2 = .015$, or image x SOA, Wilks' Lambda = .975, $F(2, 66) = 1.71$, $p = .196$, $\eta_p^2 = .025$. However, there was a significant three-way interaction between group, image, and SOA, Wilks' Lambda = .889, $F(2, 66) = 4.13$, $p = .020$, $\eta_p^2 = .111$. To explore this interaction effect further, the data at each SOA was examined

Table 2 Age, BMI and EDE-Q scores of the low shape/weight based self-worth, high shape/weight based self-worth, and eating disorder groups

	Low $n = 26$		High $n = 23$		ED $n = 20$	
	Mean	SD	Mean	SD	Mean	SD
Age	20.08	2.13	19.88	1.77	21.60	4.38
BMI	20.52	2.40	21.10	2.00	21.31	2.51
Global	1.04	.77	2.85	.94	4.29	1.21
Eating	.54	.60	2.09	1.17	4.05	1.21
Restraint	.89	.93	2.24	1.47	3.47	1.81
Shape	1.61	1.25	3.81	.93	5.03	1.16
Weight	1.12	.96	3.25	1.18	4.6	1.46

Global = EDE-Q Global scale score; Eating = EDE-Q Eating Concern subscale score; Restraint = EDE-Q Dietary Restraint subscale score; Shape = EDE-Q Shape Concern subscale score; Weight = EDE-Q Weight Concern subscale score

Table 3 IOR reaction time data for group, image type, and validity conditions (M ± SD, Milliseconds)

	Low Shape/Weight Based Self-Worth		
		700 SOA	1300 SOA
Shape/Weight	Valid	431.69 ± 45.31	404.42 ± 39.88
	Invalid	410.23 ± 37.80	397.69 ± 42.78
Animal	Valid	418.69 ± 42.01	409.95 ± 41.06
	Invalid	400.77 ± 36.72	391.00 ± 38.76
	High Shape/Weight Based Self-Worth		
		700 SOA	1300 SOA
Shape/Weight	Valid	460.35 ± 44.20	437.01 ± 46.99
	Invalid	447.22 ± 50.53	418.22 ± 44.61
Animal	Valid	467.09 ± 58.21	425.78 ± 41.53
	Invalid	441.69 ± 48.62	421.96 ± 39.27
	Eating Disorder		
		700 SOA	1300 SOA
Shape/Weight	Valid	467.90 ± 85.37	446.75 ± 71.30
	Invalid	459.70 ± 97.38	431.30 ± 85.83
Animal	Valid	464.45 ± 93.95	447.6 ± 90.77
	Invalid	452.45 ± 90.44	438.85 ± 90.35

Shape/Weight = Shape/Weight Images, Animal = Animal Images. Valid = Target in valid location, Invalid = Target in invalid location. SOA = Stimulus onset asynchrony time in milliseconds. Global = EDE-Q Global scale score; Eating = EDE-Q Eating Concern subscale score; Restraint = EDE-Q Dietary Restraint subscale score; Shape = EDE-Q Shape Concern subscale score; Weight = EDE-Q Weight Concern subscale score

separately, as is typical for IOR experiments involving multiple SOAs [11, 24].

700 ms SOA

A mixed design ANOVA revealed no significant main effect for image, Wilks' Lambda = .991, $F(1, 66) = .604$, $p = .440$, $\eta_p^2 = .009$, or group, $F(2, 66) = .760$, $p = .472$, $\eta_p^2 = .023$. Further, there was no significant interaction between image and group, Wilks' Lambda = .978, $F(2, 66) = .744$, $p = .479$, $\eta_p^2 = .022$, indicating that there was no significant difference in IOR for the shape/weight and animal images between the three groups. Figure 2 depicts the data for 700 ms SOA.

1300 ms SOA

A mixed design ANOVA revealed no significant main effects for image type, Wilks' Lambda = .983, $F(2, 66) = 1.16$, $p = .285$, $\eta_p^2 = .017$, or group, $F(2, 66) = .046$, $p = .955$, $\eta_p^2 = .001$, but did reveal a significant interaction between image type and group, Wilks' Lambda = .877, $F(2, 66) = 4.64$, $p = .013$, $\eta_p^2 = .123$, as shown in Fig. 3. To further clarify the nature of these results at the group level, paired samples *t*-tests were used to assess the difference in IOR for differing image types within the groups. The Low group exhibited significantly lower IOR, $t(25) = -2.26$, $p = .033$, for the shape/weight images ($M = 6.65$, $SD = 20.59$) than the animal images ($M = 18.73$, $SD = 28.70$). By contrast, the High group displayed significantly higher IOR, $t(22) = 2.07$, $p = .050$, for the shape/weight images ($M = 18.96$, $SD = 33.71$) than the animal images ($M = 3.87$, $SD = 26.89$). The ED group also displayed higher IOR for the shape/weight images ($M = 15.55$, $SD = 32.43$) than the animal images ($M = 5.55$, $SD = 33.17$) but this trend was non-significant, $t(19) = 1.18$, $p = .253$.

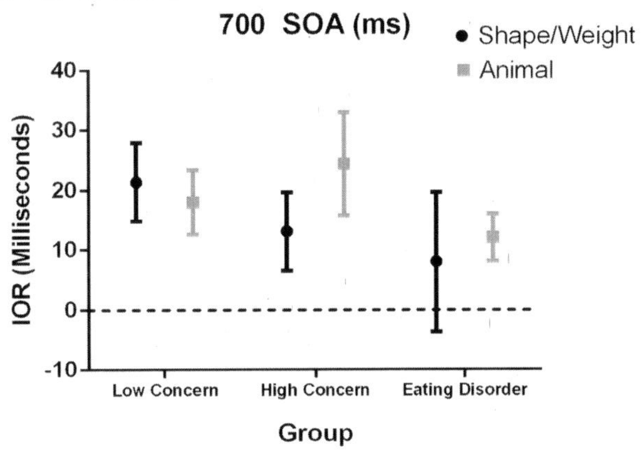

Fig. 2 IOR Indices for the Low, High and ED groups for shape/weight and animal images at 700 ms SOA. Error bars +/– one standard error of the mean

Discussion

This study aimed to investigate the nature of attentional disengagement for body shape and weight information in those with eating disorders and varying degrees of shape/weight-based self-worth. The findings indicate that, at the later (1300 ms SOA) stage of attentional processing only, different patterns in the allocation of attention were evident between the groups. As hypothesised,

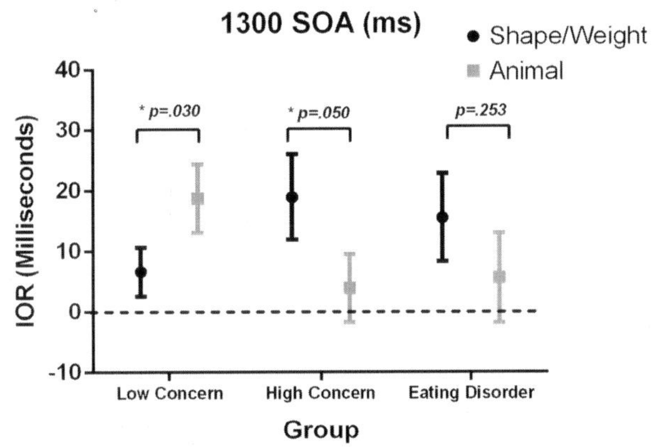

Fig. 3 IOR Indices for Low, High and ED groups for shape/weight and animal images at 1300 ms SOA. Error bars +/– one standard error of the mean

the differences in IOR between the control and body images were only observed at the longer SOA, which is to be expected since IOR typically grows as a function of SOA [22].

The attentional results revealed that the High group displayed increased IOR for shape/weight versus control images, indicating a greater level of attentional disengagement, or an avoidance response, in relation to shape/weight images. This was in the opposite direction to the hypothesised effect. It was expected that both the High and ED groups would have difficulty disengaging from disorder-relevant images (i.e., reduced IOR), a finding consistent with research using anxious and depressed populations [23, 24]. The High group instead demonstrated strong attentional disengagement from shape/weight images, which may indicate the potential occurrence of an attentional protective mechanism, as the ongoing processing of such stimuli could serve to exacerbate their shape/weight concerns. Indeed, it may be the presence of this protective cognitive mechanism that has contributed to preventing these at-risk individuals (given their tendency to base their self-worth on shape/weight) from progressing to the levels of eating disorder symptomatology evident in the eating disorder group. This is however a tentative explanation, with replication required to further inform the potential occurrence of this protective cognitive mechanism.

The ED group displayed a similar pattern of results to the High group (i.e., increased inhibition for disorder-salient information relative to non-disorder-salient information), but this did not reach significance. This result may be due to a type II error, or may be indicative of the lack of, or an insufficient, protective mechanism in their attentional processing and hence their higher endorsement of eating disorder pathology. Further, treatment may have had a beneficial role in the reduction of attentional biases, leading to the initial development of such a protective mechanism. One study found that undertaking eating disorder treatment significantly reduced biases towards eating disorder-salient information, when compared with waitlist controls and when controlling for practice effects [42]. Thus the impact of treatment may suggest a growing ability on the part of the ED group to inhibit the ongoing processing of shape/weight stimuli, increasing the potential for this to be a protective factor. Future research using individuals with eating disorders prior to commencing treatment would provide greater clarity regarding the patterns of attentional disengagement for shape/weight information in this population and the potential development of protective mechanisms.

Also contrary to the hypotheses, the Low group displayed decreased attentional disengagement from shape/weight information compared with non-shape/weight information. While unexpected, this pattern of attention is consistent with previous literature demonstrating that human body stimuli are prioritised for attentional selection relative to various types of control stimuli [43]. Importantly, a pattern of decreased disengagement in response to shape/weight images is unlikely to have adverse consequences for these individuals. As these individuals do not heavily invest in shape or weight as a basis for defining their self-worth, any processing of shape/weight images is unlikely to have adverse consequences for their self-worth and, as such, they do not require a protective mechanism.

While increased attentional disengagement from shape/weight stimuli has thus far been conceptualised as a potential protective mechanism, the converse could also be the case in that avoidance could have adverse consequences. The findings of a study that implemented attentional training either towards or away from body shape/weight words in a non-clinical undergraduate population highlight the potential adverse consequences of this pattern of attentional avoidance [44]. The results indicated that those trained to direct their attention away from body shape information subsequently reported greater concerns about their body shape, relative to those trained to direct their attention towards body shape information. Such findings are consistent with the well-established notion that avoidance of threatening stimuli exacerbates and maintains psychological symptoms and distress [45]. Further research is warranted to establish whether an attentional pattern characterised by inhibition of the ongoing processing of shape/weight stimuli elicits harmful or beneficial consequences.

In addition to the limitations and future directions for research already noted, the current study did not include stimuli representing the thin-ideal. Given the lack of clarity regarding attentional processes in relation to thin versus non-thin images, expanding the present research to examine IOR using thin-ideal images is needed. In addition, while the relatively small sample size did not permit such an analysis, further investigation into how these attentional patterns differ across eating disorder subgroups is warranted, given at least some research indicated that attentional patterns may differ across eating disorder diagnoses [46]. Finally, future research would benefit from employing the IOR task in conjunction with an eye-tracking task given that one limitation of the IOR paradigm is its inability to determine whether a decrease in IOR is indicative of reduced time to re-engage with the information or increased time to disengage. The inclusion of eye-tracking would enable researchers to investigate the exact location and duration of participants' graze duration during the IOR task (Additional file 1).

Conclusions

The present study was the first to investigate the occurrence and nature of attentional disengagement in a clinical eating disorder sample and those with differing degrees of shape/weight-based self-worth. The current findings indicate that young women without an eating disorder who base their self-worth on shape/weight display a pattern of inhibited processing of shape/weight stimuli in the later stages of attention. The impact of this attentional pattern remains unknown, highlighting the need for further research on the role of attentional avoidance in the development, maintenance, and treatment of eating disorder symptoms.

Abbreviations

ANOVA: Analysis of Variance; BMI: Body Mass Index; ED: Eating disorder; EDE-Q: Eating Disorder Examination Questionnaire; High: High shape/weight based self-worth group; IOR: Inhibition of Return; Low: Low shape/weight based self-worth group; SOA: Stimulus onset asynchrony

Acknowledgements

The authors wish to thank the staff of the ACT Health Eating Disorders Program for their assistance in participant recruitment.

Funding

The Australian National University funded this study. The funding body had no influence on the conception or execution of the study.

Authors' contributions

AC, ER, and JB conceptualised the study and methodology. AC undertook literature review, ethical approval, data collection, data analysis and preparation of the manuscript. ER and JB contributed to the content, review, and editing of the final manuscript. All authors read and approved the final manuscript.

Authors information

AC is a Clinical Psychology PhD candidate at the Australian National University. ER is AC's primary supervisor. JB is AC's secondary supervisor.

Competing interests

The authors declare that they have no competing interests.

Author details

[1]Research School of Psychology, Australian National University, Canberra, ACT 2601, Australia. [2]Research School of Psychology, Australian National University, Canberra, ACT, Australia. [3]School of Psychological Science, University of Western Australia, Perth, WA, Australia.

References

1. Amerian Psychiatric Association. Diagnostic and statistical manual of mental disorders. 5th ed. Arlington, VA: American Psychiatric Publishing; 2013.
2. Hargreaves D, Tiggemann M. The role of appearance schematicity in the development of adolescent body dissatisfaction. Cognit Ther Res. 2002;26:691–700.
3. Williamson DA, White MA, York-Crowe E, Stewart TM. Cognitive-behavioral theories of eating disorders. Behav Modif. 2004;28:711–38.
4. Vitousek KB, Hollon SD. The investigation of schematic content and processing in eating disorders. Cognit Ther Res. 1990;14:191–214.
5. Aspen V, Darcy AM, Lock J. A review of attention biases in women with eating disorders. Cogn Emot. 2012;27:820–38.
6. Cisler JM, Koster EH. Mechanisms of attentional biases towards threat in anxiety disorders: an integrative review. Clin Psychol Rev. 2010;30:203–16.
7. Faunce GJ. Eating disorders and attentional bias: a review. Eat Disord. 2002;10:125–39.
8. Dobson KS, Dozois DJ. Attentional biases in eating disorders: a meta-analytic review of Stroop performance. Clin Psychol Rev. 2004;23:1001–22.
9. MacLeod CM. Half a century of research on the Stroop effect: an integrative review. Psychol Bull. 1991;109:163–203.
10. Blechert J, Nickert T, Caffier D, Tuschen-Caffier B. Social comparison and its relation to body dissatisfaction in bulimia nervosa: evidence from eye movements. Psychosom Med. 2009;71:907–12.
11. Gao X, Li X, Yang X, Wang Y, Jackson T, Chen H. I can't stop looking at them: interactive effects of body mass index and weight dissatisfaction on attention towards body shape photographs. Body Image. 2013;10:191–9.
12. Glauert R, Rhodes G, Fink B, Grammer K. Body dissatisfaction and attentional bias to thin bodies. Int J Eat Disord. 2010;43:42–9.
13. Jansen A, Nederkoorn C, Mulkens S. Selective visual attention for ugly and beautiful body parts in eating disorders. Behav Res Ther. 2005;43:183–96.
14. Dondzilo L, Rieger E, Palermo R, Byrne S, Bell J. Association between rumination factors and eating disorder behaviours in young women. Adv Eat Disord. 2016;4:84–98.
15. Roefs A, Jansen A, Moresi S, Willems P, van Grootel S, van der Borgh A. Looking good: BMI, attractiveness bias and visual attention. Appetite. 2008;51:552–5.
16. Glashouwer KA, Jonker NC, Thomassen K, de Jong PJ. Take a look at the bright side: effects of positive body exposure on selective visual attention in women with high body dissatisfaction. Behav Res Ther. 2016;83:19–25.
17. von Wietersheim J, Kunzl F, Hoffmann H, Glaub J, Rottler E, Traue HC. Selective attention of patients with anorexia nervosa while looking at pictures of their own body and the bodies of others: an exploratory study. Psychosom Med. 2012;74:107–13.
18. Most SB, Simons DJ. Attention capture, orienting, and awareness. In: Folk CL, Gibson BS, editors. Attraction, distraction and action: multiple perspectives on attentional capture. Amsterdam: Elsevier; 2001. p. 151–73.
19. Fairburn CG, Cooper Z, Shafran R. Cognitive behaviour therapy for eating disorders: a "transdiagnostic" theory and treatment. Behav Res Ther. 2003;41:509–28.
20. Williamson DA, Muller SL, Reas DL, Thaw JM. Cognitive bias in eating disorders: implications for theory and treatment. Behav Modif. 1999;23:556–77.
21. Posner MI, Cohen Y. Components of visual orientating. In: Bouwhuis HBDG, editor. Attention and performance X: control of language processes. Abingdon: Taylor & Francis Group; 1984. p. 531–56.
22. Klein RM. Inhibition of return. Trends Cogn Sci. 2000;4:138–47.
23. Perez-Duenas C, Acosta A, Lupianez J. Attentional capture and trait anxiety: evidence from inhibition of return. J Anxiety Disord. 2009;23:782–90.
24. Dai Q, Feng Z. Deficient inhibition of return for emotional faces in depression. Prog Neuro-Psychopharmacol Biol Psychiatry. 2009;33:921–32.
25. Carters MA, Rieger E, Bell J. Reduced inhibition of return to food images in obese individuals. PLoS One. 2015;10:e013782.
26. Janelle CM, Hausenblas HA, Ellis R, Coombes SA, Duley AR. The time course of attentional allocation while women high and low in body dissatisfaction view self and model physiques. Psychol Health. 2009;24:351–66.
27. Geller J, Johnston C, Madsen K. The role of shape and weight in self-concept: the shape and weight based self-esteem inventory. Cognit Ther Res. 1997;21:5–24.

28. Geller J, Johnston C, Madsen K, Goldner EM, Remick RA, Birmingham CL. Shape-and weight-based self-esteem and the eating disorders. Int J Eat Disord. 1998;24:285–98.
29. Nijs IM, Franken IH. Attentional processing of food cues in overweight and obese individuals. Curr Obes Rep. 2012;1:106–13.
30. Fairburn C, Beglin S. Eating disorder examination questionnaire. In: Fairburn C, editor. Cognitive behavior therapy and eating disorders. New York: Guilford Press; 2008. p. 309–14.
31. Australia Beauro of Statistics: Profiles of Health, Australia, 2011–2013 (catalogue no. 4338.0). Canberra, Australia: Australian Bureau of Statistics; 2012.
32. Bradley MM, Lang PJ. The international affective picture system (IAPS) in the study of emotion and attention. In: Coan A, Allen JJB, editors. Handbook of emotion elicitation and assessment. New York: Oxford University Press; 2007. p. 29–46.
33. Fairburn CG. Cognitive behavior therapy and eating disorders. New York: Guilford Press; 2008.
34. Fairburn CG, Cooper Z. The eating disorder examination (12th ed.). In: Fairburn CG, Wilson GT, editors. Binge eating: nature, assessment and treatment. New York: Guilford Press; 1993. p. 317–60.
35. Mond JM, Hay PJ, Rodgers B, Owen C, Beumont PJ. Validity of the eating disorder examination questionnaire (EDE-Q) in screening for eating disorders in community samples. Behav Res Ther. 2004;42:551–67.
36. Aardoom JJ, Dingemans AE, Op't Landt MCS, Van Furth EF. Norms and discriminative validity of the eating disorder examination questionnaire (EDE-Q). Eat Behav. 2012;13:305–9.
37. Luce KH, Crowther JH. The reliability of the eating disorder examination-self-report questionnaire version (EDE-Q). Int J Eat Disord. 1999;25:349–51.
38. Rose JS, Vaewsorn A, Rosselli-Navarra F, Wilson GT. Test-retest reliability of the eating disorder examination-questionnaire (EDE-Q) in a college sample. J Eat Disord. 2013;1:1–42.
39. Mond JM, Hay PJ, Rodgers B, Owen C, Beumont PJ. Temporal stability of the eating disorder examination questionnaire. Int J Eat Disord. 2004;36:195–203.
40. Koelstra S, Muhl C, Soleymani M, Lee J-S, Yazdani A, Ebrahimi T, Pun T, Nijholt A, Patras I. Deap: a database for emotion analysis; using physiological signals. IEEE Trans Affect Comput. 2012;3:18–31.
41. Stoyanova RS, Pratt J, Anderson AK. Inhibition of return to social signals of fear. Emotion. 2007;7:49–56.
42. Shafran R, Lee M, Cooper Z, Palmer RL, Fairburn CG. Effect of psychological treatment on attentional bias in eating disorders. Int J Eat Disord. 2008;41: 348–54.
43. Downing PE, Bray D, Rogers J, Childs C. Bodies capture attention when nothing is expected. Cognition. 2004;93:B27–38.
44. Engel SG, Robinson MD, Wonderlich SJ, Meier BP, Wonderlich SA, Crosby RD, Steffen KJ, Mitchell JE. Does the avoidance of body and shape concerns reinforce eating disordered attitudes? Evidence from a manipulation study. Eat Behav. 2006;7:368–74.
45. Kashdan TB, Barrios V, Forsyth JP, Steger MF. Experiential avoidance as a generalized psychological vulnerability: comparisons with coping and emotion regulation strategies. Behav Res Ther. 2006;44:1301–20.
46. Giel KE, Teufel M, Friederich HC, Hautzinger M, Enck P, Zipfel S. Processing of pictorial food stimuli in patients with eating disorders—a systematic review. Int J Eat Disord. 2011;44:105–17.

What can food-image tasks teach us about anorexia nervosa?

E. Caitlin Lloyd[1*] and Joanna E. Steinglass[2,3]

Abstract

A salient feature of anorexia nervosa (AN) is the persistent and severe restriction of food, such that dietary intake is inadequate to maintain a healthy body weight. Experimental tasks and paradigms have used illness-relevant stimuli, namely food images, to study the eating-specific neurocognitive mechanisms that promote food avoidance. This systematic review, completed in accordance with PRISMA guidelines, identified and critically evaluated paradigms involving images of food that have been used to study AN. There were 50 eligible studies, published before March 10th 2018, identified from Medline and PsychINFO searches, and reference screening. Studies using food image-based paradigms were categorised into three methodologic approaches: neuropsychology, neurophysiology, and functional magnetic resonance imaging (fMRI). Paradigms were reviewed with a focus on how well they address phenomena central to AN. Across tasks, differences between individuals with AN and healthy peers have been identified, with the most consistent findings in the area of reward processing. Measuring task performance alongside actual eating behaviour, and using experimental manipulations to probe causality, may advance understanding of the mechanisms of illness in AN.

Keywords: Anorexia nervosa, Eating behaviour, Food stimuli, Eating disorders, Cognitive neuroscience, fMRI

Plain English Summary

A core feature of anorexia nervosa is the persistent limiting of calorie intake, or avoidance of eating, which results in a severely low body weight. Given the relevance of eating behaviour to anorexia nervosa, studies have often used tasks involving pictures of food to try and understand the factors that contribute to the illness. In this article, we review studies involving the presentation of food images, to highlight the approaches that have been most successful in furthering knowledge about AN. Studies to date have identified some differences among individuals with AN, but have had limited success in identifying underlying mechanisms of illness. We consider modifications to existing experimental designs that may address these limitations, in particular discussing methods that have been used to study eating behaviour in non-eating disorder populations. We conclude that when using food image tasks to develop a better understanding of anorexia nervosa, it is important to link actual eating behaviour to task outcomes, and to develop research based on more specific hypotheses.

* Correspondence: el15519@bristol.ac.uk
[1]Centre for Exercise, Nutrition and Health Sciences, School for Policy Studies, University of Bristol, Bristol, UK
Full list of author information is available at the end of the article

Background

A core feature of anorexia nervosa (AN) is disturbed eating behaviour [1]. Individuals with AN limit overall caloric intake and specifically calories derived from fat. This pattern of eating persists following weight recovery, and is associated with relapse in the longer term [2, 3]. AN is a complex illness, and there are generalized neurocognitive deficits (e.g., set shifting, central coherence) [4, 5]. Yet, maladaptive eating behavior is central to the definition of AN, leading to models and proposed neurobiological mechanisms of illness centered around aberrant brain responses to food [6]. Measures of neuropsychological processes, such as the Stroop task [7], have been adapted to include illness-specific words, which is thought to increase the attentional deficits among patients [8]. To understand maladaptive eating behaviour, experimental tasks have utilized images of food.

The primary purpose of this review is to identify and critically evaluate the food image *tasks and paradigms* that have been used in the study of AN. This systematic literature review identified neuropsychological, neurophysiological, and neuroimaging studies. Across these approaches, task domains included attention, reward, perception, and decision-making. While study findings are discussed, we primarily provide a qualitative review of the tasks themselves, and discuss how well these paradigms address phenomena central to AN.

Methods

Search strategy and eligibility criteria

PsychInfo and Medline were searched, using the search strategy shown in Fig. 1. Following deduplication, titles and abstracts were screened to determine whether the article should be included in the full-text screening stage. References in eligible studies were manually screened to identify studies not captured by database searches. Table 1 details inclusion criteria.

Data Extraction, Synthesis, and Quality Assessment

Participant details (age, AN subtype, BMI), task information (nature of task, observed variables) and study information (sample size, use of non-food control images, standardisation of pre-task intake, findings) were extracted. Studies were categorized by type (neuropsychology, neurophysiology, neuroimaging). The neuro psychology and neurophysiology tasks were further categorised by the following neurocognitive domains: attention, reward, perception, and decision-making. The qualitative review identified strengths and limitations of the tasks.

We used the Ferro and Speechley version [9] of the Downs and Black Quality Index [10] to provide a systematic assessment of study quality. A number of items were not applicable to the current review given the neurobiological nature of included studies. Consistent with an existing review [11], we removed the following items: response rate; estimates of the random variability; staff / places / facilities where patients studied representative; outcome measures valid and reliable. We also removed the confounding item given potential confounders varied substantially across studies. The final index consisted of 10 items; 10 was the maximum score (quality index item-level results available upon request).

Results

We identified 50 studies meeting eligibility criteria (Figure 2, PRISMA flow diagram). These studies are presented in Table 2.

Neuropsychology

Attention

Attention directs sensory and cognitive processing, which in turn influences behaviour [12]. An attentional bias refers to the differential allocation of attention towards one set of stimuli over another. There are three components of attentional bias: increased capture of attention by a stimulus (orienting); reduced ability to direct attention away from a stimulus once attention has been captured (disengagement); and efforts to avoid allocating attention to a stimulus (attentional avoidance) [13]. Components of attentional bias have been studied in other areas of psychopathology, such as anxiety disorders. Individuals with anxiety disorders demonstrate an enhanced orienting towards "threat-related" stimuli, along with difficulties disengaging from such stimuli [13]. These biases are related to anxiety severity [14, 15]. It has been hypothesised that individuals with AN might show similar attentional biases towards food stimuli, indicating a perceived threat, that might in turn be associated with greater dietary restriction [16]. On the other hand, attention to a food stimulus predicts consumption of that food (i.e., the opposite of dietary restriction [17])

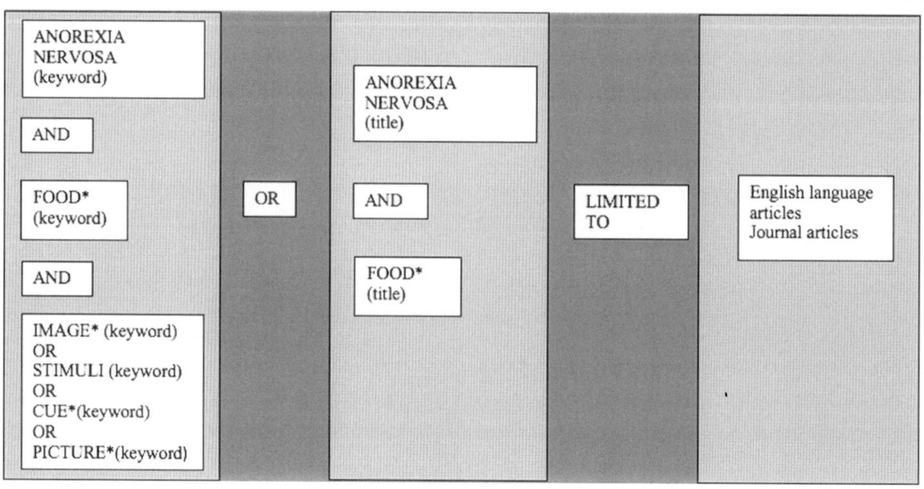

Fig. 1 Systematic Review Search Strategy

Table 1 Systematic Review Inclusion Criteria

Sample population	Study included a defined group of individuals with AN or atypical AN (acutely ill or weight-restored). AN group was analysed separately (i.e., studies with only mixed ED analyses were not included)
Study design	Administration of a paradigm involving the presentation of real food images (i.e., not cartoons)
Study type	Primary investigations only, secondary data analyses were not included
Outcome measure	Any
Date of study	Up to and including 10th March 2018
Publication type	Peer-reviewed full-text journal articles
Language	English

in healthy individuals. As such, an alternative hypothesis is that individuals with AN would show *reduced* attentional bias towards food, and that this is a mechanism that facilitates dietary restriction [18]. Attention paradigms incorporating pictures of food have been administered to individuals with AN to test these competing hypotheses, to assess whether altered attention to food underlies maladaptive dietary restriction.

In distraction paradigms (Table 2, Distraction) pictures of food are presented while participants engage in an unrelated cognitive task. The difference in task performance when food images are presented as distractor items (as compared to neutral distractors) indicates an attentional bias. Individuals with AN were less accurate than healthy controls (HC) in an attention task when distracted by food-related stimuli, with no group difference in the presence of neutral stimuli [18]. One study reported no differential effect of food versus other distractors on working memory accuracy among individuals with AN or HC [19]. However, another study reported working memory performance was compromised by food stimuli distractors among AN, but not HC [20]. In an inhibitory control task, food-image presentation was associated with decreased accuracy among HC, but not AN [20].

In visual probe detection tasks [21, 22] participants identify the location of visual probes that replace food

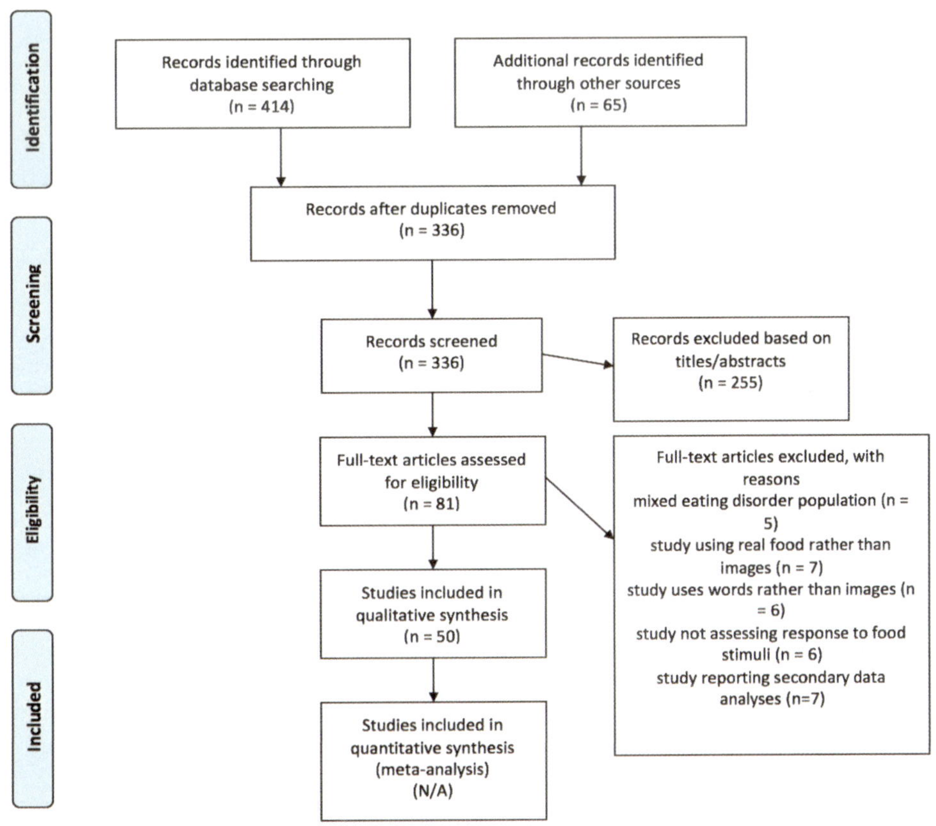

Fig. 2 PRISMA Flow Diagram

Table 2 Food-image tasks in the study of anorexia nervosa

Domain	Subdomain	Study	Paradigm & Outcome Variable(s)	Participants (AN subtype)	Mean age (SD)	Mean BMI (SD)	Non-food images presented	Meal-Task Interval Standardised	Summary of Findings	Quality Index Score
Neuropsychology: Attention	Distraction	Dickson et al., 2008 [19]	Working memory task. Effects of image presentation on reaction time and accuracy.	24 AN (R)	30.6 (9.0)	16.0 (1.0)	Yes	No	No differences AN vs HC	6
				24 HC	33.1 (8.0)	21.9 (2.0)				
		Brooks et al., 2012 [20]	Working memory and inhibitory control task. Effects of image presentation on reaction time and accuracy.	13 AN (R)	25 (11.0)	15 (1.54)	Yes	Yes	Distraction during working memory task: AN > HC Distraction during inhibitory control task: AN < HC	7
				20 HC	22 (5.0)	22.38 (2.66)				
		Neimeijer et al., 2017 [18]	Visual target detection task. Effects of image presentation on accuracy.	66 AN (57.5% R, 42.5% EDNOS AN-R)	15.25 (1.86)	15.45 (1.79)	Yes	No	Distraction AN > HC	6
				55 HC	16.14 (1.9)	20.45 (2.10)				
	Recognition	Nikendei et al., 2008 [62]	Participants view images. Recognition and recall.	16 AN (81.25% R, 18.75% BP)	22.8 (U)	14.8 (2.3)	Yes	No	No differences AN vs HC	9
				16 HC, fasted	23.6 (U)	U				
				16 HC, sated	23.1 (U)	U				
	Visual probe detection	Veenstra & de Jong 2012 [24]	Exogenous cueing task: participants detect targets that appear in one of two on-screen locations; distractor image (food or neutral stimuli) precedes tar get onset, appearing in either the same (valid trials) or opposite (in valid trials) location as the target. Response time.	88 AN (61.3% R, 28.7% EDNOS AN-R)	15.02 (1.37)	15.69 (1.90)	Yes	No	No differences AN vs HC	6
				76 HC	15.12 (1.75)	20.42 (2.37)				
		Cardi et al., 2012 [28]	Dot-probe task: Participants instructed to detect targets appearing in one of	18 AN (33% R, 11% BP, 55% EDNOS-AN)	31.5 (11.4)	17 (2.6)	Yes	No	No effect of intervention on attentional bias towards food	5
				19 HC	28.6 (8.0)	23.9 (2.8)				
		Cardi et al.,		38 AN (21%	29.9	16.2	Yes	No	Attentional bias towards food	6

Table 2 Food-image tasks in the study of anorexia nervosa *(Continued)*

Domain	Subdomain	Study	Paradigm & Outcome Variable(s)	Participants (AN subtype)	Mean age (SD)	Mean BMI (SD)	Non-food images presented	Meal-Task Interval Standardised	Summary of Findings	Quality Index Score
		2013 [27]	two on-screen locations, either replacing a food or neutral image that are presented concurrently. Response time.	EDNOS)	(7.92)	(2.35)			inpatients: pre-meal < post-meal Attentional bias towards food outpatients: pre-meal > post-meal	
		Kim et al., 2014 [23]		31 AN	23.1 (9.35)	15.15 (2.51)	Yes	Yes	No differences AN vs HC	7
				33 HC	22.18 (2.14)	20.91 (2.22)				
		Cardi et al., 2015 [29]		19 AN	31.0 (10.0)	16.7 (2.7)	Yes	Yes	No differences AN vs HC	7
				23 BN	24.4 (5.7)	23.4 (6.9)				
				36 HC	25.9 (5.0)	21.5 (2.0)				
		Leppenan et al., 2017 [26]		30 AN	26.2 (6.82)	16.3 (2.04)	Yes	Yes	Attentional bias away from food: AN > HC	8
				29 HC	26.83 (8.54)	23.25 (3.65)				
	Eye-tracking	Giel et al., 2011 [32]	Eye movements recorded while participants view pairs consisting of a food and neutral image. Number and duration of fixations on images.	19 AN (73.6% R, 26.4% BP)	24.4 (4.1)	15.8 (1.8)	Yes	Yes	Attentional bias towards food: AN < HC	7
				20 HC, sated	24.2 (2.9)	21.3 (1.7)				
				18 HC, fasted	24.4 (2.6)	21.6 (1.5)				
Neuropsychology: Reward	Explicit rating	Bossert et al., 1991 [53]	Participants view images. Palatability ratings.	9 AN (R)	21.9 (2.9)	66.1(8.5) IBW	No	No	Palatability high calorie food: AN < HC Palatability low calorie food: AN > HC	8
				20 BN	21.7 (2.9)	101.9 (12.9) IBW				
				9 HC	22.3 (1.2)	100.8 (4.8) IBW				
		Jiang et al., 2010 [46]	Participants view images. Liking and wanting ratings.	17 AN (R)	26.47 (7.12)	15.04 (1.93)	Yes	Yes	Liking: AN < HC Wanting: AN < HC	6
				29 HC	24.52 (5.58)	20.38 (1.87)				
		Krizbai et al., 2016 [52]	Participants view images. Valence, domi nance,	14 AN (R)	15.07 (1.38)	16.92 (1.73)	No	No	Positive valence: AN < HC	5
				14 HC	15.14 (1.29)	20.51 (2.50)				

Table 2 Food-image tasks in the study of anorexia nervosa *(Continued)*

Domain	Subdomain	Study	Paradigm & Outcome Variable(s)	Participants (AN subtype)	Mean age (SD)	Mean BMI (SD)	Non-food images presented	Meal-Task Interval Standardised	Summary of Findings	Quality Index Score
			arousal ratings.							
	Implicit rating	Cowdrey et al., 2013 [41]	Binary forced choice procedure: across multiple trials participants choose between two foods, each of which may be high or low calorie and sweet or savoury. Relative response time to select high and low-calorie foods (im plicit wanting).	20 AN (80% R, 20% BP) 22 AN-WR (82% R, 13% BP) 22 AN-rec (82% R, 18% BP) 41 HC	26.4 (10.56) 25.1 (6.03) 23.73 (5.76) 24.29 (6.46)	16.33 (1.1) 21.05 (1.89) 21.03 (1.53) 21.7 (1.88)	No	No	Explicit wanting high calorie food: AN < HC; AN-WR < HC Implicit wanting high calorie food: AN < HC; AN < AN-rec; AN-WR < HC Implicit wanting low calorie food: AN > HC; AN > AN-rec; AN-WR > HC	4
	Approach-Avoidance	Spring & Bulik, 2014 [51]	Affect misattribution procedure: participants briefly view food images, which are replaced by Chinese characters. Pleasantness ratings of Chinese characters (implicit liking).	9 AN 14 AN-rec 29 HC	21.4 (5.79)	U	Yes	No	Implicit liking: AN < HC	6
		Veenstra & de Jong, 2011 [54]	Manikin Task: participants move manikin towards or away from images presented on-screen de pending on orientation of image (horizontal or vertical). Errors/reaction times on approach versus avoidance trials (approach bias).	89 AN (60.7% R, 39.3% EDNOS AN-R) 76 HC	14.84 (1.70) 14.86 (1.70)	15.71 (1.87) 20.42 (2.37)	Yes	No	Approach bias: AN < HC	6
		Neimeijer et al., 2015 [56]		98 AN (64.5% AN, 45.5% EDNOS-AN)	14.97 (1.63)	U	Yes	No	Approach bias high calorie food: pre-treatment < post-treatment	8
		Paslaskis et al., 2016 [55]	Approach-avoidance task: participants push or pull computer mouse depending on	41 AN (80.5% R, 19.5% EP) 42 HC	26.85 (6.71) 24.79 (2.71)	15.29 (1.6) 21.37 (1.57)	No	Yes	Approach bias: AN < HC	6

Table 2 Food-image tasks in the study of anorexia nervosa *(Continued)*

Domain	Subdomain	Study	Paradigm & Outcome Variable(s)	Participants (AN subtype)	Mean age (SD)	Mean BMI (SD)	Non-food images presented	Meal-Task Interval Standardised	Summary of Findings	Quality Index Score
			orientation of on-screen image (horizontal or vertical). Reaction time on approach versus avoidance trials (approach bias).							
Neuropsychology: Perceptual tasks	Size perception	Yellowlees et al., 1988 [57]	Participants view real food item and adjust screen image to match perceived size. Estimated versus actual size of items.	20 AN 20 HC	22.4 (8.0) 22.0 (6.6)	U	Yes	No	Size over-estimation: AN > HC	5
		Milos et al., 2013 [58]	Participants view meals of different portion sizes. Estimates of portion size.	24 AN 27 HC	22.38 (4.10) 21.41 (2.75)	15.8 (2.01) 21.47 (2.71)	No	Yes	Portion size estimate: AN > HC	7
		Kissileff et al., 2016 [99]	Participants view meals of different portion sizes. Tolerability and expected anxiety ratings.	24 AN (87.5% R, 22.5% BP) 10 HC	15.46 (1.57) 14.6 (2.63)	17.11 (1.35) 20.6 (1.35)	No	No	Portion size tolerability: AN < HC Anticipated anxiety: AN > HC	7
	Weight-gain estimate	Milos et al., 2017 [100]	Participants view meals of different portion sizes. Estimates of weight-gain as a consequence of eating portions presented.	24 AN 27 HC	22.38 (4.10) 21.41 (2.75)	15.8 (2.01) 21.47 (2.71)	No	Yes	Estimation of weight-gain: AN > HC	7
Neuropsychology: Decision making	Food-choice	Steinglass et al., 2015 [60]	Participants select between food items varying in fat content in a binary forced choice task. Proportion of high fat food items selected.	22 AN (54.5% R, 45.5% BP) 22 HC	29.4 (11.2) 26.3 (5.8)	17.5 (1.9) 21.0 (1.7)	No	No	Preference for high-fat food items: AN < HC	6
Neurophysiology: Attention	Electroencephalography	Blechert et al., 2011 [67]	Neural activity recorded with electroencephalography	21 AN	23.2 (4.55)	16.6 (1.3)	Yes	No	Neuronal activity: AN > HC	7

Table 2 Food-image tasks in the study of anorexia nervosa *(Continued)*

Domain	Subdomain	Study	Paradigm & Outcome Variable(s)	Participants (AN subtype)	Mean age (SD)	Mean BMI (SD)	Non-food images presented	Meal-Task Interval Standardised	Summary of Findings	Quality Index Score
			(EEG) while food images viewed. Amplitude of neural response.	22 BN	26.1 (7.5)	22.6 (3.24)				
				32 HC	26.2 (5.02)	20.7 (2.41)				
		Nikendei et al., 2012 [69]		16 AN (81.25% R, 18.25% BP)	22.8 (5.2)	14.8 (2.3)	Yes	No	No differences AN vs HC	8
				16 HC pre-meal	23.1 (4.8)	22.3 (2.1)				
				16 HC post-meal	23.6 (5.2)	20.9 (1.7)				
		Novosel et al., 2014 [68]		11 AN	15.36 (1.62)	15.79 (1.87)	Yes	No	Neuronal activity: AN > HC	6
				11 HC		20.42 (1.77)				
	Magnetoencephalography	Godier et al., 2016 [33]	Neural activity recorded with magnetoencephalography (MEG) while participants think about how much they want to eat presented food images. Amplitude of neural response.	13 AN (R)	31.2 (5.3)	15.7 (1.9)	Yes	Yes	Neuronal activity at 150 ms: AN > HC; AN > AN-rec Neuronal activity at 320 ms: AN < AN-rec	6
				14 AN-rec (R)	27.1 (6.5)	20.9 (1.6)				
				15 HC	23.7 (5.4)	21.4 (1.9)				
Neurophysiology: Reward	Electromyography	Soussignan et al., 2010 [71]	Participants view food images presented following subliminal presentation of facial expressions. Activity of facial (zygomatic, corrugator) muscles index hedonic response.	16 AN (R)	26.68 (7.30)	14.97 (1.97)	No	Yes	Corrugator activity: AN > HC Zygomatic activity: AN < HC	7
				25 HC	24.6 (6.03)	20.52 (1.90)				
		Soussignan et al., 2011 [72]	Participants view food images. Activity of facial (zygomatic, corrugator) muscles index hedonic response.	17 AN (R)	26.5 (7.1)	14.9 (1.9)	Yes	Yes	Corrugator activity: AN > HC	6
				27 HC	24.7 (6.1)	20.4 (1.8)				
		Hildebrandt et al., 2015 [73]	Participants complete food-based associative learning task. Activity of facial muscles (zygomatic, corrugator, levator labii), index hedonic and disgust responses.	14 AN/EDNOS-AN (R)	15.05 (1.87)	17.52 (2.91)	No	No	Levator labii activity to food cue: AN > HC Zygomatic activity to cue for absence of food: AN > HC	5
				15 HC	17.64 (2.71)	22.49 (2.94)				

Table 2 Food-image tasks in the study of anorexia nervosa *(Continued)*

Domain	Subdomain	Study	Paradigm & Outcome Variable(s)	Participants (AN subtype)	Mean age (SD)	Mean BMI (SD)	Non-food images presented	Meal-Task Interval Standardised	Summary of Findings	Quality Index Score
		Friederich et al., 2006 [74]	Acoustic stimulus and food image presented concurrently; activity of oculomotor muscle recorded.	13 AN (84.6% R, 25.4% BP)	25.1 (3.7)	16.4 (3.7)	Yes	Yes	No differences AN vs HC	7
				15 BN	25.2 (5.1)	23.4 (3.7)				
				25 HC	25.0 (3.3)	21.8 (2.7)				
		Racine et al., 2016 [76]	Startle response indexes appetitive/aversive motivation.	19 AN (36.8% R, 63.2% BP)	25.11 (9.13)	16.72 (1.63)	Yes	No	AN unable to suppress startle response to food and negative non-food stimuli	7
		Erdur et al., 2017 [75]		33 AN (60.6% R, 39.4% BP)	28.2 (9.41)	15.8 (1.90)	Yes	Yes	No differences AN vs AN-rec vs HC	7
				15 AN-rec (33.3% R, 66.6% BP)	40.8 (6.79)	20.81 (1.93)				
				18 HC	28.95 (8.25)	21.82 (1.58)				
Neuroimaging	Passive viewing	Nagamitsu et al., 2012 [82]	Participants view images of food stimuli while brain activity measured with functional near infrared spectroscopy. Neural response.	12 AN (R)	14.4 (1.3)	15.5 (2.0)	Yes	No	No differences AN vs HC	5
				13 HC	14.3 (1.3)	18.7 (1.3)				
		Ellison et al., 1998 [78]	Participants view images of food stimuli while brain activity measured with fMRI. Neural response.	6 AN	U	15	No	No	Brain activation: AN > HC (insula, anterior cingulate gyrus, amygdala)	6
				6 HC		U				
		Santel et al., 2006 [48]		13 AN (R)	16.1 (2.0)	16.0 (1.7)	Yes	Yes	Brain activation pre-meal: AN < HC (lingual gyrus); Brain activation post-meal: AN < HC (Inferior parietal lobule)	6
				10 HC	16.8 (2.6)	20.5 (1.9)				
		Gizewski et al., 2010 [47]		12 AN (R)	27 (U)	14.1 (1.8)	Yes	Yes	Brain activation pre-meal: AN > HC (midcingulate cortex); AN < HC (ACC) Brain activation post-meal: AN > HC (L insula); HC > AN (prefrontal cortex and R insula)	6
				10 HC	25 (U)	21.4 (1.5)				
		Joos et al., 2011 [44]		11 AN (R)	25.0 (5.0)	16.2 (1.2)	Yes	No	Brain activation: AN > HC (amygdala); AN < HC (midcingulum)	6
				11 HC	26.0 (5.2)	21.1 (1.8)				
		Rothemund et al., 2011 [79]		12 AN (83.4% R, 16.6% BP)	24 (6.1)	13.6 (1.2)	Yes	Yes	Brain activation: AN > HC (precuneus)	5
				12 HC	26 (3.7)	21 (1.6)				

Table 2 Food-image tasks in the study of anorexia nervosa *(Continued)*

Domain	Subdomain	Study	Paradigm & Outcome Variable(s)	Participants (AN subtype)	Mean age (SD)	Mean BMI (SD)	Non-food images presented	Meal-Task Interval Standardised	Summary of Findings	Quality Index Score
		Holsen et al., 2012 [45]		12 AN (R) 10 AN-WF 11 HC	21.8 (2.7) 23.4 (2.3) 21.6 (1.3)	18.0 (0.8) 22.1 (2.2) 22.4 (1.3)	Yes	Yes	Brain activation pre-meal: AN < HC (amygdala, hypothalamus, in sula, hippocampus, orbitofrontal cortex); AN-WR < HC (hypothalamus, amygdala, insula) Brain ac tivation post-meal: AN < HC (insula, amygdala); AN > AN-WR (amygdala); AN < AN-WR (insula)	6
		Kim et al., 2012 [84]		18 AN (33.3% R, 66.6% EP) 20 BN 20 HC	25.2 (4.2) 22.9 (3.9) 23.3 (1.8)	16.0 (3.7) 21.6 (2.3) 19.9 (1.9)	Yes	Yes	Brain activation: AN > HC (Inferior frontal gyrus, anterior cingulate cortex, superior frontal gyrus and cerebellem); AN > BN (anterior cingulate cortex); AN < BN (middle temporal gyrus)	6
		Boehm et al., 2017 [83]		35 AN (94.2% R, 5.8% BP) 25 HC	16.25 (3.46) 16.31 (3.39)	14.59 (1.5) 20.46 (2.06)	Yes	No	Brain activation: AN > HC (superior occipital gyrus)	7
		Kerr et al., 2017 [80]		20 AN-WR (R) 20 HC	17 (3) 19.84 (0.87)	18 (3) 21.3 (1.55)	Yes	No	Brain activation correlates with interoceptive awareness in opposite directions AN vs HC	5
	Directed food tasks	Uher et al., 2003 [85]	Participants shown images of food while neural activity measured with fMRI; participants instructed to think how hungry images make them feel and whether they would like to eat the food. Neural response.	8 AN (R) 9 AN-rec (R) 9 HC	25.6 (2.8) 26.9 (5.3) 26.6 (3.3)	16.6 (1.2) 20.4 (2.1) 22.2 (3.8)	Yes	Yes	Brain activation: AN < AN-rec (Apical prefrontal cortex, dorsolateral prefrontal cortex, medial paracentral cortex, cerebellem); AN > AN-rec (occipital-lingual gyrus)	5
		Uher et al., 2004 [50]		16 AN (56.3% R, 43.2% BP) 10 BN 19 HC	26.93 (12.14) 29.80 (8.80) 26.68 (8.34)	16.04 (1.64) 22.43 (2.37) 22.41 (2.98)	Yes	Yes	Brain activation: AN > HC (medial orbitofrontal cortex, lingual gyrus, anterior cingulate); AN < HC (parietal cortex, cerebellem); AN > BN (apical prefrontal cortex, lateral prefrontal cortex, occipital lingual gyrus); AN < BN (cerebellem)	6
		Brooks et al., 2011 [81]	Participants shown images of food while neural activity measured with fMRI; participants instructed to imagine eating the food. Neural response.	18 AN (61.1% R, 38.9% BP) 8 BN 24 HC	26.0 (6.8) 25.0 (7.1) 26.0 (9.5)	U	Yes	Yes	Brain activation: AN > BN (parietal lobe, cingulate cortex); AN < BN (superior temporal gyrus, caudate, supplementary motor area); AN > HC (visual cortex); AN < HC (cerebellem)	7

Table 2 Food-image tasks in the study of anorexia nervosa *(Continued)*

Domain	Subdomain	Study	Paradigm & Outcome Variable(s)	Participants (AN subtype)	Mean age (SD)	Mean BMI (SD)	Non-food images presented	Meal-Task Interval Standardised	Summary of Findings	Quality Index Score
		Sanders et al., 2015 [49]		15 AN (60% R, 40% BP)	25.6 (5)	14.5 (1.7)	Yes	Yes	Brain activation: AN < HC (superior frontal gyrus); AN > HC (middle frontal gyrus)	6
				15 AN-rec (66.6% R, 33.3% BP)	24.3 (5)	21.1 (1.9)				
				15 HC	25.8 (5)	21.5 (2.3)				
		Scaife et al., 2016 [43]	Participants shown images of food while neural activity measured with fMRI; participants instructed to think about how much they want to eat the food at the present moment. Neural response.	12 AN (R)	29.4 (6)	15.4 (1.9)	No	Yes	Brain activation: AN < HC (postcentral gyrus, precuneus, superior parietal lobule); AN < HC (frontal pole, dorsolateral prefrontal cortex, supramarginal gyrus for low calorie food); AN > HC (frontal pole for high calorie food)	6
				14 AN-rec (R)	27 (6.5)	20.9 (1.6)				
				16 HC	24.3 (5.7)	21.2 (2)				
	Active choice	Foerde et al., 2015 [61]	Participants select between food items varying in fat content in a binary forced choice task; fMRI measures neural activity. Neural activity during food choice.	21 AN (47.6% R, 52.4% BP)	26.1 (6.5)	21.5 (1.9)	No	Yes	Brain activation: AN > HC (dorsal striatum)	6
				21 HC	22.7 (3.1)	15.7 (2.0)				

AN individuals with AN, *AN-rec* individuals recovered from AN, *AN-WR* weight recovered individuals with AN, *BP* binge-purge subtype, *EDNOS* Individuals with eating disorder not otherwise specified, *HC* healthy controls, *IBW* ideal body weight, *R* restricting subtype, *U* unreported

and non-food images (Table 2, Visual probe detection). Faster responses on food trials indicate greater attention to food stimuli (attentional bias towards food). Three studies found no evidence of differences between AN and HC in attentional bias towards food [23–25]. A fourth study found that when fasted, individuals with AN, compared with HC, displayed an attentional bias away from food stimuli [26]. Two studies of the effect of oxytocin [23, 26] and three of mealtime support interventions [27–29] explored whether attentional bias towards food mediated intervention effects on intake. Changes in attentional bias tended not to correspond with changes in food intake in AN, although small sample sizes limited detection of intervention effects in these studies.

Eye-tracking devices measure attention by monitoring the frequency and duration of gaze fixations at particular positions on a computer screen (Table 2, Eye-tracking [30, 31]). One study found AN and HC did not differ in initial fixation points when high-calorie food and household items were presented concurrently, but the duration of fixations on food-images was shorter for individuals with AN [32]. When single images of food were presented, eye-gaze measurements did not differ between AN and HC [33].

There do not appear to be robust differences in attention bias to food between AN and HC, though some studies of distraction suggest group differences. Interestingly, attention may be differentially associated with intake in the two populations.

Reward

Food is generally considered a primary reward [34], and therefore is useful for understanding how reward is assessed and processed. One approach to studying reward distinguishes separate components of liking and wanting [35, 36]. 'Liking' refers to the hedonic impact, or pleasure; 'wanting' refers to the motivation to consume a reward [37]. The rewarding properties of a food influence consumption among HC [38, 39]. This observation has resulted in the hypothesis that individuals with AN, who consume less food, do not experience food as rewarding [40], or that 'liking' or 'wanting' do not drive food consumption in the expected ways [41, 42]. To examine this, tasks have probed the reward value and processing of food by presenting images of food.

In the most straightforward behavioural paradigms, participants rate how pleasurable they find images of food, and/or how much they want to eat those foods (Table 2, Explicit rating task). Across multiple studies (behavioural and neuroimaging), individuals with AN report liking and wanting food less than HC, especially high-calorie foods [33, 41, 43–53]. A variation of this task asks individuals to rate neutral images presented immediately after food stimuli (Table 2, Implicit rating task). Neutral images that follow food images are rated as less pleasant by AN than HC [51].

In forced-choice tasks, speed of response provides a behavioural index of motivation, separate from subjective ratings (Table 2, Binary forced choice task). For example, an individual may report not wanting to eat certain foods, but then respond rapidly to these foods during a task. This rapid response is thought to indicate an implicit 'wanting' that differs from the explicit rating. Across two studies, individuals with AN were slower than HC when selecting between two high-calorie foods [41, 43], and explicit wanting scores were also lower. In one study (but not the other) individuals with AN were faster than HC to select low-calorie foods [41]; this indication of greater implicit wanting was not reflected in the explicit response.

In approach-avoidance paradigms, participants are presented with images of food and neutral items, and instructed to either move toward (approach) or away from (avoid) the image, according to image orientation (i.e., portrait vs landscape). Approach-avoidance paradigms are based on the assumption that it is easier to approach than to avoid stimuli with motivational value. Error rates and response latencies on approach trials are subtracted from avoidance trials to calculate bias (positive values reflect an approach bias). Scores in the neutral condition are subtracted from the food condition, to calculate food-specific approach/avoidance bias. One study found that individuals with AN made fewer errors than HC on avoidance food trials, resulting in a reduced approach bias to food stimuli [54]. Another study found smaller differences in response times on food approach versus avoidance trials among individuals with AN, also yielding a reduced approach bias in AN [55]. Adolescents with AN displayed an approach bias toward low-calorie, but not high-calorie, food stimuli before treatment [56]. After treatment, an approach bias was present for both types of food. These results are difficult to interpret in the absence of a HC group; one optimistic interpretation is that 'wanting' for high-calorie food increased with treatment.

The collection of findings from reward processing tasks suggest decreased value or reward of high-calorie food among individuals with AN, with mixed findings for low-calorie stimuli.

Perception

Individuals with AN often over-report caloric intake, despite under-consumption of food, raising a question about whether patients have a perceptual deficit. Some tasks test this idea by assessing perception of images of food and portion sizes (Table 2; Perceptual tasks).

In one task, individuals adjust the size of images of food and neutral items presented on screen until these are perceived to match the size of actual items. Individuals with AN over-estimated food sizes relative to HC, while estimates of neutral object size were similar between groups [57]. When presented with portions of food, individuals with AN overestimated the size of smaller (but not larger) portions [58]. Individuals with AN, but not HC, reported meal size to be larger when imagining they would eat the meal (intent to eat condition) compared to considering meal size "in general" (general condition).

These studies identified differences in assessments of portion size between AN and HC, with no overall perceptual deficits.

Decision-Making

The only food-image decision-making task administered in AN measures food-choice, or, how individuals make decisions about what to eat [59, 60]. In this task, participants rate a series of images of food for both healthiness and tastiness. One item that was rated neutral for both healthiness and tastiness is selected to be a "reference item" and participants then choose between the reference item and each of the other foods (Table 2, Decision-making). In studies of AN, the main outcome is the proportion of trials in which the individual chooses a high-fat item over the reference item. Two studies have demonstrated that this task captures the decreased selection of high-fat foods by individuals with AN, and task validity was additionally demonstrated by showing that proportion of high-fat choices correlated with actual caloric intake [60, 61]. This task can be used to examine processes contributing to maladaptive dietary restriction in AN.

Summary

Quality Index scores were most commonly affected by methods of recruitment, where the checklist is very conservative. The checklist requires studies to report enrolment either of the entire population or of consecutive patients, and a description of the source of recruitment for healthy individuals. The studies we included often did not meet these criteria for reporting, but nonetheless generally enrolled reasonable samples of individuals with AN. Some studies that did include large sample sizes also included individuals who did not meet full criteria for AN, which may limit the inferences that can be drawn [18, 24, 56]. Only one study included a power calculation [26]. Often sample sizes were small (e.g. [19, 52, 53, 62]). These factors were considered in the summary of findings.

Neuropsychological studies have captured differences in the cognitive appraisal of food in AN, and these findings have informed theoretical models of AN. Specifically, findings from reward processing tasks support the hypothesis that abnormalities in neural reward systems underlie the development and maintenance of AN [7, 63]. Differences in attention towards food between AN and HC have not been consistent; whether attention relates to eating in AN is worthy of further investigation. Decision-making (food-choice) paradigms capture the characteristic eating behaviour of individuals with AN. These paradigms, if studied in connection with actual food intake, may yield insights into mechanisms of AN.

Neurophysiology

Physiological changes can index attitudes that are outside of conscious awareness [64]. Interest in measuring physiological responses to food in AN stems from clinical observations suggesting that individuals with AN may have difficulty describing symptoms and emotions.

Attention

Event related potentials (ERPs) are fluctuations in the brain's electrical activity, or electrical potentials, that are measured via scalp electrode electroencephalography (EEG). EEG has high temporal resolution, allowing for separation of ERPs into different components [65]. An ERP recording during stimulus presentation contains distinct components of early orienting and sustained attention [66]. Three studies measured ERPs during presentation of food images (Table 2, Event-related po tential). Two studies demonstrated that when food stimuli (but not neutral stimuli) were presented, individuals with AN initially display heightened ERP amplitudes compared to HC [67, 68]. At later stages of stimulus presentation, heightened ERP amplitudes in response to low-calorie foods in AN has been reported [68], although another study found no group difference in response to food versus non-food stimuli [69]. A related technique, magnetoencephalography (MEG), measures the electromagnetic field generated by the electrical activity of neurons, indexing brain activity also with high temporal resolution [70]. The one study using this technique reported heightened early activity in response to food stimuli in individuals with AN relative to HC [33].

Reward

Electromyography (EMG) tasks involve the recording of facial muscle contractions in response to images of food (Table 2, Electromyography). The amplitude of zygomatic (smiling) and corrugator (frowning) muscles are positively and negatively associated with pleasantness evaluations, respectively. When food images were presented following emotional primes (faces displaying happy, fear, disgust and neutral expressions) zygomatic responses to food images were decreased in individuals with AN, relative to HC [71]. A second study that included neutral stimuli found reduced zygomatic activity in AN versus HC for both types of images [72]. There was some indication of greater corrugator activity specifically in response to food stimuli in AN in both studies, but this varied with state (fasted or sated) and emotional priming. These studies also measured skin conductance and heart-rate changes; differences specific to food stimuli were not observed. The only EMG study of the levator labii muscle, associated with disgust, found activity increased among AN versus HC when participants viewed cues associated with chocolate [73]. This study also found increased zygomatic activity among AN in response to cues predicting the absence of chocolate. EMG has probed the startle eye-blink response to food, by measuring contraction of the orbicularis muscle that indexes aversion. Two studies found no startle-eye blink differences between AN and HC in response to food stimuli [74, 75]. Another reported that individuals with AN had difficulties reducing their startle eye-blink responses towards food stimuli, as well as negative emotional stimuli, though there was no comparison group [76].

Summary

Quality Index scores were affected by the failure to fully report method of recruitment or failure to include exact p-values (e.g. [73]). Only one study was limited by the lack of a comparison group [76]; some studies had the added strength of comparing acutely ill patients with recovered individuals in addition to healthy individuals [33, 75]. A selection of studies had the added rigor of either standardizing or controlling for states of feeding/hunger [33, 69, 71, 72, 74, 75].

Neurophysiological approaches are less developed than neuropsychological, and may not have reached their full potential. ERP and MEG evidence suggest greater initial attention to food among individuals with AN, though sustained attention findings are inconsistent. EMG findings suggest a reduction in hedonic response to food. These physiological assessments provide another angle to examine neural mechanisms underlying responses to food.

Neuroimaging (Functional Magnetic Resonance Imaging, fMRI)

Neural correlates of illness have been examined using fMRI. One approach elicits psychiatric symptoms by presenting disorder-relevant stimuli, and measures associated neural activity (symptom provocation). Another method administers a task with known neural correlates to probe the functioning of the relevant brain system (cognitive activation probe; [77]). Food-image paradigms have been used to develop and test models of the neuropathology underlying AN.

Passive Viewing of Food

In passive viewing studies participants are asked to observe food stimuli during fMRI scanning (symptom provocation; Table 2, Passive viewing). Three studies reported altered amygdala activity among individuals with AN compared with HC [44, 45, 78], and three studies reported altered insula activation [45, 47, 78], however the direction of differences was not consistent between studies. Two studies reported alterations within visual processing areas in AN when high-calorie food was viewed, although exact loci and direction of difference was inconsistent [48, 79]. One study did not find differences in neural activity between AN and HC, but did report that neural activity during food-image viewing was differentially associated with stomach sensation ratings measured outside of the scanner in AN vs HC [80]. Collectively passive viewing studies have produced a diverse set of findings that are difficult to interpret.

Directed Food Tasks

To constrain the psychological experience when viewing food images (and in turn constrain the interpretation of findings), participants are given an instruction for how to internally process the images (symptom provocation, Table 2, Directed food tasks). When participants were asked to imagine eating presented foods, one study reported increased middle frontal gyrus activation in AN relative to HC [49], and another reported increased dorsolateral prefrontal cortex activity in AN [81]. When participants were asked to think about how hungry the presented foods made them, individuals with AN displayed greater ventromedial prefrontal cortex activity compared with HC [50]. When participants were instructed to think about how much they wished to eat each food item, increased frontal pole activity for high calorie foods was reported in AN but not HC [43]. A common finding amongst instructed viewing studies was altered frontal cortex activation in AN versus HC, though specific regions differed.

Active Food Choice

The food choice task (described in Neuropsychology) [60, 61] provides a cognitive activation probe, in that it assesses active decision-making and the neural correlates in HC are known [59]. FMRI data showed that food choice was associated with dorsal striatum activity among individuals with AN, but not HC [61]. The dorsal striatum and dorsolateral prefrontal cortex were functionally correlated, and this connectivity was related to intake among individuals with AN. By linking the task with actual eating behaviour, this study provides compelling data that dorsal frontostriatal circuit activity is associated with the maladaptive food choices observed in AN.

Summary

Quality Index scores were again affected by recruitment methods or descriptions (e.g. [79, 80, 82]). The majority of the studies involved very small numbers of participants, by current standards for fMRI investigations. Conclusions may be more robust for investigations with sample sizes greater than 20 per group (e.g. [61, 80, 83]). Some studies have the additional methodological strength of standardizing time since meals [43, 45, 47–50, 61, 79, 81, 84, 85], and of including non-food stimulus comparisons [44, 45, 47–50, 79–85].

Neuroimaging studies involving passive viewing of food have not identified consistent group differences. Adding an instruction for viewing has identified differences in frontal regions, in varying locations. Neural regions have multiple functions; various different processes may be captured during the viewing of food stimuli (even with instructions), making it difficult to draw inferences about mechanisms of illness from these paradigms. The only approach that linked neural activity with eating behaviour identified dorsal frontostriatal circuit engagement in AN. This is a promising finding that, if replicated, can open new avenues for research [86].

Discussion

Tasks using images of food have been administered in 50 different studies of AN, using neuropsychological, neurophysiological, and neuroimaging techniques. This systematic review primarily assessed the utility of the experimental approaches. Nonetheless, some conclusions can be drawn from the data. First, while attention is related to intake among healthy individuals [17], data from four studies suggest that attention and eating behaviour are dissociated among individuals with AN [23, 25–27]. While a small collection of neurophysiological evidence suggests greater attentional orienting towards food stimuli in AN as compared to HC, findings from neuropsychological studies of attention are inconsistent. Second, measures of liking, value, and choice from neuropsychological and neurophysiological studies converge to indicate that individuals with AN have a decreased preference for high-fat/calorie foods. Third, while it is one study, the only data that linked maladaptive eating with neuroimaging indicated that this behaviour is associated with dorsal frontostriatal activity [61] .

The paradigms and approaches that have been used to date have some notable strengths, as well as important weaknesses. The strengths of the neuropsychological tasks are that they have probed constructs of interest, and some have well characterized underlying neural mechanisms. For example, wanting and liking tasks have been associated with mesolimbic activity among HC, suggesting they probe reward systems [87, 88]. The strengths of the neurophysiological measures include the objectivity of the assessment, as well as temporal resolution that offers a granular study of cognitive processes (i.e., assessing components of broad cognitive processes) [65, 89]. Neuroimaging methods do not have the same temporal resolution, but do have spatial resolution that enables identification of relevant brain regions [90]. Development of paradigms within these fields may allow the parsing of distinct neurocognitive processes and circuits, for an understanding of their role in AN.

The majority of studies involved small sample sizes and specific populations that limit generalizability. The studies ranged in quality, as assessed by the checklist. While this index is the most appropriate available, it is not specifically designed for cognitive neuroscience studies and so the index score does not address the specificity of the data collected. For example, neuropsychological tasks engage multiple neurocognitive domains, even when one variable is identified as the primary outcome. Techniques like EMG and EEG have limited spatial resolution, making neurologic interpretation difficult [65, 91]. FMRI data also captures multiple processes - particularly when responses are not constrained. It is a limitation of this systematic review that the assessment of each paradigm may be influenced by the quality of the study.

The major limitation across paradigms has been the absence of information about the relationship between task variables and eating behaviour among individuals with AN. One interesting dilemma in this research is how best to utilize cognitive neuroscience when the behaviour of interest differs between groups. That is, for many of these tasks, the association between task variables and eating behaviour has been established in HC, but this relationship is not present in AN. For example, 'liking' and 'wanting' are associated with actual eating among individuals without an eating disorder [87, 88], and attention is associated with food intake among HC [17]. Yet, the association between attention and intake is not so clear in AN, as shown in the studies reviewed here. On the one hand, it is interesting and potentially important to learn that these processes are dissociated in AN. On the other hand, interpreting the finding requires additional information about the relationship between attention and the maladaptive eating behaviour characteristic of AN.

Approaches used to study eating behaviour in populations of individuals without an eating disorder may offer new ideas that can enhance the utility of existing tasks in AN. By studying the effects of experimental manipulations on food choice, causal influences on eating behaviour have been identified in healthy individuals. For example, the role of attention to particular characteristics of food was assessed by asking participants to focus specifically on one value (tastiness or healthiness) of presented foods when making choices. Receiving the instruction to focus on healthiness increased the influence of healthiness on decisions. FMRI data showed that the change in preference was associated with greater functional connectivity between the dorsolateral and ventromedial prefrontal cortices [92]. This cognitive manipulation may be useful in understanding decision-making processes in AN, again highlighting the utility of food choice paradigms.

In motor approach training, participants learn to press a button in response to particular food images presented on-screen. The comparison of food value ratings made before and after the training demonstrated that the approach training increased the reward value of the associated foods and increased choice of these foods [93]. On the flip side, with motor inhibition training individuals learn to inhibit or withhold automatic approach responses to food stimuli. Among overweight and obese participants, this resulted in decreased liking of high-calorie foods, reduced neural activity in reward-signalling regions in response to high-calorie foods, and reduced caloric intake [94 97]. Motor approach or inhibition may be useful in AN, as well, where changing value assessment and choice of foods may be therapeutic [98].

Three ideas emerge from this review that may advance research. One, the link between experimental measurements and the eating behaviour characteristic of AN is critical to establishing mechanisms of illness. Two, introducing experimental manipulations may allow for inferences about causality. Neuroimaging in conjunction with manipulations may further elucidate the neural underpinnings of maladaptive eating. Three, perhaps most importantly, clear hypotheses should guide the selection of tasks and approaches, so that research questions may be fully addressed, and in a reliable and valid manner. Much of the food-image research to date has been descriptive; it is time to begin testing the mechanistic hypotheses that have emerged.

Abbreviations

AN: Anorexia nervosa; EEG: Electroencephalography; EMG: Electromyography; ERP: Event-related potential; FMRI: Functional magnetic resonance imaging; MEG: Magnetoencephalography; HC: Healthy controls

Acknowledgements

The authors would like to thank Anne Haase and Jeff Brunstrom for reviewing the article prior to journal submission.

Funding

E.C.L. is supported by an Economic and Social Research Council [ESRC] Studentship award. J.E.S. is supported by the New York State Office of Mental Health.

Authors' contributions

E.C.L.: literature review; interpretation of existing research findings; article drafting. J.E.S.: conception and design of the review; interpretation of existing research findings; critical revision of the article. Both authors read and approved the final manuscript.

Competing interests

J.E.S. receives royalties from Up To Date.

Author details

[1]Centre for Exercise, Nutrition and Health Sciences, School for Policy Studies, University of Bristol, Bristol, UK. [2]Department of Psychiatry, Columbia University Irving Medical Center, New York, NY, USA. [3]New York State Psychiatric Institute, New York, NY, USA.

References

1. Walsh BT. The importance of eating behavior in eating disorders. Physiol Behav. 2011;104(4):525–9.
2. Schebendach JE, Mayer LE, Devlin MJ, Attia E, Contento IR, Wolf RL, Walsh BT. Dietary energy density and diet variety as predictors of outcome in anorexia nervosa. Am J Clin Nutr. 2008;87(4):810–6.
3. Schebendach J, Mayer LE, Devlin MJ, Attia E, Walsh BT. Dietary energy density and diet variety as risk factors for relapse in anorexia nervosa: a replication. Int J Eat Disord. 2012;45(1):79–84.
4. Lang K, Roberts M, Harrison A, Lopez C, Goddard E, Khondoker M, et al. Central Coherence in Eating Disorders: A Synthesis of Studies Using the Rey Osterrieth Complex Figure Test. PLOS ONE. 2016;11(11):e0165467.
5. Roberts ME, Tchanturia K, Stahl D, Southgate L, Treasure J. A systematic review and meta-analysis of set-shifting ability in eating disorders. 2007; 37(8):1075-1084.
6. Park RJ, Godier LR, Cowdrey FA. Hungry for reward: How can neuroscience inform the development of treatment for Anorexia Nervosa? Behav Res Ther. 2014;62:47–59.
7. Stroop JR. Studies of interference in serial verbal reactions. Journal of experimental psychology. 1935;18(6):643.
8. Aspen V, Darcy AM, Lock J. A review of attention biases in women with eating disorders. Cognit Emot. 2013;27(5):820–38.
9. Ferro MA, Speechley KN. Depressive symptoms among mothers of children with epilepsy: a review of prevalence, associated factors, and impact on children. Epilepsia. 2009;50(11):2344–54.
10. Downs SH, Black N. The feasibility of creating a checklist for the assessment of the methodological quality both of randomised and non-randomised studies of health care interventions. J Epidemiol Community Health. 1998;52(6):377.
11. Donnelly B, Touyz S, Hay P, Burton A, Russell J, Caterson I. Neuroimaging in bulimia nervosa and binge eating disorder: a systematic review. J Eat Disord. 2018;6:3.
12. Driver J. A selective review of selective attention research from the past century. Br J Psychol. 2001;92(Pt 1):53–78.
13. Cisler JM, Koster EH. Mechanisms of attentional biases towards threat in anxiety disorders: An integrative review. Clin Psychol Rev. 2010;30(2):203–16.
14. Van Bockstaele B, Verschuere B, Tibboel H, De Houwer J, Crombez G, Koster EH. A review of current evidence for the causal impact of attentional bias on fear and anxiety. Psychol Bull. 2014;140(3):682–721.
15. Price RB, Wallace M, Kuckertz JM, Amir N, Graur S, Cummings L, et al. Pooled patient-level meta-analysis of children and adults completing a

computer-based anxiety intervention targeting attentional bias. Clin Psychol Rev. 2016;50:37–49.
16. Cowdrey FA, Park RJ, Harmer CJ, McCabe C. Increased neural processing of rewarding and aversive food stimuli in recovered anorexia nervosa. Biol Psychiatry. 2011;70(8):736–43.
17. Werthmann J, Jansen A, Roefs A. Worry or craving? A selective review of evidence for food-related attention biases in obese individuals, eating-disorder patients, restrained eaters and healthy samples. Proc Nutr Soc. 2015;74(2):99–114.
18. Neimeijer RAM, Roefs A, de Jong PJ. Heightened Attentional Capture by Visual Food Stimuli in Anorexia Nervosa. J Abnorm Psychol. 2017;126(6):805–811.
19. Dickson H, Brooks S, Uher R, Tchanturia K, Treasure J, Campbell IC. The inability to ignore: Distractibility in women with restricting anorexia nervosa. Psychol Med. 2008;38(12):1741–8.
20. Brooks SJ, O'Daly OG, Uher R, Schiöth HB, Treasure J, Campbell IC. Subliminal food images compromise superior working memory performance in women with restricting anorexia nervosa. Conscious Cogn. 2012;21(2):751–63.
21. MacLeod C, Mathews A, Tata P. Attentional bias in emotional disorders. J Abnorm Psychol. 1986;95(1):15–20.
22. Posner MI, Snyder CR, Davidson BJ. Attention and the detection of signals. J Exp Psychol. 1980;109(2):160–74.
23. Kim YR, Kim CH, Cardi V, Eom JS, Seong Y, Treasure J. Intranasal oxytocin attenuates attentional bias for eating and fat shape stimuli in patients with anorexia nervosa. Psychoneuroendocrinology. 2014;44:133–42.
24. Veenstra EM, de Jong PJ. Attentional bias in restrictive eating disorders. Stronger attentional avoidance of high-fat food compared to healthy controls? Appetite. 2012;58(1):133–40.
25. Cardi V, Esposito M, Clarke A, Schifano S, Treasure J. The impact of induced positive mood on symptomatic behaviour in eating disorders. An experimental, AB/BA crossover design testing a multimodal presentation during a test-meal. Appetite. 2015;87:192–8.
26. Leppanen J, Cardi V, Ng KW, Paloyelis Y, Stein D, Tchanturia K, Treasure J. The effects of intranasal oxytocin on smoothie intake, cortisol and attentional bias in anorexia nervosa. Psychoneuroendocrinology. 2017;79:167–74.
27. Cardi V, Lounes N, Kan C, Treasure J. Meal support using mobile technology in Anorexia Nervosa. Contextual differences between inpatient and outpatient settings. Appetite. 2013;60(1):33–9.
28. Cardi V, Kan C, Roncero M, Harrison A, Lounes N, Tchanturia K, et al. Mealtime Support in Anorexia Nervosa: A Within-Subject Comparison Study of a Novel Vodcast Intervention. Psychotherapy and Psychosomatics. 2012; 81(1):54–5.
29. Cardi V, Leppanen J, Treasure J. The effects of negative and positive mood induction on eating behaviour: A meta-analysis of laboratory studies in the healthy population and eating and weight disorders. Neurosci Biobehav Rev. 2015;57:299–309.
30. Duc AH, Bays P, Husain M. Eye movements as a probe of attention. Prog Brain Res. 2008;171:403–11.
31. Jiang MY, Vartanian LR. A review of existing measures of attentional biases in body image and eating disorders research. Australian Journal of Psychology. 2018;70(1):3–17.
32. Giel KE, Friederich HC, Teufel M, Hautzinger M, Enck P, Zipfel S. Attentional processing of food pictures in individuals with anorexia nervosa--an eye-tracking study. Biol Psychiatry. 2011;69(7):661–7.
33. Godier LR, Scaife JC, Braeutigam S, Park RJ. Enhanced Early Neuronal Processing of Food Pictures in Anorexia Nervosa: A Magnetoencephalography Study. Psychiatry J. 2016;2016:1795901.
34. Skinner BF. Science and human behavior: Simon and Schuster; 1953.
35. Berridge KC. Food reward: Brain substrates of wanting and liking. Neurosci Biobehav Rev. 1996;20(1):1–25.
36. Robinson TE, Berridge KC. The neural basis of drug craving: an incentive-sensitization theory of addiction. Brain Res Brain Res Rev. 1993;18(3):247–91.
37. Berridge KC, Robinson TE, Aldridge JW. Dissecting components of reward: 'liking', 'wanting', and learning. Curr Opin Pharmacol. 2009;9(1):65–73.
38. Rogers PJ, Hardman CA. Food reward. What it is and how to measure it. Appetite. 2015;90:1–15.
39. De Graaf C, De Jong LS, Lambers AC. Palatability Affects Satiation But Not Satiety. Physiol Behav. 1999;66(4):681–8.
40. Davis C, Woodside DB. Sensitivity to the rewarding effects of food and exercise in the eating disorders. Compr Psychiatry. 2002;43(3):189–94.
41. Cowdrey FA, Finlayson G, Park RJ. Liking compared with wanting for high- and low-calorie foods in anorexia nervosa: aberrant food reward even after weight restoration. Am J Clin Nutr. 2013;97(3):463–70.
42. Berridge KC. 'Liking' and 'wanting' food rewards: brain substrates and roles in eating disorders. Physiol Behav. 2009;97(5):537–50.
43. Scaife JC, Godier LR, Reinecke A, Harmer CJ, Park RJ. Differential activation of the frontal pole to high vs low calorie foods: The neural basis of food preference in Anorexia Nervosa? Psychiatry Res. 2016;258: 44–53.
44. Joos AA, Saum B, van Elst LT, Perlov E, Glauche V, Hartmann A, et al. Amygdala hyperreactivity in restrictive anorexia nervosa. Psychiatry Res. 2011;191(3):189–95.
45. Holsen LM, Lawson EA, Blum J, Ko E, Makris N, Fazeli PK, et al. Food motivation circuitry hypoactivation related to hedonic and nonhedonic aspects of hunger and satiety in women with active anorexia nervosa and weight-restored women with anorexia nervosa. J Psychiatry Neurosci. 2012;37(5):322–32.
46. Jiang T, Soussignan R, Rigaud D, Schaal B. Pleasure for visual and olfactory stimuli evoking energy-dense foods is decreased in anorexia nervosa. Psychiatry Res. 2010;180(1):42–7.
47. Gizewski ER, Rosenberger C, de Greiff A, Moll A, Senf W, Wanke I, et al. Influence of satiety and subjective valence rating on cerebral activation patterns in response to visual stimulation with high-calorie stimuli among restrictive anorectic and control women. Neuropsychobiology. 2010;62(3):182–92.
48. Santel S, Baving L, Krauel K, Münte TF, Rotte M. Hunger and satiety in anorexia nervosa: fMRI during cognitive processing of food pictures. Brain Res. 2006;1114(1):138–48.
49. Sanders N, Smeets PA, van Elburg AA, Danner UN, van Meer F, Hoek HW, Adan RA. Altered food-cue processing in chronically ill and recovered women with anorexia nervosa. Front Behav Neurosci. 2015;9:46.
50. Uher R, Murphy T, Brammer MJ, Dalgleish T, Phillips ML, Ng VW, et al. Medial prefrontal cortex activity associated with symptom provocation in eating disorders. Am J Psychiatry. 2004;161(7):1238–46.
51. Spring VL, Bulik CM. Implicit and explicit affect toward food and weight stimuli in anorexia nervosa. Eat Behav. 2014;15(1):91–4.
52. Krizbai T, Csenki L, Paszthy B, Szabo P. Emotional and autobiographical memory deficits in Anorexia Nervosa. J Evid Based Psychotherapies. 2016; 16(2):191–204.
53. Bossert S, Laessle RG, Meiller C, Junker M, Ellgring H, Pirke KM. Visual palatability of food in patients with eating disorders and dieting women. Behav Res Ther. 1991;29(4):337–41.
54. Veenstra EM, de Jong PJ. Reduced automatic motivational orientation towards food in restricting anorexia nervosa. J Abnorm Psychol. 2011; 120(3):708–18.
55. Paslakis G, Kühn S, Schaubschläger A, Schieber K, Röder K, Rauh E, Erim Y. Explicit and implicit approach vs. avoidance tendencies towards high vs. low calorie food cues in patients with anorexia nervosa and healthy controls. Appetite. 2016;107:171–9.
56. Neimeijer RA, de Jong PJ, Roefs A. Automatic approach/avoidance tendencies towards food and the course of anorexia nervosa. Appetite. 2015;91:28–34.
57. Yellowlees PM, Roe M, Walker MK, Ben-Tovim DI. Abnormal perception of food size in anorexia nervosa. Br Med J Clin Res Ed. 1988;296(6638): 1689–90.
58. Milos G, Kuenzli C, Soelch CM, Schumacher S, Moergeli H, Mueller-Pfeiffer C. How much should I eat? Estimation of meal portions in anorexia nervosa. Appetite. 2013;63:42–7.
59. Hare TA, Camerer CF, Rangel A. Self-control in decision-making involves modulation of the vmPFC valuation system. Science. 2009;324(5927):646–8.
60. Steinglass J, Foerde K, Kostro K, Shohamy D, Timothy Walsh B. Restrictive Food Intake As A Choice – A Paradigm for Study. Int J Eat Disord. 2015;48(1):59–66.
61. Foerde K, Steinglass JE, Shohamy D, Walsh BT. Neural mechanisms supporting maladaptive food choices in anorexia nervosa. Nat Neurosci. 2015;18(11):1571–3.
62. Nikendei C, Weisbrod M, Schild S, Bender S, Walther S, Herzog W, et al. Anorexia nervosa: Selective processing of food-related word and pictorial stimuli in recognition and free recall tests. Int J Eat Disord. 2008;41(5):439–47.
63. Kaye WH, Fudge JL, Paulus M. New insights into symptoms and neurocircuit function of anorexia nervosa. Nat Rev Neurosci. 2009;10(8):573–84.

64. Pool E, Sennwald V, Delplanque S, Brosch T, Sander D. Measuring wanting and liking from animals to humans: A systematic review. Neurosci Biobehav Rev. 2016;63:124–42.
65. Luck SJ. An introduction to the event-related potential technique. Cambridge: MIT press; 2014.
66. Hillyard SA, Anllo-Vento L. Event-related brain potentials in the study of visual selective attention. Proc Natl Acad Sci. 1998;95(3):781.
67. Blechert J, Feige B, Joos A, Zeeck A, Tuschen-Caffier B. Electrocortical processing of food and emotional pictures in anorexia nervosa and bulimia nervosa. Psychosom Med. 2011;73(5):415–21.
68. Novosel A, Lackner N, Unterrainer HF, Dunitz-Scheer M, Scheer PJ, Wallner-Liebmann SJ, Neuper C. Motivational processing of food cues in anorexia nervosa: a pilot study. Eat Weight Disord. 2014;19(2):169–75.
69. Nikendei C, Friederich HC, Weisbrod M, Walther S, Sharma A, Herzog W, et al. Event-related potentials during recognition of semantic and pictorial food stimuli in patients with anorexia nervosa and healthy controls with varying internal states of hunger. Psychosom Med. 2012;74(2):136–45.
70. Baillet S. Magnetoencephalography for brain electrophysiology and imaging. Nat Neurosci. 2017;20(3):327–39.
71. Soussignan R, Jiang T, Rigaud D, Royet JP, Schaal B. Subliminal fear priming potentiates negative facial reactions to food pictures in women with anorexia nervosa. Psychol Med. 2010;40(3):503–14.
72. Soussignan R, Schaal B, Rigaud D, Royet JP, Jiang T. Hedonic reactivity to visual and olfactory cues: rapid facial electromyographic reactions are altered in anorexia nervosa. Biol Psychol. 2011;86(3):265–72.
73. Hildebrandt T, Grotzinger A, Reddan M, Greif R, Levy I, Goodman W, Schiller D. Testing the disgust conditioning theory of food-avoidance in adolescents with recent onset anorexia nervosa. Behav Res Ther. 2015;71:131–8.
74. Friederich HC, Kumari V, Uher R, Riga M, Schmidt U, Campbell IC, et al. Differential motivational responses to food and pleasurable cues in anorexia and bulimia nervosa: a startle reflex paradigm. Psychol Med. 2006;36(9):1327–35.
75. Erdur L, Weber C, Zimmermann-Viehoff F, Rose M, Deter HC. Affective Responses in Different Stages of Anorexia Nervosa: Results from a Startle-reflex Paradigm. Eur Eat Disord Rev. 2017;25(2):114–22.
76. Racine SE, Forbush KT, Wildes JE, Hagan KE, Pollack LO, May C. Voluntary emotion regulation in anorexia nervosa: A preliminary emotion-modulated startle investigation. J Psychiatr Res. 2016;77:1–7.
77. Breiter HC, Rauch SL. Functional MRI and the study of OCD: from symptom provocation to cognitive-behavioral probes of cortico-striatal systems and the amygdala. Neuroimage. 1996;4(3 Pt 3):S127–38.
78. Ellison Z, Foong J, Howard R, Bullmore E, Williams S, Treasure J. Functional anatomy of calorie fear in anorexia nervosa. Lancet. 1998;352:1192.
79. Rothemund Y, Buchwald C, Georgiewa P, Bohner G, Bauknecht HC, Ballmaier M, et al. Compulsivity predicts fronto striatal activation in severely anorectic individuals. Neuroscience. 2011;197:242–50.
80. Kerr KL, Moseman SE, Avery JA, Bodurka J, Simmons WK. Influence of Visceral Interoceptive Experience on the Brain's Response to Food Images in Anorexia Nervosa. Psychosomatic medicine. 2017;79(7):777–84.
81. Brooks SJ, Owen GO, Uher R, Friederich HC, Giampietro V, Brammer M, Williams SC, Schiöth HB, Treasure J, Campbell IC. Differential neural responses to food images in women with bulimia versus anorexia nervosa. PLoS One. 2011;6(7):e22259.
82. Nagamitsu S, Yamashita F, Araki Y, Iizuka C, Ozono S, Komatsu H, et al. Characteristic prefrontal blood volume patterns when imaging body type, high-calorie food, and mother-child attachment in childhood anorexia nervosa: A near infrared spectroscopy study. Brain Dev. 2010;32(2):162–7.
83. Boehm I, King JA, Bernardoni F, Geisler D, Seidel M, Ritschel F, et al. Subliminal and supraliminal processing of reward-related stimuli in anorexia nervosa. Psychol Med. 2018;48(5):790–800.
84. Kim KR, Ku J, Lee J-H, Lee H, Jung Y-C. Functional and effective connectivity of anterior insula in anorexia nervosa and bulimia nervosa. Neurosci Lett. 2012;521(2):152–7.
85. Uher R, Brammer MJ, Murphy T, Campbell IC, Ng VW, Williams SCR, Treasure J. Recovery and Chronicity in Anorexia Nervosa: Brain Activity Associated with Differential Outcomes. Biol Psychiatry. 2003;54(9):934–42.
86. Uniacke B, Timothy Walsh B, Foerde K, Steinglass J. The Role of Habits in Anorexia Nervosa: Where We Are and Where to Go From Here? Curr Psychiatry Rep. 2018;20(8):61.
87. Jiang T, Soussignan R, Schaal B, Royet JP. Reward for food odors: an fMRI study of liking and wanting as a function of metabolic state and BMI. Soc Cogn Affect Neurosci. 2015;10(4):561–8.
88. Born JM, Lemmens SG, Martens MJ, Formisano E, Goebel R, Westerterp-Plantenga MS. Differences between liking and wanting signals in the human brain and relations with cognitive dietary restraint and body mass index. Am J Clin Nutr. 2011;94(2):392–403.
89. Cacioppo JT, Petty RE. Electromyograms as measures of extent and affectivity of information processing. Am Psychol. 1981;36(5):441–56.
90. Turner R, Jones T. Techniques for imaging neuroscience. Br Med Bull. 2003;65(1):3–20.
91. Hess U. facial eMG. Methods in social neuroscience. 2009:70–91.
92. Hare TA, Malmaud J, Rangel A. Focusing attention on the health aspects of foods changes value signals in vmPFC and improves dietary choice. J Neurosci. 2011;31(30):11077–87.
93. Schonberg T, Bakkour A, Hover AM, Mumford JA, Nagar L, Perez J, Poldrack RA. Changing value through cued approach: an automatic mechanism of behavior change. Nat Neurosci. 2014;17(4):625–30.
94. Turton R, Bruidegom K, Cardi V, Hirsch CR, Treasure J. Novel methods to help develop healthier eating habits for eating and weight disorders: A systematic review and meta-analysis. Neurosci Biobehav Rev. 2016;61:132–55.
95. Lawrence NS, O'Sullivan J, Parslow D, Javaid M, Adams RC, Chambers CD, et al. Training response inhibition to food is associated with weight loss and reduced energy intake. Appetite. 2015;95:17–28.
96. Stice E, Lawrence NS, Kemps E, Veling H. Training motor responses to food: A novel treatment for obesity targeting implicit processes. Clin Psychol Rev. 2016;49:16–27.
97. Veling H, Lawrence NS, Chen Z, van Koningsbruggen GM, Holland RW. What Is Trained During Food Go/No-Go Training? A Review Focusing on Mechanisms and a Research Agenda. Curr Addict Rep. 2017;4(1):35–41.
98. Bakkour A, Foerde K, Schonberg T, Shadlen M, Walsh BT, Steinglass J, Shohamy D, editors. Cognitive mechanisms of decision making in anorexia nervosa. Society for Biological Psychiatry Annual Meeting; 2018; New York.
99. Kissileff HR, Brunstrom JM, Tesser R, Bellace D, Berthod S, Thornton JC, Halmi K. Computerized measurement of anticipated anxiety from eating increasing portions of food in adolescents with and without anorexia nervosa: Pilot studies. Appetite. 2016;97:160–8.
100. Milos G, Baur V, Schumacher S, Kuenzli C, Schnyder U, Mueller-Pfeiffer C, Martin-Soelch C. How fat will it make me? Estimation of weight gain in anorexia nervosa. Appetite. 2017;114:368–73.

Permissions

All chapters in this book were first published in JED, by BioMed Central; hereby published with permission under the Creative Commons Attribution License or equivalent. Every chapter published in this book has been scrutinized by our experts. Their significance has been extensively debated. The topics covered herein carry significant findings which will fuel the growth of the discipline. They may even be implemented as practical applications or may be referred to as a beginning point for another development.

The contributors of this book come from diverse backgrounds, making this book a truly international effort. This book will bring forth new frontiers with its revolutionizing research information and detailed analysis of the nascent developments around the world.

We would like to thank all the contributing authors for lending their expertise to make the book truly unique. They have played a crucial role in the development of this book. Without their invaluable contributions this book wouldn't have been possible. They have made vital efforts to compile up to date information on the varied aspects of this subject to make this book a valuable addition to the collection of many professionals and students.

This book was conceptualized with the vision of imparting up-to-date information and advanced data in this field. To ensure the same, a matchless editorial board was set up. Every individual on the board went through rigorous rounds of assessment to prove their worth. After which they invested a large part of their time researching and compiling the most relevant data for our readers.

The editorial board has been involved in producing this book since its inception. They have spent rigorous hours researching and exploring the diverse topics which have resulted in the successful publishing of this book. They have passed on their knowledge of decades through this book. To expedite this challenging task, the publisher supported the team at every step. A small team of assistant editors was also appointed to further simplify the editing procedure and attain best results for the readers.

Apart from the editorial board, the designing team has also invested a significant amount of their time in understanding the subject and creating the most relevant covers. They scrutinized every image to scout for the most suitable representation of the subject and create an appropriate cover for the book.

The publishing team has been an ardent support to the editorial, designing and production team. Their endless efforts to recruit the best for this project, has resulted in the accomplishment of this book. They are a veteran in the field of academics and their pool of knowledge is as vast as their experience in printing. Their expertise and guidance has proved useful at every step. Their uncompromising quality standards have made this book an exceptional effort. Their encouragement from time to time has been an inspiration for everyone.

The publisher and the editorial board hope that this book will prove to be a valuable piece of knowledge for researchers, students, practitioners and scholars across the globe.

List of Contributors

Jakob Täljemark and Maria Råstam
Lund University, Medical Faculty, Department of Clinical Sciences Lund, Child and Adolescent Psychiatry, Baravägen 1, S-221 85 Lund, Sweden

Maria Råstam
Gillberg Neuropsychiatry Centre, University of Gothenburg, Gothenburg, Sweden

Paul Lichtenstein
Department of Medical Epidemiology and Biostatistics, Karolinska Institutet, Stockholm, Sweden

Henrik Anckarsäter
CELAM (Centre for Ethics, Law and Mental Health), Institute of Neuroscience and Physiology, University of Gothenburg, Gothenburg, Sweden

Nóra Kerekes
Department of Health Sciences, University West, Trollhättan, Sweden

Nina Dittmer, Ulrich Voderholzer, Mareike von der Mühlen, Michael Marwitz, Markus Fumi, Claudia Mönch, Katharina Alexandridis and Ulrich Cuntz
Schoen Clinic Roseneck, Am Roseneck 6, Prien am Chiemsee, Germany

Nina Dittmer
Department of Clinical Psychology and E-Mental-Health, Technische Universität Dresden, Dresden, Germany

Ulrich Voderholzer
Department of Psychiatry and Psychotherapy, University Hospital of Freiburg, Freiburg, Germany

Ulrich Cuntz
Paracelsus Medical University, Salzburg, Austria

Sandra Schlegl
Department of Psychiatry and Psychotherapy, University Hospital of Munich (LMU), Munich, Germany

Haylie Smith, Marisol Perez, Michael R. Sladek, Tara K. Ohrt and Amanda B. Bruening
Psychology Department Arizona State University, 950 South McAllister Avenue Room 237, Tempe, AZ 85287-1104, USA

Carolyn Black Becker
Department of Psychology, Trinity University, Center for the Sciences and Innovation room 253, One Trinity Place, San Antonio, TX 78212, USA

Keren Fink, Paul Rhodes and Stephen Touyz
Clinical Psychology Unit, the University of Sydney, Sydney, NSW 2006, Australia

Jane Miskovic-Wheatley, Andrew Wallis, Julian Baudinet and Sloane Madden
Department of Psychological Medicine, Department of Adolescent Medicine, Eating Disorder Service, The Children's Hospital at Westmead, Sydney, NSW 2145, Australia

S. Keane, M. Clarke, M. Murphy and S. MacHale
Department of Psychiatry, Beaumont Hospital, Beaumont Road, Dublin 9,
Ireland

D. McGrath and N. Farrelly
Trinity College Health Service, Dublin, Ireland.

D. Smith
Department of Endocrinology, Beaumont Hospital, Beaumont Road, Dublin 9, Ireland

Stefania Toselli and Federico Spiga
Universita degli Studi di Bologna, Bologna, Italy

Raghad N. Saleh, Razan A. Salameh and Heba H. Yhya
Department of Medicine, College of Medicine and Health Sciences, An-Najah National University, Nablus 44839, Palestine

Waleed M. Sweileh
Department of Physiology, Pharmacology, and Toxicology, College of Medicine and Health Sciences, An-Najah National University, Nablus 44839, Palestine

Camilla Lindvall Dahlgren, Line Wisting and Øyvind Rø
Regional Department for Eating Disorders, Division of Mental Health and Addiction, Oslo University Hospital, Ullevål HF, Postboks 4950 Nydalen, 0424 Oslo, Norway

Øyvind Rø
Institute of Clinical Medicine, University of Oslo, Blindern, 0318 Oslo, Norway

Wendy Spettigue
Department of Psychiatry, Children's Hospital of Eastern Ontario, University of Ottawa, 401 Smyth Road, Ottawa, ON K1H 8L1, Canada

Mark L. Norris
Division of Adolescent Health, Department of Pediatrics, Children's Hospital of Eastern Ontario, 401 Smyth Road, Ottawa, ON K1H 8L1, Canada

Wendy Spettigue, Mark L. Norris, Alexandre Santos and Nicole Obeid
Children's Hospital of Eastern Ontario Research Institute, 401 Smyth Road, Ottawa, ON K1H 5B2, Canada

Tingting Feng
University of Oslo, Oslo, Norway

Dawit Shawel Abebe
Norwegian Social Research (NOVA), Oslo and Akershus University College of Applied Sciences, Oslo, Norway

Felipe Q. da Luz, Jessica Swinbourne and Amanda Sainsbury
The University of Sydney, The Boden Institute of Obesity, Nutrition, Exercise and Eating Disorders, Sydney Medical School, Charles Perkins Centre, Camperdown, NSW 2006, Australia

Felipe Q. da Luz, Jessica Swinbourne, Amanda Sainsbury and Stephen Touyz
The University of Sydney, School of Psychology, Faculty of Science, Camperdown, NSW 2006, Australia

Felipe Q. da Luz
CAPES Foundation, Ministry of Education of Brazil, Brasília, DF 70040-020, Brazil

Marly Palavras and Angelica Claudino
Program of Orientation and Attention of Eating Disorders, Federal University of São Paulo, São Paulo, Brazil

Phillipa Hay
Centre for Health Research, School of Medicine, Western Sydney University, Locked Bag 1797, Penrith, NSW 2751, Australia

Priyanka Thapliyal and Phillipa Hay
Translational Health Research Institute (THRI), School of Medicine, Western Sydney University, Sydney, NSW, Australia

Janet Conti
School of Social Sciences and Psychology, Western Sydney University, Sydney, NSW, Australia

L. P. MacNeill, L. A. Best and L. L. Davis
Deparment of Psychology, University of New Brunswick, Saint John, 100 Tucker Park Road, Saint John, NB E2L 4L5, Canada

Jan Alexander de Vos, Mirjam Radstaak, Ernst T. Bohlmeijer and Gerben J. Westerhof
Centre for eHealth and Well-being Research, University of Twente, Psychology, Health, and Technology, Enschede, The Netherlands

Jan Alexander de Vos
Human Concern Foundation, center for Eating Disorders, Amsterdam, The Netherlands

Andrea La Marre
University of Guelph, Department of Family Relations and Applied Nutrition, Ontario, Canada

Ernst T. Bohlmeijer
Optentia Research Focus Area, North-West University (VTC), Vanderbijlpark, South Africa

Gina Dimitropoulos and Olivia Cullen
Faculty of Social Work, Matheson Centre for Mental Health Research, University of Calgary, 4212-2800 University Way N.W., Calgary, Alberta, Canada

Ashley L. Landers
Department of Human Development and Family Science, Virginia Polytechnic Institute and State University, Falls Church, VA, USA

Victoria E. Freeman
University Health Network, Toronto General Hospital, Toronto, Ontario, Canada

Jason Novick
Department of Sociology, Mount Royal University, Calgary, Alberta, Canada

Marla Engelberg
Adolescent Eating Disorder Program, North York General Hospital, Toronto, Ontario, Canada

Cathleen Steinegger
Division of Adolescent Medicine, The Hospital for Sick Children and the University of Toronto, Toronto, Ontario, Canada

Daniel Le Grange
Department of Psychiatry, University of California, San Francisco, CA, USA

Gina Dimitropoulos
Hotchkiss Brain Institute, University of Calgary, 4212-2800 University Way N.W., Calgary, Alberta, Canada

Catherine Victoria Talbot, Jeffrey Gavin and Tommy van Steen
University of Bath, Claverton Down Road, Bath BA2 7AY, UK

Tommy van Steen and Yvette Morey
University of the West of England, Coldharbour Lane, Frenchay, Bristol BS16 1QY, UK.

Catherine Victoria Talbot
University of Exeter Medical School, College House 1.23, St Luke's Campus, Heavitree Road, Exeter EX1 2LU, UK

Line Wisting and and Øyvind Rø
Regional Department for Eating Disorders, Division of Mental Health and Addiction, Oslo University Hospital, P.O. Box 4956 Nydalen, N-0424 Oslo, Norway

Line Wisting, Torild Skrivarhaug and Knut Dahl-Jørgensen
Oslo Diabetes Research Centre, Nydalen, N-0424 Oslo, Norway
Department of Paediatric and Adolescent Medicine, Oslo University Hospital, Nydalen, N-0424 Oslo, Norway
Institute of Clinical Medicine, Faculty of Medicine, University of Oslo, Problemveien 7, N-0315 Oslo, Norway
The Norwegian Diabetic Centre, Sponhoggveien 19, N-0284 Oslo, Norway

Øyvind Rø
Institute of Clinical Medicine, Mental Health and Addiction, University of Oslo, Problemveien 7, N-0315 Oslo, Norway

Zahra Abbaspoor
Midwifery Department, Reproductive Health Promotion Research Center, Ahvaz Jundishapur University of Medical Sciences, Ahvaz, Iran

Nahid Javadifar
Reproductive Health Promotion Research Center, Ahvaz Jundishapur University of Medical Sciences, Ahvaz, Iran

Mahsa Miryan
student of nutrition, Faculty of paramedicine, Ahvaz Jundishapur University of Medical sciences, Ahvaz, Iran

Parvin Abedi
Menopause, Andropause Research Center, Ahvaz Jundishapur University of Medical Sciences, Ahvaz, Iran

Alexandra Cobb
Research School of Psychology, Australian National University, Canberra, ACT 2601, Australia

Elizabeth Rieger
Research School of Psychology, Australian National University, Canberra, ACT, Australia

Jason Bell
School of Psychological Science, University of Western Australia, Perth, WA, Australia

E. Caitlin Lloyd
Centre for Exercise, Nutrition and Health Sciences, School for Policy Studies, University of Bristol, Bristol, UK

Joanna E. Steinglass
Department of Psychiatry, Columbia University Irving Medical Center, New York, NY, USA
New York State Psychiatric Institute, New York, NY, USA

Index